FOURTH EDITION

Looking in Classrooms

Thomas L. Good
University of Missouri–Columbia

Jere E. Brophy
Michigan State University

1817

HARPER & ROW, PUBLISHERS, New York
Cambridge, Philadelphia, San Francisco, Washington,
London, Mexico City, São Paulo, Singapore, Sydney

Sponsoring Editor: Alan McClare
Project Coordination, Text Art: Caliber Design Planning, Inc.
Cover Design: John Hite
Printer and Binder: R. R. Donnelley & Sons Company

Looking in Classrooms, Fourth Edition

Library of Congress Cataloging-in-Publication Data

Good, Thomas L., 1943–
    Looking in classrooms.

    Includes bibliographies and indexes.
    1. Teaching. 2. Classroom management.
3. Observation (Educational method) I. Brophy, Jere E.
II. Title.
LB1025.2.G62   1987   371.1'02   86-33493
ISBN 0-06-042401-X

87 88 89 90 9 8 7 6 5 4 3 2

Looking in Classrooms

Contents

Preface   xi

1   Classroom Life   1

Teacher Knowledge   3
Classroom Narrative: An Elementary School
    Example   4
Analysis of the Class Discussion   7
Motivation   8
Classroom Management   9
Classroom Instruction   10
Teacher Expectations   14
Learning to Analyze Classrooms   16
A Teaching Dilemma   17
Classroom Narrative: A Secondary School
    Example   18
Conclusion   23
Suggested Activities and Questions   23
References   24

2   Classroom Complexity and Teacher Awareness   26

Classrooms Are Complex   26
Classroom Problems That May Occur Due to Lack of
    Teacher Awareness   28
Use of Time in Classrooms   34
Other Factors That Influence Achievement   37
How Students Affect Teachers   40
Why Teachers Are Unaware   43
Summary   50
Suggested Activities and Questions   50
References   51

3   Seeing in Classrooms   55

Case Study Techniques   60
Simplifying the Observational Task   68
Summary   72
Suggested Activities and Questions   73
References   73
Appendix A: A Coding Example   75
Appendix B: Brophy-Good Dyadic Interaction
    System   84
Appendix C: Emmer Observation System   88
Appendix D: Coding Vocabulary: Blumenfeld and
    Miller   92
Appendix E: Qualitative Approaches: Educational
    Ethnography   96
Appendix F: An Ethnographic Research Study Conducted
    by Susan Florio   98
Appendix G: Coding Academic Activities and
    Tasks   106
Appendix H: Combining Quantitative and Qualitative
    Procedures: Marshall and Weinstein   110

4   Teacher Expectations   116

Teacher Expectations as Self-Fulfilling
    Prophecies   117
How Expectations Become Self-Fulfilling   120
How Teachers Form Their Expectations   126
How Teachers Communicate Expectations to
    Students   128
Student Perceptions of Differential Teacher
    Treatment   130
Other Models for Indirect Mediation of Expectation
    Effects   131
Variations in Size of Expectation Effects
    Observed   135
Context and Setting Effects on Differentiation Among
    Students   135
Group, Class, and School Effects   139
Expectation Effects on Personal and Social
    Development   143
Avoiding Negative Expectation Effects   144
Basic Teacher Attitudes and Expectations   147
Summary   152
Suggested Activities and Questions   153
References   154
Appendix   161

5   Modeling   173

Awareness of Modeling   174
Teaching Through Modeling   178
Socialization Through Modeling   189
Summary   204
Suggested Activities and Questions   205
References   206

6   Management I: Preventing Problems   216

Management as Motivation and Problem
    Prevention   218
Essential Teacher Attitudes   226
General Management Principles   228
Cueing and Reinforcing Appropriate Behavior   234
Getting and Holding Attention   240
Seatwork   245
Summary   251
Suggested Activities and Questions   251
References   252

**7   Management II: Coping With Problems
Effectively   260**

Dealing with Minor Inattention and Misbehavior   260
Dealing with Prolonged or Disruptive
    Misbehavior   263
Conducting Investigations   265
Conflict Resolution   266
Effective Punishment   268
Choosing Your Role   273
The Teacher as a Socialization Agent   275
Coping with Serious Adjustment Problems   276
Other Approaches to Classroom Management   286
Analyzing Student Behavior   292
Summary   295
Suggested Activities and Questions   297
References   298

8   Motivation   305

Introduction   305
Basic Motivational Concepts   307

Essential Preconditions That Set the Stage for
  Motivational Strategies   309
Motivating by Maintaining Success Expectations   311
Inducing Students to Value Academic Activities   318
Extrinsic Motivation Strategies   319
Intrinsic Motivational Strategies   322
Strategies for Stimulating Student Motivation to
  Learn   328
Building Motivational Strategies into Instructional
  Plans   338
Summary   340
Suggested Activities and Questions   342
References   343

9   Mastery Learning, Individualized Instruction, and Open Education   352

Mastery Learning   354
Individualized Instruction/Adaptive Education   360
Open Education   374
Independent Work and Learning Centers   381
Summary   390
Suggested Activities and Questions   391
References   393

10   Teaching Heterogeneous Classes   404

Between-Class Ability Grouping (Tracking)   405
Educational Excellence and Equity   409
Within-Class Ability Grouping   415
Differentiated Instruction   419
Cooperative Learning   431
Arranging for Tutorial Assistance to Students   443
Summary   447
Suggested Activities and Questions   449
References   450

11   Instruction   459

Teacher Behavior and Student Learning   460
Adapting Instruction to Students' Individual
  Characteristics   467
Classroom Guidelines   469
The Match   470

Group Instruction   476
Questioning   486
Teaching for Conceptual Change   496
Active Student Learning   499
Providing Students With Opportunities for
    Self-Evaluation   503
Problem-Solving Strategies and Thinking Skills   504
Suggested Activities and Questions   509
References   510

12   Improving Classroom Teaching   523

The Socialization Process   524
Experimenting and Growing   526
Teaching Is Difficult   527
Self-Study   532
Opportunities to Observe and Get Feedback Can Improve
    Instruction   540
Professional Collaboration   546
Teaching Materials: Another Base for Professional
    Exchange   547
Teacher Centers   550
The Growing Importance of Staff Development   551
Staff Development in Effective Schools   552
Emerging Roles and Issues   559
Beginning Teachers   562
Induction Programs for Beginning Teachers   564
Teacher Evaluation   572
Do Look Back   575
Summary   577
Suggested Activities and Questions   582
References   583

Appendix: Practice Examples   588

Index   601

Preface

As in previous editions, *Looking in Classrooms* emphasizes classroom teaching. It is written to help teachers, principals, and supervisors develop ways of observing and describing what occurs in classrooms and also to provide strategies that teachers can use to enhance the interests, learning, and social development of their students.

Teachers are often unaware of much of their classroom behavior, and this unawareness sometimes results in inappropriate, self-defeating behavior. To help with this problem, we describe a variety of techniques that can be used to increase teachers' awareness. To the extent that teachers are cognizant of what happens in the classroom and can accurately monitor their behavior (or be assisted to do so by fellow teachers, the principal, or a supervisor), they can adapt their classroom behavior to achieve the goals that they and their supervisors have set.

In addition to helping teachers, principals, and supervisors become more skilled at classroom observation, this book also presents important knowledge, concepts, and findings that can be used to improve classroom instruction. In particular, research conducted in recent years provides compelling evidence that teachers' classroom behavior can significantly affect students' attitudes and achievement. This edition presents up-to-date reviews of research on teacher expectations, teacher modeling, classroom organization and management, student motivation, and classroom instruction.

In preparing this new edition, we have paid careful attention to work at the secondary level in addition to continuing our extensive coverage of knowledge about elementary level classrooms. Furthermore, we have included a completely new chapter on classroom motivation and thoroughly revised the chapters on classroom grouping and instruction.

We continue to believe that much of teaching is an art, and we contend that successful teachers must be able to observe, comprehend, and respond to the rapid occurrence of complex classroom behavior. Ultimately, successful teachers must also develop and continue to refine their own teaching styles. In this book, we offer teachers a method for observing, describing, and understanding classroom behavior, an important first step in developing a teaching style that is both effective and personally satisfying.

We want to express our appreciation to those individuals and institutions who have supported the development of this revision. Outstanding typing was provided by Diane Chappell at the Center for Research in Social Behavior, University of Missouri-Columbia, and by June Smith at the Institute for Research on Teaching,

Michigan State University. We also acknowledge the helpful editorial advice provided by Gail Hinkel and the editorial input provided by reviewers Dr. Phyllis Blumenfeld, University of Michigan, Dr. Ludwig Mosberg, University of Delaware, Dr. Robert Slavin, the Johns Hopkins University, Dr. Allen R. Warner, University of Houston–University Park, and Dr. Karen Kepler Zumwalt, Columbia University Teachers College. We also acknowledge the assistance of Alan McClare, sponsoring editor at Harper & Row.

Special appreciation and thanks are extended to our wives, Suzi and Arlene, and to our children—Heather, Jeff, Kate, Molly, Cheri, and Joe—for their encouragement. Finally, as in previous editions, we dedicate this book to all who teach and who attempt to structure exciting environments for students, but especially to our first and most important teachers, our parents.

Thomas L. Good
Jere E. Brophy

CHAPTER

1 Classroom Life

This book has two major purposes. The first is to help teachers and students of classroom behavior to develop ways of looking at and describing what goes on in classrooms. The second is to suggest ways in which teachers can have a positive influence on the interests, learning, and social development of their students.

Teachers are often unaware of much of what they do, and this lack of perception sometimes results in unwise, self-defeating behavior. Our intent is to show that teachers need to learn how to observe and describe classroom behavior in order to improve their teaching. To the extent that teachers can become aware of what happens in the classroom and can monitor accurately their behavior and that of their students, they can function as *decision makers*. To the extent that teachers cannot do this, they will be controlled by classroom events. When teachers fail to coordinate classroom events, students will not make optimal progress.

However, classroom decision making is not easy, in part because classrooms are complex environments in which teachers often must make quick decisions while using incomplete information. For example, Doyle (1986) cites the following aspects of classroom settings that teachers must necessarily accommodate.

1. *Multidimensionality*. Many different tasks and events exist in the classroom. Records and schedules must be kept, and work must be monitored, collected, and evaluated. A single event can have multiple consequences. Waiting a few seconds for one student to answer a question may positively affect that student's motivation but negatively influence the interest of another student who would like to respond. At the same time, it may slow the pace of the lesson for the rest of the class.
2. *Simultaneity*. Many things happen at the same time in classrooms. During a discussion, a teacher not only listens and helps improve students'

1

answers, but also monitors students who do not respond for signs of comprehension and tries to keep the lesson moving at a good pace.

3. *Immediacy.* The pace of classroom events is rapid. Sieber (1979) found that teachers evaluated pupil conduct in public on the average of 15.89 times per hour, or 87 times a day, or an estimated 16,000 times a year.

4. *Unpredictable and public classroom climate.* As Doyle notes, things often go in ways that are unanticipated. Furthermore, much of what happens to a student is seen by many other students as well. Clearly, students can infer how the teacher feels about certain students by the way the teacher interacts with them in class.

5. *History.* Doyle also states that after a class has met for several weeks or months, common norms and understandings are apt to develop. Emmer, Evertson, and Anderson (1980) show how events that happen early in the year sometimes influence how classrooms function the rest of the year. To a student teacher or observer, some classes appear easy to manage; however, events that took place earlier in the school year may explain why things run smoothly at the time of observation.

The first three chapters of this book emphasize that it is difficult for teachers or observers to monitor accurately and understand what takes place in classrooms because life in classrooms is so complex and proceeds at such a rapid pace. To make valid suggestions about how to improve classroom behavior, however, one must be able to assess what is happening in classrooms. Thus, in the first three chapters we want to help you to learn how to deal with the complexity of classrooms and to learn some strategies that will allow you to observe more carefully in classrooms. After discussing general principles that need to be followed when observing in classrooms, we will present specific instruments that can be used for recording classroom observations.

Chapters 4 through 11 provide teachers, observers, principals, supervisors, and classroom researchers with suggestions about what to look for in classrooms. These chapters discuss the role of the teacher as a model for classroom learners. In Chapter 4 more emphasis is placed on the negative aspects of teacher expectations as information is presented to indicate how teachers can communicate negative performance expectations to students in ways that lower their classroom effort and achievement. In Chapter 5 the positive aspects of teacher modeling and socialization are discussed. Chapter 6 presents strategies for preventing classroom problems and Chapter 7 discusses practical strategies for dealing effectively with misbehavior when it does occur. Chapter 8 deals with motivation; this chapter provides detailed strategies that teachers can use to make assignments more attractive to students. Chapters 9 and 10 discuss organizational aspects of education (open classrooms, individualized programs) and in particular provide advice about how various grouping strategies may aid or impede teachers who deal with a heterogeneous group of students. Chapter 11 details how recent research relevant to good classroom teaching can be applied.

Chapter 12 argues that good teachers need continuing opportunities to learn about teaching, classrooms, and students and to grow as classroom teachers. This chapter discusses strategies that teachers can use to further their professional development through personal reflection and through cooperating with other teachers to obtain needed feedback and information.

TEACHER KNOWLEDGE

We believe that many teachers fail to fulfill their potential, especially in elementary schools, not because they do not know the subject matter, but because they do not understand students or classrooms. Leinhardt and Smith (1984) distinguish between action system knowledge and subject matter knowledge. *Subject matter knowledge* includes the specific information teachers need to present content. *Action system knowledge* refers to skills for planning lessons, making decisions about lesson pace, explaining material clearly, and responding to individual differences in how students learn.

This book deals with action system knowledge. Systematic study of such knowledge will help you to understand how students learn and develop; how classrooms can be managed; and how to present information, concepts, and learning assignments effectively. This information will complement the subject matter knowledge you gain in other courses by providing you with a knowledge of classroom teaching that will help you to become a successful teacher.

Teachers who possess both action system knowledge and subject matter knowledge will be more effective than teachers who are deficient in one of these areas. Simply put, a knowledge of reading is a necessary but not a sufficient condition to be an effective reading teacher. Even with both kinds of knowledge, however, some teachers may fail because they do not apply the knowledge they possess. Such teachers may have inappropriately low expectations for students' ability to learn or for their own ability to teach. Or, they may not be active decision makers. Lacking an integrated set of theories and belief systems to provide a framework for informed decision making, such teachers do not have effective strategies for organizing information gleaned from monitoring the rapid succession of events that occur in their classrooms.

In this book, we will provide useful information about classroom teaching and help you to consider various issues related to classroom teaching and to begin to develop an integrated approach to teaching that reflects your style. However, it is important to recognize that even with good information, much teaching involves hypothesis testing. For example, we might assume that a student who has been out of his or her seat creating behavioral problems needs more structure (e.g., shorter assignments, more explicit directions, self-checking devices) to work alone productively. However, other factors may be producing the misbehavior. If the student's problem is not improved by the correction strategies suggested by the first hypothesis, other strategies will have to be used. Good planning is essential, but teachers must also be willing to examine and alter their plans as they execute them. Those who have a rich fund of action system knowledge about how students learn and develop will be able to develop better hypotheses and adapt their behavior more appropriately to the needs of their students.

Teachers must learn to manage the enduring problems or dilemmas of teaching. There are no simple answers or key solutions to such dilemmas. Teachers have to think, apply, and creatively adapt good ideas to particular groups of students. For example, teachers must necessarily teach a class or group of students much of the time but still try to respond to the needs of individuals. Similarly, teachers are constantly faced with the dilemma of covering a broad range of topics (all of American history in a given year!) but providing sufficient depth about particular topics or events so as to allow for meaningful learning. To provide you with increased awareness of the dilemmas and complexities associated with teaching, we have included many examples of classroom behavior in the text as well as practice exercises to help you learn to describe and understand classroom behavior. To illustrate classroom life, we begin with simulated dialogue from a classroom.

CLASSROOM NARRATIVE: AN ELEMENTARY SCHOOL EXAMPLE

As you read the following example, try to identify teaching behaviors that you believe are effective or ineffective. Think about what you would have done differently if you had been the teacher. Jot down your ideas as you read the material. This will give you a chance to describe and react to classroom behavior and to find out how many important factors you can identify in the example.

Mrs. Turner is a fourth-grade teacher at Maplewood Elementary School in a large university town in the South. She has 30 students in her class. Students at Maplewood come primarily from lower middle-class and working-class homes. Most are white (78 percent), and the rest (22 percent) are black. Sally Turner has taught at Maplewood since graduating from college three years ago.

The following classroom scene takes place in March. The students have been reading about Columbus. The scene begins as Sally passes out mimeographed copies of a map showing the sea routes that Columbus followed on each trip.

BILLY: (*Almost shouting*) I didn't get no map.

TEACHER: (*Calmly and deliberately*) Billy, share Rosie's map. Tim, you can look with either Margaret or Larry.

TIM: Can I look with Jill?

TEACHER: (*Slightly agitated*) Okay, but don't play around. You and Jill always get into trouble. (Most of the students turn to look at Jill and Tim.) I don't want you two fooling around today! (*Smiling but stated with some irritation*) Okay, class. Now, does everybody have a map? I wanted to pass out these maps before we start. You can see that the route of each voyage is traced on the map. It might help you to understand that there were different trips and different routes. Pay special attention during the discussion because you'll need to know the information for tomorrow's quiz. If the discussion goes well, I have a special treat for you—two filmstrips.

CLASS: (*In a spontaneous, exuberant roar*) Yea!

TEACHER: Who can tell me something about Columbus's background?

KAY: (*Calling out*) He was born in 1451 in Italy.

TEACHER: Good answer, Kay. I can tell you've been reading. Class, can anyone tell me who influenced Columbus's urge to explore unknown seas? (She looks around and calls on Jerry, one of several students who have raised their hands.)

JERRY: He'd read about Marco Polo's voyage to Cathay and about the fantastic riches he found there.

TEACHER: Okay. Jan, when did Columbus first land in America?

JAN: 1492.

TEACHER: Terrific! I know you've been reading. Good girl! Where did Columbus stop for supplies?

JIM: (*Laughingly*) But Mrs. Turner, the date was on the map you passed out.

TEACHER: (*With irritation*) Jim, don't call out without raising your hand!

BILL: (*Calling out*) The Canary Islands.

TEACHER: Okay, Bill. Now, what were the names of the three ships? (She looks around the room and calls on Biff, who has his hand up.) Biff, you tell us. (Biff's face turns red and he stares at the floor.) Biff Taylor! Don't raise your hand unless you know the answer. Okay, class, who can tell me the names of the three ships? (She calls on Andrew, who has his hand up.)

ANDREW: (*Hesitantly*) The *Santa Maria,* the *Nina,* and the . . .

TEACHER: (*Supplying the answer*) Pinta. Nancy, how long did this first voyage to the New World take?

NANCY: (*Shrugging her shoulders*) I don't know.

TEACHER: Think about it. It took a long time, Nancy. Was it less or more than 100 days? (*Silence*) The answer was on the first page of the reading material. Class, can anyone tell me how long the voyage took? (*No hands are raised.*) Class, you better learn that because it will be on the exam! Now, who can tell me why Columbus came to the New World? (Mary and two other students raise their hands.) Mary?

MARY: (*Firmly and loudly*) Because they wanted to discover new riches like explorers in the East.

TEACHER: (She pauses and looks at Max and Helen, who are talking, and at Jim, who is headed for the pencil sharpener. Max and Helen immediately cease their conversation.) Jim, sit down this minute. (*Jim heads for his seat.*) What are you doing out of your seat?

JIM: (*Smiling sheepishly*) Jan wanted me to sharpen her pencil.

JAN: (*Red-faced and alarmed*) Mrs. Turner, that's not true! (*Class laughs.*)

TEACHER: Quiet, both of you. You don't need a sharp pencil. Sit down. (*Resuming discussion*) Good answer, Mary. You were really alert. Why else, Mary? Can you think of any other reason?

NANCY: (*Calling out*) Because they wanted to find a shortcut to the Eastern treasures. The only other way was over land, and it was thousands of miles over deserts and mountains.

TEACHER: (*Proudly*) Good, Nancy! Now, who are "they"? Who wanted the riches?

BILLY: (*Calling out*) Queen Isabella and King Ferdinand. She paid for the trip because she thought Columbus would make her rich.

TEACHER: Okay, Billy, but remember to raise your hand before speaking. Why do you think Columbus was interested in making the trip? Just to find money?

CLASS: (*Calling out*) No!

TEACHER: Well, what problems did the sailors have? (She looks around and calls on Jim, who has his hand up.)

JIM: Well, they were away from home and couldn't write. Sort of like when I go to summer camp. I don't write. I was lonely the first few days, but . . .

TEACHER: (*Somewhat confused and irritated*) Well, that's not exactly what I had in mind. Did they get sick a lot? Class, does anyone know? (She looks around the room and sees Claire with a raised hand.)

CLAIRE: Well, I don't remember reading about sailors getting sick with Columbus, but I know that sailors then got sick with scurvy and they had to be careful. (*Hank approaches the teacher with great embarrassment and asks in hushed tones if he can go to the bathroom. Permission is granted.*)

TEACHER: Yes, good answer. Claire, how did they try to prevent scurvy?

CLAIRE: They carried lots of fruit . . . You know, like lemons.

TEACHER: Okay, Claire, but what special kind of fruit was important to eat? (*Claire blushes and Mrs. Turner silently forms the soft "c" sound with her mouth.*)

CLAIRE: Citrus.

TEACHER: Very good! What other problems did the sailors have? (*She calls on Matt, who has his hand up.*)

MATT: Well, they didn't have any maps and they didn't know much about the wind or anything, so they were afraid of the unknown and scared of sailing off the earth. (*Laughter*)

TEACHER: (*Noticing that many students are gazing at the floor or looking out the window, she begins to speak louder and more quickly.*) No, educated men knew that the earth was round. Don't you read very carefully?

ALICE: (*Calling out*) But even though educated men knew the earth was round, Columbus's sailors didn't believe it. They called the Atlantic Ocean the "Sea of Darkness," and Columbus had to keep two diaries. He showed the sailors the log with the fewest miles so they wouldn't get scared. But the men threatened mutiny anyway.

TEACHER: (*With elation*) Excellent answer, Alice. Yes, the men were afraid of the unknown; however, I think most of them knew that the earth was round. Okay, Matt, you made me drift away from my question: Why did Columbus want to go—what were the reasons for his trip other than money? James, what do you think? (*James shrugs his shoulders.*) Well, when you read your lesson, class, look for that answer. It's important and I might test you on it. (*With exasperation*) Tim! Jill! Stop pushing each other this instant! I told you two not to play around. Why didn't you listen to me?

TIM: (*With anger*) Jill threw the map in her desk. I wanted to use it so I could trace my own map.

JILL: But it's my map and . . .

TEACHER: (*Firmly*) That's enough! I don't want to hear any more. Give me the map and the three of us will discuss it during recess.

PRINCIPAL: (*Talking over the PA system*) Teachers, I'm sorry to break in on your classes, but I have an important announcement to make. The high school band will not be with us this afternoon. So 2:00 to 2:30 classes will not be canceled. Since I have interrupted your class, I would also like to remind you that tonight is PTA. Teachers, be sure that the boys and girls remind . . . (*During the announcement many pupils begin private conversations with their neighbors.*)

TEACHER: (*Without much emotion or enthusiasm*) It's not recess time yet. Listen, we still have work to do. Tell you what we're going to do now. I've got two filmstrips: One describes the United States space astronauts' first trip to the moon; the other describes Columbus's first trip to the New World. Watch closely when we show these films because after we see the filmstrips, I'm going to ask you to tell me the similarities between the two trips. Ralph, turn off the lights.

HANK: (*Returning from his trip to the restroom*) Hey, Mrs. Turner, why are the lights out in here? It's spooky in here!

ALICE: (*Impishly*) It's the Sea of Darkness! (*Class breaks out in a spontaneous roar.*)

TEACHER: Quiet down, class! It's time to see the filmstrips.

The example of this fourth-grade class illustrates many points, including the fact that teachers are busy and that teaching is complex. The pace of classroom life is hurried. The teacher Sally had a constant stream of student behavior to react to and she had to make a number of decisions instantaneously. Several decisions were quite complex, and on occasion you may have expressed some bewilderment—"If I were the teacher, how would I have responded?" Our goal in sharing this example with you is to illustrate that the problems of teaching that classroom teachers encounter are by no means simple to conceptualize. We hope this book will encourage you to take these problems seriously.

If you did not take notes as you read the material, you should quickly reread the example and write your reactions to the teaching incident. What were the teacher's *weaknesses* and *strengths*? If you were to discuss these observations with the teacher, what would you tell her? You may want to repeat this exercise when you finish reading the book in order to assess the information you have gained or any changes in your perspective that may occur between now and then. Complete the exercise now, then read our reactions to this teaching incident, which follow.

ANALYSIS OF THE CLASS DISCUSSION

Like most teachers, Sally Turner has some strong qualities and some weak ones. We have chosen to organize our comments around four areas of classroom teaching that are basic to most teaching/learning situations: motivation, management, instruction, and expectations. These four themes are discussed at length in separate chapters in this text; the discussion here provides an introduction to these topics.

MOTIVATION

First, Sally's attempt to breathe life into Columbus and ancient history by linking his explorations to something significant in the students' lives is notable. In the attempt to help students to identify more personally with the content, she has thought about the lesson and has gone to the trouble to order filmstrips both of Columbus's voyage (a simulation) and of the astronauts' trip to the moon. However, the astronauts' trip to the moon occurred before these students were born. It might have been more effective if the teacher had attempted to stimulate students' thoughts about the unknown with events that were more immediate to students (e.g., first trip to a soccer or scout camp, or the possibility of how future astronauts may feel on their first trip to previously unexplored points in space).

Feedback

Sally does a fair job of giving feedback to students about the correctness or incorrectness of their responses. She describes the adequacy of most students' answers. Although this may seem to be a small point, it is often highly significant. Teachers frequently fail to provide students with this information. They do not respond to student answers, or they respond in such a way as to make it difficult for some students to know if their responses are correct. An instance of such ambiguous teacher feedback is: "So, you think it's 1492?" Although many students know whether a response is right or wrong, many low-achieving students do not know unless the teacher specifically tells them. If students are to learn basic facts and concepts, they must know whether or not their answers are adequate.

Introducing the Lesson

Sally communicates certain undesirable expectations to her students. Perhaps most striking is her tendency to emphasize that the classroom recitation is important only because it will prepare students to take a test. Her behavior does not suggest that learning is enjoyable or important for its own sake and does not focus on positive learning goals (see Chapter 8). Note especially Sally's poor introduction to the lesson. She stresses that students will be tested on the material, but she provides little additional rationale for the discussion of Columbus's voyage.

Students may well appreciate hearing that material is important and will be on a quiz. Hence, there is nothing wrong with mentioning this (once!); however, Sally's introduction should have focused more on positive learning goals and less on tomorrow's quiz. At other times in the discussion, she also refers to the fact that listening is important because of future testing. Such behavior does much to convince students that learning is arbitrary, an irrelevant exercise done only to please adults or to receive high grades. (This point is expanded in Chapters 4 and 8.)

In general, Sally's attempt to make the "history" associated with Columbus's discovery of America more personal and more meaningful to students is good. However, the actual lesson itself is "dry" and students' role in the classroom recitation is relatively passive (more on this in Chapters 8 and 11).

CLASSROOM MANAGEMENT

In the area of classroom management (creating a learning environment, maintaining student involvement, etc.), Sally appears to be an average teacher. Students were generally attentive to her and to the discussion and there were few interruptions, although the students did not appear to be enthusiastically engaged. However, there are several areas in which Sally Turner could improve.

To begin with, she did not have enough maps for all the students. Equipment and material shortages inevitably lead to trouble, especially when students get to keep the material. A more careful count of the maps might have prevented both the minor delay at the beginning of the discussion and the major disruption (students fighting over a map) that occurred later.

Upon discovering the shortage and after hearing Tim's request to sit with Jill, Sally might have responded: "Okay, that's fine. Sit with Jill, because I know you and Jill can share cooperatively. Billy and Tim, I'm sorry you didn't get maps. I failed to make enough copies, but I'll draw each of you a *special* map this afternoon." This would have accomplished two important things: (1) It would have assured Billy and Tim that they would get maps and made it less likely that they would "take the law into their own hands." (As will be pointed out in Chapter 6 on management, what a teacher does to prevent misbehavior from happening is substantially more important than what is done after misbehavior occurs.) (2) This response would have encouraged more appropriate expectations, and perhaps better cooperation, from Jill and Tim. The teacher's original remark ("You and Jill always get into trouble") placed Jill and Tim in the spotlight. Such a remark may have caused them to develop an inappropriate attitude toward misbehavior. By implying that it was expected, the teacher subtly condoned misbehavior and made it more likely. The implications of the teacher attributing negative rather than positive motives to students' behavior will be discussed in Chapter 4.

Credibility

Sally has developed the bad habit of not following up on what she says. During this class discussion, she said on several occasions: "Don't call out answers, raise your hand." However, she repeatedly accepted answers that were called out. Recall this instance:

> TEACHER: (*With irritation*) Jim, don't call out without raising your hand!
> BILL: (*Calling out*) The Canary Islands.
> TEACHER: Okay, Bill . . .

As we will see in subsequent chapters, such discrepant teacher behaviors tell students that teachers do not mean what they say. Such inconsistency may lead to countless discipline problems, because it helps to convince students that teachers are not aware of much of what happens in the classroom.

Whether or not students call out answers is not the point here. There are times when calling out academically relevant responses should be encouraged, and times when students should not be allowed to respond directly to the teacher or to one another without permission. But teachers should be consistent in their demands. Teachers who do not want call-out responses should consistently communicate this fact. For example, when a student calls out an answer, the teacher should either ignore the student's response and call on someone else or acknowledge the response indirectly ("Raise your hand if you want to respond. We don't want call-out answers today.") and call on another student (who may or may not have raised a hand).

We mentioned call-out responses as being particularly desirable when a teacher wants students to respond to one another and to evaluate the adequacy of others' responses on their own. You may be prompted to ask, then, why call-out answers are sometimes undesirable. The two negative aspects of call-outs are: (1) students who are verbally aggressive dominate the discussion and (2) low-achieving students who take more time to process information may not even get a chance to think about questions because other students answer them too quickly. The purpose of questioning is not to yield quick, automatic responses but to stimulate students to think.

Rhetorical Questions

There is at least one other area in which Sally could improve her classroom management. In two different situations involving off-task behavior, she used rhetorical questions that caused needless difficulty. For example, Jim had already started to his seat (which is what the teacher wanted) when she needlessly asked, "What are you doing out of your seat?" This question evoked a more serious disruption. Similarly, in her exchange with Jill and Tim, Sally pointlessly queried, "Why didn't you listen to me?" and again the situation deteriorated and the whole class was distracted. The use of questions in discipline situations will be discussed fully in Chapters 6 and 7, but here we can say that such rhetorical, negative questions that communicate low expectations for behavior typically lead to clowning or other disruptive student behavior. Consider how you feel when someone says to you: "Why don't you listen?" "Can't you do anything right?" "Why are you always the difficult one?" These questions irritate most people.

In terms of classroom management, Sally's students are generally attentive and there are no serious misbehavior problems. Hence, her behavior management is successful—the students are participating. As we will see in Chapter 6, certain aspects of management have been neglected in this critique; however, the minimal conditions of rapport and structure have been established.

CLASSROOM INSTRUCTION

There are many aspects of classroom instruction, as will be shown in Chapter 11 (e.g., planning content, pacing lessons, making decisions about reteaching content, helping students to take notes and to understand material presented); however, the instructional aspects of this lesson are quite limited and in that sense unsatisfactory. It is difficult to understand what the instructional task is (what the teacher wants students to learn) and how this lesson fits into the overall unit (how students will use the information later). As we will see in Chapter 11, effective teaching requires that teachers plan sequences of lessons, not just isolated lessons (Clark & Peterson, 1986).

The instructional component of this lesson resides in the teacher's questions. For the most part, these appear to be rather mechanical—time filling rather than thought provoking. We now turn to a discussion of these aspects of instruction.

Teacher Questions

Table 1.1 presents the first ten questions that Sally asks. Two things seem apparent from an examination of these questions. First, most of the questions are factual (students can answer them by reading the material). Second, the questions seem more like an oral quiz than an attempt to initiate a meaningful discussion.

Unfortunately, in too many classrooms discussions are parrot-like sessions, with teachers asking a question, receiving a student response, asking a question of a new student, and so forth. Such "discussions" typically are boring and accomplish little other than the assessment of students' factual knowledge. Such assessment is important, but if that is all that is done in discussion, students may come to perceive that the teacher is interested only in finding out who knows the answers. When this occurs, discussion becomes a fragmented ritual rather than a meaningful, enjoyable process. Furthermore, students often do not perceive a clear, logical sequence to factual questions. Such questions seem more like an oral test than a lesson intended to teach content or to engage students in a meaningful discussion.

There are two major ways in which a teacher can influence students' answers: (1) by the types of questions the teacher originally asks the students and (2) by follow-up questions the teacher may pose to students after they respond. Sally Turner's initial questions were primarily factual. The students might have been more interested if they had been involved more directly in the discussion. This could have been accomplished with more questions of value and opinion, such as the following: How would you like to be isolated from your parents and friends for several days? How would you feel being in a 5 by 7 foot room and unable to leave it? Would you like to be a sailor on a ship and stay on that ship week after week, not knowing where you were going or what you would see? Would you volunteer for such a voyage? Why? What is mutiny? Is it justified? Would you have felt like mutinying if you had been a crew member on Columbus's voyage? Was it important to discover the New World? How do you feel when you are afraid or apprehensive? Would it be important to explore a new planet like Venus? Why?

Some of these questions (e.g., Was it important to discover the New World?) could be considered factual, since the book probably gives answers to them. How students react to such questions depends on the teacher. Too often teachers' questions say implicitly "Tell me what the book said." Students should be encouraged to assess facts rather than simply to accept the reasons listed in the text. Even factual questions can be used to stimulate pupil thinking. For example, Sally might

---

Table 1.1   PARTIAL LIST OF CONTENT QUESTIONS THAT SALLY ASKED

1. Who can tell me something about Columbus's background?
2. When did Columbus first land in America?
3. Where did Columbus stop for supplies?
4. What were the names of the three ships?
5. How long did this first voyage to the New World take?
6. Was it less or more than 100 days?
7. Why did Columbus come to the New World?
8. Can you think of any other reason?
9. Who wanted the riches?
10. Why do you think Columbus was interested in making the trip? Just to find money?

ask, "The book states two reasons why the Spaniards wanted to discover the New World. What were these two reasons, and what beliefs and values underlay their reasoning?" Or instead of asking "When did Columbus discover the New World?" the teacher might ask why the trip was not made before 1492.

Similarly, Sally could ask students to evaluate the social consequences of the events discussed in the lesson. Was it worth the time and money to send astronauts to the moon? What knowledge do we have now (e.g., technological and/or medical information) that was a direct result of space flights (not only the manned moon flights but also the Columbia mission and recent space ventures)? Similarly, students could discuss the risks of explorations, perhaps by noting the numerous ships that have been lost at sea or tragedies in space exploration (e.g., the explosion of the space shuttle Challenger). Some teachers might also want to comment on the expanding role of women by noting the death of Christa McAuliffe, the former classroom teacher who was the first citizen to go into space, or the contributions of Sally Ride and other female astronauts. In the teaching example, Sally used factual questions excessively and used too few questions of value and opinion that might have stimulated greater student interest in the discussion.

Teacher Questions After Student Responses

Sally seldom encouraged students to evaluate their own thinking (e.g., "Well, that's one way; what are some other ways that Columbus could have boosted his crew's morale?" "That's an accurate statement of how the crew members felt, but what about Columbus?" Do you think he was fearful?"). Nor did she ask questions to help students evaluate their classmates' answers (e.g., "Sam gave his opinion about sailing with Columbus. Bill, do you agree with him? How do you feel?" "What are some other reasons in addition to the good ones that Tim gave?"). Such opportunities to explore a particular question in depth help make a discussion more enjoyable to students, place less emphasis on obtaining simple, correct answers, and help teacher and students alike to determine whether they *really* understand material.

To reiterate, Sally did a good job of giving students feedback about the correctness of answers, and on occasion she did probe for additional information. That is, she sought an additional response from a student after the first response, for clarification (e.g., "What do you mean?" "Why do you think that is so?" "How does this relate to . . .?").

Unfortunately, the word *probe* conjures up a negative image to many teachers. They react to it as though the word meant "pick the student's answer apart." No such usage is intended here. The appropriate meaning is to help students to consider thoughtfully the implications of what they do and say—to think about the material. Probing techniques should be gentle ways to focus students' attention and to help them think. For example, an automatic response to "When did Columbus discover America?" is an unthinking "1492." However, the question "Why not 1400 or 1450?" forces a consideration of what the world was like in 1400. In the same way, the question "Why did the United States not have a manned space flight program in the 1950s?" focuses discussion on a variety of factors (national priorities, safety, etc.). Similarly, a question like "Why didn't the Columbia space voyage take place until the 1980s?" forces students to think about historical events (e.g., investment of government funds).

Factual questions are important and teachers should use them frequently when they are helping students to learn basic skills. However, factual questions should be used with other types of questions so that students also consider the implications of facts or the circumstances that produce them. Probing questions are an especially useful way to help students think more fully about material. A useful exercise for the reader would be to review the sample dialogue in Mrs. Turner's classroom and to note where probing techniques could have been useful. *Write out the probes that you would have used.*

Controlling Classroom Interaction

An especially interesting aspect of Sally's teaching was that she only called on one student who had not volunteered. If you reread the dialogue, you will see that either students call out the answer or Sally calls on students who have their hands up. However, it is often useful for teachers to call on students who do not raise their hands. First, shy students seldom raise their hands, and they need opportunities to speak in public and develop their communicative skills and self-assertion. Furthermore, low-achieving students often learn that to answer incorrectly is to receive public ridicule. Students who avoid public response opportunities need to be called on and given opportunities to learn that they can participate in successfully. Finally, when students learn that their teacher only calls on students who raise their hands, they may begin to tune out. Calling on students who do not have their hands up may increase student attention. Some teachers fall into the equally bad habit of calling on a student before asking a question (although Sally does not exhibit this problem): "Jeff, what do you think about . . .?" "Heather, state Boyle's law." This procedure tells students that they do not have to listen unless they are named.

We do not know why Sally fails to call on students who do not raise their hands during this particular lesson, but if this behavior is typical, non-hand-raisers are seldom called on in her class. A clue to explain Sally's behavior is provided by one incident. Recall that in the exchange with Biff, she scolded him for having the audacity to raise his hand without knowing the answer. This suggests that Sally wants "correct" answers, that she is more interested in establishing her point and moving on with the lesson than she is in the learning of individual students. If a teacher typically responds this way, students will learn that they are not to raise their hands unless they are absolutely sure that their answer is correct. Calling on students who know the right answer is often an unconscious teacher strategy for self-reinforcement. Teachers may delude themselves into believing that they are doing a good job because some students consistently respond with incorrect answers. Naturally, some students are more willing to take risks than other students (such as those in the example who called out answers). If teachers consistently show that they want correct answers, however, many students, especially the timid nongamblers, will be afraid to participate in class discussions.

No matter how well teachers plan, they will need to recognize that students often fail to understand in a meaningful way the ideas that are presented to them and that good teachers—often have to reteach lessons using different procedures and examples. Hence, if teachers are to make good decisions about whether or not to introduce new material or to review old material, it is necessary for them to have feedback from most, if not all, students in the class.

Student Questions

Sally did not encourage students to ask questions or to evaluate responses of classmates. However, she could have encouraged students in this way: "Today I have several questions that I want to find answers for. You have been reading the material for a week now, and you probably have some questions that weren't answered in the reading material. Maybe the class and I can help you answer these questions. Any questions that we can't answer we'll look up in the *World Book* or in the school library. I wonder why Queen Isabella picked Columbus to head the voyage? Why not some other sailor? I think that's an interesting question! Now, let's have *your* questions. We'll list them on the board and see if we have answered them at the end of the discussion."

Although it is not necessary to solicit questions for every discussion period, it is a good instructional practice to do so on occasion when teaching young children. Such teacher behavior tells pupils that the purpose of discussion is to satisfy their needs and interests as well as the teacher's. Furthermore, in asking for questions the teacher communicates to students:

1. I have important questions and I want your viewpoint.
2. You certainly must have some important questions.
3. We'll have an interesting discussion answering one another's questions.
4. If you need more information, we'll get it.

If used consistently, such an approach will in time teach students that discussion is not a quiz but a profitable and enjoyable process of sharing information. (For related information, see Chapter 5 on teacher modeling and Chapter 8 on classroom motivation.)

It is especially important that the teacher communicate enthusiasm and respect for students who ask questions. Some teachers call for student questions but then react to those questions in such a way as to discourage students from asking about issues that interest them. Such teacher comments as "Well, that is not directly related to our discussion" or "That was answered in the book" may convince a student that he or she is the only one in class who does not know the answer or that the teacher prefers that students not ask questions.

TEACHER EXPECTATIONS

There is evidence to suggest that in some classrooms the students who are believed to be more capable receive more stimulating classroom environments than do the students who are believed to be less capable (e.g., Good & Brophy, 1986; Marshall & Weinstein, 1984). As we will see in Chapters 4 and 5, teachers not only hold expectations about individual students but also hold expectations about groups and whole classes of students as well as beliefs about the particular subject matter they teach. Furthermore, teachers sometimes communicate these beliefs in their classroom behavior and assignments. This communication has both positive and negative consequences.

Much research has been focused on teachers' interactions with high and low achievers in the class. Since we do not identify the achievement level of students in the example, it is not possible for us to determine if Sally acts differently toward students she believes to be high and low performers (e.g., calls on one group more frequently than the other, asks different *types* of questions, etc.). However, we can assess her behavior toward boys and girls in the classroom and make some comments about her gender expectations.

Teacher Behavior Toward Male and Female Students

Interestingly, Sally did not praise boys but frequently praised girls. Again, it is not possible to say unequivocally that she always favors girls, but during this class discussion, she was more responsive and supportive to female students. No male student received teacher praise. Also, though Sally made few attempts to work with any of the students when they gave inappropriate responses, she more often worked with girls than with boys. When boys gave an inappropriate response, she accepted the performance and either provided the answer herself or called on another student to answer. However, on two occasions she prompted a girl who was having difficulty responding. For example, when Nancy failed to respond to the question "How long did the voyage take?", Sally first provided a clue ("It took a long time") and then reduced the complexity of the question ("Was it less or more than 100 days?"). Similarly, when Claire could not remember the word *citrus,* Sally provided a nonverbal clue.

Although we would need more information about Sally Turner's behavior toward male and female students, she may be more likely to praise the performance of girls and to work with them when they do not answer correctly. Even though Sally questions boys and girls with similar frequency (there are no differences in *quantity* of questions), the *quality* of her feedback to students' responses differs. The term *quality* refers to the way in which a teacher interacts with pupils. Does the teacher ask difficult or easy questions? How long does the teacher wait for responses? Does the teacher praise answers? Does the teacher probe for more information?

Reaction to Students' Spontaneous Comments

Sally also failed to discuss topics that students introduced spontaneously, even topics that were directly related to the class discussion. Part of Sally's plan was to get students to appreciate the sense of adventure and apprehension that explorers face. When two students mentioned their sense of fear, however, Sally failed to respond. For instance, Jim talked about his loneliness during the first few days of summer camp. Sally could have asked a variety of questions in response: "Why did you feel this way during the first few days of camp?" "How did you feel on your first day at school?" "How do you think you will feel on your first day at junior high?" "Why are we uncomfortable when we do something for the first time?" After such a discussion, the students would likely better appreciate the newness of the situation the explorers faced as well as the related stress and excitement.

A similar opportunity arose at the end of the discussion, when Hank described the spookiness of the room and Alice cleverly labeled it the Sea of Darkness. Sally could have profitably paused and pointed out that Alice's remark was a good one and perhaps have added in a quiet voice: "Okay, now listen. For one minute, no one will make a noise. Let's pretend that we are on the *Pinta*. We have been at sea for two months. It is now completely dark and there is no sound on the ship. The only noise is the roar of the sea and the creaking of the ship as it is tossed from wave to wave. We are all scared because no one has ever sailed this sea! What will we run into in the darkness? What is our destination? What will it be like when we reach it? Will the residents there be hostile?" Such techniques can involve students more centrally in class discussions. Teachers often stimulate very profitable and enjoyable discussions when they capitalize on spontaneous student examples. Teachers' spontaneous reactions help to provide direction and structure to students' perceptions. If teachers do not react positively to students' self-initiated questions and concerns, students will stop asking questions.

Outside Reading

The way in which the learning task is presented to students helps students to understand what the teacher expects them to do—in this case, to memorize facts or to understand history. Unfortunately, the classroom dialogue provides no indication that students were encouraged to do any extra reading—either about Columbus's voyage or about more general travel and exploration. For example, there are many stories that students could read and integrate into future discussions, including historical accounts of travel (Marco Polo) or literature (or movies) related to travel and exploration (e.g., *Around the World in Eighty Days, Twenty Thousand Leagues Under the Sea, Little House on the Prairie, Treasure Island*). Similarly, the teacher could read selections from Charles Darwin's travel diary or from *The Caine Mutiny*.

The point here is not that the teacher should have background reading and follow-up activities for *all* classroom assignments, but that the lesson should have some direction and continuity. Supplementary reading materials and follow-up assignments communicate to students that the teacher is interested in helping them to understand and apply ideas and concepts, not just to memorize facts. This lesson, as we mentioned earlier in our comments about the lack of sequence in Mrs. Turner's questions and her focus on learning the material in order to do well on the test, seems more an exercise to fill time than a coordinated, important learning experience.

LEARNING TO ANALYZE CLASSROOMS

In analyzing Sally's classroom, we are trying to involve you directly in the study of classrooms as complex social settings. We think that the professional role of classroom teaching is demanding and rewarding; however, we do not think that it is an easy role. You have been a classroom student for over twelve years and in this book we are encouraging you to begin to think about classrooms through the eyes of the teacher. You have seen many different teaching styles and approaches—some successful, some not—and in this book we are suggesting the need to become more reflective about the role and the duties of the classroom teacher.

Still, a brief analysis of Sally's classroom teaching yields some inferences about her classroom behavior and beliefs. Admittedly, one example of Mrs. Turner's classroom behavior is enough information on which to base only the most speculative conclusions; however, such behavior should encourage an observer to look for more information to confirm or negate the notion that she does not want students to respond unless they know the answer. Some teachers, especially beginning teachers, unwittingly fall into the trap of discouraging students from responding unless they know the answer perfectly. This is because silence or incorrect answers are difficult to respond to and are often embarrassing or threatening.

The incident with Biff illustrates two important points: (1) Teachers may encourage students not to listen by falling into ineffective but consistent questioning styles. (2) Often, we can get enough evidence from what we observe in classrooms to be able to make decisions and give firm suggestions to teachers, but at other times (e.g., the exchange with Biff), we may only note clues about the teacher's general behavior patterns or assumptions about students. These need to be checked out by talking with the teacher and/or with students or by making additional observations (more on this in Chapters 2, 3, and 12).

However, even though our examination of Sally Turner's class has been brief, we hope that the example encourages you to examine, discuss, and evaluate classroom teaching. Below we present two open-ended assignments in which we ask you to analyze classroom situations.

A TEACHING DILEMMA[1]

The following brief example describes a dilemma for the classroom teacher. As you read it, think about what you might do to resolve the problem. Do your attempts create new problems? You may want to compare your thinking with that of the author of this case (see Lampert, 1985).

> In the classroom where I teach fourth-, fifth-, and sixth-grade mathematics, there are two chalkboards on opposite walls. The students sit at two tables and a few desks, facing in all directions. I rarely sit down while I am teaching except momentarily to offer individual help. Thus, the room does not have a stationary "front" toward which the students can reliably look for directions or lessons from their teacher. Nevertheless, an orientation toward one side of the room did develop recently in the fifth-grade class and became the source of some pedagogical problems.
>
> The children in my classroom seem to be allergic to their peers of the opposite sex. Girls rarely choose to be anywhere near a boy, and the boys actively reject the girls whenever possible. This has meant that the boys sit together at the table near one of the blackboards and the girls at the table near the other.
>
> The fifth-grade boys are particularly enthusiastic and boisterous. They engage in discussions of math problems with the same intensity they bring to football. They are talented and work productively under close supervision, but if left to their own devices, their behavior deteriorates and they bully one another, tell loud and silly jokes, and fool around with the math materials. Without making an obvious response to their misbehavior, I developed a habit of routinely curtailing these distractions from the lesson by teaching at the blackboard at the boys' end of the classroom. This enabled me to address the problem of maintaining classroom order by my physical presence; a cool stare or a touch on the

[1] This material is reprinted from Lampert, M. (1985). How do teachers manage to teach? Perspectives on problems in practice. *Harvard Educational Review, 55,* 178–194.

shoulder reminded the boys to give their attention to directions for an activity or the content of a lesson, and there was no need to interrupt my teaching.

But my presence near the boys had inadvertently put the girls in "the back" of the room. One of the more outspoken girls impatiently pointed out that she had been trying to get my attention and thought I was ignoring her. She made me aware that my problem-solving strategy, devised to keep the boys' attention, had caused another, quite different problem. The boys could see and hear more easily than the girls, and I noticed their questions more readily. Now what was to be done?

I felt that I faced a forced choice between equally undesirable alternatives. If I continued to use the blackboard near the boys, I might be less aware of and less encouraging toward the more well-behaved girls. Yet, if I switched my position to the blackboard on the girls' side of the room, I would be less able to help the boys focus on their work. Whether I chose to promote classroom order or equal opportunity, it seemed that either the boys or the girls would miss something I wanted them to learn.

CLASSROOM NARRATIVE: A SECONDARY SCHOOL EXAMPLE

As you read the classroom dialogue below,[2] make notes about the effective and ineffective techniques that the teacher uses. We do not analyze this dialogue because we want you to form your own impression and to complete your own analysis. This narrative includes a number of factors associated with classroom motivation and management as well as teacher expectations and instructional effectiveness. After you have read specific chapters of this text (Chapters 4–11), it will be useful to return to this narrative to see how your reaction to it has changed. We suspect and hope that you will be able to identify both positive and negative aspects of the teaching after you have read the book.

BEGIN

1:20
1. The students are filing in. The teacher is outside by the
2. door in the hallway. The teacher pokes her head in and says
3. to the class, "You'd better be in your seats when the bell
4. rings or it's going to be demerits for you. Hurry." One
5. student runs to sharpen her pencil and says, "I can make it."

1:26
6. Another student sharpens his pencil. One student is passing
7. out folders. The teacher comes in and closes the door. The
8. bell has not rung. The teacher is at the front of the
9. room looking at the lost and found section. She says,
10. "Here are somebody's clothes," and she opens a sack. Stu-
11. dents say, "What does it have in it?" The teacher says,
12. "White corduroy slacks and a shirt." No one claims it.
13. The teacher says, "Okay," folds the clothes, puts them
14. back in the sack, and puts the sack back on the shelf.
15. The teacher says, "Now open your books. I want the
16. number of your textbook when I call your name. If you
17. don't have your textbook, you'll get a demerit." Stu-
18. dents make noises like, "Oohs, aahs, nos, Miss," from the

[2] This narrative was taken from an actual observation in the classroom management project at the Research and Development Center for Teacher Education, University of Texas, Austin, Texas. Carolyn Evertson, Ed Emmer, and Walt Doyle have provided leadership to this project.

19. class. "No, Miss, that's not fair." The teacher says,
20. "You will just have to remember from now on." She calls
21. the first two names. They have their books, and they
22. give their numbers. The teacher calls on Bruce. Bruce
23. says, "I do not have my book." The teacher says, "Then
24. you'll get a demerit." Bruce says, "Why?" The teacher
25. says, "Because you are supposed to remember to bring your
26. book to class." Bruce says, "I don't have a book." The
27. teacher says, "You need to remember to bring it." Bruce
28. says, "I don't have a book." The teacher says, "Then you
29. had better pay for the lost book and get a new one."
30. The teacher continues calling out other names. Bruce
31. says, "I don't think it's fair that I get a demerit."
32. The teacher says, "Bruce, if you can't afford to pay for
33. the book, then talk with me later and we will see what

1:28   34. can be done." Bruce says, "I can afford it." The teach-
35. er says, "Bruce, then you had better get one soon so you
36. won't get any more demerits." Bruce blurts out, "Can you
37. take that demerit off?" The teacher says, "No, Bruce."

1:30   38. Bruce goes, "Gah." The bell rings. The teacher
39. continues calling out names. Four more students get
40. demerits for not having their books. When the students
41. do not have their own books, they get demerits, but they
42. can borrow a book from the shelf to use in the class.

T—1:31   43. The teacher says, "All right, let's open our books to
44. page 44 and spend two minutes looking over the back to be
45. sure to see if there are any questions that I might ask
46. you." The teacher goes outside the door and can be heard

1:32   47. talking to a man outside the door. The observer does not
48. know who the man is or why the two are talking. While
49. the teacher is gone, five students are talking, four

1:33   50. students are looking at the book, and others are just
51. looking about the room. Eight students are talking, one
52. student is marking on her desk, six students are reading,
53. three students are looking around the room, but are

1:35   54. quiet. The teacher returns and says, "All right, you
55. should have had enough time to look over page 44." Bruce
56. goes back to the pencil sharpener and grinds away at his
57. pencil. The teacher ignores him and wipes off the trans-
58. parency that she had used in the previous class. The
59. teacher asks, "What does it tell us on the top of
60. page 44?" Three hands go up. The teacher says, "Don?"
61. Don says, "To divide." The teacher says, "So okay, we
62. are starting off with division. What does it say up
63. there in bold black type?" A student reads, "Basic
64. division facts." The teacher says, "What does 'basic'
65. mean?" Several students blurt out several different
66. answers. One student says, "Simple." The teacher says,
67. "Right, simple. The foundation of something. Okay, we
68. start off looking at the basic facts of division." The
69. teacher writes, "Division—page 44," on the overhead

1:38   70. transparency. The teacher has Bruce read the instruc-
71. tions on the first part. The teacher writes on the over-
72. head as she is explaining. Bruce reads the directions.
73. The teacher says, "Okay, let's look up here." She writes

74. the example shown to the side.

$$
\begin{array}{ccccccc}
N & N & \div & 3 & & & \\
6 & 6 & \div & 3 & = & & 2 \\
15 & 15 & \div & 3 & = & & 5 \\
12 & 12 & \div & 3 & = & & 4 \\
\end{array}
$$

75. The teacher explains that they
76. should substitute six for
77. the N, and they have their problem. "What would it be
78. if I put 15 on the left-hand side of this line? What
79. will it look like on the right-hand side?" Several stu-
80. dents raise their hands. The teacher calls on Janet.
81. She answers. The teacher says, "Yes, you're on the right
82. track, Janet, but you said it wrong." Janet repeats it.
83. The teacher says, "You said it wrong, Janet. You said
84. three divided by fifteen. There is a big difference." Janet
85. says, "What?" The teacher says, "There just is. You
86. can't—if you divided three by fifteen, you would come
87. out with a fraction. So what should it be, Janet?"
88. Janet says, "Fifteen divided by three equals five." The
89. teacher says, "Right. Let's do one more." She writes,
90. "12." "So what would we put on the right side? A stu-
91. dent answers, "Twelve divided by three equals four."
92. The teacher writes this on the transparency. She says,
93. "How about a nine?" The same hands go up. The teacher
94. says, "Let's get someone who hasn't answered yet." The
95. teacher calls on Larry. Larry answers. The teacher
96. says, "Right." The teacher continues asking for prob-
97. lems with 30, 27, and 18. She tries to call on differ-
98. ent students each time. (It seems like the same group
99. of hands go up every time. Students answer well. They
100. seem to understand this.) The teacher says, "That's the
101. way you are going to answer all the rest of the prob-
1:40 102. lems. Look at the problems one through nine, and see if
103. you have any questions." There was no response from the
104. class; no one seemed to have any questions. The teacher
105. says, "Okay, who would like to read the instructions for
106. problems ten through twenty?" Three hands go up. The teach-
107. er says, "Okay, Sarah." Sarah reads. The teacher says,
108. "Okay," and she writes "3, 21, 7" on the transparency.
109. She asks, "Can someone give me a multiplication problem
110. using these three numbers? Jeff?" Jeff answers, "Three
111. times seven equals twenty-one." The teacher says, "Very good.
112. Can anyone give me a division problem using those three
113. numbers?" Four hands go up. "Terry?" Terry says,
114. "Twenty-one divided by seven equals three." The teacher
115. says, "Very good. Let's look at one more. How about
116. the numbers seven, fifty-six, and eight? What's a good multi-
117. plication problem using those numbers? Bruce?" Bruce
118. says, "What?" Apparently Bruce was not paying attention.
119. The teacher says, "Greg, can you help Bruce out?"
120. Greg says, "Eight times seven equals fifty-six." The teacher
121. says, "Very good." She writes this on the overhead
122. transparency. Greg turns to smirk at Bruce. The teacher
123. says, "Very good. Now, who can give me a division
124. problem?" A student answers, "Fifty-six divided by
125. eight equals seven." The teacher says, "Right." There
126. is one more, which is fifty-six divided by seven equals eight."

127. The teacher writes these on the overhead transparency.
128. The teacher says, "All right, any questions on ten
129. through twenty?" There are no questions. The teacher says,
130. "You must put two multiplication and two division prob-

T—1:45 131. lems on each one of these." "Are there any questions?"
132. There are no questions. The teacher says, "All right,
133. homework for tonight is page forty-four, one through twenty. Do not
134. talk. You may begin." Students look at her with for-
135. lorn looks. The teacher says, "It's only homework if
136. you do not finish in class." The students say, "Oh,
137. yea." Students go to sharpen pencils, and they talk at
138. the pencil sharpener. The teacher says, "Let's take
139. care of those lost books as soon as possible." Students
140. settle down to work now. One student is at the teacher's

1:48 141. desk, Bruce and Greg are talking quietly, the girl in front
142. of Bruce is listening and picking her nose, all other stu-
143. dents seem to be working. The teacher leaves the light
144. of the overhead projector on so that a student can see an
145. example of what they just worked as a class. The teacher is
146. at her desk working on demerit slips. There is lots of noise

1:49 147. from the hallway and/or other classes outside this classroom.
148. The teacher flips off the overhead light. Students are work-
149. ing quietly. The teacher looks up from her desk to survey the
150. class from time to time. David is talking to the girl next
151. to him. He is having a hard time settling down to work.

1:50 152. Students work very quietly. The teacher is at her desk. She
153. does not move around to help at this time. Students go up to
154. her desk from time to time and ask for help. Bruce is copying
155. off his neighbors' papers. He tries to crane his neck around
156. to see the girl's paper who sits behind him. She has already
157. moved her desk away from his desk, and when he turns around,

1:55 158. she covers her paper automatically with her hand. Bruce gets
159. the message. He turns back around. Students go to the teach-
160. er's desk for help. All students are very quiet in the class-
161. room. All seem to be working on something. (Observer thinks
162. that the teacher is working on her demerit file. She is
163. filing cards into a cardboard box.) A student at
164. the teacher's desk asks a question. The teacher shakes her
165. head. Observer could not hear the question. The teacher
166. says, "Maybe, but we won't get to leave any earlier. We will

2:00 167. leave at 20 minutes after." The student goes back to work.
168. All is quiet again. Bruce goes to the teacher's desk to ask
169. her a question. The class is so quiet that the teacher
170. lecturing across the hall comes in loud and clear. Every now
171. and then a student in this class will look at another student
172. and laugh at something the across-the-hall teacher has said
173. to her class. She is really giving it to her students. The

2:03 174. teacher hears a lot of rustling now, and she is up and moving
175. about. Two students are up out of their desks. There is
176. no real reason for them to be out of their desks. The teacher
177. says, "Sit down," to the two students. The teacher helps one
178. student with a question; other students are working. The
179. teacher is moving about, looking over shoulders, and helping
180. where needed. A student goes to the teacher to tell her that

181. she figured a problem out. The teacher follows the student
2:09 182. back to her desk and looks at the student's paper. She says,
183. "Great," and she smiles. The student smiles and is pleased
2:10 184. with herself. The teacher returns to her desk to work.
185. Another student follows the teacher there with a question,
186. then another student goes to her with a question. (Observer
187. feels that maybe the teacher sat down too soon.) A third
188. student goes to her desk to ask the teacher a question. The
189. second student now returns to the teacher's desk with book and
190. folder in hand. The teacher and student are going to grade
191. one of the student's past papers that had been turned in for
192. makeup work. Bruce is playing with a ruler. Greg blurts
193. out, "Miss, may I go home?" The teacher does not say anything
194. because she is helping two students. (Observer thinks that
195. maybe she did not even hear the comment. Observer feels that
2:12 196. Greg might as well go home because he has only written three words
197. on his paper.) Don asks the teacher what do they do when they
198. are finished. The teacher says, "Then you don't have any
199. homework." He says, "Then we just sit here?" The teacher
200. says, "No, go to the extra-credit box and get something to
201. work on." A girl goes to the box, and she returns to her
202. desk, she blurts out, "Miss, can we write on these papers?"
203. The teacher says, "What paper?" The student points to the
2:13 204. extra-credit box. The teacher says, "Yes, they are yours."
2:14 205. The teacher is very busy helping two students at a time.
206. Several students finish. There is a murmur in the class.
207. It's quiet, but there are still murmurs. There is loud pencil
208. sharpening. A student stops at the observer and asks, "Do you
209. write Spanish?" The observer answers, "Just fast and sloppy."
210. The student smiles and goes on. The teacher is now helping
211. a boy and girl at her desk. Students are quiet, but there are
2:18 212. lots of restless body movements. Two students are talking and
213. laughing, one student is talking to the teacher about the
214. bottle that is on the teacher's desk. Greg is sitting and
215. staring, others are sitting quietly and still working. Greg
T—2:18 216. says, "Miss, it's time to clean up." The teacher says, "Let's
217. pass folders up to the front. Bruce, let me have my ruler
218. back." The teacher repeats, "Let's pass our folders up to the
219. front. No talking," but there is still talking. It is quiet
2:19 220. talking, but there is talking in the classroom. The teacher
221. is busy helping students put up folders. The teacher says,
222. "Everybody in their chairs now so we can go when the bell
223. rings." One girl goes over to look at the metric poster.
224. (Observer feels maybe she just does this out of spite to the
225. teacher.) Two girls are taking up the folders. Others are
226. sitting in their desks. The bell rings. The teacher says,
227. "First and second row may go." A student blurts out, "First
228. and second from what side?" The teacher points to the first
229. and second row by the door. She says, "Okay, the third row
230. may go." The teacher pauses to let the fourth and fifth rows
231. get quiet. The teacher says, "Okay, fourth and fifth rows may
232. go. Bye-bye, you all have a nice evening." The students say
233. bye-bye to the teacher as they leave class.

CONCLUSION

We have presented our reactions to a discussion in an elementary classroom. We hope that the narrative and our comments have caused you to consider teaching behavior carefully. Perhaps you noted strengths or weaknesses that we did not address or took exception to some of our comments. If so, that's fine! The purpose of the chapter is to involve you in the process of looking at classroom behavior. Classrooms are complex environments, and careful observation and analysis of teacher and student behavior can yield greater insight about effective instructional procedures. However, the dilemmas of teaching are not easy to resolve. To illustrate this we have shared with you an example of a teaching dilemma and have asked you to respond to the situation as though you were the classroom teacher. We also provided a narrative of events in a secondary classroom, and we encouraged you to consider the relative strengths and weaknesses of this teacher with regard to classroom management, motivation, expectations, and instructional effectiveness.

In the Appendix to the book, you will find five additional narratives from elementary and secondary classrooms. You may want to read these now in order to raise more questions about teaching behavior. However, these materials will likely be most useful after you have read the entire text, because analyzing the cases will allow you to practice the skills and to use the information you obtain from the book.

There are additional questions that observers of classroom life must address: Are most teachers unaware of certain aspects of their classroom behavior and of its consequences? If so, why are they unaware? How can they become aware of what they do in the classroom and more knowledgeable about how their behavior affects students? We turn to these questions in the next two chapters.

SUGGESTED ACTIVITIES AND QUESTIONS

1.1. After reading the secondary classroom narrative, how would you describe the teacher's relative strengths and weaknesses? Based on your experience in schools, how would you rate this teacher (average, below average, above average)? Why?

1.2. If you were going to talk to the secondary teacher about the classroom, what would you want most to talk about? Why?

1.3. From reading the teaching dilemma facing the teacher who works with fourth-, fifth-, and sixth-grade students, how would you respond to the problem? How does your answer compare to that of your classmates? What explains these differences of opinion?

1.4. If you had a chance to talk with Mrs. Turner about her lesson, what questions would you ask? Why? How might additional information change your opinion of her teaching?

1.5. If Mrs. Turner's classroom was composed entirely of students from an inner-city neighborhood, how would you assess her instruction? Does teaching have to be adjusted to the characteristics of students? Explain your answer.

1.6. Reread the questions that Mrs. Turner asks in class. How could you improve on these fragmented questions? Write ten questions of your own. Why are your questions better than Mrs. Turner's?

1.7. Watch a videotape or film of classroom behavior with a group of fellow students or teachers. List the major strengths and weaknesses of teacher behavior that you see and compare your list with others' lists.

1.8. If films are not available, select one of the case studies in the Appendix at the end of the book. As you read the class description, evaluate the teaching. Compare your assessment with those of others. How similar or dissimilar are the reactions to the teaching behavior?

1.9. Watch four or five 5-minute teaching segments of different teachers. View the teaching segments with at least three other observers. After watching the films, rank-order the teachers on the following criteria:

a. I would feel most comfortable in this class.

b. I would learn the most in this class.

c. This teacher would be least likely to criticize me.

See if the teachers in the films were given the same rank order by all observers. Try to identify the teaching characteristics that made you respond as you did. What, for example, led each of you to think that you would feel comfortable in a particular teacher's classroom? If individuals feel differently about the teachers (and they may), try to identify the characteristics that attracted some observers but not others.

1.10. Consider the grade that you teach (or plan to teach) and identify the ten most important skills, attitudes, and/or behaviors that a teacher must possess in order to instruct students effectively at this grade. Keep this list so that you can compare it with a list that you make after you have read the entire book.

1.11. Reread the example of Mrs. Turner's fourth-grade class and identify four instances in which she could have probed for student responses. Write the questions you would have used. Read some of the case studies presented in the Appendix at the end of the book and identify places where teachers could have asked probing questions.

1.12. We critiqued Mrs. Turner's teaching. What additional teaching strengths or weaknesses did you identify that we did not mention? Explain why these behaviors are strengths or weaknesses.

1.13. Assume that you are an observer in Mrs. Turner's classroom. During recess she asks "Well, you watched the explorer unit today. What are my two major teaching strengths and my two major weaknesses?" How would you respond? Why do you believe that the strengths and weaknesses you suggest are the most important or basic?

1.14. We criticized Mrs. Turner's introduction to the lesson. Improve the introduction by writing your own. In general, what steps should a good introduction include? Why?

1.15. Why do teachers have a difficult time being aware of everything that occurs in classrooms?

1.16. We suggested that before conducting a class discussion, it is often a good idea to solicit questions from students. Why? Under what circumstances might this be a poor approach?

REFERENCES

Clark, C., & Peterson, P. (1986). Teachers' thought processes. In M. Wittrock (Ed.), *Handbook of research on teaching* (3rd ed.). New York: Macmillan.

Doyle, W. (1986). Classroom organization and management. In M. Wittrock (Ed.), *Handbook of research on teaching* (3rd ed.). New York: Macmillan.

Emmer, E., Evertson, C., & Anderson, L. (1980). Effective classroom management at the beginning of the school year. *Elementary School Journal, 80,* 219–231.

Good, T., & Brophy, J. (1986). *Educational psychology: A realistic approach* (3rd ed.). New York: Longman.

Lampert, M. (1985). How do teachers manage to teach? Perspectives on problems in practice. *Harvard Educational Review, 55,* 178–194.

Leinhardt, G., & Smith, D. (1984). Expertise in mathematics instruction: Subject matter knowledge. Paper presented at the annual meeting of the American Educational Research Association, New Orleans.

Marshall, H., & Weinstein, R. (1984). Classrooms where students perceive high and low amounts of differential teacher treatment. Paper presented at the annual meeting of the American Educational Research Association, New Orleans.

Sieber, R. (1979). Classmates as workmates: Informal peer activity in the elementary school. *Anthropology and Education Quarterly, 10,* 207–235.

CHAPTER

2

Classroom Complexity and Teacher Awareness

Our brief glimpse into Sally Turner's classroom reveals that it is exceedingly busy and that she is probably unaware of much of her behavior and its effects on students. The junior high mathematics teacher who is featured in the other narrative is also probably unaware of certain aspects of classroom interaction.

In this chapter, we discuss research that supports the assertion that classrooms are *complex,* that the fast pace observed in Sally Turner's class is common, that teachers are unaware of much of their classroom behavior, and that teachers sometimes behave in self-defeating ways. We argue that teachers do not perceive many classroom events because (1) classroom interaction involves fast and complex communication, (2) teachers are not trained to monitor and study their behavior, and (3) teachers rarely receive systematic or useful feedback about their behavior. In particular, we argue that many factors affect how teachers interact with students and that teachers must resolve many questions (How long should I wait for a student to respond to a question? Is it fair or appropriate to wait longer for some students than others?). Finally, we emphasize that neither teachers nor observers are likely to understand classroom behavior unless they know how to collect classroom information, know what behaviors to look for, and have a conceptual or theoretical framework to use in analyzing their observations.

CLASSROOMS ARE COMPLEX

In a single day, an elementary teacher may engage in more than 1000 interpersonal exchanges with students (Jackson, 1968). Teachers in secondary schools may have interactions with as many as 150 different students a day. Not only do teachers have numerous interactions with students, they must also *interpret* complex classroom behavior on the spot (Anderson-Levitt, 1984; Brophy et al., 1981). It is not surprising that most teachers are hard pressed to keep track of the number and the substance of contacts that they share with each pupil. It may not be important for a teacher to remember all classroom contacts; however, teachers must recall certain information (the ten students who did not get a chance to present their class reports; a student who had trouble with vowel sounds during reading, etc.).

Because teachers constantly respond to immediate needs while they teach, they have little time during teaching to consider what they are doing or planning to do. Unless teachers look for signs of student disinterest or difficulty, they may not see them. Teachers are so absorbed in their work that it is difficult for them to get a perspective on what happens in their classrooms. Gloria Channon (1970), an elementary teacher in New York City, describes it this way:

> The teacher, like the doctor in the midst of an epidemic, is so busy with the daily doings that she finds it hard to get some distance between herself and her functions, to see what is happening. As a result she is vulnerable to each day's experience in a special transient way.

Other teachers note that they are not only busy but also alone. Freedman, Jackson, and Boles (1983, p. 270) quote one teacher who describes the problem: "We never had any administrative encouragement to work together. There was never any time, there was never any made, there were very few group decisions. It's a very individual thing. If you found someone you wanted to share materials with you did it on your own. No, nobody has ever encouraged that route. . . ."

Furthermore, as Spencer (1984a, 1984b) notes, the personal lives of teachers are often filled with so many demands and commitments that it is difficult for teachers to analyze and reflect on events in the teaching day during their spare time. Hence, it is necessary that teachers improve their ability to monitor their classroom behavior as it occurs as well as have opportunities at school to observe and discuss teaching with their colleagues. (Teachers also need time at school to meet, study, and discuss with other teachers—a point we will return to in Chapter 13.)

Classrooms also have social aspects that reach beyond the classroom doors. Anderson-Levitt (1984, pp. 334–335) puts it this way:

> Finally, an evaluation is more than the sum of the crucial, socially constructed "facts" . . . the note to the parents, the comment to a colleague, or the official report to the principal is a many-tiered speech act. At one level, teachers are simply making a statement about a student's progress. But at other levels, they may be trying to persuade the school inspector that they merit a raise, to get the child who needs a special class placed in special education, to communicate deference to a well-educated and assertive parent, to build a sense of solidarity with a fellow teacher at the end of a hard year. . . .

Much happens in the classroom, and teachers have to be able to deal with the complexities of teaching in a social setting.

Teacher Perceptions of Classroom Behavior

What proof do we have that teachers are often unaware of or misinterpret their behavior in classrooms? Some particularly revealing information is provided by the minicourse training experiences at the Far West Laboratory (Borg et al., 1970). That laboratory has prepared a number of in-service courses designed to help teachers develop specific teaching skills. For example, their minicourse on independent work activity is designed to help teachers develop skills in (1) discussing with pupils the meaning of working alone, (2) discussing the assigned independent learning task, (3) eliciting potential problems and solutions, (4) establishing standards for what to do when finished, (5) providing delayed responses to completed student work, and (6) evaluating pupils' success in working independently. These skills appear to be clear, and it seems that teachers would know whether or not they had performed such behaviors in their teaching. Such was not the case. Borg et al. (1970) report that the majority of teachers felt that they had included the skills presented in the minicourse on independent work; however, an analysis of data from observations of teachers teaching small groups of students in minicourse laboratory sessions showed that this was not usually true. If teachers cannot accurately describe their performance in laboratory teaching, it is unlikely that they could accurately describe their behavior when teaching an entire class.

Emmer (1967) also presents evidence that classroom teachers are unaware of much of their teaching behavior. He reports that teachers were unable to describe accurately even simple classroom behaviors, such as the percentage of time that they and their students talked. Most teachers grossly underestimated the amount of time they talked.

These two studies suggest that teachers sometimes behave in ways of which they are unaware. We do not have proof that teachers in both studies were unaware of their behavior, because these and similar studies collected only information about teacher (or student) behavior and did not assess teachers' (or students') awareness of their behavior.

A study conducted by Good and Brophy (1974), however, provides clear evidence that teachers are unaware of their classroom behavior. These researchers found that teachers differed widely in the extent to which they stayed with students in failure situations (repeated or rephrased a question, asked a new question, and so on) or gave up on them (gave an answer or called on someone else). Interviews with teachers showed that they were largely unaware of the extent to which they generally gave up or stayed with students and of their behavior toward certain students. It appeared that teachers were so preoccupied with running the classroom that awareness of this dimension of classroom life eluded them.

Other researchers have reached similar conclusions. Indeed, even a seemingly simple aspect of teacher-child interaction can turn out to be a complex perceptual problem in a fast moving, complex social setting such as a classroom. For example, Martin and Keller (1974) note that teachers usually do not accurately recall the extent to which they call on boys or girls, the frequency with which students approach them, the number of private contacts they initiate with students, or the amount of class time they spend on procedural matters.

CLASSROOM PROBLEMS THAT MAY OCCUR DUE TO LACK OF TEACHER AWARENESS

In the sections that follow, we want to describe classroom problems that occur in part because of lack of teacher awareness and information. Most of the problems presented here are discussed later in the book. The material in this chapter is designed to help you to begin thinking about factors that affect teacher behavior and student achievement. In this chapter, we discuss a variety of classroom issues, including interactions with students. We note that classroom organization (e.g., seat location, independent seatwork) affects how teachers monitor students and thus leads to different patterns of teacher-pupil interaction. Furthermore, we argue that time usage, curriculum appropriateness, and what students do in other instructional programs (e.g., supplementary programs) and at home affect the teacher's ability to instruct effectively. Teachers must be cognizant of the effects of these factors on pupil and teacher behavior. Teachers who have accurate information are better able to instruct.

Classroom Communication

Research done some time ago indicates that teachers monopolize communication in the classroom. Adams and Biddle (1970) conclude that teachers are the principal actors in 84 percent of classroom communication episodes. Hudgins and Ahlbrand (1969) report similar figures. These findings suggest that teachers dominate classroom discussion, even though they sometimes do not want to and may not be aware that they behave this way. Cuban (1984) reports that the basic structure of classrooms, with a heavy reliance on teacher-student recitation, has remained unaltered for many years.

We believe that teachers can talk too much or too little and that both types of teachers may be unaware of their behavior. Nevertheless, *quality* of teacher talk is much more important than quantity.

Emphasis On Meaning

The basic issue concerns primarily what teachers talk about, not the amount of talk per se. Durkin (1978–1979) found after 300 hours of observation in reading and social studies classrooms that less than 1 percent of the time was devoted to comprehension instruction. Two studies indicate that mathematics teachers who actively instruct and emphasize the meaning of concepts obtain higher achievement from students than teachers who use instructional time for other purposes (e.g., transitional activities) or assign considerable independent work without much teaching (Good, Grouws, & Ebmeier, 1983; Evertson, Emmer, & Brophy, 1980). Thus, unless teachers are *aware* of how and why they use time as they do, they are unlikely to be effective. Although awareness alone is not sufficient for effective teaching (information on alternate teaching strategies is also needed, see Chapters 4–11), we do believe that awareness is the first step in improving teaching.

Teachers' Questions

Researchers have also examined the effects of teachers' questions (Borg et al., 1970; Winne, 1979). Borg et al. summarize this literature and suggest that the types of questions teachers ask pupils have not changed in more than half a century, despite the demonstrated need for a variety of questions. Factual questions help teachers to determine whether or not students know the basic information. However, teachers use many more factual questions than they probably realize. We are not advocating that all teachers use more thought questions (questions that place higher level cognitive demands on students). Our point is that many teachers who utilize largely factual questions are unaware of the *types* of questions they ask, which prevents them from changing their behavior. We discuss teachers' questions at length in Chapter 11. There we argue that the usefulness of a question depends on *why* the question is asked and at what lesson stage. As we will see in the following section, some teachers also do not realize which students they call on.

Motivation

After over 100 hours of observation in six intermediate grade classrooms, Brophy and Kher (1986) found that only a third of the teachers' task introduction statements included comments judged likely to have positive effects on student motivation. These few comments usually consisted of general predictions that students would enjoy a task or do well on it. Indeed, Brophy and Kher found only *nine* attempts to explain to students why it was important to learn material, and none at all suggesting that students could derive personal satisfaction from learning relevant skills or knowledge. Brophy and Kher suggest that teachers make few attempts to motivate students because they have not been taught strategies for doing so. We suggest such strategies in Chapter 8.

Seat Location

Sometimes the way a teacher groups or assigns students to seats influences communication. Adams and Biddle (1970) discovered the existence of an "action zone" in the classroom. This zone included students who sat in the middle-front-row seats and in seats extending directly up the middle aisle. These students received more opportunities to talk than did other students, possibly because teachers tended to stand at the front of the classroom, where their attention was focused on students nearby. In any case, students seated in this zone received more teacher attention. Other researchers have identified action zones where certain students monopolize classroom discussion, although the form of some action zones is quite different from that reported by Adams and Biddle (see, e.g., Alhajri, 1981).

Other seating patterns can influence communication and affect peer relations. Teachers often group students by ability in order to reduce the range of individual differences within each group and to instruct more effectively. Some teachers completely segregate low- and high-ability students by seating them apart. The top readers sit at the same table, the next best group sits together, and so on. Such seating patterns are likely to create status differences among students and engender an attitude of inferiority in low achievers that will remove them from the mainstream of classroom life. We suspect that many teachers are largely unaware of how seat assignments and grouping practices influence student behavior.

Seatwork

Many students spend considerable classroom time doing seatwork while the teacher instructs another group of students. During such times some students may engage in off-task behavior that escapes teacher attention. Indeed, Anderson, Brubaker, Alleman-Brooks, and Duffy (1985) suggest that in addition to death and taxes, seatwork in elementary schools should be included in a list of inevitable events. Despite the fact that students in some classes spend 70 percent of class time doing seatwork (i.e., reading or writing tasks completed without direct teacher supervision), little formal study of seatwork has been completed.

Anderson et al. (1985) conducted one of the few studies of seatwork that examines in depth what students do during seatwork and how they attempt to understand and complete assigned work. Results showed that the 32 students studied in first-grade classes spent from 30 to 60 percent of time allocated to reading instruction doing some type of seatwork. Furthermore, an average of 50 percent (but in some classes virtually 100 percent) of seatwork assignments utilized commercial products such as workbooks, dittos, and reading material. Although there were some differences from class to class in seatwork assignments, within each class assignments were similar across time, with the same form of assignment often used two to five times a week (e.g., Read a sentence and then choose one of three to four pictures that represents the meaning of the sentence, or Copy sentences with blanks and choose the correct word from several options). Anderson et al. found that teacher instruction related to seatwork assignments seldom included statements about what would be learned and how the assignment related to other things that the students had learned. When teachers did pay attention to students who were doing seatwork, they most often monitored student behavior but not student understanding or task performance.

Differential Teacher-Student Interaction

The teacher is the principal actor in many classrooms. When teachers do allow students to speak, however, which ones do they call on? Jackson and Lahaderne (1967) indicate that student contact with the teacher varies widely within the same classroom. Observing four sixth-grade classrooms for about ten hours each, they found that teachers interacted with some students as few as 5 times and with others as often as 120 times.

Although Carew and Lightfoot (1979) did not find evidence that teachers discriminated on the basis of race or gender, they did find that teachers' affective reactions to students resulted in uneven attention. A study by Brophy et al. (1981) also indicates that teachers' affective reactions (attachment, concern, indifference, rejection) influence their behavior toward pupils. However, this influence is complex. Some teachers attempt to hide feelings of attachment or rejection, whereas others express their preferences more openly. In general, research suggests that teachers vary widely in terms of how they behave toward boys and girls and students who differ in ethnicity or ability (some teachers discriminate but others do not; see Wilkinson & Marrett, 1985, for an extended discussion).

Student Achievement Levels

Perhaps the most consistent finding concerning teacher interaction with students is the tendency for teachers to call on students believed to be better students more frequently than they call on students they believe are less capable. Some teachers show this more than others. However, many teachers call on high- and low-achieving students equitably and some even call on low-achieving students more often than on the high-achieving. In Chapter 4 we present a detailed review of the literature concerning teacher differential behavior toward students that teachers believe to be more and less capable.

Brophy and Good (1970) studied the classroom behavior of four first-grade teachers toward high- and low-achieving students. They reported only minor differences in the *frequency* of teacher contact with students of different achievement levels but found important variations in the *quality*. Teachers were much more likely to praise high-achieving students, even when differences in the correctness of students' answers were taken into account.

When high-achieving students gave a right answer, they were praised 12 percent of the time. Low-achieving students were praised only 6 percent of the time following a right answer. Even though they gave fewer correct answers, low-achieving students received proportionately less praise. Similarly, low achievers were more likely to be criticized for wrong answers. They were criticized 18 percent of the time, and high achievers were criticized 6 percent of the time. Furthermore, teachers were twice as likely to stay with high-achieving students (repeat the question, provide a clue, ask a new question) when they made no response, said "I don't know," or answered incorrectly. More recent research (e.g., Cooper & Good, 1983) illustrates that some teachers still show differential interaction patterns.

It is important to note that not all teachers behave differently towards high- and low-achieving students. After reviewing a number of our own studies and the work of others, it became apparent that teachers vary widely in the extent to which they are influenced by expectations and treat low-achieving students inappropriately. Many teachers develop appropriate expectations for low achievers and treat them fairly (Brophy & Good, 1974; Cooper & Good, 1983; Good & Brophy, 1986). Many others, however, especially those who are unaware of their behavior, favor high achievers (more on this in Chapter 4).

Student Gender

That patterns of school achievement differ for boys and girls is an undeniable fact (Hyde, 1981; Maccoby & Jacklin, 1974). However, gender differences in intellectual functioning that are reported in the literature are quite small. Thus, there is no reason to believe that boys and girls cannot succeed equally well in different school subjects or subsequently in different vocational fields.

Although boys and girls do achieve in somewhat different ways, available evidence clearly indicates that it is unreasonable to explain differential levels of achievement on the basis of innate biological differences. Performance differences between the sexes are for the most part learned behaviors (induced by societal expectations and the behaviors of adults). For example, the tendency for girls to read better than boys in elementary school but to avoid advanced mathematics classes in secondary school appears to be due to motivational factors related to social expectations and experiences (Good & Findley, 1985).

Some teachers overreact to student gender either by forming unwarranted perceptions or by treating students differently as a function of their gender. A number of studies demonstrate that teachers tend to perceive male and female students differently. Motta and Vane (1977) examined teachers' perceptions of students' creativity, aggression, dependence, and achievement orientation. They found that teachers viewed girls as more dependent, creative, and achievement-oriented, while boys were seen as more aggressive. Simmons (1980) also measured teachers' perceptions of a number of personality traits. She found that teachers expected boys to be more aggressive, independent, and to have better physical skills. In addition, teachers expected girls to be more emotional, intuitive, ambitious, and empathetic.

Student gender also affects the quantity and quality of students' communication with teachers. Studies consistently show that boys have more interactions with teachers than do girls (Brophy & Good, 1974; Cooper & Good, 1983). However, the magnitude of this difference varies with the nature of communication, being greatest for disciplinary exchanges and smallest for instructional messages. Morse and Handley (1985) studied seventh- and eighth-grade students during science instruction over two consecutive years and found that in the seventh grade, 41 percent of the student-to-teacher academic interactions were initiated by girls; in the eighth grade, these same girls initiated only 30 percent of the interactions. Thus, as they matured, girls initiated interactions less often in science classes. In contrast, the boys' initiation of interactions increased over the two years.

Subject matter may also affect teachers' treatment of boys and girls. Leinhardt, Seewald, and Engel (1979) studied teacher-student interactions in 33 second-grade classrooms and found that in reading, girls had a higher percentage of academic contacts with teachers and received somewhat more instructional time than boys. In mathematics, however, boys received more academic contacts and instructional time with teachers than did girls. In all classrooms, boys had more management contacts with teachers than did girls. These researchers note that differential instructional behavior and student achievement were related in reading. Although there were no differences in initial abilities, significant gender differences were found in end-of-year standardized achievement testing. Presumably, the fact that teachers spent relatively more time with girls in reading was associated with girls' higher reading achievement.

Bossert (1981) notes that when students are assigned mixed-gender projects or experiments, boys are likely to manipulate objects and set up equipment, whereas girls are likely to watch and listen or to perform note-taking duties for the group. Bossert argues that teachers need to be aware of the different interests that students bring to the classroom and to encourage all student to participate in a variety of classroom work. As Bossert notes, teachers may treat boys and girls differently partly because boys and girls have varied interests and behave differently in the classroom. That is, although teachers may not assign girls to act as recorders, most girls may assume these duties because of their interests and skills. Similarly, Fennema and Peterson (1985) argue that gender-related differences in mathematics achievement may exist in part because of subtle differences in students' participation in mathematics over time. They argue that one learns to do high-level math tasks by choosing, persisting, and succeeding at high-level tasks.

There is evidence that at least some teachers socialize young girls to be responsible and dependable but not to be assertive and initiating (Grant, 1985). It is likely that some secondary mathematics and science teachers tend to favor boys over girls. For example, Morris and Handley (1985) found that secondary science teachers spent more time reinforcing and/or rewarding questions for males than for females. They also found that teachers gave males more feedback that prolonged interaction between teacher and student than females received. They conclude that such interactions reflect higher teacher expectations for boys than for girls. Still, it is clear that differential teacher behavior toward male and female students is an individual variable. Although some teachers differentiate content and interaction on the basis of student gender, other teachers show little of such behavior (e.g., see Eccles & Blumenfeld, 1985).

Furthermore, student behavior influences teacher behavior. Brophy et al. (1981, p. 118) conclude: "Boys misbehaved much more often and more disruptively, but were not more likely than girls to be alienated from the teachers or to express negative affect toward them. Nor were teachers alienated from them, although they were slightly more likely to express negative affect in interactions with boys than in interactions with girls. All in all, the sex difference data reviewed here reinforce and extend the patterns observed in earlier research: Teachers perceive girls more positively than boys and share more positive patterns of interaction with them, but most, if not all, of these differences are attributable to differences in the behavior of the students themselves and not to significant teacher favoritism of girls or rejection of boys."

It is also important to note that students have a variety of characteristics and that interactions are based not only on gender but on other characteristics such as race (see Grant, 1985). Leacock (1969) found that teachers generally rated black students less favorably than they rated white students, and that teachers showed particular hostility and rejection toward the *brightest* black students. This is a reversal of the usual finding in studies involving white students. Teachers need to be aware of certain differences in students that they may overreact to if they are not careful (see Brophy et al., 1981; Grant, 1985; Wilkinson & Marrett, 1985, for a review of this literature).

USE OF TIME IN CLASSROOMS

Allocated Time

There is evidence that teachers vary widely in how they use instructional time. Some elementary school teachers spend a great deal of time on mathematics, but others spend relatively little time on this subject. Some subjects generally receive less attention than do other subjects. For example, Ebmeier and Ziomek (1983) studied 75 teachers in Grades 2–6 and found that an average of only 15 minutes *per week* was spent on science in second-grade classes. By fifth grade, this time had increased to 43 minutes. Often there were differences in how instructional time was allocated to particular subjects even between two fifth-grade classrooms in the same school. Berliner (1979) also found that teachers vary widely in time allocations. For example, time allocated for second-grade math ranged from a low of 24 minutes to a high of 61 minutes. The range for second-grade reading was from 32 to 131 minutes. Some students may receive as much as four times more instructional time in a given subject than other students in the same grade.

Variations in time utilization are found in secondary classrooms as well. Some teachers use 40 minutes of a 45-minute period to develop concepts; in other classrooms only 20–25 minutes will be used for developing subject matter content. Stallings (1980) studied 87 secondary classrooms and reports that teachers who obtained relatively poor achievement from students used more class time for non-interactive instruction. During class these teachers graded papers or made lesson plans while students worked on written assignments or read. Stallings also found that achievement was poor in classrooms that had considerable off-task behavior involving non-academic interaction, behavior problems, uninvolvement, or excessive transition time.

Engaged Time

Increased time allocated to a subject does not always correlate with increased achievement. For example, Caldwell, Huitt, and Graeber (1982) note that time given to reading group work with no adult supervision was related negatively to reading achievement in second grade. A growing number of researchers suggest that *quality* (how time is used) is more important than how much time is allocated.

Recent studies indicate that student engaged time, or time on task, and academic learning time are more sensitive predictors of achievement than allocated time (see Berliner, 1979). *Student engaged time* is the amount of time that an average student is actively engaged in or attending to academic instruction or tasks. Researchers define engaged time as allocated time multiplied by engagement (observational measures of whether students appear to be on task). For example, if 75 minutes are assigned for a mathematics lesson and students are estimated to be on task 75 percent of the time, the average student engaged time would be approximately 56 minutes. Student engaged time correlates more positively with achievement than does allocated time. However, even student engaged time does not always relate to achievement, in part because students who are on-task may look as though they are off-task (e.g., listening to a story while gazing out the window) and vice versa (see Peterson & Swing, 1982).

Academic Learning Time

Fisher et al. (1978) introduced a new time measure called *academic learning time,* which they define as the amount of time a student spends performing relevant academic tasks with a high level of success (e.g., 80%). Although this measure is not always associated with student achievement, variations in academic learning time are reasonably good predictors of student achievement. Good and Hinkel (1982) argue that measures of engaged time tend to show at least some correlation with student achievement because even superficial task involvement suggests that (1) the teacher possesses minimal managerial skills, (2) the teacher has elicited some compliance from students, (3) there is some apparent agreed-upon direction and purpose to the class, and (4) at least *some* of the time, students reflect on assigned work.

Academic learning time varies widely from classroom to classroom. For example, Fisher et al. (1978) found that some second-grade pupils spend as little as

3 minutes a day working successfully on reading, whereas others spend as much as 42 minutes. Some teachers who allocate less time for a subject have considerably higher rates of academic learning time because they involve students more in appropriate tasks that allow the students to experience higher rates of success.

Teachers' Beliefs and Time Utilization

We suspect that most teachers are not aware of how their time allocations to particular subjects differ from those of other teachers. Furthermore, most teachers probably have little knowledge of what percentage of their allocated time is academic learning time and how their classrooms compare with other teachers'. Indeed, Stallings (personal communication) says that the biggest problem she had in training teachers to be more effective in their use of time was getting them to become *aware* of and to accept the fact that their management of time was relatively poor. Still, teachers make some decisions about time only after planning and reflection.

Some research suggests that teachers allocate time to various subjects partly on the basis of their attitudes toward subject matter. Schmidt and Buchmann (1983) found that teachers who enjoyed teaching reading more than writing tended to stress reading over language arts instruction and that teachers who enjoyed mathematics more than social studies allocated more time to mathematics. Indeed, the teachers who enjoyed teaching mathematics spent over *50 percent* more time teaching math than teachers who did not. Thus, in addition to making teachers aware of how they spend time, it may also be necessary to alter teachers' knowledge of, and attitudes toward, subject matter so that they feel comfortable teaching all subjects.

Attitudes teachers held towards various subjects (e.g., importance, ability to teach it) were associated with how teachers used time in the classroom. Table 2.1 shows how much time teachers actually allocated to particular subject areas. As Schmidt and Buchmann note, these data suggest that teachers' judgments about content emphases and enjoyment of teaching a subject account for some of the variation in how time is allocated to subjects.

Table 2.1   TEACHERS' TIME ALLOCATIONS (IN MINUTES) TO DIFFERENT SUBJECT MATTER AREAS

Teacher	Reading	Mathematics	Language arts	Science	Social studies
A	67.4	43.7	53.7	2.0	2.4
B	50.6	29.1	48.1	6.7	13.3
C	80.3	32.0	25.3	43.2	43.2
D	95.5	49.9	41.1	10.6	6.0
E	32.0	30.6	46.5	25.7	30.5
F	26.5	34.6	72.0	3.7	26.5

Note. Figures given are the average number of minutes spent in each subject matter area by the typical child on the typical day for each individual teacher.

Source: Schmidt, W., & Buchmann, M. (1983). Six teachers' beliefs and attitudes and their curricular time allocations. *Elementary School Journal, 84,* 162–172.

OTHER FACTORS THAT INFLUENCE ACHIEVEMENT

Teachers' allocation of classroom time to different subject-matter areas is just one factor determining student learning. Student opportunity to learn is another factor. Different teachers teaching obstensibly the same curriculum will present varied information, assignments, and activities to their students, so that even where time allocation is equal, students will be exposed to different information and learning opportunities for good or ill. Much of this will occur as a result of conscious decision making by teachers, but some of it also will occur without teacher awareness. Brophy (1982) argues that teachers play a key role in determining the curriculum that students actually receive even where clear curriculum guidelines and adopted materials are in place, and that this enacted curriculum is further modified by the students themselves when their efforts to make sense of what they are learning cause them to interpret information differently from the way that the teacher intended (see Figure 2.1).

Many school districts use standardized *achievement tests* that are poorly matched to textbooks or to the instructional approach of a particular teacher (see Freeman et al., 1983, for a discussion of the relationship between various standardized mathematics achievement tests and five textbook series). Hence, it is possible to find high academic learning time and apparently poor achievement in the same class because the test used is dissimilar to the curriculum and instruction that students receive. Clearly, unless the curriculum and the test are aligned, incorrect conclusions are likely to be drawn about the effects of schooling. In our opinion, curriculum goals should determine the test used and not vice versa.

Related problems occur when curriculum materials that teachers assign are inappropriate for students. Jorgenson (1978) reports that in some classes 85 percent of students used learning materials that were too difficult. Teachers probably were unaware of this mismatch or of its deleterious effects on students' motivation to learn. Problem recognition must precede improvement efforts (e.g., Wyne & Stuck, 1982).

Pull-Out Instruction

We have argued that time allocations may appear to be satisfactory but may not characterize effective learning if either the curriculum or the evaluation is inappropriate. We have seen that attempts to improve student achievement by allocating more time may not work in a given classroom if quality of time is not considered. Furthermore, increased instructional time (e.g., extra time for reading and mathematics) may not produce more learning for students if the additional time is not carefully planned and coordinated. If the regular classroom teacher is not aware of what happens in other settings (e.g., assignments, behavior management strategies), extra teaching may be of limited value.

Ironically, some students may receive less and/or inappropriate instruction when schools attempt to provide them with extra assistance. Hill and Kimbrough (1981) studied pull-out instruction programs (students are taken out of their regular classes for supplementary instruction) and found that such programs posed problems for students who received special assistance as well as for regular teachers. In some schools, children were out of classes for categorical programs so frequently

1. The official curriculum (A) is adopted at the state or district level.

2. Local (school level) changes are introduced by the principal or a committee of teachers. These include both deletions (A_0) from and additions (B) to the official curriculum (A).

3. This yields the school level curriculum (C) adopted unofficially but formally within each school ($C = A + B - A_0$).

4. Each teacher further alters the school level curriculum (C) by making additional deletions (C_0) and additions (D), based on personal preferences and beliefs about student needs.

5. This yields each individual teacher's intended curriculum (E) ($E = C + D - C_0$), which differs from both the official (A) and unofficial (B) adopted curricula.

6. In the process of teaching the intended curriculum (E), however, teachers make further deletions (E_0) due to time constraints, and also teach some parts in distorted or incorrect fashion (F), so that students are exposed to misleading or incorrect information.

7. Of the material that is actually taught to the students, whether correctly (E), or incorrectly (F), some will be learned and retained in the form in which it was taught (E_1, F_1), some will be taught too briefly or vaguely to allow learning retention (E_2, F_2), and some will be distorted by students as they filter it through erroneous preconceptions (E_3, F_3). Of these subsets, only E_1 represents successful teaching of the intended curriculum (E).

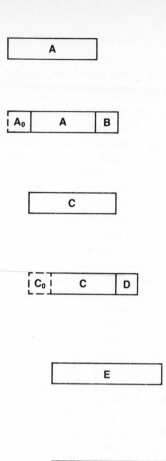

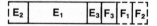

Figure 2.1 The transformation of content from curriculum adoption through teaching to learning. (*Source:* From Brophy, J. (1982). How teachers influence what is taught and learned in classrooms. *Elementary School Journal, 83,* 1–14.)

that teachers had their total classes only one and a half hours daily and therefore were unable to implement the state-mandated curriculum. Fragmented instruction was especially a problem for Hispanic students because they qualified for so many special programs (six or seven daily!). Indeed, even though the Hispanic students had attended school for five years, many had received *no* formal instruction in science or social studies. Special programs were *replacing,* not supplementing, the core curriculum for many students.

Students who received both regular and supplemental instruction were still not well-served. Hill and Kimbrough found that in several cases incompatible teaching *methods* and *materials* were used in special and regular classrooms. Many children became confused by conflicting approaches taken by special and regular teachers. Conceptual learning would be especially difficult for students who receive conflicting information (i.e., it is hard enough to learn about fractions without being taught conflicting conceptualizations at the same time).

The disruptive effects of pull-out instruction and other "outside intrusions" are described in one class in an ethnographic study by Florio (1978, pp. 145–148):

> Ms. Wright's classroom presents evidence of the gradual establishment of contextual expectations among children even during events like worktime in which the constituent contexts are not discussed by participants. As has been suggested above, the expectations are most visible when they are violated. Recall, for example, that Ms. Wright's class exists within a Title I school where there are many opportunities for tutorial help and enrichment outside regular class activities. Children come and go from the room with great frequency and in large numbers for bilingual class, remedial reading and math, speech and physical therapy. At first glance such comings and goings would not appear to disrupt an event which is as "open" as worktime. However, we now know enough about the subtle, complex organization of worktime to recognize that it can, indeed, be interrupted. The teacher's resistance to interruption and what happens when interruption occurs serve to illustrate the contextual expectations that teacher and children come to share in the course of a year of worktimes.
>
> > Worktime was interrupted this morning by a trip to a bake sale held by some older children in another part of the school. Ms. Wright mentioned the bake sale during the first circle. However, at 9:40, while the children were engaged in working activities, Ms. Wright attempted to call everyone together to get their money and leave for the bake sale. She said, "All right, would everyone go and sit on the rug for a sec?" At this point some children did go to the rug, but many did not. They began to clean up instead, even though their activities had barely gotten started. Ms. Wright had to remind them that they would be returning to worktime after they had finished visiting the bake sale (Field Notes, 10/21/75).
>
> On another day, an anticipated interruption of worktime made it difficult for the children to become focused on their worktime tasks. Although the teacher does not talk about worktime having a focused time, she lamented its absence explicitly on this day:
>
> > Today, the teacher and children knew in advance that their worktimes would be interrupted by a trip to the auditorium where class photographs would be taken. They were informed by the principal that he would call over the public address system when the photographer was ready for them. The children had come to school dressed for the occasion. They were reminded by Ms.

Wright that, since they were dressed in good clothes, they should be careful during worktime. As a result, worktime was physically subdued. It appeared that the impending interruption of worktime was making it difficult for Ms. Wright and the children to focus on activities and to get involved in them. The level of ambient noise was high, and there was a lot of wandering. Finally, in an exasperated tone of voice, Ms. Wright said, "I wish I knew what time they're gonna do this so I could *plan* something!" (Field Notes, 3/5/76).

Finally, even when the special activity which will interrupt worktime occurs right in the classroom, it is potentially troublesome. The following incident is an example:

> A math tutor whom Ms. Wright had never met came in during worktime today to announce that several students would be receiving extra help in the room during two mornings each week. Ms. Wright, who has frequently voiced objection to the removal of so many of her students to work with specialists at the expense of their opportunity to engage in activities with their own teacher and classmates, was likewise resistant to the idea of in-class help. Although the math tutor said, "I've worked in open classrooms before, it will be no problem!" Ms. Wright disagreed. She cited the following objections:
>
> (1) it would be "too noisy and distracting" for the special students as well as for the rest of the class;
> (2) it would be "breaking up [her] time" with the class;
> (3) she said, in concluding, "I know Clarice [the school psychologist] wants people in the room, but. . . ."
>
> The tutor recalled the initial objections of other teachers, but insisted that "open classrooms" posed no such problems. Ms. Wright reiterated that there were times of the day which "shouldn't be interrupted." They adjourned having decided that the children would be tutored out of the room and at a more opportune time. Ms. Wright, however, told me that she was determined to take the matter "to the office" (Field Notes, 11/18/75).

Given what we know about the organization of worktime, we can understand Ms. Wright's objections. They are not instances of arbitrary resistance to the tutor's help. We see that Ms. Wright is attempting to protect the integrity of an important interactional event in her room, an event which she and the children are managing as a series of contexts about which there are shared expectations. To preserve worktime as it has come to be known by the students, she must insure that the contexts through which children pass in its course continue to exist. Personnel and social relations as well as activity in physical space play important roles in the nature of those contexts.

HOW STUDENTS AFFECT TEACHERS

The way students present themselves to teachers may make teaching decisions more difficult. Spencer-Hall (1981) illustrated in an ethnographic study that some students are much better at impression management than others. These students were better able to maintain a favorable evaluation by teachers and peers because they misbehaved in ways that escaped the teacher's attention. One student was selected by teachers at the end of the school year for a good citizenship award, despite the fact that the student had often engaged in disruptive behavior when teachers were nearby.

She notes that some pupils were adept at misbehaving when the teacher had her back turned but were capable of looking appropriately involved when the teacher was monitoring classroom behavior. She noted that these same students were occasionally caught when their misbehavior became so absorbing that they forgot to continue looking for the teacher's movement. However, when caught, they were likely to grin, giggle, or show embarrassment rather than to appear indifferent or defiant. Consequently, they continued to be perceived by the teacher as cooperative, but subject to an occasional lapse into understandable childish behavior.

There are many clinical examples of the influence of individual students or classes of students on teachers and on classroom procedures. Most students and teachers are aware of students who have successfully manipulated their instructors into giving them extra time and help. One of our favorite examples was provided by Myron Dembo (personal communication). As a teacher at the University of Southern California, he talks frequently with students about influence strategies that they use. He reports that the key aspect of successful manipulation by one student to get *extra time* involved contacting instructors and requesting permission to take exams *early* (due to a supposed conflict). Instructors typically preferred (for purposes of test security) that she take the exam late, however, and often gave her the same exam that was given to the class. Hence, she often received extra time and knew the test content. Furthermore, instructors often viewed the student favorably because of her "willingness" to take the exam early.

Some students appear more interested in class discussions and may be more likely to get a clue or a second chance than students who seem to be less attentive. Students' self-presentations and worksheets may therefore lead teachers to make erroneous assumptions about students' knowledge and motivation, especially when teachers have to make rapid decisions in a complex classroom setting.

Carter and Doyle (1982) provide an excellent example of how a teacher and students mutually influenced one another during a writing assignment in a junior high language arts class. When the teacher's lesson was a familiar one (e.g., a grammar lesson), the class moved in a smooth and predictable fashion; however, when the class focused on writing, work periods were slow to begin and were frequently interrupted by student-initiated questions about requirements and procedures.

According to Carter and Doyle, much of the students' behavior during complex writing tasks was directed at trying to get more information from the teacher about what an acceptable product would be. Some of the more sophisticated student attempts to get teachers to give more exact information about a good piece of work included:

1. "Trying out" answers for assignments, to get teacher reactions
2. "Guessing" to elicit prompts from the teacher
3. Responding incorrectly, to secure answers from the teacher
4. Bringing work in progress to the teacher for suggestions and corrections
5. Bargaining as a group for information about accomplishing a task
6. "Contracting" with one student (with a history of success) to get answers from the teacher

Their research suggests that when some students are asked to make new and somewhat unpredictable responses, they will attempt to make the assignment more routine and more predictable.

Students' Reactions to Classroom Tasks

In earlier work, Doyle (1979a; 1979b; 1980) argues that various class assignments or academic tasks are associated with different levels of ambiguity and risk. Memory tasks (e.g., What happened in 1588? What is the product of 9 × 8?) are low in ambiguity because answers are known to students in advance. On the other hand, students must construct rather than simply reproduce answers for tasks that involve understanding.

Risk refers to the likelihood that students will be able to produce an answer on a given occasion. Although memory tasks are typically low in ambiguity, they can be high or low in risk, depending on the amount of information to be recalled. Academic tasks that require understanding are at least moderately high in ambiguity and tend to be high in risk. Carter and Doyle point out that this is because the precise answer cannot be predicted in advance and the constructive process is problematic. They also note that an accountability system has to be operating for risk to be an important variable. That is, if a teacher accepts any answer, then there is no risk. The work of Doyle (1979a) and Carter and Doyle (1982) illustrates that students tend to work to reduce risk and ambiguity.

Carter and Doyle's study also demonstrates the powerful influence of the teacher's grading system on classroom behavior. They write (1982):

> Many of the teacher's comments on graded writing assignments were directed to grammar and mechanics and grades for those aspects of written work were typically lower than those for content. In turn, students' questions most often focused on mechanics and grammar elements while most of the teacher's instructions and suggestions about content were ignored. In other words, grammar actually carried more weight in writing assignments (although this policy was not explicitly stated by the teacher) and students directed their efforts to this facet of the task.

We suspect that teachers often make decisions and behave in ways that they do not intend because of students' responses to classroom realities. It appears that teachers do not perceive some student influences on their behavior.

Students' Reports of Their Classroom Experiences

It is important to realize that there are multiple perspectives for viewing classroom life and these viewpoints are often strikingly different. Sometimes it is easy to believe that a discrepancy between a classroom observer's viewpoint and the teacher's viewpoint indicates a weakness on the part of the teacher. However, observers can be wrong and can draw inappropriate conclusions about what occurs in classrooms (more on this in Chapter 3).

Also, it is clear that students often see things differently than their teacher does, so there are multiple interpretations of what is taking place in the classroom. For example, Peterson and Swing (1982) studied the relationships among student thought processes, time on task, and subsequent classroom achievement. These investigators reported that students' descriptions of their attention (active listening) to teacher presentations were better predictors of achievement than were observers' ratings of students' time on task during teacher presentations. Interestingly, observer reports of student attending behaviors were not related to students' self-reports of attention. Similarly, Weinstein and Middlestadt (1979), Weinstein (1982), and Rohrkemper (1985) have demonstrated the utility of getting information from students. As Rohrkemper (1985) argues, information describing how students actively process and interpret their experiences in the classroom is a prerequisite to accurate interpretation of observed classroom interactions (more on this will appear in Chapter 3 where we present ideas for conducting case studies of students).

Communication With Parents

Clearly, what students do at home (Do they have difficulty completing assigned homework?) is an important source of information that may help teachers to understand student performance more fully. A full discussion of issues related to parent involvement in school activities is beyond the scope of this book (for discussion see Becker & Epstein, 1982; Epstein & Becker, 1982). However, it is clear that some teachers have more access to parents and have better skills in working out collaborative arrangements with parents. Hence, some teachers have access to more resources for understanding student behavior. Some of the variation in teachers' use of parents is suggested by Figure 2.2 taken from Becker and Epstein (1982). Teachers' beliefs about parents' influence, how teachers interact with parents, and what they request of parents ultimately affect teachers' awareness of individual students.

WHY TEACHERS ARE UNAWARE

We have discussed certain behaviors teachers engage in without full awareness, and also noted that teachers are aware of their behavior but not of its effects. We believe that teachers' lack of awareness about what they do or the effects of their behavior lessens their classroom effectiveness. In this section, we want to discuss some of the reasons why teachers are unaware of certain aspects of their behavior (or that of students) and of other factors associated with classroom learning (e.g., the readability of materials).

The most fundamental factor making it difficult for teachers to assess classroom behavior is that so much happens so rapidly that they cannot be aware of everything they do. This problem can be solved in part through training. Awareness of everything that occurs is impossible, but with practice teachers can become more aware of their classroom behavior.

A second factor limiting teachers' awareness is that teacher training programs seldom equip teachers with specific teaching techniques or provide them with skills for analyzing and labeling classroom behavior. Too often they give teachers global advice (e.g., treat the whole child, individualize instruction) without linking it to specific behaviors. Although many teacher education programs have begun to stress teachers' ability to examine specific behaviors, many others still do not. Most inservice teachers are not able to describe accurately what occurs in their classrooms. *Conceptual labels* are powerful tools for helping us to be aware of what we do. For example, the Brophy and Good (1970) study reported that teachers gave up on low-achieving students who had difficulty responding to questions. However, the teachers did not view their behavior as giving up. Rather, they said they were

Evaluation Categories:

Unrealistic to expect parent cooperation

No support

Parents do not have sufficient skills

Workable, but did not use this year

Passive support

Used a few times this year

Used *many times* this year

Active support

The *most satisfying* parent involvement technique

ACTIVITIES EMPHASIZING READING

Ask parents to read to their child regularly or to listen to the child read aloud.

Loan books, workbooks, etc. to a parent to keep at home for short periods as extra learning material.

Ask parents to take their child to the library.

LEARNING THROUGH DISCUSSION

Ask parents to get their child to talk about what he/she did that day in your classroom.

Give an assignment that requires the children to ask their parents questions – for example, that children write about their parent's experiences.

Ask parents (one or more) to watch a specific television program with their child and to discuss the show afterwards.

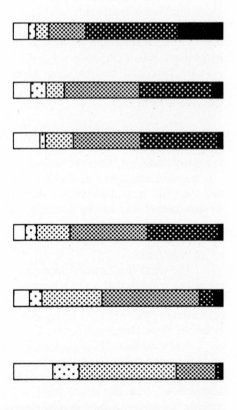

Figure 2.2 Fourteen techniques for involving parents in teaching activities at home — evaluations by Maryland teachers. (*Source:* From Becker, H., & Epstein, J. (1982). Parent involvement: A survey of teacher practices. *Elementary School Journal, 83,* 85–102.)

INFORMAL LEARNING ACTIVITIES AT HOME

Suggest ways for parents to incorporate their child into their own activities at home that would be educationally enriching.

Send home suggestions for game or group activities related to the child's schoolwork that can be played by parent and child.

Suggest how parents might use the home environment (materials and activities of daily life) to stimulate their child's interest in reading, math, etc.

CONTRACTS BETWEEN TEACHER AND PARENT

Establish a formal agreement where the parent supervises and assists the child in completing homework tasks.

Establish a formal agreement where the child provides rewards and/or penalties based on the child's school performance or behavior.

DEVELOPING TEACHING AND EVALUATION SKILLS IN PARENTS

Ask parents to come to *observe* the classroom (not to "help") for part of a day.

Explain to parents certain techniques for teaching, for making learning materials, or for planning lessons.

Give a questionnaire to parents so they can evaluate their child's progress, or provide some other "feedback" to you.

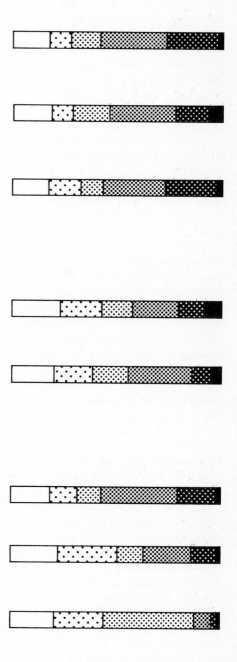

Figure 2.2 *(Continued)*

embarrassed by the silence, they thought that the students were embarrassed, or they wanted to keep the discussion moving. Similarly, we suspect that teachers in the Rowe (1969) study did not realize that they were giving low-achieving students less time to respond and thereby making a response more difficult, and that teachers in the Leinhardt, Seewald, and Engel (1979) study were not aware of their differential behavior toward male and female students.

These findings suggest that teacher training institutions and in-service programs in schools have not given teachers ways of labeling and monitoring their behavior. This is not to say that teachers should never give up on students in recitation sequences, for there are times when it is appropriate to move on. However, teachers should be aware that they are giving up and should know how often they do this with low-achieving students. Otherwise, they will teach such students that the easiest way of reacting to a teacher's question is to make no response.

Similarly, teachers should know the alternative responses they can make when students make no response or respond incorrectly: providing clues, probing, asking a simpler question, repeating the question, and so forth. Teachers can learn alternative responses if they are trained to identify and label specific teaching situations and the skills that can be used in responding to these situations. Being able to label teaching skills and concepts helps teachers to be more aware of what they do in the classroom and to respond appropriately (see, e.g., Pambookian, 1976).

A third obstacle to awareness is that there is no formal, useful system of providing teachers with information about what they do. Pambookian (1976) and McNeil (1971) point out that teachers are most likely to change when provided with information that shows a discrepancy between what they want to do and what they are doing. Teachers are unlikely to get this information unless they meet with their supervisors several times during the year or have the chance to observe in other classrooms and to exchange information with fellow teachers. However, teachers rarely see their supervisors. A survey by the National Education Association reveals that only 34 percent of secondary teachers in the United States are observed even once during the year for a period of 5 minutes or longer. The median number of observational visits in secondary schools is one and the median in elementary schools is two, and only half of these visits are followed by a conference (McNeil, 1971). Unless they have unusual principals or supervisors, teachers seldom receive direct, useful feedback about their teaching.

Fortunately, as we shall see in Chapter 12, change is beginning to occur in some school districts; however, increased principal classroom visitation is typically more for purposes of evaluating teaching than it is for helping teachers to become more aware of their behavior or to improve instruction. Evaluation must occur, but we believe that teachers need information about what they are doing and suggestions for improvement as well (more on this in Chapter 11).

Under the present supervisory structure of schools, teachers may view feedback from supervisors with suspicion and hostility. Teachers usually know that supervisors' ratings are unreliable. Also, teachers' most frequent disagreements with supervisors are over goals (McNeil, 1971). Tuckman and Oliver (1968) found that teacher behavior was not substantially changed by feedback from supervisors. In fact, when supervisor feedback was the only information teachers received, they changed their behavior in the direction opposite to that suggested by the supervisor. Feedback from students, though, had a positive effect. Apparently, the *source* of advice and the *basis* on which it is given are of concern to teachers. If teachers feel that supervisors do not spend enough time in the classroom to assess their behaviors adequately, employ vague or irrelevant criteria, or lack the necessary subject matter knowledge, teachers may reject supervisors' advice.

Although some school districts have increased the opportunity for teachers to be observed by helpful supervisors and for teachers to observe one another and to exchange valuable information, in too many instances observation is evaluative in nature and fails to stimulate collegial exchange. Freedman, Jackson, and Boles (1983, p. 271) lament the fact that feedback, when it is provided, tends to focus on problems. "Rather than working on problems together, teachers—and pupils—are labeled, categorized, and divided. . . ."

Interestingly, there is reason to believe that teachers value and want more frequent communication and feedback about their performance in the classroom, particularly when teachers have had some ability to affect the criteria for evaluation. Indeed, one of the sources of teacher dissatisfaction is infrequency of evaluation (see, for example, Natriello & Dornbusch, 1980–1981; Wise et al., 1985).

Considering the recent interest in making teaching more of a profession and in creating master teachers (Griffin, 1985) and career ladders (Rosenholtz & Smylie, 1984), we hope that in the next few years there will be a significant increase in opportunities for teachers to obtain useful feedback (see Chapter 12 for an extended discussion).

Student Teachers

Student teachers in university training programs also seldom receive direct, useful feedback. In the following account, Medley (quoted in Burkhart, 1969) describes one supervisor's technique for providing a student teacher with information. Although the example may be extreme, it does suggest what we suspect to be a frequent problem in training programs: Candidates do not learn specific teaching skills or a conceptual language for describing classroom behavior.

> This particular woman said, "Well, I didn't say anything to the student teacher because this is a very sensitive area. But when she did something that was particularly bad, I looked at her, and she understood." . . . we also interviewed the students, and believe it or not, one of the students said, "Well, Mrs. So-and-so didn't talk much. We just looked at this film, and when there was something that I had done particularly well, she looked at me, and I knew."

In this same source, Medley also reports findings about the classroom behavior of student teachers. His major conclusion was that supervision and video feedback, as implemented in his study, had no effect on student teachers' behavior. Students and supervisors did not talk about *specific* behavior of mutual interest. He writes:

> The most important substantive finding is that the seminal problem in improving teaching may be perceptual in nature; that the key to helping teachers change their behavior may lie in helping them to see behavior—see what they themselves, and others as well, are doing.

Ironically, many student teachers fail to receive meaningful feedback about their teaching even though they are presumably learning how to teach and feedback is widely acknowledged as being critical to any learning! For example, Griffin (1983) found that during supervisory interactions there was little attention paid to developing a knowledge base that would help student teachers subsequently when they had their own classrooms. Supervisory interactions focused in large measure on immediate, specific issues and a "let's see if this works" style of offering suggestions. Unfortunately, a rationale for practice typically was not provided and there were few references to learning theory, child development, instructional models, etc.

Griffin (1983) notes that supervisory interactions were dominated by the cooperating teacher, who selected the topics for conversation and controlled how those topics were discussed. Conversations usually focused on a particular classroom at a certain time; they seldom considered alternate ways to understand and respond to classroom events.

Feedback to Teachers About Classroom Behavior

Typically, there are only three ways teachers can obtain systematic and reasonably reliable feedback about their behavior:

1. Certain information can be collected from students. This alternative is not very useful for primary-grade teachers, however, because young children are not capable of providing complex feedback. Intermediate-level students in elementary schools and secondary students can provide useful feedback, and teachers should seek their opinions.
2. Fellow teachers can be asked to observe and code behavior during a free period. This source of feedback presupposes, of course, that fellow teachers have a free period and have the necessary observation skills. A strategy for creating reciprocal visits and exchanging information is provided in the last chapter of this book.
3. Teachers can develop a conceptual system for labeling their own behavior.

The ability to describe one's own behavior heightens awareness of behavior as it unfolds in the classroom. A conceptual system allows teachers to classify what they are doing as they do it, making it possible for them to be aware of what they do and to remember how they have behaved. Many school districts now have video equipment so that teachers can see themselves in action. At first glance, videotaping seemed like a real learning aid—what better way for teachers to improve than to see themselves as others do? Unfortunately, studies report that after teachers have viewed tapes, the changes in their teaching behavior are not very impressive.

Seeing a film of oneself teaching is like sitting in a classroom watching another teacher. The behavior on the film is still rapid and complex. If teachers do not know what to look for, they will not see very much. Research demonstrates, however, that when teachers view tapes with a consultant who can provide specific feedback or with materials describing what to look for, positive change occurs. If used appropriately, videotapes can help teachers to analyze and improve their behavior. Reviews of the literature on the use of video and audiotape in helping teachers to improve their classroom behavior conclude that such materials are effective only if specific teaching behaviors are highlighted and discussed (Fuller & Manning, 1973).

The terms *conceptual* and *observational tools* refer to a descriptive vocabulary. Every social organization, game, or system has a language of its own. Some are simple; others, like the language of the classroom, are complex. For example, bridge has a unique descriptive vocabulary, as does football. Persons who do not understand such terms as "three no-trump" or "first down" cannot understand the games. We want to make teachers more familiar with the language of the classroom so that they will be able to describe and understand what they do there.

In this book we will present many research findings and concepts. We hope this information will encourage you to look more closely at classroom teaching and to respect the complexity and difficulty of effective classroom teaching. In this chapter we have discussed some of the complexities of classroom life and have suggested a few types of classroom behavior that teachers may be unaware of.

Although we believe that it is possible for teachers to improve their awareness of classroom behavior, to develop improved instructional techniques, and to instruct students more effectively, we do not believe that there are any simple ways to do this. Good teaching takes study, practice, and dedication. One way to become a better teacher is to develop a way of looking at and thinking about classroom behavior.

To repeat, research findings and concepts provide a way of thinking about classroom instruction, but they are not rules for classroom behavior. A good example of the need to use classroom research findings as tools rather than as answers can be seen in Adams and Biddle's (1970) discussion of the "action zone." As noted earlier in the chapter, they found that students who sat in the middle-front-row seats and in seats extending directly up the middle aisle received more opportunities to talk in class than did other students. We view the action zone as an exciting concept that provides a useful way for identifying possible problems in the classroom. Adams and Biddle's work suggests that there may be areas of a classroom where students receive more response opportunities than do students in other areas. However, if interpreted too literally, the work of Adams and Biddle would suggest that teachers and/or classroom observers should pay most attention to what takes place in the front row and the middle of the class.

Recent data collected by Alhajri (1981) show the utility of viewing the action zone as a concept rather than as a generalized phenomenon. In 32 classrooms, Alhajri found only one class that had an action zone like that described by Adams and Biddle; on the other hand, some kind of action zone was present in many classrooms. If observers or teachers were monitoring classes only for one type of action zone, they would not have perceived the zones that took a different form.

We discuss research findings in order to present concepts that enable teachers to examine classrooms. Research results do not provide answers because they must be applied to particular classrooms and individual teachers and students. We believe that research concepts can enable educators rapidly to observe more behaviors. For example, as we noted earlier, Rowe (1969) found that teachers wait longer for students believed to be more capable to respond than they do for students believed to be less able. The concept of wait-time not only allows us to be more aware of one aspect of classroom behavior (i.e., How long will the teacher wait for a student to respond?), but also encourages us to consider types of teacher and student communication that were not part of the original research (e.g., Is the teacher more likely to accept the "excuse" of a student believed to be a high achiever by allowing an extension of an assignment while denying similar opportunities to students believed to be less capable? Can we wait too long as well as too briefly for students to respond?).

SUMMARY

In this chapter we have argued that teachers are not aware of everything that goes on in the classroom and that this lack of awareness may interfere with their effectiveness. This problem exists for at least three basic reasons:

1. Teacher preservice and in-service training programs spend too little time training teachers to perform specific behaviors or to describe specific teaching behaviors.
2. Classrooms are busy places, and teachers (and students as well) are so busy responding that they have little time to think about what they are doing. The chapter lists some of the factors that contribute to classroom complexity.
3. Teachers are seldom observed on any systematic basis. Consequently, they seldom get valuable information about ways to increase their effectiveness, and when they are observed it is typically for purposes of evaluation.

Teaching is more likely to be effective if teachers' goals and classroom behavior are in agreement. We have suggested that often there is a gap between what teachers do and what they think they do or want to do. There is no such thing as one appropriate teaching style. The correctness of any teaching style depends on the objectives of the learning exercise and to some extent on the personality of the teacher and the characteristics of the students themselves.

We have posited that teachers need to develop skills for examining classroom behavior. Preservice teachers also need insight into their own behavior when they do practice observations and student teaching. A major goal of this book is to help teachers acquire a language for describing behavior and develop new ways of structuring classroom learning experiences.

SUGGESTED ACTIVITIES AND QUESTIONS

2.1. Read one of the Classroom Narratives that appear in the Appendix at the end of the book. What are the relative teaching strengths and weaknesses represented? If you could make three suggestions to improve the teacher's behavior, what would they be? Why? To what extent do you think this teacher is aware of classroom behavior? If you could interview the teacher and students in that class, which three or four questions would you ask? Why?

2.2. After reading this chapter, do you have any questions about the ideas, facts, or concepts presented? Are there topics that you would like more information about? If so, write two or three questions of your own and turn them in to your instructor for feedback, or trade questions with fellow teachers or students.

2.3. The chapter has stressed that sometimes teachers are not aware of all of their classroom behaviors. When you teach (whether micro, simulated, or real), attempt to monitor your teaching behavior (e.g., the ratio of fact to thought questions) and see how your mental record compares with the actual record taken by a coder (a classroom observer) and with what you hear when you play back your tape-recorded lesson. Practice monitoring your behavior, listening to what you say as you teach, and comparing your mental list with objectively recorded lists. Most of us find it difficult to monitor our teaching behavior initially (we are so busy thinking about what we will ask next that we do not hear completely what we say), but improvement comes with practice.

2.4. Give two examples to illustrate how a teacher's lack of awareness about what he or she does in the classroom might result in inefficient or self-defeating behavior.

2.5. How can teachers improve their ability to see behavior in classrooms?

2.6. When entering a classroom, why is it important that an observer have a conceptual system for describing behavior and for noticing significant occurrences?

2.7. Describe the potential ill effects of placing students in learning groups on the basis of achievement or intelligence test scores. What possible advantages can be gained by grouping students?

2.8. Teachers obviously want low-achieving students to do well, but some low-achieving students receive less teacher contact and help than high achievers. How could teachers improve their interaction patterns with low achievers without reducing their effectiveness with other students?

2.9. Why is the use of video equipment (allowing teachers to see themselves teach) relatively ineffective unless it is combined with specific directions concerning what to look for or descriptions of what took place?

REFERENCES

Adams, R., & Biddle, B. (1970). *Realities of teaching: Explorations with video tape*. New York: Holt, Rinehart and Winston.

Alhajri, A. (1981). *Effect of seat position on school performance of Kuwaiti students*. Unpublished doctoral dissertation. Columbia: University of Missouri.

Anderson, L., Brubaker, N., Alleman-Brooks, J., & Duffy, G. (1985). A qualitative study of seatwork in first-grade classrooms. *Elementary School Journal, 86,* 123–140.

Anderson-Levitt, K. (1984). Teacher interpretation of student behavior: Cognitive and social processes. *Elementary School Journal, 84,* 315–337.

Becker, H., & Epstein, J. (1982). Parent involvement: A survey of teacher practices. *Elementary School Journal, 83,* 85–102.

Berliner, D. (1979). Tempus educare. In P. Peterson & H. Walberg (Eds.), *Research on teaching: Concepts, findings, and implications*. Berkeley, CA: McCutchan.

Borg, W., Kelley, M., Langer, P., & Gall, M. (1970). *The mini-course: A micro-teaching approach to teacher education*. Beverly Hills, CA: Macmillan Educational Services.

Bossert, S. (1981). Understanding sex differences in children's classroom experiences. *Elementary School Journal, 81,* 255–268.

Brophy, J. (1982). How teachers influence what is taught and learned in classrooms. *Elementary School Journal, 83,* 1–14.

Brophy, J., Evertson, C., Anderson, L., Baum, M., & Crawford, J. (1981). *Student characteristics and teaching*. New York: Longman.

Brophy, J., & Good, T. (1970). Teachers' communication of differential expectations for children's classroom performance: Some behavioral data. *Journal of Educational Psychology, 61,* 365–374.

Brophy, J., & Good, T. (1974). *Teacher-student relationships: Causes and consequences*. New York: Holt, Rinehart and Winston.

Brophy, J., & Kher, N. (1986). Teacher socialization as a mechanism for developing student motivation to learn. In R. Feldman (Ed.), *Social psychology applied to education.* New York: Cambridge University Press.

Burkhart, R. (Ed.). (1969). *The assessment revolution: New viewpoints for teacher evaluation.* National symposium on evaluation in education. New York State Education Department and Buffalo State University College.

Caldwell, J., Huitt, W., & Graeber, A. (1982). Time spent in learning: Implications from research. *Elementary School Journal, 82,* 471–480.

Carew, J., & Lightfoot, S. (1979). *Beyond bias.* Cambridge, MA: Harvard University Press.

Carter, K., & Doyle, W. (1982). Variations in academic tasks in high and average ability classes. Paper presented at the annual meeting of the American Educational Research Association, New York.

Channon, G. (1970). *Homework.* New York: Outerbridge and Dienstfrey.

Cooper, H., & Good, T. (1983). *Pygmalion grows up: Studies in the expectation communication process.* New York: Longman.

Cuban, L. (1984). *How teachers taught: Constancy and change in American classrooms 1890–1980.* New York: Longman.

Dembo, M. (personal communication).

Doyle, W. (1979a). Classroom tasks and students' abilities. In P. Peterson & H. Walberg (Eds.), *Research on teaching: Concepts, findings, and implications.* Berkeley, CA: McCutchan.

Doyle, W. (1979b). *The tasks of teaching and learning in classrooms.* Report No. 4103, Research and Development Center for Teacher Education, University of Texas at Austin.

Doyle, W. (1980). *Student mediating responses in teaching effectiveness.* Final report of National Institute of Education Grant NIE-G-76-0099. North Texas State University, Denton.

Durkin, D. (1978–1979). What classroom observations reveal about reading comprehension instruction. *Reading Research Quarterly, 14,* 481–533.

Ebmeier, H., & Ziomek, R. (1983). *Student academic engagement rates.* Final report of National Institute of Education Grant NIE-G-0-0892. Wheaton, Illinois Public Schools.

Eccles, J., & Blumenfeld, P. (1985). Classroom experiences and student gender: Are there differences and do they matter? In L. Wilkinson & C. Marrett (Eds.), *Gender influences in classroom interaction.* New York: Academic Press.

Emmer, E. (1967). *The effect of teacher use of student ideas on student verbal initiation.* Unpublished doctoral dissertation. Ann Arbor: University of Michigan.

Epstein, J., & Becker, H. (1982). Teachers' reported practices of parent involvement: Problems and possibilities. *Elementary School Journal, 83,* 103–114.

Evertson, C., Emmer, E., & Brophy, J. (1980). Predictors of effective teaching in junior high mathematics classrooms. *Journal of Research in Mathematics Education, 11,* 167–178.

Fennema, E., & Peterson, P. (1985). Autonomous learning behavior: A possible explanation of gender-related differences in mathematics. In L. Wilkinson & C. Marrett (Eds.), *Gender influences in classroom interaction.* New York: Academic Press.

Fisher, C., Filby, N., Marliave, R., Cahen, L., Dishaw, M., Moore, J., & Berliner, D. (1978). *Teaching behaviors, academic learning time, and student achievement.* Final report of Phase III-B Beginning Teacher Evaluation Study. San Francisco: Far West Laboratory for Educational Research and Development.

Florio, S. (1978). *Learning how to go to school: An ethnography of interaction in a kindergarten-first-grade classroom.* Unpublished doctoral dissertation, Cambridge, MA: Harvard University.

Freedman, S., Jackson, J., & Boles, K. (1983). Teaching: An imperilled "profession." In L. Shulman & G. Sykes (Eds.), *Handbook of teaching and policy*. New York: Longman.

Freeman, D., Kuhs, T., Porter, A., Floden, R., Schmidt, W., & Schwille, J. (1983). Do textbooks and tests define a national curriculum in elementary school mathematics? *Elementary School Journal, 83,* 501–513.

Fuller, F., & Manning, B. (1973). Self-confrontation review: A conceptualization for video playback in teacher education. *Review of Educational Research, 43,* 469–528.

Good, T., & Brophy, J. (1974). Changing teacher and student behavior: An empirical investigation. *Journal of Educational Psychology, 66,* 390–405.

Good, T., & Brophy, J. (1986). *Educational psychology: A realistic approach* (3rd ed.). White Plains, NY: Longman.

Good, T., & Findley, M. (1985). Sex role expectations in achievement. In J. Dusek (Ed.), *Teacher Expectations*. Hillsdale, NJ: Erlbaum.

Good, T., Grouws, D., & Ebmeier, H. (1983). *Active mathematics teaching: Empirical research in elementary and secondary classrooms*. New York: Longman.

Good, T., & Hinkel, G. (1982). *Schooling in America: Some descriptive and explanatory statements*. Technical Report No. 301, Center for Research in Social Behavior, University of Missouri-Columbia.

Grant, L. (1983). The socialization of white females in classrooms. Paper presented at the annual meeting of the American Educational Research Association, Montreal, Canada.

Grant, L. (1985). Race-gender status, classroom interaction, and children's socialization in elementary school. In L. Wilkinson & C. Marrett (Eds.), *Influences in classroom interaction*. New York: Academic Press.

Griffin, G. (1983). *Student teaching and the commonplaces of schooling (Report No. 9038)*. Austin: University of Texas, Research and Development Center for Teacher Education.

Griffin, G. (1985). The school as a workplace and the master teacher concept. *Elementary School Journal, 86,* 1–16.

Hill, P., & Kimbrough, J. (1981). *The aggregate effects of federal education programs*. The Rand Publication Series. Santa Monica, CA: The Rand Corporation.

Hudgins, B., & Ahlbrand, W., Jr. (1969). *A study of classroom interaction and thinking*. Technical Report Series No. 8. St. Ann, MO: Central Midwestern Regional Educational Laboratory.

Hyde, J. (1981). How large are cognitive gender differences? *American Psychologist, 36,* 892–901.

Jackson, P. (1968). *Life in classrooms*. New York: Holt, Rinehart and Winston.

Jackson, P., & Lahaderne, H. (1967). Inequalities of teacher-pupil contacts. *Psychology in the Schools, 4,* 204–208.

Jorgenson, G. (1978). Student ability—material difficulty matching: Relationship to classroom behavior. Paper presented at the meeting of the American Educational Research Association, Toronto, Canada.

Leacock, E. (1969). *Teaching and learning in city schools*. New York: Basic Books.

Leinhardt, G., Seewald, A., & Engel, M. (1979). Learning what's taught: Sex differences in instruction. *Journal of Educational Psychology, 71,* 432–439.

Maccoby, E., & Jacklin, L. (1974). *The psychology of sex differences*. Stanford, CA: Stanford University Press.

Martin, R., & Keller, A. (1974). Teacher awareness of classroom dyadic interactions. Paper presented at the annual meeting of the American Educational Research Association, Chicago.

McNeil, J. (1971). *Toward accountable teachers: Their appraisal and improvement*. New York: Holt, Rinehart and Winston.

Morse, L., & Handley, H. (1985). Listening to adolescents: Gender differences in science classroom interaction. In L. Wilkinson & C. Marrett (Eds.), *Gender influences in classroom interaction*. New York: Academic Press.

Motta, R., & Vane, J. (1977). An investigation of teacher perceptions of sex-typed behaviors. *Journal of Educational Research*, 363–368.

Natriello, G., & Dornbusch, S. (1980–1981). Pitfalls in the evaluation of teachers by principals. *Administrator's Notebook, 29*(6).

Pambookian, H. (1976). Discrepancy between instructor and student evaluation of instruction: Effect on instruction. *Instructional Science, 5*, 63–75.

Peterson, P., & Swing, S. (1982). Beyond time on task: Students' reports of their thought processes during classroom instruction. *Elementary School Journal, 82*, 481–491.

Rohrkemper, M. (1985). The influence of teacher socialization style on students' social cognitions and reported interpersonal classroom behavior. *Elementary School Journal, 85*, 245–275.

Rosenholtz, S., & Smylie, M. (1984). Teacher compensation and career ladders. *Elementary School Journal, 85*, 149–166.

Rowe, M. (1969). Science, silence, and sanctions. *Science and Children, 6*, 11–13.

Schmidt, W., & Buchmann, M. (1983). Six teachers' beliefs and attitudes and their curricular time allocations. *Elementary School Journal, 84*, 162–172.

Simmons, B. (1980). Sex role expectations of classroom teachers. *Education, 100*(3), 249–253.

Spencer, D. (1984*a*). The home and school lives of women teachers. *Elementary School Journal, 84*, 283–298.

Spencer, D. (1984*b*). The home and school lives of women teachers: Implications for staff development. *Elementary School Journal, 84*, 299–314.

Spencer-Hall, D. (1981). Looking behind the teacher's back. *Elementary School Journal, 81*, 281–290.

Stallings, J. (1980). Allocated academic learning time revisited, or beyond time on task. *Educational Researcher, 9*, 11–16.

Stallings, J. (Personal communication).

Tuckman, B., & Oliver, W. (1968). Effectiveness of feedback to teachers as a function of source. *Journal of Educational Psychology, 59*, 297–301.

Weinstein, R. (May 1982). Students in classrooms. *Elementary School Journal* (special issue).

Weinstein, R., & Middlestadt, S. (1979). Student perceptions of teacher interactions with male high and low achievers. *Journal of Educational Psychology, 71*, 421–431.

Wilkinson, L., & Marrett, C. (Eds.) (1985). *Gender influences in classroom interaction*. New York: Academic Press.

Winne, P. (1979). Experiments relating teachers' use of higher cognitive questions to student achievement. *Review of Educational Research, 49*, 13–49.

Wyne, M., & Stuck, G. (1982). Time and learning: Implications for the classroom teacher. *Elementary School Journal, 83*, 67–75.

CHAPTER
3

Seeing in Classrooms

Benefits of Observation

We believe that providing you with concepts that describe classroom processes will help you to monitor more of your behavior. Knowledge of variables such as *wait time* can help you to increase the amount of time you wait for students to respond under some conditions. Similarly, awareness of a tendency to *give up* on students with presumed lesser ability may allow you to ask more new questions, provide clues, rephrase questions and generally to demand more performance from such students.

Furthermore, teachers who are trying to understand their behavior can apply the observational techniques presented in this book. For example, consider the "Sea of Darkness" example that was presented and discussed in Chapter 1. If the teacher had tape recorded this lesson, most of the dimensions discussed in our analysis might have become evident to her (the high rates of asking factual questions, the lack of a clear pattern to the questions, different reactions toward boys and girls, and so forth). Teachers who occasionally tape record their lessons (e.g., once every two weeks) could derive many of the same benefits as having an observer in the classroom. However, neither teachers nor observers are likely to understand classroom behavior unless they know how to collect classroom information, know what behaviors to look for, and have a conceptual or theoretical framework to use in analyzing classroom behavior. Thus, in addition to a willingness to understand, teachers must also have concepts and particular methods for analyzing instruction.

We stress observation skills for two other reasons as well. First, it seems plausible that increasing numbers of teachers will have the opportunity to observe other teachers and in return to be observed by peers. As more school districts adopt master teacher or career ladder plans (see Griffin, 1985; Zumwalt, 1985), teachers will be provided with release time so that they can observe and provide constructive feedback to other teachers. Thus, we stress skills for observing in order to allow you (1) to observe skillfully in other teachers' classrooms, and (2) to interpret the comments of supervisors and other teachers who observe in your classroom. As you examine and modify your teaching style, observational feedback from others will usually be of immense assistance; however, you need to be aware that all observations have some error.

Problems With Observing

We have discussed the problems teachers have in perceiving classroom behavior and the difficulty of monitoring classroom behavior that is both rapid and complex. Research shows that teachers' perceptions of classroom behavior differ, at least in certain respects, from those of students and observers (Cooper & Good, 1983; Ehman, 1970; Weinstein, 1983; Wolfson & Nash, 1969).

Why should teacher perception be at odds with the views of other observers? After all, students and observers are seldom trained to rate specific behaviors, and they too must observe rapidly occurring events. Part of the answer is that teachers and observers may miss some classroom occurrences because events happen so quickly. The purpose of this chapter is to discuss another reason: teachers and observers can and do *misinterpret* classroom behavior. That is, the problem of observing in classrooms is a bit more complex than we have described so far. Although it is true that a fast classroom pace and not knowing what to look for reduce one's ability to perceive behavior in the classroom, another problem is that on occasion what we think we see is not congruent with reality. Our past experiences, biases, and prejudices can lead us to interpret what we see incorrectly rather than to objectively see, describe, and analyze what really happened.

As Posner (1985) notes, people who support various theories of teaching may actually interpret what they see in classrooms differently. For example, those who hold a didactic view of teaching believe that teaching is primarily aimed at transmitting knowledge and providing clear explanations or demonstrations that show how the knowledge operates. In contrast, a discovery view of teaching focuses on student experimentation, with a minimum of teacher structure and explanation, and the opportunity to learn inductively from direct observation. In contrast, according to Posner, the interactionist view holds that there is a necessary interaction among students' naive ideas, their empirical observation, and the curriculum content. This view argues that students arrive in the classroom with well-formed, although often incorrect, ideas. Didactic teaching rejects or ignores these ideas, whereas discovery teaching allows students to develop further and supports ideas that are not true. Thus, an observer who prefers a didactic approach to learning may have difficulty in fairly assessing a teacher who uses a discovery approach. In addition to the problems discussed earlier (speed, complexity, lack of conceptual vocabulary for describing classroom behavior), we see that personal bias (values, preferences) may distort what we see in the classroom.

Persons who wish to observe accurately must identify and examine their biases. For instance, a classroom observer who is irritated by assertive, highly verbal teachers may see such teachers as punitive and rigid, whereas another observer may view them as well organized and articulate. Similarly, a classroom teacher may view two students who are performing the same behavior yet perceive the students' behavior differently. Imagine the following situation. Mr. Fulton, who teaches tenth-grade American history, is talking when Bill calls out, "Why are we talking about this?" Mr. Fulton, knowing Bill to be a troublemaker, assumes that Bill wants to waste time or provoke an argument. Therefore, he responds aggressively, "If you would pay attention, you'd know what we're doing. Pay attention!" Compare this response with Mr. Fulton's reply to a different student. Jim calls out the same words in the same tone: "Why are we talking about this?" But because Mr. Fulton "knows" that Jim is a good, dependable student, he views Jim's words not as a threat, but as a serious question. He reasons that if Jim does not understand the purpose of the discussion, nobody does. He responds, "Jim, I probably haven't made this clear. Last Friday we discussed. . . ."

On occasion teachers react not only to what they hear, but to their *interpretation* of what students say. Teachers' past experiences with a student often influence their interpretation of what the student seems to be saying (see Chapter 4 this volume). We do not suggest that teachers should not interpret student comments, but argue that teachers should be *aware* of when they do so. Some teachers fall into the unconscious trap of expecting a student to behave in a certain way and then systematically coloring their interpretations of the student's behavior, so that the behavior appears to fulfill the teacher's expectation. Often the distinction between observed behavior and the teacher's interpretation of that behavior is lost.

This chapter argues that anyone who tries to observe behavior will have to guard against his or her tendency to let personal biases color what is seen. An exercise to help readers identify their classroom biases is provided at the end of the chapter. After you become more aware of various teacher and student behaviors and your attitudes toward them, you will be able to interpret classroom behavior more objectively. Suggestions are also presented to help observers gather classroom data without unduly influencing the behavior of teachers and students.

Selective Perception: An Example

Teachers often perceive classroom behavior according to their own experience. The following illustration taken from the book *Problem Situations in Teaching* (Greenwood, Good, & Siegel, 1971) shows how the process might operate. As you read the example, note how Mr. Smith's attitudes influence his interpretations.

. . . consider Mr. Smith, who has frequently observed two students, Jean and Shirley, in his senior civics class whispering together in the back of the room. He has always ignored this behavior, hoping it would disappear. The two girls are very physically attractive to Mr. Smith, and very popular among their classmates. He wanted to befriend them, but they seemed to make fun of him at times. Once when he tripped over a wastebasket, they seemed to laugh louder and longer at him than anyone else in the room. At other times, they would whisper together, look in his direction, and begin to giggle.

Mr. Smith was not very popular when he was a student in high school. He was shy around girls, dated very little, and did not participate in varsity athletics, although he wanted to be admired and popular. He became a teacher, although he wanted to be a medical doctor, primarily because he felt that the local teacher's college was the only place that he could financially afford to attend and feel reasonably sure of being able to do the academic work required of him.

On the day in question, another teacher had hurt his feelings by criticizing the tie that he had worn to school. The other teacher had said, "Man, you are never going to be a swinger as long as you wear square ties like that." During second period civics class, Jean and Shirley once again whispered together in the back of the room, looked in Mr. Smith's direction, and began to laugh. Mr. Smith inferred from their behavior that they were talking about him. He told them to go to the Dean of Girls' office.

The Dean of Girls later told Mr. Smith that the girls had been telling one another jokes. Mr. Smith didn't really believe this "story" of the girls and told them in no uncertain terms that he was going to move them away from one another and that the next time they talked he would cut their grades. Both girls had confused and bewildered expressions on their faces and Jean began to cry. Shirley said, "Why are you treating us this way, Mr. Smith? We really thought that you were the one teacher that we have who really understands us!"

You can probably think of a great number of things that you would like to find out about Jean, Shirley, Mr. Smith, and others, before you begin to diagnose this case. A good starting point is to consider Mr. Smith's objectivity. Was he objective in examining the data? From a measurement standpoint, objectivity of this kind refers to the amount of agreement between observers. If two other teachers had observed the same behavior as Mr. Smith observed, would they have made the same inferences from the behavior of Jean and Shirley?

If Mr. Smith could remove his perceptual blinders for a moment, what would he have actually observed about Jean and Shirley's behavior and what would he have inferred? He had definitely seen the two girls whispering together, glancing at him, and laughing at him from time to time. He could probably even guess how many times they have engaged in this behavior, if it were important. He did hear and see them laugh loudly when he tripped over the wastebasket. Further, the Dean of Girls said the girls explained that they were telling jokes on the day that he sent them out of the class. Finally, we know precisely what the girls said to Mr. Smith when he talked to them later because we have an exact quote. We can't see the girls' faces or hear the way in which Shirley said what she did to Mr. Smith. Our data have many limitations, but they do provide some clues and suggest the need to collect additional information.

What kinds of inferences did Mr. Smith make from the behavioral data? Are there other interpretations that could be made? First, he seemed to feel that the girls saw him as an inadequate male. Second, he inferred that they were whispering and giggling about him and his inadequacies. After the incident was reported, Mr. Smith later said he refused to accept Shirley's statement concerning his adequacy as an understanding teacher. Are other inferences concerning the girls' behavior possible? Did Mr. Smith respond to the behavior that he observed, or did he respond to inferences that he drew from this behavior? Imagine Mr. Smith at some future time with some other teachers in the lounge during their "planning period." Imagine another teacher saying, "I have Jean Sinders and Shirley Merrick in my class this semester. Boy, what lookers! Hey, George, didn't you have some trouble with them last semester?" Mr. Smith: "Did I ever! They were always disrupting the class. Every time I turned my back they were whispering and giggling and making all kinds of noise."

Teacher Anxiety: A Source of Bias

The example presented above illustrates how a teacher's anxiety can lead to a distorted view of classroom events. Teachers who are insecure and who possess a poor teaching self-concept are especially unlikely to seek information about themselves and likely to distort "threatening" information when they receive it. Insecure teachers often prefer to interpret problems in ways that suggest that factors other than personal competency are the source of instructional difficulties ("TV has spoiled students." "Students don't like me." "You can't motivate them anymore.").

It is known that many teachers report considerable tension and anxiety while engaged in teaching activities (see, for example, Coates & Thoresen, 1976). It is less clear how teacher anxiety influences teacher behavior and the anxiety and classroom behavior of students. Still, it would seem difficult for teachers who are excessively concerned about themselves to actively monitor interactions in order to see how others are *affected* by classroom events.

Student teaching is often a stressful event because of poor communication between the student teacher and the cooperating teacher. If self-concerns are excessive, however, student teachers should seek advice and help from the college teaching staff. People who are uncomfortable in the teaching act will have a difficult time in accurately seeing what is happening in their classrooms and helping students to fulfill their needs. To be a successful teacher, one has to develop technical competence and the self-confidence to use those skills.

Observe Behavior Before Making Interpretations

The teaching incident involving Mr. Fulton also illustrates that inferences should be made *after* we have collected and examined descriptive information. Our own background, particularly our experiences as a student and our personal definitions of a good teacher, can lead us to draw erroneous conclusions. If the teacher does something we especially like (e.g., asks questions before calling on students), we may rate him or her high in all areas. Similarly, if the teacher does something we particularly dislike (e.g., humiliates a student who provides a wrong answer), we may evaluate him or her low on all dimensions of classroom behavior even if other aspects are positive. Thus, when we view teacher behavior it is important not to evaluate behavior as positive or negative independent of its effects upon students. For example, the teacher we see as hypercritical may be seen by students as a person who sets high standards because he or she cares about them. As a case in point, see Kleinfeld (1975).

It is difficult for an observer to sit in a classroom and note the behavior that occurs without attempting to *interpret* what the behavior means. Observers should concentrate on observing and coding, however, because time spent speculating about the possible motivation behind a student's or teacher's behavior increases the chances that the observer will miss significant aspects of classroom interaction. It is preferable to hypothesize about the causes of classroom behavior only *after* objectively describing that behavior, particularly because hypotheses made while we are still observing in the classroom lock us into a narrow viewpoint. When we are looking for something, we are likely to find it. Remember the example of Mr. Smith and recall how his perceptual blinders caused him to interpret behavior to make it conform to his view.

Looking for specific behaviors in the classroom is one way to minimize the degree to which our attitudes and biases will color what we see. For example, if we believe a teacher to be caustic and ineffectual, it is less likely that such an attitude will interfere with our description of classroom life when we pay attention to behavior (e.g., how often the teacher calls on low-achieving male students) than it will when we attempt to describe the teacher in global, inferential terms (how warm, friendly, fair, etc., the teacher is).

However, a focus on behavior does not in itself guarantee that one will see accurately. Behavior will be seen accurately only if the observer wants to do so and is willing to practice and to compare his or her observations with those of others. Nevertheless, a focus on behavior is a useful starting point for trying to see and describe classroom life.

Other common sources of errors that can occur during observation appear in Table 3.1. As Evertson and Green (1986) note, these issues need attention if one is to observe accurately in the classroom.

CASE STUDY TECHNIQUES

One useful way to improve observational skills is by doing case studies that focus on one student or a few students. Case studies that involve the reporting of observed behaviors are particularly helpful. Such assignments facilitate one's ability to observe and describe behavior accurately, and these skills are necessary to the generation of effective, concrete plans for dealing with students. Traditional case studies are excellent analytical tools for expanding one's ability to see and to interpret student behavior.

Readers who seek more detailed advice about ways to conduct scientific inquiries using case studies and qualitative field notes can profitably consult other sources for more detailed information (e.g., Erickson, 1986). Here, our focus is on practical techniques for studying students in one's own classroom.

Table 3.1   SOURCES OF ERROR IN OBSERVATIONAL RESEARCH

Type of error	Definition
1. Central tendency	When using rating scales, the observer tends toward the subjective midpoint when judging a series of stimuli.
2. Leniency or generosity	When using rating scales for which a "yes," "sometimes," "rarely," or "no" is required, the observer tends to be lenient or generous.
3. Primacy or recency effects	Observers' initial impressions have a distorting effect on later judgments (primacy). Observers' ratings may be unduly influenced by their most recent observations (recency).
4. Logical errors	Observer makes judgment errors based on theoretical, experiential, or commitment-based assumptions (e.g., the assumption that because a teacher shows warmth to a class, she/he is also instructionally effective).

Table 3.1   **(Continued)**

Type of error	Definition
5. Failure to acknowledge self	The influence of the observer on the setting is overlooked. The investigator's role may lead to the establishment of particular expectations. Judgments can be made in accordance with these expectations.
6. Classification of observations	Construction of macro categories loses fine distinctions. Such categories permit quantification but lose information about the process and fine-grained differences.
7. Generalization of unique behavior	Judgments may be based on evidence from an unrepresentative sample. Can lead to false conclusions or incorrect classifications of people or events.
8. Vested interests and values of observer	Findings become value-laden or otherwise distorted because of unchecked personal bias.
9. Failure to consider perspective of the observed	For investigators interested in a clear picture of everyday life, failure to obtain participants' perspectives may lead to identification of unvalidated factors, processes, or variables.
10. Unrepresentative sampling	Errors may occur based on samples which do not represent the general group of behaviors, that do not occur frequently enough to be observed reliably, or are inconsistent with the theory guiding the observations.
11. Reactions of the observed	Reactions of participants being observed can distort the process or phenomena being observed (e.g., teachers who are anxious about being observed may behave differently than they would at a calmer time).
12. Failure to account for situation or context	Leads to incorrect conclusions from assumptions of functional equivalents (e.g., reading time 1 = reading time 2). Can lead to overlooking what is being taught, changes in activities, variations in rights and obligations for participation, hence can distort conclusions.
13. Poorly designed observation systems	Leads to problems with reliability and validity.
14. Lack of consideration for the rapid speed of relevant action	Errors may occur based on the omission of crucial features because of the rapidity of actions in the classroom.
15. Lack of consideration for the simultaneity of relevant action	Errors may occur based on failure to account for more than one activity occurring at a time; more than one message being sent at a time (e.g., use of different channels—verbal and nonverbal); and more than one function of a message at a time.
16. Lack of consideration of goal-directed or purposive nature of human activity	False conclusion that a behavior lacks stability because of failure to consider the purposes of human behavior.
17. Failure to insure against observer drift	Errors caused by changes in the way the observer uses a system as time goes on. Can lead to obtaining descriptions that do not match the original categories or that vary from each other.

Source: Adapted from Evertson, C., & Green, J. (1986). Observation as inquiry and method. In M. Wittrock (Ed.), *Handbook of research on teaching* (3rd ed.). New York: Macmillan.

Discovering Bias

We have noted that observers and teachers often misinterpret behavior because their own backgrounds and biases lead them to color classroom behavior and because they attempt to interpret behavior prematurely. The first step in changing this undesirable behavior is to become aware of its presence and consequences. Teachers need awareness of both *behavior* (e.g., the teacher criticizes some students almost every time they give a wrong answer) and its *consequences* (e.g., the students volunteer less, begin to avoid the teacher, or hand in fewer homework assignments).

When we become aware of our attitudes, we can often control our behavior more optimally. For example, the teacher who unhesitantly says, "I am a fair grader. I am never influenced by the student as a person, and I grade only the paper," is often an extremely unfair grader. The fact is that knowing who wrote a paper does influence most graders. With certain students, teachers tend to *read more into the answer* than is really there (especially with students perceived as highly competent). We demand more proof from other students (e.g., although a student's first paragraph in an essay is excellent, the teacher suspects that this student does not really know the material).

Similarly, quality of handwriting may influence the way we grade an essay exam (Chase, 1968), or the ways that students present themselves orally to the teacher when making a request may affect the teacher's response (e.g., Anderson-Levitt, 1984; Spencer-Hall, 1981). Once teachers realize that they do have *biases* that interfere with grading fairly, they can take steps to reduce the effects of those biases. For example, teachers can mask the identity of the student who wrote the paper before grading it, can grade all papers on the first question before going to the next question, and can score only content and not handwriting.

In the same way, one can improve other weak spots if one becomes aware of them. Self-study is difficult to conduct. The most pervasive problem is the difficulty of admitting certain feelings and reactions because we feel that they are unprofessional or inappropriate. For example, we tend not to accept the fact that we react differently to different students.

Greenberg (1969) describes some of the myths that frequently produce teacher problems, such as the myth of "liking all students equally," and notes that such magnanimous behavior is impossible. Teachers will treat students in equally fair and facilitating ways if and when they are aware of their feelings about the students. This does not mean identical teacher behavior, however, because some students need more teacher contact, others need more opportunity to work on their own, and so forth. As human beings, teachers experience the full range of human emotions: they will distrust some students, they will be proud of certain others, some will delight them, and others they will want to avoid. Similarly, observers will have different reactions toward different teachers. If we are not careful, these feelings will interfere with our ability to see accurately. Too often teachers do not have collegial support groups that allow them to express their feelings in a supportive environment (Spencer, 1984*a*, 1984*b*).

Once we identify our feelings, it is possible to monitor classroom behavior more objectively. For example, if we realize that a student makes us uneasy because of physical ugliness, filth or smell, embarrassing questions, or shyness, we can take steps to make the student more attractive to us. However, if we only think "I love all students," we are unlikely to identify our differential behavior toward students whom we dislike. The assignment outlined below will help you to identify some of your attitudes and preferences toward students.

Case Study: Self-Study

The case study assignment that follows will provide you with a direct opportunity to study your personal values, preferences, and attitudes. This case study forces you to consider the types of students (or teachers) whom you find fun and exciting to work with and to identify the types who annoy, bore, or disgust you.

From the following list, select two contrast groups for study—any two except pair 1 and 4. If you are not in an observation course, pick peers who are in your class or pick two different college instructors and analyze their differential behavior. Better yet, arrange to observe in a class similar to the one you teach or will be teaching.

1. Select the two students with whom you most enjoy working; that is, if you were the classroom teacher, which two students in the class would you select first to be in your own room? (*Positive feelings*)
2. Select the two students whom you dislike the most in the classroom. (*Negative feelings*)
3. Select two students for whom you have no strong feeling whatsoever. Use the class roster here so that you will not forget about anyone. (*Apathy, indifference, do not notice when they are absent*)
4. Select two students (one boy, one girl) who best represent the child you would want your son or daughter to be like at this age. (*Identification*)

After selecting the four students, begin to observe them more closely during class activities. If you are observing in public schools and you choose to take notes during class, be sure to obtain the teacher's permission and let him or her know that the notes are about students and not the teacher. Some of you will be busy teaching during the day, so your notes will have to be made after class ends. The notes are for your own use, so their form is completely open. Bear in mind that any information you record in classrooms is confidential; students should never be identified by name. Even notes that you take in class should include no *actual* student names (notes are often lost). For this case study, it is *not* necessary to collect data from the school files, which might influence the observation anyway. Normal classroom behavior is sufficient.

Analyze the similarities and differences among the four students. This analysis should provide you with clues regarding the types of student behavior that are likely to touch off positive or negative responses in your own behavior as a teacher. You will then be in a better position to understand why you behave as you do and to learn to interact more positively with students who irritate you. You will want to raise some of the following questions when you compare and contrast the students:

1. What are the students like physically? How do they look? Do they have nice clothes? Are they attractive? Clean? Are they large or small for their age? Are they male or female?

2. What are their favorite subjects? What lessons bore them? What are their strong and weak points as students? As persons?
3. What are their most prominent behavioral characteristics? Do they smile a lot? Do they thank you for your attention? Do they seek you out in the classroom—more or less than the average student? Do they raise their hands to answer often? Can they be depended on to do their own work? How mature are they? Are they awkward or clumsy?
4. What are their social characteristics? What socioeconomic level do they come from? What is their ethnic background?

The goal of this exercise is not to put you through an intensive self-analysis. It is to start you thinking about the possible linkages between your feelings about students and the way students treat you and you treat them in the classroom. A valuable parallel exercise would be to list the teacher behaviors that provoke your interest or boredom. The purpose of such activities is to make you more aware of what you like and dislike, so that these attitudes will not interfere with your classroom observation and teaching.

Case Study: Some General Comments

If you are puzzled about particular students, or even just interested in learning more about them, concentrated and sustained observation usually will reveal new insights and suggest interpretations and explanations. Case studies help teachers to overcome the tendency to see students only within the student role. Attention is focused on students as unique individuals, and an attempt is made to empathize with them. This involves trying to see the classroom environment as students see it and to develop an understanding of what they are trying to accomplish when they respond to it.

First, who are the students? What are their background characteristics (age, sex, birth order, family background)? What are their orientations toward school? Toward the teacher? Toward classmates? What are their hobbies and interests? Their strengths and weaknesses as individuals? As students? Thinking about such questions and jotting down tentative answers are helpful in developing an open mind toward students and learning to look at them in new ways. These steps may help you improve your knowledge of a particular student before you even spend any time observing that student. For example, if you cannot name several strengths *and* weaknesses, your view of the student is probably biased. In our desire for simplicity and consistency in our perceptions, we tend to overstress things that fit together and reinforce our biases and to slight things that do not.

No special preparation or equipment is required to observe a student systematically. An ordinary notebook and pen or pencil will do. You should be near enough to see and hear the student, but not so close as to be inhibiting. Ideally, the student should not know that you are observing him or her systematically. If possible, make observations of the student outside class as well, during recess, at lunch, and between classes, when the student's behavior is likely to be more characteristic than it is when constricted by the student role.

If the student presents a problem, try to formulate the problem as specifically as you can, using terms that translate into observable behavior. Include any relevant qualifiers relating to the contexts in which behavior occurs (subject matter, size of group, time of day, type of situation). Such patterns in the student's behavior may help you to increase your understanding. You also might notice important differences between situations in which the student is and is not a problem (degree of interest in the topic, degree of structure in the activity, involving vs. quiet activity, type of antecedent experience, presence of peers or other distractors, etc.). Whatever the activity, focus on the student, including times when he or she is a passive spectator. There is a tendency to observe the teacher or whoever else is the center of attention at times like these, but when you are doing a case study, it is important to concentrate on the student of interest.

Keep a running log of the student's behavior during periods of observation. Observations should be dated, each clearly separated from others, and subdivided into natural units according to what was going on at the time (class periods and breaks between periods, different activities and settings within classes, etc.). The log should contain narrative descriptions of behavior along with interpretations about its possible meanings. It is important to keep objective descriptions of behavior separate from subjective interpretations concerning meaning, because interpretations may change as more information is collected. Probably the easiest way to do this is to use only the left half of the page for keeping the log of behavior. Interpretations can be written on the right half of the page later, when you review your notes and think about what you have observed.

If you have the chance to interview students, you may find that students' beliefs about school subjects and other topics may be somewhat different from what you had concluded on the basis of your observation. Students can be excellent sources of information about how classrooms work. Interview techniques are beyond the scope of this book, but excellent suggestions about the use of student interviews as well as how to conduct them can be found elsewhere (Rohrkemper, 1981, 1985; Spradley, 1979; Weinstein, 1983).

When recording for a case study, the goal is to include as much pertinent and interpretable information as possible, but to stick with the facts and avoid unsupportable and perhaps incorrect interpretations. This is not difficult to do, but it may take some practice to learn to separate vague information from interpretable facts, and interpretable facts from interpretations themselves. For example, suppose an observer were watching Ron, a white student, at a time when he became involved in an incident with Ralph, a black student:

Ralph taps Ron, points, and speaks. Ron replies, shaking head. Ralph gestures, speaks. Ron strikes Ralph and a fight starts.

This information is factual, but it is too vague and sketchy to be much good. Even if the words of the boys are not heard, their gestures and the general nature of their interaction can be described much more clearly. Let's look at another example:

Ron is working quietly until bothered by Ralph. He listens, then refuses. Ralph becomes angry and abusive. Ron becomes aggressive, triggering a major racial incident.

Assuming that the observer could not hear what was said, this is not so much an observation as an interpretation. Ron may or may not have "refused" whatever

Ralph wanted, Ralph may or may not have "provoked" Ron, and the incident may or may not be "racial." These are interpretations. They fit the facts and may be true, but this also can be said of many other possible interpretations. A good observation would have recorded the facts as follows:

> Ralph taps Ron on shoulder, shows his assignment, points to something, speaks. Ron looks, shakes head no, says something. Ralph replies with disgusted look, downward gesture of arm. Turns away when finished speaking. Ron says something to Ralph from behind, then slaps Ralph's head. Ralph responds as if attacked, fight begins.

This is about as much useful information as could be recorded without becoming interpretive. About all that is missing is a description of Ron's facial expression and general manner when slapping Ralph. This information would be helpful in judging whether the head slap really was meant as an attack (if so, it would be an unusual behavior).

The interpretation of this information would raise questions about its meaning. Who actually started the trouble, and what started it? Is it accurate to call this a "racial incident," or is the fact that one boy is black and the other white irrelevant? What really happened?

Ordinarily, the observer would get answers to these and related questions, because interactions as intense as fights usually involve loud talk, which is easy to hear. However, without more information, the interpretation of these facts would have to be confined to speculation. The first fact is that Ralph interrupted Ron by tapping his shoulder, pointing to the assignment, and saying something. The shoulder tap apparently did not bother Ron, because he did not show any reaction to it. In fact, he did not appear angry until later. The fact that Ralph showed the assignment and pointed to something suggests that he was seeking help or information about it or was expressing an opinion. However, it is possible that Ralph did these things just to give the appearance of discussing the assignment and that what he had to say to Ron had nothing to do with the assignment. If so, he could have made a provocative statement, but not necessarily.

Ron responded by shaking his head no and saying something. This could have been a refusal to listen, a refusal of a request, or an answer to Ralph's question, among other things. If Ralph had expressed an opinion, this could have been a disagreement by Ron. In any case, it is clear that Ron responded negatively to whatever Ralph asked or said.

Ralph's gesture and facial expression in his reply suggest disgust and/or anger. However, it is not at all clear whether he provoked Ron in some way. He might have, but he might also have been expressing his own frustration with whatever Ron had said. He might even have been giving an opinion. For example, he might have originally pointed out what he considered to be a stupid question and asked Ron if he understood it. Ron might have said that he did not understand it either, and Ralph might have responded with a gesture and look of disgust while saying something like, "Why do they ask us stuff like this?"

Just as Ralph's behavior may or may not have involved provocation, Ron's behavior may or may not have involved aggression. It could have been an attack on Ralph, perhaps in retaliation for something Ralph said. However, it also could have been horseplay. Boys frequently poke or slap one another as a way of teasing (but not attacking), and that could be what happened.

With a little imagination, we can think of several other interpretations of what occurred between Ron and Ralph, but the above is enough to indicate the difference between factual observations and interpretations. Ambiguous situations like this are common when classroom observations are collected in case studies, which is why it is important to physically separate factual observations from interpretations of these observations. The factual observation record will remain constant even when interpretations change in the light of new evidence. Even when you are not formally entering observations in a case study record, the distinction between fact and interpretation should be kept in mind. The ability to maintain and be aware of this distinction is an important part of learning to be accurate when looking in classrooms.

You may have to experiment a bit in order to find the right level of generality for behavioral description. You should not attempt to record literally everything that you see, partly because this would not be possible and partly because you would be recording a great deal of trivial information about momentary behaviors and expressive mannerisms that have no interpretive importance. On the other hand, in the interest of objectivity, it is important that you record observable behaviors. Thus, it would be appropriate to note that the student smiled or even smiled at the teacher, but it would be an interpretation to say that the student showed friendly warmth (as opposed to happy self-satisfaction, for example). Similarly, it would be appropriate to state that the student spent time apparently absorbed in thinking and problem solving, but it would be an interpretation to say that the student *was* thinking and problem solving. Perhaps he or she has learned to give this appearance while daydreaming (e.g., Peterson & Swing, 1982; Spencer-Hall, 1981).

Naturally, in making notes you will want to highlight information relevant to your concerns about the student. However, your record should keep everything in proper perspective, even if it differs in the degree of specificity included about various episodes. For example, if you are watching a student who gets into trouble with peers, it would be appropriate for you to have detailed descriptions of what happened on the two occasions that he or she became involved in arguments during the observation period. On the other hand, it should be clear from the record that the two instances of peer conflict involved only a few minutes, and the record should provide a running account of what the student was doing during the rest of the period. In fact, when you observe problem children, it can be helpful to keep the question "What does the student do when not misbehaving?" in the back of your mind. This will help cue your attention to behavior representative of the positive self that you have to learn about, build on, and ultimately begin to think about when you think about this student. To develop this information, it is important to fight the tendency to let halo effects structure your perceptions. Just as outstanding students have weaknesses, problem students have strengths.

Behavioral records should be reviewed and checked for completeness and accuracy at the first opportunity. At this time, you can also fill in initial interpretations, add clarification, and generally edit your notes to make them as useful as possible in the future. You may or may not be able to interpret everything you see, but your notes should be as complete and unambiguous as possible concerning what actually happened. In addition to a description of what transpired, there should be information about the qualitative or process aspects of the behavior (Was it random or purposeful? Was there anything unusual or noteworthy about it?) and explanations about reasons for the behavior (Why did the behavior occur? What stimulated it? What was its purpose? What was its function?).

In reviewing behavioral comments, look for correlations and contradictions. Try to identify repeated patterns. Are they well known, or do they suggest new insights? Look for places where a particular pattern might have been expected but did not occur. These could be keys to understanding the explanations for patterns or to developing ideas about how to get the student to change. If your notes suggest certain hypotheses but do not contain enough information to allow you to evaluate them, try to identify what information you need. You might be able to identify specific situations that you could observe in the near future. For example, suppose the student challenged the teacher on each of two occasions when asked to read aloud. This could be a defense mechanism used in an attempt to avoid reading, perhaps because the student cannot read. You cannot tell from only two instances, but you could watch for this in the future whenever the class is involved in oral reading, and you could see the student individually and try to obtain more information about his or her reading achievement level. Information gleaned from these supplementary activities then can be added into the log at appropriate places dealing with the interpretation of the behavior.

SIMPLIFYING THE OBSERVATIONAL TASK

In this chapter, emphasis has been placed on the need to study observer and teacher biases to prevent them from interfering with assessment. However, another major obstacle hinders perception in classrooms: the sheer physical complexity of the classroom can, at times, prevent us from seeing certain events. While the teacher instructs a reading group, four students may be at the science table, three listening to tapes at the listening post, four reading at their desks, and three writing at the blackboard. No observer can monitor everything that takes place in the classroom. Even relatively simple tasks may be impossible to code simultaneously. For instance, if an observer wants to code the number of hands raised when a teacher asks a question and whether or not the student called on by the teacher has a hand up, the observer may still be counting hands when the teacher calls on the student and will thus be unable to determine whether or not the student has a hand up.

One useful way to break down the physical complexity of the classroom is to study the behavior of a few students. Such students can be studied intensively, and their behavior will mirror what is taking place in the entire classroom. For example, the observer can choose to focus on a few students (perhaps two high, two middle, and two low achievers; one female and one male at each achievement level) or on a particular group of students (low achievers). Then a record can be made of everything these students do. For example, it might be useful to look at these differences between high, middle, and low achievers:

1. How often do low, middle, and high achievers raise their hands?
2. Do all students approach the teacher to receive help, or do some students seldom approach the teacher?
3. How long does the reading group last for each group of achievers?

4. Are the students involved in their work? How long do they work independently at their desks?

5. How often are students in different groups praised?

These questions represent a few of the many you can examine. Our purpose is not to suggest what to look for (this will come later) but to examine ways and procedures that will facilitate looking. Studies of representative students are an excellent way of reducing the complexity of looking in classrooms. These studies allow one to focus attention upon the teacher and only a few students, rather than trying to code everything that takes place in a large classroom. This focus on a few students is especially useful when you first begin to observe in classrooms.

Another strategy for aiding ability to observe in classrooms is simply to *limit* the number of behaviors that you look for at one time. The student observer, or teachers participating in self-evaluation or in-service programs, will do well to restrict their attention *initially* to only five to ten behaviors at any one time. When one attempts to measure too many things, one becomes confused and cannot measure objectively. It would be better for an observer to concentrate on certain behaviors for a couple of days and then start to code a new set of behaviors.

Reliability of Observations

In addition to realizing their own biases and limiting the number of students and behaviors observed, observers should learn to estimate their ability to code class-room behavior accurately by comparing their observations with those collected by other observers. Perhaps this is the easiest way to determine if you are observing what happens and not allowing your personal biases to interfere with your observing. (A fuller description of reliability is appended at the end of the chapter. The reader desiring more information on reliability is referred to this material. Furthermore, the reader who wishes additional information can profitably consult Evertson & Green, 1986; Linn, 1986; Shavelson, Webb, & Burstein, 1986.)

In general, the observation forms presented in this book can be used reliably with very little practice. After discussing observation scales for a short time period (5–20 minutes, depending upon the scale), students should be able to achieve general agreement (60–90 percent agreement) and thus be able to use the scale reliably to code classroom behavior. Let us discuss agreement further. If observers are watching a videotape and coding the number of academic questions that a teacher asks, we may find that one observer tallied 16 instances of academic questions while another observer tallied only 10. The agreement between two observers can be estimated using a simple formula suggested by Emmer and Millet (1970).

$$\text{agreement} = 1 - \frac{A - B}{A}$$

The formula tells us to subtract the difference between the two observers' counts and to divide them by the sum of the two observers' counts. The A term is always the larger number. Thus the agreement in this example would be:

$$1 - \frac{16 - 10}{16 + 10} = 1 - \frac{6}{26} = 1 - 0.23 = 77\%$$

Evertson and Green (1986) have detailed a number of reliability problems—and ways to respond to those problems. A summary of some of the issues they raise appears in Table 3.2.

General Plan for Looking in Classrooms
What you look at in a classroom will vary from situation to situation and from individual to individual. Some observers will be able to focus on six behaviors;

Table 3.2 PRACTICAL QUESTIONS AND ISSUES RELATED TO ASSESSING RELIABILITY

Questions	Related Issues
When should observer agreement be measured?	1. Prior to data collection. 2. Training does not guarantee against observer skill deterioration as data collection proceeds. 3. Calculations of degree to which observer disagreement limits reliability should be done after study.
On what kinds of data should observer agreement be calculated?	1. Agreement should be computed using same unit(s) of behavior to be used in data analysis. 2. Agreement should be computed on subcategories of behavior as well as larger, subsuming categories.
With whom should agreement be obtained?	1. High interobserver agreement may not mean agreement with original categories, because systematic misinterpretation can exist even with high agreement. 2. Observers' scores should also be compared with criterion. This is known as criterion-related agreement.
Under what conditions should agreement be calculated?	1. Coding the setting may differ from coding of unambiguous samples in laboratory or training session. 2. Ways to heighten observer vigilance and maintain accountability should be considered.
How can agreement be measured?	1. *Interclass correlation coefficients.* Useful after a study is completed, but impractical during or before. Highly affected by variance between subjects. 2. *Simple percentage agreement.* Drawbacks are that low frequencies in some categories and high frequencies in others may make interpretations ambiguous. Does not account for false inflation due to chance agreement.
Which agreement coefficient is appropriate?	1. Dependent upon type of observation system, number of categories, type of data, unit(s) of analysis, and purpose. 2. If nominal comparisons cannot be obtained, then marginal agreement methods should be used. 3. If only a few categories and/or frequency distributions are unequal, then correction for chance agreement should be made. 4. Definition of "items" changes with system. Probability of occurrence of items must be considered.

Source: Adapted from Evertson, C., & Green, J. (1986). Observation as inquiry and method. In M. Wittrock (Ed.), *Handbook of research on teaching* (3rd ed.). New York: Macmillan.

others may be able to code ten. Some observers may be in the classroom eight hours a week, some only four. Some observers may see two or three different teachers, while others will remain in the same room. Despite such situational differences, there are some general principles to bear in mind when looking in classrooms.

First, observers often try to reduce the complexity of classroom coding by focusing their attention exclusively upon the behavior of the teacher. This is particularly true of teachers in training, who are still trying to determine what teachers do in the classroom. This is misplaced emphasis. *The key to looking in classrooms is student response.* Are the students actively engaged in worthwhile learning activities?

Earlier, mention was made of the fact that some observers may see a teacher as punitive and rigid, whereas others see the same teacher as well organized and articulate. A good way to reduce your own bias in viewing teacher behavior is to supplement your observations with attention to the effects of teacher behavior upon student behavior. When you code in the classroom, reduce the number of things you look at to a small, manageable set, but look at both teacher and student behaviors. Students influence teachers as teachers influence students. If classrooms are to be understood, the social aspects of classrooms must be dealt with.

Classroom teachers who want to receive relevant feedback about their behavior and that of their pupils, and observers who want to see what life in a classroom is like, must be careful not to disturb the *natural* flow of behavior in the classroom. By *natural* we simply mean the behavior that would take place in the classroom if the observer were not present. Students, especially young ones, will adjust quickly to the presence of an observer if teachers prepare them properly and if observers follow through with appropriate behavior. The teacher should make a brief announcement to explain the observer's presence, so that the students will not have to wonder about the observer or try to question him or her to find out for themselves. For example, a second-grade class might be told: "Mr. Ramon will be with us today and the rest of the week. He is learning about being a teacher. Mr. Ramon will not disturb us because we have many things we want to finish, and he knows how busy we are. Please do not disturb him because he too is busy and has his own work to do."

The observer can help the teacher by avoiding eye contact with the students and by refusing to be drawn into long conversations with them or aiding them in their seatwork—unless, of course, the observer is also a participant in classroom life. (Some university courses call for students to serve as teacher aides before they do their student teaching.)

Observers should not initiate contact with students or do anything to draw special attention to themselves (e.g., frequently ripping pages out of a notebook). It is especially important when two observers are in the same room that they do not talk with each other, exchange notes, and so forth. Such behavior bothers both the teacher and the students and causes attention to be focused on the observers, so that natural behavior is disturbed.

When students approach you while you are observing a classroom, you should appear to be busy and avoid eye contact unless the student speaks to you. In most situations, you can politely but firmly remind the student that he or she should be sitting down and working, and you can tell the student that you are very busy with your own work. Requests for help should simply be referred to the teacher: "I'm sorry, I can't help you. Ask your teacher, Mrs. Brown."

If children bring pictures that they have drawn especially for you, react to such gifts pleasantly, but with minimal response, and then send the children back to their seats.

Occasionally, the student may ask a question that the observer cannot redirect to the teacher. For instance, if the student asks, "Are you writing about me?" you need only make a minimal response ("I'm very busy writing about everything in the room and I have to keep at my work") and then direct the student back to his or her seat.

In advance of coming into a classroom, observers should talk with teachers about where they will sit in the room, how they should be introduced to the students, and how they should respond when individual students approach them. Without such preparation, both teachers and observers frequently are paralyzed when students approach the observer. Teachers are embarrassed because students are out of their seats, and they are indecisive about what to do because they do not know whether the observer wants to inspect the students' work or would prefer not to be bothered. Observers are often unskilled at dealing with students. They are not sure how to act when approached, except that they do not want to be a rude guest. These difficult moments in coding will be reduced if observers meet with teachers before the coding begins to discuss what they want to do and how they should be introduced. Mutual agreement should be reached about how to deal with students who are bent upon making themselves known to the coder. At such meetings, observers can also obtain curriculum materials and information about the students (seating chart, achievement ranking). Such information is necessary if the observer plans to conduct an intensive study of only a few children at different achievement levels. The basic information needed for using the rating systems that appear at the end of each chapter has been presented in this chapter. Students who wish detailed information about more advanced coding systems can profitably consult the appendixes at the end of this chapter.

SUMMARY

This chapter has stressed the fact that objective coding of behavior is the way to guard against our biases and gain the most benefit from classroom observations. In particular, stress has been placed upon reducing our personal bias in observing by (1) becoming aware of our preconceptions; (2) looking for specific behavior, to break down the complexity of classroom activity; and (3) checking our observations against the observations of others. Exercises have been suggested to help you observe your own or another's behavior objectively. Procedures for minimizing the observer's effect on the classroom have been discussed, along with techniques for observing unobtrusively in the classroom. These considerations should be borne in mind when you use end-of-chapter forms for classroom observation.

This chapter, in combination with the previous two chapters, has identified many of the factors that may limit your perception of classroom behavior. In these introductory chapters we have also discussed ways in which we can reduce problems of bias and complexity, as well as ways in which we can observe more objectively in the classroom. In the following chapters, we will develop the theme of looking in classrooms by providing detailed comments about *what* to look for in classrooms. The following chapters provide a focus on what could be and should be occurring in classrooms. Furthermore, the forms at the end of each chapter contain rating scales that can be used to code or look for the presence or absence of the teaching behaviors that are discussed in the chapter.

SUGGESTED ACTIVITIES AND QUESTIONS

3.1. Visit a classroom or watch a videotape of a classroom discussion and try to tally the number of times that the teacher
   a. asks a question
   b. responds to a student's answer
   c. praises a student
   Compare your tallies with those of another observer by calculating the percent of agreement between your observations.

3.2. Try some simple observation with one or two other observers and attempt to code behavior reliably. For example, attempt to keep track of three goldfish. After five minutes of observation, can you agree on which is fish 1, 2, or 3? Can you agree upon which fish moves the most? Which is the fastest when it does move? Which fish is the most aggressive or most playful? Most observers will find this seemingly simple task to be quite complex when they first attempt it. Do a similar exercise for a group of five nursery school children or five older students. Which child is the most aggressive? Which child is busiest? (Add other questions of your own.)

3.3. Examine the classroom observation systems that appear in the appendixes at the end of this chapter. Which system seems most helpful to you? Why?

3.4. Which of the observation systems would be the most difficult to use reliably in the classroom?

3.5. Think about all the teachers you have ever had and list the major characteristics of your favorite teacher. What was he or she like as a person? What were the chief elements of his or her teaching style?

3.6. Similarly, list the distinguishing factors of your least liked or least effective teacher. Why were you more comfortable, more stimulated in one class than the other? Was it because of the teacher, the subject matter, the students in the class, or a combination of factors?

3.7. Identify the ten student characteristics or behaviors that will delight you most when you are a teacher. What does this list tell you about your personal likes and your teaching personality?

3.8. List the ten student characteristics or behaviors that are most likely to irritate you or make you anxious. Why do these behaviors bother you? How can you deal fairly with students who exhibit behaviors that are bothersome to you?

3.9. Why should classroom observers be attuned to student behavior as well as to teacher behavior?

3.10. What can observers do to minimize their disruption of the natural flow of classroom events?

REFERENCES

Anderson-Levitt, K. (1984). Teacher interpretation of student behavior: Cognitive and social processes. *Elementary School Journal, 84,* 315–337.
Brophy, J., & Good, T. (1970). The Brophy-Good Dyadic Interaction System. In A. Simon & E. Boyer (Eds.), *Mirrors for behavior: An anthology of observation instruments*

continued, Supplement (Vols. A and B). Philadelphia: Research for Better Schools, Inc.

Chase, C. (1968). The impact of some obvious variables on essay test scores. *Journal of Educational Measurement, 5,* 315–318.

Coates, T., & Thoresen, C. (1976). Teacher anxiety: A review with recommendations. *Review of Educational Research, 46,* 159–184.

Cooper, H., & Good, T. (1983). *Pygmalion grows up: Studies in the expectation communication process.* New York: Longman.

Doyle, W. (1983). Academic work. *Review of Educational Research, 53,* 159–199.

Doyle, W. (1986). Classroom organization and management. In M. Wittrock (Ed.), *Handbook of research on teaching* (3rd ed.). New York: Macmillan.

Ehman, L. (1970). A comparison of three sources of classroom data: Teachers, students, and systematic observation. Paper presented at the annual meeting of the American Educational Research Association, Minneapolis.

Emmer, E. (1986). *Academic activities and tasks in first-year teachers' classes. Report No. 6025.* Austin: University of Texas, Research and Development Center for Teacher Education.

Emmer, E., and Millet, G. (1970). *Improving teaching through experimentation: A laboratory approach.* Englewood Cliffs, NJ: Prentice-Hall.

Erickson, F. (1986). Qualitative methods in research on teaching. In M. Wittrock (Ed.), *Handbook of research on teaching* (3rd ed.). New York: Macmillan.

Evertson, C., & Green, J. (1986). Observation as inquiry and method. In M. Wittrock (Ed.), *Handbook of research on teaching* (3rd ed.). New York: Macmillan.

Goetz, J., & LeCompte, M. (1984). *Ethnography and qualitative design in educational research.* New York: Academic Press.

Greenberg, H. (1969). *Teaching with feeling.* New York: Macmillan.

Greenwood, G., Good, T., & Siegel, B. (1971). *Problem situations in teaching.* New York: Harper & Row.

Griffin, G. (1985). The school as a work place and the master teacher concept. *Elementary School Journal, 86,* 1–16.

Gump, T. (1982). School settings and their keeping. In D. Duke (Ed.), *Helping teachers manage classrooms.* Alexandria, VA: Association for Supervision and Curriculum Development. (pp. 98–114).

Kleinfeld, J. (1975). Effective teachers of Eskimo and Indian students. *School Review, 83,* 301–344.

Linn, R. (1986). Quantitative methods in research on teaching. In M. Wittrock (Ed.), *Handbook of research on teaching* (3rd ed.). New York: Macmillan.

Marshall, H., & Weinstein, R. (1984). Classroom factors affecting students' self-evaluations: An interactional model. *Review of Educational Research, 54*(3), 301–326.

Marshall, H., & Weinstein, R. (1986). *Classroom dimensions observation system: Revised manual.* Berkeley: University of California.

Peterson, P., & Swing, S. (1982). Beyond time on task: Students' reports of their thought processes during classroom instruction. *Elementary School Journal, 82,* 481–491.

Posner, G. (1985). *Field experience: A guide to reflective teaching.* New York: Longman.

Rohrkemper, M. (1981). *Classroom perspectives study: An investigation of differential perceptions of classroom events.* Unpublished doctoral dissertation. East Lansing: Michigan State University.

Rohrkemper, M. (1985). The influence of teacher socialization style on students' social cognitions and reported interpersonal classroom behavior. *Elementary School Journal, 85,* 245–275.

Shavelson, R., Webb, N., & Burstein, L. (1986). Measurement of teaching. In M. Wittrock (Ed.), *Handbook of research on teaching* (3rd ed.). New York: Macmillan.

Spencer-Hall, D. (1981). Looking behind the teacher's back. *Elementary School Journal, 81,* 281–290.

Spencer, D. (1984*a*). The home and school lives of women teachers. *Elementary School Journal, 84,* 283–298.

Spencer, D. (1984*b*). The home and school lives of women teachers: Implications for staff development. *Elementary School Journal, 84,* 299–314.

Spradley, J. (1979). *The ethnographic interview.* New York: Holt, Rinehart and Winston.

Spradley, J. (1980). *Participant observation.* New York: Holt, Rinehart and Winston.

Weinstein, R. (1983). Student perceptions of schooling. *Elementary School Journal, 83,* 287–312.

Wolfson, B., & Nash, S. (1969). Perceptions of decision making in elementary school classrooms. *Elementary School Journal, 69,* 89–93.

Zumwalt, K. (1985). The master teacher concept: Implications for teacher education. *Elementary School Journal, 86,* 45–54.

APPENDIX A: A Coding Example

Subsequent chapters in this book are followed by forms that you can use to observe and record classroom behavior objectively. Before you can do so profitably, you will need to acquire certain basic coding habits and skills and to learn to check your coding reliability. These skills are not difficult to learn, but they do require some concentration and practice.

A good way for you to begin is to carefully study the following example. It contains coding instructions and coding sheets adapted from the authors' dyadic interaction observation system (Brophy & Good, 1970), and shows the coding of Arlene and Suzi, two observers who coded in the same classroom at the same time. By using this system to code classroom interaction with one or more friends and by computing agreement percentages as shown for Arlene and Suzi, you can obtain necessary practice and assess your reliability as a coder.

The coding system shown in Figure 3.1 is similar to those presented later in the book, in that it applies only to certain kinds of teacher-student interactions; it is not used continually. You may have seen or used a different coding system that involved continual coding—recording information every 30 seconds, for example, regardless of what was going on at that time. The coding approach taken in this book is different. Instead of presenting a general system to be used continually, we provide a variety of forms tailored for use in specific situations. Certain forms are used when teachers are lecturing, for example, while others are used when they are giving seatwork directions, and still others when they are dealing with management problems.

Thus, you do not code continually with these forms. You use a given observation form only when the appropriate behavior is present (i.e., when *codable instances* are observed). When no codable instances are present, you do not code anything, or else you use a different observation form appropriate to the present situation.

CODING QUESTION-ANSWER-FEEDBACK SEQUENCES

In this example, teacher and student behaviors are coded during question-and-answer interchanges. Whenever the teacher asks a question and calls on a student to respond, the observers code information about whether the student is male or female, about the quality of the student's response, and about the nature of the teacher's feedback reaction to the student. If you have not done so already, study the coding instructions in Figure 3.1 before continuing.

Coding sheets are prepared so that this information can be quickly recorded by entering check marks in appropriate places on the coding sheet. No writing or note taking is required. The coding sheet is organized to follow the time sequence involved in coder decision making,

STUDENT SEX

SYMBOL	LABEL	DEFINITION
M	Male	The student answering the question is male.
F	Female	The student answering the question is female.

STUDENT RESPONSE

+	Right	The teacher accepts the student's response as correct or satisfactory.
±	Part right	The teacher considers the student's response to be only partially correct or to be correct but incomplete.
—	Wrong	The teacher considers the student's response to be incorrect.
0	No answer	The student makes no response or says he or she doesn't know (code student's answer here if teacher gives a feedback reaction before he or she is able to respond).

TEACHER FEEDBACK REACTION

++	Praise	Teacher praises student either in words ("fine," "good," "wonderful," "good thinking") or by expressing verbal affirmation in a notably warm, joyous, or excited manner.
+	Affirm	Teacher simply affirms that the student's response is correct (nods, repeats answer, says "Yes," "OK," etc.).
0	No reaction	Teacher makes no response whatever to student's response—he or she simply goes on to something else.
—	Negate	Teacher simply indicates that the student's response is incorrect (shakes head, says "No," "That's not right," "Hm-mm," etc.).
—	Criticize	Teacher criticizes student, either in words ("You should know better than that," "That doesn't make any sense—you better pay close attention," etc.) or by expressing verbal negation in a frustrated, angry, or disgusted manner.
Gives Ans.	Teacher gives answer	Teacher provides the correct answer for the student.
Asks Other	Teacher asks another student	Teacher redirects the question, asking a different student to try to answer it.
Other Calls	Another student calls out answer	Another student calls out the correct answer, and the teacher acknowledges that it is correct.
Repeats	Repeats question	Teacher repeats the original question, either in its entirety or with a prompt ("Well?" "Do you know?" "What's the answer?").
Clue	Rephrase or clue	Teacher makes original question easier for student to answer by rephrasing it or by giving a clue.
New Ques.	New question	Teacher asks a new question (i.e., a question that calls for a different answer than the original question called for).

Figure 3.1 Coding categories for question-answer-feedback sequences.

so that in coding a given interchange, the coders move from left to right across the page (see Figures 3.2–3.4). As soon as they recognize that a codable interchange is occurring (i.e., the teacher has asked a question and is calling on a student to respond), the coders begin recording the information. When the teacher selects a student to respond, coders record his or her sex by entering a check mark under M or F. Then, after noting the student's response and the teacher's reaction to it, they code the quality of the response by entering a check mark under +, ±, −, or 0. Finally they code the teacher's feedback reaction by entering one or more check marks in the appropriate teacher reaction columns. For example, if the teacher simply affirmed that a correct response was correct and then went on to another question and another student, coders would enter a check mark in the + column. However, if the teacher had praised the response and then asked the same student another question, coders would have entered check marks in both the + + and the New Ques. columns.

To see if you understand, try to code the following sequence:

TEACHER: Which is heavier, a pound of lead or a pound of feathers? George?
GEORGE: Neither one—they're both a pound!
TEACHER: That's right—good thinking, George!

To code this sequence correctly, you would:

1. Enter a check under M—George is a male student.
2. Enter a check under +—he answered the question correctly.
3. Enter a check under +—the teacher affirmed the answer ("That's right").
4. Enter a check under ⁺₊—the teacher also praised the student ("Good thinking").

Once the teacher's response to the student's answer (or failure to answer) has been coded, the information for that particular question-answer-feedback sequence is complete, and coders drop down to the next row and move back to the left side of the coding sheet to be prepared for coding the next sequence. The next sequence may be with the same student (if the teacher has repeated the question or rephrased it, given a clue, or asked a new question, thus giving the student a second opportunity to respond), or it may be with a new student.

Thus each row contains information about a single question-answer-feedback sequence, and this interaction can be reconstructed from the coding sheets. Both Arlene's and Suzi's sheets (Figures 3.2 and 3.3, respectively) show that in the first observed codable interchange: (1) the teacher called on a female student to respond, (2) the student responded correctly, (3) the teacher affirmed that her response was correct. Inspection of the second row on each sheet shows that Arlene and Suzi agree that the teacher directed the second question to a male student and that he also answered correctly. However, the coders are in disagreement about the teacher's feedback reaction. Arlene felt that the teacher's reaction was simply affirmation of the correctness of the student's answer, but Suzi saw the teacher's reaction as more intense or positive, and so she coded it as praise. This is the first of several coding disagreements between Arlene and Suzi.

How serious are these disagreements? Can the coders' interpretations be trusted? To answer such questions, objective methods of assessing coders' reliability are required. An objective analysis of Arlene's and Suzi's reliability is presented below.

ESTABLISHING RELIABILITY

To establish reliability, you will need to code in the company of at least one other person. This will allow you to assess reliability by comparing your codes with another's and will provide the basis for clearing up ambiguities and misunderstandings through discussion of disagreements. Once good reliability is established, you can code semi-independently. However, it is wise to continue to check reliability periodically, even after initial proficiency has been established. This will help guard against the tendency to gradually drift into un-

	STUDENT SEX		STUDENT RESPONSE				TEACHER FEEDBACK REACTION									
NO.	M	F	+	±	−	0	++	+	0	−	− − −	GIVES ANS.	ASKS OTHER	OTHER CALLS	RE-PEATS	CLUE	NEW QUES.
1		✓	✓					✓									
2	✓		✓					✓									
3	✓					✓	✓									✓	
4	✓		✓					✓									
5	✓		✓														
6		✓			✓						✓						✓
7	✓		✓				✓										
8	✓		✓						✓								
9	✓					✓			✓		✓	✓					
10	✓																
11																	
12																	
13																	
14																	
15																	

Figure 3.2 Arlene's codes.

Figure 3.3 Suzi's codes.

NO.	STUDENT SEX M	STUDENT SEX F	STUDENT RESPONSE +	STUDENT RESPONSE ±	STUDENT RESPONSE −	STUDENT RESPONSE 0	FEEDBACK ++	FEEDBACK +	FEEDBACK 0	FEEDBACK −	FEEDBACK −−	GIVES ANS.	ASKS OTHER	OTHER CALLS	RE-PEATS	CLUE	NEW QUES.
1		✓	✓					✓									
2	✓		✓				✓									✓	
3	✓					✓	✓										
4	✓		✓				✓										
5	✓		✓				✓										
6		✓									✓		✓				✓
7		✓	✓		✓		✓										
8	✓		✓		✓				✓								
9	✓		✓						✓								
10	✓					✓					✓	✓					
11	✓																
12																	
13																	
14																	
15																	

desirable observation and coding habits over time. Even the use of structured, standardized observation instruments cannot guarantee against coding inaccuracies. Thus, even the most experienced coders need to recheck their reliability occasionally if they want to be sure that their observations can be trusted. This is especially important, of course, in research situations.

Two or more coders can check their reliability either by visiting in a classroom together or by coding the same film or videotape of classroom interaction. When films or videotapes are available, it is often advisable to use them in the initial stages of learning to code. Any number of coders can all code the same films or videotapes, which can be replayed to refresh everyone's memory when disagreements are discussed.

At first, the major source of disagreement between coders usually is speed. That is, if one or both coders fall behind while trying to make up their minds about a code or trying to find the correct place on the coding sheet to record it, they may fail to observe or record one or more instances of codable interaction that occurred while this was going on. Such problems disappear rapidly with practice, however, and coders soon learn to keep up with the pace of classroom interaction.

After this is accomplished, disagreements between coders usually will occur not because one coder coded an interaction that the other one missed, but because both coders coded an interaction but coded it differently. That is, the two coders disagree in their observation of the instance in question. By analyzing and discussing these instances of disagreement, coders can usually identify common or repeated causes. For example, one coder may always code "good" as praise, while another coder might not consider "good" to be praise. Thus, the first coder would code many more instances of praise in the classroom of a teacher who frequently said "good." By identifying and coming to agreement about how to resolve those reported sources of disagreement, coders can eliminate most unreliability.

COMPUTING CODER AGREEMENT PERCENTAGES

Arlene and Suzi show general agreement, but they have several disagreements. To assess their agreement precisely, they could compute agreement percentages. The computations are shown below.

Assessment of coder agreement in using this type of observation scheme requires getting answers to two questions: (1) When a codable interchange appeared, did both coders code it? (2) When both coders did code an interchange, did their coding agree? The first question deals with coding speed, the ability of the coders to keep up with the pace of classroom interaction. The second deals with coder agreement on how particular interchanges should have been coded.

Coder speed can be assessed with the formula given in the chapter. This formula can be used whenever agreements on frequency, or number of codes, are being measured. In our example, Suzi coded 11 interchanges, while Arlene coded 10. Applying the formula for agreement between two observers, we have:

$$1 - \frac{A - B}{A + B} = 1 - \frac{11 - 10}{11 + 10} = 1 - \frac{1}{21} = 1 - 0.05 = 95\%$$

Thus, Arlene and Suzi showed good, but not perfect, agreement. Arlene missed 1 of 11 codable interchanges, while Suzi coded all 11. It is possible that both coders missed one or more other codable interchanges, but we cannot tell from the data. If the coders knew that they both had missed additional coding, they would have to take this into account in interpreting their agreement data. In this case, the 95 percent figure would be deceptively high.

To assess coder agreement on how particular interchanges should be coded, we turn our attention to those interchanges that both Arlene and Suzi coded. Suzi's extra coding (the seventh row on her coding sheet) is not used in this analysis because we do not know how Arlene would have coded this interchange, and therefore, we have nothing to compare with Suzi's coding. To facilitate comparison, Figure 3.4 shows Arlene's codes superimposed on Suzi's coding sheet (skipping Suzi's seventh row, because Arlene does not have a parallel set of codes; Arlene's seventh row belongs with Suzi's eighth row, and so on).

Coder agreement is computed separately for the three decisions that each coder had to make concerning each interchange: (1) the sex of the student, (2) the quality of the student's response, and (3) the nature of the teacher's feedback reaction. The method to be used in computing agreement is (1) establish the number of *coding decisions* that were made and (2) compute the percentage of these decisions on which the two coders agreed.

Since ten interchanges were coded by both coders, each coder had to note the student's sex ten times. Agreement between Arlene and Suzi on these decisions about student sex was perfect (10/10 = 100 percent agreement).

There were also ten student responses to be coded as right, part-right, wrong, or no response. Arlene and Suzi also agreed on all ten of these coding decisions (100 percent agreement).

Disagreements appeared in the coding of the teacher's feedback reactions to students. Twice Arlene coded "affirm" while Suzi coded "praise"; otherwise, the two coders agreed in coding a total of ten teacher feedback reactions. Thus, they agreed in 10 out of 12 (83 percent) of the instances in which they both coded an aspect of the teacher's feedback. (There are 12 codes here rather than 10, because the teacher showed two different categories of feedback on each of two occasions.)

Overall, Arlene and Suzi's agreement is quite good. One clear pattern of disagreement does show up: Suzi tends to code "praise" at times when Arlene codes "affirm." This occurred twice out of the five times that this particular distinction had to be made (i.e., their agreement for the praise vs. affirm decision was only 60 percent). We cannot tell from the data which coder is correct, if either is. Arlene and Suzi would have to discuss these instances of disagreement to discover the reason for them.

INTERPRETING CLASSROOM CODING

The example is too short to allow firm conclusions, but we can make some tentative hypotheses about the teacher on the basis of it. First, note that the majority of questions are answered by boys. If this proves to be a reliable finding, it suggests that the teacher is not calling on girls as much as would be desirable. This could be brought to the teacher's attention for discussion and possible action.

The students' answers show an appropriate success rate. The difficulty of teachers' questions should be such that most, but not all, are answered correctly. This way the difficulty level is adjusted to student ability. Students can follow the lesson and respond without great difficulty, but at the same time the questions are not so old or easy that they present no challenge.

When the students in this example did not respond correctly, they tended not to respond at all. If this happens often, it may mean that the teacher is not waiting long enough to allow students to formulate a response, or that he or she is overly critical in response to wrong answers, so that the students hesitate to answer unless they are sure they are right. In any case, it usually is better that students make some response rather than remain silent when stuck. If they remain silent, it is likely that inappropriate teacher behavior is the reason.

A tendency to criticize students when they do not respond correctly has shown up in this teacher's codes; it may be part of the explanation for the students' tendency to remain silent when stuck. *Criticism is almost never appropriate in these instances.* However, note that the teacher also tends to praise frequently. Taken together, these codes suggest that the teacher may be generally overreacting to student performance. He or she might do better to be more problem-centered and less personal in feedback reactions.

TEACHER FEEDBACK REACTION

STUDENT SEX | STUDENT RESPONSE

NO.	M	F	+	+/-	-	0	++	+	0	-	-/-	GIVES ANS.	ASKS OTHER	OTHER CALLS	RE-PEATS	CLUE	NEW QUES.
1																	
2																	
3																	
4																	
5																	
6																	
7																	
8																	
9																	
10																	
11																	
12																	
13																	
14																	
15																	

Figure 3.4 Arlene's codes superimposed over Suzi's codes.

The pattern of praise and criticism suggests that the teacher may be playing favorites and/or may prefer boys to girls, although much more data would be needed to find out for sure.

APPROPRIATE USE OF FREQUENCY DATA

Production of frequency data involves counting the number of behaviors in a category that occur during a lesson or a week of observation. Most of the scales and ratings sheets presented in this book involve such counting. Your thinking about what happens in classrooms will be stimulated by information gotten just from looking at count totals.

However, if you have a research purpose, or if comparisons are to be made between teachers or students, it may be more appropriate to use a common frame of reference for comparisons. *Rates* (the number of behaviors per hour) and *percentages* (actually observed rates expressed as percentages of the total number of times that the behavior could have occurred) are two convenient ways to summarize data.

We often observe for unequal amounts of time in different classrooms. If we observe in Classroom A once for two hours and once for three hours, and in Classroom B on two occasions for one hour each, it will be misleading to compare Teacher A and Teacher B in terms of frequency. Teacher A may total more thought questions, discipline problems, and so on, simply because we spent more time in that classroom.

However, Classrooms A and B can be compared meaningfully in terms of events per hour (rate). Assume that students approached the teacher to seek feedback about their work 30 times in Classroom A and 20 times in Classroom B. Rate measures reveal that students in Classroom B approached the teacher more often in work-related situations,

$$\frac{20}{2} = \text{ten times per hour}$$

than students in Classroom A,

$$\frac{30}{5} = \text{six times per hour}$$

Converting frequency data into percentages and rates will help you avoid misinterpreting. For example, some teachers may appear to have few private contacts with certain students, but only because they have few contacts with students generally. Some teachers may have 200 or more private contacts with students a day; others may have fewer than 25. When describing differences between teachers in the number of contacts, the specific numbers are important and should be noted in frequency terms (200 vs. 25). However, when we talk about differential teacher treatment of students, it would help to use percentage data. (What percent of the 200 or the 25 contacts went to high or to low achievers?)

In some situations, frequencies will not provide the information desired. This is likely to occur when you are interested in the regularity with which one behavioral act precedes or follows another. For example, if you wanted to know if teachers praised high- and low-achievement students differentially, it would *not* be possible to use frequencies (high-achievement students may get more praise because they answer more questions correctly). To examine the question of differential behavior, it would be necessary to determine what percent of low-achievement students' correct answers are followed by teacher praise (When low-achievement students do answer correctly, are they praised?) compared to the percent of time that the correct answers of high-achieving students are followed by praise.

CONCLUSIONS

The extended example presented in this appendix shows how you would establish coder agreement and use coded information to draw inferences about teaching. The principles involved are applicable to any coding in the classroom. To check agreement on frequency or number of codes, use the formula

$$\text{Agreement} = 1 - \frac{A - B}{A + B}$$

To check agreement on how interchanges should have been coded, compute a percentage by dividing the number agreed upon by itself plus the number not agreed upon (i.e., agreements divided by total decisions).

To interpret coded information, look for patterns that give clues about appropriate and inappropriate teacher behavior (this will be discussed at length in the following chapters). Remember, though, that interpretations based on one or just a few observations are tentative and suggestive. Do not make judgments on the basis of insufficient evidence. At times, more meaningful comparisons can be made when frequencies are converted to rates or percentages.

APPENDIX B: Brophy-Good Dyadic Interaction System

There are many observational systems that one can use to code classroom behavior. All systems are selective and code certain behaviors while ignoring other aspects of the classroom. Hence, the usefulness of a particular observation system depends upon one's goal. In this appendix, one observation system, the Brophy-Good Dyadic Interaction System, is briefly presented. If more information about the system is desired, the complete manual (with extended discussion of variables and terms, and examples) can be obtained from the Research and Development Center, Education Annex, University of Texas, Austin, Texas 78712, Report No. 0043).

In this particular system, the goal is to determine if individual students receive more or less of certain behaviors than do other students (e.g., Are high-achieving female students treated differently than low-achieving male students?). After you read the definitions and examine the coding sheets that follow, go back to Chapter 1 and examine the long classroom scene. Do the teachers provide equal opportunity for all students? Coding systems like the Brophy-Good system help us to be more systematic in our observations.

BRIEF DEFINITIONS OF VARIABLES CODED IN BROPHY-GOOD DYADIC INTERACTION SYSTEM

The coding sheet (see Figure 3.5) uses the definitions that appear below. Definitions are presented in the order that they appear on the coding sheet. For an extended discussion of these definitions and coding examples see Brophy and Good (1970).

Student-initiated question. A student asks the teacher a question in a public setting.

Reading or recitation. Student is called upon to read aloud, go through an arithmetic table, and so on.

Discipline question. The discipline question is a unique type of direct question in which the teacher uses the question as a control technique, calling on the student to force him or her to pay better attention rather than merely providing a response opportunity in the usual sense.

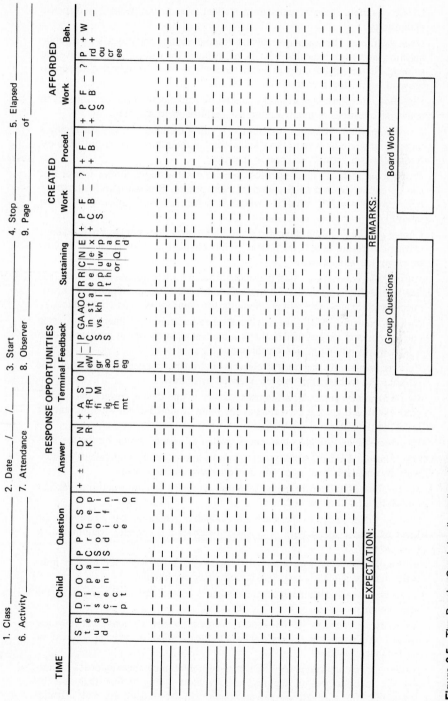

Figure 3.5 The Brophy-Good dyadic coding sheet.

Direct question. Teacher calls on a student who is not seeking a response opportunity.

Open question. The teacher creates the response opportunity by asking a public question and also indicates who is to respond by calling on an individual student, but the teacher chooses one of the students who has indicated a desire to respond by raising a hand.

Call-outs. Response opportunities created by students who call out answers to teachers' questions without waiting for permission to respond.

Process question. Requires students to explain something in a way that requires them to integrate facts or to show knowledge of their interrelationships. It most frequently is a "why?" or "how?" question.

Product question. Product questions seek to elicit a single correct answer that can be expressed in a single word or short phrase. Product questions usually begin with "who?," "what?," "when?," "where?," "how much?," or "how many?"

Choice question. In the choice question, the student does not have to produce a substantive response but may instead simply choose one of two or more implied or expressed alternatives.

Self-reference question. Asks the student to make some nonacademic contribution to classroom discussion ("show-and-tell," questions about personal experiences, preferences, or feelings, requests for opinions or predictions, etc.).

Opinion question. Much like a self-reference question (i.e., there is no single correct answer) except that it elicits a student opinion on an academic topic ("Is it worth putting a man on the moon?").

Correct answer. If the student answers the teacher's question in a way that satisfies the teacher, the answer is coded as correct.

Part-Correct answer. A part-correct answer is one that is correct but incomplete as far as it goes or correct from one point of view but not what the teacher is looking for.

Incorrect answer. A response that is treated as simply wrong by the teacher.

Don't know. Student verbally says "I don't know" (or its equivalent) or nonverbally indicates that he or she doesn't know (shakes head).

No response. Student makes no response (verbally or nonverbally) to teacher question.

Praise. Praise refers to the teacher's evaluative reactions that go beyond the level of simple affirmation or positive feedback by verbally complimenting the student.

Affirmation of correct answers. Affirmation is coded when the teacher indicates that the student's response is correct or acceptable.

Summary. Teacher summarizes the student's answer (generally as part of the affirmation process).

No feedback reaction. If the teacher makes no verbal or nonverbal response whatever following the student's answer to the question, the teacher is coded for no feedback reaction.

Negation of incorrect answer. Simple provision of impersonal feedback regarding the incorrectness of the response, without going farther than this by communicating a negative personal reaction to the student. As with affirmation, negation can be communicated both verbally ("No." "That's not right." "Hmm-mm.") and nonverbally (shaking the head horizontally).

Criticism. Evaluative reactions that go beyond the level of simple negation by expressing anger or personal criticism of the student in addition to indicating the incorrectness of the response.

Process feedback. Coded when the teacher goes beyond merely providing the right answer and discusses the cognitive or behavioral processes that are to be gone through in arriving at the answer.

Gives answer. This category is used when the teacher gives the student the answer to the question but does not elaborate sufficiently to be coded for process feedback.

Asks other. Whenever the student does not answer a teacher question and the teacher moves to another student in order to get the answer to that same question, the teacher's feedback reaction is coded for *asks other*.

Call out. The call-out category is used when another student calls out the answer to the question before the teacher has a chance to call on someone.

Repeats question. Teacher asks a question, waits some time without getting the correct answer, and then repeats the question to the same student.

Rephrase or clue. In this feedback reaction, the teacher sustains the response opportunity by rephrasing the question or giving the student a clue as to how to respond to it.

New question. When the first question is not answered or is answered incorrectly, the teacher asks a new question that is different from the original, although it may be closely related. A question requiring a new answer is coded as a new question.

Expansion. Teacher responses to vague or incomplete statements that ask the student to provide more information ("I think I understand, but tell me . . .").

DYADIC TEACHER-STUDENT CONTACTS

The preceding material has dealt primarily with the coding of response opportunities and reading and recitation turns.

Dyadic teacher-student contacts differ from response opportunities and reading and recitation turns in that the teacher is dealing privately with one student about matters idiosyncratic to him or her rather than publicly about material meant for the group or class as a whole.

Dyadic teacher-student contacts are divided into procedural contacts, work-related contacts, and behavioral or disciplinary contacts. They are also separately coded according to whether they are initiated by the teacher (teacher-afforded) or by the student (student-created). The coding also reflects certain aspects of the teacher's behavior in such contacts.

Work-Related Contacts

Work-related contacts include those teacher-student contacts that have to do with the student's completion of seatwork or homework assignments. They include clarification of the directions, soliciting or giving help concerning how to do the work, or soliciting or giving feedback about work already done. Work-related interactions are considered *student-created* if the student brings his or her work up to the teacher to talk about it, raises a hand, or otherwise indicates a desire to discuss it with the teacher. Work-related interactions are coded as *teacher-afforded* if the teacher gives feedback about work when the student has not solicited it (the teacher either calls the student to come up to his or her desk or goes around the room making individual comments to the students). *Created* contacts are not planned by the teacher and occur solely because the student has sought out the teacher; *afforded* contacts are not planned by the student and occur solely because the teacher initiates them. Separate space is provided for coding *created* and *afforded* work-related interactions on the coding sheets, and the coder indicates the nature of an individual dyadic contact by where the interaction is coded.

In addition to noting the interaction as a work interaction and as an interaction that is student-created or teacher-afforded, the coder also indicates the nature of the teacher's feedback to the student during the interactions. He or she indicates this by using one or more of the five columns provided for coding teacher's feedback in work-related interaction: praise (+ +), process feedback (pcss), product feedback (fb), criticism (−), or "don't know" (?). The first four of these categories have the same meaning as they have in other coding of teacher feedback. The additional "don't know" category is added for this coding because frequently the individual teacher-student interaction that occurs in the dyadic contacts will be carried on in hushed tones or across the room from the coder, where it is not possible to hear the content of the interaction. In such cases, the coder notes the occurrence of the work-related interaction and the fact that it was either teacher-afforded or student-created but enters the student's identification number in the "don't know" column (identified by the question mark on top).

Procedural Contacts

The category of *procedural contacts* includes all dyadic teacher-student interactions that are not coded as work-related contacts or as behavioral contacts. Thus it includes a wide range of types of contacts, most of which are initiated on the basis of the immediate needs of the teacher or student involved. Procedural contacts are *created* by the student for such purposes as seeking permission to do something, requesting needed supplies or equipment, reporting some information to the teacher (tattling on other students, calling attention to a broken desk or pencil, etc.), seeking help in putting on or taking off clothing, getting permission or information about how to take care of idiosyncratic needs (turning in lunch money, delivering a note from the parent to the principal, etc.), as well as a variety of other contacts. In general, any dyadic interaction initiated by the student that does not fit the definition of *work-related contacts* is coded as a *procedural contact*.

Behavioral Contacts

Behavioral contacts are coded whenever the teacher makes some comment on the student's classroom behavior. They are subdivided into *praise, warnings,* and *criticism.* The coder notes the information by entering the student's identification number under the appropriate column. Behavioral evaluation contacts are considered to be teacher-*afforded*, although they usually occur as reactions to the student's immediately preceding behavior. Nevertheless, they are teacher-afforded in the sense that the student usually does not want and does not expect the interaction and that the teacher chooses to single the student out for comment.

APPENDIX C: Emmer Observation System

In Appendix B, we examined parts of the Brophy-Good Dyadic Interaction System and we have seen that it allows us to code and/or think more systematically about the two classroom scenes presented in Chapter 1. However, teachers do more than interact with individual students, and we need ways to classify and think about these aspects of classroom interaction as well.

One interesting and useful observational manual has been prepared by Ed Emmer at the University of Texas. We can present but a small part of this system here; the reader interested in more of the observational scales included in the manual and in details of training and reliability can consult Emmer (1973), and the entire manual can be purchased from the Research and Development Center, Education Annex, University of Texas, Austin, Texas 78712.

Emmer recommends that the scales should be used approximately every 15 minutes, because longer time periods may reduce reliability by placing too much reliance on the observer's memory and shorter intervals may fail to provide sufficient information to use the scale. He also suggests that the observer should sit where he or she can observe the teacher and students and be in a position to see the faces of as many students as possible.

What follows are examples of five of the twelve scales that appear in the Emmer system.

LEVEL OF ATTENTION

Attention as defined for this scale refers to pupil orientation toward the teacher, the task at hand, or whatever classroom activities are appropriate. If pupils are attending to inappropriate activities or are engaged in self-directed behavior when they are supposed to be engaged in a class activity, this behavior is not considered attentive. Therefore, you should look for behavior that is focused on or engaged in whatever activity is appropriate, be it individual seatwork, group discussion, or listening to the presentation of information. Cues that are useful in recognizing attentive behavior include eye contact, body orientation, response to questions or other eliciting cues, and participation in class activity. Cues that are useful in recognizing inattentiveness include inappropriate social interaction, repetitive body movement, visual wandering, and engagement in behavior other than the sanctioned class activity. At times, it will be difficult to determine whether a student is being attentive, such as when the teacher presents information and the student sits facing the teacher, with no observable behaviors indicating inattention. In such instances, the pupils are considered attentive until they behave otherwise.

To code behavior on this scale, scan the class on several occasions during each 15-minute observation period. Note how many pupils appear attentive or inattentive at a given time. After some practice you will find it easier to keep in mind your estimate of the number of inattentive students. Average your estimates of attention and record this average using the scale below.

1. Fewer than half of the students are attentive most of the time.
2. One-half to three-fourths of the students appear attentive most of the time; the remainder are attentive only some of the time.
3. Most of the students are attentive, but several (four to six) are attentive only some of the time.
4. Nearly all students are attentive, but a few (one, two, or three) are attentive only some of the time.
5. All of the students are attentive most of the time.

Note—the phrase "most of the time" means at least 75 percent of the time the observer checks the pupils for attentiveness.

Some examples from which inattention or attention may be inferred:

Inattention: Moving around the room at an inappropriate time

Reading a book during class discussion

Two students whispering

Sitting with elbows on desk, fingers holding eyelids open

Doodling with a pencil

Laying head on desk

Asking a question unrelated to the activity of the class

Staring fixedly at an object not related to class activity

Attention: Raising hand to volunteer a response

Maintaining eye contact, following teacher's movements

Turning to watch another student who is contributing to the class activity

Working on assigned activity

If a free-activity period, pupils engaged in some task

Teacher Presentation

This scale measures only one type of behavior. The observer's task is to estimate the relative amount of class time occupied by teacher presentation of substantive information. *Teacher presentation* means substantive (content-oriented) verbal or nonverbal behavior that provides information and does not imply or require pupil response or evaluate pupil behavior. Thus, teacher questions, procedural directions, praise, and criticism are not instances of teacher presentation. Lecturing, reading to the class, answering pupil questions, and any other activity in which the teacher gives information are all instances of teacher presentation.

To use this scale, observe the teacher's behavior and note the amount of teacher presentation as compared to the total of all teacher behavior, pupil behavior, and periods of seatwork or other activities in which there is no verbal interaction.

1. Teacher presentation occurs 0–20 percent of the period.
2. Teacher presentation occurs 21–40 percent of the period.
3. Teacher presentation occurs 41–60 percent of the period.
4. Teacher presentation occurs 61–80 percent of the period.
5. Teacher presentation occurs 81–100 percent of the period.

Note that in order for a 5 to be scored, the observation period must be taken up almost entirely by teacher information-giving. Even a small amount of discussion or other activity will be likely to cause the rating to be a 4 or less. On the other hand, a score of 1 will occur only when there is a very small amount of teacher information giving (less than 20 percent of the time).

Teacher presentation should not be confused with *teacher talk*, since the former may be only a small part of the latter. Although a question-and-answer session might contain 70 percent teacher talk, much of it may be teacher questions and evaluation rather than presentation. Be sure to distinguish teacher presentation from other teacher behaviors.

The two scales presented above, like most of those included in the Emmer system, require that one look for specific behaviors and estimate the frequency of their occurrence. The three scales that follow call for classroom observers to make inferential judgments.

TASK ORIENTATION

This scale is a measure of the degree to which the teacher works toward content-related, substantive goals. Low task orientation occurs when class sessions place little emphasis on student attainment of content objectives, as indicated by wandering discussions, wasting time with procedural activities, busywork assignments, and unproductive activity. High task orientation occurs when there is a definite emphasis on student attainment of content objectives, when class activities appear to be carefully planned, and when discussions are substantive and focused.

1. Very low task orientation. There is much wasted time and discussion, many pointless activities, and little substantive progress is attempted by the teacher.
2. Low task orientation, but neither very low or moderate.
3. Moderate task orientation. Attainment of content objectives is usually, but not always, the main purpose of class activities; class activities and procedures are occasionally a waste of time and effort.
4. High task orientation, neither moderate nor very high.
5. Very high task orientation. Emphasis clearly is on student attainment of content objectives; class activities appear to be carefully planned; discussions are fruitful; a minimum of time is lost to procedural activity.

In using this scale, you will find it helpful to adopt the perspective that it is primarily the *teacher's* task orientation you are assessing, and only secondarily, the *class's*. Time wasted by the students when they have been given an assignment by the teacher does not count for a low rating, although failing to help the students get on with the task does count toward a low rating. The latter rating depends on the observer's judgment that the need for such help was or should have been apparent to the teacher. Assignments given just to keep pupils busy (admittedly, a subjective judgment) get lower ratings than assignments that relate clearly to the content objectives that are the focus of the lesson. Remember, however, that you are not observing a Marine Corps drill team or an automobile assembly line, so a small amount of "wasted" time and motion is to be expected in even the most task-oriented teacher's classroom or learning center.

CLARITY

Clarity refers to the degree to which the teacher's presentation of material and substantive interactions with students are understood by them. Low clarity means that the teacher is vague, confusing, or "over the heads" of pupils. High clarity means that the pupils appear to understand the teacher. The observer must use many cues to make this rating, noting particularly the pupils' reactions to the teacher's presentation and instructions as well as the teacher's actual behavior. When observing the teacher for clarity, check for behaviors such as stating the objectives of the activity or assignment, giving directions that do not require constant repetition, giving several examples or using different media to illustrate a point, checking with students at various times to verify their understanding, and summarizing main points from discussions or lessons. Other than the absence of the above characteristics of clarity, indicators of low clarity include looks of bewilderment on the faces of the pupils, statements that they do not understand or that they are confused, frequent incorrect pupil responses to the teacher's questions, teacher statements that use qualifiers (e.g., maybe, sometimes, not always) without seeking or supplying the salient qualifying attributes, and vague or evasive teacher responses to pupil questions.

1. Very low clarity. Pupils seem very confused by the presentation. The teacher cannot answer the pupils' questions, or answers them in an unclear manner by using concepts and terms that pupils are apparently unfamiliar with or by being overly complex and ambiguous.
2. Low clarity, between very low and moderate.

3. Moderate clarity. The teacher seems to be understood by most pupils, but not all of the time. Sometimes the teacher is confusing and vague.
4. High clarity, between moderate and very high.
5. Very high clarity. The teacher's explanations are easy to understand and pupil questions are adequately answered. The teacher seems aware of the pupils' levels, sensing problems they are having or may have in the future.

ENTHUSIASM

This scale is used to judge the extent to which the teacher displays interest, vitality, and involvement in subject and instruction.

1. Very low enthusiasm. The teacher's behavior is lethargic, dull, routine; there is a minimum of vocal inflection, gesturing, movement, or change in facial features. The teacher appears to lack interest in what he or she is doing.
2. Low enthusiasm, between very low and moderate.
3. Moderate enthusiasm. Occasionally the teacher seems interested and involved; there is some display of activity, such as gesturing. Sometimes the teacher is dull, routine, and lacking in vigor.
4. High enthusiasm, between moderate and very high.
5. Very high enthusiasm. The teacher is stimulating, energetic, and very alert. He or she seems interested and involved in teaching; moves around, gestures, inflects voice.

Although some of these scales are not useful for analyzing classroom dialogue (such as the examples presented in Chapter 1), they do extend the range of behaviors that we can consider when we think about classrooms. Obviously, to use a scale like enthusiasm, one would have to see and hear the classroom participants. However, some of the scales in the Emmer system are useful in analyzing classroom transcripts as well as actual classroom behavior. As a case in point, the presentation scale helps us to examine the extent to which the teacher is using time to develop subject matter aspects of the lesson. Read the dialogue and narrative in Chapter 1 and determine how much emphasis is placed on content in the two scenes.

As was mentioned in Chapter 2, teachers are known to vary widely in how they allocate time to particular subjects. The presentation scale is a tool that can help one look at time decisions both within and across subjects. Similarly, the attention scale can assist one in thinking about the effects of teaching (e.g., high and low levels of teacher presentation paired with high and low clarity) on students (i.e., Are they engaged in tasks?). As we have stated often in this book, much happens quickly, and classroom coding systems may be of great benefit if they are used to clarify what actually happens in classrooms and if they stimulate thought. If they are used to support generalities about teaching (teachers should always have a "high" level of presentation), then they are of little value.

APPENDIX D: Coding Vocabulary: Blumenfeld and Miller

There has been a rapid growth in the use of observation systems in training and research and the types of systems used to code classroom behavior have become more varied in the past few years (Evertson & Green, 1986). The following material was prepared by Phyllis Blumenfeld and Samuel Miller for their students at the University of Michigan. It is a very effective device for describing different means of collecting narrative and frequency count information.

NARRATIVE STRATEGIES

Anecdotal Record

Characteristics:
a. Provides a brief sketch or illustration about a student's behavioral pattern or learning style (e.g., several brief anecdotes might be used to illustrate how a student reacts to a particular situation).
b. Indicates that students have mastered or applied concepts (e.g., brief anecdotes might be used to illustrate that students used knowledge from a subtraction lesson to solve a problem in another subject or outside of class).

Procedure:
a. Write down the incident as soon after it occurs as possible.
b. Identify the basic action of the key person and what was said.
c. Include a statement that identifies the setting, time of day, and basic activity.
d. In describing the central character's actions or verbalizations, include the responses or reactions of other people in the situation.
e. Whenever possible note exact words used, to preserve the precise flavor of the conversation.
f. Preserve the sequence of the episode.
g. Be objective, accurate, and complete (i.e., do not interpret).

Running Record

Characteristics:
a. Running records are used to record the situation in a manner that lets someone else read the description later and visualize the scene or event as it occurred.
b. As opposed to anecdotal records, which provide a brief illustrative episode on a student, running records provide a detailed, continuous, or sequential descriptive account of the behavior and its immediate environmental context (eyewitness account par excellence).
c. Running records can be used to help locate the source of the problem or pattern of behavior. (If you wanted to know whether the teacher used effective questioning strategies you could collect running records of lessons and later go to the records to pinpoint instances of the teacher using effective and ineffective questions.)

Procedure:
a. Describe the scene as it is when the observer begins the description.
b. Focus on the subject's behavior and whatever in the situation itself affects this behavior.
c. Be as accurate and complete as you can about what the subject says, does, and responds to within the situation.
d. Put brackets around all interpretive material generated by the observer so that the description itself stands out clearly and completely.
e. Include the "how" for whatever the subject does (e.g., teacher said to be quiet in a high voice while pointing her right hand at the students vs. the teacher said to be quiet).
f. Give the "how" for everything done by anyone interacting with the subject (e.g., emphasis on the details not on inferences).
g. For every action report all the main steps in their proper order.
h. Describe behavior positively, rather than in terms of what was NOT done.
i. Use observational tools whenever possible (tape recorders, cameras, or videotape).

Comparison of Anecdotal and Running Records

Comparison is related to the following points:

a. *Length of Observation.* Anecdotal records require shorter periods of time and are normally completed after the event has occurred whereas running records are recorded as events occur and usually continue for extended periods of time.

b. *Amount of Detail.* Running records demand a greater number of details than anecdotal records require. Additionally, compared to anecdotal records, running records place little emphasis on impressions or interpretations (whenever they occur they are set off by brackets).

c. *Breadth of Focus.* While both records are targeted on a particular student(s) or event(s), the running record includes much more information on the environmental context than does the anecdotal record. Anecdotal records are less sophisticated than are running records—they are similar to a diary whereas the running record is similar to a verbatim report.

d. *Systematicness.* Anecdotal records do not provide generally systematic evidence. They are brief illustrative sketches of incidents rather than evidence collected across situations and at different times.

FREQUENCY COUNTS

Two frequency count approaches will be presented—time sampling and event sampling. Read the characteristics and procedures for conducting each in order to understand the similarities and differences between the two approaches.

Time Sampling

Characteristics:
a. In time sampling behaviors are observed over repeated intervals for different periods of time (e.g., 3 recordings of a behavior per ten minutes for 4 one-hour periods).
b. Time sampling is appropriate only for behaviors that occur fairly frequently, at least once every fifteen minutes on average.
c. This behavior is then looked upon as a "sample" of the person's usual behavior(s).

Procedure:
a. Identify behaviors that occur regularly and define the behavior so that others will agree with what the focus of the observation will be (e.g., on-task behavior which may be defined as (1) on-task, engrossed, (2) on-task, at work but not engrossed, (3) off-task, quietly disengaged, or (4) off-task, disruptive).
b. Decide how long the observation period will be and how many observations are needed within this period (e.g., 3 one-hour observation periods during math where the observer codes on-task behavior of 5 children for 3 minutes, waits 7 minutes, records behavior during another 3-minute period, waits 7 minutes, etc.). If the behavior occurs during an observer wait period it is not recorded.

Event Sampling

Characteristics:
a. In event sampling, the observer waits for the selected behavior to occur and records it (e.g., all selected behaviors which occur are recorded).

Procedure:
a. Clearly identify the kind of behavior you want to study (e.g., how students get the teacher's attention during seatwork).

    b. Determine what kind of information you want to record (e.g., call the teacher's name, hold an object in front of his/her face, stand in front of teacher, ask teacher for assistance, cause a disruption, etc.).

    c. Decide how many times you will observe and how long you will observe during each time (e.g., 10 40-minute seatwork classes).

Comparison of Time Sampling and Event Sampling

    a. Both event and time sampling are useful for determining the frequency of behaviors or events and both allow for the collection of a large number of observations in a relatively short period of time.

    b. Time sampling is limited to frequently or regularly occurring behaviors and counts only those behaviors that occur during a recording interval. Event sampling counts all instances of the behavior's occurrence and the behavior does not have to occur regularly frequently.

    c. With both approaches the observer must determine what behaviors are to be observed, when they are to be observed, and for how long they are to be observed to obtain a sample set of behaviors typical of the student(s) in question.

Method	Focus	Advantages/disadvantages
Case study narratives	Single student	+ Provides a rich detailed account of an individual's actions + Allows for an in-depth examination of a single problem − Descriptions may be affected by the observer's biases − Conclusions may not apply to the same student in other classes or to other students
Frequency counts	Single student Small groups	+ Gives actual number of behaviors per unit of time, which allows for comparisons among students or across classes + Allows teacher to receive immediate information on a problem without having to receive extensive training − Actual behaviors recorded may not explain all facets of the problem − Apart from the behavior in question the teacher will not know what students are doing during the observation time
Classroom observation scale (COS)	Single student Small groups Whole class	+ Gives actual number of behaviors per unit of time, which allows for comparisons among students or across classes − Usually involves more observer training than do other methods − Apart from the behavior in question the teacher will not know what students are doing during the observation time
Questionnaire	Single student Small groups Whole class	+ Allows for the collection of information on a variety of topics in a relatively short period of time + Since students respond to the same set of questions, questionnaires allow for comparisons among individuals or across classes

Method	Focus	Advantages/disadvantages
		− Question construction is more difficult than it may appear (e.g., responses may be affected by how questions are worded)
		− Responses may not truly represent what students will do in actual situation (validity)
		− Responses may differ if questionnaire was given at another time (reliability)
Interview	Single student Small groups	+ Yields more student information than do other methods
		+ Allows greater flexibility to probe a student's response more deeply
		− Since students give more information comparisons among students may be difficult
		− Responses given may be affected by student biases
		− Usually will take longer to conduct than will other methods
Ethnography	Whole class	+ Relative to other methods it provides more information on the social context of the classroom
		− Since the purpose is to interpret behaviors, the analysis may be affected by observer bias
		− Since the focus is not on a particular set of behaviors for all students, comparisons among students or across classes are difficult
		− The purpose is not to answer specific questions but to describe the norms governing interactions in social settings—therefore, the information collected may not be appropriate for answering specific questions

APPENDIX E: Qualitative Approaches: Educational Ethnography

Recently researchers have become interested in more qualitative approaches to the collection of classroom data and in the interpretation of these data. Although there have been qualitative studies in educational research in the past, the use of qualitative inquiry has become especially popular in the past few years (Goetz & LeCompte, 1984). In general, qualitative studies attempt to describe particular classroom situations as richly as possible. Descriptions of classroom situations include not only observation of behavior (as in quantitative studies), but also interviews with teachers and students, and the attempt is to understand how individual classroom participants see and interpret behavior.

Goetz and LeCompte (1984) note that the general goal of educational ethnography is to provide rich, descriptive data about the contexts, activities, and beliefs of participants in educational settings with an emphasis on trying to study the whole setting. However, just as there are differences between qualitative and quantitative approaches, there are also differences within the qualitative tradition, making it difficult to define in any simple way what the qualitative tradition is. Although the techniques used are varied, educational ethnography is characterized by an approach to studying problems—an approach that emphasizes rich, descriptive data.

We introduce the distinction here between quantitative and qualitative research because it is one that readers will increasingly see as they read the educational literature in the next few years. Neither approach is inherently superior and either done well will yield valuable information.

In general, quantitative studies allow for collection of a narrow range of information in many classrooms, whereas the same resources would allow investigators to conduct a qualitative study of a broader range of issues but in only one or two classrooms. Quantitative studies suggest general patterns of behavior (e.g., How do fourth-grade teachers get achievement gains?), whereas qualitative studies help to explain why something occurs in a particular classroom.

In this book, part of the difference between quantitative and qualitative approaches can be seen by comparing the classroom narrative presented in Chapter 1 with the observation scales presented in Appendices B and C. The narrative record that appears at the end of Chapter 1 is an attempt to collect classroom data as broadly as possible and hence allows for more discovery and description than do the Brophy-Good Dyadic Interaction System and Emmer Classroom Observation System. In this sense, then, the narrative record is more qualitative than the instruments presented in Appendices B and C (obviously, the narrative approach would be more qualitative if it combined teacher and student interviews with the narrative coding).

To collect such qualitative data reliably and accurately requires careful training. We noted earlier the need for concern with reliability when using quantitative methods. Such concern is equally important when using qualitative procedures. To illustrate the difference that a well-trained coder can make, compare the narrative that follows with the one taken from Chapter 1. It is especially instructive to note in the following example how little information is provided about the first ten minutes of the class.

CLASSROOM NARRATIVE
BEGIN

1:25	1.	The bell rings. The teacher walks into the classroom and
	2.	says, "Class, would you get out your homework." One stu-
	3.	dent says, Homework?" The teacher says, "Yes, homework.
	4.	Who would like to call out the answers?" One student
	5.	raises his hand. "Okay, Pat." The class continues working
	6.	the problems in this manner. The teacher calls out the
	7.	problem and a student's name, and the student gives the
	8.	answer to that particular problem. The students are very
1:35	9.	orderly. This activity ends, and the teacher says, "Okay,
	10.	very good. Now I want to talk to you about something.
	11.	How many of you want to pass your math class?" The stu-
	12.	dents raise their hands. "Okay, how many of you did your
	13.	homework last night?" Thirteen students raise their hands.
	14.	"Okay, now some of you didn't raise your hands, but the
	15.	rest of you I am very proud of. Now I guarantee that
	16.	if you do your homework you will pass this class. If your
	17.	average is 59 and you turn in all your homework, you will
	18.	pass; but if your average is 59 and you have not turned
	19.	in your homework, you are not going to pass my course.
	20.	A zero in homework can hurt your grade an awful lot."
1:38	21.	The teacher ends this procedure of explaining to the stu-
T—1:38	22.	dents how they can pass her course. "Okay, I want you
1:39	23.	to turn to page 12 in your math books." The students are
	24.	walking up to the teacher's desk to ask questions. The
	25.	teacher says, "Okay, if you will look at your text on page

26. 12, you can see that it is easy to add figures if you group
27. the numbers. Let's say we have a problem of eight plus
28. two plus four plus nine plus six. You should group in
29. tens, and you will see that you have two groups of ten,
30. because eight plus two is ten and six plus four is ten.
31. You then only have a nine left over. So it's easier to
32. see that the answer is 29. Two groups of ten, and one
33. group of nine, so that is 29. Okay, now let's remember
34. that there should be no talking. I'll give you a few
35. minutes to begin working, and then I'll come around and

1:49   36. see if you need help." The students begin working. The
1:54   37. students are going to the teacher's desk when they have
      38. problems. The students are working very quietly. This
2:01   39. teacher has one student who is non-English speaking. The
      40. teacher has assigned one student to sit with the Spanish-
2:09   41. speaking student to help her as time goes on. The students
2:13   42. are continuing their math assignment. The bell rings,
2:20   43. and the class is dismissed. (This teacher runs her class
      44. very strictly, very firmly, very orderly. Her methods appear
      45. to work. When the students are noisy, she asks, "What are
      46. our listening skills?" The students immediately say, "Sit
      47. straight, put your pencils down, and look at your speaker."
      48. When there is talking in the classroom, the teacher very
      49. hurriedly stops it. She calls the name of the student and
      50. tells him or her to meet her at the end of school.)

APPENDIX F: An Ethnographic Research Study Conducted by Susan Florio

Some qualitative researchers study a single classroom for a long time in order to describe and understand its unique characteristics and functioning. The article that appears below provides one example of how qualitative researchers conduct classroom inquiry. Notice that this research attempts to describe and understand both the social and cognitive tasks of classroom. For more details describing the method of qualitative research, see Erickson, 1986; and Goetz and LeCompte, 1984; Spradley, 1979, 1980.

The Problem of Dead Letters: Social Perspectives on the Teaching of Writing[1]

SUSAN FLORIO

Institute for Research on Teaching, Michigan State University, East Lansing, Michigan

Dead letters! does it not sound like dead men? Conceive a man by nature and misfortune prone to a pallid hopelessness, can any business seem more fitted to heighten it than that of continually handling these dead letters . . . ?

HERMAN MELVILLE,
Bartleby the Scrivener [1]

[1] From Susan Florio, "The problem of dead letters . . .," *Elementary School Journal*, 80 (1979), 1–7. Reprinted with permission.

Why is it so hard to get students writing in school? Of the language arts, writing is the most troublesome. While the value of literacy is unquestioned by educators and researchers alike, writing, as part of literacy, is typically slighted in the course of a day in school and in research on the basic skills (2).

In attempting to account for this neglect, some have noted that writing—and its pedagogy—require hard work. Thus it could be argued that teachers and students assiduously avoid difficult tasks, and so they avoid writing. Yet, all of us can think of difficulty endured in the pursuit of a valued goal. What is more, from the ranks of the few who have taken a look at the teaching of writing comes a recommendation that is disturbing in its simplicity. We are advised, in a variety of voices, that the best way to teach writing is simply to let students do it! (2, 3, 4).

Why, then, is it so hard to get students writing in school?

When researchers at the Institute for Research on Teaching set out to address this question, they were confronted with much the same finding as the lawyer who set out to discover the roots of Bartleby the Scrivener's "derangement." The problem, in each case, was the lack of meaningfulness. At the heart of a student's successful engagement in the complex and difficult task of writing, experienced teachers told us, was the requirement that the writing task have meaning. Writing requires having something to express, an intended audience, and a chance for some kind of response (4). Apparently the teachers with whom we spoke had shared just about enough of Bartleby's experience to abhor it.

Bartleby's first job involved reading and sorting letters that were undeliverable—dead letters. From that job he went to work as a scribe, or copier of the manuscripts of others, for a lawyer. Is it any wonder that, after years of such meaningless interaction with truncated human communication, his only response when asked by the lawyer to perform written tasks was, "I prefer not to"? Teachers told us that they preferred not to read "dead letters" from their students—exposition going nowhere and written only to fulfill academic requirements. Similarly, the teachers preferred not to ask their students merely to put their own words to someone else's ideas. The teachers knew that the perseverance and the practice needed to master a craft as complex as writing were likely to be present only when school writing tasks had meaningful communicative functions in the lives of their students.

The teachers' insight suggests that writing may be avoided in school not simply because of its inherent difficulty, but also because writing, as one of many tasks in a busy school day, typically is not connected to anything or anyone else in the lives of students or teachers. If this is true, then "letting children write" may amount to far more than pedagogical laissez faire. The teaching of writing may require vigilant attention to the learning environments in which writing occurs to insure that written expression is motivated and that it goes somewhere.

Perhaps teachers can best serve the acquisition of writing by structuring both for and with students social occasions in which writing functions meaningfully as communication. The possibility parallels what we know about the acquisition of speaking, another complex communicative skill. Both research and experience tell us that spoken language is acquired literally "in the doing." Children are welcomed as communicators even before their first words are uttered. Early in life, children find that their moves and sounds elicit action from other people. Children, in effect, practice the use of language not as preparation or training for social life, but as social life itself (5).

Research on language acquisition has shown us that requisite grammatical skills are seldom taught directly to children by the adults with whom they communicate. For teachers of writing, an essential lesson from research on language acquisition is that even the most flawed and rudimentary communicative attempts of novices are functional in that they have social meaning. Critical to acquiring language is the social fact that a child's emergent and stumbling efforts are heeded by others. Early talk is meaningful by virtue of the child's membership in the family, the first community.

Classrooms contain the stuff of community, too, and therein lies potential that writing done in them will be meaningful. Classrooms are located in organized social worlds where meanings are shared and values held, and at the same time classrooms individually constitute small communities with cumulative histories, shared beliefs, and rights and responsibilities of membership.

To learn more about the acquisition of writing skills and the ways in which writing in school can be meaningful to students, researchers at the Institute for Research on Teaching have been looking closely at one second-grade classroom in central Michigan. The classroom is notable because children do a great deal of writing there and because a strong sense of community can be found there as well.

To get to Mrs. Frank's second grade you must travel to the small community of Haslett, Michigan. The town of nearly seven thousand is located in the shadow of the state capitol and a large public university. Although some of the residents are farmers, the parents of most of the children in Mrs. Frank's room are employed in one of the area's major activities—state government, education, and manufacturing.

Mrs. Frank's students attend the Ralya School, one of three elementary schools in Haslett. The contemporary school building houses about 170 students and contains one room for each grade from Kindergarten through Grade 5. Approaching Mrs. Frank's room, you already have a sense of why she is well known in and around Haslett and why children look forward to being in her class. The classroom literally spills out into the corridor with bright colors and activity. Upon entering the classroom, you encounter yet another small community, one that the children have dubbed, "Betterburg."

As the map in Figure 3.6 drawn by one of Mrs. Frank's students illustrates, the child-sized, cardboard buildings of Betterburg dominate the physical space of the classroom. We have found that Betterburg dominates as well the social life and the attendant writing that is done in that physical space.

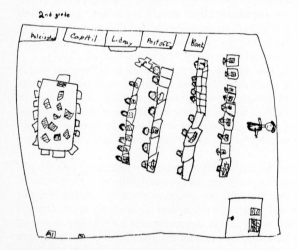

Figure 3.6 Map drawn by students on 6/2/78. Instructions were to fill in "important things and places—as many as you can remember."

The members of Mrs. Frank's class populate Betterburg, filling its civil offices and making its laws. Betterburg has all the accoutrements of a community—law enforcement, cultural activities, commerce, welfare and, most important for our purposes, a postal system. Of course, the room also has all the other features of standard classrooms—blackboards, desks, bookshelves, and the like; but the dominance of the town is clear. One day upon leaving the class the children were asked to draw maps of the important things and places in the room. The children's maps included, often in considerable detail, each aspect of the town. The content of their drawings is summarized in Table 3.3.

During the year that the children in Mrs. Frank's class were observed, they wrote often and produced a wide variety of documents. Table 3.4 displays the written products and the occasions when writing occurred on March 15, 1978, a typical day in the classroom. Activities recorded in Table 3.4 include everything from the practice of motor skills, spelling, and the rules of punctuation to the use of metaphor, simile, and the complex rhetoric of persuasion. Table 3.4 also illustrates the fact that the variety of writing activities done in this classroom involves the practice of a wide range of skills. Sometimes spelling and punctuation are in the foreground for teacher as well as students. At other times, self-expression is most highly valued, and correct spelling is incidental. Such changes in emphasis are accompanied by changes in the behaviors of teacher and students. The teacher's role may vary from that of helper or resource to that of editor or critic. Similarly, what children need to do to complete adequately the various kinds of writing activities changes depending on the particular activity in which they are engaged.

Table 3.3 CLASSROOM AREAS AND OBJECTS AND PERCENT OF STUDENTS NAMING THEM IN CLASSROOM MAPS

Area or object	Percent of children including area or classroom map
→ Capitol building	83
→ police station/jail	78
student desks	78
→ post office*	74
→ Department of Health, Education & Welfare	70
library	70
teacher's desk	70
→ bank	65
→ mailboxes*	55
reading table	35
other tables	35
chairs	22
blackboard	13
plants	13
coatrack	13
toys	13
bulletin board, art work, books, shelves, cabinets, wastebasket, school bell, wall	

→ town-related area
* area related to letter writing

Table 3.4   **PRODUCTS AND OCCASIONS FOR WRITING**

Field notes, March 15, 1978

I. Writing Headlines: Teacher as Scribe

It is a typically busy morning in the second-grade classroom. First, the children who have brought in articles from the previous evening's newspaper share them with the class. The teacher acts as scribe, making a headline out of each article.

> N. M. builder recycles tin cans into households. Until recently U.S.'s spendthrifts didn't conserve nation's resources.

> We're expecting a blackout because miners haven't obeyed President Carter's demands.

> Bicycles and motorcycles aren't safest, insurance company reports. They're larger than children and teen-agers can handle, and we've got record highway injuries.

At the end of the presentation of news, children volunteer to come to the board and circle in the headlines instances of abbreviations, compound words, prefixes, suffixes, contractions, and the like. The noise level rises as children wave their hands in the air, jump up and down, and call "Me! I know it!"

II. Expository Writing and Editorial Work

Later in the morning some of the children work on the manuscript of a book the class is writing. The book is intended for very young children and their parents. It is going to be about becoming a good and happy person. Children have written entries and have drawn pictures to illustrate them. Now the task of layout—the spacing and matching of pictures and words—remains. Some of the entries with which children are working include the following:

> Don't be crool to people because they mite be crool to you because you're teaching them to be crool.

> It's like planning how to make a building. You have to think how you want it before you start if you want it to be a beautiful building.

> The teacher comments about the manuscript that is taking shape, "It came out real well considering how much they agonized over it."

III. Writing Answers on Worksheets

While the teacher spends the better part of an hour working with reading groups, children work quietly at their desks. Some of them catch on their reading—from primers or from library books. Others work busily on dittoed worksheets, circling, marking with x's and writing an occasional word in answer to a fill in the blank question.

IV. Writing Letters

During seatwork, some of the children are polishing up letters that they have written to companies manufacturing their favorite toys and candies. Because the entire class is planning to have a store this spring, the children have decided to solicit help from the companies. Children have written to makers of Flair pens, Cracker Jacks, Mounds, DC Comics. Here is an example:

> Dear Parker Brothers,
> Hi! My name is Marnie at Ralya School in second grade and we have a town in our classroom. Our town's name is Betterburg because we want to make things better. We'll have a store in our town. We have a police station, Bank, capitol, Library, H.E.W. and a Post Office. My teacher said I could sell anything in the world I wanted to and I chose you because we have some of your games and we play with

Table 3.4 *(Continued)*

them all the time and we like them alot. I always want to buy the games but we don't get enough money. When I'm over to somebody's house I look at the games. If I find a Parker Brothers game I want to play it but if they don't have a Parkers Brother game I don't want to play a game. I have to buy your good games at a good wholesale price or we won't make any money. Please, please give us it at a good wholesale price. We really need it bad. Just send the games and bill. We'll be sure to pay the bill if you send the games with the letter. Thank you for reading my letter.

Your friend,
Marnie

V. "Meta Writing" Spelling Words, Making Concrete Sentences

After the children return from recess, the teacher, standing at the front blackboard, asks them to clear their desks and take out pencils and spelling books. She draws lines on the blackboard. Then she says, "We've been *neglecting* your spelling words." She asks them to pick out the two hardest words from this week's spelling list and write a sentence using each word. "In order to be a sentence, it has to *tell* something. I'm not going to spell any words for you: just sound them out. It isn't a spelling test. The only word I care about your spelling correct is the spelling word."

The children write quietly at their desks. As they finish, a few of them bring their sentences up to the teacher. She tells them, "Sit down." Finally, as the whispering and shifting in seats increases, the teacher says, "Stand up if you are ready." The teacher calls on children standing at their desks to read their sentences. Here is a bit of what follows:

Teacher calls on Christy.
CHRISTY: Do you want to clean your room now?
TEACHER: I should have . . . OK you can either *tell* something or *ask* something. She asked. What did she put at the end of her sentence?
CHILDREN: A question mark!
Another child is called on.
KRISTINA: I clean my room every day.
TEACHER: Oh, you do really? Is she telling or asking?
CHILDREN: Telling.
TEACHER: I'm going to ask your mother about that, Kristina!
JACK: I clean the living room every day.
TEACHER: He *told* you right. Jack, would you like to come over to my house tonight?
CHILDREN: Laughter.
SAM: He is sleeping.
TEACHER: What did Sam do to the word? He put the *ing* on a suffix. Don't do that on the spelling test tomorrow, but it's all right.

VI. Cursive Writing Practice

After many children have shared their sentences, the teacher turns to the lines she has drawn on the blackboard. She says as she does this in brisk, clipped speech. "Up, up! Sit up! Feet on floor. When I say 'ready,' what do you do?" The students reply, "Do we have to write in *cursive?*" The teacher, smiling says, "Yup." What follows is a lesson in cursive writing in which students use the spelling words from their sentences. The teacher coaches in colorful language—each motion of the pen corresponds to a phrase that the children know. Some of them talk along with her: "Rainbow up, straight back. Rocker, come around, straight, rocker." As children finish their words, they are asked to bring them up to show to the teacher.

VII. Imaginative Writing

After the children finish their cursive writing, the teacher asks them to sit in a circle at her feet at the front of the room. It is nearing St. Patrick's day, and the teacher has

Table 3.4 (Continued)

brought in a story about leprechauns. The children listen quietly. Sometimes the teacher stops to ask questions about the story. The children answer in chorus. After the story there is just time enough before lunch for the children to do one more thing. The teacher, in a soft voice, says, "I want you to think. Shut your eyes. You're a leprechaun now, hiding under your mushroom and you're thinking. 'If I were a leprechaun, what magic would I play?' What magic would you play if you were a leprechaun?"

As the children open their eyes and are sent back to seats, the teacher passes out bright green paper shamrocks. She asks them to write down on lined paper the trick they thought of to play. She says that after writing them, the children will paste them onto the shamrocks and put them in the hall "for everyone to see." She also says they can copy them over into St. Patrick's Day cards to bring home to their mothers.

After the assignment is made, the room is alive with whispering and children leaning over one another's papers. The teacher stands at the board, and as children call out words she spells them for them on the board. As children finish, they bring their tricks up to the teacher. One student reads his aloud to the teacher, "If I were a leprechaun, I'd use my magic finger to turn trash into flowers because I'd like to make the world into a better place." The teacher replies, "He accomplished something with his trick. It wasn't wasted."

On the day that information for Table 3.4 was compiled, one of the most daring and most sustained writing activities was the writing of letters to manufacturers of the children's favorite games and candies. Betterburg was establishing a store, and the children needed to acquire goods to sell in the store. To turn a profit, it was necessary to buy the goods at the wholesale price. Despite inexperience with the nuances and the intricacies of spelling, punctuation, and sentence structure, the children undertook the sophisticated task of writing persuasively. They needed to interest their readers in the doings of Betterburg. To this end, the children needed to take the perspective of someone who had never heard of the classroom town. Writing from this point of view, the students had to weave into their letters sufficient information to make subsequent requests for goods sensible. It might be said that the children were out of their depth in such a task but, like young children acquiring speech, they were learning in the doing.

In Betterburg the performance of such complex social and linguistic operations through the medium of the letter was typical. Letter-writing was observed almost daily over months of field work in the classroom, and when the children were interviewed at the end of the year about their activities, the only writing activity on which they commented in detail was letter-writing. Here are excerpts from the interviews:

INTERVIEWER: I want to know about all the things you wrote this year.
STUDENT 1: Yeah, we wrote people to come to our store.
STUDENT 2: Letters.

STUDENT 3: Oh, yeah. We wrote to our moms and dads and wrote to kids in our class.
STUDENT 4: Our post office would get mail.

Additional evidence of the importance of letter-writing in this classroom community can be found in Table 3.3. The post office is among the places most frequently included in the classroom maps. The mailboxes—the one outside the post office as well as those fastened to the children's desks—are included in the maps of more than half the students. Finally, when Mrs. Frank and the students recorded the history of Betterburg in a yearbook, the text was made up almost entirely of the letters that had been written during the existence of the town.

The celebration of community in the classroom in the form of Betterburg appears to be related powerfully to the use of letter-writing as an expressive activity. Dewey suggests that education fundamentally involves the child, whose "understandings are primarily personal and concrete," and the transmission of "values incarnate in the mature experience of the adult" (6:4). From this perspective, teaching of writing can be thought of as occurring at the place where the personal world and the wider community meet. Writing is the private struggle of an individual with pen and paper, and writing is the social activity of communication with another. Furthermore, writing occurs within communities. A pedagogy of writing that slights any of these features risks engaging students in the generation of dead letters rather than in communication.

Betterburg enables immediate and explicit sharing of classroom membership, and the town is a powerful organizer of the students' personal experiences. The classroom town also provides the occasion for students to venture outside its borders into the wider adult community. This movement is fundamental to writing. It constitutes, in the words of Elsasser and John-Steiner, a

> critical shift in the consciousness of the learner, a shift of attention from an immediate audience that shares the learner's experience and frame of reference to a larger, abstract, and unfamiliar audience [7:358].

In the classroom community of Betterburg, there is need for discourse across the boundaries. Because Betterburg operates, in microcosm, very much like Haslett, students write to government officials in the town and in the nearby state capital for guidance in the establishment and the enforcement of laws. Similarly, Betterburg, as we have already seen, has a commerce. Haslett and other nearby towns are potential markets for the goods that children sell in their store. Haslett citizens are reached by means of letters to individuals and to the local newspaper.

Because letters are a meaningful medium for Mrs. Frank's class, the postal system of Betterburg is important. In a sense, the postal system epitomizes Betterburg's integrity and links the class to the wider world. The system insures that letters can leave the confines of the classroom, that responses can be distributed, and that letters can be noted officially. Mailboxes serve as a tangible reminder that it is possible to communicate with someone who is not physically present. Perhaps even more dramatically, however, the post office of Betterburg stands for the potential efficacy of the students in the world of communication. An address is not only a place from which to express oneself, it is also a place where one can be reached when someone wants to respond.

Some educators say that one writes if one can realistically expect a response, if one does not feel isolated and powerless. But one does not feel isolated and powerless because one writes and is responded to (7, 8). Bartleby the Scrivener was immobilized by a social order that stymied both the chance for expression and the opportunity for response. Although Mrs. Frank's classroom is perhaps novel in its design, it paints in bold strokes a community spirit that is potentially available in all classrooms. That community spirit stems from recognition both of shared classroom meanings and of access of the class to a world beyond itself by means of the written word. Understanding and using the classroom as a community can rescue children from academic writing activities that are mere copying or expressions falling on deaf ears. As one child in Mrs. Frank's class put it, reflecting on the writing he had done in Betterburg, "I made my own words, and I didn't copy people. The more I learned to write good letters, the better they got."

NOTES AND REFERENCES

The work reported here is sponsored by the Institute for Research on Teaching, College of Education, Michigan State University. The Institute for Research on Teaching is funded primarily by the Teaching Division of the National Institute of Education, United States Department of Health, Education, and Welfare. The opinions expressed in this article do not necessarily reflect the position, policy, or endorsement of the National Institute of Education. (Contract No. 400-76-0073)

HERMAN MELVILLE. "Bartleby the Scrivener," in *Eight Great American Short Novels*, p. 52. Edited by Philip Rahv. New York, New York: Berkeley Publishing Company, 1963.

DONALD H. GRAVES. *Balance the Basics: Let Them Write*. New York, New York: The Ford Foundation, 1978.

KENNETH KOCH. *Wishes, Lies, and Dreams*. New York, New York: Chelsea House, 1970.

JAMES MOFFETT. *Teaching the Universe of Discourse*. New York, New York: Houghton Mifflin, 1968.

COURTNEY B. CAZDEN. *Child Language and Education*. New York, New York: Holt, Rinehart, and Winston, 1972.

JOHN DEWEY. *The Child* and *the Curriculum and The School and Society*. Chicago, Illinois: The University of Chicago Press, 1956.

NAN ELSASSER and VERA P. JOHN-STEINER. "An Interactionist Approach to Advancing Literacy," *Harvard Educational Review*, 47 (August, 1977), 355–69.

PAULO FREIRE. *Cultural Action for Freedom*. Harvard Educational Review and Center for the Study of Development and Social Change, Monograph Series No. 1. Cambridge, Massachusetts: Harvard Educational Review and Center for the Study of Development and Social Change, 1970.

APPENDIX G: Coding Academic Activities and Tasks[1]

In the past few years following the wave of enthusiasm for coding teacher-student interaction in the classroom, there has been a growing interest in coding other aspects of classroom life. Doyle (1983, 1986) has argued the need to code the task structure in the classroom and elsewhere has outlined procedures for coding classroom tasks.

Emmer (1986) has outlined the practical value of coding task structures in classrooms, illustrating that the variations from classroom to classroom can be quite striking. Emmer, studying the classrooms of first-year teachers following Gump (1982), coded classroom activities (lesson segments) in order to describe how time and behavior were organized and studied the structure of academic tasks (Doyle, 1983) to determine how the teacher transforms curriculum content and goals into assignments and work activities for students.

During each observation an observer made notes describing all classroom academic activities and other information pertinent to task descriptions. After the observation, the observer dictated a narrative record using both the observation notes and an audiotape recording of the class. Based on this material, lesson segments were labeled according to the predominant activity (whole-class presentations, group work, transitions, etc.). Furthermore, all academic tasks were (i.e., products students generated, reports, worksheets, etc.) along with resources that teachers made available to students (handouts, etc.).

These activity and task structures are shown for two of the teachers in Tables 3.5 and 3.6.

As Emmer (1986) notes, striking differences are found in the activities and tasks used by these teachers. Teacher 5 used a varied set of activities that included short recitation formats, numerous classwork assignments, lab activities, and presentations. The assignments and activities in this class seemed well integrated. In contrast, Teacher 6 used lengthy seatwork and teacher presentation segments, along with a relatively restricted set of tasks. Furthermore, some of the tasks and activities lacked integration (e.g., seatwork assignments

---

[1] This material is taken from Emmer (1986) and reprinted with the author's permission. [Emmer, E. (1986), *Academic activities and tasks in first-year teachers' classes. Report No. 6025*. Austin: University of Texas, Research and Development Center for Teacher Education.]

Table 3.5 ACTIVITY SEQUENCES FOR TEACHER 5 (GRADE 8 SCIENCE, 24 STUDENTS) AND TEACHER 6 (GRADE 6 SCIENCE, 21 STUDENTS) MARCH 26–28

	Teacher 5			Teacher 6	
Date	Elapsed time (min.)	Description	Date	Elapsed time (min.)	Description
3/26/85	4	*Teacher presentation.* The teacher provides introductory information for the next activity.	3/26/85	2	*Seatwork.* Students write answers to a question based on the preceding day's lesson.
	35	*Seatwork.* Students read an article on energy and write answers to 20 worksheet questions.		3	*Checking/recitation.* Students check the seatwork exercise.
	9	*Recitation.* The teacher reviews answers to the first 10 worksheet questions.		8	*Presentation.* Teacher describes components of electrical circuits.
3/27/85	7	*Recitation.* Continuation of the class activity from 3/26.		5	*Presentation.* Teacher distributes a hand-out illustrating AC and DC concepts and explains it.
	29	*Presentation.* Renewable energy resources is the topic; students copy overhead projector information into spiral notebooks.		11	*Recitation/seatwork.* Electrical current concepts; students write answers to questions on worksheets.
	3	*Recitation.* A few questions relating to the previous presentation.		20	*Presentation.* How cells and batteries produce direct current.
	8	*Dead time.* Students are permitted to converse; no expectation for academic work.	3/27/85	2	*Seatwork.* Students write answers to two questions based on the preceding day's presentations.
3/28/85	5	*Seatwork.* Students write responses to five factual questions based on the 3/27 presentation.		3	*Checking.* Students check the seatwork exercise.
	6	*Recitation.* Review based on the five questions from the preceding activity.		11	*Recitation.* Review of basic electrical concepts; batteries and cells.

Table 3.5 ACTIVITY SEQUENCES FOR TEACHER 5 (GRADE 8 SCIENCE, 24 STUDENTS) AND TEACHER 6 (GRADE 6 SCIENCE, 21 STUDENTS) MARCH 26–28 *(continued)*

Teacher 5

Date	Elapsed time (min.)	Description
	33	*Presentation.* Continuation of the presentation from 3/27, on renewable energy resources.
	6	*Seatwork.* Worksheet on energy costs, not related to preceding activities.

Teacher 6

Date	Elapsed time (min.)	Description
	9	*Presentation.* The teacher gives instructions for a laboratory activity on wiring DC circuits.
	21	*Laboratory activity/seatwork.* Students work with wires, bulbs, and batteries to test circuits.
3/28/85	5	*Test.* Pop quiz on cells and batteries.
	3	*Checking.* Students check quiz papers.
	2	*Procedural.* The teacher collects the preceding day's laboratory assignment.
	13	*Presentation/recitation.* Review of concepts of direct current and alternating current.
	4	*Presentation.* The teacher demonstrates production of alternating current with a magnet and copper coil generator.
	15	*Presentation/recitation.* How an electric power plant operates.
	4	*Seatwork.* Students answer questions on AC, generation of electricity.

Source: Emmer, E. (1986). Academic activities and tasks in first-year teachers' classes. Report No. 6025. Austin: University of Texas, Research and Development Center for Teacher Education.

Table 3.6 SUMMARY OF ACADEMIC TASKS IN TWO SCIENCE CLASSES, MARCH 26–28

Tasks	Student product	Resources provided by the teacher	Accountability
Teacher 5			
1. Worksheet Qs on energy article.	Answers to 20 Qs based on a Nat. Geographic article on energy.	Minimal. A short—4 min.—introduction to the article was presented.	Low. (The T collected but did not grade the worksheet; recorded completion only.)
2. Worksheet Qs on energy costs.	Answers to 19 items on cost of electricity.	Minimal. Worksheet not related to preceding activities. T did respond to individual Ss requests for assistance.	Low. (T usually collected classwork, but checked it only for completion.)
3. Notebook keeping.	Ss copied class notes into spiral notebooks.	T presented a detailed outline of class material using the OP and chalkboard.	Moderate. (Earlier in the year the T periodically collected, graded NBs, but had not for 12 weeks.)
4. (Unit test)			
Teacher 6			
1. Warm-up assignments (2).	Answers to one or two review Qs based on previous day's lesson.	Presentations or assignments on the preceding day.	High. Ss checked their answers; the T recorded points.
2. Classwork assignments (2).	Written answers to Qs on handouts.	Presentations and discussions of concepts. Also, T provided answers to some Qs during recitations.	Low. Not checked or graded. Ss were expected to complete these assignments during class and include them in their NBs.
3. "Pop" quiz.	Answers to seven Qs over the previous day's lesson.	Assignments—Task 2—and related presentations and discussions.	High. Corrected immediately and grades were recorded.
4. Notebook keeping.	A notebook containing classwork, handouts, and other material.	Assignments—Task 2—and related presentations and discussions. (T described the expected product.)	High. (Collected and checked for completion and order every 6 weeks. Occasional spot checks.)
5. Laboratory assignment.	Answers to Qs on direct current circuits.	Presentations and demonstrations of DC circuits; assignments (Task 2); materials—wires, cells, bulbs.	High. Assignment sheet was collected for grading by T.
6. (Unit test)			

Source: Emmer, E. (1986). Academic activities and tasks in first-year teachers' classes. Report No. 6025. Austin: University of Texas, Research and Development Center for Teacher Education.

on calculating unit costs of electricity were not supported by any previous teacher presentation). In general, Teacher 6 placed students in a passive, primarily receptive mode of learning.

Thus, it seems evident that examinations of activity and task structures can lead to very important comparisons of classrooms.

APPENDIX H: Combining Quantitative and Qualitative Procedures: Marshall and Weinstein

Although quantitative and qualitative research methods have distinct purposes and traditions, there is growing interest in trying to combine the two techniques, at least in some areas of inquiry and research (see Evertson & Green, 1986). The work of Marshall and Weinstein represents an instance of combining quantitative and qualitative procedures to study classroom expectations.

Marshall and Weinstein (1986) have developed an observation system that utilizes both methods to investigate classroom influences on the development of students' achievement expectations. Features of their system are excerpted in this appendix and based on their revised coding manual (Marshall & Weinstein, 1986).

The Classroom Dimensions Observation System was developed to investigate factors within the classroom environment, including structuring, instructional strategies, and teacher-student interactions, that may be related to the development of students' self-concepts of ability and self-evaluations. Due to its unique features, the observation system and modifications of it may be used for other purposes as well.

UNIQUE FEATURES

The Classroom Dimensions Observation System includes five unique features: (1) uses both quantitative and qualitative methods, (2) varies the depth and breadth of focus, (3) allows for quantitative coding from narrative records, (4) accounts for interpersonal and subject-matter context, and (5) uses both low- and higher- inference items.

Use of Quantitative and Qualitative Methods

This system utilizes both qualitative and quantitative methods to investigate classroom influences on the development of students' self-concepts of ability and self-evaluations. The procedure of utilizing qualitative (narrative) records and field notes in conjunction with a quantitative categorical system has the advantage of overcoming a major drawback of most quantitative observation systems. Much useful information that would otherwise be lost in the process of only recording quantitative codes during the observation can be retrieved for further analysis or explanatory purposes. The use of qualitative records and field notes complements and enhances the quantitative coding scale in two ways. First, the coded quantitative data can be placed in context by referring to the transcripts of the qualitative record and field notes. The contextual information from the qualitative record can help explain the results of the quantitative data. Second, additional information not initially included in the quantitative scale can be coded from the transcripts at a later time. Using both quantitative and qualitative data in this manner has the additional advantage of reducing the initial time and cost of sifting, analyzing, and coding open-ended field notes.

Focus Through Multiple Lenses

The second and related feature of this system stems from the conception that the classroom functions as a whole and that effects on students are multiply determined by different factors within the classroom. This conception is different from a more behavioristic approach to classroom research where the influence of a single variable or set of classroom variables, e.g., praise, is investigated. Instead, the conception reflected in this system is that classroom events are embedded in the larger classroom context as a whole (and that the classroom is embedded in the context of the school and so on). Within the larger classroom context, certain factors may compensate for or negate the effect of other factors in an interactive manner (see Marshall & Weinstein, 1986 for more details). That is, the effect of one factor may be attenuated by other factors operating within the larger classroom context. Viewed in this manner, it may be misleading to investigate a limited set of categories without considering the larger context of the classroom as a whole. Consequently, this observation system allows the observer/researcher to shift focus to different widths and depths of the classroom reality so as to better consider the parts in relationship to each other and in relationship to the whole. To this end, the qualitative narrative record and field notes and the first section of the quantitative scale show what is happening in the classroom as a whole. More detailed notes and a second section of the quantitative scale focus more closely on the teacher and the individual(s) he or she is working with. Thus, one can move from a wide-angle lens that focuses broadly on the whole classroom to a lens that provides more detail on a narrow segment of events and then expand again to the wider context, if desired (see Evertson & Green, 1986).

Quantitative Coding From Transcripts

A third unique feature of this system is that much of the quantitative coding is done from the transcripts of the narrative record rather than live in the classroom. The narrative account and the field notes serve as a concrete record to which the observer refers in completing the quantitative coding of both the broad overall classroom structure and the more specific and narrowly focused teacher behaviors. Thus, in addition to allowing retrieval of explanatory and contextual information, the qualitative record permits more accurate counting and coding of the events observed. By referring to the records, observers have time to reflect on the context of their observations and consider whether the behaviors actually fit the definition. Since the coding is done by the observers themselves, subtle nuances that occurred in the setting but may not have been completely recorded can also be taken into consideration. Furthermore, this system allows for more accurate retrieval of instances and discussion with others in checking accuracy and reliability.

Interpersonal and Subject Matter Context

The fourth unique feature of this system is that the observer codes whether the teacher is interacting with an individual alone, an individual in a group or a whole class setting, a group, or the whole-class. Subject matter is also noted. Recording these aspects of context permits separate analyses of interactions in the context of individual students, the group (and different types of groups), and the whole class as well as in different subject matter content areas.

Inference Level

In the first two parts of the Classroom Dimensions Scale (CDScale), observers rate the occurrence of a broad spectrum of clearly observable verbal and nonverbal behaviors. These behaviors have been selected and specifically defined so as to require the observer to make only minimal inferences regarding evidence or interpretation of them. Because low-inference behaviors are rated or counted, the halo effect common to high-inference rating scales is avoided, yet the frequency and intensity of behaviors can be indicated. In contrast, items on the third part of the CDScale require a somewhat higher level of inference, because the frequency and intensity of two more global behaviors are rated.

DESCRIPTION OF THE SYSTEM

The Classroom Dimensions Observation System consists of two sections: (1) the qualitative narrative records and field notes and (2) the quantitative CDScale.

Qualitative Section

The qualitative section is comprised of (*a*) the narrative record or running account of events in the classroom recorded as they occur (transcripts of the observations) and (*b*) the observer's field notes (personal observations, impressions, and interpretations). The observer focuses on the teacher and those students with whom the teacher is interacting, recording the teacher's statements as closely to verbatim as possible (except for subject matter content). Particular attention is paid to statements concerning motivation, evaluation, feedback, responsibility, relationships, and expectations and attributions. Observers also record the teacher's tone of voice and that of the student(s) who is the focus of the teacher's interaction.

Quantitative Section

The items on the quantitative CDScale were determined by the model of classrooms that influences the development of students' self-evaluations. The notion that the classroom is more than a sequence of teacher-student-teacher behavior also influenced the construction of the scale (see Marshall & Weinstein, 1984).

The CDScale itself is subdivided into three parts, each coded in a different way for different purposes. The codes on Part I provide a broad overview and summary of the structure of the tasks, grouping, and evaluation, and which create the context for learning during the observation period. Part II describes more specifically the nature of the teacher's interaction with individual students, groups of students, or the whole class. Unlike some interaction analysis systems where codes are recorded every three to five seconds, each instance of a specific behavior is recorded (counted) from the narrative record, providing the exact number of times the behavior occurs. On Part III of the scale, higher inference variables of warmth and irritation are rated. Examples of the type of quantitative data generated in this system are provided in Tables 3.7–3.9.

Table 3.7 ASSESSING CLASSROOM EVALUATION

Evaluation: Code the predominant type of T evaluation of St work.

Definitions	Examples
1. *T checks completed work.* T checks off or corrects completed work. Or T says she is collecting to correct. Or T turns back corrected work. Includes Sts bringing work to T to be checked or raising hands and T going to St to check work. Does not include Sts checking own or each other's work. Does not include T checking ongoing progress while Sts are still working. Clues include T collecting work after checking, or st filing work after checking.	T collects and checks off assignment turned in. Sts bring completed work to T. T checks and collects it.
2. *T leads correction of students' own work.* T leads sts in correcting their own work, either whole class, group, or individuals. T calls for or reads answers. Sts check to see if own answer agrees. T may or may not have previously completed troublesome problems worked out on board.	T has sts exchange papers, then reads correct answers. T has sts take turns reading answers as they correct their own papers.
3. *T checks work as sts work (in progress).* T checks individuals' progress on work as they are carrying out their tasks or checks work problem by problem. This does not refer to checking completed work or completed problems. This includes listening to st reading individually. The checking can be either for written or oral work. Includes questions for comprehension on new reading. Does *not* refer to *discussion* of new material (as opposed to review and checking of ideas.)	T stops and asks Joan to read a paragraph, so she can see how Joan's reading is coming. T looks at Tom's math and points out those problems he needs to check over. T has st do problem while T watches. T has math group do one problem at a time and checks each one as sts complete it.
4. *No T evaluation observed.*	

Source: Marshall, H., & Weinstein, R. (1986). *Classroom Dimensions Observation System: Revised Manual.* Berkeley: University of California.

Table 3.8   ASSESSING CLASSROOM TASKS ASSIGNED TO STUDENTS

Task within the group or within the class. Code whether all sts within the group or in the class are working on the same or different task.

Definitions	Examples
1. *Same exact task.* All sts are working on the same exact task at the same time. (Limited.) If sts are working on same task, but start something else when they finish, code what start with.	All sts are working on same story in reading or same pages in workbooks.
2. *Same broad topic (type of task) in series.* Sts are working on the same type of task but are in a different place in the series of learning materials.	Different pages in same workbook or different workbook in series. Computation +, −, ×—regardless of type of materials. Science experiments in series.
3. *Different activities but tasks within content areas are in sequence.* Sts are working on two or more types of activities but tasks are sequential within content areas. Sts may complete tasks at own pace. Sts may or may not be working on same subject matter at same time or in same order.	Assignments for reading, math, and spelling are posted. Sts complete at own pace such that some are working on different tasks at the same time. T gives sts packet of seatwork consisting of math, spelling, phonics that they complete at own pace. One group works on geometry. Another group works on multiplication ditto.
4. *Same broad topic (type of task), not in series.* Sts are working on same type of tasks and materials, but tasks are not organized into a series of learning materials and have no consecutive order that all must follow. May or may not relate to common goal.	Reading from trade (library) books. Geoboards, puzzles. Creative writing story stems. Art—e.g., drawing, collage, mural. Science experiments not in series. Sts paint on mural and cut out figures. Sts meet in committees to plan and work for class picnic. Sharing. Reading games.
5. *Different activities (nonsequential, unrelated).* Sts are working on two or more different activities that are unrelated to each other and are not completed in a sequence.	Ten sts are working in math workbook, 7 sts are using beansticks, 6 are playing dominoes. Some sts read, some write stories, some illustrate. Some do math ditto, some creative writing.

Source: Marshall, H., & Weinstein, R. (1986). *Classroom Dimensions Observation System: Revised Manual.* Berkeley: University of California.

Table 3.9   ASSESSING TEACHER-STUDENT INTERACTION (EXAMPLES OF ITEMS FROM PART II OF CD SCALE)

Code each item as to *context* of whether the interaction is with the Class as whole, as Individual within the Class, a Group, an Individual within a Group, or an Individual Alone.

Definitions	Examples

Motivation

Cooperative behavior
T structures for or sts display cooperation, helpfulness on nonacademic tasks.

St drops crayon box. Several others help put them back.

Competitive behavior
T structures for or sts exhibit competitive behavior in nonacademic sphere, such as which table is quietest, cleanest. (See above re limited resources.)

"Let's see which table works the most quietly." (At beginning of period.) (Code group level.)

If all can win or receive reward, do not code as competitive, e.g., "Let's see who is quiet and can watch the slides."

"Points for the first row ready."

Responsibility

T encourages self-evaluation
T helps sts evaluate own work, to find out what is wrong or how to make it better.

T tells st to look at the story again to see if the answer is correct.
T asks st to recheck addition.

T helps sts compare work to own past performance. (Note different from *T* making comparison—item 22.)

T asks st to compare handwriting to that done last month.

Different from T probing where T guides through content questions.

T goes over st's story, asking him if he can find capitalization errors.

Evaluation

Praise: academic
T mentions or emphasizes sts' academic successes.

"I really like the way you're doing that!"

T tells sts individually and/or as a group what a good job they are doing, etc. Does *not* include standard phrases, e.g., "O.K.," "uh, uh," "right."

"That's a great idea!"

Do *not* code "good" as praise if it is used for closure purposes (indicating that it's time to go on with next student or subject), or if it indicates routine correctness.

"You're absolutely right!"
"You've been working so hard."

Praise deviates from T's routine or standard or usual way of affirming—either in change of words or tone of voice.

"Nice job. Good for you." (= one instance)

Buffered criticism: academic
T softens critical statements about academic performance and buffers impact either through tone of voice, dialect; phrasing it with a positive statement or through humor.

"Your work is usually very good, but what happened today? You tired?"
"It's not quite right, but I don't think I explained that very well."

Relationships

Fairness
T makes deliberate attempt to be fair to all. More than routine class management or politeness.

"We need some more girls to make it even."
"Someone from table 3 needs to have a chance."

Source: Adapted from Marshall, H., & Weinstein, R. S. (1986). *Classroom Dimensions Observation System: Revised Manual.* University of California, Berkeley.

CHAPTER

4

Teacher Expectations

Teachers' behavior is goal-directed, and thus shaped by their beliefs and expectations about how to accomplish their goals. In planning for and interacting with the class as a whole, with small groups, and with individuals, teachers are guided by their beliefs about what students need and by their expectations about how students will respond if treated in particular ways. As argued in Chapter 2, the more accurate these beliefs and expectations, the more likely that teachers will achieve their goals.

A great deal of research has been done in the last 20 years on the effects of teacher expectations on teacher-student interaction and student performance. *Teacher expectations* are defined here as inferences that teachers make about the future behavior or academic achievement of their students, based on what they know about these students now. *Teacher expectation effects* are student outcomes that occur because of the actions that teachers take in response to their own expectations.

Researchers have examined two types of teacher expectation effects (Cooper & Good, 1983). The first is the *self-fulfilling prophecy effect* in which an originally erroneous expectation leads to behavior that causes the expectation to become true. Merton (1948), who coined the term, gave bank failures as an example. He noted that a false rumor that a bank was about to fail could cause depositors to panic and flock to the bank to clear out their accounts. If enough depositors acted on this unfounded rumor and demanded their money, the bank's financial position would deteriorate rapidly and the rumored failure would occur, even though it would not have occurred if the false rumor had not circulated in the first place. As a classroom example, consider the first-grade teacher who decides that her student Karen will be one of the best readers in the class, because last year Karen's older sister, Amy, was a brilliant first-grade reader. Let us assume that Karen is actually a student with average potential, but that the teacher warms up to her right away, expresses confidence that she will be a good reader, calls on her often in class, and arranges for her to practice at home with Amy. Chances are that this treatment will make Karen one of the best readers in the class before long, even though this would not have happened if the teacher had not treated her specially. Karen's rapid progress in reading can be seen as a self-fulfilling prophecy effect of her teacher's expectations and related instructional decisions.

The second type of expectation effect is the *sustaining expectation effect*. Here, teachers expect students to sustain previously developed behavior patterns, to the point that they take these behavior patterns for granted and fail to see and capitalize on changes in student potential. The findings described in Chapter 2 on teachers' differential treatment of high versus low achievers (Cooper & Good, 1983; Rowe, 1969) are examples of sustaining expectation effects. To the extent that teachers wait longer for high achievers to respond to questions, provide them with more second chances following initial failures, and react to their answers with more praise and less criticism, they are likely to sustain (and probably increase somewhat) the achievement differences between the two groups.

Self-fulfilling prophecy effects are more powerful than sustaining expectation effects because they induce significant change in student behavior instead of merely minimizing such change by sustaining established patterns. Self-fulfilling prophecy effects can be powerful and dramatic when they occur, but the more subtle sustaining expectation effects probably occur much more often. This chapter is organized around the concept of self-fulfilling prophecies, but both forms of expectation effect are important and provide useful concepts for examining classroom events.

TEACHER EXPECTATIONS AS SELF-FULFILLING PROPHECIES

Robert Rosenthal and Lenore Jacobson's *Pygmalion in the Classroom* (1968) created wide interest in and controversy about self-fulfilling prophecies. Their book describes research in which they manipulated teacher expectations for student achievement to see if these expectations would be fulfilled. The study involved several classes in each of the first six grades at Oak School. Expectations were created by claiming that a test (actually a general achievement test) had been developed to identify students who were about to bloom intellectually and therefore could be expected to show unusually large achievement gains during the coming school year. A few students in each class were identified to the teachers as such "bloomers." Actually, they had been selected randomly rather than on the basis of test scores, so there was no real reason to expect unusual gains from them.

Yet, the "bloomers" did score relatively higher than other students on achievement tests given at the end of the school year (although the effects were confined primarily to the first two grades). Rosenthal and Jacobson interpreted these results in terms of the self-fulfilling prophecy effects of teacher expectations. They reasoned that the expectations they created had somehow caused the teachers to treat the "bloomers" differently, so that they did make unusually high achievement gains that year.

At first, this conclusion was accepted enthusiastically, and secondary sources sometimes even made exaggerated claims that went far beyond those made by

Rosenthal and Jacobson. For example, one ad in the Readers' Digest read: "Actual experiments prove this mysterious force can heighten your intelligence, your competitive ability, and your will to succeed. The secret: Just make a prediction! Read how it works." Soon, however, critics began to attack the study (Snow, 1969; Taylor, 1970) and a replication attempt failed to produce the same results (Claiborn, 1969), leading to debates over the merits of the Oak School experiment. Meanwhile, other investigators did related studies using a variety of approaches, and attention shifted from debates over the original study to attempts to make sense of a growing literature on teacher expectation effects and related topics (Braun, 1976; Brophy & Good, 1974; West & Anderson, 1976). This process has continued in the nearly two decades since the Oak School experiment, leading to a consensus that teacher expectations can and sometimes do affect teacher-student interaction and student outcomes, along with the recognition that the processes involved are much more complex than originally believed (Brophy, 1983; Cooper & Good, 1983; Dusek, 1985; Marshall & Weinstein, 1984).

To make sense of the research, one must distinguish between two types of studies. The first type, which includes the Rosenthal and Jacobson study, involves experimental attempts to manipulate or induce teacher expectations. Here, the investigators try to create expectations by identifying "late bloomers," using phony IQ scores, or providing some other fictitious information about students. The second type of study uses the expectations that teachers form naturally on the basis of whatever information they have available (test scores and cumulative folder information, information from other teachers, previous experience with the family, etc.). A few examples of each type of study follow.

Effects of Induced Expectations

Studies conducted in quite different settings have shown that student achievement can be affected by expectations induced in instructors. Beez (1968), studying adult tutors teaching Headstart children; Burnham (1968), studying swimming instructors teaching preadolescents how to swim; and Schrank (1968) working with Air Force mathematics instructors, all obtained similar results. In each study, expectations were manipulated by causing certain teachers to believe that the students or classes they would work with had unusually high learning potential, when in fact the groups had been matched or selected randomly. Nevertheless, in each study, the students of instructors who had been led to hold high expectations achieved more than the students of other instructors.

Beez (1968) monitored teacher behavior in his study and found that achievement differences were a direct result of differences in how much was taught. Tutors with high expectations tried to teach more material than the tutors with low expectations, and succeeded in doing so.

Many studies involving teacher expectations have not produced positive results, apparently because the teachers did not acquire the expectations that the experimenters were trying to induce. The most obvious case is one in which the teachers knew that the expectations were not true, as in Schrank's (1970) adaptation of his earlier study of Air Force mathematics courses. For this second study, Schrank merely simulated the manipulation of teacher expectations; the teachers knew that their students had been grouped randomly rather than by ability levels, but were asked to pretend that they were teaching a higher ability group. Similar negative results were reported by Fleming and Anttonen (1971), who tried to induce expectations using falsely inflated IQ scores but found that teachers did not accept the phony IQs and thus did not allow them to affect their treatment of students.

Such mixed results are typical of induced expectation studies. Some such studies have produced clear-cut positive results demonstrating that teacher expectations can have self-fulfilling prophecy effects on student achievement, and a few have produced information about the processes that mediate these effects. Along with data from studies linking teachers' naturally formed expectations to their classroom interactions with students, such research provides information about how teachers' expectations can become self-fulfilling. Self-fulfilling prophecy effects can be demonstrated scientifically only through experiments involving induced expectations. They cannot be shown through studies of teachers' naturally formed expectations; sometimes such expectations are based on real differences in student potential and thus are merely accurate predictions rather than actual causes of student outcomes.

Effects of Naturally Formed Expectations

In this type of study, teachers' expectations are assessed either prior to their interactions with their students (ideally) or early in the term before the teachers have had a chance to collect much first-hand information and develop firm opinions. Various measures of teachers' naturally formed expectations have been developed (Cooper & Tom, 1984), but usually teachers are asked to rank or rate their students on either current achievement levels or expected improvement over the term. Student outcome data are then examined for differences between groups of students rated low versus high by their teachers.

Palardy (1969) studied the reading achievement levels produced by two groups of first-grade teachers. Using a questionnaire, he identified 10 teachers who believed that their boys could make just as much progress in first-grade reading achievement as their girls, and another 14 teachers who expected the girls to do better. Five teachers from each group were selected for further study. All taught in middle-class schools, used the same basal reading series, and worked with three reading groups in heterogeneously grouped, self-contained classrooms.

The two groups did not differ on reading readiness tests given in September. However, on reading achievement tests given in March, boys whose teachers believed that they could achieve as well as girls averaged 96.5, but boys whose teachers believed that they could not perform as well as girls averaged only 89.2. The girls in these classes averaged 96.2 and 96.7, respectively. Thus, the boys did, indeed, have lower achievement scores in classes taught by teachers who thought that boys could not progress as rapidly as girls.

Doyle, Hancock, and Kifer (1972) asked first-grade teachers to estimate the IQs of their pupils shortly before an IQ test was given. Later comparisons showed that the teachers tended to overestimate the IQs of girls and underestimate those of boys, and that these IQ estimates were related to reading achievement. Even though there was no statistically significant gender-related difference in IQ, the girls showed higher reading achievement scores. Furthermore, within both sexes, students whose IQs had been overestimated by their teachers had higher reading achievement scores than students whose IQs had been underestimated.

Most studies of teachers' naturally formed expectations have related such expectations to teacher-student interaction rather than to student outcomes. Such studies typically demonstrate that teachers interact differently with high-expectation students than they do with low-expectation students, and they suggest the mechanisms that mediate sustaining expectation effects.

HOW EXPECTATIONS BECOME SELF-FULFILLING

Teacher expectation effects in classrooms are just special cases of the more general principle that any expectation can become self-fulfilling. (See Jones, 1977, for a discussion of other expectation effects.) Although it is not true that "wishing can make it so," our expectations affect the way we behave, and the way we behave affects how other people respond. Sometimes our expectations about people cause us to treat them in ways that make them respond just as we expected they would.

For example, look ahead (or back) to your first teaching assignment. Unless they already know the situation, most new teachers want to find out as much as possible about the school and the principal with whom they will be working. Suppose you spoke to a friend already teaching at the school who said, "Mr. Jackson is wonderful. You'll love working for him. He's very warm and pleasant, and he really takes an interest in you. Feel free to come to him with your problems; he's always glad to help." If you heard this about Mr. Jackson, how do you think you would respond to him when you met him? Think about this for a few moments, and then consider a different situation. Suppose your friend had said, "Mr. Jackson? Well, uh, he's sort of hard to describe. I guess he's all right, but I don't feel comfortable around him; he makes me nervous. I don't know what it is exactly, just that I get the feeling that he doesn't want to talk to me, that I'm irritating him or wasting his time." How do you think that you would act when meeting Mr. Jackson after you had heard this?

If you are like most people, your behavior would differ depending on which description you heard. If you had received the positive information, you probably would look forward to meeting Mr. Jackson and would approach him with confidence and a friendly smile. Among other things, you would likely tell him that you had heard good things about him and were happy to be working with him and looking forward to getting started. Having heard the other description, however, you probably would not look forward to the meeting, and you might well be nervous, inhibited, or overly concerned about making a good impression. You might approach with hesitation, wearing a serious expression or a forced smile, and speak in rather reserved, formal tones. Even if you said the same words, the chances are that they would sound more like a prepared speech than a genuine personal reaction.

Now, put yourself in Mr. Jackson's place. Assume he knows nothing about you as a person. Take a few moments to think about how he might respond to these two disparate approaches. Chances are, Mr. Jackson would respond positively to the first approach. Faced with your warmth, friendliness, and genuine-sounding compliments, he likely would respond in kind. Your behavior would put him at ease and cause him to see you as a likeable, attractive person. When he smiled and said he would be looking forward to working with you too, he would really mean it.

But what if you took the nervous, formal approach? Again, Mr. Jackson probably would respond in kind. Your behavior would likely make him feel nervous and formal, if he were not already. He would respond in an equally bland and formal manner, and this probably would be followed by an awkward silence that would make you both increasingly nervous. As the authority figure and host, he probably would feel compelled to make the next move. In view of your behavior, attempts at small talk would be risky, so he might just get down to business and begin to speak in his capacity as principal, talking to you in your capacity as teacher.

Brophy and Good's Model

The example shows that it is not just the existence of an expectation that causes self-fulfillment; it is the behavior that this expectation produces. This behavior then affects other people, making them more likely to act in the expected ways. In our early research on teacher expectation effects on individual students (Brophy & Good, 1970), we suggested the following model for how the process might work in the classroom:

2. Consistent with these differential expectations, teachers behave various toward different students.
3. This treatment tells students something about how they are expected to behave in the classroom and perform on academic tasks.
4. If the teacher treatment is consistent over time, and if students do not actively resist or change it, it will likely affect their self-concepts, achievement motivation, levels of aspiration, classroom conduct, and interactions with teachers.
5. These effects generally will complement and reinforce teachers' expectations, so that students will come to conform to these expectations more than they might have otherwise.
6. Ultimately, this will affect student achievement and other outcome measures. High-expectation students will be led to achieve at or near their potential, but low-expectation students will not gain as much as they could have gained if taught differently.

Self-fulfilling prophecy effects of teacher expectations can occur only when all of the elements in the model are present. Often, however, one or more elements is missing. A teacher may not have clear-cut expectations about every student, or those expectations may change continually. Even when expectations are consistent, the teacher may not necessarily communicate them to the student through consistent behavior. In this case, the expectations would not be self-fulfilling even if they turned out to be correct. Finally, students might prevent expectations from becoming self-fulfilling by counteracting their effects or resisting them in a way that makes the teacher change them.

Practice Examples

We have provided some practice examples you can use to improve your understanding of the self-fulfilling prophecy concept. Read each example and determine whether you think a self-fulfilling prophecy is involved. If so, you should be able to identify: (1) the original expectation, (2) behaviors that consistently communicate this expectation in ways that make it more likely to be fulfilled, and (3) evidence that the original expectation has been confirmed. If the example does not contain all three elements, it does not illustrate a self-fulfilling prophecy.

1. Coach Winn knows that Thumper Brown is the son of a former All-American football star. Although he has never seen Thumper carry the ball, he predicts, "That boy will help our team in his sophomore year." In practice sessions, Winn treats Thumper like all the other runners. He carries the ball the same number of times in drills, and the coach praises him only when his performance deserves it. Thumper wins a starting position in his sophomore year, becomes an outstanding player, and is named to the all-conference team.

2. Mr. Wilson, a tenth-grade social studies teacher, believes that Sharon Canter and Jim Davis can be better students. Although they have earned only average grades, he has seen flashes of insight in them that suggest higher potential. Furthermore, their aptitude test scores are higher than their achievement profiles. However, he has noted that both students have poor work habits. Neither spends much time working on seatwork assignments and it is not uncommon for Jim and Sharon to fail to hand in homework two or three times a week. Mr. Wilson "knows" that both students can do better if he can motivate them to work harder, so he begins to call on them more often and to provide more detailed feedback on their seatwork and homework papers. By December, he has seen no progress. Nevertheless, he continues his efforts, and by May, Jim is performing at a much higher level, although Sharon's classroom behavior and test scores have not improved.

3. Mrs. Explicit is giving directions to John Greene, a second grader who is frequently in trouble. She has no confidence in John's sense of responsibility, so she gives him detailed instructions: "John, take this note to Mrs. Turner's room. Remember: Don't make noise in the hall, don't stop to look in other classrooms, and above all, don't go outside." John responds with an obviously pained look, "Mrs. Explicit, don't you trust me?"

4. As the school year begins, Tom Bloom is assigned to Dean Helpful for academic counseling. The dean knows that Tom will probably flunk out at the end of the semester. He has low entrance scores and poor writing skills. He is also socially withdrawn and shy, making it unlikely that he will get to know his instructors very well or receive much help from them. The dean tells Tom that he may encounter academic difficulty and urges him to enroll in the study skills clinic and to devote extra time on weekends to his studies. In addition, he has Tom report to his office once a week. Tom realizes that the dean expects him to have trouble unless he works hard, so he works as hard as he can for the whole semester. When the grade slips are mailed in January, Tom has two Bs and three Cs.

5. Mr. Graney knows that Beth Burton will be a problem. He had her older sister the year before and she was uncontrollable. Trying to keep Beth out of trouble, Mr. Graney seats her at a table away from the other third graders in the room. Before long, though, Beth begins to throw things at her peers to attract their attention.

6. Tom Burton teaches a consumer business course at Mill Tour High School. He believes that students need and want to perform enjoyable drill activities in class but are not interested in tasks that require higher-order thinking. Therefore, in his taxation unit he emphasizes how to fill out tax forms and quick ways to check for computation errors. His other units also emphasize practical exercises involving much drill and practice but comparatively little analysis (Why are taxes collected? How legitimate is the present system? What are alternative taxation plans that would yield the same revenue but distribute the burden differently?).

7. Judy Jones, a seventh-grade mathematics teacher, used tests emphasizing speed rather than pure ability to group students for mathematics instruction. At the beginning of the year she taught new material to the high group (students who did well on the speed test) but required the slow group to review sixth-grade material in order to build up their speed. However, in the early weeks, the slower students worked only a few of the review problems because they knew how to do them and because they wanted to listen to the teacher work with the high group so that they would be ready to do the work. This failure to complete assigned work during the class period strengthened the teacher's belief that these students still needed more drill work. In time, the slow-group students became bored with the easy, repetitive drill work; did even fewer problems; and became less interested in listening to the teacher work with the high group (in part because they did not get to work on similar problems). By the end of the year, many slow-group students were engaging in disruptive behavior.

8. Miss Ball is concerned about the peer-group adjustment of Dick Stewart, one of her second-grade boys. Dick had participated all year long in the races and group games conducted during recess, but he began to withdraw from the group in the spring, when she started the children playing baseball. Although Dick has good physical coordination, he had not played much baseball and had difficulty hitting and catching the ball. As a result, he was usually one of the last children chosen when teams were selected. After this happened a few times, Dick began to withdraw, claiming that he did not want to play because he had a headache or a sore foot. This did not fool Miss Ball, who recognized that embarrassment was the real reason.

To help Dick compensate for his deficiencies and to see that he did not lose peer status, Miss Ball began allowing him to serve as umpire for ball games. This gave him an important active role which she reinforced by praising and calling other children's attention to his umpire work. In private contacts, she reassured Dick that he should not feel bad because he was not playing and that there could not be a ball game without an umpire.

In the last few days of school, Miss Ball decided to let Dick play again, now that his confidence was built up. She was gratified to see that he was picked earlier than usual by the team captain. However, his batting and catching were just as bad as before. The next day, he was the last one chosen and he begged off, complaining of a headache.

Responses

Let us see how well you were able to identify self-fulfilling prophecies. If we have been successful in describing the process, you should have identified each example correctly.

In Example 1, Coach Winn's original expectation about Thumper is fulfilled. However, there is no evidence that Winn caused this through special behavior toward Thumper. Thus, the coach's prediction did not act as a self-fulfilling prophecy, even though his prediction was accurate.

Example 2 is a self-fulfilling prophecy for Jim but not Sharon, even though the teacher believed that both students could do better. Mr. Wilson's determined teaching apparently has been successful in changing Jim's perceptions and beliefs ("I can do math." "I should do it." "I want to."), thus improving his behavior and achievement. However, Mr. Wilson's behavior did not improve Sharon's performance (perhaps she viewed his increased questioning as nagging or as a lack of confidence in her ability). Students, as well as teachers, interpret classroom behavior.

In Example 3, the teacher gives Johnny explicit instructions because she fears that he will take advantage of the situation and misbehave. She subconsciously communicates this expectation in her behavior toward him, and he picks it up. However, there is no evidence that his behavior changes accordingly, so this is not an example of a self-fulfilling prophecy. If Mrs. Explicit were to continue to treat Johnny this way, though, he might begin to behave as she expects. At this point, her expectation would have become self-fulfilling.

Example 4 is especially interesting and instructive. The dean fears that Tom will flunk, and he communicates this expectation. Tom gets the message, but he reacts by working as hard as he can to prove himself. He ends up doing well, despite the dean's original expectation. This occurs because the dean communicates a serious concern, but then follows this up with attempts to deal with the problem (referring Tom to the study skills clinic, calling for extra study time, scheduling regular counseling appointments). In effect, the dean works against his own expectation by engaging in what might be called "counterprophetic compensation" behaviors (Brophy, 1985) designed to prevent the feared outcome. If, instead, the dean had communicated hopelessness and done nothing to change the situation, his expectation probably would have been fulfilled.

Goldenberg (1985) presents two case studies from a first-grade classroom that include a series of events remarkably parallel to those involving our fictional Tom Bloom. Goldenberg contrasts what occurred with Marta and Sylvia, two girls toward whom the teacher had contrasting expectations at the beginning of the year. Marta began the year with low test scores and was assigned to the lowest reading group. The teacher also perceived her as having a poor attitude—doing her work hurriedly, poorly, and carelessly. She also was something of a behavior problem due to immaturity, laughing and playing in class, and acting silly with other children. Concerned about these problems, the teacher acted early in the year by telling Marta that she expected a better effort from her and by contacting Marta's mother to enlist her support in improving Marta's attitudes and behavior. These actions led to an immediate change in Marta's classroom behavior and achievement. She began paying consistent attention to lessons, worked at a good pace, and made steady progress, to the point that the teacher's perceptions of her changed dramatically. She was moved to a higher reading group as the year progressed, and ended up reading at grade level.

Marta's classmate Sylvia showed nearly the opposite pattern. The teacher began with high expectations for her and maintained these expectations for much of the year. In part, this was because Sylvia was an eager participant who frequently raised her hand during lessons and answered correctly when called on. Early in the year, Sylvia made steady progress and turned in all of her assignments. By December, however, Sylvia's work pace had slowed. The work she did do was done neatly and correctly, but she was falling behind in her work because she spent a lot of time staring out the window or attending to events elsewhere in the room. She did not actively misbehave, however, so that she did not come to the teacher's attention during these times. The teacher was aware that Sylvia was not performing up to expectations. She did not feel the need to intervene because Sylvia was not causing disruptions and her being behind was partly a result of missing a week of school. The teacher simply assumed that Sylvia had fallen into some temporary funk from which she would emerge on her own. However, Sylvia's progress continued to lag until almost the end of the year, when a classroom observer called the teacher's attention to Sylvia and suggested that intervention was needed. Sylvia's pace picked up considerably once the teacher intervened.

Goldenberg's case studies of actual students illustrate that students sometimes can benefit from initially low teacher expectations if those expectations cause the teacher to take action intended to counteract the feared consequences, and also that students can suffer negative consequences from initially high teacher expectations if those expectations cause the teacher to fail to notice changes that call for corrective action.

Example 5 is a classic illustration of a self-fulfilling teacher expectation. Mr. Graney expects Beth to be a problem and begins to treat her as one. His treatment involves separating her from her peers, which leads her to misbehave to get attention and causes his expectation to become fulfilled.

Example 6 is an interesting example to analyze. First, we do not know whether Tom's expectation is correct or not. It is likely that many of his students do prefer drill and practice tasks over those that require higher-order thinking (so his expectation is correct for these students). However, other students may want to know why things exist and how they operate. If these students' attitudes change over the year and they develop a preference for concrete, repetitive activities, then a self-fulfilling prophecy will have occurred. From the material given in the example, it is not possible to tell.

From another perspective, Tom's behavior can be seen as communicating low and inappropriate expectations for classroom performance, expectations that would at least *sustain* undesirable student behavior and attitudes. That is, even if he does not cause students to alter their preferences by confining the course to drill and practice activities, he will have denied students the chance to develop a broader understanding of the topic through higher-order thinking activities.

Example 7 parallels the findings of one of the studies presented in Chapter 2.

It is not a self-fulfilling prophecy, although it has many of the same characteristics. First, it involves an inappropriate teacher belief, that students' slowness is due largely to low ability rather than to motivational factors. Second, the teacher does engage in differential teacher behavior. However, this stems from the teacher's attempt to provide each group with the curriculum and instruction that she thinks they need rather than from a tendency to "write off" the slow group as hopeless. Nevertheless, the end result is much like a teacher-expectation effect (the gap between the slow and the fast students is widened), because the teacher's beliefs about student needs are incorrect and lead to counterproductive slow-group teaching.

Example 8 illustrates how a teacher's expectation can be self-fulfilling even though it is unformulated and unrecognized by the teacher. Miss Ball intends to build Dick's confidence so that he will participate in ball games. However, her approach takes into account only his attitude and not his need for practice in hitting and catching the ball. Although she does not think about it this way, her approach reflects the expectation that Dick cannot hit or catch and, therefore, needs some alternate role. This is very different from the idea that Dick cannot hit or catch and, therefore, needs to be taught to do so. Miss Ball's attempt to solve the problem involves many good things for Dick but not the things he needs most: practice hitting and catching the ball. As a result, by the end of the year he is even farther behind his classmates in these skills than he was earlier.

The last two examples are among many that could have been given of teachers who adopt inappropriate strategies because they define the problem improperly. Teachers who worry about their students' self-concepts often do this because they think that they have to improve self-concept before ability will improve. Usually, the opposite is true (Eccles & Wigfield, 1985). Low self-concept results from low ability, and improvement in ability will produce improvement in self-concept. When students show handicaps, inhibitions, or lack of skill, the appropriate teacher strategy is to provide remedial instruction and extra practice or opportunities to learn. Although well meant, attempts to make students feel better by providing compensation in other areas rather than dealing directly with their problems are not helpful.

HOW TEACHERS FORM THEIR EXPECTATIONS

We will now consider some of the research on teacher-expectation effects, along with its implications for teachers. Most of this research has focused on teachers' expectations for student achievement rather than for other student outcomes (motivation, conduct, social adjustment), and most has focused on expectations about individual students rather than groups or classes as a whole. Therefore, we will begin with research on teachers' expectations for individual student's achievement, considering it in terms of the steps in the Brophy and Good model.

The model begins with the statement that teachers form differential achievement expectations for individual students at the beginning of the school year. Investigators have studied the nature of the information that teachers use to form these expectations and the degree to which the expectations are accurate.

One body of literature consists of experimental studies of expectation formation in which subjects (not necessarily teachers) are given only carefully controlled information about, and little or no opportunity to interact with, the "students" (usually fictional) about whom they are asked to make predictions. In such a study, for example, all of the subjects might be given cumulative record forms containing identical test scores, grades, and comments presumably written by previous teachers, but half of the forms would be accompanied by a picture of a white child and the other half by a picture of a black child (to see if knowledge about the fictional student's race would affect predictions about his or her achievement). Such experiments have shown that expectations can be affected significantly by information about test performance, performance on assignments, track or group placement, classroom conduct, physical appearance, race, socioeconomic status, ethnicity, sex, speech characteristics, and various diagnostic or special education labels (see reviews by Baron, Tom, & Cooper, 1985; Braun, 1976; Brophy & Good, 1974; Dusek & Joseph, 1985; Persell, 1977; Peterson & Barger, 1985; Rolison & Medway, 1985).

These findings are not surprising, given the very limited information that experimental subjects had to work with. Unfortunately, however, such findings often are generalized to discussions about teachers' formation of expectations concerning their actual students, to the point of making teachers appear to be both extremely gullible (willing to accept whatever phony information someone gives them) and extremely prejudiced (tending to jump to conclusions based on race, sex, etc.). In reality, studies focusing on real teachers' expectations concerning their actual students, conducted under more natural conditions, suggest a much more positive picture. First, teachers will not passively accept phony information if it is contradicted by other information from more credible sources or from their own tests, assignments, or interactions with the students (Bognar, 1982; Fleming & Anttonen, 1971; Raudenbush, 1984). Furthermore, studies of in-service teachers' achievement expectations for their actual students do not reveal much evidence of grossly biased judgment. Instead, teachers' perceptions of students are largely accurate and based on the best available information, and most inaccuracies are corrected when more dependable information becomes available (Borko et al., 1979; Brophy & Good, 1974; Shavelson, Cadwell, & Izu, 1977; Short, 1985).

Most of the information in school records is accurate and likely to induce accurate expectations in teachers who read it, and most of the impressions that teachers form from interacting with their students are based primarily on student participation in academic activities and performance on tests and assignments, rather than on physical or other status characteristics. Thus, teachers' predictions about student achievement are usually quite accurate, sometimes even more accurate than predictions based on test data (Egan & Archer, 1985; Hoge & Butcher, 1984; Mitman, 1985; Monk, 1983; Pedulla, Airasian, & Madaus, 1980).

In summary, in-service teachers are usually quite accurate in developing expectations about their actual students, and these expectations tend to become further corrected as more or better information becomes available. This limits the possibilities for self-fulfilling prophecy effects (which are based on false or unjustified expectations), although it still leaves a great deal of room for sustaining expectation effects. Self-fulfilling prophecy effects are especially likely to occur when students are new to their teachers because it is early in the school year (especially in kindergarten and first grade and in the first year of middle school, junior high, or high school) or because they have transferred from another school.

HOW TEACHERS COMMUNICATE EXPECTATIONS TO STUDENTS

Given that teachers have formed differential expectations for different students, the next step of the Brophy and Good model postulates that teachers communicate these differential expectations through their behavior toward students. Researchers have addressed this issue by documenting the ways that teachers interact with students who differ in current or expected achievement levels.

Rosenthal (1974) reviewed the research on mediators of teacher expectation effects and identified four general factors. Focusing on positive self-fulfilling prophecy effects, he suggested that teachers will maximize student achievement if they:

1. Create warm social-emotional relationships with their students (climate).
2. Give them more feedback about their performance (feedback).
3. Teach them more (and more difficult) material (input).
4. Give them more opportunities to respond and to ask questions (output).

This four-factor model is a useful summary, but we prefer to offer a more lengthy list of potential mediating mechanisms, for three reasons. First, teachers and teacher educators can use each of the items in a more detailed list as a basis for observing classroom interaction. Second, we want to complement Rosenthal's emphasis on enhancing student achievement through positive expectation effects with an emphasis on ways that teachers might minimize the learning progress of low-expectation students through negative or undesirable expectation effects. Unfortunately, research suggests that teachers are more likely to be affected by information leading to negative expectations than by information leading to positive expectations (Mason, 1973; Persell, 1977; Seaver, 1973). Third, we want to emphasize that teachers can communicate their expectations in a variety of ways, including some that are much more subtle than the direct ways summarized in Rosenthal's model. Reviews of the literature (Brophy & Good, 1974; Brophy, 1983; Good, 1981) suggest that the following behaviors sometimes indicate differential teacher treatment of high and low achievers:

1. Waiting less time for lows to answer (Allington, 1980; Bozsik, 1982; Rowe, 1974a, 1974b; Taylor, 1979).
2. Giving lows answers or calling on someone else rather than trying to improve their responses by giving clues or repeating or rephrasing questions (Brophy & Good, 1970b; Jeter & Davis, 1973).
3. Inappropriate reinforcement: rewarding inappropriate behavior or incorrect answers by lows (Amato, 1975; Fernandez, Espinosa, & Dornbusch, 1975; Graham, 1984; Kleinfeld, 1975; Meyer et al., 1979; Natriello & Dornbusch, 1984; Rowe, 1974a; Weinstein, 1976; Taylor, 1977).
4. Criticizing lows more often for failure (Brophy & Good, 1970; Cooper & Baron, 1977; Good, Cooper, & Blakey, 1980; Good, Sikes, & Brophy,

1973; Jones, 1971; Medinnus & Unruh, 1971; Rowe, 1974*a;* Smith & Luginbuhl, 1976).

5. Praising lows less frequently than highs for success (Babad, Inbar, & Rosenthal, 1982; Brophy & Good, 1970; Cooper & Baron, 1977; Firestone & Brody, 1975; Good, Cooper, & Blakey, 1980; Good, Sikes, & Brophy, 1973; Martinek & Johnson, 1979; Medinnus & Unruh, 1971; Rejeski, Darracott & Hutslar, 1979; Spector, 1973).

6. Failing to give feedback to the public responses of lows (Brophy & Good, 1970; Good, Sikes, & Brophy, 1973; Jeter & Davis, 1973; Willis, 1970).

7. Generally paying less attention to lows or interacting with them less frequently (Adams & Cohen, 1974; Blakey, 1970; Given, 1974; Kester & Letchworth, 1972; Page, 1971; Rist, 1970; Rubovits & Maehr, 1971).

8. Calling on lows less often to respond to questions (Davis & Levine, 1970; Mendoza, Good, & Brophy, 1972; Rubovits & Maehr, 1971), or asking them only easier, nonanalytic questions (Martinek & Johnson, 1979).

9. Seating lows farther away from the teacher (Rist, 1970).

10. Demanding less from lows. This differential treatment is evidenced by a variety of behaviors. Beez (1968) found that tutors with high expectations not only taught more words but also taught them more rapidly and with less extended explanation and repetition of definitions and examples. The studies of inappropriate reinforcement mentioned above indicate that teachers may accept low-quality or even incorrect responses from lows. Graham (1984) suggests that excessive teacher sympathy or offers of gratuitous, unsolicited help may communicate low expectations, especially if these behaviors occur instead of behaviors designed to help low achievers meet success criteria.

11. Interacting with lows more privately than publicly, and monitoring and structuring their activities more closely. Brophy and Good (1974) discuss these differences in detail.

12. Differential administration or grading of tests or assignments, in which highs but not lows are given the benefit of the doubt in borderline cases (Cahen, 1966; Finn, 1972; Heapy & Siess, 1970).

13. Less friendly interaction with lows, including less smiling and fewer other nonverbal indicators of support (Babad, Inbar, & Rosenthal, 1982; Chaikin, Sigler, & Derlega, 1974; Kester & Letchworth, 1972; Meichenbaum, Bowers, & Ross, 1969; Page, 1971; Smith & Luginbuhl, 1976) and less warm or more anxious voice tones (Blanck & Rosenthal, 1984).

14. Briefer and less informative feedback to questions of lows (Cooper, 1979; Cornbleth, Davis, & Button, 1972).

15. Less eye contact and other nonverbal communication of attention and responsiveness (forward lean, positive head nodding) in interaction with lows (Chaikin, Sigler, & Derlega, 1974).

16. Less use of effective but time-consuming instructional methods with lows when time is limited (Swann & Snyder, 1980).

17. Less acceptance and use of lows' ideas (Martinek & Johnson, 1979; Martinek & Karper, 1982).

Several points should be made about these forms of differential treatment that have been documented in various studies. First, they do not occur in all teachers' classrooms. Teachers differ considerably in how much they differentiate their treatment of students for whom they hold different expectations (more on this later).

Second, sometimes these treatment differences are due mostly or even entirely to the students rather than to the teacher. For example, if lows seldom raise their hands it will be difficult for the teacher to insure that they get as many response opportunities as highs, and if their contributions to the lesson are of lower quality it will be difficult for the teacher to accept and use their ideas just as frequently.

Third, some of these forms of differential treatment may be appropriate at times and may even represent good individualizing of instruction by the teacher rather than inappropriate projection of negative expectations. Lows appear to require closer monitoring of their work and more structuring of their activities, for example, and one could argue that it makes sense to interact with them more privately than publicly or to ask them easier questions. It is difficult to distinguish seatwork monitoring that includes just the right degree of extra structuring and assistance from seatwork monitoring that amounts to giving students the answers without requiring them to think and learn. Similarly, it may be difficult to determine whether a teacher is challenging a student below, at, or above the optimal level. Thus, one should not assume that the forms of differential treatment described above are necessarily inappropriate whenever they are observed.

On the other hand, they are danger signals, especially if the differentiation is large and encompasses many of these variables rather than just one or two. Such a clear pattern of differentation suggests that the teacher is merely going through the motions of instructing low-expectation students without genuinely trying to encourage their academic progress.

Note also that some of these forms of differential treatment would have direct effects on students' opportunity to learn. To the extent that teachers provide lows with less information and less feedback than they provide to highs, the lows are almost certain to make less progress than the highs. This will occur regardless of whether or not the lows are aware of the differential treatment and its implications about their teacher's expectations for them.

In addition to these expectation effects that occur directly through differences in exposure to content, there may be indirect effects that occur through teacher behavior that affects students' self-concepts, motivational levels, performance expectations, or attributions (inferences about why they succeed or fail). This brings us to Step 3 of the Brophy and Good model, which postulates that students perceive differential treatment and its implications about what is expected of them.

STUDENT PERCEPTIONS OF DIFFERENTIAL TEACHER TREATMENT

Are students aware of differences in teachers' patterns of interaction with various students in the class? Research by Weinstein (1983, 1985) and her colleagues indicates that they are. Interviews with elementary school students indicate that they see their teachers as projecting higher achievement expectations and offering more opportunity and choice to high achievers, while structuring the activities of low achievers more closely and providing them both with more help and with more negative feedback about both academic work and classroom conduct (Weinstein et al., 1982). Furthermore, students see these differences as applying to their own personal treatment from their teachers, not just to the treatment of others (Brattesani, Weinstein, & Marshall, 1984).

Cooper and Good (1983) reported similar findings. Compared to low-expectation peers, elementary students for whom their teachers held high expectations reported themselves as engaging more often in teacher-initiated public interactions but less often in teacher-initiated private interactions, supplying correct answers more frequently, and receiving more praise and less criticism from their teachers. Actual observed differences were in the same directions but less extreme, suggesting that students not only perceive differential treatment but exaggerate the degree of differentiation that exists.

Combining their student interview findings with classroom observation findings on teachers' patterns of interaction with students who differ in expectation or achievement level, Good and Weinstein (1986) produced the summary shown in Table 4-1. To the extent that such differentiation exists in a teacher's classroom, expectation effects on student achievement are likely to occur both directly through opportunity to learn (differences in the amount and nature of exposure to content and opportunities to engage in various academic activities) and indirectly through differential treatment likely to affect student self-concept, attributional inferences, or motivation.

Individual differences among students will also affect the size of teacher expectation effects. Some students may be more sensitive than others to voice tones or other subtle communication cues, so that they may decode teachers' communications of expectations more often and accurately (Conn et al., 1968; Zuckerman et al., 1978). Younger and more teacher-dependent students may also be more susceptible to teacher-expectation effects (Persell, 1977; West & Anderson, 1976).

OTHER MODELS FOR INDIRECT MEDIATION OF EXPECTATION EFFECTS

Considering that the teacher forms differential expectations for different students, that the teacher acts on these expectations by treating students differently, and that the students perceive this differential treatment and infer implications about what is expected of them, the stage is set for teacher-expectation effects on student achievement mediated through effects on self-concept, motivation, expectations, and attributions. The remaining steps in the Brophy and Good model suggest that such effects occur but do not say much about how the process might work. However, others have developed models to offer such explanation.

Darley and Fazio's Model

Darley and Fazio (1980) have outlined a model for conceptualizing expectation effects in general social interactions. Paraphrased to refer specifically to teacher expectation effects on students, the model is similar to the Brophy and Good model but includes more explicit attention to causal attributions and other information-processing mechanisms that become involved when teachers and students interpret the meanings of each others' behavior:

Table 4.1 **GENERAL DIMENSIONS OF TEACHERS' COMMUNICATION OF DIFFERENTIAL EXPECTATIONS AND SELECTED EXAMPLES**

	Students believed to be MORE capable have:	Students believed to be LESS capable have:
Task Environment Curriculum, procedures, task definition, pacing, qualities of environment	More opportunity to perform publicly on meaningful tasks.	Less opportunity to perform publicly, especially on meaningful tasks (supplying alternate endings to a story vs. learning to pronounce a word correctly).
	More opportunity to think.	Less opportunity to think, analyze (since much work is aimed at practice).
Grouping Practices	More assignments that deal with comprehension, understanding (in higher-ability groups).	Less choice on curriculum assignments—more work on drill-like assignments.
Locus of Responsibility for Learning	More autonomy (more choice in assignments, fewer interruptions).	Less autonomy (frequent teacher monitoring of work, frequent interruptions).
Feedback and Evaluation Practices	More opportunity for self-evaluation.	Less opportunity for self-evaluation.
Motivational Strategies	More honest/contingent feedback.	Less honest/more gratuitous/less contingent feedback.
Quality of Teacher Relationships	More respect for the learner as an individual with unique interests and needs.	Less respect for the learner as an individual with unique interests and needs.

1. The teacher develops a set of expectations about the student (based on the student's status characteristics, information about past behavior or accomplishments, and observations of present behavior or accomplishments).
2. These expectations influence the teacher's interactions with the student.
3. The student interprets the teacher's actions. To the extent that these actions are seen as responsive to factors specific to the student (rather than being attributed to the teacher's general predispositions or typical responses to situations that the student happened to be in), the student will come to expect similar treatment from the teacher in the future.
4. The student will respond to the teacher's behavior, as he or she interprets this behavior. Usually the student's behavior will bear some reciprocal relationship to the teacher's actions, so as to confirm the teacher's expectations. This is especially likely if the expectations implied by the teacher's behavior are congruent with the student's self-image or at least are acceptable to the student. Where this is not the case, the student may respond in ways that disconfirm the teacher's expectations.

5. The teacher interprets the student's response. Most people are biased toward maintaining their expectations once they have been formed, so that student responses that confirm expectations are likely to be attributed to the dispositional qualities of the student and thus taken as confirmation of expectations, whereas disconfirming responses are likely to be attributed to situational factors and thus not necesarily taken as evidence that expectations are incorrect. Repeated and salient disconfirmation may be necessary to change an entrenched expectation.

6. Finally, the student interprets his or her own response to the teacher. One frequent interpretation will be that the response is self-revealing, that it gives the student more information about what he or she is like. To the extent that the student has understood the teacher's expectation or responded with behavior that confirms that expectation, the student's self-image may change in the direction implied by the teacher's expectation.

Cooper's Model

Cooper (1979, 1985) suggests that teachers' needs to retain predictability and control over classroom interaction cause them to treat low achievers in ways that may erode their achievement motivation. He notes that predictability and control are especially important issues to teachers in public interaction situations, where a student's unexpected words or actions may disrupt lesson continuity and produce classroom management problems. Because low achievers are the most likely students to cause such problems, teachers who fear loss of control may minimize these students' potential for disrupting public interaction settings by squelching their initiations and calling on them only for very brief and tightly controlled contributions. In order to exert such control, these teachers may treat low-achieving students less warmly. In particular, they may tend not to praise strong efforts by low achievers because such praise might encourage these students to initiate interactions more often, and they may criticize the low achievers' weak efforts more often because such criticism would increase their control over the lows' behavior. Meanwhile, high achievers would be treated more warmly, because the teacher has less to fear from encouraging them to initiate public interactions and has less need to criticize them in order to retain control over their behavior.

Such a difference in teacher warmth would likely affect student motivation all by itself. In addition, however, this differential treatment might affect student motivation by decreasing the low achievers' belief in a direct relationship between academic effort and achievement outcomes. Whereas highs would be praised or criticized in direct response to their levels of effort (praised when efforts are strong and criticized when they do not try hard enough), lows sometimes would be praised or criticized more because of the teacher's desire to control their public interactions than for reasons having to do with their levels of effort. For them good efforts would often go unrecognized and poor efforts would often be allowed because the teacher was more concerned about discouraging them from disrupting lessons than about reinforcing their learning efforts. Over time, highs would develop a clear sense that their learning efforts paid off, but lows would see a less clear relationship between effort and outcome. In theory, this should lead directly to a reduction in lows' achievement motivation, and indirectly to a reduction in achievement itself.

Good's Model

Good (1981) suggests that certain forms of treatment by teachers will induce passivity in low-achieving students. He suggests two mechanisms for this. First, many teachers call on low achievers less often, wait less time for them to respond, give them answers rather than try to help them improve their responses if they answer incorrectly, and are less likely to praise their successes but more likely to criticize their failures. Considering that they are less likely to be able to answer correctly in the first place and that their mistakes occur in public, low achievers must face considerably more than the usual degrees of ambiguity and risk that are built into classroom interactions (Doyle, 1983) when they participate actively in lessons. Under the circumstances, a good strategy for them is to remain passive—not to volunteer and not to respond when called on.

A second factor that might lead toward their passivity is that low achievers apparently must adjust to more varied teacher expectations than other students must. Their teachers might treat them inconsistently over the course of the school year, trying one approach after another in an attempt to find something that works. They may have more teachers at a given time (if they are involved in remedial or special education), and teachers differ in their strategies for trying to work with low achievers. Some teachers minimize interactions with them and treat them coolly when they do interact, but others seek them out frequently and provide a great deal of encouragement and support. Some teachers call on them frequently in an attempt to get them to participate more often, but others mostly avoid them. Some rarely praise their successes but others praise almost everything they do, even responses that are not correct. Student passivity is a likely outcome of such diversity of treatment and expectations. Not knowing what to do, low achievers may learn to avoid initiations and wait for the teacher to structure their behavior.

Attribution Theory Models

Others (Dweck & Elliott, 1983; Eccles & Wigfield, 1985; Graham, 1984) have suggested that expectation effects are mediated by teachers' influences on students' attributional thinking about the reasons for their successes and failures. Ideally, students will believe that they have the ability to succeed at academic tasks if they apply reasonable effort ("I can succeed if I try."). However, some students, especially low achievers, fall into a failure syndrome/learned helplessness pattern ("I can't do the work—I'm dumb."). Such students are prone to discount their successes ("I was lucky.") and to attribute their failures to lack of ability rather than to insufficient effort or reliance on an ineffective strategy. Eventually, they come to believe that nothing they can do will enable them to succeed consistently, so they give up. Various authors have suggested that teacher communication of low expectations encourages low achievers to develop this pattern of attributional thinking. Teachers usually do not directly suggest that students do not have the ability to succeed (Blumenfeld et al., 1983), but they may suggest this indirectly by minimizing demands on them, overreacting to minor successes, treating failures as if they were successes, or responding to failures with pity or excessive sympathy instead of diagnosis and remedial instruction.

VARIATIONS IN SIZE OF EXPECTATION EFFECTS OBSERVED

Let us summarize what we have said so far in our review of research on the effects of the expectations that teachers develop for individual students in their classes. First, the factors needed to set the stage for expectation effects appear to be in place: Teachers do form differential expectations quickly at the beginning of the year, teachers do treat high- and low-expectation students differently, and students appear to be aware of this differential treatment. Thus, mechanisms exist for mediating expectation effects on student achievement, either directly through differences in how much is taught or indirectly through teacher behaviors that affect students' self-concepts, motivation, expectations, or attributions. Finally, experimental studies have shown that expectation effects can occur through these mechanisms (Rosenthal, 1976; Smith, 1980).

We have also noted, though, that in-service teachers are neither as gullible nor as prejudiced in developing expectations about their actual students as writers generalizing from artificial laboratory experiments sometimes make them out to be, and that their expectations are generally accurate, based on good information, and likely to be modified as new or better information becomes available. These factors limit the possibilities for sizeable expectation effects, especially self-fulfilling prophecy effects that can occur only when teachers develop and sustain significantly inaccurate expectations. So what does research indicate about teacher expectation effects on students' individual achievement in typical classroom settings?

First, it shows that such effects do occur. Even though measures of student ability or prior achievement available at the beginning of a school year are highly accurate predictors of the students' achievement at the end of the year, adding measures of teacher expectations will produce significant increases in the level of accuracy of prediction that can be achieved (Brattesani, Weinstein, & Marshall, 1984; Crano & Mellon, 1978; Humphreys & Stubbs, 1977; Smith, 1980). Such data suggest that teacher expectation effects cause students to achieve more or less than they might have achieved otherwise. Second, research shows that significant expectation effects do not occur in all classrooms, and that there is great variability in the size of such effects when they do occur. The strength and direction (positive or negative) of teacher expectation effects that are likely to appear will vary with the nature of the classroom context and (especially) with the kind of person that the teacher is.

CONTEXT AND SETTING EFFECTS ON DIFFERENTIATION AMONG STUDENTS

Different school contexts and settings provide opportunities for differential teacher-student interaction patterns, and thus opportunities for expectation effects to occur. Grade level is one such factor. Other things being equal, greater expectation effects would be expected in the early grades before students' records of academic achievement and their academic self-concepts and attribution patterns become firmly established. This is in fact the pattern that Raudenbush (1984) found in his review of the findings of 18 experiments on induced teacher expectations. Effects were stronger in grades one and two than in grades three through six. Then they became strong again at grade seven, the first year of junior high school for most students. The latter finding suggests that strong effects might also be seen in the first year of high school, college, or graduate school, or whenever students are new to the institution and the instructors who will be teaching them.

Differences between the elementary and secondary grades also create differences in the patterns of treatment of students that are likely to be observed. In the elementary grades, students have the same teacher all day long and often interact with that teacher individually. In the secondary grades, however, students see most of their teachers for only an hour or less per day and do not spend much time interacting with them individually. Consequently, in the early grades expectations are likely to be communicated through qualitative aspects of individualized teacher-student interaction (the teacher interacts frequently with all students but may treat highs and lows in quite different ways), but in the secondary grades differentiation is more likely to occur through the sheer quantity of individualized teacher-student interactions (the teacher interacts with highs much more often than with lows, because highs contribute to lessons more often).

Time of year is another relevant context factor. Greater expectation effects would be expected early in the year (Brophy & Good, 1974). More specifically, such effects should be most evident from the second week, when stable expectations are becoming established, through the second month, when most of the significant shifts in perception and expectations that are going to occur have already occurred, and teachers and students settle into routine interaction patterns (Cooper, 1985). As the year progresses, teachers may pay relatively less attention to within-class differences among individuals or subgroups and begin to pay more attention to the progress of the class as a whole, adjusting their pace of instruction to suit the potential of the class as they have come to perceive it (Cooper & Good, 1983).

Subject matter is another significant context variable. Smith (1980) reported larger expectation effects on reading achievement than on math achievement. This may be because a greater variety of grouping and instructional practices tends to be used in teaching reading than in teaching math, so that there is more room for teachers to translate differential expectations into differential treatment of students.

Interaction patterns also differ according to whether the setting is private and oriented primarily toward teaching the material to individual students or public and oriented primarily toward group recitation, review, or performance of skills taught previously (Bossert, 1979; Cooper, 1979; Horn, 1984). Finally, the most important context factor is probably the nature of the learning environment that the teacher establishes. The potential for expectation effects (especially for undesirable effects of low expectations) is greatest in classrooms that feature uniform rather than multiple goals, a narrow rather than a broad range of activity structures, norm-referenced achievement standards, a competitive atmosphere, public performance evaluation, emphasis on achievement rather than effort, and frequent publicly perceived differential treatment of high and low achievers (Rosenholtz & Simpson, 1984; Rosenholtz & Wilson, 1980; Thomas, 1980; Weinstein, 1983).

Effects of Teachers' Personal Characteristics

More important than context and setting factors in determining teacher expectation effects are individual differences in teachers themselves, especially in personal characteristics and beliefs about teaching and learning. Some teachers are especially likely to show sizeable self-fulfilling prophecy effects, especially negative effects that result in reduced student achievement gains.

For example, Brattesani, Weinstein, and Marshall (1984) studied achievement outcomes in classrooms where the students described the teachers as differentiating considerably in their treatment of high vs. low achievers and in classrooms where the students reported little such differentiated treatment. They found that including teacher expectation measures added 9–18 percent to the variance in year-end achievement beyond what could be predicted from prior achievement in the high-differentiation classes, but added only 1–5 percent in the low-differentiation classes. Thus, "high-differentiating" teachers produced sizeable expectation effects, but "low-differentiating" teachers did not. Monk (1983) also reports differences in outcomes related to differences in teachers' tendencies to make public comments about their students' achievement progress and classroom behavior.

Noting such differences among teachers observed in our own studies, we (Brophy & Good, 1974) suggested that teachers can be thought of as being on a continuum from proactive through reactive to overreactive. *Proactive* teachers are guided by their own beliefs about what is reasonable and appropriate in setting goals for the class as a whole and for individual students. If they set realistic goals and have the needed skills, they are likely to move their students systematically toward fulfilling the expectations associated with these goals. Proactive teachers are the most likely to have positive expectation effects on their students.

At the other extreme are *overreactive* teachers who develop rigid, stereotyped perceptions of their students based on prior records or on first impressions of student behavior. Overreactive teachers tend to treat their students as stereotypes rather than as individuals, and they are the most likely to have negative expectation effects on their students.

Most teachers fall in between these extremes and are classified as *reactive* teachers who hold their expectations lightly and adjust them to take note of new feedback and emerging trends. Reactive teachers have minimal expectation effects on their students, tending merely to maintain existing differences between high and low achievers (although these differences will increase slightly because of varied behavior by the students themselves that teachers do not compensate for).

Subsequent research supports these distinctions, but with an important qualification: Unfortunately, it appears that most sizeable teacher expectation effects on student achievement are negative ones, in which low expectations lead to lower achievement than might have been attained otherwise (Brophy, 1983). There is little evidence that even proactive teachers significantly augment the achievement of individual students by projecting positive expectations, but much evidence that overreactive teachers minimize student progress by projecting low expectations. Work by other investigators has shown that these overreactive teachers differ from other teachers in being more rigid, authoritarian, and prone to bias and prejudice.

Taylor (1983) found that teachers with negative attitudes toward Black English dialect assigned lower reading comprehension scores to a reader who spoke in Black dialect than to a reader who spoke standard English, even though there was no actual difference in quality of responses to comprehension questions. Teachers who did not have negative attitudes toward Black English dialect did not assign differential grades. Tom, Cooper, and McGraw (1984) showed that teachers who scored highly on a test of authoritarian attitudes were more likely than other teachers to be affected by race and socioeconomic status information in making predictions about the academic achievement of fictional students. Babad, Inbar, and Rosenthal (1982) found that "high-bias" physical education student teachers (so-classified because they took family social status into account when grading drawings made by students) interacted quite differently with high-expectation students compared to low-expectation students in their physical education classes. In contrast, "no-bias" student teachers did not take family background into account when grading drawings and tended to interact similarly with high- and low- expectation students in their physical education classes.

These studies were unusual in that simple interview or personality measures were effective for identifying overreactive or high-bias teachers. Babad et al. (1982) reported no difference between "high-bias" and "no-bias" student teachers on a variety of self-report measures: educational ideology, dogmatism, political views, defensiveness, locus of control, extroversion, impulsiveness, and performance on an embedded figures test. If anything, the "high-bias" student teachers described themselves as *more* rational, objective, and reasonable than the "no-bias" student teachers. However, qualitative analyses of their self-report data showed that the "high-bias" student teachers gave more extreme responses and showed more indicators of conventionalism, rigidity, intolerance of ambiguity, and other aspects of authoritarianism or dogmatism. They also wrote more dogmatic statements and showed more concern about authority and failure issues in responses to open-ended questions about hypothetical classroom events, and when observed in the classroom they were described as more autocratic, rigid, distant, impulsive, and preferential, and as less trusting in their interactions with students.

More generally, Babad (1985) reviewed the literature and found that teachers prone to expectation effects usually cannot be identified through average scores on standardized self-report instruments, but can be identified if their responses are checked for patterns indicating extreme scores and defensiveness, if they are given more open-ended instruments on which they can express their attitudes at length and in their own words, or if they are observed in the classroom. As an example of the extreme response pattern, he cites data indicating that teachers who expressed mixed and moderate views of the effectiveness of integration efforts were less prone to expectation effects than teachers who either declared that those efforts had been highly successful or rejected them as completely unsuccessful.

In summary, although it is not always obvious from administration of self-report instruments, one cluster of traits likely to be found in overreactive or "high-bias" teachers is a tendency toward conventionalism, authoritarianism, or dogmatism. Other personal traits are less well documented but seem likely on logical grounds: (1) a tendency to maintain expectations rigidly once they are formed (Brophy, 1983); (2) a teacher role definition that minimizes the teacher's personal responsiblity for insuring that students master the curriculum (Brophy & Evertson, 1976); (3) a tendency to view student ability as unitary and fixed rather than as multiple and open to improvement through instruction and practice (Dweck & Elliott, 1983; Eccles & Wigfield, 1985; Swann & Snyder, 1980); (4) a tendency to notice, think about, and comment on the differences rather than the similarities between students, and to take these into account when planning instruction; (5) a tendency to repress or rationalize teaching failures rather than recognize or attempt to overcome them; and (6) poorly developed classroom management and instructional skills (which would give the teacher more to be defensive about and thus more to repress or rationalize).

These personal characteristics of teachers will interact with the teachers' beliefs about appropriate curriculum and instruction to determine the nature and strength of expectation effects on the achievement of individual students that may be observed in their classes. For example, teachers with all of the above listed characteristics probably would have powerful (and mostly negative) expectation effects, including self-fulfilling prophecy effects, on substantial numbers of their students if they were teaching in the primary grades using approaches that maximized the time that they spent with individuals and small groups but minimized the time spent with the class as a whole. In contrast, these same teachers might have only relatively minor sustaining expectation effects if they were teaching mathematics to high school students and relying exclusively on a whole-class approach that provided the same instruction, tasks, and requirements to all students and minimized the time that the teacher spent with individuals. Thus, a major factor determining expectation effects on students is the time spent with individuals.

GROUP, CLASS, AND SCHOOL EFFECTS

The previous point serves as a reminder that so far we have been discussing expectation effects on different individuals within the same classroom, because most of the research has concentrated on expectation effects at this level. However, expectation effects can operate at the level of groups, classes, or entire schools. Much less research is available on such expectation effects, but they appear to be at least as important as within-classroom effects on individuals. If Mr. Defeated is a fourth-grade teacher who decides that three of his students just do not have the aptitude needed to learn fourth-grade mathematics, any undesirable effects of these low expectations will apply only to those three students. However, if Mr. Defeated is a ninth-grade teacher who believes that students admitted to his algebra sections have mathematical aptitude but students admitted to his general math sections do not, he may make only half-hearted attempts to teach mathematics in the general math sections, thus having sizeable direct expectation effects on all of the students in these sections.

Group Effects

Expectation effects at the group level are possible whenever teachers use a small-group approach to instruction, and especially if the groups have been formed according to ability or achievement level, as is the common practice for elementary reading instruction. For example, Weinstein (1976) showed that reading group membership information added 25 percent to the variance in mid-year reading achievement that could be predicted beyond what was predictable from readiness scores taken at the beginning of the year. Placement into high groups accelerated achievement rates, but placement into low groups slowed them down (relative to the differences that would have been expected anyway due to variations in readiness levels).

Research comparing instruction in different reading groups (reviewed by Hiebert, 1983) suggests some possible reasons for this. Teachers tend to give longer reading assignments (Pflaum et al., 1980), to provide more time for discussion of the story (Bozsik, 1982), and to be generally more demanding (Haskett, 1968) with high groups than with low groups. They are quicker to interrupt low-group students when they make reading mistakes (Allington, 1983) and more likely to just give them the word or prompt them with graphemic (phonetic) cues rather than to offer semantic or syntactic cues that might help them recognize the word from its context (Allington, 1980; Pflaum et al., 1980). Teachers are also less likely to ask low groups higher level comprehension questions (Bozsik, 1982).

The nature and extent of such differential treatment vary from teacher to teacher, and at least some of the variation can be seen as appropriate differential instruction (Brophy, 1983; Haskins, Walden, & Ramey, 1983). However, as is the case with differential treatment of individual students, consistently widespread and powerful patterns of such differential treatment of groups are cause for concern. Too often, low groups continually get less exciting instruction, less emphasis on meaning and conceptualization, and more rote drill and practice activities (Good & Marshall, 1984).

Eder (1981) provides an interesting detailed example of the problems that can develop. She compared instruction in the high and the low reading groups in a first-grade classroom in a school serving a relatively homogeneous middle-class population. None of the students could read prior to entering first grade, and given their relative homogeneity of background, it is not clear that ability grouping was needed at all (the teacher probably would have wanted to teach beginning reading in small groups, but these could have been randomly formed groups progressing at the same pace rather than high, middle, and low groups progressing at different paces).

The teacher did use "ability grouping," however, basing her assignments on kindergarten teachers' recommendations. These recommendations, in turn, were based on the maturity levels of the students in addition to their perceived ability levels. Consequently, a major reason that the low group progressed slowly was that it contained a high percentage of immature, inattentive students whose disruptive behavior frequently interrupted lesson continuity. Compared to the high group, the low group spent almost twice as much time off task, and when they were paying attention, were more likely to read out of turn or call out words or answers that were supposed to be supplied by other students. Thus, the achievement progress of low-group members can be slowed not only by factors associated with low teacher expectations but also by factors associated with the undesirable social contexts that develop when groups are short on academic peer leaders and long on attention and conduct problems.

There is some reason to believe that a "low-group psychology" develops wherever ability grouping is practiced, even in schools whose low-group students would be high-group students somewhere else. Often, these students are taught at a slower pace and exposed to less interesting and varied activities than they are capable of handling, and the fact that they have been placed into low groups even though they have considerable reading ability may unnecessarily embarrass them or their parents, or cause them to suffer subtle criticism ("Are you not trying hard enough?"). Such students may be prime candidates to become "underachievers," because it may be easier for them to remain passive and to feign indifference rather" than to risk failure by trying their best. One wonders how much potential and creativity are wasted by unnecessary and premature assignments to ability groups in first-grade classes.

Suggestions for avoiding undesirable expectation effects on low-ability groups are given in Chapter 10, which deals with classroom grouping at length.

Class Effects

Brophy and Evertson (1976) found that a "can-do" attitude was associated with teachers' relative levels of success in eliciting achievement gains from their students. The most successful teachers believed that their students were capable of mastering curriculum objectives and that they (the teachers) were capable of meeting the students' instructional needs. These expectations were associated with behaviors such as augmenting or even replacing the curriculum materials or evaluation instruments if these did not appear to be suited to the needs of the students.

Ashton (1985) reported similar findings for teachers who differed in *sense of efficacy*. Sense of efficacy was measured by the teachers' responses (on five-point scales from "strongly agree" through "strongly disagree") to the following two statements:

1. When it comes right down to it, a teacher really can't do much because most of a student's motivation and performance depends on his or her home environment.
2. If I really try hard, I can get through to even the most difficult or unmotivated students.

Teachers who rejected the first of these statements but agreed with the second were classified as high in sense of efficacy: They believed that they were capable of motivating and instructing their students successfully. In contrast, teachers with low efficacy response patterns believed either that no teachers could have important motivational or instructional effects on their students or that some teachers could have such effects but they personally could not (presumably because they lacked needed knowledge or skills).

Research done in 48 basic level (i.e., low-achieving) mathematics and communication classes in four high schools revealed relationships between teachers' sense of efficacy, patterns of teacher-student interaction, and student achievement gains. Compared to teachers with a low sense of efficacy, teachers with a high sense of efficacy were more confident and at ease in their classrooms, more positive (praising, smiling) and less negative (criticizing, punishing) in interactions with their students, more successful in managing their classrooms as efficient learning environments, less defensive, more accepting of student disagreement and challenges, and more effective in producing student achievement gains. Low-efficacy teachers revealed low expectations and a tendency to concentrate on rule enforcement and behavior management, whereas high-efficacy teachers concentrated on instructing the students in the curriculum and interacting with students about academic content. These data are correlational, but the fact that they come from parallel sections of the same courses taught to similar students in the same schools suggests that they were caused by differences among teachers rather than students.

Cooper and Good (1983) found that teachers who held lower expectations for their classrooms as a whole tended to teach easier lessons, to spend less time on rigorous academic activities, and to accept less than perfect performance from their students before moving on to new material. Sedlak et al. (1985) reported that many teachers, especially at the high school level, develop implicit "bargains" with students, in which the teachers minimize their work demands (i.e., stick with easy, routine, and predictable tasks) in exchange for student cooperation and good will.

Teacher expectation effects at the class level are especially likely to appear in schools using tracking systems. For example, Evertson (1982) identified several ways in which the behavior of students in low-track classrooms slowed down academic pacing and shifted time allocation from academic to procedural or behavioral matters. However, she also noted differences in how the same teachers taught their high- and low-track classes that suggest teacher expectation effects in addition to student effects on teachers. Compared with their behavior in high-track classes, many teachers were observed to be less clear about their objectives, to introduce content less clearly or completely, to make fewer attempts to relate the content to students' interests or backgrounds, to be less reasonable in their work standards, to be less consistent in their discipline, and to be less receptive to student input in low-track classes.

Other research suggests that most teachers prefer to teach high-track classes and will compete with one another to get such classes (Finley, 1984), that they tend to plan and implement more independent projects and to introduce more high-level and integrative concepts in these classes (Heathers, 1969), but that they stress more structured assignments dealing with basic facts and skills in low-track classes (Borko, Shavelson, & Stern, 1981). In addition, teachers appear to plan more thoroughly for their high-track classes in order to be prepared for the academic challenges that these classes present, but they are likely to be less well prepared for low-track classes and to spend more time allowing students to do activities of their own choosing rather than to spend time teaching academic content (Brookover et al., 1979; Keddie, 1971; Leacock, 1969; Rosenbaum, 1976).

Good and Weinstein (1986) offer the following suggestions for improving classrooms that feature low expectations and boring, unchallenging routines.

1. **Broaden the goals of lessons and activities.** Students need to practice and master basic content and skills, but they also need application opportunities. Something is wrong if students are usually working on phonics skills exercises but rarely reading, usually practicing penmanship or copying spelling words but rarely writing, or usually working on arithmetic computation exercises but rarely attempting to formulate and solve problems.
2. **Pay more attention to students' ideas and interests and encourage students to play a larger role in assessing their own performance.** Students are often much more passive and teacher-dependent in their learning efforts than they need to be.
3. **Increase opportunities for students to participate actively and use materials in meaningful ways.** Teacher-led lessons should require more than just quiet listening, and follow-up assignments should require more than just working through highly structured and routinized seatwork assignments.
4. **Besides asking routine factual questions, ask students questions that require them to think, analyze, synthesize, or evaluate ideas.**

Include questions that have no single correct answer or that can be answered at a variety of levels and from a variety of points of view in order to encourage a greater range of students to participate and experience success.

5. Focus on the positive aspects of learning. Be encouraging and reinforcing by noting group progress toward learning goals. Minimize public comparisons of students with one another, discouraging criticisms of the class as a whole or suggestions that the material to be learned is overly difficult or unrewarding.

School Effects

Studies of school effectiveness and school improvement programs (reviewed by Good & Brophy, 1986) indicate that high expectations and commitment to bringing about student achievement are part of a pattern of attitudes, beliefs, and behaviors that characterize schools that are successful in maximizing their students' learning gains. Brookover et al. (1979), for example, found that teachers in effective schools not only held higher expectations but acted on them by setting goals expressed as minimally acceptable levels of achievement rather than using prior achievement data to establish ceiling levels beyond which students would not be expected to progress. Such teachers responded to failure as a challenge, requiring students to redo failed work (with individualized help as needed) rather than writing them off or referring them to remedial classes. They responded to mistakes and response failures during class with appropriate feedback and reinstruction rather than with lowering of standards or inappropriate praise. Similar findings have been reported by Edmonds (1979) and by Rutter et al. (1979).

In response to such findings, school improvement programs (Proctor, 1984) and professional development programs for in-service teachers (Farley, 1982; Kerman, 1979) have begun to incorporate elements designed to reduce negative expectation effects on student achievement.

EXPECTATION EFFECTS ON PERSONAL AND SOCIAL DEVELOPMENT

This chapter has concentrated on teacher expectation effects on student achievement, because most of the research on expectation effects has concentrated on this topic. However, there is reason to believe that teacher expectation effects might play a significant role in shaping students' personal and social development, at least within the school setting.

Various experiments in the direct labeling of children by adults (Grusec, Kuczynski, Rushton, & Simutis, 1978; Kraut, 1973; Lepper, 1973; Miller, Brickman, & Bolen, 1975; Toner, Moore, & Emmons, 1980) have shown that children labeled as possessing prosocial traits such as patience or generosity are more likely to demonstrate these traits in follow-up test situations than control children who were not so labeled. Unfortunately, less desirable outcomes such as learned helplessness can also result from direct labeling effects (Langer & Benevento, 1978).

Other investigators have shown that self-perceptions and behavior can be affected by expectations communicated indirectly. Hauserman, Miller, and Bond

(1976) found that children's self-concepts could be improved by stimulating them to make positive statements about themselves each day. Riggs et al. (1983) have shown that self-perceptions can even be induced indirectly (people who were asked questions implying that the experimenter believed them to be introverted described themselves as more introverted following this treatment than people who had been asked questions suggesting that they were considered extroverted). Brophy et al. (1983) showed that students were less engaged in classroom activities that teachers introduced in ways suggesting negative expectations (that the activities would be very difficult or unenjoyable) than they were in other classroom activities.

Such research illustrates that beliefs, attitudes, expectations, and behavior can be socialized, both directly through deliberate actions and indirectly through communication of the socializing agent's beliefs, attitudes, or expectations. This suggests that the success of a teacher's classroom management efforts probably is determined in part by the kinds of expectations that the teacher communicates about student conduct; that the interpersonal atmosphere in the classroom probably depends in part on the kinds of expectations that the teacher communicates about student cooperation and interpersonal relationships; and that student responsiveness to lessons and assignments probably depends in part on the kinds of expectations that the teacher communicates about the meaningfulness, interest, or practical value of school activities. Thus, besides affecting student achievement, teacher expectations can be expected to affect students' attitudes, beliefs, attributions, expectations, motivational patterns, and classroom conduct.

AVOIDING NEGATIVE EXPECTATION EFFECTS

How can teachers avoid having negative expectation effects and perhaps arrange to have positive expectation effects on their students?

Some authors have suggested that teachers should avoid forming any expectations at all: by refusing to discuss students with their previous teachers and ignoring cumulative records and test information. We reject this suggestion, for two reasons.

First, expectations cannot be suppressed or avoided. We remember experiences that make an impression on us. When events occur repeatedly, they are seen as expected and normal, and these expectations are reinforced with repetition. Thus, teachers form expectations simply from interacting with students, even if they try to avoid other sources of information. Second, whether other sources of information are examined is not as important as *how information is used*. Information about students will create expectations about them, but these expectations can be useful in planning individualized instruction to meet their specific needs. A teacher should try to get information and use it in this way rather than avoid obtaining information.

Other authors have suggested that teachers should have only highly positive expectations. This idea is superficially appealing, because confidence and determination are important teacher qualities and a "can-do" attitude helps cut problems down to workable size. However, this attitude must not be carried to the point of distorting reality. Students show large individual differences in learning abilities and interests, and these cannot be eliminated through wishful thinking. Teachers will only frustrate both themselves and their students if they set unrealistically high standards that students cannot reach.

Expectations should be *appropriate* rather than necessarily high, and they should be followed by appropriate instructional behavior; that is, planned learning experiences that move students through the curriculum at a pace they can handle. An appropriate pace allows continued success and improvement and varies for different students. Teachers should not feel guilt or feel that they are stigmatizing slower learners by moving them along at a slower pace. As long as students are working up to their potential and progressing at a steady rate, a teacher has reason to be satisfied.

Regular repetition of student behavior will build up strong expectations in all teachers, including (and perhaps especially) teachers who try to deny or suppress expectations. Inevitably, some of these expectations will be pessimistic. However, teachers can avoid undesirable self-fulfilling prophecy effects if they remain alert to the formation of, and changes in, their own expectations and if they monitor their behavior to see that negative expectations are not communicated. To the extent that such expectations do exist, they should be of the helpful variety, ones that encourage teachers to combine expressions of concern with behavior designed to remediate difficulties. Saying that a student needs help is bad only if the teacher does not provide that help in a positive, supportive way.

Keeping Expectations Flexible and Current

Expectations created as a result of recurring classroom events can be very compelling. If Susan frequently fails to do homework assignments, her teacher may gradually stop trying to change Susan's work habits and begin to accept her poor performance as "to be expected." To avoid falling into this rut, teachers need to keep their expectations flexible and bear in mind their role as instructors. If expectations are allowed to become too strong or too fixed, they can distort perception and behavior. Teachers may notice only those behaviors that fit their expectations and as a result may deviate from good teaching practice.

Once formed, expectations tend to be self-perpetuating for students as well as teachers because expectations guide both perceptions and behavior. When we expect to find something, we are much more likely to see it than when we are not looking for it. For example, most people do not notice counterfeit money or slight irregularities in clothing patterns. However, treasury department officials and inspectors for clothing manufacturers, who have been trained to look for such deviations, will notice them. Hidden abilities and aptitudes also may not be noticed except by those who are on the lookout for them. This is part of the reason why teachers often fail to notice the strengths of students who are frequent discipline problems in the classroom. When expecting misbehavior, teachers may miss many of these students' accomplishments or positive contributions that someone else might have noticed and reinforced.

Expectations not only cause us to notice some things and fail to notice others, but they also affect the way we *interpret* what we do notice. The optimist, for example, notices that the glass is half full, while the pessimist observes that it is half empty. Mistaken beliefs about other people can be difficult to correct because of their tendency to influence how we interpret what we see. If we are convinced that a person has particular qualities, we often see these qualities when we observe this individual.

Consider the teacher who asks a difficult question and then gives students some time to think about the answer. After a while he calls on Johnny Bright, whom he sees as an intelligent and well-motivated student. Johnny remains silent, pursing his lips, knitting his brow, and scratching his head. The teacher knows that he is working out the problem, so he patiently gives him more time. Finally, Johnny responds with a question, "Would you repeat that last part again?" The teacher is happy to do so, because this indicates that Johnny has partially solved the problem and may be able to do it by himself with a little more time. He repeats and then waits eagerly, but patiently, for Johnny to respond again. If someone interrupted the teacher at this point to ask what he was doing, he might respond that he was "challenging the class to use creativity and logical thinking to solve problems."

Suppose, however, that the teacher had called on Sammy Slow instead. The teacher knows that Sammy is a low achiever, and he does not think Sammy is very well motivated, either. When called on, Sammy remains silent, although the teacher notes his pursed lips, his furrowed brow, and the fact that he is scratching his head. This probably means that Sammy is hopelessly lost, although it may mean that he is merely acting, trying to give the impression that he is thinking about the problem. After a few seconds, the teacher says, "Well, Sammy?" Now Sammy responds, but with a question instead of an answer, "Would you repeat that last part again?" This confirms the teacher's suspicions, making it clear that any more time spent with Sammy on this question would be wasted. After admonishing Sammy to listen more carefully, he calls on someone else. If interrupted at this point and asked what he was doing, the teacher might respond that he was "making it clear that the class is expected to pay close attention to the discussion so that they can respond intelligently when questioned."

In this example, the teacher's expectations for these two students caused him to make different inferences about the students' behavior than a more neutral observer would have made. Although the behavior of the two boys was the same, and they made the same response to the initial question, the teacher interpreted the behavior quite differently by reading initial meaning into it. His interpretations about the two boys may have been correct, but we (and he) cannot tell for certain because he did not verify them. Instead, he acted as if his interpretations were observable facts, so that his treatment of Sammy may have been grossly inappropriate.

Although the need to continually review and adjust expectations may seem obvious, it can be difficult to do in everyday life as well as in the classroom. (For example, the widely advertised brand is not always better than the unknown brand; the more expensive item is not necessarily better than the cheaper one; and the large economy size is not always a better bargain than the regular size. Yet every day, most people automatically accept such things without verifying them.)

Similarly, the fact that a student could not do something yesterday does not mean that he or she cannot do it today, but the teacher will not find out unless the student is given a chance. Expectations stress the stable or unchanging aspects of the world. Teachers, however, are agents of change who are trying to make students into something different from what they are today. Therefore, teachers must keep their expectations in perspective. To the extent that they are negative, expectations represent problems to be solved, not definitions of reality to which a teacher must adapt.

Emphasizing the Positive

The implication of all this seems to be that teachers should form and project expectations that are as positive as they can be while still remaining realistic. Such expectations represent genuine beliefs about what can be achieved and therefore are taken seriously as goals toward which to work in instructing the students. Brophy (1983) suggests that teachers might accomplish this through the following steps:

1. In planning your instruction, concentrate on teaching (and where necessary, reteaching) the material to the class or group as a whole rather than worrying too much about individual differences.
2. Keep expectations for individual students current by monitoring their progress closely; stress present performance over past history.
3. Set goals for the class and for individuals in terms of floors (minimally accepted standards), not ceilings. Let group progress rates rather than limits adopted arbitrarily in advance determine how far the class can go within the time available.
4. When individualizing instruction and giving students feedback about their performance, stress their continuous progress relative to previous levels of mastery rather than how they compare with other students or with standardized test norms. In planning and delivering instruction, concentrate on students' present levels of understanding and mastery (and the implications of these for present instructional needs) rather than on who the students are individually or how they are doing relative to one another.
5. In responding to student performance, do not confine yourself to evaluating success or failure. In addition, provide students with the feedback or additional instruction that they will need in order to meet the objectives.
6. When students have not understood an explanation or demonstration, think in terms of diagnosing their learning difficulty and following through by breaking down the task or reteaching it in a different way rather than merely repeating the same instruction or giving up in frustration.
7. In general, think in terms of stretching the students' minds by stimulating them and encouraging them to achieve as much as they can and not in terms of "protecting" them from failure or embarrassment.

BASIC TEACHER ATTITUDES AND EXPECTATIONS

The above list of suggestions is confined to issues surrounding student individual differences in achievement. Expectation effects can occur in other aspects of the teachers' role as well, however. Therefore, we conclude the chapter with a consideration of other teacher beliefs, attitudes, and expectations that we think are basic in setting the stage for teachers to do their jobs effectively.

Teachers Should Enjoy Teaching

Teaching brings many rewards and satisfactions, but it is a demanding, exhausting, and sometimes frustrating job. It is hard to do well unless you enjoy doing it.

Teachers who enjoy their work show it in their classroom behavior. They come to class prepared and present lessons in ways that suggest interest and excitement in promoting learning. Student difficulties and confusion are perceived as challenges to be met with professional skills, not as irritations. When students do achieve success, the teacher shares in their joy. In general, teachers who enjoy their work see themselves as benevolent resource persons for their students and not as wardens or authority figures.

A Teacher's Main Responsibility Is to Teach

The teacher's job involves many roles besides that of instructing students. At times, a teacher serves as a parent surrogate, entertainer, authority figure, psychotherapist, and record keeper, among other things. All of these roles are necessary. However, they are subordinate to, and must help to support, the major role of teaching. They must not be allowed to overshadow the teacher's basic instructional role.

Some teachers become more concerned with nurturing or entertaining students than with teaching them. In their classes, much of the day is spent reading stories, playing games, working on arts and crafts projects, singing and listening to records, playing show-and-tell, and participating in enrichment activities. Such teachers do not like to spend much time teaching the curriculum and feel they must apologize to students or bribe them when lessons are conducted. These teachers are meeting their own needs, not those of the students. By the end of the year, their students will have acquired negative attitudes toward the school curriculum and will have failed to achieve at levels close to their potential.

In the higher grades, failure to teach is sometimes seen in teachers who have low expectations about their classroom management abilities or the learning abilities of certain classes. Where homogeneous grouping is practiced, teachers assigned to low-achieving classes may sometimes abandon serious attempts to teach. They may perhaps attempt to entertain their classes or else merely act as proctors who are interested only in seeing that noise does not get out of hand. Such behavior indicates that teachers lack confidence, either in their ability to motivate and control their classes or in students' abilities to learn or to become interested in the subject matter. Failure to teach is surrender to failure expectations (for related research, see Evertson, 1982; Metz, 1978).

The Crucial Aspects of Teaching

Failure to understand the crucial aspects of teaching—task presentation, diagnosis, remediation, and enrichment—characterizes teachers who favor high achievers over low achievers or who pay more attention to answers than to thought processes. Such teachers apparently believe that students should learn on their own with no help from them. If a student does not understand immediately after one demonstration or does not do work correctly after hearing the instructions one time, they react with impatience and frustration (e.g., see Duffy & McIntyre, 1982).

Such behavior represents a fundamental failure to appreciate the teacher's basic role. The teacher is in the classroom to instruct, which involves more than just giving demonstrations or proctoring learning experiences. Instruction also means giving additional help to those who are having difficulty, diagnosing the sources of their problems, and providing remedial assistance. It means conducting evaluation with an eye toward identifying and correcting difficulties and not merely as a prelude to praising or criticizing. It means keeping track of students' individual progress so that they can be instructed in terms of what they learned yesterday and what they should learn tomorrow. For the teacher, it means finding satisfaction in the progress of slower students as well as brighter ones.

Many behaviors indicate whether or not teachers clearly understand what they are supposed to be doing with students. The handling of seatwork and homework assignments is one good indicator. The purpose of such assignments is to provide students with practice on the skills they are learning and to provide teachers with information about students' progress. Teachers should monitor students' performances on seatwork and homework, noting error patterns that occur. These error patterns suggest the nature of the students' learning problems and the remedial actions that teachers should take. However, some teachers simply pass out work and then collect and score it, without following the scoring with remedial teaching.

Teachers can create negative attitudes toward seatwork assignments if the assignments are inappropriate or if they are not adjusted to individual differences among students. Teachers sometimes create this attitude in otherwise well-motivated and bright students, who tend to do seatwork quickly and correctly. If a teacher's method of handling students who finish quickly is to assign them more of the same kind of exercises, students will learn to work more slowly or hide the fact that they have finished. Teachers would do much better to assign more challenging work or to allow the students to select alternative activities.

Another indicator is the way teachers respond to right and wrong answers. When teachers have the appropriate attitude, they accept either type of response for the information it gives about student knowledge. They become neither overly elated about correct answers nor overly disappointed about incorrect answers. They use questions as a way to stimulate thought and to acquire information about a student's progress.

Inappropriate expectations can even be communicated through praise. Although praise and encouragement are important, they should not interfere with basic teaching goals. If a teacher responds with overly dramatic praise every time a student answers a simple question, the class will likely be distracted from the content of the lesson. A contest in which the more confident and outgoing students compete for teacher recognition and approval will probably result. A better strategy is to follow a simple correct answer with simple feedback to acknowledge that it is correct. The teacher should then advance the discussion by asking another question or adding information to expand on the previous one. Praise can be saved for times when it can be given more effectively and meaningfully, especially during private contacts with individual students. Criticism, of course, should usually be omitted. In general, the teacher's behavior during question-and-answer sessions should say, "We're going to discuss and deepen our understanding of the material," not "We're going to find out who knows the material and who doesn't."

Teachers Need to Assess Students' Understanding

There may be disparity between what teachers think they have communicated and what students actually heard. Teachers should regularly monitor the work of their students and talk to them about their understanding of classroom instruction. Unfortunately, many teachers become relatively passive during seatwork and deny themselves the opportunity to discover gaps or confusion in student understanding. It is important for teachers to assess the effects of instruction immediately (rather than waiting for an exam), to prevent students from practicing errors and developing misunderstandings.

As a case in point, one of the authors observed a secondary English class on paragraph composition. The teacher emphasized three times that students should use personality descriptors, not behavioral descriptors, to describe the person they were writing about. During the lesson, the teacher wrote, with the students' help, a sample paragraph on the board. In part because of the rapid nature of the interaction that took place during this writing, the teacher included some behavioral descriptors in the sample paragraph. Students then had to decide whether to follow the original instructions (don't use behavioral descriptors) or to follow the model paragraph on the board. Other discrepancies also occurred during the lesson. The teacher did not monitor the students' work or talk to them once they started to write their paragraphs so a golden opportunity for correcting misunderstandings was lost.

Students Should Meet Minimum Objectives

Although all students cannot be expected to do equally well, teachers can establish reasonable minimal objectives for each class. Naturally, most students will be capable of going considerably beyond minimal objectives, and should be encouraged to do so. However, teachers must not lose sight of basic priorities. Remedial work with students who have not yet met minimal objectives should not be delayed in favor of enrichment activities with those who have. Ways that teachers can use grouping, peer tutoring, and other techniques to make time for such remediation are discussed in Chapter 9.

Teachers with appropriate attitudes will spend extra time working with students who are having difficulty, and they will be supportive, patient, and confident when interacting with these students. In contrast, teachers with inappropriate attitudes will often spend less time with the students who are most in need of extra help. When they do work with these students, they often do so in a halfhearted way that communicates disappointment and frustration. Such teachers are often overly dependent on achieving easy success and eliciting many right answers. They need to change this attitude if they are to conduct effective remedial teaching with slower learners.

Students Should Value Learning

This is one of the most common areas where teacher expectations can become self-fulfilling. When teachers do have the appropriate attitude toward schoolwork, they present it in ways that make their students see it as meaningful and interesting. Tasks and assignments are given without apology, as activities valuable in their own right. Comments about upcoming assignments stress the specific ways in which they build on present knowledge and skills. Comments about present work reinforce the students' sense of progress and mastery. Teachers should not expect students to enjoy learning in the same way they enjoy a ride on a roller coaster. Instead, there should be quiet but consistent satisfactions and feelings of mastery that come with the accumulation of knowledge and skills.

Teachers with negative attitudes see learning activities as unpleasant but necessary drudgery. If they believe in a positive approach toward motivation, they will be apologetic and defensive about assignments and will frequently resort to bribery, attempting to generate enthusiasm through overemphasis on contests, rewards, and other external incentives. If they are authoritarian and punitive, they will present assignments as bitter pills that students must swallow or else. In either case, the students will acquire a distaste for school activities, thus providing reinforcement for teacher expectations.

Other evidence of inappropriate teacher attitudes toward school activities includes: emphasizing the separation of work and play, with work pictured as unpleasant activity that one endures in order to get to play; introducing assignments as something the class *has* to do rather than merely as something they are going to do; the use of extra assignments as punishments; and practices such as checking to make sure that everyone has signed out one or more books from the library. Teachers with negative attitudes also discuss academic subjects in a way that presents them as dull and devoid of content. For example, they might say, "We're going to have history," instead of, "We're going to discuss the voyage of Columbus," or "Read pages 17 to 22," instead of, "Read the author's critique of Twain's novel." All these behaviors tell students that the teacher does not see school activities as very interesting or pleasant. Unfortunately, sometimes comments like the following make it clear that teachers feel that academic tasks do not have intrinsic value: "Finish your assignment and then you can do something you want to do."

Teachers Should Expect to Deal With Individual Students

As a rule, teachers should think, talk, and act in terms of individual students. This does not mean that teachers should not practice grouping. It does mean keeping a proper perspective about priorities. Grouping must be used as a means of meeting the individual needs of each student.

The way teachers talk about students in their classes is an indication of how they think about them. Teachers who continually mention groups to the exclusion of individuals may have begun to lose sight of individual differences within groups and to overemphasize variation between groups. It is likely that such teachers rarely change the group membership in their classes, that groups are seated together and spend most of the day together, and that these teachers spend more time with highs than with lows.

Although labels and stereotypes are often helpful in thinking about ways to teach individuals better, teachers should avoid using oversimplified, stereotyped labels (immature, discipline problem, mentally retarded, etc.) to describe students. A teacher may react more to a stereotype than to a student's individual qualities and may well fail to notice behavior that does not fit the stereotype. For example, a teacher might label or criticize a student directly, describe problems without trying to do anything about them, or treat a student on the basis of untested assumptions rather than observed behavior. These behaviors suggest that the stereotyped label has begun to structure the teacher's perception of the student.

Teachers Should Assume Good Intentions and a Positive Self-Concept

Teachers must communicate to all of their students the expectations that the students want to be, and are trying to be, fair, cooperative, reasonable, and responsible. This includes even those who consistently present the same behavior problems. The rationale here is that teachers' basic faith in the students' abilities to change is a necessary (even if not sufficient) condition for such change. If students see that teachers do not have this faith in them, they will probably lose whatever motivation they have to keep trying. Thus, teachers should be very careful to avoid suggesting that students deliberately hurt others or enjoy doing so, that they cannot and probably will not ever be able to control their own behavior, or that they simply do not care what they do. Even in cases where such assessments might actually be true, there is nothing to be gained and much to be lost by voicing them. Such statements will only establish or help reinforce a negative self-concept and lead to even more destructive behavior ("If they think I'm bad now, wait until they get a load of this.").

Teachers Should Expect to Be Obeyed

Some teachers have serious discipline problems of their own making. Usually, the cause is failure to observe one of the principles for establishing classroom rules that are discussed in Chapter 6. Obedience is usually obtained rather easily by teachers who establish fair and appropriate rules, who are consistent in what they say, who only say what they really mean, and who regularly follow up with appropriate action whenever it is necessary. Such procedures produce credibility and respect; the students are clear about what the teacher expects of them and know that they are accountable for meeting these expectations.

There are many observable teacher behaviors that damage teachers' credibility and, therefore, their ability to command obedience. Among these behaviors are: inconsistency about rules; playing favorites or picking on certain students; making threats or promises that are not kept; failure to explain conduct rules or expectations, so that behavioral reactions appear to be arbitrary and inconsistent to the students; indecisiveness or hesitancy in giving instructions; failure to listen to the whole story or get all the facts, so that hasty and ill-conceived solutions have to be retracted and changed; and failure to respond to serious defiance that simply cannot be ignored. These behaviors will convince students that teachers do not know what they want, do not mean what they say, or do not expect to be taken seriously and obeyed. This will tend to make students question and test instructions rather than accept and obey them. Such reactions can be prevented if teachers show students that they are quite serious about what they say, well aware of what they are saying when they say it, and seriously intent on seeing it carried out.

SUMMARY

In this chapter, we have shown how teachers' attitudes and expectations about different students can lead them to treat the students differently, sometimes to the extent of producing self-fulfilling prophecy effects. A particular danger is that low expectations combined with an attitude of futility will be communicated to certain students, leading to erosion of their confidence and motivation for school learning. This will confirm or deepen the students' sense of hopelessness and cause them to fail even when they could have succeeded under different circumstances.

Expectations tend to be self-sustaining. They affect both perception, by causing teachers to be alert for what they expect and to be less likely to notice what they do not expect, and interpretation, by causing teachers to interpret (and perhaps distort) what they see so that it is consistent with their expectations. In this way, some expectations can persist even though they do not fit the facts (as seen by a more neutral observer).

Sometimes low expectations exist because the teacher has given up on certain students and accepts failure rather than trying to do anything further with them. In these instances, rationalization or other defense mechanisms are used to take the teacher's mind off the problem or to explain it away ("Johnny's limited intelligence, poor attitude, and cumulative failure in school have left him unable to handle eighth-grade work; he belongs in a special education class."). This attitude psychologically frees the teacher from continuing to worry about the student's progress and from seeking new and more successful ways to teach the student.

Once a teacher and student become locked into such a circle of futility, they tend to stay there. The teacher's behavior causes the student to fall even father behind than he or she might have otherwise, which in turn reinforces the teacher's already low expectations.

Teachers can avoid such problems by adopting appropriate general expectations about teaching and by learning to recognize their specific attitudes and expectations about individual students and to monitor their treatment of individual students. In particular, it is essential that teachers remember that their primary responsibility is to teach, to help all students reach their potential as learners. It is natural that teachers form differential attitudes and expectations about different students, because each student is an individual. To the extent that these are accurate and up to date, they are helpful in planning ways to meet each student's needs. However, they must constantly be monitored and evaluated to insure that they change appropriately in response to changes in the student. When teachers fail to monitor and evaluate their attitudes, expectations, and behavior toward students, they can easily get caught in the vicious circle of failure and futility described above.

Remember, teaching attitudes and expectations can be your allies and tools if properly maintained and used. However, if accepted unquestioningly and allowed to solidify, they can become defense mechanisms that lead you to ignore or explain away problems rather than solve them. Therefore, learn to control your attitudes and expectations—don't let them control you!

SUGGESTED ACTIVITIES AND QUESTIONS

4.1. Which students in your preservice teacher education courses (or teachers at your school) are the brightest? What behavioral evidence and information have you used to form your opinions? How accurate do you think your estimates are?

4.2. When teachers form expectations about how students will perform in their classes, do you think that teachers tend to underestimate or overestimate the following types of learners: loud, aggressive males; quiet, passive males; loud, aggressive females; quiet, passive females; students who are neat and who follow directions carefully; students with speech impediments; and students who complain that school work is dull and uninteresting? Why do you feel that teachers tend to overestimate or underestimate the ability of these student types?

4.3. Analyze your own attitudes about classroom learning. As a student, did you find school assignments enjoyable? If so, why? Was it just because you did well, or for other reasons? What reasons? When learning was unrewarding, was it due to particular teachers or subjects?

4.4. What can you do as a teacher to make learning more rewarding for your students?

4.5. Write an original example of a self-fulfilling prophecy, based on something that happened to you, a relative, or a classmate. Be sure that you include each of these three steps: an original expectation, behaviors that consistently communicated this expectation, and evidence that the original expectation was confirmed.

4.6. Role-play the beginnings and endings of lessons. (You be the teacher and let class-mates play students at a specific grade level.) Try to communicate appropriate expectations.

4.7. Read one or two of the case studies in the Appendix at the back of the book and list instances when teachers communicate positive or negative expectations. Compare your lists with those made by others.

4.8. How can a teacher's overemphasis on praise of right answers interfere with student learning?

4.9. Should teachers hold expectations for student performance?

4.10. Why should expectations be appropriate rather than necessarily positive and that they must be followed up with appropriate behavior?

4.11. How do teachers form their expectations about students?

4.12. Explain in your own words why expectations, once formed, tend to be self-perpetuating.

4.13. Discuss ways in which inappropriate teacher expectations may lead to inappropriate teacher behavior.

4.14. In particular, how might a teacher's use of homework and seatwork assignments communicate undesirable expectations to students?

4.15. Select two of the forms at the end of this chapter that are designed to measure behaviors that communicate teacher expectations and use them to rate real teachers or videotaped teaching situations.

REFERENCES

Adams, G., & Cohen, A. (1974). Children's physical and interpersonal characteristics that affect student-teacher interactions. *Journal of Experimental Education, 43,* 1–5.

Allington, R. (1980). Teacher interruption behaviors during primary grade oral reading. *Journal of Educational Psychology, 72,* 371–377.

Allington, R. (1983). The reading instruction provided readers of differing reading ability. *Elementary School Journal, 83,* 548–559.

Amato, J. (1975). Effect of pupils' social class upon teachers' expectations and behavior. Paper presented at the annual meeting of the American Psychological Association, Chicago.

Ashton, P. (1985). Motivation and the teacher's sense of efficacy. In C. Ames & R. Ames (Eds.), *Research on motivation in education. Vol. II: The classroom milieu.* Orlando, FL: Academic Press.

Ashton, P., & Webb, R. (1986). *Making a difference: Teachers' sense of efficacy and student achievement.* New York: Longman.

Babad, E. (1985). Some correlates of teachers' expectancy bias. *American Educational Research Journal, 22,* 175–183.

Babad, E., Inbar, J., & Rosenthal, R. (1982). Pygmalion, Galatea, and the Golem: Investigations of biased and unbiased teachers. *Journal of Educational Psychology, 74,* 459–474.

Baron, R., Tom, D., & Cooper, H. (1985). Social class, race, and teacher expectations. In J. Dusek (Ed.), *Teacher expectancies.* Hillsdale, NJ: Erlbaum.

Beez, W. (1968). Influence of biased psychological reports on teacher behavior and pupil performance. *Proceedings of the 76th Annual Convention of the American Psychological Association, 3,* 605–606.

Blakey, M. (1970). The relationship between teacher expectancy and teacher verbal behavior and their effect upon adult student achievement. *Dissertation Abstracts International, 31,* 4615A.

Blanck, P., & Rosenthal, R. (1984). Mediation of interpersonal expectancy effects: Counselor's tone of voice. *Journal of Educational Psychology, 76,* 418–426.

Blumenfeld, P., Hamilton, V., Bossert, S., Wessels, K., & Meece, J. (1983). Teacher talk and student thought: Socialization into the student role. In J. Levine & M. Wang (Eds.), *Teacher and student perceptions: Implications for learning.* Hillsdale, NJ: Erlbaum.

Bognar, C. (1982). Dissonant feedback about achievement and teachers' expectations. *Alberta Journal of Educational Research, 28,* 277–287.

Borko, H., Cone, R., Russo, N., & Shavelson, R. (1979). Teachers' decision making. In P. Peterson & H. Walberg (Eds.), *Research on teaching: Concepts, findings, and implications.* Berkeley, CA: McCutchan.

Borko, H., Shavelson, R., & Stern, P. (1981). Teachers' decisions in the planning of reading instruction. *Reading Research Quarterly, 16,* 449–466.

Bossert, S. (1979). *Tasks and social relationships in classrooms: A study of instructional organization and its consequences.* New York: Cambridge University Press.

Bozsik, B. (1982). A study of teacher questioning and student response interaction during pre-story and post-story portions of reading comprehension lessons. Paper presented at the annual meeting of the American Educational Research Association, New York.

Brattesani, K., Weinstein, R., & Marshall, H. (1984). Student perceptions of differential teacher treatment as moderators of teacher expectation effects. *Journal of Educational Psychology, 76,* 236–247.

Braun, C. (1976). Teacher expectation: Sociopsychological dynamics. *Review of Educational Research, 46,* 185–213.

Brookover, W., Beady, C., Flood, P., Schweitzer, J., & Wisenbaker, J. (1979). *School social systems and student achievement: Schools can make a difference.* New York: Bergin.

Brophy, J. (1983). Research on the self-fulfilling prophecy and teacher expectations. *Journal of Educational Psychology, 75,* 631–661.

Brophy, J. (1985). Teachers' expectations, motives, and goals for working with problem students. In C. Ames & R. Ames (Eds.), *Research on motivation in education. Vol. II: The classroom milieu.* Orlando, FL: Academic Press.

Brophy, J., & Evertson, C. (1976). *Learning from teaching: A developmental perspective.* Boston: Allyn and Bacon.

Brophy, J., & Good, T. (1970). Teachers' communication of differential expectations for children's classroom performance: Some behavioral data. *Journal of Educational Psychology, 61,* 365–374.

Brophy, J., & Good, T. (1974). *Teacher-student relationships: Causes and consequences.* New York: Holt, Rinehart and Winston.

Brophy, J., & Good, T. (1986). Teacher behavior and student achievement. In M. Wittrock (Ed.), *Handbook of research on teaching* (3rd ed.). New York: Macmillan.

Brophy, J., Rohrkemper, M., Rashid, H., & Goldberger, M. (1983). Relationships between teachers' presentations of classroom tasks and students' engagement in those tasks. *Journal of Educational Psychology, 75,* 544–552.

Burnham, J. (1968). *Effects of experimenters' expectancies on children's ability to learn to swim.* Unpublished master's thesis. West Lafayette, IN: Purdue University.

Cahen, L. (1966). *An experimental manipulation of the halo effect.* Unpublished doctoral dissertation. Stanford: Stanford University.

Chaikin, A., Sigler, E., & Derlega, V. (1974). Nonverbal mediators of teacher expectation effects. *Journal of Personality and Social Psychology, 30,* 144–149.

Claiborn, W. (1969). Expectancy effects in the classroom: A failure to replicate. *Journal of Educational Psychology, 60,* 377–383.

Conn, L., Edwards, C., Rosenthal, R., & Crowne, D. (1968). Perceptions of emotion and response to teachers' expectancy by elementary school children. *Psychology Reports, 22,* 27–34.

Cooper, H. (1979). Pygmalion grows up: A model for teacher expectation communication and performance influence. *Review of Educational Research, 49,* 389–410.

Cooper, H. (1985). Models of teacher expectation communication. In J. Dusek (Ed.), *Teacher expectancies.* Hillsdale, NJ: Erlbaum.

Cooper, H., & Baron, R. (1977). Academic expectations and attributed responsibility as predictors of professional teachers' reinforcement behavior. *Journal of Educational Psychology, 69,* 409–418.

Cooper, H., & Good, T. (1983). *Pygmalion grows up: Studies in the expectation communication process.* New York: Longman.

Cooper, H., & Tom, D. (1984). Teacher expectation research: A review with implications for classroom instruction. *Elementary School Journal, 85,* 77–89.

Cornbleth, C., Davis, O., & Button, C. (1972). Teacher-pupil interaction and teacher expectations for pupil achievement in secondary social studies classes. Paper presented at the annual meeting of the American Educational Research Association, Chicago.

Crano, W., & Mellon, P. (1978). Causal influences of teachers' expectations on children's academic performance: A cross-lagged panel analysis. *Journal of Educational Psychology, 70,* 39–49.

Darley, J., & Fazio, R. (1980). Expectancy confirmation processes arising in the social interaction sequence. *American Psychologist, 35,* 867–881.

Doyle, W. (1983). How order is achieved in classrooms. Paper presented at the annual meeting of the American Educational Research Association, Montreal, Canada.

Doyle, W., Hancock, G., & Kifer, E. (1972). Teachers' perceptions: Do they make a difference? *Journal of the Association for the Study of Perception, 7,* 21–30.

Duffy, G., & McIntyre, L. (1982). A naturalistic study of instructional assistance in primary-grade reading. *Elementary School Journal, 83,* 15–23.

Dusek, J. (Ed.). (1985). *Teacher expectancies.* Hillsdale, NJ: Erlbaum.

Dusek, J., & Joseph, G. (1985). The bases of teacher expectancies. In J. Dusek (Ed.), *Teacher expectancies.* Hillsdale, NJ: Erlbaum.

Dweck, C., & Elliott, E. (1983). Achievement motivation. In P. Mussen (Ed.), *Handbook of child psychology, Vol. IV: Socialization, personality, and social development (4th ed.).* New York: Wiley.

Eccles, J., & Wigfield, A. (1985). Teacher expectations and student motivation. In J. Dusek (Ed.), *Teacher expectancies.* Hillsdale, NJ: Erlbaum.

Eder, D. (1981). Ability grouping as a self-fulfilling prophecy: A micro-analysis of teacher-student interaction. *Sociology of Education, 54,* 151–161.

Edmonds, R. (1979). Effective schools for the urban poor. *Educational Leadership, 37,* 15–18.

Egan, O., & Archer, P. (1985). The accuracy of teachers' ratings of ability: A regression model. *American Educational Research Journal, 22,* 25–34.

Evertson, C. (1982). Differences in instructional activities in higher- and lower-achieving junior high English and math classes. *Elementary School Journal, 82,* 329–350.

Farley, J. (1982). Raising student achievement through the affective domain. *Educational Leadership, 39,* 502–503.

Fernandez, C., Espinosa, R., & Dornbusch, S. (1975). *Factors perpetuating the low academic status of Chicano high school students.* (Memorandum No. 13). Stanford, CA: Center for Research and Development in Teaching, Stanford University.

Finley, M. (1984). Teachers and tracking in a comprehensive high school. *Sociology of Education, 57,* 233–243.

Finn, J. (1972). Expectations and the educational environment. *Review of Educational Research, 42,* 387–410.

Firestone, G., & Brody, N. (1975). Longitudinal investigation of teacher-student interactions and their relationship to academic performance. *Journal of Educational Psychology, 67,* 544–550.

Fleming, E., & Anttonen, R. (1971). Teacher expectancy or My Fair Lady. *American Educational Research Journal, 8,* 214–252.

Given, B. (1974). Teacher expectancy and pupil performance: The relationship to verbal and non-verbal communication by teachers of learning disabled children. *Dissertation Abstracts International, 35,* 1529A.

Goldenberg, C. (1985). The paradox of expectations: Two case studies. Paper presented at the annual meeting of the American Educational Research Association, Chicago.

Good, T. (1981). Teacher expectations and student perceptions: A decade of research. *Educational Leadership, 38,* 415–423.

Good, T. & Brophy, J. (1986). School effects. In M. C. Wittrock (Ed.) *Handbook of research on teaching* (3rd ed.). New York: Macmillan.

Good, T., Cooper, H., & Blakey, S. (1980). Classroom interaction as a function of teacher expectations, student sex, and time of year. *Journal of Educational Psychology, 72,* 378–385.

Good, T., & Marshall, S. (1984). Do students learn more in heterogeneous or homogeneous achievement groups? In P. Peterson & L. Cherry-Wilkinson (Eds.), *Student diversity in the organization process.* New York: Academic Press.

Good, T., Sikes, J., & Brophy, J. (1973). Effects of teacher sex and student sex on classroom interaction. *Journal of Educational Psychology, 65,* 74–87.

Good, T., & Weinstein, R. (1986). Teacher expectations: A framework for exploring classrooms. In K. K. Zumwalt (Ed.), *Improving teaching.* (The 1986 ASCD Yearbook). Alexandria, VA: Association for Supervision and Curriculum Development.

Graham, S. (1984). Teacher feelings and student thoughts: An attributional approach to affect in the classroom. *Elementary School Journal, 85,* 91–104.

Grusec, J., Kuczynski, L., Rushton, J., & Simutis, Z. (1978). Modeling, direct instruction, and attributions: Effect on altruism. *Developmental Psychology, 14,* 51–57.

Haskett, M. (1968). An investigation of the relationship between expectancy and pupil achievement in the special education class. *Dissertation Abstracts, 29,* 4348A–4349A.

Haskins, R., Walden, T., & Ramey, C. (1983). Teacher and student behavior in high- and low-ability groups. *Journal of Educational Psychology, 75,* 865–876.

Hauserman, N., Miller, J., & Bond, R. (1976). A behavioral approach to changing self-concept in elementary school children. *Psychological Record, 26,* 111–116.

Heapy, N., & Siess, T. (1970). Behavioral consequences of impression formation: Effects of teachers' impressions upon essay evaluations. Paper presented at the annual meeting of the Eastern Psychological Association, Atlantic City.

Heathers, G. (1969). Grouping. In R. Ebel (Ed.), *Encyclopedia of educational research* (4th ed.). New York: Macmillan.

Hiebert, E. (1983). An examination of ability grouping for reading instruction. *Reading Research Quarterly, 18,* 231–255.

Hoge, R., & Butcher, R. (1984). Analysis of teacher judgments of pupil achievement level. *Journal of Educational Psychology, 76,* 777–781.

Horn, T. (1984). The expectancy process: Causes and consequences. In W. Straub & J. Williams (Eds.), *Cognitive sport psychology.* Lansing, NY: Sport Science Association.

Humphreys, L., & Stubbs, J. (1977). A longitudinal analysis of teacher expectation, student expectation, and student achievement. *Journal of Educational Measurement, 14,* 261–270.

Jeter, J., & Davis, O. (1973). Elementary school teachers' differential classroom interaction with children as a function of differential expectations of pupil achievements. Paper presented at the annual meeting of the American Educational Research Association, New Orleans.

Jones, R. (1977). *Self-fulfilling prophecies: Social, psychological, and physiological effects of expectancies.* Hillsdale, NJ: Erlbaum.

Jones, V. (1971). *The influence of teacher-student introversion, achievement, and similarity on teacher-student dyadic classroom interactions.* Unpublished doctoral dissertation, University of Texas at Austin.

Keddie, N. (1971). Classroom knowledge. In F. Young (Ed.), *Knowledge and control: New directions for the sociology of education.* London: Collier-Macmillan.

Kerman, S. (1979). Teachers' expectations and student achievement. *Phi Delta Kappan, 16,* 716–718.

Kester, S., & Letchworth, J. (1972). Communication of teacher expectations and their effects on achievement and attitudes of secondary school students. *Journal of Educational Research, 66,* 51–55.

Kleinfeld, J. (1975). Effective teachers of Eskimo and Indian students. *School Review, 83,* 301–344.

Kraut, R. (1973). Effects of social labeling on giving to charity. *Journal of Experimental Social Psychology, 9,* 551–562.

Langer, E., & Benevento, A. (1978). Self-induced dependence. *Journal of Personality and Social Psychology, 36,* 886–893.

Leacock, E. (1969). *Teaching and learning in city schools.* New York: Basic Books.

Lepper, M. (1973). Dissonance, self-perception, and honesty in children. *Journal of Personality and Social Psychology, 25,* 65–74.

Marshall, H., & Weinstein, R. (1984). Classrooms where students perceive high and low amounts of differential teacher treatment. Paper presented at the annual meeting of the American Educational Research Association, New Orleans.

Martinek, T., & Johnson, S. (1979). Teacher expectations. Effects on dyadic interaction and self-concept in elementary-age children. *Research Quarterly, 50,* 60–70.

Martinek, T., & Karper, W. (1982). Canonical relationships among motor ability, expression of effort, teacher expectations, and dyadic interactions in elementary age children. *Journal of Teaching and Physical Education, 1,* 26–39.

Mason, E. (1973). Teachers' observations and expectations of boys and girls as influenced by biased psychological reports and knowledge of the effects of bias. *Journal of Educational Psychology, 65,* 238–243.

Medinnus, G., & Unruh, R. (1971). Teacher expectations and verbal communication. Paper presented at the annual meeting of the Western Psychological Association.

Meichenbaum, D., Bowers, K., & Ross, R. (1969). A behavioral analysis of teacher expectancy effects. *Journal of Personality and Social Psychology, 13,* 306–316.

Merton, R. (1948). The self-fulfilling prophecy. *Antioch Review, 8,* 193–210.

Metz, M. (1978). *Classrooms and corridors: The crisis of authority in desegregated secondary schools.* Berkeley, CA: University of California Press.

Meyer, W., Bachmann, M., Biermann, U., Hemplemann, M., Ploger, F., & Spiller, H. (1979). The informational value of evaluative behavior: Influences of praise and blame on perceptions of ability. *Journal of Educational Psychology, 71,* 259–268.

Miller, R., Brickman, P., & Bolen, D. (1975). Attribution versus persuasion as a means for modifying behavior. *Journal of Personality and Social Psychology, 31,* 430–441.

Mitman, A. (1985). Teachers' differential behavior toward higher and lower achieving students and its relation to selected teacher characteristics. *Journal of Educational Psychology, 77,* 149–161.

Monk, M. (1983). Teacher expectations? Pupil responses to teacher mediated classroom climate. *British Educational Research Journal, 9,* 153–166.

Natriello, G., & Dornbusch, S. (1984). *Teacher evaluative standards and student effort.* New York: Longman.

Page, S. (1971). Social interaction and experimenter effects in the verbal conditioning experiment. *Canadian Journal of Psychology, 25,* 463–475.

Palardy, J. (1969). What teachers believe—what children achieve. *Elementary School Journal, 69,* 370–374.

Pedulla, J., Airasian, P., & Madaus, G. (1980). Do teacher ratings and standardized test results of students yield the same information? *American Educational Research Journal, 17,* 303–307.

Persell, C. (1977). *Education and inequality: The roots and results of stratification in American schools.* New York: Free Press.

Peterson, P., & Barger, S. (1985). Attribution theory and teacher expectancy. In J. Dusek (Ed.), *Teacher expectancies.* Hillsdale, NJ: Erlbaum.

Pflaum, S., Pascarella, E., Boswick, M., & Auer, C. (1980). The influence of pupil behaviors and pupil status factors on teacher behaviors during oral reading lessons. *Journal of Educational Research, 74,* 99–105.

Proctor, C. (1984). Teacher expectations: A model for school improvement. *Elementary School Journal, 84,* 469–481.

Raudenbush, S. (1984). Magnitude of teacher expectancy effects on pupil IQ as a function of the credibility of expectancy induction: A synthesis of findings from 18 experiments. *Journal of Educational Psychology, 76,* 85–97.

Rejeski, W., Darracott, C., & Hutslar, S. (1979). Pygmalion in youth sport: A field study. *Journal of Sports Psychology, 1,* 311–319.

Riggs, J., Monach, E., Ogburn, T., & Pahides, S. (1983). Inducing self-perceptions: The role of social interaction. *Personality and Social Psychology Bulletin, 9,* 253–260.

Rist, R. (1970). Student social class and teacher expectations: The self-fulfilling prophecy in ghetto education. *Harvard Educational Review, 40,* 411–451.

Rolison, M., & Medway, F. (1985). Teachers' expectations and attributions for student achievement: Effects of label, performance pattern, and special education intervention. *American Educational Research Journal, 22,* 561–573.

Rosenbaum, J. (1976). *Making inequality.* New York: Wiley-Interscience.

Rosenholtz, S., & Simpson, C. (1984). Classroom organization and student stratification. *Elementary School Journal, 85,* 21–37.

Rosenholtz, S., & Wilson, B. (1980). The effect of classroom structure on shared perceptions of ability. *American Educational Research Journal, 17,* 75–82.

Rosenthal, R. (1974). *On the social psychology of the self-fulfilling prophecy: Further evidence for Pygmalion effects and their mediating mechanisms.* New York: MSS Modular Publications.

Rosenthal, R. (1976). *Experimenter effects in behavior research* (2nd ed.). New York: Irvington.

Rosenthal, R., & Jacobson, L. (1968). *Pygmalion in the classroom: Teacher expectation and pupils' intellectual development.* New York: Holt, Rinehart and Winston.

Rowe, M. (1969). Science, silence, and sanctions. *Science and Children, 6,* 11–13.

Rowe, M. (1974a). Pausing phenomena: Influence on quality of instruction. *Journal of Psycholinguistic Research, 3,* 203–224.

Rowe, M. (1974b). Wait-time and rewards as instructional variables, their influence on language, logic, and fate control: Part 1: Wait-time. *Journal of Research in Science Teaching, 11,* 81–94.

Rubovits, P., & Maehr, M. (1971). Pygmalion analyzed: Toward an explanation of the Rosenthal-Jacobson findings. *Journal of Personality and Social Psychology, 19,* 197–203.

Rutter, M., Maughan, E., Mortimore, P., Ouston, J., & Smith, A. (1979). *Fifteen thousand hours: Secondary schools and their effects on children.* Cambridge, MA: Harvard University Press.

Schrank, W. (1968). The labeling effect of ability grouping. *Journal of Educational Research, 62,* 51–52.

Schrank, W. (1970). A further study of the labeling effect of ability grouping. *Journal of Educational Research, 63,* 358–360.

Seaver, W. (1973). Effects of naturally induced teacher expectancies. *Journal of Personality and Social Psychology, 28,* 333–342.

Sedlak, M., Wheeler, C., Pullin, D., & Cusick, P. (1985). High school reform and the "bargain" to learn. *Education and Urban Society, 17,* 204–214.

Shavelson, R., Cadwell, J., & Izu, T. (1977). Teachers' sensitivity to the reliability of information in making pedagogical decisions. *American Educational Research Journal, 14,* 83–97.

Short, G. (1985). Teacher expectation and West Indian underachievement. *Educational Research, 27,* 95–101.

Smith, F., & Luginbuhl, J. (1976). Inspecting expectancy: Some laboratory results of relevance for teacher training. *Journal of Educational Psychology, 68,* 265–272.

Smith, M. (1980). Meta-analysis of research on teacher expectation. *Evaluation in Education, 4,* 53–55.

Snow, R. (1969). Unfinished Pygmalion. *Contemporary Psychology, 14,* 197–199.

Spector, P. (1973). *The communication of expectancies: The interaction of reinforcement and expectancy instructions.* Unpublished manuscript. St. Louis: Washington University.

Swann, W., & Snyder, M. (1980). On translating beliefs into action: Theories of ability and their application in an instructional setting. *Journal of Personality and Social Psychology, 38,* 879–888.

Taylor, C. (1970). The expectations of Pygmalion's creators. *Educational Leadership, 28,* 161–164.

Taylor, D. (1977). *Second grade reading instruction: The teacher-child dyadic interactions of boys and girls of varying abilities.* Unpublished masters thesis. New Brunswick, NJ: Rutgers University.

Taylor, J. (1983). Influence of speech variety on teachers' evaluation of reading comprehension. *Journal of Educational Psychology, 75,* 662–667.

Taylor, M. (1979). Race, sex, and the expression of self-fulfilling prophecies in a laboratory teaching situation. *Journal of Personality and Social Psychology, 37,* 897–912.

Thomas, J. (1980). Agency and achievement: Self-management and self-reward. *Review of Educational Research, 30,* 213–240.

Tom, D., Cooper, H., & McGraw, M. (1984). Influences of student background and teacher authoritarianism on teacher expectation. *Journal of Educational Psychology, 76,* 259–265.

Toner, I., Moore, L., & Emmons, B. (1980). The effect of being labeled on subsequent self-control in children. *Child Development, 51,* 618–621.

Weinstein, R. (1976). Reading group membership in first grade: Teacher behaviors and pupil experience over time. *Journal of Educational Psychology, 68,* 103–116.

Weinstein, R. (1983). Student perceptions of schooling. *Elementary School Journal, 83,* 287–312.

Weinstein, R. (1985). Student mediation of classroom expectancy effects. In J. Dusek (Ed.) *Teacher expectancies.* Hillsdalle, NJ: Erlbaum (329–350).

Weinstein, R., Marshall, H., Brattesani, K., & Middlestadt, S. (1982). Student perceptions of differential teacher treatment in open and traditional classrooms. *Journal of Educational Psychology, 74,* 678–692.

West, C., & Anderson, T. (1976). The question of preponderant causation in teacher expectancy research. *Review of Educational Research, 46,* 613–630.

Willis, B. (1970). The influence of teacher expectation on teachers' classroom interaction with selected children. *Dissertation Abstracts, 30,* 5072A.

Zuckerman, M., DeFrank, R., Hall, J., & Rosenthal, R. (1978). Accuracy of nonverbal communication as determinant of interpersonal expectancy effects. *Environmental Psychology and Nonverbal Behavior, 2,* 206–214.

APPENDIX

Observation forms for measuring teacher behavior related to the basic teacher attitudes and expectations discussed in the chapter are presented in this appendix. Each form has a numbered title, a definition of the classroom situations in which it should be used, and a description of its purpose. Although all the forms share these common properties, they differ from one another in several ways. Some are confined to strictly behavioral categories and require simple counting of observed events, while others require the coder to make inferences or judgments and score the teacher on more global rating scales. Also, some call for only a single coding for a single event, while others involve coding several items of information about series of events that occur in sequences.

Skilled coders can use many of the observation forms during a single observation, so long as they do not attempt themselves to code two things at the same time. At the beginning, however, it is best to start with one or two forms while you acquire basic observation and coding skills.

The observation forms define the applicable classroom situation and then list several alternative ways in which the teacher could respond in the situation. The different teacher behaviors listed are most often mutually exclusive, but sometimes more than one could occur in a given situation. To use the observation forms correctly, you must be able to: (1) recognize when relevant situations are occurring that call for use of the form, (2) accurately observe the teacher's handling of the situation, and (3) accurately record this information on the form. If the teacher shows more than one codable behavior in the situation, simply number consecutively the different behaviors that the teacher shows. This will preserve not only the information about different techniques that were used but also the sequence in which they were used.

USING CODING SHEETS

An example (Figure 4.1) of how the coding sheet would be used and how the information recorded on it can be recovered later is presented on page 162. This example includes the form used for teacher behavior when introducing lessons or activities or making assignments (Form 4.1). This form is used to measure the teacher's motivation attempt (if any) as opposed to specificity or completeness in presenting the assignment (the latter is covered on a different form).

On this form, the observer would note carefully what attempt the teacher made to build up interest or *motivate* the students to look forward to or to work carefully on the lesson or assignment; this information is numbered by categories, and these numbers are used to record the behavior in the coding columns.

In the example, the coding sheet shows that three such instances were observed by the coder (the coding sheet has room for 50 instances). Note that the first code entered is a 4. This indicates that the teacher began a lesson or gave an assignment with no attempt at all to motivate or build up interest. Some directions may have been given to get the group started, but no attempt was made to promote to the activity ("Yesterday we finished page 53. Open your books to page 54. Mark,

MOTIVATION ATTEMPT, INTRODUCING ACTIVITIES	EVALUATIONS AFTER ACTIVITIES	INDIVIDUAL PRAISE	INDIVIDUAL CRITICISM
1. Gushy build-up	1. Praises specific progress	1. Perseverance, effort	1. Poor persistence, effort
2. Enjoyment	2. Criticizes specifically	2. Progress	2. Poor progress
3. New information, skills	3. Praises general progress	3. Success	3. Failure
4. No motivation attempt	4. Criticizes general performance	4. Good thinking	4. Faulty thinking, guessing
5. Apologizes	5. Ambiguous praise	5. Imagination, originality	5. Triteness
6. Promises reward	6. Ambiguous criticism	6. Neatness, care	6. Sloppiness, carelessness
7. Warns of test	7. Praises good behavior	7. Obedience, attention	7. Breaks rules, inattentive
8. Threatens to punish	8. Criticizes misbehavior	8. Prosocial behavior	8. Antisocial behavior
9. Gives as punishment	9. No group evaluation	9. Other (specify)	9. Other (specify)
10. Other (specify)	10. Other (specify)		

CODES		CODES		STUDENT NUMBERS AND CODES		STUDENT NUMBERS AND CODES	
_4_ 1.	___ 26.	_5_ 1.	___ 26.	_14_ 1. 3	___ 26.	_16_ 1. 3	___ 26.
_43_ 2.	___ 27.	_5_ 2.	___ 27.	_23_ 2. 3,4	___ 27.	_21_ 2. 3	___ 27.
_43_ 3.	___ 28.	___ 3.	___ 28.	_6_ 3. 3	___ 28.	_5_ 3. 3,4	___ 28.
___ 4.	___ 29.	_9_ 4.	___ 29.	_18_ 4. 3	___ 29.	_12_ 4. 3	___ 29.
___ 5.	___ 30.	___ 5.	___ 30.	___ 5.	___ 30.	___ 5.	___ 30.
___ 6.	___ 31.	___ 6.	___ 31.	___ 6.	___ 31.	___ 6.	___ 31.
___ 7.	___ 32.	___ 7.	___ 32.	___ 7.	___ 32.	___ 7.	___ 32.
___ 8.	___ 33.	___ 8.	___ 33.	___ 8.	___ 33.	___ 8.	___ 33.
___ 9.	___ 34.	___ 9.	___ 34.	___ 9.	___ 34.	___ 9.	___ 34.
___ 10.	___ 35.	___ 10.	___ 35.	___ 10.	___ 35.	___ 10.	___ 35.
___ 11.	___ 36.	___ 11.	___ 36.	___ 11.	___ 36.	___ 11.	___ 36.
___ 12.	___ 37.	___ 12.	___ 37.	___ 12.	___ 37.	___ 12.	___ 37.
___ 13.	___ 38.	___ 13.	___ 38.	___ 13.	___ 38.	___ 13.	___ 38.
___ 14.	___ 39.	___ 14.	___ 39.	___ 14.	___ 39.	___ 14.	___ 39.
___ 15.	___ 40.	___ 15.	___ 40.	___ 15.	___ 40.	___ 15.	___ 40.
___ 16.	___ 41.	___ 16.	___ 41.	___ 16.	___ 41.	___ 16.	___ 41.
___ 17.	___ 42.	___ 17.	___ 42.	___ 17.	___ 42.	___ 17.	___ 42.
___ 18.	___ 43.	___ 18.	___ 43.	___ 18.	___ 43.	___ 18.	___ 43.
___ 19.	___ 44.	___ 19.	___ 44.	___ 19.	___ 44.	___ 19.	___ 44.
___ 20.	___ 45.	___ 20.	___ 45.	___ 20.	___ 45.	___ 20.	___ 45.
___ 21.	___ 46.	___ 21.	___ 46.	___ 21.	___ 46.	___ 21.	___ 46.
___ 22.	___ 47.	___ 22.	___ 47.	___ 22.	___ 47.	___ 22.	___ 47.
___ 23.	___ 48.	___ 23.	___ 48.	___ 23.	___ 48.	___ 23.	___ 48.
___ 24.	___ 49.	___ 24.	___ 49.	___ 24.	___ 49.	___ 24.	___ 49.
___ 25.	___ 50.	___ 25.	___ 50.	___ 25.	___ 50.	___ 25.	___ 50.

Figure 4.1 Sample coding sheet combining four observation forms.

begin reading with the first paragraph."). The teacher also did not promise rewards or threaten punishment for good or bad performance in the activity.

The teacher's behavior the second time he or she introduced a lesson or activity is coded in the next row. Here the coder has entered both a 1 and a 3. This indicates that the teacher began with a gushy buildup but later also mentioned the information or skills that would be learned in the activity.

The third row also shows a 1 followed by a 3, indicating again that the teacher introduced a lesson or activity with an excessive buildup followed by mention of the information or skills to be learned.

Although not enough instances are recorded to make interpretations with great confidence, a pattern is noticeable in the three instances coded. The teacher appears to be basically positive in the presentation of lessons and activities. No negative motivation attempts (apology, threat of test, or punishment) appear. However, in attempting to provide positive motivation, the teacher may be over-doing it in that the observer coded two instances of overdramatic buildup.

If this did indeed develop as the teacher's stable pattern, some guidelines for

---

FORM 4.1. Introducing Lessons, Activities, and Assignments

USE: When the teacher is introducing new activities or making assignments
PURPOSE: To see whether or not the teacher pictures school work as worth-
while or enjoyable
Observe teacher behavior when introducing activities and making assign-
ments. For each codable instance observed, record the numbers (consecutive-
ly) of each category applicable to the teacher's behavior.

BEHAVIOR CATEGORIES

1. Gushes, gives overdramatic build-up
2. Predicts that group will enjoy the activity
3. Mentions information or skills the group will learn
4. Makes no attempt to motivate; starts right into activity
5. Apologizes or expresses sympathy to group ("Sorry, but you have to . . .")
6. Bribes, promises external reward for good attention or work
7. Warns group, or reminds them, about test to be given later
8. Threatens punishment for poor attention or work
9. Presents the activity itself as a penalty or punishment
10. Other (specify)

NOTES:

CODES

1. _4_	26. ___
2. _1,3_	27. ___
3. _1,3_	28. ___
4. ___	29. ___
5. ___	30. ___
6. ___	31. ___
7. ___	32. ___
8. ___	33. ___
9. ___	34. ___
10. ___	35. ___
11. ___	36. ___
12. ___	37. ___
13. ___	38. ___
14. ___	39. ___
15. ___	40. ___
16. ___	41. ___
17. ___	42. ___
18. ___	43. ___
19. ___	44. ___
20. ___	45. ___
21. ___	46. ___
22. ___	47. ___
23. ___	48. ___
24. ___	49. ___
25. ___	50. ___

additional questions and observations would emerge. What would be the effects of this overdramatizing on the class? Would it tend to amuse them or cause them to lose respect for the teacher? Would it train them to begin to complain or suspect unenjoyable activities if the teacher failed to give the coming activity a big buildup? If there was evidence that the teacher's overacting was having these kinds of effects on the class, he or she might be advised to tone down the motivation attempts. If there appeared to be no adverse effects on the class, it might be advisable for the teacher to continue the present style of motivating the class and instead work on changing problem behaviors that appear to have negative consequences.

The observation forms in this appendix, as well as all of the forms following subsequent chapters, will be partially filled in to show how they look after being used in the classroom. However, we will no longer add our interpretations of the data shown on these sample coding sheets. Studying the partially filled in coding sheets will help you quickly grasp what is involved in using each observation form. In addition, it will provide a basis for practicing interpretation of coded data. If possible, compare your interpretations of these data with those of a friend or colleague. Discuss any disagreements in detail to discover the reasons for them and

---

FORM 4.2. Evaluations After Lessons and Activities

USE: *When teacher ends a lesson or group activity*
PURPOSE: *To see whether the teacher stresses learning or compliance in making evaluations*
When the teacher ends a lesson or group activity, code any summary evaluations he or she makes about the group's performance during the activity.

BEHAVIOR CATEGORIES

1. Praises progress in specific terms; labels knowledge or skills learned
2. Criticizes performance or indicates weaknesses in specific terms
3. Praises generally good performance, for doing well or knowing answers
4. Criticizes generally poor performance (doesn't detail the specifics)
5. Ambiguous general praise ("You were very good today.")
6. Ambiguous general criticism ("You weren't very good today.")
7. Praises good attention or good behavior
8. Criticizes poor attention or misbehavior
9. No general evaluations of performance were made
10. Other (specify)

NOTES:

Teacher uses stock phrase ("You were really good today; I'm very pleased").

* 13 cut off by bell; might have praised otherwise.

1= Homework Review

2 = Division Facts Drill

3 = Board Work

CODES

1.	5	26.	
2.	5	27.	
3.	9	28.	
4.		29.	
5.		30.	
6.		31.	
7.		32.	
8.		33.	
9.		34.	
10.		35.	
11.		36.	
12.		37.	
13.		38.	
14.		39.	
15.		40.	
16.		41.	
17.		42.	
18.		43.	
19.		44.	
20.		45.	
21.		46.	
22.		47.	
23.		48.	
24.		49.	
25.		50.	

to determine what additional information (if any) would be needed to resolve the matter with confidence. Your instructor or in-service leader can help you to resolve coding difficulties.

The observation forms are divided so that each measures just one or only a small number of related teacher behaviors. Thus, each form is a self-contained observation instrument that can be used independently of the others. Once you have acquired some skill as a coder, however, you will want to observe several aspects of teacher behavior, using several different forms. To do this, you may find it convenient to combine several forms onto a single coding sheet. There are many ways to do this, and personal preferences and convenience are the primary criteria for deciding whether or not a given method is desirable. To show how this can be done, we have provided a sample coding sheet in Figure 4.1 that combines Forms 4.1, 4.2, 4.3, 4.4.

The four forms were compressed onto a single coding sheet by using only key terms rather than the full behavior category descriptions that appear on the originals. Use and purpose descriptions are omitted entirely, since it is assumed that the coder

---

FORM 4.3. Individual Praise

USE: *Whenever the teacher praises an individual student*
PURPOSE: *To see what behaviors the teacher reinforces through praise, and to see how the teacher's praise is distributed among the students Whenever the teacher praises an individual student, code the student's number and each category of teacher behavior that applies (consecutively).*

BEHAVIOR CATEGORIES	STUDENT NUMBER	CODES
1. Perseverance or effort, worked long or hard	_14_	1. _3_
	_23_	2. _3,4_
2. Progress (relative to the past) toward achievement	_6_	3. _3_
	_18_	4. _3_
3. Success (right answer, high score), achievement	_8_	5. _1_
4. Good thinking, good suggestion, good guess or nice try	_8_	6. _1_
	_8_	7. _1_
5. Imagination, creativity, originality	____	8. __
6. Neatness, careful work	____	9. __
7. Good or compliant behavior, follows rules, pays attention	____	10. __
8. Thoughtfulness, courtesy, offering to share; prosocial behavior	____	11. __
9. Other (specify)	____	12. __
	____	13. __
	____	14. __
	____	15. __
NOTES:	____	16. __
All answers occurred during social studies discussion.	____	17. __
	____	18. __
	____	19. __
	____	20. __
Was particularly concerned about	____	21. __
#8, a low-achieving male	____	22. __
	____	23. __
	____	24. __
	____	25. __

is already familiar with the four original forms. The result is a sheet with spaces to code up to 50 instances of each of the four teacher behaviors. A coder would use this sheet until all 50 spaces were used for one of the four behaviors and then switch to a new sheet.

Figure 4.1 shows only one of many ways that these four forms could be combined onto a single coding sheet. Feel free to create coding sheets that meet your own preferences and needs. There is no single ideal coding sheet; the one that you like and that does the job is the one you should use.

Generally, all the information you need to code is on the sheet. For example, in Figure 4.1, column one, you can see that most of the ways a teacher can motivate students when introducing a lesson have been summarized into nine categories; if the teacher's behavior cannot be described in one of these nine categories, use the tenth category. Occasionally, users will have to supply some information of their own. Notice scales representing Forms 4.3 and 4.4 (individual praise and individual criticism) in Figure 4.1. When individual students must be identified, as in these

---

FORM 4.4. Individual Criticism

USE: *Whenever the teacher criticizes an individual student*
PURPOSE: *To see what behaviors the teacher singles out for criticism, and to see how the teacher's criticism is distributed among the students*
    Whenever the teacher criticizes an individual student, note the student's name or number and code the behavior that is criticized.

BEHAVIOR CATEGORIES	STUDENT NUMBER	CODES
1. Lack of effort or persistence, doesn't try, gives up easily	16	1. 3
2. Poor progress (relative to expectations), could do better, falling behind	21	2. 3
3. Failure (can't answer, low score), lack of achievement	5	3. 3,4
4. Faulty thinking, wild guess, failure to think before responding	12	4. 3
5. Trite, stereotyped responses, lack of originality or imagination	5	5. 1
6. Sloppiness or carelessness		6.
7. Misbehaves, breaks rules, inattentive		7.
8. Selfish, discourteous, won't share; antisocial behavior		8.
9. Other (specify)		9.
		10.

NOTES:
All answers during social studies discussion.
Teacher sharply critical of student #5; seems irritated with her generally.

11. __ 12. __ 13. __ 14. __ 15. __ 16. __ 17. __ 18. __ 19. __ 20. __ 21. __ 22. __ 23. __ 24. __ 25. __

FORM 4.5. Teacher's Use of Tests

USE: When the teacher gives a quiz or test
PURPOSE: To see if the teacher uses tests appropriately as diagnostic tools
and teaching aids, rather than merely as evaluation devices
Code items A, B, and C when the teacher gives the test. If possible,
code items D, E, and F after observing how test results are used.

BEHAVIOR CATEGORIES
A. Test content
   1. Test mostly requires integration or application of knowledge or skills
   2. Test is balanced between memory and integration or application
   3. Test is mostly rote or factual memory; no thinking or application involved
B. How is test presented to students?
   1. Test presented as a diagnostic aid to the teacher—assesses strengths and weaknesses
   2. Test presented without explanation, rationale, or discussion of follow-up
   3. Test presented as a threat or hurdle to the class—to find out who knows the answers and who doesn't
C. What expectations are communicated in the teacher's directions to students?
   1. Teacher gives positive directions (eyes on your paper, guess if you're not sure)
   2. Teacher gives negative directions (no cheating or else, no guesswork)
D. Is the test reviewed with the class?
   1. Test is reviewed and discussed with class
   2. Test scored by teacher, not reviewed with class
E. How does the teacher follow up with students who scored poorly?
   1. Teacher arranges for remediation with those who do not meet minimal standards and retests to see that they reach those standards
   2. Some remediation attempted, but teacher doesn't retest to ensure mastery
   3. No evidence of remedial efforts with those who perform poorly
F. How does the teacher follow up if the whole class scores poorly? (code NA if Not Applicable)
   1. Teacher reviews or reteaches material that was not mastered and retests to ensure mastery
   2. Some remediation attempted, but teacher doesn't retest to ensure mastery
   3. No evidence of remedial efforts when material was not mastered

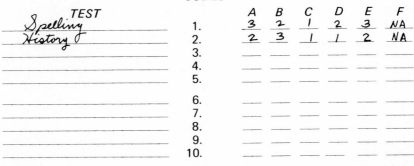

TEST		A	B	C	D	E	F
Spelling	1.	3	2	1	2	3	NA
History	2.	2	3	1	1	2	NA
	3.	—	—	—	—	—	—
	4.	—	—	—	—	—	—
	5.	—	—	—	—	—	—
	6.	—	—	—	—	—	—
	7.	—	—	—	—	—	—
	8.	—	—	—	—	—	—
	9.	—	—	—	—	—	—
	10.	—	—	—	—	—	—

CODES

FORM 4.6. Teacher's Use of Time

USE: Whenever activities are introduced or changed
PURPOSE: To see if the teacher spends time primarily on activities related to teaching and learning
Record starting time and elapsed time for the following teacher activities (when more than one activity is going on, record the one in which the teacher is involved). Totals for the day are entered in the blanks in the lower left corner of the page.

BEHAVIOR CATEGORIES
1. Daily rituals (pledge, prayer, song, collection, roll, washroom, etc.)
2. Transitions between activities
3. Whole-class lessons or tests (academic curriculum)
4. Small-group lessons or tests (academic curriculum)
5. Going around the room checking seatwork or small-group assignments
6. Doing preparation or paperwork while class does something else
7. Arts and crafts, music
8. Exercises, physical and social games (nonacademic)
9. Intellectual games and contests
10. Nonacademic pastimes (reading to class, show-and-tell, puzzles and toys)
11. Unfocused small talk
12. Other (specify)

NOTES:

\# 3, 5, 7 = *Reading Groups*
\# 11, 13 = *Math lesson & seatwork*
\# 9 = *outside recess (free play)*

TOTAL TIME PER CATEGORY

BEHAVIOR CODE	TOTAL MINUTES
1.	20
2.	24
3.	38
4.	88
5.	30
6.	
7.	
8.	15
9.	
10.	
11.	
12.	

CODES FOR EACH NEW ACTIVITY

	STARTING TIME	BEHAVIOR CODE	ELAPSED TIME
1.	8 : 15	1	15
2.	8 : 30	2	3
3.	8 : 33	4	27
4.	9 : 00	2	5
5.	9 : 05	4	25
6.	9 : 30	2	4
7.	9 : 34	4	36
8.	10 : 10	2	5
9.	10 : 15	8	15
10.	10 : 30	2	2
11.	10 : 32	3	38
12.	11 : 10	2	5
13.	11 : 15	5	30
14.	11 : 45	1	5
15.	11 : 50	Lunch	
16.	:		
17.	:		
18.	:		
19.	:		
20.	:		
21.	:		
22.	:		
23.	:		
24.	:		
25.	:		
26.	:		
27.	:		
28.	:		
29.	:		
30.	:		
31.	:		
32.	:		
33.	:		
34.	:		
35.	:		
36.	:		
37.	:		
38.	:		
39.	:		
40.	:		
41.	:		
42.	:		
43.	:		
44.	:		
45.	:		
36.	:		
47.	:		
48.	:		
49.	:		
50.	:		

examples, users will have to supply their own identification codes. In the first instance, under *individual praise,* we see that student 14 received teacher praise for successful accomplishment (category 3).

Thus, depending on their coding goals, users will have to supply appropriate code numbers. For example, if a coder is interested in how teachers praise male and female students, respectively, then he or she need only use a 1 when girls are praised and a 2 when boys are praised. Obviously, in Figure 4.1 the coder is coding the entire class, because, in the second instance of a teacher praising an individual student, the student's number is 23. If you are interested in coding the behavior of an entire class, simply assign each student a unique number and use this number whenever interactions involving that student are coded.

PREDICTIONS, EXPECTATIONS, AND UNTESTED ASSUMPTIONS

The following list of predictions and interpretations illustrates decisions that teachers have made about students. In each case observed, the interpretation was simply assumed to be true—it was not tested or verified. Even if verified, however, such interpretations should not be verbalized to the students because of the undesirable incidental learning that may result. Read the list to help establish what is meant by an *untested assumption* about a student. As you observe additional examples in classrooms, add them to the list for future reference. The key is that the teacher behaves as if the assumption is true, without first testing it.

1. The student is not ready for a particular book or problem.
2. The student can't be trusted or believed and, unless proven innocent, is guilty.
3. The student can't be allowed to use special equipment because it will only be broken.
4. The student must be isolated from others because he or she has no self-control.
5. The student will cheat unless you take precautions to prevent it.
6. The student can't talk quietly and, therefore, should not be allowed to talk at all.
7. The student won't like (or understand) the activity coming up next.
8. The student obviously knows the answer because he or she is smart (or obedient, or has a hand up).
9. The student will need help in finding the page (or other things the student can easily do indepentently).
10. The student will cause trouble unless seated next to the teacher.
11. The student will need a "crutch" to be able to do this exercise and, therefore, should be given one.
12. The student is daydreaming, not thinking about schoolwork.
13. If Johnny or Sally Bright doesn't know the answer, no one will.
14. The student will fail next week's test.
15. It's Friday afternoon, so the class will be rowdy.
16. The student just doesn't care about schoolwork.
17. All you can do for this student is see that he or she gets lots of sunlight, water, and air.

FORM 4.7. Positive Expectations Communicated to the Class

USE: At any time
PURPOSE: To document the frequency and nature of the teacher's
communication of positive expectations for the class as a whole
If the teacher's remarks made to the class as a whole include positive
expectations or statements about the class, check the type of statement
made and record the statement in the space below the checklist.

_____ 1. General goodness of class (they are a fine group of students, the teacher enjoys working with them, etc.)

_____ 2. Intelligence/ability (the students are bright, alert, sharp, etc.)

_____ 3. Careful work (they work carefully on their assignments)

_____ 4. Good ideas/thoughtful (they ask good questions and make good comments about the content; write interesting essays, etc.)

_____ 5. Eager to learn (they are curious, interested in the content, eager to master skills, etc.)

_____ 6. Steady progress (they are making steady progress in mastering material and approaching long term goals)

_____ 7. Improvement (their work shows notable improvement over earlier levels).

_____ 8. Mature/responsible (they know how to act, use good judgment, can assume responsibility, live up to the teacher's confidence in them, etc.)

_____ 9. Achievement oriented (they work hard because they want to do their best)

_____ 10. Cooperative with teacher (they want to cooperate by following the teacher's and the school's rules, and in general, conducting themselves appropriately)

_____ 11. Prosocial attitudes and behavior (they are, or are striving to be, kind, considerate, and helpful in their dealings with peers and with people generally)

_____ 12. Other (indicate)

NOTES:

FORM 4.8. Treatment of Low Achievers

USE: When the teacher has been observed frequently enough so that
reliable information can be coded
PURPOSE: To document evidence of appropriate attitudes, expectations,
and behavior toward low achievers, especially evidence that the
teacher is proactively reaching out to low achievers and trying to
assist their learning efforts
Which of these behaviors are evident in this teacher's classroom?
(Check any that apply.)

_____ 1. Seat assignments: low achievers are disbursed randomly or seated near the teacher, rather than being seated farthest away from the teacher

_____ 2. Response opportunities: low achievers are called on frequently during recitations and discussions

_____ 3. Waiting for answers: patient, willing to give students time to think when they cannot answer immediately

_____ 4. Affirms correct answers: consistently provides affirmative feedback or occasional praise following correct answers, but does not overreact or patronize

_____ 5. Negates incorrect answers: states clearly but matter-of-factly that wrong answers are incorrect, rather than either acting as if they are correct or overreacting with intense or personal criticism

_____ 6. Asks for explanation: when the thinking that led to an incorrect answer is not clear, the students are asked to explain their answers

_____ 7. Elicits improved responses: where feasible, sustains the interaction with the original respondent and attempts to elicit improved response by repeating or simplifying the question, giving clues, or identifying the reason for the error and inviting correction

_____ 8. Seatwork monitoring: makes sure low achievers know what to do and how to do it before releasing them to work on assignments, monitors progress closely, provides help and encouragement but does not do the work for the students

_____ 9. Response to student initiations: listens carefully and responds respectfully to low achievers' questions and comments about the content

_____ 10. Remedial work: provides additional instruction to students having difficulty; requires or at least allows these students to do additional work, redo assignments, and retake tests to improve their grades

_____ 11. Commitment to specific goals: commits self to making sure that all students master basic knowledge and skills objectives identified as essential

_____ 12. Task variety: even with a mastery emphasis, makes sure that low achievers experience a variety of cognitive levels, not just drill and workbook exercises

_____ 13. Responsibility/autonomy: sees that low achievers get their share of opportunities to fulfill monitor roles and other classroom responsibilities and to exercise autonomy in choosing or planning work on assignments

_____ 14. Nonverbal communication: nonverbally as well as verbally, the teacher communicates warmth, encouragement, patience, positive expectations, etc. during interactions with low achievers

_____ 15. Other (describe)

NOTES:

FORM 4.8. (_Continued_)

FORM 4.9. Teacher's Predictions and Untested Assumptions About Students

USE: Whenever the teacher makes a prediction about an individual or group
PURPOSE: To see what kinds of expectations the teacher communicates
    directly
    Record what the teacher says when making a prediction or directly
communicating an expectation about an individual or group, or when acting
upon an untested assumption. What does he or she predict (about whether
they can or cannot succeed, for example)? What untested assumption does
he or she act upon?

GROUP OR INDIVIDUAL	PREDICTION, EXPECTATION, OR UNTESTED ASSUMPTION
# 5	Can't read Astronaut's supplementary reader.
# 14	"Won't know this one" on Friday's test

CHAPTER

5 Modeling

Janice Taylor is an ambitious senior at Compton College, majoring in social studies. She plans to teach after graduating and eventually to combine that career with marriage and a family. Presently, she is doing her student teaching at Oak Junior High School. The students at Oak come from middle-class homes, and this pleases Janice because as a student she attended a similar school and came from a middle-class home. At times, however, she feels quite apprehensive. She has not been in a junior high school for several years, and although she gained some useful information in her college classes, she has not taught. Will students obey her? Can she make them enjoy schoolwork? Doubts about her ability as a teacher become prevalent as the time for her to assume teaching responsibility nears. She has been observing Mrs. Woodward's class for two weeks. One more week to observe, and then Janice is to become the teacher for the second-period (a slow class) and sixth-period (an average class) social studies classes.

Janice watches Mrs. Woodward intently because this is the first opportunity she has had to observe a junior high school teacher, and she wants to learn how to get the students to respond and to obey. Janice likes Mrs. Woodward and feels that she is a good teacher who treats the students fairly and is respected by them. However, Janice is basically a shy and soft-spoken person and frequently becomes nervous when she is around loud, assertive people. Consequently, she is often upset by the forceful way in which Mrs. Woodward runs the class. She speaks in a booming voice, and if students are misbehaving, she does not hesitate to give them a "tongue lashing" or to send them out of the room. Mrs. Woodward's favorite tactic when students are disruptive is to boom out, "I'm telling you once and for the last time (Alice and Ted, or whomever), listen to your classmates when they talk." Students typically stop after Mrs. Woodward pinpoints their misbehavior.

One week later, when Janice is teaching the class, she loudly addresses some misbehaving students in the same way, "I'm telling you once and for the last time, listen to your classmates. . . ." Think about these two questions:

1. Why did Janice imitate Mrs. Woodward's teaching style?
2. How might Janice have taught if she had taught with a different cooperating teacher?

In the previous example, the student teacher learned many things from observing a supervising teacher. (Indeed, this example is a rather common one. Several research studies have shown that the cooperating teacher greatly influences the teaching style of the student teacher.) Not all of the things Janice learned were directly connected with teaching, and relatively few of them were deliberately taught by Mrs. Woodward. Janice picked up beliefs, attitudes, and habits simply by observing them.

How does this happen? Research has shown that many things are learned without deliberate instruction by the teacher or deliberate practice by the learner. Much emphasis has been placed upon observational learning by social learning theorists, who argue and present data to illustrate that people can learn vicariously. Albert Bandura (1969, 1977) is been among the writers and researchers who contend that much learning occurs through observation. Bandura and other researchers have found that observers often are able to imitate entire sequences of behaviors on their first attempt, without practice or reinforcement. Thus, it is clear that students can and do learn even when no formal attempts are being made to instruct them. The learner only needs to see the behavior demonstrated by someone else to be able to imitate it. A person who demonstrates the behavior is called the *model,* and this form of learning is often called *modeling.*

When used purposefully, modeling can be a powerful teaching tool. Many things can be learned much more easily through observation and imitation than by trying to understand and respond to verbal explanations and instructions. This is especially true for younger students, whose abilities to follow complex verbal instructions are limited.

AWARENESS OF MODELING

Most teachers recognize the power of prepared demonstrations as teaching tools. However, they are usually less aware of the more general modeling effects that occur in the classroom and less likely to take advantage of them through deliberate, planned modeling behavior. We all know how bad examples can lead to misbehavior, but we are less aware of the power of a good model's example to influence behavior positively. Children learn many things by imitating models rather than by being instructed in a systematic fashion. They learn to speak their native tongue this way, as well as most of their attitudes, values, problem-solving strategies, and social behavior. In fact, behavioral example is usually a more powerful influence than verbal instruction.

If there is a discrepancy between our preaching and our practice, students will tend to do what we do, not what we say. This was shown in an experiment with children's altruism (Bryan & Walbek, 1970). Each child in the study played a game with an adult model. The game was designed so that each model and child could win money by succeeding at it. Unknown to the children, the experimenter controlled the results so that each model and each child won a specific amount. As part of the experiment, a box requesting donations for poor children was placed in the room where the game was conducted. Each adult model made mention of this donation box. Some of the adult models spoke in favor of donating, saying that it was a good thing to help the poor and that people should donate. With other children, the adult models complained about the donation box. They stated that their winnings should be their own and that nobody should ask them to donate part of their winnings to someone else. Half of the time when the models preached in favor of donating, they followed up by donating part of their winnings. The other half of the time they did not donate, despite their words. Similarly, half of the time the adult models who spoke against donating did not donate; the other half of the time, they donated some of their winnings even after speaking against it resentfully.

The results of the experiment show clearly that the children's donating behavior was affected much more by what the adults *did* than by what they *said*. Children who observed the model donate part of his or her winnings tended to do the same, regardless of whether the model had spoken for or against donating. Similarly, children who saw that the adult did not donate tended not to donate themselves, even if the model had spoken in favor of donation. The children clearly took their cue from what they saw the models do, not from what they heard the models say.

The same thing happens in the classroom. If students perceive discrepancies between what a teacher says and practices, they will ignore what is said. Also, if they see discrepancies between what is demanded and what is actually allowed, they will guide their behavior according to what is allowed. For example, students will obey the teacher for the first few days if they are told to do their seatwork quietly and on their own. However, if it gradually becomes clear that the teacher does not intervene in any way when students do not work quietly or when they copy from one another, they will come to see that the teacher does not mean what he or she says.

This points up the need for teachers to be aware of their behavior in the classroom. Modeling effects can occur at any time, not just at those times when the teacher is deliberately trying to serve as a model. Remember, all that is required is that the students *see* the behavior modeled before them. The potential for modeling effects exists at all times; it is not something the teacher can turn on or off at will. What students learn from watching the teacher as a model may be either desirable or undesirable. Teachers are responsible for living up to their own ideals, and they must remain aware of their roles as models in order to insure that most of what the students learn from observing them is positive and desirable.

What Is Learned From Models

Exposure to a model can result in either or both of two responses by the learner: imitation and incidental learning. *Imitation* is the simplest: the learner observes the model's behavior and then imitates it to make it his or her own. Often this is used as a teaching technique, as when students observe their teacher perform a zoology dissection or a chemistry or physics experiment and then repeat the process on their own. Unfortunately, unplanned and sometimes undesirable imitation also occurs.

Students will often pick up distinctive expressions, speech patterns, or gestures that their teachers use, whether or not they are used consciously. They will also take their cue from the teacher in learning how to react in ambiguous situations. If the teacher responds to student embarrassment with tact and sympathy, the class will tend to follow suit. However, if the teacher reacts with insensitive sarcasm or ridicule, the students will probably laugh and call out taunts of their own.

Besides imitation, observation of a model produces *incidental learning,* sometimes called inferential learning. The learner observes the model's behavior and on the basis of these observations makes inferences about the model's beliefs, attitudes, values, and personality characteristics. Here the learner is making inferences about why the model is behaving that way or about what type of person the model is. This is often called incidental learning because it involves acquisition of information in addition to or instead of what the model was trying to convey.

For example, suppose a teacher calls on a student to go to the blackboard and work out a mathematical equation. The teacher will serve as a model in the way he or she reacts to a mistake made by the student. One teacher might point out the mistake and ask the student to look at the problem again to try to find the error. Another teacher might inform the student of the mistake and then call on someone else to go to the board and do the problem correctly. Both teachers would be teaching the mathematical content, specifically, the question of how to solve the particular problem involved. However, the incidental learning acquired by the student called to the board and by the rest of the class in this situation would differ with the two teachers.

In the first case, the students learn: "The teacher is friendly and helpful. It is safe to make a mistake. You will have a chance to correct yourself if you can do so, or will get some help if you can't." In the second teacher's class, the students learn: "You had better be ready to perform when you get called to the board. The teacher wants to see the problem done correctly and has limited patience with anybody who can't do it right. If you know the answer, raise your hand and try to get called on to go to the board. If you're not sure, try to escape the teacher's attention so that you don't get embarrassed."

Incidental learning of this type goes on whenever students observe their teachers reacting to errors. The teachers probably are not trying to teach the information that is learned incidentally; in fact, some of it is undesirable information that they would avoid if they knew about it. Nevertheless, the students will learn these things by observing them. How to do mathematics is only one of the things the students will learn in these situations.

Factors Affecting What Is Learned From Observing a Model

The potential for modeling effects exists whenever learners observe a model. The amount and kind of learning that result from such observation, however, depend on several other factors that influence whether the learners are likely to imitate a model and whether the information they learn incidentally is desirable from the model's viewpoint. These factors and their effects on learning are summarized here. (For a more detailed treatment, see Bandura, 1969, 1977).

One important factor that affects learning from a model is the situation in which the modeling occurs. Modeling effects are more likely to occur in new situations or situations where the expected behavior of the learner is unclear. Like Janice Taylor in the example at the beginning of the chapter, when we enter a new situation and are unsure about what to do, we tend to "do as the Romans do," by observing and imitating models. In this sense, the behavior of the models we observe in such situations defines the situation for us. It tells us what is normal or expected. This was shown in a fascinating series of experiments on emotional reactions by Schachter (1964). He administered stimulating drugs to subjects in his experiments, but he did not tell the subjects what kinds of reactions they might expect from the drugs. He then put the subjects in rooms with models (confederates of the experimenter) to see how they would be affected by the models' behavior. Some models displayed anger and aggression; others showed a giggling euphoria. Most subjects assumed that the effect of the drug was to make them feel like the model appeared to feel, so that subjects exposed to aggressive models tended to become aggressive, while those exposed to euphoric models tended to become euphoric.

Because modeling effects are strongest in ambiguous situations where people do not know what to expect and tend to observe models in order to find out, modeling effects in the classroom are likely to be especially strong at the beginning of the year. Based on contacts with their new teachers, students make inferences about the teachers and decide whether or not they like them; what kind of people they are; and whether they invite or discourage questions and comments, mean what they say, are interested in individual problems, are patient and helpful or frustrated and discouraged in dealing with slow learners, seem reasonable and open-minded or opinionated and unapproachable; and many other things. Also, teachers' behavior early in the school year tends to set the tone for classroom climate variables, such as competitiveness, pressure and tension felt by the students, organization and order, and the degree to which students are responsible for their own behavior.

It is especially vital that teachers model appropriate behavior early in the school year. Opportunities to teach through modeling are greater at this time because rules and procedures are amenable to change (Doyle, 1986; Emmer, Evertson, & Anderson, 1980). Indeed, recent research suggests that teachers who have well-managed classrooms throughout the year take time early in the year to explain and to model their classroom expectations. Later, when both the teacher and the class settle into predictable routines, it will be more difficult to effect change. Once patterns are established, they tend to persist, and firmly established expectations tend to lead to self-fulfilling prophecy effects such as those discussed in the previous chapter.

In addition to situational factors, modeling effects vary with the personality and behavior of the models themselves. Students will imitate a warm, enthusiastic teacher whom they like. The students are likely to adopt many of the teacher's attitudes and beliefs and to imitate his or her behavior. Students are less likely to imitate a teacher whom they dislike or do not respect, especially in the sense of adopting or conforming to the teacher's beliefs. Much undesirable incidental learning will occur from the observation of such teachers, but relatively few desirable modeling effects are likely.

The model's actual behavior and the consequences of that behavior are also important. Students are likely to imitate behavior that they see as relevant or effective or behavior that has been rewarded. Behavior that is ineffective or has been punished is not likely to be imitated. Reward and punishment can be powerful factors that sometimes lead students to imitate undesirable behavior, even when modeled by teachers that they do not like or respect. This is why hostile, sarcastic, or hypercritical teachers usually produce a destructive classroom climate. Students imitate such teachers even though they dislike them, because the teachers not only model, but also reward such behavior.

Teacher rewards and punishments also influence students' reactions to one another. When students observe the teacher praise or reward a classmate for a particular behavior, or when they discover through incidental learning that the teacher holds the classmate in high regard, they are likely to adopt the classmate as a model and imitate him or her. On the other hand, if they see their teacher reject or mistreat a classmate, they may imitate the teacher and begin to mistreat the classmate.

Other factors, such as the degree to which the student's attention is focused on the relevant behavior and the degree to which the student is given instructions and time to practice the relevant behavior, also affect the kind and amount of learning that take place through modeling. These factors are discussed in later sections of this chapter, which list several positive attitudes and behaviors that teachers can present through modeling. Teachers preach some of these factors but do not always practice them consistently. There are also other factors which are not usually thought of as being at work in the classroom, but can be utilized by teachers who are aware of their role as models. We will suggest how teachers can increase desirable outcomes through deliberate modeling and point out behaviors that teachers should avoid because they tend to produce undesirable incidental learning effects.

TEACHING THROUGH MODELING

The most obvious use of modeling as a teaching device occurs in deliberate demonstrations that are given as parts of lessons. In teaching many skills, especially to younger students, demonstration is the method of choice. Teachers differ in their skills as demonstrators, however, so that some demonstrations are more successful than others. Guidelines for effective demonstrations are presented in the following section.

In addition to formal demonstrations of skills, there are many other ways teachers can instruct or stimulate cognitive development through modeling. Especially important, for example, is teacher modeling of logical thinking and problem solving for students. Students cannot observe their teachers performing such operations unless the teachers share them by thinking out loud. Suggestions on how teachers can use modeling to stimulate development of these abilities in their students are given below, following the section on demonstrations.

Effective Demonstrations

Some things can be demonstrated with little or no verbalization. Demonstrations are usually much more effective, though, if they are accompanied by verbal explanations. This is especially true for the kinds of things that are demonstrated by teachers. Usually, these demonstrations provide examples of more general principles or rules that the teacher wants the students to learn. Thus, the teacher should not focus simply on getting the students to be able to do the immediate problem; the focus should be on helping the students to learn the more general rule. Thus, a demonstration should not only show the students the physical movements involved in solving a problem, it should also include explanations of the thinking that lies behind the movements.

To say that demonstrations need explanations may seem obvious, but research shows that people usually leave out important pieces of information when explaining or demonstrating something to someone else (Flavell et al., 1968; Hess et al., 1971), and that some teachers' demonstrations are more active and meaningful than others' (Good, Grouws, & Ebmeier, 1983). People tend to assume that the listener sees the situation the same way they do, so they often forget that certain things need to be explained. You have probably discovered this for yourself if you have ever sought out a friend or relative for driving lessons, swimming lessons, or instructions about how to cook a complicated dish. Professional instructors can teach these skills to beginners with ease and efficiency. Most other people cannot, though, even if they are able to drive, swim, or cook very well.

What's the trick? Expert instructors have broken the process down into step-by-step operations. They assume no knowledge in the learner. Instead, they define each term that they introduce and point to each part as they label it. They describe what they are going to do before each step and describe what they are doing as they do it. They have the learner master one step at a time rather than try to do the whole job at once. They take their time and give corrections in a very patient tone so the learner can concentrate on the task at hand and not worry about working quickly enough.

The things that teachers demonstrate in school are not usually so complex as the examples above, but the principles for effective demonstrations remain the same. Teachers will need to bear this in mind when demonstrating new skills (e.g., word attack, mathematical operations, art projects, and science experiments) and when giving instructions for seatwork or homework. Such strategies are especially important when doing remedial work with students who clearly do not understand how to perform the steps involved in solving problems. A good demonstration should proceed as follows:

1. Focus attention. Be sure that all are attentive before beginning, and see that their attention is focused in the right place. Hold up the object or point to the place you want them to look at.
2. Give a general orientation or overview. Explain what you are going to do so that the students will have a general idea of what is going to happen. This will get them mentally set to observe the key steps as you go along.
3. If new objects or concepts are introduced, be sure to label them and have the students repeat the labels until you are sure they understand. A student cannot follow an explanation if he or she does not know what some of the words mean.
4. Go through the process step by step. Begin each new step with an explanation of what you are going to do next and then follow through by describing your actions as you do them. Think out loud throughout the demonstration.
5. Perform each action slowly and with exaggerated motions to help insure that the students follow.

6. Have a student repeat the demonstration so you can observe and give corrective feedback. If the demonstration is very short, you can have the student do the whole thing and wait until the end to give feedback. If the demonstration is longer or complex, break it into parts and have the student do one part at a time.

7. In correcting mistakes, do *not* dwell on the mistake and the reasons for it, but instead redemonstrate the correct steps and have the students try again.

These principles form guidelines for observing demonstrations. When a demonstration does not succeed, it is likely that one or more of these principles have not been followed.

Thinking out loud at each step is crucial, especially when the task is primarily cognitive and the physical motions involved are relatively minor or nonessential. If you only demonstrate procedures such as pouring a substance into a test tube, placing a number on the board, or making an incision during a dissection, students will not be able to follow you (unless they already knew what to do and therefore did not need a demonstration in the first place!). While the students watch you, they will need to hear you describe how you are filling the test tube exactly to the 10-ml line, how you get the sum by carrying two 10 units and adding them to the rest of the numbers in the 10s column, or how you begin your incision at the breastbone and stop short of the hipbones. Unless you verbalize the thinking processes going on in your mind as you work through a problem or demonstration, the processes will be hidden from the students. And unless they know enough to figure out each step independently, watching your demonstration may give them no more information about what you are doing and how you are doing it than they would get from watching a magician perform a baffling trick.

Perrott (1982) suggests that clear presentations feature continuity, simplicity, and explicitness. She suggests the following criteria for judging these clarity factors:

CONTINUITY

1. *Sequence of discourse.* The lesson should follow a planned sequence that is made obvious to the students. Diversions from this structure should be kept to a minimum, and where they do occur (usually in response to student questions or comments), it should be made clear to the students that they are diversions.

2. *Fluency.* The teacher should speak in easily intelligible grammatical sentences, seldom leaving sentences unfinished or having to interrupt in order to reformulate a statement.

SIMPLICITY

1. *Avoid grammatical complexity.* The teacher should keep sentences short, minimize multiple qualifying clauses, and use visual means, such as diagrams, tables, and models, to communicate complex relationships that are difficult to understand from a verbal presentation.

2. *Vocabulary.* The teacher should use simple language that is within the students' normal vocabulary for effective communication. Only those technical terms needed for adequate comprehension of material should be introduced during the lecture, and they should be defined or explained adequately.

EXPLICITNESS

1. *Inclusion of all the elements of an explanation.* Explanations should include both identification of the components (objects, events, processes) to be related and specific description of the relationship between these components (causal, justifying, interpreting, etc.).
2. *Explicit explanation statements.* The teacher should also explain links that clarify the causal or logical relationships between the components being related.

If a lecture or demonstration is lengthy, the teacher can help the students use chunking strategies by explicitly noting subparts and the transitions between them and by including internal summaries at the end of each subpart. If the continuity of the presentation has been broken by student questions or discussion, the teacher can help reestablish the desired learning set before continuing by reminding the students of the overall structure of the presentation and of the place at which it is being resumed.

Modeling Logical Thinking and Problem-Solving Behavior

Teachers should regularly think out loud when trying to solve problems so that students can see them model the thought processes involved. Much of the school curriculum, especially in the first few years, is devoted to teaching simple facts and basic skills that are learned through rote memory and practice. Partly because of this, many children begin to assume that everything is learned this way—that you either know an answer or you do not. The possibility that they might arrive at an answer by thinking about the problem and working it out for themselves is not always recognized. This leads to a preoccupation with finding out what the right answer is at the expense of learning how to cope with particular types of problems. Instead of developing effective problem-solving strategies to use in these situations, some students develop strategies for covering up their ignorance. Teachers can help avoid these problems by modeling good problem-solving strategies and by encouraging the development of them in their students.

The basic method of modeling for this purpose is to think out loud when problem solving. Often, this can be done in connection with lessons in the curriculum. In giving directions about how to do seatwork or homework, for example, and in doing remedial work with students who are having difficulty, teachers should verbalize each step in their thinking processes from beginning to end. Verbalizing will help students see the way the problem is approached and help them see that the answer is a logical conclusion following a chain of reasoning rather than something that the teacher just knew and that the student must commit to memory.

Although this may seem obvious, we have observed many teachers who do not teach this way. Instead, they tend to ask "Who knows the answer?" rather than "How can we find the answer?" They fail to stress the thinking and problem-solving processes that the problem is supposed to teach. Among other things, such teachers spend more time with and are more rewarding toward students who are succeeding, and they are less accessible and less supportive toward those who most need their help. Other telltale behavior occurs in instances when students give answers that are acceptable but are not the ones the teacher was looking for.

Instead of modeling respect for good thinking by complimenting the student on the answer ("That's right, I hadn't thought of that"), such teachers tend to reject these answers as if they were totally wrong. Unless the students are mature and secure enough to see this teacher behavior as unreasonable, it will tend to make them distrust their own problem-solving abilities, and they will begin to think in terms of guessing what the teacher has in mind rather than attempting to work through a problem rationally. It will also tend to depress student curiosity, creativity, and initiative.

Perhaps the best way to observe the degree to which a teacher models concern for the thinking process is to watch the way he or she handles errors in reading, seatwork, and homework exercises. Except for the relatively few things that are purely matters of rote memory, errors in reading and in working out assigned problems are evidence that the student has not mastered the principles involved. The appropriate teacher response in such situations is to help the learner master these principles, not merely to give the right answer to a particular problem. Yet many teachers typically respond to reading failures by simply giving the student the correct word (or calling on someone else), and they grade work assignments merely by marking answers correct or incorrect. Neither of these responses is usually of much help to the student.

Merely providing the correct answers in these single examples will not help the student to learn to cope with similar problems involving the same principles. He or she needs to know why the answer is correct, not merely to know what the answer is. The teacher needs to model the application of the principles by describing the process out loud, being sure to include each step in the problem-solving process.

Teachers can also model problem-solving processes in areas outside the regular curriculum. Opportunities to do so are presented whenever plans have to be changed, repairs or substitutions have to be made, or immediate problems have to be solved. These may include stuck drawers, equipment that will not function properly, science demonstrations that do not work, broken items that need fixing, and special events that require change in plans or schedules. When things like these happen, teachers should share their thinking with the students. They should first define the problem, since it may not be obvious to the students. Then they should verbalize their thoughts about solutions, or better yet, solicit suggestions from the group if time permits. This will come as a genuine revelation to certain students, who on their own would not think of fixing something that is broken or substituting for something that is missing.

Many spontaneous student questions—even those that involve a degree of hostility—can be good starting points for teachers who want to model appropriate beliefs about subject matter and have a willingness to make classroom assignments meaningful to students. Consider the following example:

Classroom example   Mr. Starford teaches an honors section of world history to sophomores at Riverside High, an inner-city school with 1000 students. He has taught in this school district for eight years. He believes that a teacher should personalize history and make it come alive. Concluding a unit assignment, he states, "When we're finished with the unit on Egypt, you can show how much you learned in this unit by writing either a children's book on Egypt or a letter that a Phoenician sailor would have written to his girlfriend while he was aboard a ship. In conveying your knowledge, try to teach it or represent it by using language and ideas that are appropriate to your audience. Describe what is important in everyday Egyptian life and compare and contrast that with what you believe are readers' understandings of their own hometowns."

Tim, one of the best students in the class who sits in the back of the room, raises his hand. "Why do we have to do an assignment like this? Why couldn't we just take tests? I really enjoy reading history, but it seems to me that you often have these little 'Mickey Mouse' assignments that get in the way of learning." Although the student's language is extreme, he raises his question in a reasonable fashion; the teacher views it as legitimate and responds in the following way: "Without a good knowledge of history, I don't think you can understand events that are currently occurring. For example, many of you are bussed to school. I don't think you can understand why you're bussed and what's happening today without understanding slavery, the Civil War, Jim Crow laws, Martin Luther King, Jr., and the civil rights movement. Furthermore, if you can understand what it was like to be on a Phoenician slave ship, and English common law and Roman civil law, you will have a much better chance of understanding the issues of freedom and basic rights."

The student responds with interest, "Yeah, I sort of understand what you're saying and I agree with that. I like history and in general I find this course interesting; however, I still think all these little activities are pointless. Why do I have to write a letter pretending I'm on a Phoenician ship when I understand the issues without going to the trouble to give this information back to you in a particular form?"

Mr. Starford replies, "I understand what you're saying too, and I lament the fact that many students don't have the concerns that you have. It seems appalling to me that a recent survey shows that one-third of high school seniors do not know that Columbus sailed to American before 1750 and that over one-half could not say within 50 years when World War I occurred!

"My only point in asking you to do some of these exercises is to personalize history and to try to make it more meaningful to you. However, I agree that the formats that I am using on this assignment are simply ways of presenting information. The type of format is not that important. If there is a better way—one that is more constructive and more useful for you personally—I certainly would consider an alternate assignment for you."

Although we do not recommend changing assignments just because students voice some concern, we believe that teachers' willingness to discuss their beliefs about subject matter and their thinking about particular assignments can be helpful to students. Students benefit from such discussions because they can see the thinking and rationale behind assignments and rules.

Many students, especially those from disadvantaged backgrounds, fail to develop adequately what some psychologists call an "internal locus of control"—an appreciation of their own potential for affecting the world through goal-oriented thinking and problem solving (for more information, see Fanelli, 1977; Rotter, 1966). Such students tend to feel helpless in the face of frustration and adversity, so that they often accept them passively instead of trying to cope with them more actively and effectively. They have learned to think in terms of accepting their fate rather than shaping it. Teachers can help combat this outlook by modeling rational problem solving and by encouraging and rewarding it in their students. As was argued in the chapter on teacher expectations, some teachers' behaviors inadvertently encourage low achievers to become *passive* learners.

Another way to model thinking and problem-solving strategies is through the use of games such as Password or 20 Questions. The following example shows how.

TEACHER: Today we are going to play a game called 20 Questions. John, you can help us get started. In a minute, I'm going to go over to the window and turn my back while you point to something in the room. When everybody has seen what you are pointing to, go back to your seat and call me. Then I'll come back and start asking you questions to see if I can figure out what you pointed to. I'll have to ask you questions that you can answer either "yes" or "no." If I'm smart enough to figure out what you pointed to in 20 questions or fewer, I win. Now, let's see if you can stump me. Remember, you can point to anything in the room that you want, as long as it is visible—something I can see.

JOHN: Okay, we're ready.

TEACHER: All right, I'm going to turn around now. Don't give me any hints by looking at what John pointed to. (Teacher turns around.) Well, let's see. There's no point in guessing, because there are too many things it could be. I think I'd better try to narrow it down some. Now, what's a question that would narrow it down for me? I know—I'll find out where it is in the room. (Teacher walks to the center of the room and points to the left side.) I'm in the center of the room now. Is it somewhere on this side of where I'm standing?

JOHN: No, it isn't.

TEACHER: Good, now I know that it is somewhere on the right side of the room. I'll have to narrow it down some more. Let's see, Ralph is seated about halfway back there. Is it in front of where Ralph is sitting?

JOHN: No.

TEACHER: Okay, now I know that it is on the right side of the room somewhere in back of Ralph. Let's see, it could be something on the walls, it could be one of you, it could be something on a desk, it could be something that you're wearing . . . I'd better narrow it down some more. Is it a person or a part of the body?

JOHN: No.

TEACHER: Well, now I know it must be an object of some kind. Is it something that someone is wearing or that is on someone's desk?

JOHN: Yes.

TEACHER: Good, that eliminates all those things along the wall. Well, let's find out if it's something somebody's wearing or if it's on a desk. Is it something on a desk?

JOHN: No.

TEACHER: Hummm, then it has to be something that one of these six students is wearing. Is it worn by a boy?

JOHN: No.

TEACHER: Well! Now we know that it is something that either Janice or Mary is wearing. Let's see, is it an article of clothing?

JOHN: No.

TEACHER: Good, that really narrows it down. It must be their jewelry or accessories. Let's see, it is worn on the head or the neck?

JOHN: No.

TEACHER: Ah! Now we're getting close. It looks as though it has to be either Janice's ring or Mary's wristwatch. Now I'm ready to make a guess. Is it Mary's wristwatch?

JOHN: Yes.

TEACHER: Well! I win! I did it in only nine or ten questions. I thought I'd probably win, because I had it pretty well narrowed down after five or six questions.

By thinking out loud this way, the teacher models problem-solving strategies for the students. In addition, the teacher's reactions to "no" answers help reinforce the idea that such answers provided valuable information and were not a cause of disappointment. Overemphasis on getting right answers and underemphasis on thinking processes have conditioned many students to believe that they have failed or have asked a dumb question simply because the answer to a question was "no."

After modeling as in the above example, the teacher could follow through by having the students play the game themselves. Besides games such as 20 Questions and Password, riddles and brain teasers can be used to model and practice problem solving, as can exercises in which the problem and answer are given and the students are asked to show how the answer is reached. In all such activities, the teacher can model methods of approaching the problem efficiently and systematically and can acknowledge and reinforce these methods when they are used by the students. Similarly, in secondary classrooms, teachers can encourage gamelike explanations that challenge students to think ("I'm thinking of a likely candidate for President in 1992. Who can. . . .?").

Teachers Model Their Beliefs About Subject Matter

It was mentioned in Chapter 2 that teachers' beliefs about particular subjects are sometimes associated with how much time and emphasis are assigned to a subject. Such teacher behaviors (e.g., more time, more excitement, more frequent testing) will communicate in subtle ways teachers' perceptions of the importance of particular subjects to students. Teachers model many ways of thinking about a subject, and teachers are often unaware of the various attitudes they communicate to students. Consider the following dialogue:

TEACHER: One, two, three. I want someone to take my 15 links and divide them into groups of three. Mike? Groups of three. If divided into groups of three, you get how many groups?

MIKE: Five.

TEACHER: Five groups. Okay, isn't that something like we had up there yesterday? Take a look at these sentences, they're kind of alike aren't they?

STUDENT: They're backwards (referring to the two matched sentences that the teacher has put on the board: $3 \times 5 = 15$, $15 \div 5 = 3$).

TEACHER: They're backwards. Do they remind you of anything else in math?

STUDENT: Adding.

TEACHER: Adding and what?

STUDENT: Subtracting.

TEACHER: Adding and subtracting? Can anyone give me two sentences for adding and subtracting that are like these? Okay, Heather, do you want to write them? Why don't you write over there in the clean space. You don't have to use my same numbers, you can use your own if you want. (Student writes $12 + 3 = 15$.) Okay, that's the addition of it. Can you give me a subtraction sentence while you're up there that is like that? Just leave that one up and write the other one under it. (Student writes $15 - 3 = 12$.) Are those related to each other? (Heather nods head affirmatively.) That's the way it is with division and multiplication sentences. If you want, you can turn it around and write a division sentence. We've still got 15 links up here haven't we? (She points to the overhead picture projected on the wall.) Okay, I'm going to add three more. How many do I have now?

STUDENT: Eighteen.

TEACHER: Eighteen links. I want someone to come up and put them into groups of three links. While you're doing that, I want you to think about how many groups they're in. Let's see, if we started out with 18 and divided them into groups of three, how many groups are we going to get? Jonathan?

JONATHAN: Six.

TEACHER: Six groups. You're right. Or we could say six groups of three make 18, right? Okay, this time, boys and girls, let's say I'm going to take away one, how many would I have then? Seventeen. I want someone to come up and put these into groups of two. You have 17 and you are putting them into groups of two, how many do you end up with?

STUDENT: Eight groups plus one left over.

TEACHER: Can't you put it in with one of the others? Well, how many groups of two do we have? Okay, we counted eight groups of two, but what else have we got?

STUDENT: One left over.

TEACHER: One left over. Okay, in math want do we call a leftover?

STUDENT: A remainder.

TEACHER: Right. So this problem is a little more interesting—we have a remainder.

This teacher models a number of things in this brief dialogue (e.g., that the process is as important as the right answer); however, we will focus on but one point in teaching. Ostensibly, the teacher is instructing a third-grade class in the concept of division with remainders. However, the teacher is also implicitly teaching attitudes about mathematics as well. For example, often when students are introduced to a concept, it is with a sense of futility or irritation ("You don't know what to do now, do you?" "That's too bad, a remainder. Now we have to spend more time on this problem."). Such behaviors, if consistent, will teach students to view division as complicated. This teacher appears to present the concept of remainders in a positive and problem-solving fashion. If the teacher continues to present this attitude to students, they are likely to view mathematics with interest and a "can-do" attitude.

Modeling Curiosity and Interest in Learning for Their Own Sakes

By the very nature of their jobs, teachers are, or should be, committed to learning. This commitment should come across in their classroom behavior. They should model not only a specific interest in curriculum subject matter, but a general commitment to learning and knowledge.

One important situation in which teachers can do this is in responding to students' questions, especially questions that are not covered in a textbook. Questions from the class are a sign of interest in the topic. They indicate that the students are participating actively in the discussion and thinking about problems rather than just listening passively. These are the "teachable moments" when the students are most receptive to new learning.

At these times, teachers should be sure to respond in a way that shows that questions are welcome and valued. First, the question itself should be acknowledged or praised: "That's a good question, John. It does seem strange that the Boston people would want to throw that tea in the water, doesn't it?" Then the teacher should attempt to answer the question or should refer it to the class for discussion: "How about it, class? Why would they throw the tea in the water instead of taking it home with them?"

If the question is one that neither the teacher nor the class is prepared to answer, some strategy should be adopted to find the answer. A relevant question should not be simply dropped or brushed aside as an unwelcome intrusion. The teacher should promise to get the answer, or better yet, assign the student who asked the question to go to the library (or other resource) to find the answer and then report it to the class the following day. If necessary, the teacher should give the student guidance about how to get the desired information. This behavior helps to reinforce the idea that learning is interesting and worth pursuing for its own sake. It communicates the implicit assumption that students will want to know everything they can about American history, not just the particular facts in their textbooks. This helps place the book in context as a means rather than an end in itself.

Teachers do not have to wait until a student asks a question in order to model curiosity and interest in learning. This can be done in many different ways. Interest in reading can be modeled directly when the class goes to the library. Teachers can check out books at this time, too, and follow up later by giving their reactions to them in class. During class discussions, teachers can model curiosity in the way they respond to questions for which they do not have ready answers. They not only should respond warmly to the question itself, but also should follow up by sharing their thinking through verbalizing their thoughts: "I never thought about that before. Why didn't they take the tea home with them? I doubt that they just didn't think about it. That tea was very valuable, and they must have considered stealing it. So they must have decided not to steal it but to throw it in the water instead. How come?" The teacher could continue in this vein or else invite the class to make suggestions at this point.

Curiosity and interest in learning can also be modeled in the information the teacher gives the class about his or her private life. Although an interest in books, newspapers, magazines, and other educational resources can be stimulated through class assignments and projects, it can also be generated, perhaps more effectively and with greater generality, through teacher modeling. When the teacher reads a book, magazine article, or newspaper item of interest, he or she should mention it to the class so they can read it themselves if they wish. Ideally, the teacher should have the item available to pass around so the students can note the reference or borrow the item if they wish to. The teacher should also distribute announcements of coming television programs, museum exhibits, entertainment events, and other special events of educational or cultural value. Here again, a written announcement can help when passed around the class for individual reference.

It is important that references to out-of-school educational and cultural events be made in a way that leaves the decision of whether to attend completely up to the students. There should be no hint that the teacher is pressuring the students to take part or is planning to check up on them later to see if they did. (When *assignments* of the latter sort are made, they should be labeled as such, whether they are required of everyone or are voluntary projects for extra credit. Such assignments are valuable and useful, but they should not be confused with the kinds of totally voluntary activities advocated here.)

The teacher should give many suggestions for totally voluntary activities in addition to whatever projects or assignments are made. This is because it is important to model an interest in learning for what it contributes to one's quality of life (completely free of any connection with school tests or school credit) and to show that the teacher assumes that students also will have this interest. There will usually be a strong temptation after the announced event to check up on the students to see how many participated, but this temptation should be resisted. Comments volunteered by students should be acknowledged and encouraged, but there should be no head count to see who participated and who did not. The teacher can give personal impressions if he or she participated—specific statements about the most intriguing or interesting aspects, not general reports about how worthwhile the whole experience was. If the teacher did not participate, he or she should say so if asked: "Unfortunately, I had to miss it, but I'd like to hear about it."

The teacher can also reinforce curiosity and interest in learning through the asides and comments made in passing during class conversations. Without belaboring the point unnecessarily, the teacher can get across to the class that he or she regularly reads the newspaper ("I read in the paper last night that . . ."), watches the news ("Last night on the six o'clock news they showed . . ."), and participates in other outside educational and cultural pursuits. The students should also be made aware that their teacher thinks carefully about elections and participates in them, keeps abreast of major news developments, and otherwise shows evidence of an active, inquiring mind.

SOCIALIZATION THROUGH MODELING

The previous sections described how teachers can use their role as a model to teach curriculum content and to stimulate thinking and curiosity. These uses of modeling are closely related to the teacher's role as an instructor.

However, teachers also socialize their students through modeling. That is, they shape the values, attitudes, and behavioral standards that their students adopt. Students' ideas about appropriate and inappropriate behavior and about how they should look upon themselves and others are affected by what they see when they observe their teachers.

Research on moral development (reviewed in Hoffman, 1970; Rest, 1983) shows that children progress to successively higher levels of moral knowledge as they grow older. (For related information on moral development and curriculum application, see Brophy & Willis, 1981; Kohlberg, 1980; Lickona, 1976; Mosher, 1980.) Young children tend to have a hedonistic or punishment-avoidance orientation. Their behavior responds more to their own desires and fears of punishment than to an intellectual moral system. By the time they reach elementary school, children have developed moral codes. However, these tend to be in the form of overgeneralized rules acquired from adults—a list of dos and don'ts followed without any real understanding. Some children never really develop much past this stage, so that even as adults, their moral thinking is mostly confined to a set of overgeneralized, rigid rules.

Where conditions for moral development are more favorable, school children gradually develop a higher level of moral knowledge. Rules become less rigid as the child learns to take into account situational factors and to separate motives, intentions, and actions. By adolescence, these rules usually are organized into a coherent, general moral system, so that the student not only can identify the most just or moral way of behaving in a given situation but also can explain the choice by relating it to general principles of morality.

Although the situations producing good inner self-control and a highly developed moral sense are complex and not completely understood, at least two things appear to be important: (1) Children must see ideal behavior patterns modeled by the adults around them, and (2) they must come to see that rules are supported by rationales based on logic and consideration of the general welfare of people (Hoffman, 1977; Perry & Perry, 1983). Rules should not be seen as arbitrary demands to be followed only because they may be enforced by a powerful authority figure.

Teachers are in a good position to foster this development through the thinking and behavior they model in the classroom. They may be the primary influence in this area for many students, since many parents rarely use the child-rearing techniques that foster good moral development (Hess, 1970; Maccoby & Martin, 1983). Students who have been reared by arbitrary and punitive parents who make and enforce but do not explain their demands are likely to remain at an immature stage of moral development unless they are sufficiently exposed to other, more effective, adult models. When another adult does succeed in breaking the child away from a moral code featuring rigid rules and punishment avoidance, that adult is likely to be a teacher.

Some of the major ways teachers can use their positions as models to socialize their students are discussed in the following sections.

Teachers' Credibility With Their Students

Credibility is vital in all human relationships. We tend to like and accept another person if we see that person as honest and reliable. Conversely, we are uncomfortable if we feel that the person does not know what he or she is talking about, does not tell the truth, or fails to keep promises. Only a few instances of these kinds can create mistrust, since most people believe that someone who has lied or otherwise proved to be unreliable in the past will repeat such behavior in the future.

The need for teachers to protect their credibility is even more important when working with young children than with older students or adults. Children tend to take things literally and to see things in a polarized, either-or fashion. They have difficulty making fine distinctions and taking into account extenuating circumstances. Thus, they will take teachers' threats and promises literally, even though these may contain exaggerations or figures of speech that the teacher does not mean literally. Promises or threats that are not followed through tend to be seen as lies or at least as evidence that the teacher does not mean what he or she says. Once children begin to perceive their teacher this way, they will tend not to believe threats or promises until they see them come true. They will also tend to test any teacher rule or control statement (this is discussed at greater length in the following chapter).

Problems in this area can be prevented if the teacher carefully monitors what he or she says to the class. Nothing should be promised or threatened that the teacher does not have every intention of carrying out. When unforeseen circumstances cause a change in plans, the reasons for the change should be fully explained to the class so that the teacher's credibility is maintained.

All teachers can expect problems in this area early in the year. Because of their experience with teachers during the previous year, or because of a history of unfortunate experiences with adults generally, some students automatically will doubt or even discount what a new teacher tells them. They will tend to be skeptical about threats and promises and may interpret teacher behavior as something other than what it is. Praise, for example, may be seen as an attempt by the teacher to "butter them up," or to "con" them out of some ulterior motive. A few may even believe that only a fool would trust a teacher or take what is said at face value.

With these students, teacher credibility must be established, not merely maintained. Teachers not only may have to model appropriately by practicing what they preach, they also may have to call the students' attention to their own credibility. This may mean discussing the subject directly and pointing to the record: "George, you've got to understand that I mean what I say. I'm not playing games or talking just to hear myself talk. Think—have I misled you or made a promise I didn't keep? . . . Well, try to remember that. It's frustrating for me to know that you always think I'm trying to fool you or put something over on you. Maybe other people have let you down in the past, but I'm not them, and you've got to try to remember that. I try to give you and everybody else in the class a square deal, and in return I expect all of you to respect me and trust me. If I ever do anything to let you down, you let me know about it right away so we can straighten it out."

It is sometimes helpful to use the local slang or street language in talking to students, especially adolescents. This should be done, however, only if the teacher knows this language and feels comfortable using it. Students will understand more formal English, even though they might not use it themselves if they were trying to say the same thing. Furthermore, they will be aware that the teacher is struggling to communicate something very important in his or her own way of speaking. All of this helps reinforce the teacher's credibility. If the teacher were to affect the local slang or use it inappropriately, the students probably would pick this up and interpret it as more evidence that the teacher was trying to "con" them. Thus, the degree to which communication is honest and direct is much more important than the particular language in which it is phrased.

Rational Control of Behavior

Another area to be stressed through modeling, especially by teachers working with younger students, is the importance of a rational approach to coping with the world and its problems. Piaget (1983), among others, has shown that young children often assume people's actions to be conscious and deliberate and think that they do things "because they want to." They have difficulty with concepts such as accidents and random events, tending to assume that someone deliberately made them happen. Because they are often treated with authoritarianism by the school and by their parents, they often do not see or understand the reasons behind rules and may ascribe them to the whims of the rule makers. This confusion may persist through adolescence in students raised in authoritarian home backgrounds. Furthermore, almost all adolescents tend to resent and resist rules to some degree, as part of the process of becoming independent and self-regulating.

Thus, teachers at all levels should regularly spell out the rationales underlying their decisions and rules. There will be good reasons for a rule or decision if it is rational in the first place, and these reasons should be explained to the class. This sort of modeling has a double payoff. First, it stimulates the students intellectually, helping them to link causes to their consequences and to see rules as a means of achieving larger goals rather than as goals in their own right. Second, it tends to motivate students, to make them more willing to accept the rule or decision. Like anyone else, students are more willing to accept and internalize rules they can understand.

Teachers cannot assume that students will figure out the rationales underlying rules by themselves. They need to be told. Without such explanation, many students will assume the teacher is acting arbitrarily, perhaps just to flaunt authority or indulge a personal whim. By carefully explaining rationales, teachers can help the class to see rules and decisions as carefully thought-out attempts to solve observable problems. Once the class learns to think this way, they will be capable of establishing their own rules on such matters as how limited resources can be shared fairly and how noise and disruptions can be minimized without undue restrictions on everyone.

For example, consider a third-grade teacher who has just acquired a View-Master for use in the classroom:

TEACHER: Now that you all know how to use the View-Master, I'm going to keep it here in the cabinet where you can get it and use it by yourselves. I think we need to talk about this, though, because there is only one View-Master and I know most of you will want to use it. We need to work out ways to see that everyone gets a chance.

JOHN: Why not let us sign up so we can take it home with us one day at a time?

TEACHER: No, we can't do that, because it has to stay at school. There is too much danger of damage if we let people take it home with them. Also, I'd hoped to develop a plan so that many of you could use it on the same day. If only one of you had it each day, some would have to wait almost a month before getting a chance.

MARY: We could look at it together.

TEACHER: Well, I hadn't thought about that, but I guess you could if it didn't get too noisy. Remember, there will be a group lesson and seatwork going on while the View-Master is being used.

GEORGE: Well, it wouldn't be too noisy if just a few of us used it and if we went back in the corner.

TEACHER: Yes, I agree. I think that would work. But how will we decide who uses it at a given time?

SALLY: The first ones to finish their seatwork should use it.

TEACHER: I don't know about that, Sally. I wouldn't want you all to start racing through your work so you could be first to get at the View-Master. I want you to think about your work and do it carefully without being distracted or trying to work very quickly. Also, I want to make sure that everyone gets a chance.

JOHN: We could just make a list and take turns.

TEACHER: Well, maybe we could make three lists, John. One for each reading group. How about if we divide each reading group into three groups of three or four students each, and then have each group take turns with the View-Master? The first group could use it one day, the second group the next day, and the third group the third day. Then the first group would get its turn again.

MARY: Who decides what pictures to look at?

JOHN: Just take turns, naturally.

CHUCK: Yeah.

TEACHER: Yes, you and the other people in your group could decide on your order. When it's your turn, you would decide what pictures to look at. Does this plan sound good to you then? (*Class agrees.*) Okay, let's see if we've got this straight now. Each reading group will divide up into three groups, with three or four in each group. Every day, one of the three groups will use the View-Master during self-chosen activity time. The group will meet at the small table back in the corner. One person at a time will decide what pictures to look at next. Is that it? (*Class agrees.*) Okay, remember to handle the View-Master carefully. Also, feel free to talk about the pictures, but keep the conversation quiet enough so that it doesn't disturb the rest of the class.

As a footnote to the above example, we might add one additional point: To model rationality successfully, teachers must apply the same standards to themselves as they do to their students. This means being ready to abandon a rule if there is no good reason for it or if the reasons that led to its inception have since disappeared. In our example, it is likely that the rule about using the View-Master would be needed for only a few weeks. By that time, many of the students would no longer be interested in using the View-Master every time their turn came up. At that point, it would make sense to take into account this change in demand and modify the rule. The students should be allowed to work out the new rule themselves within whatever restrictions are needed to maintain classroom order. Teachers who adhere strictly to the rules they have established, even when the students can manage such behavior on their own, miss an important opportunity to allow students to develop enhanced skills for self-management. Rules for using other equipment such as a microcomputer may have to remain in effect longer, but the goal will remain the same—to remove the rule when it is no longer necessary.

Teachers' language and general socialization style can have strong effects on student behavior (Brophy & Rohrkemper, 1981; Rohrkemper, 1985). Rohrkemper (1985) found in one study that students whose teachers use a behavior modification style, in contrast to students whose teachers use a more inductive managerial style, develop sophistication about behavioral action-reaction linkages but not about the motives and intentions that underlie these behaviors. Teachers who emphasize only rules and their consequences are apt to have less desirable effects on students than teachers who also emphasize, model, and explain the reasons for the rules.

Respect for Others

Good teachers model respect for others by treating their students politely and pleasantly and by avoiding behavior that would cause anyone to suffer indignities or "lose face" before a group. Many well-intentioned attempts to help students learn politeness and good manners are undermined by teachers' failures to model the behavior they preach.

Respect for others must be presented effectively in the first place. Guidelines for social behavior should be presented as aspects of the Golden Rule ("Do unto others as you would have them do unto you"), not as rituals to be practiced for their own sake. Teachers should stress that in using politeness and good manners, one shows concern for the feelings of others and respect for their personal dignity. Students will find this more meaningful and will be more willing to cooperate than if they are asked to show good manners merely to please the teacher or to "be nice."

Teachers must then back up their verbal explanations and rationales with appropriate modeling. This often can be difficult, since teachers have responsibility for their classrooms and are continually exerting authority. Because of this, it is easy for them to slip into the habit of giving orders brusquely or of criticizing in nagging, strident tones. This is especially likely with younger students, who are sometimes treated by teachers and other adults as if they have no feelings or cannot understand what is said to or about them. Usually, they do understand, of course, and they feel hurt or resentful when treated badly. This is why it is usually not only appropriate but desirable that teachers treat even the youngest students with the same respectful manner and tone of voice that they use when dealing with another teacher. This holds also for interaction with hall guards, monitors, secretaries, janitors, bus drivers, and other school personnel.

As much as possible, directions should be given in the form of requests rather than orders. The words *please* and *thank you* should be used regularly. Tone and manner are also important. When directions are shouted or delivered in a nagging voice, the teacher's manner tends to distract from the verbal content and may cause anxiety or resentment.

What is said *about* students can be just as beneficial or destructive as what is said *to* them. Many teachers will regularly criticize a student in front of the class or publicly comment about him or her to classroom visitors. For example, on our visits to classrooms, teachers have pointed at specific students while they explained the sordid details of a problem family background, listed the student's typical forms of misbehavior, or stated that they were having the student tested so he or she could be moved to a classroom for the mentally retarded. Sometimes such statements were made loudly in front of the entire class, while at other times the teacher spoke in more hushed tones intended only for our ears. Even in the latter cases, however, the student involved usually heard what was said, as did much of the rest of the class. Naturally, all of the students were watching and listening carefully to what the teacher was telling us. Instead of modeling concern and respect for their students, these teachers were setting themselves up as "the enemy."

For whatever reason, adults will apparently make all sorts of statements when speaking to another adult about children and adolescents that they would never make to the student directly. In an extreme case known to the authors, a teacher who was leaving at midterm introduced her successor to the class by having each student stand in turn while she gave a lengthy description of his or her personal idiosyncrasies. Although such callous disregard for students' feelings is fortunately rare, instances like those mentioned above are commonplace. Apparently, the inhibiting factors that prevent us from treating people callously when we speak directly *to* them do not work as efficiently when we are speaking *about* them, even if they are clearly within earshot. In view of this, the safest policy probably is to avoid discussing individual students at all with visitors to the class. Visitors should be requested to save their questions until the students have gone home or at least are outside the classroom.

When the teacher does choose to speak to classroom visitors during class time, he or she should take advantage of the opportunity to model and reinforce desirable behavior. In describing class activities, for example, care can be taken to stress the skills that students are learning and the progress they are making. This should be done with reference to the class as a whole or to a subgroup within it rather than to an individual singled out for specific attention. The teacher could also take the opportunity to state publicly that he or she holds the class in high regard and is proud of them. Rather than describe to visitors what individuals are doing, the teacher could invite the visitor to question the students themselves. This invitation will reinforce the idea that the teacher has pride and confidence in the students and will avoid putting them in the uncomfortable position of being talked about in a conversation between the teacher and the visitors. If a student is asked to do something or make some sort of presentation for the visitors, he or she should be asked politely rather than directed and should be thanked when finished. The student also should be introduced by name to the visitor.

Comments made about individuals should be restricted to their positive individual traits and their present activities or the goals they are presently working toward ("Richard is a talented artist. He's making a poster for the class bulletin board right now."). Public comparisons with other students should be avoided ("Jane is one of our brightest students."). These are some of the ways teachers can show respect for the dignity and individuality of their students when visitors come to the classroom. Basically, this involves extending to students the same degree of courtesy and respect that would be extended to fellow teachers if the visitors were being taken on a tour of the school instead of just one classroom. Courtesy and respect should be modeled at all times, of course, not just when visitors come.

Fostering a Good Group Climate

Ideally, the group climate in the classroom is one of friendliness and cooperation. Some classes, however, are notable for jealousy, hostility, and unhealthy aggressive competition. When this occurs, the teacher is almost always contributing to the situation both through direct modeling and through teacher behaviors that indirectly foster ill will among the students.

Direct modeling includes sarcasm, vindictiveness, scapegoating, and other overreactions to misbehavior. If students see their teacher regularly react this way to frustrations or annoyances, they are likely to begin to do so themselves. The teacher's behavior will raise frustration levels in the students and, at the same time, will provide them with a model for dealing with it by taking it out on others.

Extreme forms of this classroom climate have been observed by Henry (1957), who speaks of "the witch hunt syndrome." Henry describes classrooms that are notable for destructive and hostile criticism of students by the teacher and by fellow students; for negative competitiveness, in which one student's loss is another's gain; for frequent accusations and attempts to elicit public confessions of wrongdoing; and for evidence of docility and powerlessness in the victims, who tend to accept such treatment rather than rebel against it.

Most of this negative classroom behavior was directly traceable to the behavior of teachers. For example, they would initiate and maintain public witch hunts, in which students would be asked to publicly tattle on or criticize other students. The tattling would be followed by public criticism and punishment of the victim. Group hostility was further developed through practices such as emphasizing destructive criticism in the comments made about students' responses or work and making it clear that similar comments were expected when students were asked to comment about one another's work. One teacher even organized a witch hunt formally by conducting a weekly hearing in which each student's behavior for the week was publicly reviewed and criticized.

There are other less extreme, but more common, teacher behaviors that also promote ill will in a group (see, for example, Carew & Lightfoot, 1979; Good & Brophy, 1986). Foremost among these are playing favorites and rewarding activities (such as tattling) that pit one student against another. Students should be praised and rewarded for their good work, but not in ways that make one student gain at the expense of another (or even make it seem that way). At times, praise of individual students or of parts of the group is useful and appropriate as a means of motivating other students. These comments should be confined to praise, however ("Good job,

Johnny—those transition sentences really tie the theme together."). There should be no blaming of others and no invidious comparisons ("John's desk is nice and clean, but look at the rest of yours. Why can't you be more like him?").

Behavior of this sort will only cause resentment, both against the teacher and against the student being praised. Encouraging students to tell on one another or rewarding them for doing so can have the same effect. So can putting a particular student in charge while the teacher leaves the room, telling him or her to write down the name of anyone who misbehaves. So can passing out papers so that students grade one another's work and then call out the score of the person whose paper they have graded (public reporting focuses too much attention on individuals' grades and invites problems such as ridicule and resentment). In general, anything that places a student in the position of being against a classmate or of profiting from other's problems can cause harm to everyone involved. The class will resent this teacher behavior, and the victim will probably resent the behavior of the other students. The "teacher's pet" is in a bad position also, since this student probably will become isolated from peers.

When a teacher inherits a class that is highly competitive and hostile (usually because the previous teacher acted as described above), he or she should do as much as possible to eliminate these qualities by fostering friendly, cooperative relations. Peer tutoring and group project assignments can help, along with making very clear how much individual integrity and success are valued and how little interest there will be in assessing guilt or punishment. It will also help to verbalize and model individualized standards ("Did I do my best?") and to couple recognition of individual differences with positive expectations ("Some people will take more time to learn this than others, but you will all learn it if you keep at it.").

Showing Interest in the Students

The behavior of many teachers says "don't bother me" to their classes. Sometimes this is communicated directly, as when a teacher greets a student who wants to ask a question by saying, "Now what do you want?" This is especially common with younger students. Teachers often expect these students to have the same social sophistication as adults, including the ability to discriminate between when to approach the teacher and when to wait. Young children are less inhibited than older ones and are less aware of how an adult might react when interrupted while talking or doing paperwork. They are quite sensitive to hostility, however. Unless the teacher is very careful, a message that is intended to say, "Please don't interrupt me now; I'll be with you in a minute," can be perceived as "Don't bother me—go away." Usually, only a few such responses are required before students follow the directions as they see them.

To avoid this undesirable incidental learning, teachers must be emotionally prepared to deal with student questions and concerns as they arise. If there are times when the teacher does not want to be interrupted (such as when conducting small-group lessons), this should be stated clearly and explained to the class. Whenever students do come to the teacher, the teacher should respond with concern and interest. Even if the student must be put off because something more pressing has to be handled immediately, this can be done in a way that reflects such concern. Tone and manner are more important than the exact words used. The teacher should speak in a soft, friendly tone, use the student's name, and include a positive statement about when the problem will be handled, "Not right now, Sally. Come back when reading group is over." This short statement recognizes the student individually, shows concern for her problem, and states a willingness to deal with it at a specific time. Compare this with: "Now now—we don't bother teacher during reading group." This reminds Sally of the rule but does not show concern for her or reassure her that she is welcome to come back later.

A similar type of incidental learning often occurs when students come to the teacher to show their work or creations or to tell something personal. Even if the student is not put off in a negative fashion, he or she often is dismissed quickly with an empty comment such as "Really?" or "How nice." Although these may be meant as positive responses, only the most dependent and attention-starved students will accept them as such. Show-and-tell and similar activities often produce this type of response in teachers who are not really listening to the students or watching what they do. Such teachers will occasionally give themselves away by saying something like "That's nice" after a student has told a sad story. If a student is relating a story or showing and describing an object, the teacher should pay careful attention and ask relevant questions or make relevant comments.

Teachers can respond appropriately in these situations without getting into a long and detailed discussion with the student. A brief response will usually do just as well, provided it is a meaningful statement that is relevant to what the student has said or done. This means, of course, that the teacher must pay attention to what the student is saying or doing in order to respond appropriately. The response, then, should be meaningful and specific. When the student shows an artistic creation, for example, the teacher can ask the student to describe it (or can label it if it is clear what it is) or make some specific comments about it. When the student shows seatwork or homework, the teacher should point out any mistakes and review them with the student or ask the student to try to correct them. If there are no mistakes, the teacher should compliment the student not merely for the paper itself but also for the skill it represents ("That's good work, Jeff. You're really learning how to multiply.").

Even deliberate, well-meant comments by the teacher can sometimes cause unintended negative reactions. Inappropriate praise is probably the most frequent of these. Praise that is delivered in a straightforward, direct manner and is specific to the accomplishment being praised will be perceived as genuine by students and will be valued by them. Other sorts of praise, while well-intended, may have a different reception. One type is the vacuous or empty "That's good" or "How nice," especially when delivered in an insincere or uninterested manner. This is not truly praise, since the teacher has not really paid much attention to what the student has said or done. It is essentially a way of brushing the student off, and it will be perceived this way by most students.

Overdramatized praise is equally undesirable (Brophy, 1981). Students tend to be realistic about their accomplishments, since their peers are their severest critics. They monitor one another's schoolwork and creations, and they know roughly where they stand in each area. Therefore, they will react with healthy skepticism when a teacher sucks in breath and gushes, "Isn't that wonderful!" This praise may be accepted as genuine but perceived as overdone and perhaps embarrassing. Furthermore, consistent praise of this sort usually will cause the teacher one of two kinds of trouble. First, if a minority of the class tends to be favored with such praise, jealousy and hostility will be engendered among the others. A different sort of problem will arise if everyone is praised this way: a demand for it will be created. The students will see overdramatized praise as the way this teacher praises and will no longer be satisfied with ordinary praise. Credibility will be damaged because the students will begin to wonder if the teacher really means what he or she says when saying something without gushing. Respect will be undermined because even kindergarten children know that such behavior is appropriate only for infants, if at all. Thus, while they may view the teacher as warm and loving, they will also tend to see him or her as a comic figure to be laughed at or manipulated rather than respected. Suggestions on how to praise appropriately are given in Chapter 6.

Modeling Good Listening and Communication Habits

The phrase "teacher talk" conjures up in many people an image of long-winded, righteous nagging. The word *lecture* has a similar meaning for some people. These images usually are one result of experience with a teacher who talked *at* students rather than *to* them. Some teachers talk at their students regularly, and too many teachers do so more often than they realize.

Ideally, teachers should use a normal conversational tone in most situations. Their manner in giving explanations or asking questions in class should be the same as it would be if they were in the company of a group of friends. While a little acting is valuable at times, it should not replace teachers' natural style of behavior. They should not have one way of speaking with their students and a different way of speaking with adults, nor should they frequently use either a syrupy or a severe tone. These are phony and even very young children know so.

Questions should be genuine ones, requiring answers, and not merely rhetorical, seeking compliance or agreement. Most questions should require substantive answers, not merely "yes" or "no." Discussions should be true interchanges of knowledge and opinions and not merely monologues in which teachers ask and then answer their own questions. When questions are asked, teachers should wait for students to respond in their own words and not try to put words in their mouths. When students make responses or contribute to a discussion, teachers should model careful listening and hear them out, not cut them off as soon as they mention a key phrase the teacher wanted to hear.

In general, teachers must be good listeners and follow the same rules for polite discussion that they would follow in the company of other adults. If they do not, the students will quickly get the message and will begin to respond to their behavior by trying to figure out what they want and then giving it to them, instead of by listening to and thinking about their questions. The students may also imitate teachers' rudeness by butting in on one another or calling out answers when a classmate pauses to think.

Modeling Emotional Control

One of the major problems facing growing children is achieving an optimal relationship between emotions, feelings, and impulses, on the one hand, and conscience, or beliefs about correct and appropriate behavior, on the other. Infants start with little emotional control, but they acquire it gradually as they develop and learn about parental and societal expectations. When socialization is incomplete or unsuccessful, the result is an immature adult who lacks effective emotional control. Depending on the prominent emotions displayed, he or she may appear happy but overly loud and socially inept, may be very dependent on someone else for reassurance or guidance, may respond to frustration or anxiety by withdrawing or turning to alcohol or drugs, or may act out anger and hostility by attacking other people. These are just a few of the behavior patterns observed in adults who have not learned to express their emotions in mature and socially acceptable ways.

A different type of adult emerges from a socialization pattern that has been too "successful," a pattern that has led the person to reject his or her emotions or to keep them under rigid control. Such people tend to be stern, sober, overcontrolled, and inhibited about their own emotions and feelings.

The optimum is somewhere between these two extremes of emotional immaturity and emotional overcontrol. To the extent that problems exist in a given individual, they are likely to be mostly in one direction or the other. Teachers and other educated people generally are more likely to have problems with overcontrol of their emotions. Young children and many older students, especially those who come from disadvantaged areas, often have poor emotional control. This in itself can cause problems, especially if an overcontrolled teacher is teaching in a lower-class school.

To the extent that teachers are comfortable and in control of their emotions, they can be valuable models to students. This is especially true in regard to negative emotions, such as anger, hostility, fear, or frustration. By showing or reporting these emotions, the teacher helps to communicate that they are normal and understandable. This will be reassuring to some students, who may feel compelled to try to deny or repress their own, similar emotions because they think they are dishonorable or seriously abnormal. Because of the way they have been reared, these students have difficulty distinguishing between the feeling or experience of emotion and the way it is expressed in behavior. For example, instead of realizing that anger and aggression are normal emotions that must be controlled and expressed in acceptable ways, they may feel that they are never justified in becoming angry or that aggressive feelings must be repressed or denied. Fear is another emotion that is often denied. Many boys especially feel ashamed to admit that they are afraid, because they see fear as something unacceptable rather than as a normal reaction to be controlled and overcome.

Teachers can help break down tendencies to deny natural emotional reactions by freely discussing their own feelings and by taking advantage of opportunities to point out that unpleasant emotions are normal in some situations. Discussions of history and current events, for example, provide many such opportunities. By discussing the feelings of Columbus and his sailors or, better yet, by role-playing these individuals, students can learn much about experiencing and dealing with strong negative emotions. If these reactions do not come out spontaneously, the teacher can point out that such emotions were natural and understandable under the circumstances.

This same thing can be done more directly in discussions about appropriate and inappropriate social behavior. This is especially valuable for junior high and high school students, who tend to develop inhibitions and fears about social acceptability by their peers. Fear of ridicule before a group becomes very strong at these ages, and students often inhibit impulses or actions or decline to ask questions because they are afraid of being laughed at. They will take pains to cover up inhibitions and areas of ignorance rather than admit to them. This can lead to what Sullivan (1953) has called "delusions of uniqueness," in which the students come to believe that they may be the only one of their peers who has the fears, doubts, or inhibitions that they have.

Role-Playing Techniques

Teachers can be a big help in such cases by discussing and role-playing some of the situations their students deal with in the peer group every day: reacting to half-serious jokes and jibes about personal appearance or habits, dealing with conflicts between what the group is urging and what conscience dictates, responding to flirtations from the opposite sex, fear of losing face before the group, and so forth. These activities will help bring the fears and self-doubts in these situations out in the open and will help students see that they are not alone in having such experiences.

To set up this kind of role-playing exercise, the teacher should define each role in a hypothetical situation and briefly sketch the interactions that are to take place. Then the teacher should assign a student to each role, perhaps also taking a role personally. Role-playing exercises like the one that follows, if done appropriately, can help students to learn about emotional reactions.

> TEACHER: Janice and Matt, let's role-play a situation where one of the guys gives you a bad time. Pretend we're part of a big group at a pizza place. Matt, you're a guy who's interested in Janice and trying to make conversation with her to get to know her better. I'll be a friend of yours who keeps butting in with smart remarks. Janice, you pretend that we're two guys that you know well enough to say hello to, but that's all.

Leyser (1982) provides excellent guidelines for implementing role-playing in the classroom. Building on the work of Stanford (1974), Leyser notes that there are six major problems that teachers have to overcome when they use role-playing in the classroom: (1) students who are not well acquainted and comfortable with one another, (2) students' inhibitions and self-conciousness, (3) students' lack of necessary skills, (4) students not properly prepared for role-playing activities, (5) teachers' passivity, and (6) students' tendency to expect role-playing to be entertaining rather than a serious learning endeavor.

According to Leyser, role-playing seems to work best when sessions are carefully planned and the classroom teacher carefully follows a sequence of steps. In general, Leyser recommends that teachers include seven steps when they use role-playing techniques. The first step is the warm-up activity. This step recognizes that students have not had many opportunities to perform in front of other students and that it is important for the teacher to have ice-breakers that are relatively easy on students, such as simple exchanges of information: How do you feel when you watch someone else being put down? How do you feel in the classroom when you can't answer a teacher's question? Why is it that some people don't like ice cream?

A variety of suggestions for warm-up activities are presented in Roark and Stanford (1975).

The second step involves selection and presentation of the problem. The problem could be role-played or enacted if selected and presented. Situations for role-playing may include real-life problems, such as incidents of physical agression or unfinished problem stories that are written especially for role-playing activities (see, for example, Dinkmeyer, 1973; Shaftel & Shaftel, 1967).

In the third step recommended by Leyser, the teacher explains the physical situation and selects the location in the classroom as well as the needed props. For example, a desk and four chairs might be placed in front of the classroom with the comment, "Here is the principal's office and here are three students who are petitioning to delay the basketball season until the soccer season has ended."

The fourth step involves choosing actors and explaining their roles. Leyser recommends that students not be forced to participate and that the teacher ask for volunteers. After students have been exposed to role-playing activities in the classroom, the teacher can gradually include more and more students in these activities. However, when role-playing activities are first introduced, it is important to involve students gradually in these activities, especially if teachers in preceeding grades have not used role-playing techniques. After recruiting students for the role-playing activity, the teacher may give a few general guidelines about the roles students are expected to enact. For example, one might point out that students should not use physical agression, should not threaten the principal, and might even urge students to develop a few specific reasons about why delaying basketball until after the soccer season would be beneficial not only for students involved but also for others (including parents, teachers, and other students at the school).

The fifth step involves explaining the role to the audience. If students are to learn from role-playing, they need to listen carefully so they can participate in the discussion and analysis that follow. Members of the audience need to know specifically what notes they should take and the criteria that they should apply as they consider the activity that is presented. Some of the students, for example, may listen to the plausibility of the arguments; other students may serve as consultants and provide suggestions that the actors can utilize the next time they present the role. The audience's most important task is not to critique the skill and precision with which roles are enacted, but to provide realistic feedback about how a principal or another adult listening to the presentation might react.

The sixth step is the actual enactment of the role playing. This is the performance or presentation stage. Some student actors may be inhibited, especially the first time these activities are presented. Teachers' help in the form of a demonstration or guiding questions might be useful before the first performance. The teacher could carefully organize and practice (as one would with a school play) the first one or two role plays. However, more emphasis should subsequently be placed on changing information because the value of the role-playing activity is not in presenting a careful, well-delivered drama but simply in getting students to talk and to share strategies about topics that they may find difficult to discuss.

In terms of specific enactment strategies, Leyser recommends:

1. *Role reversal.* Role players exchange roles to get a better understanding of the other point of view.

2. *Multiple enactments.* The scene is enacted again with different players.
3. *The consultant.* Group members are assigned as consultants to an actor, helping him/her to improve the role either before the first presentation or afterwards.
4. *Multiple role players.* Two students play a character and together help each other in the enactment and in working out the solution.

Step seven is the discussion stage and is the heart of the role-playing activity. During this step, class members who serve as the audience are expected to discuss the feelings, needs, thoughts, and behaviors of the characters or actors and to speculate on alternative behaviors and solutions to the problem. The discussion can take one of several formats: large groups, small groups, or even pairs of students.

After students have developed some capacity for role-playing techniques, the activities can be used from time to time to help students understand various subjects; for example, in understanding how laws enacted by the British Parliament and sponsored by the King might have been viewed by British citizens versus Americans. Similarly, when a school problem arises it may be helpful to use role-playing techniques to enable students to identify the problem, understand their feelings associated with the problem, and develop realistic strategies for responding to the problem. For example, the teacher might provide students the opportunity to develop techniques for responding to aggression that audiences at school sporting events express: "Assume that you have been shoved during half-time at a basketball game by someone who is considerably bigger than you are and someone who you suspect might physically abuse you. After the person shoves you he says, 'Want to do anything about this? Are you too scared to do anything about it?' How might you respond to this problem?"

Used occasionally to portray sensitive topics, role-playing techniques may help students to develop insights into human behavior and to expand their repertoires for dealing with various feelings and emotions they experience in school. Teachers who plan these activities well and help students to play roles successfully can enable students to deal better with real problems in their daily lives. By leading discussions about how people feel in situations that are role-played and about how the participants could or should react, teachers can help students develop insight into their emotions and confidence in their abilities to cope with stressful situations.

Teachers need to show that emotions are not only acceptable but also controllable. This can be modeled directly, for example, in situations where the teacher has become angry: "Look, I've had about as much of this as I can take. I've tried to be patient and give you time to straighten yourself out, but you've kept bugging me for several days now and I'm starting to get angry. If you don't cut it out and begin to treat me with more respect, I'm going to be forced to resort to punishment. I don't want to do this, but you're not leaving me much choice." In this example, the teacher communicates anger, but in a nondestructive and controlled way.

Anger and misunderstandings between students can be dealt with by encouraging the students to verbalize their anger and the reasons for it rather than to express it physically. The technique of role reversal (Johnson, 1970) is especially useful here. Each student involved can be asked to take the role of the other student as a means of helping him or her to see the other students' point of view ("Now if you were George, how would you feel after everybody laughed?"). This promotes better understanding of the situation and gives the students practice at verbalizing and controlling hostility instead of expressing it directly. Suggestions for handling disputes between students are given in greater detail in Chapter 7.

Teachers must be comfortable with their own emotions if they are to discuss certain taboo subjects productively. Many students never ask the questions they would like to ask about sex or drugs, for example, because they know their teachers cannot tolerate objective discussions of these matters. Discussion is closed off because the teacher has made it clear that no decent person would even consider masturbation, fornication, or pornography and that anybody who uses drugs is a dope fiend. Other teachers inhibit discussion by overreacting to what they consider to be obscene language. In these classes, students can ask what they want only if they are capable of using terms such as "penis," "vagina," or "copulation." If they know only the slang or street language substitutes for these words, and if they know that the teacher will not allow use of this terminology, they will not ask their questions.

Teachers should try to evaluate objectively their own emotional tolerance in taboo areas. If they can handle discussions in these areas without becoming flustered or upset, they can be a valuable resource to their students. If they cannot, it is probably better to avoid getting into such discussions, since it is not likely that flustered teachers will do much good, and they may well spread some of their inhibitions to their students.

If it is possible to do so without penalty, teachers should also avoid situations in which they try to inculcate values or standards that they do not believe or accept themselves. Teachers are often put in this position when asked to implement a school's sex or drug "education" program, when the program is more propaganda than education. Generally, it is better for teachers to leave out those parts of the program that they cannot accept or to ask the principal to provide a substitute who can argue for them convincingly (if the principal or school board absolutely insists that these ideas be presented). If the teacher does try to present the ideas, the students will almost certainly detect that he or she does not believe them, and the teacher's credibility will be damaged.

Observers may notice teachers communicating negative emotions without realizing they are doing so. Noticeable anxiety may appear, for example, when the principal or some visitor enters the room or when a particular child acts up. Disgust may be registered by shrinking away from physical contact with a student or by a horrified expression following mention of a taboo subject.

Observers can be of help to teachers by calling their attention to such evidence of negative emotion. This must be done with caution, however, because the teachers' behavior is a conditioned reaction that may be very difficult for them to change or even discuss. Fear or rejection of specific individuals can usually be dealt with effectively by calling the teacher's attention to it, discussing the problem, and suggesting some remedial steps. Changing the teacher's behavior in relation to taboo topics can sometimes be more difficult, however, since this behavior may be connected with a larger pattern of inhibition or neurosis. When this is true, the teacher may strongly resist getting into a discussion of his or her feelings on the subject. Even here, though, some discussion of how the teacher should behave in these situations in the future should be carried out. This is because certain students will be fascinated or amused by the teacher's negative reaction and may regularly do things calculated to produce it. At the same time, other students pick up the teacher's unhealthy negative emotions about the subject through imitation of the teacher as a model. Thus, some remedial plan of action is needed to prevent things from getting worse.

SUMMARY

In this chapter, we have pointed out that students learn from their teachers simply by observing them. Two types of observational learning that result from exposure to a teacher model were described: (1) imitation, in which the students copy what their teachers say or do; and (2) incidental learning, in which students observe what teachers say and do and then use this information to make inferences about teachers' beliefs, attitudes, values, and personal qualities.

When students like and respect their teachers, they imitate them in order to be more like them and to earn their respect and affection. If the students do not like or do not respect their teachers, they are less likely to imitate them, although they will develop a picture (mostly negative) of teachers' personalities by observing them.

Unfortunately, students may imitate rejecting and punitive teachers if they fear their wrath. This is not the positive kind of imitation that liked and respected teachers induce; it is a frantic attempt to "get on the teacher's good side" and escape or minimize punishment. The students, at least at first, imitate such teachers' behavior not because they think it is good or effective but because they think the teachers will reward them if they do or will punish them if they do not. However, if bad habits originally learned this way become well established, they can persist long after the students escape the teachers who caused them in the first place.

Students may learn from observing their teachers model at any time, since all that is necessary for such learning to occur is the chance to observe the model. Teachers cannot choose to model at some times and not others; they cannot turn the process on or off at will. However, by learning to monitor their behavior more closely and to consciously and systematically model when opportunities arise, teachers can use modeling as a teaching tool and can help insure that most of what their students learn from observing them is beneficial.

The most obvious use of deliberate modeling is in a lecture or demonstration. By learning to give clear and effective demonstrations, teachers can minimize their students' learning problems as well as the time they need to spend repeating and reteaching.

There are other ways, however, for teachers to educate through deliberate modeling. Thinking and problem-solving skills can be taught this way if teachers share their thinking by verbalizing aloud each step involved in the process of solving a problem. This modeling should illustrate not only the logic and actions involved but also the use of such good scientific practices as thinking about alternatives before responding and checking each step in a long process before going on to the next.

Intellectual curiosity and the valuing of learning can be modeled through comments and behavior that show that teachers are interested in the subject matter and not just in covering the textbook; that they value and will help find answers to students' questions; and that they read, keep abreast of current events, and have intellectual interests outside the school setting.

Teachers not only educate (in a more narrow sense) through modeling, they also socialize their students by modeling attitudes and values about behavior. Teachers who model rationality, emotional maturity, politeness and good manners, and personal respect in their classroom behavior tend to induce these qualities in students. In contrast, hostile, sarcastic, or critical teachers produce a class atmosphere marked by these undesirable qualities.

In general, teachers have little hope of inducing positive qualities in students if they do not model them. Students rightfully become cynical and resentful when they see a double standard of behavior (one for the teacher, another for them) or when they see a clear discrepancy between what the teacher says and does. A basic factor determining where a teacher stands with students is the teacher's personal credibility, a quality that often is hard-won and easily lost.

Remember, if you want to command positive respect (not fear) from students, you must model the behaviors and attitudes you espouse. Students looking for a model who embodies the qualities their teacher holds as ideals should find that model in the teacher.

SUGGESTED ACTIVITIES AND QUESTIONS

5.1 Assume that you are a teacher beginning a new year with a group of students. Outline the points that you plan to make in order to convey your interest in the students.

5.2 Define the situation you plan to teach in (subject content, type of student, grade level, etc.) and role-play Activity 5.1 with classmates or other teachers. Seek feedback from observers concerning how sincere they felt you were and how interested they were in what you had to say.

5.3 Use the observation forms (Forms 5.1–5.8) at the end of the chapter to observe the modeling behavior of real teachers or apply them to videotapes. Identify positive and negative instances of teacher modeling and attempt to pinpoint any incidental learning that may be taking place. If films are not available, read the narrative that appears at the end of Chapter 1 and the case studies in the Appendix at the end of the text and list positive and negative instances of modeling. Compare your list with those that others make.   5.1–5.8

5.4 Why does the cooperating teacher often exert a powerful influence on the student teacher's classroom style?

5.5 In the example at the beginning of the chapter, Janice Taylor was student teaching in a school that was composed of students who came from homes that were similar (same socioeconomic level, etc.) to Janice's. To be a good model, should a teacher necessarily have the same socioeconomic background or be of the same race as his or her pupils? What are possible advantages or disadvantages in matching teachers and students this way? Should students be exposed to teachers who have personalities similar to theirs, or will they learn more by being with teachers whose personalities differ markedly?

5.6 Why is it relatively useless to tell people to "Do as I say, not as I do"?

5.7 Why are the most powerful effects of modeling likely to occur at the beginning of the year?

5.8 Describe in your own words the steps that are included in effective demonstrations.

5.9 How can a teacher model curiosity and interest in learning?

5.10 Explain the following statement: "What is said *about* students can be just as destructive as what is said *to* them."

5.11 Why do the authors suggest that when students make errors, the teacher must do more than give them the correct answers?

5.12 In what ways can you as a teacher become more credible to your students? Be explicit.

5.13 Explain in your own words how you can help your students to learn that emotions are acceptable and controllable.

REFERENCES

Bandura, A. (1969). *Principles of behavior modification*. New York: Holt, Rinehart and Winston.

Bandura, A. (1977). *Social learning theory*. Englewood Cliffs, NJ: Prentice-Hall.

Brophy, J. (1981). Teacher praise: A functional analysis. *Review of Educational Research, 51*, 5–32.

Brophy, J., & Rohrkemper, M. (1981). The influence of problem ownership on teachers' perceptions of and strategies for coping with problem students. *Journal of Educational Psychology, 73*, 295–311.

Brophy, J., & Willis, S. (1981). *Human development and behavior*. New York: St. Martin's Press.

Bryan, J., & Walbek, N. (1970). Preaching and practicing generosity: Children's actions and reactions. *Child Development, 41*, 329–353.

Carew, J., & Lightfoot, S. (1979). *Beyond bias*. Cambridge, MA: Harvard University Press.

Dinkmeyer, D. (1973). *Developing understanding of self and others*. Manual, DUSO D-2. Circle Pines, MN: American Guidance Service.

Doyle, W. (1986). Classroom organization and management. In M. Wittrock (Ed.), *Handbook of research on teaching* (3rd ed.). New York: Macmillan.

Emmer, E., Evertson, C., & Anderson, L. (1980). Effective classroom management at the beginning of the school year. *Elementary School Journal, 80*, 219–231.

Fanelli, G. (1977). Locus of control. In S. Ball (Ed.), *Motivation in education*. New York: Academic Press.

Flavell, J., Botkin, P., Fry, C., Wright, J., & Jarvis, P. (1968). *The development of role-taking and communication skills in children*. New York: Wiley.

Good, T., & Brophy, J. (1986). *Educational psychology: A realistic approach* (3rd ed.). White Plains, NY: Longman.

Good, T., Grouws, D., & Ebmeier, H. (1983). *Active mathematics teaching: Empirical research in elementary and secondary classrooms*. New York: Longman.

Henry, J. (1957). Attitude organization in elementary school classrooms. *American Journal of Orthopsychiatry, 27*, 117–133.

Hess, R. (1970). Social class and ethnic influences on socialization. In P. Mussen (Ed.), *Carmichael's manual of child psychology* (3rd ed., Vol. 2). New York: Wiley.

Hess, R., Shipman, V., Brophy, J., & Bear, R. (1971). Mother-child interaction. In I. Gordon (Ed.), *Readings in research in developmental psychology*. Glenview, IL: Scott, Foresman.

Hoffman, M. (1970). Moral development. In P. Mussen (Ed.), *Carmichael's manual of child psychology* (3rd ed., Vol. 2). New York: Wiley.

Hoffman, M. (1977). Moral internalization: Current theory and research. In L. Berkowitz (Ed.), *Advances in experimental social psychology* (Vol. 10). New York: Academic Press.

Johnson, D. (1970). *The social psychology of education*. New York: Holt, Rinehart and Winston.

Kohlberg, L. (1980). Moral education: A response to Thomas Sobol. *Educational Leadership, 38*, 19–23.

Leyser, Y. (1982). Role playing in the classroom: A threat or a promise? *Contemporary Education, 53*, 70–74.

Lickona, T. (Ed.). (1976). *Moral development and behavior: Theory, research, and social issues*. New York: Holt, Rinehart and Winston.

Maccoby, E., & Martin, J. (1983). Socialization in the context of the family: Parent-child interaction. In P. Mussen (Ed.), *Handbook of child psychology* (4th ed., Vol. IV). New York: Wiley.

Mosher, R. (Ed.). (1980). *Moral education: A first generation of research*. New York: Praeger.

Perrott, E. (1982). *Effective teaching: A practical guide to improving your teaching*. New York: Longman.

Perry, D., & Perry, L. (1983). Social learning, causal attribution, and moral internalization. In J. Bisanz, G. Bisanz, & R. Kail (Eds.), *Learning in children: Progress in cognitive development research*. New York: Springer-Verlag.

Piaget, J. (1983). Piaget's theory. In P. Mussen (Ed.), *Handbook of child psychology* (4th ed., Vol. I). New York: Wiley.

Rest, J. (1983). Morality. In P. Mussen (Ed.), *Handbook of child psychology* (4th ed., Vol. III). New York: Wiley.

Roark, A., & Stanford, G. (1975). Role playing and action methods in the classroom. *Group Psychotherapy, Psychodrama and Sociometry, 28*, 33–49.

Rohrkemper, M. (1985). The influence of teacher socialization style on students' social cognitions and reported interpersonal classroom behavior. *Elementary School Journal, 85*, 245–275.

Rotter, J. (1966). Generalized expectancies for internal versus external control of reinforcement. *Psychological Monographs, 80,* 1–28.

Schachter, S. (1964). The interaction of cognitive and physiological determinants of emotional state. In L. Berkowitz (Ed.), *Advances in experimental social psychology* (Vol. 1). New York: Academic Press.

Shaftel, F., & Shaftel, G. (1967). *Role playing for social values*. Englewood Cliffs, NJ: Prentice-Hall.

Stanford, G. (1974). Why role playing fails. *English Journal, 63*, 50–54.

Sullivan, H. (1953). *The interpersonal theory of psychiatry*. New York: Norton.

FORM 5.1. Getting Help from Students

USE: *When teacher requests a student to run an errand or perform a duty*
PURPOSE: *To see if teacher models politeness and respect for students*
    For each codable instance, code whether or not the teacher shows each of the four behaviors.

BEHAVIOR CATEGORIES

CODES

	1		2		3		4	
	YES	NO	YES	NO	YES	NO	YES	NO

1. Calls student by name
2. Asks rather than tells. Uses interrogative rather than imperative language form
3. Says "please"
4. Says "thank you"

	1	YES	NO	YES	NO	YES	NO	YES	NO
1.		✓	—	✓	—	—	✓	✓	—
2.		✓	—	✓	—	—	✓	✓	—
3.		✓	—	✓	—	—	✓	—	✓
4.		✓	—	✓	—	—	✓	✓	—
5.		—	✓	✓	—	—	✓	—	✓
6.		✓	—	✓	—	—	✓	✓	—
7.		✓	—	✓	—	—	✓	✓	—
8.		—	—	—	—	—	—	—	—
9.		—	—	—	—	—	—	—	—
10.		—	—	—	—	—	—	—	—
11.		—	—	—	—	—	—	—	—
12.		—	—	—	—	—	—	—	—
13.		—	—	—	—	—	—	—	—
14.		—	—	—	—	—	—	—	—
15.		—	—	—	—	—	—	—	—
16.		—	—	—	—	—	—	—	—
17.		—	—	—	—	—	—	—	—
18.		—	—	—	—	—	—	—	—
19.		—	—	—	—	—	—	—	—
20.		—	—	—	—	—	—	—	—
21.		—	—	—	—	—	—	—	—
22.		—	—	—	—	—	—	—	—
23.		—	—	—	—	—	—	—	—
24.		—	—	—	—	—	—	—	—
25.		—	—	—	—	—	—	—	—

NOTES:

Doesn't say "please" but asks in polite manner.

Students appear eager to help her.

FORM 5.2. Teacher's Response to Students' Questions

USE: When a student asks the teacher a reasonable question during a discussion or question-answer period
PURPOSE: To see if teacher models commitment to learning and concern for students' interests
Code each category that applies to the teacher's response to a reasonable student question. Do not code if student wasn't really asking a question or if he or she was baiting the teacher.

BEHAVIOR CATEGORIES
1. Compliments the question ("Good question")
2. Criticizes the question (unjustly) as irrelevant, dumb, out of place, etc.
3. Ignores the question, or brushes it aside quickly without answering it
4. Answers the question or redirects it to the class
5. If no one can answer, teacher arranges to get the answer or assigns a student to do so
6. If no one can answer, teacher leaves it unanswered and moves on
7. Other (specify)

NOTES:

#7 Explained that question would be covered in tomorrow's lesson.

CODES

1.	4	26.	
2.	4	27.	
3.	1,4	28.	
4.	4	29.	
5.	4	30.	
6.	3	31.	
7.	4	32.	
8.	4	33.	
9.	7	34.	
10.	4	35.	
11.	4	36.	
12.		37.	
13.		38.	
14.		39.	
15.		40.	
16.		41.	
17.		42.	
18.		43.	
19.		44.	
20.		45.	
21.		46.	
22.		47.	
23.		48.	
24.		49.	
25.		50.	

FORM 5.3. Teacher's Response to Unexpected Answers

USE: *When a student answers the teacher's question in a way that is reason-*
able but unexpected
PURPOSE: *To see if teacher models respect for good thinking when a ques-*
tion doesn't lead to the expected response
For each codable instance, code each applicable behavior category
shown by the teacher in reacting to a reasonable but unexpected answer.

BEHAVIOR CATEGORIES	CODES	
1. Compliments ("Why, that's right! I hadn't thought of that!")	1. _3_	26. __
2. Acknowledges that the answer is correct or partially correct	2. _4_	27. __
	3. _3_	28. __
3. Gives vague or ambiguous feedback ("I guess you *could* say that...")	4. _3_	29. __
	5. _4_	30. __
4. Responds as if the answer were simply incorrect	6. _3_	31. __
5. Criticizes the answer as irrelevant, dumb, out of place, etc.	7. _3_	32. __
	8. _3_	33. __
6. Other (specify)	9. _4_	34. __
	10. _3_	35. __

NOTES:

Tends to respond minimally – looking
ahead to the expected answer. Teacher
actually reading Teacher's Manual a
couple of times while children are
responding.

11. _4_	36. __
12. _4_	37. __
13. _3_	38. __
14. __	39. __
15. __	40. __
16. __	41. __
17. __	42. __
18. __	43. __
19. __	44. __
20. __	45. __
21. __	46. __
22. __	47. __
23. __	48. __
24. __	49. __
25. __	50. __

FORM 5.4. Personal Relationships with Students

USE: *When teacher has been observed frequently enough so that reliable in-*
     formation is available
PURPOSE: *To see if teacher models an interest in individual students*
         Note any information relevant to the following questions:

1. Do students seek out this teacher for personal contact? Do they show
   things, make small talk, seek advice? *No. They usually come to him
   only when they need something (permission, help, supplies).*

2. Does the teacher actively seek out individual students for informal personal
   contacts or must they come to the teacher? *No informal contacts
   observed.*

3. Is the teacher accessible to students before, during, and after school hours?
   Yes but see #1

4. When students tell the teacher things, does he or she listen carefully and
   ask questions, or respond minimally and cut short the conversation? *He often
   responds curtly or cuts short the conversation by giving a direction.*

5. When the teacher questions students in informal contacts, does he or she
   ask open-ended questions seeking their opinions, or leading or rhetorical
   questions that elicit only cliché responses or compliance?
   No informal questions observed.

6. How does the teacher react when students mention taboo topics? Does he
   or she tolerate discussion or quickly close it off? *Not observed.*

7. In general, does the teacher talk *to* students, or *at* them? Does he or she
   use a natural voice, or a special "teacher tone"?

   *Teacher is cold, standoffish. Students avoid him. He is
   "strictly business" in dealing with them. Much
   "teacher talk."*

FORM 5.5. Overemphasis on Misbehavior

USE: *When teacher has been observed frequently enough so that reliable information can be coded*
PURPOSE: *To see if teacher is fostering undesirable incidental learning about how he or she expects students to behave*
Check any of the following observations that are evident in this teacher's class :

_____   1. Students not allowed to use resource or reference books because they might harm them.

_____   2. Audiovisual self-teaching devices cannot be used without teacher supervision because students might harm the devices otherwise.

_____   3. Students must spend at least a specified minimum time on seatwork, because they won't do neat work if allowed to do something else when they finish early.

___√___   4. Students never allowed to correct their own tests.

_____   5. When teacher leaves room, a student is assigned to take down names of anyone who misbehaves.

___√___   6. Teacher dwells too much on cheating and takes elaborate precautions to prevent it.

_____   7. Teacher spies on students, searches for forbidden objects, etc.

Note any other observations concerning rigid rules and restrictions or other overemphasis on misbehavior.

Allows no talking during seatwork (because students might " cheat") During a short quiz, the teacher told students, " Move your desks apart so you won't be tempted to cheat."

FORM 5.6. Group Climate

USE: *When teacher has been observed frequently enough so that reliable information can be coded*
PURPOSE: *To see if teacher models respect for individuals and avoids practices that foster destructive group climates*
  Check any behavior categories that apply to this teacher's classroom behavior.

BEHAVIOR CATEGORIES

POSITIVE

✓ 1. Makes a point of forbidding ridicule or hostile criticism; insists on respect for others
___ 2. Uses peer tutoring, team learning, or other methods involving cooperation among students
___ 3. Speaks well of class to visitors
✓ 4. Publicly acknowledges and praises prosocial behavior (sharing, helping others, showing sympathy and good will)
✓ 5. Other (specify) *Frequently uses subtle means of promoting good atmosphere (speaks of "sharing" answers and ideas," "helping" others solve problems, "working together" on projects, etc.)*

NEGATIVE

___ 1. Encourages or rewards tattling
___ 2. Publicly compares students or groups, causing embarrassment to one or both
___ 3. Encourages or rewards destructive, hostile criticism of fellow students
___ 4. Uses types of competitive practices that allow some students to gain at others' expense
___ 5. Punishes boys by making them stay with girls (and vice versa)
___ 6. Allows students to call out answers or insulting remarks when someone can't respond
✓ 7. Has "pets" that get preferential treatment (rewards, privileges, helper roles, etc.)
___ 8. Picks on certain students, or uses them as scapegoats
___ 9. Other (specify) *While generally positive, tends to hold up students #6 and #10 as examples to others.*

FORM 5.7. Positive Modeling

USE: *When teacher has been observed frequently enough so that reliable information can be coded*
PURPOSE: *To see if teacher takes advantage of opportunities to teach through deliberate modeling*
Record any information relevant to the following questions:

MODELING THINKING
When the teacher must solve a problem or think through a question, does he or she think out loud? Does the teacher allow students to hear the steps he or she goes through, or explain them after giving the answer?

Does this well when reviewing seat work and homework, but often doesn't explain rationale when she answers students questions during discussion.

Does the teacher include activities that allow students to practice thinking and problem solving (20 questions, brain teasers, solving hypothetical problems)?

Uses drill-like games and contests but none that promotes thinking and problem solving

MODELING COMMITMENT TO LEARNING
Does the teacher give evidence of a continuing active interest in learning (discuss newspaper or magazine articles, books, TV programs, special events, educational activities of teacher)? *Only in response to a question or comment from class.*

FORM 5.8. The Teacher's Credibility

USE: When teacher has been observed frequently enough so that reliable information can be coded
PURPOSE: To see if teacher's behavior undermines his or her credibility with students
Below is a list of teacher behaviors that tend to undermine the teacher's credibility with students. Check those behaviors that are observable in this teacher.

_____ 1. Teacher is gushy, overdramatic, unconvincingly "warm."

✓ 2. Teacher's praise is unconvincing because he or she continually uses a stock phrase or fails to specify what is being praised.

_____ 3. Teacher insists on "nice" or "acceptable" motives and thoughts, or tends to deny or explain away taboo problems rather than deal with them.

_____ 4. Teacher will resort to obviously false or exaggerated "reasons" in defending rules, decisions, or opinions, rather than admit mistakes.

_____ 5. Teacher promises when still uncertain whether he or she can deliver or fails to follow through on announced intentions.

_____ 6. When students express fears or suspicions, teacher responds with vague or unconvincing reassurances rather than investigations or detailed explanations.

_____ 7. Teacher cannot tolerate differences of opinion on matters of taste or values; tends to foist his or her own values on the students.

_____ 8. Teacher will not admit areas of ignorance or acknowledge mistakes.

_____ 9. Teacher tends to talk down to students, sermonize, or repeatedly harp on pet topics or gripes, to the extent that students are alienated or amused.

✓ 10. Teacher clearly favors or picks on certain students.

_____ 11. Students have learned that they can get teacher to change rules, decisions, or assignments by badgering or complaining.

_____ 12. Teacher's assumptions about students' home backgrounds, values, interests, or life styles are grossly inaccurate.

_____ 13. Teacher brushes aside questions on complex or touchy issues by repeating platitudes or oversimplified "reasons" or "solutions."

✓ 14. Teacher sometimes appears not to believe what he or she is saying (specify).

_____ 15. Other (specify)

NOTES:

Overuses, "Very good, John."

6 Management I: Preventing Problems

Classroom management is of major concern to almost everyone connected with education (Doyle, 1986). New teachers often fear that their students will not respect them. Even experienced teachers usually say that classroom management is a major goal in the first few weeks of the year. Principals give low ratings to teachers who cannot control their classes. Indeed, even students expect teachers to provide leadership, discipline, and to manage classrooms effectively. Nash (1976) found six main themes in elementary students' attitudes and expectations concerning teachers: (1) keeping order (strict rather than lenient; punishes if necessary); (2) teaching (keeps you busy); (3) explaining (can be understood, gives help if you need it); (4) interesting (provides variety, not boring); (5) treating fairly (consistent, does not play favorites or pick on anyone); and (6) acting friendly (kind or nice, talks gently rather than shouts, can laugh when appropriate).

To manage classrooms effectively, teachers need both clear expectations about how students should spend their time and knowledge about what to do when their expectations are not being met. Expectations define classroom management goals and guide decisions about creating, maintaining, and restoring desirable student behavior. Teachers who have clear expectations about what their students should be doing can organize the classroom and plan activities accordingly, articulate these expectations clearly to students, and recognize when discrepancies between expectations and actual student behavior are unacceptably large. Such discrepancies indicate a need for action, at which point the teacher must call on knowledge of general principles of classroom management and of the needs and characteristics of the particular students involved to decide what to do.

Taken together, teachers' expectations about appropriate student activities and behavior can be called the *student role*. Elements that make up the student role include: (1) mastery of basic skills; (2) development of interest in and knowledge about the topics included in the formal curriculum; and (3) participation, usually as a member of a group, in extracurricular activities. Extracurricular activities like assemblies or fire drills are considered necessary for efficient institutional functioning. Most, however, are designed either to support the program of instruction (e.g., field trips or music programs) or to develop qualities believed important for all citizens (e.g., physical education and the pledge of allegiance).

As Jackson (1968) and Doyle (1986) note, the following factors are identified with the student role: regimentation of activity, restriction of movement, and subordination of individual desires to the personal authority of the teacher and the less personal but often restrictive school and classroom rules. The rules help provide for an orderly and reasonably satisfactory group living experience within an institutional setting, but they do so at a price. Behavior considered natural and appropriate elsewhere, such as boisterous talk and play, is forbidden at schools; to help a friend is sometimes considered cheating in school, but to fail to help a friend in a social setting is treachery!

We shall approach classroom management with a kind of cost/benefit analysis, considering management techniques with an eye toward what they are designed to accomplish, what they do in fact accomplish, and what side effects they may have. Certain practices are inappropriate because they are not essential to any worthwhile goal or because their positive effects are outweighed by negative ones (persistent authoritarian and punitive practices, for example, requiring students to remain absolutely silent at all times unless addressed by the teacher).

In our discussion of management we will stress problem prevention; however, we will also provide strategies for dealing with misbehavior when it does occur. Furthermore, we will discuss how teachers can manage classroom groups as well as help individual students (Doyle, 1986).

Approaches to classroom management depend on teachers' attitudes toward learning and the relationships they establish with students. Four commonly observed types of classrooms are the following:

1. This class is in continual chaos and uproar. The teacher spends much of the day trying to establish control but never fully succeeds. Directions and even threats are often ignored, and punishment does not seem to be effective for long.

2. This class is also noisy, but the atmosphere is more positive. The teacher tries to make school fun for the students by introducing games and recreational activities, reading stories, and including lots of arts and crafts and enrichment activities. Still, there are problems. Many students pay little attention during lessons, and seatwork often is not completed or not done carefully. This occurs even though the teacher holds academic activities to a minimum and tries to make them as pleasant as possible.

3. This class is quiet and well-disciplined because the teacher has established many rules and makes sure that the rules are followed. Infractions are noted quickly and cut short with stern warnings, or with punishment when necessary. The teacher spends a lot of time doing this, partly because he is so quick to notice any misbehavior. He appears to be a successful disciplinarian because the students usually obey him. However, the class atmosphere is uneasy. Trouble is always brewing just under the surface, and whenever the teacher leaves the room, the class "erupts."

4. This class seems to run by itself. The teacher spends most of her time teaching, not handling discipline problems. The students follow instructions and complete assignments on their own, without close supervision. Those involved in seatwork or enrichment activities interact with one another, so noise may be coming from several sources at the same time. However, these are the controlled and harmonious sounds of students productively involved in activities, not the disruptive noises of boisterous play or disputes. When noise does become disruptive, a simple reminder from the teacher is usually effective. Observers in this class sense a certain warmth in the atmosphere and go away positively impressed.

These four very different types of classrooms are found in almost every school, whatever its socioeconomic status, so their differences cannot be attributed entirely to the types of schools or students involved. Furthermore, many teachers have similar patterns year after year. Some have chronic control problems. Others regularly gain respect and obedience with little apparent effort, even from students who were problems the year before. We have described four familiar types. The first "can't cope," the second "bribes the students," the third "runs a tight ship," and the fourth "has few control problems." Before reading on in this chapter, take time to think about these four teachers. Assume that all four have roughly equivalent groups of students to work with at the beginning of the year. List three attitudes or behaviors for each teacher that might help explain why the classrooms have evolved along the lines described. What might be their expectations and assumptions about students and about the learning process? What might their students learn from observing them as models?

Also, reread the narrative at the end of Chapter 1 and characterize the teacher in terms of the four managerial styles described above. Does one of these styles describe that teacher?

MANAGEMENT AS MOTIVATION AND PROBLEM PREVENTION

The purpose of the preceding exercises was to help you focus on the teacher's role in shaping the learning environment or atmosphere in the classroom. There is no clear-cut atmosphere at first. It develops gradually, in response to the teacher's communication of expectations, modeling of behavior, and approach to classroom management. As is seen in schools where classes are taught by more than one teacher, the same class that is interested and attentive with one teacher can be bored or rebellious with another.

Generally, the most important determinant of classroom atmosphere is the teacher's method of classroom management, especially techniques for keeping the class attentive to lessons and involved in productive independent activities. This is why this chapter's title refers to management rather than to discipline or control. The latter terms have a connotation that we wish to avoid: the idea that motivating students is mostly a matter of handling their misbehavior successfully.

Although classroom management is often discussed in terms of dealing with misbehavior, research on classroom discipline (Kounin, 1970) and on behavior modification generally (Bandura, 1969; O'Leary & O'Leary, 1977) suggests that this approach puts the cart before the horse. Trying to control behavior problems through emphasis on punishment is ineffective and usually counterproductive.

In the 1960s it was popular to equate classroom management with classroom discipline and considerable emphasis was placed on what to do *after* students misbehaved. However, research initiated by Kounin (1970) and validated and expanded by a number of researchers in the past few years illustrates that good classroom managers do not react to student misbehavior very differently from poorer managers (Brophy & Good, 1986; Doyle, 1986). Rather, the key behaviors that distinguish good from poor managers are techniques that *prevent* misbehavior by eliciting student cooperation and involvement in assigned work.

Generally, it is much more effective to focus on desirable behavior, using management techniques that prevent problems from emerging, than it is to try to deal with problems after they emerge. The key to success lies in the things the teacher does to create a good learning environment and a low potential for trouble.

This was shown originally in a series of studies on classroom discipline by Kounin and his associates (Kounin, 1970). These investigators studied many different teachers, using interviews, on-the-spot note-taking, and the coding of videotapes. They did not conduct an experiment or try to influence the teachers. Instead, they simply observed in classrooms and developed information about relationships between teacher and student behavior. Surprisingly, the findings of several studies indicated that the teachers' methods of responding to discipline problems were unrelated to the frequency and seriousness of such problems. That is, teachers who minimized discipline problems appeared no different from those who had frequent and serious discipline problems, *on measures of teacher response to student misbehavior.*

The teachers did differ in other ways, however, that were related to their success in classroom management. These key differences were in teacher behaviors involved in minimizing the frequency with which students became disruptive in the first place by maximizing the time that students spent profitably involved in academic activities and by resolving incidents of minor inattention before they developed into major disruptions. Some of these teacher behaviors are as follows:

With-it-ness. Effective managers monitored their classrooms regularly. They positioned themselves so they could see all of the students and they continuously scanned the classroom to keep track of what was going on, no matter what else they were doing at the time. This continuous monitoring let the students know that the teachers were "with it"—aware of what was happening at all times and likely to detect inappropriate behavior early and accurately. This enabled them to nip problems in the bud before they could escalate into serious disruptions.

Overlapping. Effective managers could do more than one thing at a time when necessary. When teaching reading groups, for example, they responded to students from outside the group who came to ask questions, but at times and in ways that did not disrupt the activities of the reading group. When circulating to check on seatwork progress, they conferred with individual students but still kept an eye on the rest of the class. In general, they handled routine housekeeping tasks and met individual needs without disrupting the ongoing activities of the class as a whole.

Signal continuity and momentum in lessons. Effective managers were well prepared to teach their lessons and thus able to move through them at a brisk pace. They seldom had to interrupt the flow in order to consult the manual to see what to do next or to obtain a prop that should have been prepared earlier, and they seldom confused the students with false starts or backtracking to present information that should have been presented earlier. They ignored minor, fleeting inattention but dealt with serious inattention before it escalated into disruption, using methods that were not themselves disruptive. Thus, they moved near inattentive students, used eye contact when possible, directed a question to them, or cued their attention with a brief comment. They knew that students tend to be attentive (and their inattention tends to be fleeting) when they have a continuous academic signal to attend to. When teachers deliver extended reprimands or otherwise overreact to minor inattention, they lose the *momentum* of the lesson and break the *signal continuity* that provides focus for student attention. Typically, problems multiply and escalate in intensity when students are left without such a focus.

Variety and challenge in seatwork. Students spent much (often a majority) of their time working independently rather than under the direct supervision of the teacher. If they were to remain continuously engaged in seatwork tasks, the tasks had to be familiar and easy enough for them to do successfully and yet offer enough challenge and variety to maintain interest and motivation.

Subsequent work by other investigators indicates that these teacher behaviors are keys to successful classroom management and that they are associated with student learning gains in basic skills. Furthermore, other researchers have elaborated on Kounin's findings, especially by showing how successful managers implement their methods at the beginning of the year. (This is especially illustrated in the work of several projects carried out at the University of Texas. See, for example, Anderson, Evertson, & Emmer, 1980; Emmer, Evertson, & Anderson, 1980.)

Emmer, Evertson, and Anderson (1980) began by observing in 28 third-grade classrooms, visiting frequently during the first few weeks of the school year and occasionally thereafter. Observers took detailed notes about what rules and procedures the teachers introduced, how they did so, and how they followed up when it became necessary to use the procedures or enforce the rules. In addition, they scanned the classroom every 15 minutes to record the percentage of students who were engaged in lessons, academic tasks, or other teacher-approved activities.

This research showed that the seemingly automatic, smooth functioning of the classrooms of successful managers results from thorough preparation and organization at the beginning of the year. Room arrangement, materials storage, and other physical factors were prepared in advance, and teachers spent much time introducing rules and procedures in the early weeks. On the first day and throughout the first week, there was special attention to matters of greatest concern to the students (information about the teacher and their classmates, review of the daily schedule, times and procedures for lunch and recess, where to put personal materials, when and where to get a drink). Classroom routines were introduced gradually as needed so as not to overload the students with too much information at one time.

Effective managers not only told their students what they expected, but also modeled correct procedures for them, took time to answer questions, and, if necessary, arranged for the students to practice the procedures and get feedback. In short, key procedures were formally taught to students, just as academic content is taught.

Although implementing classroom rules and procedures involved more instruction than "control," effective managers were also thorough in following up on their expectations. They reminded students about procedures shortly before they were to carry them out, and they scheduled additional instruction and practice activities when students did not carry out procedures properly. Consequences of appropriate and inappropriate behavior were clear in their classrooms and sanctions were applied consistently. Inappropriate behavior was stopped quickly. In general, the effective managers showed three major clusters of behavior.

> *Behaviors that convey purposefulness.* Students were held accountable for completing work on time (after being taught to pace themselves by using the clock, if necessary). Regular times were scheduled each day to review briefly independent work, and the teachers regularly circulated to check on progress during seatwork. Completed papers were returned to students promptly, with feedback. In general, effective managers tried to maximize use of the time available for instruction and to see that their students learned the content (not just that they remained quiet).
>
> *Behaviors that teach students appropriate conduct.* Effective managers were clear about what they expected and what they would not tolerate. They focused on what students should be doing and taught them how to do it when necessary. This included not only conduct and housekeeping guidelines, but also learning-related behaviors such as how to read and follow directions for seatwork. When students failed to follow procedures properly, the teachers' responses stressed specific corrective feedback rather than criticism or threat of punishment.
>
> *Skills in maintaining students' attention.* Effective managers continuously monitored students for signs of confusion or inattention and were sensitive to their concerns. Seating was arranged so students could easily face the point in the room where they most often needed to focus attention. Variations in voice, movement, or pacing were used to refocus attention during lessons. Daily activities were scheduled to coincide with students' readiness to pay attention versus their need for physical activity, and these activities had clear beginnings and endings, with efficient transitions in between. The active attention of all students was required when important information was given.

Effective managers followed up this intensive activity in the early weeks by consistently maintaining their expectations. They no longer needed to devote much time to procedural instruction and practice, but they continued to give reminders and occasional remedial instruction, and they remained consistent in enforcing their rules.

A related study of junior high school teachers revealed similar findings about effective classroom management, as well as a few differences. In particular, junior high teachers did not need to spend as much time teaching their students how to follow rules and procedures. They did, however, have to communicate expectations clearly and monitor students for compliance. Procedures for maintaining student responsibility for engaging in and completing work assignments were especially important at the junior high level (Evertson & Emmer, 1982*b*).

Evertson and Emmer (1982*b*) list the following as characteristic of effective managers at the junior high school level.

> *Instructing students in rules and procedures.* All teachers had rules and procedures, but the effective managers described their rules more completely and installed their procedures more systematically. They were especially likely to be more explicit about desirable behavior (the dos, not just the don'ts).
>
> *Monitoring student compliance with rules.* The better managers monitored their students' compliance with rules more consistently, intervened to correct inappropriate behavior more often, and mentioned the rules or described desirable behavior more often when giving feedback at these times.
>
> *Communicating information.* The better managers were clearer in presenting information, giving directions, and stating objectives, and they were better able to break down complex tasks into step-by-step procedures.
>
> *Organizing instruction.* Effective managers wasted little time getting organized or accomplishing transitions between activities, and they maximized student attention and task engagement during activities by maintaining signal continuity and momentum in lessons, overlapping their own activities, and using the other techniques identified earlier by Kounin.

Subsequent work by Evertson, Emmer, and their colleagues involved training teachers in effective classroom management techniques. This work showed that teachers could learn these techniques and thereby decrease classroom disruptions and increase student engagement in academic activities. This teacher training was accomplished using extremely detailed manuals that describe desired behaviors in detail and provide examples, checklists, and step-by-step instructions telling teachers how to implement these procedures in their classrooms. An outline of the content used in these training programs can be found in Table 6.1. One manual has been prepared for elementary teachers (Evertson, Emmer, Clements, Sanford, & Worsham, 1981), and another for junior high teachers (Emmer, Evertson, Sanford, Clements, & Worsham, 1982). The latter is generally appropriate for use by senior high teachers as well.

A Management Experiment in Secondary Classrooms

Classroom management is correlated with pupil achievement. Studies in elementary schools (Anderson, Evertson, & Brophy, 1979; Brophy & Evertson, 1976) as well as those in secondary schools (Evertson, Anderson, Anderson, & Brophy, 1980; Evertson & Emmer, 1982*a*) consistently provide evidence that teachers who are effective in promoting student achievement generally have better organized class-

Table 6.1 MAJOR COMPONENTS PRESENTED IN BEGINNING-OF-YEAR TREATMENT

1. *Readying the classroom.* Be certain your classroom space and materials are ready for the beginning of the year.

2. *Planning rules and procedures.* Think about what procedures students must follow to function effectively in your classroom and in the school environment: decide what behaviors are acceptable or unacceptable; develop a list of procedures and rules.

3. *Consequences.* Decide ahead of time consequences for appropriate and inappropriate behavior in your classroom, and communicate them to your students; follow through consistently.

4. *Teaching rules and procedures.* Teach students rules and procedures systematically; include in your lesson plans for the beginning of school sequences for teaching rules and procedures, when and how they will be taught, and when practice and review will occur.

5. *Beginning-of-school activities.* Develop activities for the first few days of school that will involve students readily and maintain a whole-group focus.

6. *Strategies for potential problems.* Plan strategies to deal with potential problems that could upset your classroom organization and management.

7. *Monitoring.* Monitor student behavior closely.

8. *Stopping inappropriate behavior.* Handle inappropriate and disruptive behavior promptly and consistently.

9. *Organizing instruction.* Organize instruction to provide learning activities at suitable levels for all students in your class.

10. *Student accountability.* Develop procedures that keep the children responsible for their work.

11. *Instructional clarity.* Be clear when you present information and give directions to your students.

Source: Evertson, C., Emmer, E., Sanford, J., & Clements, B. (1983). Improving classroom management: An experiment in elementary school classrooms. *Elementary School Journal, 84,* 173–188.

rooms and fewer student behavior problems. As Evertson (1985) argues, effective classroom management begins on the first day of school, and teachers must use a systematic approach and proactive planning.

More recent experimental field studies show that teachers' classroom management and student achievement are closely related and demonstrate that recommendations and suggestions for teachers based on correlational data can be used to improve teacher and student classroom performance. Recent research (Borg & Ascione, 1982; Emmer, Sanford, Clements, & Martin, 1981; Evertson, Emmer, Sanford, & Clements, 1983) shows that training that enables teachers to plan rules and procedures early in the year, to present these rules and procedures to students along with expectations for appropriate work, to maintain a systematic approach through monitoring student academic work and behavior, and to provide feedback to students can result in improved student involvement in classroom activities.

Evertson (1985) demonstrates that staff development personnel in school districts can be trained and taught observational skills and techniques that help teachers to improve their management skills and lead to increased task involvement in students. Thus, the training procedures developed by various classroom researchers can be used in local district training programs.

Evertson (1985) conducted research in 102 classrooms drawn from six school districts. Although her sample included both elementary and secondary schools, we will limit our comments here to the findings from the secondary-school classrooms. Because the study was designed to examine both the content and the processes involved in developing a model for classroom management training, personnel within each district were trained to carry out the research using materials adapted from previous work (Sanford, Clements, & Emmer, 1981). These materials contained case studies, procedures, and activities that teachers could use in their classrooms. Teachers' manuals that had been produced in earlier work were also used (Emmer et al., 1982; Evertson et al., 1981).

Observers (11 school district administrative staff members) were trained to collect data. Observational measures included narrative records used to gather qualitative data about classroom activities and behaviors of both teachers and students. Student engagement rates indicating the extent to which students were involved in seatwork were also recorded. After each observation, the observer used a set of classroom ratings of various aspects of classroom management and student conduct. Table 6.2 summarizes the content that was presented in the training program and Table 6.3 summarizes the observational measures used to compare treatment and control teachers.

The results of the observation indicated that of the 35 five-point ratings of teachers' management practices, 22 (61%) were significantly in favor of the treatment group who had received the training. In addition, treatment group means

Table 6.2   OUTLINE OF CONTENT PRESENTED IN THE EVERTSON (1985) SECONDARY SCHOOL MANAGEMENT STUDY

I. Planning (before school starts)
   A. Use of space (readying the classroom)
   B. Rules for general behavior
   C. Rules and procedures for specific areas
      1. Student use of classroom space and facilities
      2. Student use of out-of-class areas
      3. Student participation during whole-class activities/seatwork
      4. Student participation in daily routines
      5. Student participation during small-group activities
   D. Consequences/incentives for appropriate/inappropriate behavior
   E. Activities for the first day of school
II. Presenting rules, procedures, and expectations (beginning of school)
   A. Teaching rules and procedures
      1. Explanation
      2. Rehearsal
      3. Feedback
      4. Reteaching
   B. Teaching academic content
III. Maintaining the system (throughout the year)
   A. Monitoring for behavioral and academic compliance
   B. Acknowledging appropriate behavior
   C. Stopping inappropriate behavior
   D. Consistent use of consequences/incentives
   E. Adjusting instruction for individual students/groups
   F. Keeping students accountable for work
   G. Coping with special problems

Source: Evertson, C. (1985). Training teachers in classroom management: An experimental study in secondary school classrooms. *Journal of Educational Research, 79,* 51–58.

Table 6.3 SPECIFIC COMPARISONS MADE BETWEEN EXPERIMENTAL AND CONTROL TEACHERS IN THE EVERTSON (1985) SECONDARY MANAGEMENT STUDY

Instructional management	*Managing student behavior*
Describes objectives clearly	Restrictions on student movement
Variety of materials	Rewards appropriate performance
Materials are ready	Signals correct behavior
Clear directions for assignments	Consistency in managing student behavior
Waits for attention	Effective monitoring
Assignments for different students	
Appropriate pacing of the lesson	*Student misbehavior*
Clear explanations	Amount of disruptive behavior
Monitors student understanding	Amount of inappropriate behavior
Consistently enforces work standards	Stops inappropriate behavior quickly
	Ignores inappropriate behavior
Room arrangement	
Suitable traffic patterns	*Classroom climate*
Good visibility	Conveys value of the curriculum
	Task-oriented focus
Rules and procedures	Relaxed, pleasant atmosphere
Efficient routines	
Appropriate general procedures	*Miscellaneous*
Suitable routines for assigning and checking work	Listening skills
	Avoidance behavior during seatwork
	Participation in class discussions
Meeting student concerns	
High degree of student success	*Percentage of students engaged*
Level of student aggressiveness	Percent of students off-task
Attention spans considered	Percent of students probably on-task
Activities related to students' interests	Percent of students on-task

Source: Adapted from Evertson, C. (1985). Training teachers in classroom management: An experimental study in secondary school classrooms. *Journal of Educational Research, 79,* 51–58.

exceeded control group means in the predicted direction for all of the variables but one. Thus, the teachers who were trained in management procedures used these procedures much more consistently than teachers who had not received training.

In the area of instructional management, all 11 differences favored the treatment group, and eight of these differences were statistically significant. Similarly, in the area of managing student behavior, all five differences favored the treatment group, and four of these were significant. As Evertson (1985) notes, the training had strong effects on the direct management of student behavior, including the restriction of students' freedom of movement around the classroom. Still, such restriction did not affect classroom climate, which was also rated highly. The treatment teachers received significantly higher ratings on all of the classroom climate variables.

In terms of student behavior, treatment teachers had less inappropriate behavior in their classes and were less likely to ignore it when it did occur. They also had significantly fewer students off-task and more students involved in assigned work.

Furthermore, classroom observers judged assignments in the treatment classrooms to be more appropriate (not too hard or too easy) and noted that students cooperated in getting seatwork done quickly. These students were kept accountable for their work assignments by the teachers.

Thus, the data collected by Evertson suggest that effective management techniques can be taught to a large number of teachers by local school personnel and, assuming that certain training procedures are followed, that students' involvement can be enhanced in ways that do not undermine classroom climate.

Other experimental research has also illustrated that teachers can be taught specific techniques that allow them to reduce off-task behavior and discipline problems in their classrooms. For example, Borg and Ascione (1982) found that teachers who were trained in the Utah State University Classroom Management Program learned to use the specific skills emphasized in the training program and that students' classroom behavior was favorably affected. Hence, there is growing evidence that research and development activities can be applied in ways that help teachers to manage classrooms more effectively.

Summary: Management Research

In summary, until recently, advice to teachers about classroom management was based mostly on untested theory or unsystematic individual testimonials about "what works best for me." Much of it was contradictory and very little was based on solid evidence. In the past 15 years or so, research in classrooms has established clearly that some approaches are more effective than others and in particular that *the key to successful classroom management is preventing problems before they occur* (Brophy & Putnam, 1979; Evertson & Emmer, 1982a, 1982b). This is not the whole story, of course. Problems occur in all classrooms, and some students are disturbed enough to require special treatment. Suggestions for dealing with some of these problems are made in Chapter 7, after more general management techniques are discussed here.

ESSENTIAL TEACHER ATTITUDES

Effective classroom management cannot be reduced to simple cookbook recipes. However, there are general principles that apply to most situations. If practiced systematically, they will prevent or resolve most problems, and at the same time, they will leave the teacher well positioned to handle the problems that do require special solutions. Before suggesting specific techniques, we wish to stress certain key teacher attitudes that must be present if those techniques are to succeed. *The attitudes and behaviors to be described complement one another to form a systematic approach. Attempts to use parts of this system as isolated techniques or gimmicks will not succeed for long.*

Many teacher attitudes and personal qualities basic to successful management have been discussed in previous chapters. They are reviewed here briefly insofar as they relate to making the teacher someone whom students will respect and want to please, not merely obey. First, teachers must like their students and respect them as individuals. They need not be overdramatic or even particularly affectionate; enjoyment of students and concern for their individual welfare will come through in tone of voice, facial expressions, and other everyday behavior. We have had clear evidence for some time that even young children adjust quickly to a teacher's personality (Anderson & Brewer, 1945), so there is no need for quiet or undemonstrative teachers to emote in order to impress their students with their concern.

It is important, however, to get close to students during private interactions. A teacher who is standoffish will be perceived as cold and will seem to be talking at rather than to the students, despite good intentions. In the early elementary grades, gestures such as patting the back or resting the hand on the shoulder are often effective ways for teachers to communicate concern or affection nonverbally when conferring with, praising, or encouraging students. Preschool and early elementary school teachers can use these techniques regularly. Older students may resent or be embarrassed by such physical contact, however, and it may be threatening for adolescents striving toward independence and autonomy. In any case, all teachers should regularly bend close to students and deal with them at their level during private contacts and should make an effort to get to know them individually. Students who like and respect their teachers will want to please them and will be more likely to imitate their behavior and adopt their attitudes. They also will be more likely to sympathize when the teachers are challenged or defied, instead of allying with the defiant students.

Teachers must also establish and maintain credibility, because most students have been exposed to discrepancies between what adults preach and what they practice. Some may even automatically assume that the teacher is trying to "con" them, seeing genuine expressions of concern as attempts to manipulate them for ulterior motives. Credibility is established largely by making sure that words and actions coincide and by pointing out this modeling to the class when necessary. Once teachers are established as respectable, likable people who can be believed, they will be in a position to practice the classroom management techniques described.

Credibility provides structure that students want and need. If they can depend on what teachers say, they will be less likely to test them constantly. Teacher credibility also helps enable students to accept responsibility for their own behavior. When teachers establish fair rules and enforce them consistently, rule breakers can get angry only at themselves. However, if teachers make empty threats or enforce rules inconsistently, rule breakers who are punished will likely feel picked on ("Johnny did it yesterday and you didn't do anything.").

Appropriate expectations are also involved in establishing credibility. Students tend to conform not so much to what teachers say as to what they actually expect. If students learn that "No talking over there" really means "Keep the noise down to a tolerable level," they will respond to the second message, not the first. This would be all right, except that sometimes the teacher really means "Keep quiet." At these times, the students will react in the usual way, and misunderstanding and resentment may result.

To avoid this, teachers must think through what they really expect from their students and then see that their own behavior is consistent with those expectations. Such self-monitoring will help eliminate empty, overgeneralized, or inconsistent statements. Observers can be helpful, since teachers are often unaware of inappropriate expectations. Teachers who bribe students to learn provide one example. They think of school-related tasks as unrewarding drudgery and do not expect students to enjoy them. This expectation is picked up by the class, who learns to wince, sigh, or protest at the mention of assignments. Their behavior reinforces the teachers' expectations, making teachers more likely to minimize demands and to bribe students by promising them rewards if they will cooperate. Such teachers are not positive influences on students, even though they may have their affection and, to a degree, their respect. The students will achieve poorly, and their next teacher will be faced with a rehabilitation job in motivating them for school.

In summary, to establish the groundwork for successful classroom management, teachers must: (1) have the respect and affection of the students; (2) be consistent and, therefore, credible and dependable; (3) assume responsibility for the students' learning; (4) value and enjoy learning and expect the students to do so, too; (5) communicate these basic attitudes and expectations to students and model them in behavior.

GENERAL MANAGEMENT PRINCIPLES

If teachers have these personal qualities, what specific steps can they take to establish good classroom management? The rest of this chapter and the one that follows address this question, moving from general to specific situations and from techniques that help prevent problems to techniques used in remediating problems after they have appeared.

The recommendations in this section all concern general principles of classroom organization. These principles are based on one or more of the following assumptions:

1. Students are likely to follow rules that they understand and accept.
2. Management should be approached with an eye toward maximizing the time students spend in productive work rather than from a negative viewpoint stressing control of misbehavior.
3. The teacher's goal is to develop the students' inner self-control, not merely to exert control over them.
4. Discipline problems are minimized when students are regularly engaged in meaningful work geared to their interests and aptitudes.

Establish Clear Rules Where Rules Are Needed

Certain aspects of classroom management are part of the daily routine. These include storage of clothing and personal belongings, use of the toilets and drinking fountains, access to paper and other supplies, use of special equipment (supplementary readers, audiovisual aids, art or science supplies, etc.), and behavior during periods of independent work (e.g., what students who finish their seatwork should do while the teacher is still busy with a lesson group).

In these or other situations where a rule is required, the rule should be explicit and the rationale for it should be explained. Explanation is especially important at the beginning of the year and with students in kindergarten or first grade who are new to school. Some will never have used or even seen pencil sharpeners, audiovisual equipment, or certain arts and crafts equipment, so that verbal explanation alone may not be enough. A demonstration followed by the opportunity to practice the use and care of such equipment may be required before some students can meet expectations.

Demonstrations and practice will be less necessary with older students, although still important for introducing new responsibilities (such as the use and care of laboratory equipment). Older students still will need thorough discussions of rules, however. Each new grade adds experiences that they have not been through before. More importantly, last year's teacher may have demanded behavior that differs from what this year's teacher wants, especially on the matter of what things the student must seek permission to do and what may be done without permission. Therefore, each teacher should specify rules clearly and demonstrate if necessary.

Rules should be kept to a minimum and should be clearly stated. If a rule does not have a convincing rationale, it should be discarded or revised. Rules should be presented to the class as means, not ends in themselves. For example, the rationale underlying rules about behavior during seatwork times might stress that students should not disrupt group lessons that the teacher is conducting or distract other students who are still involved in seatwork. There is a range of activities that students who finish seatwork can engage in without disturbing either the teacher or classmates who are still at work (read a supplementary reader, begin an art project, examine a science display, work on homework, talk quietly with another student who has also finished, etc.). An overgeneralized rule such as "When you finish your seatwork you will remain quiet and not talk to anyone or leave your seats for any reason," would not be justifiable. This is much more restrictive than it should be and will cause more problems than it solves. Instead, the teacher should stress the basic goal of avoiding disturbances to students involved in lessons or seatwork and then list examples of acceptable and unacceptable behavior.

Earlier reference was made to the classroom management manuals that were produced in the Texas Classroom Management Project. Examples of the usefulness of this work can be seen in Table 6.4, which outlines some of the procedures secondary teachers will need to establish at the start of the school year. As Emmer et al. (1981) argue, teachers who establish these procedures and communicate them to students will save much time for instruction by avoiding lengthy discussions about classroom procedures.

Table 6.4 PROCEDURES FOR BEGINNING CLASS IN JUNIOR HIGH SETTINGS

Things to ask yourself	Suggestions
Administrative Matters	
1. What administrative matters need efficient handling by you at the beginning of the period? Where will you handle them?	You will want to handle such tasks as roll call and filling out the absence slip as quickly and efficiently as possible. Choose a location where the seating chart, roll book, and absence slips can be used easily (such as at a podium or table), preferably near the door where the slip is put out.
2. If a student was absent on the previous day, what should she or he do?	If you have a particular location for roll call, you can have the student leave his/her absence excuse slip there for you to sign, or bring it to you to sign while you are checking roll. It is the teacher's responsibility to see that students who were absent have an office excuse (permit to enter class). In order to keep track of previous absences, you will need a record that you can check. Many teachers use their grade book, marking in pencil an "a" for absent and "t" for tardy.

Table 6.4 (Continued)

3. If a student will be leaving during the period, what should she or he do?

First find out what your school requires. You will want to know at the beginning of the period if anyone must leave class. The student can inform you while you are taking roll. It will simplify matters to have only one system for these kinds of contacts.

4. What is the procedure for students who are tardy?

Find out the school policy and follow it. If there is no specific school policy, you will need to have a procedure of your own. Some schools require the student to sign a slip when tardy, and after a certain number of "tardies" the student receives a detention. Some teachers require students to stay in before or after school each time they are tardy. You will need to have a recordkeeping system for this and keep it handy, so that it will take little time to handle.

Student Activities

1. When the tardy bell rings, what are students supposed to do?

When the bell rings, most effective managers expect talking to stop. A good idea is to have a regular beginning class routine for the first four or five minutes of class. Students should begin the activity as soon as the bell rings.

2. If PA announcements come on, what is expected of the students?

Tell the students specifically what their expected behavior is during announcements (e.g., no talking, stop, or continue working).

3. What materials are students expected to bring to class and/or have ready when the bell rings? If these vary from day to day, how will you let them know?

Most effective managers expect students to have all of their materials ready to use when the bell rings. This includes sharpened pencils, headings on papers (if needed), homework papers, textbooks, project materials, etc. Having this requirement also discourages tardiness.

4. What procedures will you use for checking out books to students?

You will want to have something for students to do while you are recording book numbers. This may be either an academic activity such as a worksheet or exercise from the chalkboard, or a procedural activity, such as covering the books or filling out forms. Determine ahead of time where and how you will record book numbers. Take as little time as possible in this activity.

5. What procedures will you use for distributing supplies and equipment?

If students will be using books or supplies that are kept in the room, you will need a system whereby students pick up their own materials, or monitors pass them out. Monitors may be specially chosen students or the first or last person in each row. Make sure your directions to monitors are clear and specific.

6. What responsibilities do you want students to have in taking care of materials or equipment?

If there are specific instructions for the care and use of equipment or materials, the instructions should be given and demonstrated, if appropriate, prior to passing them out. You may also wish to have a chart with step-by-step directions for students to follow in dealing with materials.

Source: Adapted from Emmer, E., Evertson, C., Clements, B., Sanford, J., & Worsham, M. (1981). *Organizing and managing the junior high classroom.* Austin: University of Texas, Research and Development Center for Teacher Education.

Emmer et al. (1981) also provide valuable advice about procedures to use during instructional activities and procedures for ending the class. The point here is that teachers who plan carefully and who communicate their plans to students can eliminate the need for endless discussions about procedures.

When rules are no longer needed or no longer do the job they were meant to do, they should be modified or dropped. Teachers should explain the reasons for any such changes and not just announce them. Sometimes it may be worthwhile to explain the problem and invite students to suggest solutions. In summary, good classroom management involves: establishing clear rules when rules are needed, avoiding unnecessary rules, reviewing rules periodically and changing or dropping them when appropriate, and involving students to some degree in establishing and changing rules.

Let the Students Assume Independent Responsibility

There is no reason for teachers to do what students can do for themselves. With proper planning and instruction, even the youngest children can take out and replace equipment, sharpen pencils, open milk cartons, pass out supplies, carry chairs, and form orderly lines. Older students can also work independently or in small groups and can check their own work. Some teachers do these things themselves or control them by calling on students one by one. This only creates delays, diverts teachers from teaching tasks, and retards students' development of independent responsibility.

Teachers will sometimes say, "I tried to get them to do it themselves, but they couldn't." Often students only need a demonstration lesson or an opportunity to practice the behavior. Time spent in explanation and patience in response to slowness and mistakes early in the year pays great dividends later.

Some teachers adopt overly rigid rules on the grounds that they are needed to prevent waste or vandalism ("If I let them sharpen their pencils, they'll sharpen them right down to the eraser." "If I put out supplementary readers, they'll steal them." "If I allow them to work in groups, they'll just copy from one another or waste time."). This attitude represents an avoidance of the problem rather than an attempt to solve it. It also communicates negative expectations to the students (who are treated as if they were infants). When students understand the rationales underlying rules and know they are expected to follow the rules, they will do so.

Needless rituals and delays can be avoided by letting students assume classroom management functions they can handle on their own. This will minimize the disruptions that often begin when students are idle during lulls in activities. It will also help students develop independence and responsibility. As we argue in Chapter 8, it is also important for teachers to teach students specific strategies for becoming more autonomous and more able to evaluate their own learning (Corno & Rohrkemper, 1985).

Minimize Disruptions and Delays

Management problems start and spread more easily when students are idle or are distracted by disruptions than when everyone is involved in productive activity. There are many things teachers can do to minimize delays, disruptions, and distractions.

Thorough daily planning is important. Problems often begin when teachers break the flow of a lesson because they need to prepare equipment that could have been readied earlier or to refer to the manual. In general, minimize waiting time (situations in which students must idly wait for something, with no clear focus for their attention). Unless there is no alternative, the entire class should never be lined up to do something at one time. Instead, break the class into subgroups or appoint assistants to help.

The time needed for distributing supplies can be cut down by having one student from each row or table pass things out. Items should be stored where students can get them unaided. In the early grades, supplies should be stored low enough for students to reach them and arranged neatly for easy identification and replacement. In all grades, items should be stored as close as possible to where they typically are used (to cut down on traffic and reduce spillage).

Use of storage space should be determined by convenience. Store frequently used items where they can be taken out and returned most conveniently. Items that are used rarely or at a different time of the year can be stored in the harder-to-reach areas.

The room should be arranged to promote free and easy traffic flow. Heavily used traffic lanes (areas around the door, the drinking fountain, the coatrack, or lanes between the students' usual seats and special areas for group lessons) should not be obstructed. Traffic lanes should be wide enough for students to move freely without bumping into the furniture or one another.

Delays frequently result when there is high demand for something that is in short supply, as when the entire class must use paste from a single jar or get supplies from a single container. Much time can be saved by storing small items (crayons, paste, pencils, etc.) in several containers instead of a single, large container.

Much dead time in junior high and high school classes can be prevented through advance preparation. Unless it is important for the teacher to model the motions involved, complicated diagrams, maps, or mathematical computations should be prepared on the chalkboard or overhead before class begins or distributed on mimeographed sheets rather than constructed during class. Similarly, many science experiments and other demonstrations can be partially prepared ahead of time when the preparations themselves do not need to be demonstrated. Or students can help with these preparation activities, especially when they must be done during class time. This will speed up the job and at the same time allow students to participate more actively.

Bear in mind that when students must wait with nothing to do, four things can happen, and three of them are bad: (1) students may remain interested and attentive; (2) they may become bored or fatigued, losing interest and ability to concentrate; (3) they may become distracted or start daydreaming; or (4) they may actively misbehave. Therefore, plan room arrangement, equipment storage, preparation of equipment and illustrations, and transitions between activities to avoid needless delays and confusion.

Plan Independent Activities as Well as Organized Lessons

Usually students spend a good part of their school day working at their seats on assignments or on activities they have selected for themselves. Disruptions often originate with students who are not working on their assignment or who have finished it and have nothing else to do. Teachers who fail to provide worthwhile seatwork or to have backup plans prepared for times when seatwork is completed more quickly than anticipated have more classroom management problems than their better prepared colleagues (Kounin, 1970).

Seatwork is (or should be) a basic part of the curriculum, not merely a time filler. It should provide students with opportunities to practice skills they are learning or to apply them in solving problems. If properly designed and used, it also provides teachers with good information about how each student is progressing. Therefore, teachers should plan seatwork as carefully as they plan their lessons and should make its importance clear to students when assigning it.

The assignment should be specific (the teacher should assign particular exercises, not just provide busywork without caring how many or which problems are done), and the work should be used for diagnosis and remediation (the teacher should check it and follow up with students who do not understand). Checking seatwork helps insure that students are held accountable for the assignment and makes it likely that the assignment will have its desired effects.

In addition to being specific about the seatwork assignments, the teacher should provide clear expectations about what students should do when they finish. These may involve additional specific assignments (e.g., reviewing the story they are going to study later in the reading group). Or there may be a range of optional activities (educational games, supplemental readers, etc.) to select from. In any case, students should know what options are available if they finish seatwork early. They should not have to interrupt the teacher to ask what to do next or to find out if something is permissible.

Nor should students have to interrupt their seatwork frequently to get help. Recent research indicates that teachers often give students tasks that are too difficult for them (Fisher et al., 1980; Gambrell, Wilson, & Gantt, 1981; Jorgenson, 1977). Assigning students work that is too difficult not only impedes their learning progress (see Chapter 11), but also invites classroom management problems, especially when the teacher is trying to work with a small group while the rest of the students do independent work at their seats. In this situation, the students who are supposed to work independently must understand what to do and be able to do it with little or no help. Teachers can accomplish this by assigning seatwork that is appropriate in the first place and by reviewing the directions with the students and checking to see that they understand them before "turning them loose" to work independently.

Assignments should be written on the board or available in some other place so students who are not sure about what to do can check for themselves rather than interrupt the teacher. There should also be clear procedures for students to follow when they know what to do but not how to do it. Different teachers will prefer different procedures (ask your neighbor, ask a designated tutor or assistant, come up to the teacher but wait quietly until the teacher signals readiness to hear your question, etc.). In any case, whatever procedure is adopted should be made clear to the students.

Disruptions may occur frequently, even during whole-class seatwork times when the teacher is circulating around the room, if students must wait for long periods before the teacher gets to them (Fisher et al., 1980). Sometimes (when everyone seems to need help) the problem is inappropriately difficult seatwork. At other times problems occur because the teacher becomes absorbed with individual students to the point of neglecting the rest of the class. In addition to monitoring the classroom continuously ("with-it-ness") at these times, teachers need to perfect the art of keeping themselves in circulation and available to give immediate help to students who need it (Brophy & Evertson, 1976; Fisher et al., 1980). Interactions with individuals should be brief. The teacher should provide them with enough guidance to keep them going on the assignment but should not necessarily cover everything they eventually will need to know (the teacher can return again after the student does the next few problems). When many students seem to have the same question or misconception, it is probably worthwhile to briefly clarify the problem to the class as a whole. Otherwise, it is usually best to provide private help to those who need it while allowing the rest of the students to move through the assignment without interruption.

In summary, students must be provided with appropriate seatwork and other independent activities during times when the teacher is busy with small-group instruction. Students should know what their assignments are, what to do if they need help, and what they can or should do when they finish. These activities will provide a basis for responsible self-guidance and will minimize problems resulting from idleness or confusion about what to do.

CUEING AND REINFORCING APPROPRIATE BEHAVIOR

Previous sections have discussed how to arrange the classroom to minimize management problems and to establish effective rules and procedures. However, rules will not fit all situations, and teachers need to know how to give on-the-spot instructions when they are needed. These are likely to be effective to the extent that they clearly specify the desired behavior.

Stress Positive, Desirable Behavior

Like everyone else, students find learning easier and more pleasant when someone is showing them what *to* do rather than what *not* to do. This is why most lessons begin with a demonstration. Teachers would not think of teaching addition by naming all the sums that $2 + 2$ do not equal. In general, learning from direct instruction is easier than learning by trial and error.

Most teachers realize the value of the direct, positive approach in teaching school subjects, but they (and adults generally) often do not appreciate that it is just as important in socializing behavior. A string of "don'ts," with emphasis on what students should *not* be doing, may create anxiety in students or resentment against the teacher. Therefore, teachers must train themselves to specify desirable behavior in positive terms, as in the following examples.

Positive Language	**Negative Language**
Close the door quietly.	Don't slam the door.
Try to work these out on your own without help.	Don't cheat by copying from your neighbor.

Quiet down—you're getting too loud.	Don't make so much noise.
Sharpen your pencils like this (demonstration).	That's not how you use the pencil sharpener.
Carry your chair like this (demonstration).	Don't make so much noise with your chair.
Sit up straight.	Don't slouch in your chair.
Raise your hands if you think you know the answer.	Don't yell out the answer.
When you finish, put the scissors in the box and bits of paper in the wastebasket.	Don't leave a mess.
These crayons are for you to share—use one color at a time and then put it back so others can use it too.	Stop fighting over those crayons.
Use your own ideas. When you do borrow ideas from another author, be sure to acknowledge them. Even here, try to put them in your own words.	Don't plagiarize.
Speak naturally, as you would when talking to a friend.	Don't just read your report to us.
Note the caution statements in the instructions. Be sure to check things mentioned there before proceeding to the next step.	Take your time when doing this experiment or you'll mess it up.
Be ready to explain your answer—why you think it is correct.	Don't just guess.

Sometimes negative statements are appropriate, as when a student is doing something that must be stopped immediately (fighting, causing a major disruption). Even in those cases, however, negative remarks should be followed with positive statements about what to do instead. Teachers should phrase instructions in positive, specific language that indicates the desired behavior clearly.

Recognize and Reinforce Desired Behavior

Most sources of advice to teachers urge them to recognize and reinforce students' good conduct, contributions to lessons, or academic work. The idea is that students' accomplishments should be rewarded not only with high grades but also with frequent verbal praise and other rewards such as public recognition (hanging examples of good work for public display, describing accomplishments in the school bulletin), symbolic rewards (stars, happy faces, stickers), extra privileges or activity choices, or material rewards (snacks, prizes). Social learning theorists and behavior modifiers see reinforcement as essential in providing both motivation and guidance to learners: Behavior that is reinforced is likely to be repeated, but behavior that is not reinforced is likely to be extinguished. Other writers see reinforcement as desirable, if not essential, on the grounds that it helps students to appreciate their successes, develop positive self-concepts, boost motivation, or develop a sense of accomplishment. Whatever their rationale, most writers state or at least imply that reinforcement is highly desirable and should occur regularly in classrooms.

We accept the validity of the general principle of reinforcement (behaviors that are reinforced will be retained; behaviors that are not reinforced will be extinguished), but we question some of the suggestions that have been made for implementing this principle in classrooms. We believe that too much emphasis has been placed on quantity or frequency of reinforcement and not enough on quality and questions such as whom to reinforce, under what conditions, and with what kinds of reinforcement. We believe that teachers' attempts to reinforce are valuable under certain circumstances, but ineffectual or even counterproductive under other circumstances.

Let us begin by noting that a great deal of reinforcement of student behavior occurs simply as a natural consequence of performing that behavior. Attention to the teacher and devotion of effort to assignments typically lead to success (correct performance), which in turn leads to high grades and feelings of satisfaction. More generally, succeeding in school and gaining the respect of teachers and peers are important goals to most students, so that any behaviors that students recognize as supporting progress toward those goals will be reinforced automatically. Thus the issue is not whether reinforcement should occur in the classroom, but whether (and if so, how much) the teacher should inject additional reinforcement beyond that which occurs as a natural consequence of student behavior. Our position is that such additional reinforcement is not necessary, although it may be appropriate.

It is not necessary because, unlike lower animals, humans learn through a variety of mechanisms in addition to the mechanism of shaping behavior through reinforcement. Our thinking and speaking abilities enable us to learn by observing a model and by being instructed, making us less dependent on shaping through reinforcement. Also, we respond to a great many motives (self-actualization, cognitive consistency, curiosity, etc.) in addition to, and sometimes instead of, the desire to be reinforced. Furthermore, even when reinforcement is a primary motive, reinforcement from sources other than the teacher (winning a competition with a peer, for example, or gaining peer acceptance or attention) may be more important than anything the teacher does. Thus, reinforcement from the teacher is only one of many factors influencing students' behavior.

Even when reinforcement from the teacher is relevant, there are limits on how much such reinforcement is productive. Overly frequent reinforcement is unnecessary to sustain behavior and may become intrusive. Too much of even a good thing is still too much.

Another complicating factor is individual differences in students' motivational systems. Eden (1975) has shown that for a given person and situation, certain motives will be relevant and others will not, so that the success of a motivational effort will depend on how well it fits with the person's present motives. In the classroom, for example, teachers are likely to produce a significant increase in students' motivation to perform desired behavior only if they deliver some *relevant* motivational consequence following the performance of a desired behavior. If they should deliver a consequence that is irrelevant to the students' presently operating motives, there is likely to be a small but real decrease in overall motivation to continue the behavior. Thus, even well-intended motivational efforts may have (slightly) negative effects when they are based on incorrect assumptions about students' motives. Teachers need to monitor their students' responses to consequences intended to be reinforcing and not just assume that all students actually experience these consequences as reinforcing. Students bring a variety of motives to the classroom—some prefer to work alone while others prefer cooperative opportunities. Balancing the various motivational needs of students through providing a variety of classroom activities and organizational structures is a complicated teaching task (Ames & Ames, 1985).

Some educational theorists (Montessori, 1964; Moore & Anderson, 1969; Piaget, 1952) oppose reinforcement even in principle. These writers urge teachers to capitalize and build on students' intrinsic motivation for learning, without trying to supplement it through extrinsic reinforcement (including praise). Several recent studies by attribution theorists support this view to some extent (attribution theorists are concerned about what happens when we try to explain our successes or failures to ourselves—when we *attribute* our performance to causes). It has been shown that if you begin to reward people for doing what they already were doing spontaneously, you decrease their intrinsic motivation to continue the behavior in the future (Deci, 1975; Lepper & Greene, 1978). Furthermore, to the extent that their attention becomes focused on the reward rather than the task itself, their performance tends to deteriorate (Condry & Chambers, 1978). They develop a piecework mentality, doing whatever will garner them the most rewards with the least effort rather than trying to do the job as well as they can to create a high-quality product.

For a time, it was thought that these undesirable effects were inherent in the use of extrinsic reinforcement, including praise. More recently, it has become clear that the effects (both desirable and undesirable) of reinforcement depend on the nature of the reinforcement used and especially on how it is presented. Decreases in performance quality and in intrinsic motivation for subsequent repetition of the behavior are most likely when reinforcement has the following characteristics:

High salience (large or highly attractive rewards, or rewards presented in ways that call attention to them)

Noncontingency (rewards are given for mere participation in activities rather than being contingent on achieving specific performance objectives)

Unnatural/unusual (rewards are artificially tied to behaviors as control devices rather than being natural outcomes of the behaviors)

In short, reinforcement is likely to undermine students' intrinsic motivation when it implies that their behavior is controlled externally—that they are engaging in an activity only because they must do so in order to earn a reward (Deci & Ryan, 1980; Kruglanski, 1978). Actually, this effect will occur not only with reinforcement but also with any factor that leads students to attribute their behavior to external pressures rather than their own intrinsic motivation. Other examples include teacher reminders to students that they are under surveillance and student awareness of pressure to meet a deadline (Lepper, 1982).

The data reviewed in this section suggest that reinforcement of student behavior is likely to be effective only to the extent that the consequences intended for use as reinforcers are actually experienced as reinforcing by the student, that they are contingent on the student achieving specific performance objectives, and that they are awarded in a way that complements rather than undermines the development of intrinsic motivation and other natural outcomes of behavior. More specific guidelines about reinforcing effectively are given in the following section on effective praise. We have chosen to concentrate on praise because most teachers will use this form of reinforcement much more frequently than other forms. However, most of the guidelines for praising effectively also apply to the effective administration of other kinds of rewards.

Praising Effectively

Praise is usually described as a form of reinforcement, although it does not always have this effect (Brophy, 1981). Sometimes teachers do not even intend their praise to be reinforcing, as when they use praise in an attempt to build a social relationship with an alienated student ("I like your new shirt, John"). Even when teachers do intend their praise to be reinforcing, some students will not perceive it that way. In particular, public praise may be more embarrassing than reinforcing to certain students, especially if it calls attention to conformity rather than to some noteworthy accomplishment. This is especially likely when teachers try to shape the behavior of onlookers by praising peers ("I like the way that Susie is sitting up straight and ready to listen"). Susie is unlikely to feel reinforced by such "praise," especially if it leads to taunts from peers. In summary, praise has been oversold to teachers as a form of reinforcement, partly because reinforcement in general has been oversold, but also because praise does not always function as reinforcement.

Writers interested in humanizing education also tend to stress praise. They usually contrast it with criticism. It is true that emphasis on the positive is preferable to emphasis on the negative, and that teachers who frequently criticize their students usually have trouble controlling their classrooms and minimal success in fostering student learning (Brophy & Evertson, 1976; Dunkin & Biddle, 1974; Rosenshine, 1976). However, correlations between teachers' rates of praise and their students' learning gains are not always positive and in any case are usually too low to be of practical importance (Brophy, 1981). Students usually express positive attitudes toward teachers who praise frequently, but neither teachers nor students see teacher praise as an important or powerful reinforcer (Ware, 1978). In general, teachers' strategies for eliciting desirable student behavior in the first place are much more important than their praising such behavior after it appears. To the extent that praise is important, the key to its effectiveness lies in its quality rather than its frequency. Effective teachers know both when and how to praise.

Effective praise calls attention to students' developing learning progress or skill mastery. It expresses appreciation for students' efforts or admiration for their accomplishments in ways that call attention to the efforts or accomplishments themselves rather than to their role in pleasing the teacher. This helps students to learn to attribute their efforts to their own intrinsic motivation rather than to external manipulation by the teacher and to attribute their successes to their own abilities and efforts rather than to dependency on the teacher, lack of challenge in the task, or sheer luck.

Unfortunately, praise and reinforcement do not conform to the above guidelines in most classrooms. Perhaps this is because attribution research is very recent, and few teachers have received good information about how to praise effectively. In any case, much teacher praise is directed more toward controlling students than toward expressing admiration for their efforts or accomplishments.

Also, much teacher praise functions not so much as reinforcement but as an indication of teachers' expectations or attitudes. Brophy, Evertson, Anderson, Baum, and Crawford (1981) found that teachers were credible and spontaneous when praising students whom they liked, often smiling as they spoke and praising genuine accomplishments. However, although they praised students whom they disliked just as often, they usually did so without accompanying spontaneity and warmth and often with reference to appearance or behavior rather than to academic accomplishments. Dweck, Davidson, Nelson, and Enna (1978) found that teachers were likely to praise boys only for objectively successful performance but sometimes praised girls for neatness, for following instructions to the letter, for answering in the proper form (not merely giving correct content), or for other issues of form rather than substance. Several studies have found that teachers often praise incorrect answers (Anderson, Evertson, & Brophy, 1979; Bellack, Kliebard, Hyman, & Smith, 1966; Mehan, 1974). Such inappropriate praise is especially likely to be directed toward the lowest achievers (Brookover et al., 1978; Kleinfeld, 1975; Natriello & Dornbusch, 1984; Weinstein, 1976).

No doubt inappropriate praise often is part of a well-intentioned attempt to encourage low achievers or build better relationships with alienated students. It is dangerous, however, because it may undermine credibility and confuse or depress the students, especially if they realize that they are being treated differently from their classmates. Meyer et al. (1979), for example, found that effusive teacher praise for essentially minor accomplishment led both onlookers and recipients to conclude that the teacher felt sorry for the recipients because they were not very bright.

Furthermore, research by Blumenfeld, Pintrich, Meece, and Wessels (1982) suggests that there is little point in teachers trying to shield students from classroom realities. Younger students (in the early elementary grades) tend to think of themselves as successful as long as they complete their work successfully (regardless of what other students are doing), and older students are aware of how their performance compares to that of others, even when their teachers try to hide this. Students (especially those who are struggling) need encouragement, but they also need accurate feedback about their performance.

The implication is that praise is most likely to be effective when delivered as spontaneous, genuine reaction to student accomplishment rather than as part of a calculated attempt to manipulate the student. Other guidelines for effective praise are given below, and a summary is given in Table 6.5.

1. Praise should be simple and direct, delivered in a natural voice, without gushing or dramatizing. Even very young students will see theatrics as insincere and phony.

2. Praise in straightforward, declarative sentences ("That's interesting, I never thought of that before.") instead of gushy exclamations ("Wow!") or rhetorical questions ("Isn't that wonderful?"). The latter are condescending and more likely to embarrass than reward.

3. Specify the particular accomplishment being praised and recognize any noteworthy effort, care, or perserverance ("Good! You figured it out all by yourself. I like the way you stuck with it without giving up"—instead of—"Good"). Call attention to new skills or evidence of progress ("I notice you've learned to use different kinds of sentences in your compositions. They're more interesting to read now. Keep up the good work.").

4. Use a variety of phrases for praising students. Overused stock phrases soon begin to sound insincere and give the impression that the teacher has not really paid much attention to the student.

5. Verbal praise should be backed with nonverbal communication of approval. "That's good" is not very rewarding when said with a deadpan expression, a flat tone of voice, and an air of distraction or apathy. The same phrase is much more effective when delivered with a smile, a tone communicating appreciation or warmth, or gestures such as a pat on the back.

6. Avoid ambiguous statements like "You were really good today." Students may take them as praise for compliance rather than for learning. Instead, praise in a way that specifically rewards learning efforts: "I'm very pleased with your reading this morning, especially the way you read with so much expression. You made the conversation between Billy and Mr. Taylor sound very real. Keep up the good work."

7. Ordinarily, individual students should be praised privately. Public praise will embarrass some students and may even cause problems with the peer group. It is difficult to praise students publicly without sounding as though you are holding them up as examples to the rest of the class. Delivering praise during private interactions avoids this problem and also helps show the student that the praise is genuine.

When used systematically and appropriately, teacher attention and praise can reinforce desired behavior in students. They help students to know that their efforts and progress are seen and appreciated, especially if praise is delivered in natural, genuine language that includes a description of the specific behavior being commended.

GETTING AND HOLDING ATTENTION

So far we have discussed general personal qualities and behavior that can help teachers establish a good classroom atmosphere and maximize the time and effort students devote to learning. In this section we will suggest techniques for dealing with everyday problems of minor inattention and disruption caused by boredom, fatigue, or situational distractions. Techniques for dealing with more serious problems are discussed in the next chapter.

Kounin's (1970) research suggests that the most successful way to handle situational inattention and distraction is to prevent it from happening, or if it does occur, to check it before it becomes more serious. This is accomplished mostly with

Table 6.5 GUIDELINES FOR EFFECTIVE PRAISE

Effective praise	Ineffective praise
1. Is delivered contingently	1. Is delivered randomly or unsystematically
2. Specifies the particulars of the accomplishment	2. Is restricted to global positive reactions
3. Shows spontaneity, variety, and other signs of credibility; suggests clear attention to the student's accomplishment	3. Shows a bland uniformity that suggests a conditioned response made with minimal attention
4. Rewards attainment of specified performance criteria (which can include effort criteria, however)	4. Rewards mere participation, without consideration of performance processes or outcomes
5. Provides information to students about their competence or the value of their accomplishments	5. Provides no information at all or gives students information about their status
6. Orients students toward better appreciation of their own task-related behavior and thinking about problem solving	6. Orients students toward comparing themselves with others and thinking about competing
7. Uses student's own prior accomplishments as the context for describing present accomplishments	7. Uses the accomplishments of peers as the context for describing student's present accomplishments
8. Is given in recognition of noteworthy effort or success at difficult (for this student) tasks	8. Is given without regard to the effort expended or the meaning of the accomplishment
9. Attributes success to effort and ability, implying that similar success can be expected in the future.	9. Attributes success to ability alone or to external factors such as luck or (easy) task difficulty
10. Fosters endogenous attributions (students believe that they expend effort on the task because they enjoy the task and/or want to develop task-relevant skills)	10. Fosters exogenous attributions (students believe that they expend effort on the task for external reasons—to please the teacher, win a competition or reward, etc.)
11. Focuses students' attention on their own task-relevant behavior	11. Focuses students' attention on the teacher as an external authority figure who is manipulating them
12. Fosters appreciation of, and desirable attributions about, task-relevant behavior after the process is completed	12. Intrudes into the ongoing process, distracting attention from task-relevant behavior

Source: Brophy, J. (1981). Teacher praise: A functional analysis. *Review of Educational Research, 51,* 5–32.

techniques that minimize disruptions by causing students to attend at all times, not merely when they are called on.

Focus Attention When Beginning Lessons

Teachers should establish that they expect each student's full attention to lessons at all times. They should first have everyone's attention before beginning lessons. Some teachers fail to do this, or even deliberately start the lesson in a loud voice in an attempt to get students to pay attention. This is inconsistent with several ideas that teachers should be trying to promote. Briefly, it connotes rudeness; it involves talking *at* rather than talking *to* students; it reinforces the idea that one gains attention by loudly breaking into conversations; and it causes many students to miss the beginnings of lessons.

For these reasons, teachers should never launch into lessons without first gaining full attention. The teacher should have a standard signal that tells the class "We are now ready to begin a lesson." The particulars of this signal will vary with teacher preferences. One teacher might prefer "All right, let's begin," while another might say, "Everyone turn to page 62." Whatever the method, teachers should develop a predictable, standard way of introducing lessons. This will tell students that the transition between activities is over and a new activity is about to begin.

After giving the signal, teachers should pause briefly to allow it to take effect. Then, when they have attention, they should begin briskly. Ideally, they should start by describing what will be done. This overview will help the class focus their attention and will provide motivation for learning.

The pause between giving the signal and beginning the lesson should be brief, just long enough for students to focus their attention. If the pause is too long, some students will lose this sharp focus. Therefore, the teacher should act quickly if a few students do not respond. If the students are looking at the teacher, expressions and gestures can be used to indicate that they should pay attention. If they are not looking, the teacher should call their names. Usually this will be enough by itself; if not, a brief focusing statement can be added ("Look here.").

Keep Lessons Moving at a Good Pace

Teachers often begin with good attention but lose it by spending too much time on minor points or by causing everyone to wait while students respond individually, while equipment is passed out individually, and so forth. Attention will wander when students are waiting or when something they clearly understand is being discussed needlessly. Review lessons are often abused in this way. When students clearly know the material, the review should be cut short. There is no need to ask the next 35 questions simply because they are in the teacher's manual. If only a few students need further review, work with them individually or form them into a special group rather than require all the others to go through the review too.

Monitor Attention During Lessons

Teachers should regularly scan the class or group throughout the lesson. Students are much more likely to maintain attention if they know the teacher regularly watches everyone (both to see if they are paying attention and to note signs of confusion or difficulty). In contrast, teachers who bury their nose in the manual, rivet their eyes on the board, or look only at the student who is reciting are asking for trouble.

Stimulate Attention Periodically

When things become too predictable and repetitive, the mind tends to wander. There are several things teachers can do to help insure continual attention as a lesson or activity progresses.

The teacher's own variability is one important factor. There is no need for theatrics, but lectures delivered in a dull monotone with few facial expressions or gestures soon produce yawns. Teachers should speak loudly enough for everyone to hear and should modulate their tone and volume to break monotony. It also helps to use a variety of techniques so that lessons are not overly repetitive or predictable. Lectures should be mixed with demonstrations, group responses with individual responses, and reading or short factual questions with thought-provoking discussion questions.

Even extended presentations usually can be broken into several parts. By changing voice inflections or using transitional signals ("All right," "Now," etc.) teachers can stimulate attention by cueing students that they are moving into a new phase.

In addition to these more subtle techniques, attention can be stimulated directly. For example, the teacher can challenge the class, "Now, here's a really hard question—let's see if you can figure it out," or create suspense, "Now we come to the tricky part—be alert." When the type of question changes, this can be noted in a statement that not only calls attention to the change, but also stimulates interest: "All right, let's see if we understood the story." "All right, you seem to know the theory, now let's see if you can apply it to a practical problem."

Techniques for stimulating attention should be used in ways that do not call attention to themselves or distract attention from the content. Teachers ordinarily should not say, "Remember, I might call on you at any time to tell me what's happening, so pay attention." It would be better just to use this technique without calling attention to it, meanwhile stimulating interest in the topic and communicating expectations for attention in more positive ways as well.

Maintain Accountability

All students should be accountable for attending to lessons and learning all of the material, not just the parts they recite or demonstrate. Several techniques are useful with students whose attention tends to wander. One is to develop variety and unpredictability in asking questions (Kounin, 1970). Students should know that they may be called on at any time, regardless of what has gone on before. Teachers should occasionally question students again after they have answered an earlier question or ask them to repeat an answer just given by another student, to state whether the answer was correct, or to comment about it ("Paul, do you agree with Ted's answer?"). In using these techniques to insure accountability, teachers must be careful to avoid threatening students. The techniques are intended to challenge the class, stimulate interest, and avoid predictability, not to catch inattentive students in order to embarrass or punish them. If misused this way, they will cause resentment and probably not have the desired positive effects.

Note the emphasis on *occasional* use of these accountability devices; they may be counterproductive if used too often or in the wrong situations. Good and Grouws (1975) found that teachers who used accountability devices moderately were more successful than those who used them either too often or not often enough. This is not surprising, because accountability devices are essentially methods of recapturing lost attention, so that frequent use implies that the teacher either is not doing enough of the fundamental things that establish and maintain good attention in the first place or is unnecessarily diverting student attention and learning time from a focus on lesson content to a focus on accountability concerns.

Situational differences are also important. Accountability devices may be more necessary in whole-class than in small-group situations. In the first place, small-group lessons usually have better signal continuity and momentum, so there is less inattention. Also, because teachers work with students at close quarters in small groups, it is easier for them to stimulate attention using the verbal and nonverbal techniques described above.

In the early grades, such accountability devices are not as important as careful monitoring, because the problems facing teachers are not so much accountability as anxiety, confusion, or short attention spans. In fact, Brophy and Evertson (1976) and Anderson, Evertson, and Brophy (1979) found that teachers who had students read in a predictable order during reading groups got better results than those who called on students to read "randomly." It is not clear why this was so. Possible reasons include reduced anxiety (the predictable pattern provided structure that helped students follow the lesson and minimized fears of being called on unexpectedly) and elimination of competition for response opportunities (young students tend to wave their hands and try to get teachers to call on them when there is no clear turn-taking pattern). In any case, it appears that the main problem facing teachers in the early grades is helping students to be *able* to follow lessons, not making sure that they *choose* to follow them. This is accomplished through such techniques as teaching the children in small groups, having them follow with their finger or a marker, monitoring them regularly to see that they have their place, and so on. Here, predictability is probably helpful.

When students become able to keep track without help, and especially when they learn to anticipate what they will be held accountable for and practice it ahead of time, teachers will have to call on them in less predictable patterns. Notice that we do not say "random" patterns. This is because most investigations of distribution of recitation opportunities by teachers indicate that presumably "random" patterns are not random at all. The brighter and more assertive students seek response opportunities and get called on often, but reticent students rarely get called on at all. To prevent this, teachers should keep track of who has responded and who has not. All students need not get exactly the same number and kinds of response opportunities, but these opportunities should not be monopolized by a few students. Teachers can monitor this by checking or tallying response opportunities in a logbook (in fact, using a simple coding system, they also can keep track of success and failure in handling questions of varying difficulty levels).

Continuing attention can also be fostered by putting questions to the class as a whole and allowing time for thinking before calling on a student to respond. Students who know they may be called on to answer are likely to think about the question and try to form an answer if given time to do so. On the other hand, if the teacher names a student to answer a question before asking it, the rest of the students will know they are not going to be called on. This may cause some of them to turn attention elsewhere.

Other potentially undesirable things that students, especially older ones, can learn from observing predictable patterns are: "The teacher only calls on students who raise their hands." "The teacher always begins with someone in the front row." "If I answer one question, I won't be called on again." "If I raise my hand and give the impression that I understand, the teacher won't check me out." "When we have practice examples on the board, the teacher always takes them in the same order that they are in the book."

Predictable teacher behavior of this sort probably will be noticed up by the students who are searching for ways to "beat the system." This means less attention and, in the long run, less learning.

Terminate Lessons That Have Gone on Too Long

When the group is having difficulty maintaining attention, it is better to end the lesson early than to doggedly continue. This is especially important for younger students, whose attention span for even the best lesson is limited. When lessons go on after the point where they should have been terminated, more of the teacher's time is spent compelling attention and less of the students' time is spent thinking about the material.

Teachers usually know this but sometimes pursue lessons anyway because they do not want to get off schedule. This attitude is self-defeating, because students do not learn efficiently under these conditions and the material will probably have to be retaught. The wise teacher tailors the schedule to the needs of the students.

Teachers sometimes prolong an activity needlessly because they want to give each student a chance to participate individually. This intention is usually laudable, but it may not apply to certain recitation lessons or to activities such as show-and-tell. When recitation becomes boringly repetitive or when show-and-tell becomes stilted and predictable, the teacher should move on to something else. Students who did not get their chance to participate on a particular day can (and should) do so later in the week.

Some teachers deliberately prolong repetitive activities in order to use them as time fillers or opportunities to do paperwork. For this reason, show-and-tell may go on for an hour in certain primary classrooms and older students may be asked to read aloud from readers or to make repetitive recitations when these activities are not really needed or useful. Students know that if activities are really important, teachers will participate actively and pay careful attention to what is happening. If teachers only pay minimal attention or do paperwork, even very young students will become bored. They know an uninterested baby-sitter when they see one.

SEATWORK

The typical elementary school teacher conducts a daily language arts/reading period that lasts for approximately two hours. During reading most teachers instruct small groups of students for about 20 minutes each. Few teachers teach entire classes during the reading period, although it is clear that during language arts most students spend a great deal of time working independently without the direct supervision of the teacher. In order to have time for sustained interaction with small groups during reading (in which the teacher must closely attend to the behavior of individual students), a teacher must organize the class so that students can work productively on their own. Students in most secondary classes spend much time in seatwork activities (e.g., writing essays, solving proofs, etc.). In this section we want to discuss some of the special management problems that are associated with seatwork supervision. We will use the elementary school as a setting for this discussion although the problems are similar (conceptually) at the secondary level.

As noted in Chapter 2, Anderson et al. (1985) conducted one of the few studies of seatwork that examines in depth what students do during seatwork and how they attempt to understand and complete assignments. Results showed that students spent from 30 to 60 percent of time allocated to reading instruction doing some type of seatwork. Furthermore, an average of 50 percent (but in some classes virtually 100 percent) of seatwork assignments used commercial products such as workbooks, dittos, and reading material. In many cases these materials were all from the same basal series.

Although there were some differences from class to class in seatwork assignments, within each class the assignments were very similar across time, with the same form of assignment often used two to five times a week (e.g., "Read each sentence and then choose the picture that represents the meaning of the sentence," or copying sentences with blanks and choosing the correct word from several options).

In six of the eight classes, over half of the seatwork assignments were given to the whole class. Thus, despite the fact that some students were assigned to different groups, they still completed the same seatwork assignment.

Teacher Directions/Explanations

Anderson et al. found that teacher instruction related to seatwork assignments seldom included statements about what would be learned and how the assignment related to other things that students had learned. When teachers did pay attention to students who were doing seatwork, they most often monitored student behavior but not student understanding or performance. For instance, when providing feedback, teachers' comments and explanations were usually procedural (e.g., "Read the sentence and then pick the word that completes the sentence"), with little attention to the cognitive demands of the task (i.e., strategies for selecting the appropriate word). Likewise, much teacher feedback focused on correctness of answers or neatness of work.

Low Achievers' Seatwork

Anderson et al. were especially aware of the inappropriateness of many seatwork assignments that low achievers received (see related discussion in Chapter 4: students perceived as less talented often receive less stimulating and less interesting assignments). These students frequently did poorly on their assignments and often derived answers by using strategies that allowed them to complete assignments without understanding what they were supposed to be learning. For example, one six-year-old student commented as he finished his seatwork, "There! I didn't understand that, but I got it done."

In these classrooms teachers generally emphasized keeping busy and finishing assigned work rather than understanding what was being taught. Anderson et al. suggest that poor seatwork habits developed in first grade may contribute to a subsequent passive learning style. Low achievers, who often work on assignments they do not understand, may come to believe that schoolwork does not have to make sense and that consequently they do not need to obtain additional information or assistance. In contrast, high-achieving students seldom have difficulty with seat-work, so that any problems they have are likely to motivate them to take steps to reduce confusion and to obtain additional information (see the discussion of Good's Passivity Model in Chapter 4).

Others, too, have commented on the need for special care in assigning workbook tasks to low-achieving students because these students spend so much time working on practice activities. However, as Osborn (1984) notes, much of what appears in workbooks is confusing or trivial. Teachers who are effective instructional managers can prevent much wasted time by carefully reviewing work-book and other seatwork assignments and identifying tasks that require additional instruction, tasks that can be completed quickly, and so forth. Table 6.6 gives guidelines (Osborn, 1984) that teachers can use to evaluate workbook assignments.

Because many primary-age students spend 300–400 hours a year doing seatwork during language arts classes, it is imperative that teachers find strategies and activities that enable students to use this time well. Successful seatwork activities have the following characteristics: (1) allow students to work successfully and independently, (2) are interesting and reflect variety both in terms of the type of the assignment and how it is completed, (3) frequently allow students to read for comprehension and pleasure, and (4) occasionally relate to students' personal lives.

Success

From time to time it is necessary for teachers to work in a concentrated, sustained manner with small student groups based on ability or interest. Much seatwork must therefore be designed so that it can be completed successfully by individual students who will not need to interrupt the teacher during group instruction. Successful seatwork does not have to be dull or mechanical, although it is clear that much seatwork assigned in school appears insipid or designed more to fill time than to allow students to develop skills or to gain new insights. Furthermore, students often do not understand the procedures required to do assigned work, despite the relative-ly superficial nature of many seatwork assignments.

Workbooks

An examination of activities included in workbooks illustrates that many assign-ments require only a limited level of reading. These exercises seldom ask students to draw conclusions or reason about the material they read. As the Commission on Reading (Anderson et al., 1985) notes, few workbook activities foster fluency or

Table 6.6   GUIDELINES FOR WORKBOOK TASKS

1. A sufficient proportion of workbook tasks should be relevant to the instruction in the rest of the unit or lesson.

2. Another portion of workbook tasks should provide for a systematic and cumulative review of what has already been taught.

3. Workbooks should reflect the most important (and workbook-appropriate) aspects of what is being taught in the reading program. Less important aspects should remain in the teacher's guide as voluntary activities.

4. Workbooks should contain, in a form that is readily accessible to students and teachers, extra tasks for students who need extra practice.

5. The vocabulary and concept level of workbook tasks should relate to those of the rest of the program and to the students using the program.

6. The language used in workbook tasks must be consistent with that used in the rest of the lesson and in the rest of the workbook.

7. Instructions to students should be clear and easy to follow; brevity is a virtue.

8. The layout of pages should combine attractiveness with utility.

9. Workbook tasks should contain enough content so that there is a chance a student doing the task will *learn* something and not simply be *exposed* to something.

10. Tasks that require students to make discriminations must be preceded by a sufficient number of tasks that provide practice on components of the discriminations.

11. The content of workbook tasks must be accurate and precise; workbook tasks must not present wrong information or perpetuate misrules.

12. At least some workbook tasks should be fun and have obvious benefits.

13. Most student response modes should be consistent from task to task.

14. Student response modes should be the closest possible to reading and writing.

15. The instructional design of individual tasks and of task sequences should be carefully planned.

16. Workbooks should contain a finite number of task types and forms.

17. The art that appears on workbook pages must be consistent with the prose of the task.

18. Cute, nonfunctional, space- and time-consuming tasks should be avoided.

19. When appropriate, tasks should be accompanied by brief explanations of purpose for both teachers and students.

20. English-major humor should be avoided.

Source: Osborn, J. (1984). Workbooks that accompany basal reading programs. In G. Duffy, L. Roehler, & J. Mason (Eds.), *Comprehension instruction: Perspectives and suggestions.* New York: Longman.

strategic reading. Almost none requires extended writing. Rather, responses usually involve placing a word in a blank, circling or underlining a particular word, or selecting one of several choices. The exercises often have difficult-to-understand directions and drill students on skills that have little value in learning to read. Furthermore, workbook activities are often unrelated to the current reading lesson.

Classroom research consistently shows that the amount of time devoted to worksheets is unrelated to students' year-to-year gains in reading proficiency. This is not surprising, given the typically low level of these assignments. For these reasons, teachers either need to improve workbook assignments and to supplement them with more meaningful activities or to use such materials less frequently in their classrooms.

Variety and Interest

Although most assigned work consists of workbook tasks that students complete individually, there are countless other tasks that students can complete alone (read, read and answer questions, write an alternate ending to a story, write a story, write an ending for a story that another student started). To allow variety in lessons, teachers should occasionally have students work together to complete seatwork (e.g., two or more students may debate issues in a story or compare and contrast endings that they have written independently). Older elementary students in particular benefit from the chance to work with and learn from peers. Giving students choices among sound academic alternatives is another way to increase students' work involvement.

Assignments that students are interested in may also encourage sustained effort over a long period of time. For example, one of the authors observed a small group of fifth-grade students write and rewrite with great enthusiasm and intensity their descriptions of a baseball bubble gum card during several free time periods over two weeks. Students displayed considerable imagination in their writing (e.g., detailed records of players' accomplishments with various baseball clubs) and had a chance to practice several skills (organizing and editing information) during an enjoyable activity.

Reading for Pleasure

Although students need decoding skills and some practice developing those skills, they should often be allowed to read a variety of books, including books of personal interest. Unfortunately, in too many reading classes, especially at the primary level, students have inadequate time to engage in silent reading for pleasure. Most second graders and some first graders will benefit from brief periods during which they can read books that they choose. Obviously, students in the upper elementary grades will benefit from more frequent silent reading.

Meaningful Assignments

Although it may not be necessary to have many assignments that allow students to influence other persons and future classroom events, teachers should schedule such activities occasionally. Allowing third- and fourth-grade students to prepare and to share stories with kindergarten and first-grade students can promote valuable associations and insights and provide older students with a real audience. Similarly, third- and fourth-grade students will benefit from seeing or reading plays written by sixth graders and the chance to write letters in response (of thanks, seeking specific information, or providing critiques). Similarly, kindergarten students can learn from communicating with others (e.g., preparing valentines for parents or senior citizens) and gain satisfaction from oral and written communication. Students enjoy and become involved in activities that allow them to influence classroom events (e.g., responding to themes like, "If I could be the teacher for the day . . .").

Considering the limited time available in most classrooms for independent reading and for writing, it is likely that reading instruction could be improved in many classrooms by allowing students more time to write and to read independently rather than having them fill out drillsheet after drillsheet. Skill drills are needed, but spending 70 percent of reading instruction time on drillsheets is inappropriate; teachers might want to reduce this figure to perhaps 25 percent and spend the remaining time on other activities.

Similarly, increasing the time available for independent reading would be a helpful way to improve reading instruction. Reading a book, in contrast to doing computer drills or filling out workbook pages, provides an opportunity for students to practice all aspects of reading. Students decode, but also anticipate and compare their thoughts with those of the author. Students who read independently get considerable practice in reading, and this practice, combined with a high level of interest, helps to explain why children who read independently make more progress in reading than do students who do not read silently.

According to the Commission on Reading, an examination of schools that are successful in promoting independent reading reveals that one important factor is ready access to books. However, 15 percent of American schools do not have libraries and most schools have small libraries, averaging about 13 volumes per student. Furthermore, many of these books are quite old and thus of limited interest to today's students. Teachers could promote independent reading by developing their own classroom libraries (perhaps sharing materials with other teachers at their grade levels) in order to have challenging, interesting materials available to their students.

The priority that classroom teachers give to independent reading can also affect students' reading outside of school. The Commission on Reading recommends that two hours a week of independent reading should be expected by the time children are in the third or fourth grade. However, if students are to do this, they will need ready access to books and guidance in choosing appropriate and interesting books. Some of the homework that students are assigned could involve having students read books and then share their new knowledge and understandings with others (e.g., writing a letter to a friend about the important message in a book as opposed to always writing a dry book report).

We have discussed reading and language arts as a special instance of seatwork/management issues that teachers face. However, it is clear that at all levels of schooling and in all subjects, students spend considerable time in independent seatwork activities. For example, in an intensive analysis of narrative records from junior high school English classes, Doyle (1984) found that successful managers established an activity system early in the year and closely supervised the system, ushering it along and protecting it from intrusion or disruption. During seatwork for the first three weeks, for example, contacts with individual students were brief and the teachers circulated around the room maintaining a whole-group perspective. They tended to promote the curriculum and talk about work rather than misbehavior. Less successful managers, on the other hand, focused public attention on misbehavior by their frequent reprimands, so that eventually all work ceased. By November of the school year, observations indicated that if a work system was established effectively, a successful teacher often spent less time supervising the class and more time with individual students. By this point, the work system itself seemed to maintain order and the teacher was free to attend to other classroom events.

If independent work is to be productive, teachers must insure that the work is meaningful and appropriate for all students. Teachers who structure classroom assignments so that they are meaningful to students and in such ways that students can obtain information, resources, and direction as needed will have done much to guarantee that students will be involved in assigned work.

SUMMARY

The key to successful classroom management is prevention—teachers do not have to deal with misbehavior that never occurs. Many problems originate when students are crowded together, forced to wait, or idle because they have nothing to do or do not know what to do.

Crowding can be minimized in several ways. Classroom management and equipment storage should be planned so that traffic is minimized and needed items are accessible. Problems that occur when everyone needs the same item can be reduced by stocking several items rather than just one or by storing materials in several small containers rather than in one large one. Waiting can be minimized by allowing students to handle most management tasks on their own, by eliminating needless rituals and formalities, by simultaneously assigning various jobs to different subgroups rather than having the whole class tackle one job at a time, and by establishing rules where needed. Confusion and idleness can be minimized by preparing appropriate independent work assignments in sufficient quantity and variety and by seeing that students know what to do if they finish or if they need help.

It is important that teachers specify desired behavior in positive terms, provide instruction and opportunities to practice routines, monitor students for compliance with expectations, and praise individual students for meeting those expectations. Teaching strategies should maximize student attention to lessons and involvement in productive activities. Teachers should establish clear signals to gain students' attention and alert them to the fact that an activity is beginning. Next they should provide a brief overview or advance organizer to tell students what is coming and help them prepare for it. Then teachers should keep the activity moving at a brisk pace, avoiding unnecessary delays. If an activity has gone on too long, it should be terminated. When it is necessary to hold students accountable for material and to stimulate their continuing attention, teachers should vary their questioning patterns and avoid falling into repeated, predictable patterns that tempt certain students to try to "beat the system."

Teachers who consistently apply the strategies presented in this chapter will maximize productive student activity and minimize the time students spend "in neutral" or misbehaving. All aspects of good management must occur in combination and mutually reinforce one another to be maximally effective. Attempts to use isolated techniques are unlikely to succeed, especially over a long period.

SUGGESTED ACTIVITIES AND QUESTIONS

6.1. Teachers should attend to desirable student behavior. Why do many teachers spend too much time reacting to misbehavior, especially of a minor sort?

6.2. Table 6.5 lists some of the procedures that a junior high teacher should establish at the beginning of the year. What other procedures might an elementary school teacher want to establish early in the school year?

6.3. In one section in this chapter, advice is given for making positive requests. The examples used on page (234) are primarily elementary school examples. Write five examples of positive language that would be appropriate at the high school level.

6.4. Teachers should make learning rewarding rather than teach students that school assignments are done only to get rewards, adult approval, opportunity to play a game, a high grade, and so forth. Teachers sometimes conduct useful and enjoyable learning activities only to undermine their efforts to foster intrinsic motivation by telling students such things as "You've done so well today that I am going to give you a free hour after lunch so you can do the things you really want to do." What guidelines should teachers follow when they summarize learning activities? Apply your ideas to the case study of Mrs. Turner in Chapter 1. What would be an effective way to end the lesson she presented? Write out your ending in a few sentences and compare it to the endings written by others.

6.5. Describe in your own words how teachers can praise appropriately. What type of student will be most difficult for *you* to praise? Why?

6.6. Why is it suggested that teachers show variety and unpredictability in asking questions? Watch a videotape of a teacher conducting a class discussion and determine whether the teacher's questioning style is unpredictable.

6.7. Think about the grade level you teach or plan to teach and specify the minimum set of rules that will be observed in your room. Be sure to state your rules in positive terms. Are your rules really essential for establishing a good learning climate? Why?

6.8. Describe how you will establish rules and procedures in your classroom and what criteria you will use for adding or deleting them as the year progresses.

6.9. Why is it important to prevent discipline problems before they occur? What preventive steps can teachers take to reduce the number of discipline problems they will face?

6.10. While conducting a reading group, a teacher notices two students talking loudly at table 1. Three other students at table 1 are busily engaged in independent activities. Should the teacher stop the misbehavior? If so, how? Should the teacher focus on desirable or undesirable behavior? After you read Chapter 7, return to this question and see if you would answer it in the same way.

6.11. Using the criteria given in this chapter for praising effectively, describe how you should respond to these situations:
   a. The class as a whole, except for two students, does very well on a test.
   b. One of your slowest students struggles but eventually succeeds in doing a relatively easy math problem at the board, in front of the class.
   c. One of your alienated underachievers does very well on a test, but you suspect cheating or lucky guessing.
   d. Mary and Joel turn in perfect papers again this week, as they have all term long.
   e. Randy asks a question that is relevant to the topic and indicates interest and good thinking on his part, although he would have known the answer to his question if he had read the assignment.
   f. Your lowest reading group finally finishes a reader that the other groups finished weeks ago.
   g. Dull, methodical Bernie turns in a composition that is trite but neat and error-free. Creative but erratic Linda turns in one that contains exciting content written sloppily with many spelling errors.

6.12. Think about seatwork assignments you will make. What kinds are appropriate for the subject/grade you will teach? Why?

REFERENCES

Ames, C., & Ames, R. (1985). *Research on motivation in education: Vol. 2: The classroom milieu.* New York: Academic Press.

Anderson, H., & Brewer, H. (1945). Studies of teachers' classroom personalities. I: Dominative and socially integrative behavior of kindergarten teachers. *Applied Psychological Monographs.*

Anderson, L., Brubaker, N., Alleman-Brooks, J., & Duffy, G. (1985). A qualitative study of seatwork in first-grade classrooms. *Elementary School Journal, 86,* 123–140.

Anderson, L., Evertson, C., & Brophy, J. (1979). An experimental study of effective teaching in first-grade reading groups. *Elementary School Journal, 79,* 193–223.

Anderson, L., Evertson, C., & Emmer, E. (1980). Dimensions in classroom management derived from recent research. *Journal of Curriculum Studies, 12,* 343–356.

Anderson, R., Hiebert, E., Scott, J., & Wilkinson, I. (1985). *Becoming a nation of readers: The report of the Commission on Reading.* Washington, DC: National Institute of Education.

Bandura, A. (1969). *Principles of behavior modification.* New York: Holt, Rinehart and Winston.

Bellack, A., Kliebard, H., Hyman, R., & Smith, F. (1966). *The language of the classroom.* New York: Teachers College Press.

Blumenfeld, P., Pintrich, P., Meece, J., & Wessels, K. (1982). The formation and role of self-perceptions of ability in elementary classrooms. *Elementary School Journal, 82,* 401–420.

Borg, W., & Ascione, F. (1982). Classroom management in elementary mainstreaming classrooms. *Journal of Educational Psychology, 74,* 85–95.

Brookover, W., Schweitzer, J., Schneider, J., Beady, C., Flood, P., & Wisenbaker, J. (1978). Elementary school social climate and school achievement. *American Educational Research Journal, 15,* 301–318.

Brophy, J. (1981). Teacher praise: A functional analysis. *Review of Educational Research, 51,* 5–32.

Brophy, J., & Evertson, C. (1976). *Learning from teaching: A developmental perspective.* Boston: Allyn & Bacon.

Brophy, J., Evertson, C., Anderson, L., Baum, M., & Crawford, J. (1981). *Student characteristics and teaching.* New York: Longman.

Brophy, J., & Good, T. (1986). Teacher behavior and student achievement. In M. Wittrock (Ed.), *Handbook of research on teaching* (3rd ed.). New York: Macmillan.

Brophy, J., & Putnam, J. (1979). Classroom management in the elementary grades. In D. Duke (Ed.), *Classroom management. (Seventy-eighth yearbook of the National Society for the Study of Education, Part II.)* Chicago: University of Chicago Press.

Condry, J., & Chambers, J. (1978). Intrinsic motivation and the process of learning. In M. Lepper & D. Greene (Eds.), *The hidden costs of reward: New perspectives on the psychology of human motivation.* Hillsdale, NJ: Erlbaum.

Corno, L., & Rohrkemper, M. (1985). The intrinsic motivation to learn in classrooms. In C. Ames & R. Ames (Eds.), *Research on motivation in education. Vol. 2: The classroom milieu.* New York: Academic Press.

Deci, E. (1975). *Intrinsic motivation.* New York: Plenum.

Deci, E., & Ryan, R. (1980). The empirical exploration of intrinsic motivational processes. In L. Berkowitz (Ed.), *Advances in experimental social psychology* (Vol. 13). New York: Academic Press.

Doyle, W. (1984). How order is achieved in classrooms: An interim report. *Journal of Curriculum Studies, 16,* 259–277.

Doyle, W. (1986). Classroom organization and management. In M. Wittrock (Ed.), *Handbook of research on teaching* (3rd ed.). New York: Macmillan.

Dunkin, M., & Biddle, B. (1974). *The study of teaching.* New York: Holt, Rinehart and Winston.

Dweck, C., Davidson, W., Nelson, S., & Enna, B. (1978). Sex differences in learned helplessness: II. The contingencies of evaluative feedback in the classroom; III. An experimental analysis. *Developmental Psychology, 14,* 268–276.

Eden, D. (1975). Intrinsic and extrinsic rewards and motives: Replication and extension with Kibbutz workers. *Journal of Applied Social Psychology, 5,* 348–361.

Emmer, E., Evertson, C., & Anderson, L. (1980). Effective classroom management at the beginning of the school year. *Elementary School Journal, 80,* 219–231.

Emmer, E., Evertson, C., Sanford, J., Clements, B., & Worsham, M. (1982). *Organizing and managing the junior high classroom.* Report No. 6151. Austin: University of Texas, Research and Development Center for Teacher Education.

Emmer, E., Sanford, J., Clements, B., & Martin, J. (1981). *The design of the Junior High Management Improvement Study.* Report No. 6150. Austin: University of Texas, Research and Development Center for Teacher Education.

Evertson, C. (1985). Training teachers in classroom management: An experimental study in secondary school classrooms. *Journal of Educational Research, 79,* 51–58.

Evertson, C., Anderson, C., Anderson, L., & Brophy, J. (1980). Relationships between classroom behaviors and student outcomes in junior high mathematics and English classes. *American Educational Research Journal, 17,* 43–60.

Evertson, C., & Emmer, E. (1982a). Effective management at the beginning of the school year in junior high classes. *Journal of Educational Psychology, 74,* 485–498.

Evertson, C., & Emmer, E. (1982b). Preventive classroom management. In D. Duke (Ed.), *Helping teachers manage classrooms.* Alexandria, VA: Association for Supervision and Curriculum Development.

Evertson, C., Emmer, E., Clements, B., Sanford, J., & Worsham, M. (1981). *Organizing and managing the elementary school classroom.* Report No. 6060. Austin: University of Texas, Research and Development Center for Teacher Education.

Evertson, C., Emmer, E., Sanford, J., & Clements, B. (1983). Improving classroom management: An experiment in elementary classrooms. *Elementary School Journal, 84,* 173–188.

Fisher, C., Berliner, D., Filby, N., Marliave, R., Cahen, L., & Dishaw, M. (1980). Teaching behaviors, academic learning time, and student achievement: An overview. In C. Denham & A. Lieberman (Eds.), *Time to learn.* Washington, DC: National Institute of Education, U.S. Department of Education.

Gambrell, L., Wilson, R., & Gantt, W. (1981). Classroom observations of task-attending behaviors of good and poor readers. *Journal of Educational Research, 74,* 400–405.

Good, T., & Grouws, D. (1975). *Process-product relationships in fourth-grade mathematics classrooms.* Final report of the National Institute of Education Grant NIE-G-00-3-0123. Columbia: University of Missouri.

Jackson, P. (1968). *Life in classrooms.* New York: Holt, Rinehart and Winston.

Jorgenson, G. (1977). Relationship of classroom behavior to the accuracy of the match between material difficulty and student ability. *Journal of Educational Psychology, 69,* 24–32.

Kleinfeld, J. (1975). Effective teachers of Eskimo and Indian students. *School Review, 83,* 301–344.

Kounin, J. (1970). *Discipline and group management in classrooms.* New York: Holt, Rinehart and Winston.

Kruglanski, A. (1978). Endogeneous attribution and intrinsic motivation. In M. Lepper & D. Greene (Eds.), *The hidden costs of reward: New perspectives on the psychology of human motivation.* Hillsdale, NJ: Erlbaum.

Lepper, M. (1982). Extrinsic reward and intrinsic motivation: Implications for the classroom. In J. Levine & M. Wang (Eds.), *Teacher and student perceptions: Implications for learning.* Hillsdale, NJ: Erlbaum.

Lepper, M., & Greene, D. (1978). *The hidden costs of reward: New perspectives on the psychology of human motivation.* Hillsdale, NJ: Erlbaum.

Mehan, H. (1974). Accomplishing classroom lessons. In A. Cicourel, K. Jennings, S. Jennings, K. Lieter, R. MacKay, H. Mehan, & D. Roth (Eds.), *Language use and school performance*. New York: Academic Press.

Meyer, W., Bachmann, M., Biermann, U., Hempelmann, M., Ploger, F., & Spiller, H. (1979). The informational value of evaluative behavior: Influences of praise and blame on perceptions of ability. *Journal of Educational Psychology, 71,* 259–268.

Montessori, M. (1964). *The Montessori method.* New York: Schocken.

Moore, O., & Anderson, A. (1969). Some principles for design of clarifying educational environments. In D. Goslin (Ed.), *Handbook for socialization theory and research.* Chicago: Rand McNally.

Nash, R. (1976). Pupils' expectations of their teachers. In M. Stubbs & S. Delamont (Eds.), *Explorations in classroom observation.* New York: Wiley.

Natriello, G., & Dornbusch, S. (1984). *Teacher evaluative standards and student effort.* New York: Longman.

Osborn, J. (1984). Workbooks that accompany basal reading programs. In G. Duffy, L. Roehler, & J. Mason (Eds.), *Comprehension instruction: Perspectives and suggestions.* New York: Longman.

O'Leary, K., & O'Leary, S. (Eds.). (1977). *Classroom management: The successful use of behavior modification* (2nd ed.). New York: Pergamon.

Piaget, J. (1952). *The origins of intelligence in children.* New York: International Universities Press.

Rosenshine, B. (1976). Classroom instruction. In N. Gage (Ed.), *The psychology of teaching methods. (Seventy-fifth yearbook of the National Society for the Study of Education.)* Chicago: University of Chicago Press.

Sanford, J., Clements, C., & Emmer, E. (1981). *Communicating results of classroom management research to practitioners.* Report No. 6051A. Austin: University of Texas, Research and Development Center for Teacher Education.

Ware, B. (1978). What rewards do students want? *Phi Delta Kappan, 59,* 355–356.

Weinstein, R. (1976). Reading group membership in first grade: Teacher behaviors and pupil experience over time. *Journal of Educational Psychology, 68,* 103–116.

FORM 6.1. Transitions and Group Management

USE: *During organizational and transition periods before, between, and*
after lessons and organized activities
PURPOSE: *To see if teacher manages these periods efficiently and avoids*
needless delays and regimentation
How does the teacher handle early morning routines, transitions be-
tween activities, and clean-up and preparation time?

Record any information relevant to the following questions:

1. Does the teacher do things that students could do for themselves?

2. Are there delays caused because everyone must line up or wait his turn?
   Can these be reduced with a more efficient procedure?

3. Does the teacher give clear instructions about what to do next before
   breaking a group and entering a transition? *Students often aren't clear*
   about assignment so they question her during transitions and while
   she is starting to teach next group.

4. Does the teacher circulate during transitions, to handle individual needs?
   Does he take care of these before attempting to begin a new activity?
   Mostly, problem is poor directions *before* *transition, rather*
   than failure to circulate here.

5. Does the teacher signal the end of a transition and the beginning of a
   structured activity properly, and quickly gain everyone's attention?
   Good signal but sometimes loses attention by failing to
   start briskly. Sometimes has 2 or 3 false starts.

Check if applicable:

_____ 1. Transitions come too abruptly for students because teacher
              fails to give advance warning or finish up reminders when
              needed

_____ 2. The teacher insists on unnecessary rituals or formalisms that
              cause delays or disruptions (describe)

___✓___ 3. Teacher is often interrupted by individuals with the same prob-
              lem or request; this could be handled by establishing a general
              rule or procedure (describe) *See # 3 above.*

___✓___ 4. Delays occur because frequently used materials are stored in
              hard to reach places *Pencil sharpener too close to*
              reading group area, causing frequent distractions.

_____ 5. Poor traffic patterns result in pushing, bumping, or needless
              noise

_____ 6. Poor seating patterns screen some students from teacher's view
              or cause students needless distraction

_____ 7. Delays occur while teacher prepares equipment or illustrations
              that should have been prepared earlier

FORM 6.2. Poor Attention to Lessons

USE: *When teacher is having difficulty keeping students attentive to a lesson*
PURPOSE: *To identify the probable cause of the poor attention*
     When students are notably inattentive to a lesson or activity, what is the apparent reason? (Check any that apply)

_____   1. Activity has gone on too long
_____   2. Activity is below students' level or is needless review
_____   3. Teacher is continually lecturing, not getting enough student
                 participation
___✓___   4. Teacher fails to monitor attention—poor eye contact
___✓___   5. Teacher overdwells, needlessly repeating and rephrasing
_____   6. Teacher calls on students in an easily predictable pattern
_____   7. Teacher always names student before asking question
___✓___   8. Activity lacks continuity because teacher keeps interrupting
                 (specify cause for interruption)
_____   9. Activity lacks variety, has settled into an overly predictable or
                 boring routine
_____   10. Other (indicate)

Frequent delays while teacher finds place in manual. This is also main reason for poor eye contact. #5 often asks teacher for attention (and gets it) but then instead of teaching the teacher elaborates for 30-40 seconds on why the students should listen and when he ends the sermon and begins the lesson several students have "drifted" away.

FORM 6.3. Seatwork Quality and Management

USE: Whenever sufficient information is available
PURPOSE: To assess the effectiveness of the seatwork assignments and
of the teacher's seatwork management and accountability systems
Given the subject matter and the students, how effective is the
seatwork component of the teacher's total instructional program? (check all
that apply).

_____ 1. Assignments are pitched at the right level of difficulty
(students can achieve high levels of success if they put forth
reasonable effort)
_____ 2. If necessary, different students are given different
assignments
_____ 3. The work involves useful practice or application of concepts
or skills being taught
_____ 4. The work is challenging enough to be worthwhile
_____ 5. The work is varied enough to be interesting
_____ 6. The students are required to show calculations rather than
just answers, and to compose verbal responses rather than
just circle, underline, or fill in single words
_____ 7. The teacher prepares the students for the assignment before
releasing them to work on it independently
_____ 8. Assignments are posted for reference by students who are
not sure about what to do or when it needs to be turned in
_____ 9. Unless busy teaching a small group, the teacher circulates to
supervise and assist the students during seatwork times
_____ 10. Immediate help is available to students who get stuck
_____ 11. The students know when and how to get help if they need it
_____ 12. The students know what options are available to them if they
finish their assignment early
_____ 13. Assignments are routinely checked and reviewed with the
class
_____ 14. The teacher has articulated a clear accountability system
informing students of the consequences of failure to turn in
assignments or turning in incomplete or late work
_____ 15. Students who do not meet criteria must redo assignments or
complete alternate assignments
_____ 16. There are clear expectations regarding make-up work by
students who have been absent

NOTES:

FORM 6.4. Classroom Rules and Routine

USE: Whenever sufficient information is available
PURPOSE: To assess the adequacy of the teacher's system of classroom
   rules and routines
   Students should be clear about each of the following issues. Check
each issue that is handled adequately through classroom rules or routines,
and explain the problem when the issue is not handled adequately.

———— 1. What books and supplies are to be brought to class routinely
———— 2. Where to sit and store personal belongings
———— 3. Precisely when class begins and what is expected at that
         time (in terms of attention to the teacher and advance
         preparation of materials)
———— 4. When and for what purposes students may leave their seats
———— 5. When and for what purposes students may converse with
         one another
———— 6. Rules for participation in whole-class or small group lessons
         (when, if at all, it is allowable to call out responses without
         first raising one's hand and being recognized)
———— 7. When it is permissible to approach the teacher with personal
         concerns and when the teacher should not be interrupted
         except for emergencies
———— 8. What to do if you enter the class late or leave it early
———— 9. Rules regarding use of equipment and learning centers
———— 10. Procedures for distributing and collecting work or supplies
———— 11. What forms of student cooperation in working on
         assignments are allowed or encouraged
———— 12. Due dates for assignments and penalties for unexcused late,
         incomplete, or missing work
———— 13. What will be taken into account in assigning grades
———— 14. Other (sources of student confusion or managerial difficulty
         that could be eliminated by clarifying rules or procedures)

NOTES:

7 Management II: Coping With Problems Effectively

Consistent use of the techniques discussed in the previous chapter will minimize inattention and misbehavior, especially if activities are enjoyable and appropriate to students' needs and interests. Some problems will occur, however, and teachers must be prepared to cope with them. The present chapter contains suggestions on how to analyze such problems when they occur, identify their causes accurately, and respond effectively.

DEALING WITH MINOR INATTENTION AND MISBEHAVIOR

Techniques for dealing with minor inattention or misbehavior are designed to achieve a single goal: *eliminate the problem quickly and with minimal distraction of other students*. These techniques should be used whenever students are engaged in minor mischief and the teacher wants to return their attention to work as quickly as possible.

Monitor the Entire Classroom Regularly

Kounin (1970) stressed that successful classroom managers showed "with-it-ness"—their students knew that these teachers always "knew what was going on" in their classrooms. Teachers who regularly scan the classroom are able to respond to problems effectively and nip most of them in the bud. Those who fail to notice what is going on are prone to such errors as failing to intervene until a problem becomes disruptive or spreads to other students, attending to a minor problem while failing to notice a more serious one, or rebuking a student who was drawn into a dispute instead of the one who started it. Teachers who make such errors regularly convince students that the teachers do not know what is happening. This will make the students more likely to misbehave and also to test teachers by talking back or trying to confuse them.

Many conflicts between students begin when one student "starts something" while the teacher's back is turned. Once a student becomes inattentive it is likely that at least some other students will be drawn off-task. For example, Felmlee, Eder, and Tsui (1985) present evidence that distracting inattention on the part of one student significantly affects the rate at which other students are inattentive. Thus, it is important for teachers to monitor their classrooms regularly, even while conducting small-group lessons, writing on the board, or talking with individual students.

Seating patterns should be arranged so that this is possible. Teachers should always be able to see all students. During small-group activities, the teacher should sit facing most students who are involved in seatwork, and students in the small group should sit facing the teacher, with their backs to the rest of the class. In this way, the teacher can monitor the whole class and distractions to students in the group will be minimized.

Ignore Minor, Fleeting Misbehavior

Teachers should not intervene every time they notice a problem, because intervention may be more disruptive than the problem itself. When this is true, it is better for the teacher to delay action or simply ignore the problem. For example, teachers may notice that a student has dropped a pencil or neglected to replace some equipment that should be put away. Such incidents usually require action, but rarely immediate action. Teachers should wait until they can deal with these problems without disrupting the class. Stopping a lesson to tell a student to pick up a pencil or put away a book will only cause more problems.

Much minor misbehavior can be ignored, especially when it is fleeting. If the group is distracted because someone accidentally drops a book, or if two students briefly whisper and then return attention to the lesson, it is usually best to take no action at all. The students' attention is already back on the lesson, and there is nothing to be gained by disrupting the lesson to call attention to minor misbehavior that is already completed.

Stop Sustained Minor Misbehavior Without Disrupting Activity

When minor misbehavior is repeated or intensified, or when it threatens to spread or become disruptive, teachers cannot simply ignore it; they must take action to stop it. Unless the misbehavior is serious enough to call for investigation (and it seldom is), teachers should use techniques designed to eliminate it as quickly and nondisruptively as possible. These techniques should be used in preference to more disruptive ones when the goal is simply to return inattentive students to work and avoid distracting other students.

1. *Eye contact.* When it can be established, simple eye contact will compel attention. To make sure the message is received, teachers can add head

nods or gestures such as looking at the book the student is supposed to be reading. Eye contact is doubly effective in stopping minor problems for teachers who regularly scan the room. When students know that their teacher regularly scans the room, they will tend to look at the teacher when misbehaving (to see if the teacher is watching). This makes it easier for the teacher to intervene through eye contact.

2. *Touch and gesture.* When the students are close by, as in small-group situations, teachers do not need to wait to establish eye contact. Instead, they can use touch or gesture to gain attention. A light tap, perhaps followed by a gesture toward the book, delivers the message without need for verbalization.

Gestures are also helpful in dealing with events going on elsewhere in the room. If eye contact can be established, teachers may be able to communicate by shaking their heads, placing their fingers to their lips, or pointing. Such gestures are less disruptive than leaving the group or speaking to students across the room. In general, touch and gesture are most useful in the early grades, where much teaching is done in small groups and distraction is a frequent problem. Also, some adolescents resent any touching by teachers.

3. *Physical proximity.* When teachers are checking seatwork or moving about the room, they often can eliminate minor misbehavior simply by moving close to the students involved. If students know what they are supposed to be doing, the teacher's physical presence will motivate them to get busy. This technique is especially useful with older elementary students.

4. *Asking for responses.* During lessons, the simplest method of capturing students' attention may be to ask them questions or call for responses. Such requests automatically compel attention and do so without mentioning the misbehavior.

This technique should be used with care, however, because it can backfire. If used too often, students may perceive it as an attempt to "catch" them. Also, the questions must be ones that students can answer. Questions that students cannot meaningfully respond to (because they were not paying attention to the previous question) should not be asked. Such questions only embarrass the students and force them to admit that they were not paying attention (thereby violating an important principle by focusing on the misbehavior instead of the lesson) or, if they dare, to respond with a sarcastic or aggressive remark. Thus, it would not be appropriate to ask a clearly inattentive student, "John, what did Tom just say?" Acceptable alternatives would be to move toward John, to call his name and gesture, or to ask him a question that he can respond to even if he did not hear the previous one ("John, Tom says that the villain was motivated by jealousy—what do you think?").

In summary, these are several techniques that enable teachers to eliminate minor problems without disrupting activity or calling attention to the misbehavior. Eye contact, touch and gesture, and physical proximity require no verbalization and are especially effective with younger students. Calling on the student to answer a question is effective if not done too often and if the response request is reasonable.

DEALING WITH PROLONGED OR DISRUPTIVE MISBEHAVIOR

What should teachers do when techniques for preventing inattention and dealing with minor misbehavior have not worked or when misbehavior is serious enough to require intervention? Suggestions for dealing with these more serious matters are presented in this section.

Stopping Misbehavior Through Direct Intervention

When misbehavior is dangerous or seriously disruptive, teachers will have to stop it directly by calling out the students' names and correcting them. Because such direct intervention is itself disruptive, it should be used only when necessary.

Also, like the techniques described in the previous section, *direct intervention should be used only when no information is needed*—when both the teacher and the disruptive students know what the students are supposed to be doing and the nature of the misbehavior is obvious to the teacher. This includes such behavior as loud socializing, shooting wads of paper or rubber bands, and copying during a test. In situations like these, where teachers can see that students have become distracted from well-defined tasks, they do not need additional information to be able to act. They only need to stop the misbehavior and return the students to the task.

In more ambiguous situations where students cannot reasonably be expected to know what they are supposed to be doing or in situations where the teacher is not sure what is going on (e.g., two students are talking but may or may not be discussing the problem as directed), the teacher may need to get more information and make some decisions before intervening with direct instructions.

There are two basic ways for teachers to intervene directly. First, they can *demand appropriate behavior*. Such demands should be short, direct, and to the point, naming the students and indicating what they should be doing. The teacher should speak firmly and loudly enough to be heard but should not shout or nag. Commands such as "John! Get back to your seat and get to work" and "Mary, Laura! Stop talking and pay attention to me" unnecessarily label the misbehavior or call attention to it. Instead, a brief direction telling the students what to do will be sufficient: "John, finish your work" and "Mary and Laura, look here."

A second direct intervention technique is to *remind students of rules and expectations*. If clear rules have been established, with thorough explanation or discussion of the reasons for them, teachers can then use brief reminders of these rules to prevent or stop misbehavior. Quick rule reminders can serve these purposes without requiring teachers to sermonize excessively or embarrass students unnecessarily. During independent work periods, reminders are often the best responses to misbehavior, especially loudness and disruption. When the class has become noisy, rather than naming the offenders, it may be simplest for the teacher to say, "Class, you're getting too loud. Remember, talk only about the assignment, and speak softly."

As with other forms of direct intervention, rule reminders should be brief and firm. Usually they are preferable to demanding appropriate behavior because they help students internalize behavioral control. When students are clear about rules and the reasons for them, rule reminders help them see their responsibility for their own misbehavior and help keep down conflict ("Linda, if you have finished your assignment you can choose another activity, but don't bother Betty. Remember, we don't disturb people who are busy working").

In summary, situations in which students know what to do but are not doing it because they are engaged in *disruptive* misbehavior call for intervention. Such intervention should be brief and direct, stressing appropriate behavior rather than misbehavior. Sometimes this can be done through a simple rule reminder; other times the teacher will have to indicate appropriate behavior in more specific detail.

Inappropriate Intervention

There are several things that teachers should *not* do in response to easily interpretable misbehavior. *First, teachers should not ask questions about obvious misbehavior*. This situation is clear and the goal is simply to return the misbehaving students to productive work; there is no need to conduct an investigation. Also, the questions asked in such situations tend to be counterproductive, rhetorical questions. The essential meaninglessness of these questions and the tone in which they are asked show that they are not really questions at all. Instead, they are attacks on the student: "What's the matter with you?" "How many times do I have to tell you to get busy?" Such questions do no good and may cause embarrassment, fear, or resentment.

Teachers should also *avoid unnecessary threats and appeals to authority*. By simply stating how they want the students to behave, teachers communicate the expectation that they will be obeyed. However, if they add a threat ("Do it or else . . ."), they not only create conflict with the students but also suggest indirectly that they are not sure the students will obey.

If the students should ask why teachers are telling them to do something, teachers should give reasons. Teachers who become defensive and appeal to authority ("You'll do it because I say so!") will only produce anger and resentment. Such behavior constitutes a direct challenge to students and may cause them to lose face before their peers, so it may even produce an outburst against the teacher. Furthermore, if onlookers feel that the teacher is acting unfairly, the teacher's relationship with them will suffer too.

Finally, teachers must *avoid overdwelling on the misbehavior itself* (nagging). In a direct intervention situation, there is no reason to describe the present misbehavior in detail or to catalog the student's misbehavior during the past week, month, or year. Here again, this constitutes an attack on the student rather than a corrective measure, places the teacher in conflict with the student, and endangers credibility and respect. If a teacher does this regularly, students may come to see it as funny. Some may even begin to provoke the teacher deliberately, just to see if they can trigger a new or more spectacular response.

Teachers sometimes forget to stress desired behavior and get into the rut of just describing misbehavior instead of changing it. In effect, they tell students that they have given up hope of change ("Mary, every day I have to speak to you for fooling around instead of doing your work. It's the same again today. How many times do I have to tell you? You never learn."). Chances are that it will be the same story tomorrow and the day after too, unless the teacher begins to focus on changing Mary's misbehavior. Instead of merely nagging Mary, the teacher should try to isolate the cause of her misbehavior and to develop a solution. Perhaps the seatwork is too easy, too difficult, or otherwise inappropriate for her. Or Mary may have developed a "fooling around" relationship with a classmate, so that a conference, and possibly a new seating arrangement, is required. In any case, rather than let the situation continue, the teacher should discuss it with Mary, come to an agreement with her about the future, and follow through with appropriate treatment (discussed in the following sections).

There are three responses that teachers should avoid when dealing with easily interpretable misbehavior: (1) rhetorical or meaningless questions, (2) threats and arbitrary displays of authority, and (3) overdwelling on misbehavior (nagging). These reactions do no good and may cause needless anxiety or resentment.

CONDUCTING INVESTIGATIONS

When situations are not clear enough to allow teachers to act without additional information, they will need to question one or more students. Unfortunately, many teachers (and other adults) question children and adolescents in ways that fail to get information or that produce negative side effects.

Questions should be genuine attempts to get information, not rhetorical questions of the type described in the preceding section. They should be direct, to the point, and addressed to matters of *fact* that students can answer. Questions about students' *intentions* should not be asked unless the teacher seriously needs the information. Some questions about intentions help establish what the student was doing and why ("Why did you leave the room?" "Why haven't you turned in your homework?"). However, students should not be berated ("Did you think you could get away with it?") or confused with questions about intentions that they cannot answer ("Why didn't you remember to be more careful?").

When questioning to establish the facts in a dispute, it usually is best to talk to each student privately and to confine the discussion to the students directly involved. This avoids putting individuals on the spot in front of the group and thus minimizes their need to save face with lies or confrontations. When questioning students in a group, teachers should insist that each individual be allowed to respond without interruption. If teachers allow others to jump in, or if they address questions to the group, the students are likely to argue over who did what first to whom.

When responses conflict or when one student appears to be lying, teachers must guard against making snap judgments or accusations. They should point out the discrepancies and perhaps indicate that they find certain statements hard to believe. This avoids rejecting anyone's statement out of hand and leaves the door open for someone to change his or her story.

Teachers should make it clear that they expect the truth and should back their words with credible actions that cast them as helpers who want the best for all concerned and not as authority figures interested only in assessing guilt. There must be no reward for lying and no punishment for telling the truth.

The facts need not always be established in detail. If the goal is to promote long-run development of integrity and self-control, not merely to "settle" an individual incident, it may be desirable to leave contradictions unresolved or even to accept a lie or exaggeration without labeling it as such. This is especially true when teachers suspect that students are not telling the truth but are unable to prove it.

Even when such students are guilty, they will respond poorly to a teacher who insists that they are lying. They may conclude that the teacher is picking on them or perhaps that the teacher has such a low opinion of them that they are expected to lie. Thus, teachers confronted with unresolvable discrepancies should: remind the students that they try to treat them fairly and honestly and expect them to reciprocate, state that they "just don't know what to think" in view of the discrepancies and contradictions, state that there is no point in further discussion without new information, and restate behavioral expectations or give specific instructions. This procedure will be most successful in achieving long-run goals. It avoids accusations and punishment, and it increases the probability that students who lied will recognize and feel guilty about their lies.

CONFLICT RESOLUTION

Most misbehavior can be either prevented or handled on the spot with the techniques described so far. However, certain students with chronic personality or behavioral problems will require more intensive treatment. Two approaches to such treatment are Gordon's "Teacher Effectiveness Training" and Glasser's "Ten Steps to Good Discipline."

Gordon

Gordon (1974) advocates what he calls the "no-lose" approach to solving problems and resolving conflicts. He begins by analyzing the degree to which parties to a conflict "own" the problem. The teacher owns the problem when the teacher's needs are being frustrated (as when a student persistently disrupts class by socializing with friends). Conversely, students own the problem when their needs are being frustrated (as when a student is rejected by the peer group through no fault of the teacher). Finally, teachers and students share problem ownership whenever each is frustrating the needs of the other.

Gordon believes that student-owned problems call for the teacher to provide sympathy and help, especially in the form of *active listening*. Like ordinary listening, active listening involves listening to students describe their side of a conflict and trying to understand it from their point of view. In addition, active listening involves reflecting students' statements back to them to show that they have been understood accurately and also listening for the personal feelings and reactions that students express to the events being described, and reflecting these as well.

When the teacher owns the problem, Gordon believes the teacher should explain it to the student using *"I" messages* that explicitly describe the student's behavior, show how it frustrates the teacher's needs, and specify the effects of this on the teacher's feelings (e.g., discouragement, frustration). The idea is to get the student not only to recognize the problem behavior but also to see its effects on the teacher, and yet to do so without blaming or rejecting the student.

Gordon believes that active listening and "I" messages will help teachers and students to achieve shared rational views of problems and to assume a cooperative, problem-solving attitude. When conflicts are involved, he advocates following the six-step "no-lose" method for finding the solution that best satisfies all concerned:

1. Define the problem.
2. Generate possible solutions.
3. Evaluate those solutions.
4. Decide which is best.
5. Determine how to implement the best solution.
6. Assess the effectiveness of the solution after it is implemented (a new agreement must be negotiated if the solution is not working satisfactorily to all concerned).

Glasser

Glasser's (1977) ten-step approach is intended for use with students who persistently violate rules that are reasonable and fairly administered by teachers who maintain a positive, problem-solving stance in dealing with those students. It emphasizes showing students that they will be held responsible for their in-school behavior. The ten steps are as follows. Starting with step 4, each new step escalates reaction to the problem, so new steps are not taken unless previous steps have not solved the problem.

1. Select a student for concentrated attention and list typical reactions to the student's disruptive behavior.
2. Analyze the list to see what techniques do and do not work, and resolve not to repeat the ones that do not work.
3. Improve your relationship with the student by providing extra encouragement, asking the student to perform special errands, showing concern, or implying that things will improve.
4. Focus the student's attention on the disruptive behavior by requiring the student to describe what he or she has been doing. Continue until the student describes the behavior accurately, and then request that it be stopped.
5. Call a short conference and again have the student describe the behavior. Then have the student state whether or not the behavior is against the rules or recognized expectations and ask the student what he or she should be doing instead.
6. Repeat step 5, but this time add that the student will have to formulate a plan to solve the problem. The plan must be more than a simple agreement to stop misbehaving, because such agreements have not been honored in the past. The plan must include commitment to positive actions designed to eliminate the problem.
7. Isolate the student from the class and require him or her to devise a plan for insuring that the rules will be followed in the future. Continue isolation until the student has devised such a plan, gotten it approved, and made a commitment to follow it.
8. If this does not work, the next step is in-school suspension. Now the student must deal with the principal or someone other than the teacher, but this person will repeat earlier steps in the sequence and press the student to devise a plan that is acceptable. The student will either follow the reasonable rules in effect in the classroom or continue to be isolated outside of class.

9. If students remain out of control or do not comply with in-school suspension rules, their parents are called to take them home for the day and they resume in-school suspension the next day.

10. Students who do not respond to the previous steps are removed from school and referred to another agency.

There is little systematic research available on the approaches advocated by Gordon and Glasser. The general principles underlying their approaches were supported by Brophy and Rohrkemper's (1981) study of teachers' strategies for coping with students who present chronic personality or behavior problems. Two general factors were associated with principals' and observers' ratings of teacher effectiveness in dealing with such students. The first was a willingness to assume responsibility for solving the problem. Teachers rated as effective tried to deal with such problems personally, whereas teachers rated ineffective often disclaimed responsibility or competence to deal with the problem and tried to refer it to the principal or counselor. Secondly, the effective teachers used long-term, solution-oriented approaches to problem solving, whereas the ineffective teachers concentrated on controlling misbehavior in the immediate situation, often by relying on threat or punishment. Effective teachers concentrated on helping their students understand and cope with the conflicts or problems that caused their symptomatic behavior. These teachers usually did not find it necessary to punish problem students, although punishment was sometimes needed as part of the larger solution strategy. The following section offers suggestions about how to punish effectively when punishment becomes necessary.

EFFECTIVE PUNISHMENT

Teachers who rely heavily on punishment can achieve only narrow and temporary success at best. Like the teacher described in the previous chapter who "runs a tight ship," they may achieve grudging compliance, but only at the cost of chronic group tension and frustration. Such teachers are continually in conflict with their students, who may obey them out of fear when they are present but will go out of control when they are not in the room. Punishment is sometimes necessary, however, and teachers should use it when circumstances call for it. To use it properly, they will need to know when to punish, what punishment to use, and how to apply it.

When to Punish

Generally, punishment is used only in response to *repeated* misbehavior. It is a treatment of last resort for students who persist in the same kinds of misbehavior despite continued expressions of concern and explanations of the reasons for rules. It is a way to exert control over students who will not control themselves.

Teachers should not resort to punishment lightly, because it signifies that neither they nor the students can cope with the problem. It communicates lack of confidence in the students, indicating that the teacher thinks that they are not trying to improve or that their misbehavior is deliberate. This can damage students' self-concepts as well as reduce the chances for solving the problem.

Thus, punishment is inappropriate for dealing with isolated incidents, no matter how severe, if there is no reason to believe that the student will repeat the action in the future. Even with repeated misbehavior, punishment should be avoided when students are trying to improve. Teachers should give students the benefit of the doubt by assuming their good will and should express confidence in their ability to improve. Punishment should be used only as a last resort, when students repeatedly fail to respond to more positive treatment.

What Punishment Does

The effects of punishment are limited and specific. A great body of evidence (reviewed in Bandura, 1969) shows that *punishment can control misbehavior, but by itself it will not teach desirable behavior or even reduce the desire to misbehave.* Thus, punishment is never a solution by itself; at best, it is only part of a solution.

Using Punishment for the Right Reasons

When used, punishment should be employed consciously and deliberately, as part of a planned response to repeated misbehavior. Even though it is a last resort, it should not be applied unthinkingly or vengefully. When teachers use punishment to deal with their own frustrations or anger, the punishment is usually accompanied by statements or thoughts like "We'll fix your wagon" or "We'll see who's boss." Such statements do not indicate use of punishment as a deliberate control technique; they are emotional outbursts indicating poor self-control and emotional immaturity.

Inappropriate Punishment

Abusive Verbal Attacks   These are never appropriate. Severe personal criticism cannot be justified on the grounds that the student needs it. It has no corrective function and will only cause resentment, both in the victim and in the rest of the class.

Physical Punishment   We do not recommend physical punishment, even where it is legal, for several reasons. First, by its very nature, it places the teacher in a position of attacking students, physically if not personally. This can cause injury, and in any case, it will undermine the teacher's chances of dealing with the students effectively in the future.

Although physical punishment still exists in many schools and often is defended by principals and teachers, research (summarized in Hyman & Wise, 1979) reveals that it typically is used: ineffectively and counterproductively, mostly by inexperienced or poorly trained personnel who lack effective alternatives; most often against younger students from lower-class and minority groups, who are unlikely to defend themselves physically or legally; and for such offenses as tardiness, unfinished homework, or forgotten gym clothing rather than for physical aggression or insubordination. In short, it is used by the ineffective to take out their frustrations on the weak and vulnerable.

Second, physical punishment is intense and focuses attention on the punishment itself rather than on the misbehavior that led to it. Third, despite this intensity, physical punishment is over quickly and has an air of finality about it, so that it usually fails to induce guilt or personal responsibility for misbehavior in the offenders. They are more likely to be sorry for having gotten caught than for having misbehaved. Fourth, physical punishment is only temporarily effective at best. The least-controlled, most hostile students usually come from homes where their parents beat them regularly. Criminals convicted of assault and other violent crimes almost always have home backgrounds in which physical punishment was common. In general, physical punishment teaches people to attack others when angry. It does not teach them appropriate behavior, which is the purpose of discipline.

Extra Work   Some teachers punish by assigning extra work or by having the students write sentences like "I must not talk in class" a certain number of times. We do not recommend assigning extra schoolwork as punishment because this may cause students to view schoolwork as drudgery. Both teachers and students should see work assignments as useful opportunities to practice or apply skills, not as punishments.

Requiring students to copy rules or write compositions about them may or may not be effective punishment, depending on how it is handled. Writing "I must not disrupt the class" five or ten times might help students remember the rule. However, requiring them to write it 50 or 100 times calls attention more to the punishment than the rule and seems likely to cause students to resent this form of punishment or think it funny.

Ordinarily, it is more effective to ask older students to write a composition about how they should behave. This will force them to think about the rationales underlying the rules rather than just copy the rules in rote fashion. The teacher should follow up by discussing the composition with the students. The punishment itself is only part of the treatment.

In summary, abusive criticism, physical punishment, and assignment of extra schoolwork should not be used as punishment. Compositions about classroom rules and the reasons for them may be appropriate, if kept short and followed up with a conference.

Effective Punishment

More important than the type of punishment is the way the teacher presents it to the students. Punishment should be threatened before actually being used, so students have fair warning. It should be clear that punishment will be used as a last resort and not because the teacher wants to get even or enjoys punishing. The students should see that their own behavior will bring on the punishment because they leave the teacher no other choice.

Tone and manner are very important. The teacher should avoid dramatizing ("All right, that's the last straw!" "Now you've done it!") or implying a power struggle ("I guess we'll have to show you who's boss"). Instead, the need for punishment should be stated in a quiet, almost sorrowful voice, using a tone and manner that communicate a combination of deep concern, puzzlement, and regret over the student's behavior. Whether or not it is stated overtly, the implied message should be "You have misbehaved continually. I have tried to help with reminders and explanations, but your misbehavior has persisted. I cannot allow this misbehavior to continue, however. If it does, I will have to punish you. I don't want to, but I must if you leave me no choice."

If punishment becomes necessary, it should be related to the offense. If students misuse materials, for example, it may be most appropriate to restrict or suspend their use of them for a while. If they continually get into fights during recess, they can lose recess privileges or be required to stay by themselves. If they are continually disruptive, they can be excluded from the group.

The teacher should explain why students are being punished and what they must do restore normal status. This involves making a clear distinction between students' unacceptable behavior and their overall acceptance as persons. Students should know that they are being punished solely because of their unacceptable behavior and that they can regain normal status by changing this behavior.

In contrast, inflexible punishments ("You'll stay after school for a week . . . get an 'F' in conduct . . . have to get special permission to leave your seat from now on") are inappropriate overreactions that leave teachers stuck with either enforcing them or taking them back. Either way teachers lose. If they follow through and "execute the sentence," they will deepen the student's discouragement or resentment. If they back off, they will appear inconsistent or wishywashy, and will "lose face."

Withdrawal of privileges and exclusion from the group should be tied closely to remedial behavior whenever possible. This means telling students not only why they are being punished, but also what they may do to regain their privileges or rejoin the group. This explanation should stress that punishment is only temporary and that they can redeem themselves by showing improved behavior ("When you share with the others without fighting." "When you pay attention to the lesson"). Students should have only themselves to blame for their punishment, but they should also be given a way to redeem themselves, to focus their attention on positive behavior and provide an incentive for changing.

This is in contrast to the "prison sentence" approach ("You have to stay here for ten minutes." "No recess for three days.") and the "I am the boss" approach ("You stay here until I come and get you." "No more crayons unless I give you permission."). These statements include no explicit improvement demands, and they make it easy for the student to get angry or feel picked on.

Punishment that is closely related to the offense is more easily seen as fair. Students can blame only themselves if they lose a privilege because they have abused it, but they can easily feel picked on if the teacher punishes by imposing restrictions in an entirely unrelated area. An especially bad practice of this type is to lower the students' academic grades as punishment for misbehavior. Students who misbehave frequently are often low achievers as well, and lowering their grades as punishment is likely to further alienate or discourage them from academic efforts. Except where the punishment is *directly related* and *proportional* to the offense, as when a student who cheats on a test is given a failing grade for that test (and only that test), students should *not* be punished by having their grades lowered.

Exclusion From the Group

If not handled properly, exclusion from the group may actually function as a reward rather than a punishment. Ideally, the place designated for excluded students should be located so that students sent there will be excluded psychologically as well as physically. They should be placed behind the other students, where they cannot easily attract their attention. To help insure a feeling of exclusion, the excluded student can be placed facing a corner or a wall. In combination with the techniques for explaining the punishment described above, this will help insure that the exclusion is experienced as punishment and has the desired effects on behavior.

Exclusion should be terminated when excluded students indicate that they are ready to behave properly. Stated intentions to behave should be accepted without "grilling" the students to extract specific promises ("You'll stop calling out answers without raising your hand? "You'll stop talking to your neighbor during the lesson?").

Also, when students request readmittance, the teacher should respond in ways that clearly accept them back into the group. Vague phrases like "Well, we'll see" should be avoided. Instead students should be shown that the teacher has heard and accepted their intention to reform and then be instructed to rejoin the class ("Well, John, I'm glad to hear that. I hate to exclude you, or anyone, from the class. Go back to your seat and get ready for math.").

Sometimes, excluded students may offer only halfhearted or tongue-in-cheek pledges to reform. In such cases, especially if there has been a previous history of failure to take exclusion seriously, the teacher may wish to hold out for a more credible commitment. This should be done with caution, since it is usually better to give students the benefit of the doubt than to risk undermining reform efforts. When a plea is rejected, the reasons must be made clear. The students must see that the teacher is acting on the basis of observed behavior ("I'm sorry, John, but I can't accept that. Several times recently you promised to behave and then broke that promise as soon as you rejoined the group. I don't think you realize how serious this problem has become. Go back to the corner and stay there until I get a chance to come and talk to you about this some more.").

Punishment as a Last Resort

We cannot stress too strongly that punishment is a measure of last resort, appropriate only as a way to curb misbehavior in students who know what to do but refuse to do it. It should not be used when misbehavior is not disruptive or when problems exist because students do not know what to do or how to do it.

This does not mean that any nondisruptive behavior should be allowed to continue. Withdrawal, daydreaming, or sleepiness can be serious problems if they are characteristic and continuing. However, punishment is not an appropriate response to such behavior. Nor is it helpful for problems such as failure to answer questions or to do assigned work. Students who fail to turn in work should be made to complete it during free periods or after school but should not be punished in addition. Finally, when students do not know what to do or how to do it, they need instruction, not punishment.

Bear in mind that punishment places attention and emphasis on undesirable behavior, and it tends to reduce work involvement and raise the level of tension in the room (Kounin, 1970). Using it to handle one control problem may contribute to causing several others. This is part of the reason why teachers who rely on punishment have more, not fewer, control problems. They try to treat problems with a stopgap control measure instead of prevention and cure. Meanwhile, they undermine their chances of gaining the cooperation and respect needed to treat problems successfully.

CHOOSING YOUR ROLE

Although certain management duties are necessary in all teaching situations, students' age and developmental level make it much more likely that teachers at various grade levels will deal with different management problems. Prior to discussing specific techniques teachers can use to cope with serious student adjustment problems, it is useful to provide some general background regarding the problems of students at different developmental levels.

As students progress through school, their personal and social development affects the role of the teacher and the goals and techniques of classroom management. Brophy and Evertson (1978) identified four developmental stages:

1. *Kindergarten and the early elementary grades.* Here students are socialized into the student role and instructed in basic skills. Most still consider adults as authority figures, are predisposed to do what they are told, and are likely to feel gratified when they please teachers and upset when they do not. They turn to teachers for directions, encouragement, solace, assistance, and personalized attention. Serious classroom disturbances usually do not yet occur. Consequently, teachers function primarily as instructors and trainers. The emphasis is on teaching students what to do rather than on getting them to comply with familiar rules. These instructional or socialization aspects of classroom management are basic to the teacher's job in the early grades; indeed, it probably is not possible to teach young children effectively without spending considerable time on these tasks.

2. *The middle elementary grades.* Time spent handling classroom management concerns is reduced and teachers are able to concentrate on instructing students in the formal curriculum. This stage starts when basic socialization to the student role is completed and continues as long as most students remain adult-oriented and relatively compliant. Students are familiar with most school routines and the serious disturbances seen frequently in later years are not yet common. Creating and maintaining an appropriate learning environment remain central to teaching success, but these tasks consume less teacher time.

3. *The upper elementary and lower high school grades.* As more and more students change their orientation from pleasing teachers to pleasing peers, they begin to resent teachers who act as authority figures. Maintaining control of a class can be difficult at times. Certain students become more disturbed and harder to control than they used to be. As a result, classroom management again becomes a prominent part of the teacher role, perhaps even more important than teaching the formal curriculum. Many students have mastered basic skills and can manage much of their learning on their own. The teacher's primary problem now is motivating them to behave as they know they are supposed to, not instructing them in how to behave, as in the first stage.

4. *The upper high school grades.* As many of the most alienated students drop out of school and the rest become intellectually and socially more mature, classrooms once again assume an academic focus. Classroom management requires even less time than it did during the second stage because students assume almost complete responsibility for their behavior at school. Teaching at this level is mostly a matter of instructing students in the formal curriculum. Classroom management remains important but requires little time, except during the first few class meetings. The socialization that does occur is mostly informal, occurring during out-of-class contacts with individual students (but mostly within the school setting, however).

These developmental aspects of classroom management should be considered when thinking about the grade level one is preparing to teach at. Teachers who enjoy working with young children, who like to provide nurturant socialization as well as instruction, and who have the patience and skills needed for socializing young children into the student role would be especially effective in the primary grades. Elementary teachers who want to concentrate mostly on instruction would be best placed in the middle grades. Grades seven to ten would be best for teachers who enjoy or at least are not bothered by the misbehavior of adolescents and who see themselves as socialization agents and models at least as much as instructors. The upper high school grades are best for teachers who want to function mostly as subject-matter specialists.

There has been much debate, but little research and certainly no conclusive evidence, about how to handle the most serious problems: racial and other group tensions; severe withdrawal and refusal to communicate; hostile, antisocial acting-out; truancy; refusal to work or obey; vandalism; and severe behavioral disorders or criminality. Psychotherapists have not achieved much success in dealing with behavior disorders, and neither they nor correctional institutions have achieved even modest success in dealing with severe delinquency and criminality. Yet teachers typically are asked to cope with such problems while at the same time coping with any problems that other students may present (five times as many in junior high and high school); instructing all these students in the school's curriculum; and dealing with the conflicting pressures presented by the school district, the principal, other teachers, the students themselves, the parents, and their own personal lives. Some teachers respond to this challenge with determination to solve whatever problems come along. We hope that their energy and optimism hold out indefinitely. If so, they probably will succeed.

Other teachers respond by concluding that it is better to concentrate on a few tasks and perform them well than to try to accomplish all of them. We find this position quite understandable. A teacher with little interest in pupil socialization who recognizes this predisposition and chooses to teach at grades where socialization is a minimal problem and to concentrate on becoming highly skilled at teaching subject matter probably is making a wise decision. Such teachers, who recognize their own limitations and work within them, will have less extensive effects on students than will teachers who deal with the entire spectrum of responsibilities. Still, their effects will tend to be positive and probably greater in the long run than they would have been if these teachers had tried to do everything and ended up doing nothing very well.

Teachers who choose to minimize socialization activities can do so, although they cannot eliminate them entirely. If they are content with a primarily instructional role, they can get by with classroom management strategies that are effective for maintaining an orderly classroom but not for changing severely disturbed students. Such teachers can legitimately take the position that changing such students is not their job and can let school counselors or other treatment experts assume this function, confining their own efforts with such students to instructional activities.

THE TEACHER AS A SOCIALIZATION AGENT

Teachers who want to socialize students can accomplish this goal, but they will need to understand the commitment involved in this decision and the frustrations to be encountered because of rules and regulations, uncooperative school officials or parents, and students who fail to respond to their best and most persistent efforts. A teacher who makes a commitment to deal with student problems in addition to providing instruction in the formal curriculum also may need:

> To invest time and energy to cultivate close personal relationships with students that go far beyond those necessary for purely instructional purposes
>
> To spend considerable time outside regular school hours dealing with students and their families, perhaps to even be "on call" as a counselor to students who have no one else to turn to
>
> To receive no extra financial compensation for such efforts and perhaps even some opposition from school officials
>
> To deal with the wrath of a student's parents or another person who may be involved in the situation
>
> To deal with complex problems that have developed over a period of years

Difficulties of Socialization

Teachers typically do not have special training in methods of dealing with serious personality or behavior disorders. Neither do they have the luxury of being able to interact with students by taking a friendly, nonauthoritarian therapist's role. Indeed, they have to find ways to reach disturbed students while still playing the role of authority figure and dealing with them every day in class. As a result, even the most energetic, determined, and skilled teachers will have only limited success. This is not bad in itself because the success rates even of professionally trained therapists are not impressive. However, it does mean that in addition to possessing all the qualities listed above, teachers who want to help students who have serious problems must be able simultaneously to expect the best and yet be prepared for the worst. Teachers who expect to succeed consistently or to be rewarded with expressions of love and gratitude will be disappointed. Rewarding experiences occur, but so do frustrations. Many students will not respond at all, despite continued and appropriate attempts to reach them. Others will respond and make initial progress only to regress and end up worse than when they started. Furthermore, relatively few "success cases" will respond with overt gratitude or other direct reinforcement of the teacher.

Even the most talented and determined teachers can work successfully with only so many students at one time. Overcommitment will cause diminishing returns. Therefore, teachers will have to be selective about their "caseloads," holding them within a manageable limit, if they are to expect success.

If you think that you can try to reach students persistently despite a steady diet of frustrations, you probably have a good chance to be a successful socialization agent. In fact, if you find the prospect exciting and challenging rather than dismal, you might consider teaching any of the grades between six and ten, where student socialization needs are most frequent and intense.

As Brophy (1985) argues, teachers' potential for successful socialization effects in general and for self-fulfilling prophecy effects in particular is even greater in the personal, social, and moral areas than in the area of academic achievement. Hence, the potential for influence by teachers who choose a socialization role is great; however, such influence takes a great amount of work and must be balanced with the teacher's academic role (for additional discussion, see Prawat & Nickerson, 1985).

COPING WITH SERIOUS ADJUSTMENT PROBLEMS

Most classrooms have students whose serious and continuing problems require individualized treatment beyond that suggested so far. This section presents suggestions for dealing with them.

General Considerations

Although different problems require different treatment, certain general considerations apply to all of them.

Do Not Isolate Students or Label Them as Unique Cases.   Because expectations and labels can act as self-fulfilling prophecies, it is important that problem students not be labeled or treated as special, different from the rest of the class. This is doubly important for continuing behavior problems because they are harder to eliminate once they become labeled as characteristic of the student. Labels place undue attention on the misbehavior and suggest that more of the same is expected. Interactions with these students concerning their behavior should be as private as possible, to cut down their need for face-saving behavior and their attempts to use misbehavior to gain attention.

Stress Desired Behavior.   Teachers should stress desired behavior, not the misbehavior the student is showing. Stress on the positive must be more than verbal. Teachers must not only talk this way, but also think and act in a manner consistent with the intention of moving the student toward desired behavior. This even applies to such behaviors as stealing or destroying property. If property destruction is due to impulsiveness or carelessness, the teacher can instruct the student about how to handle property carefully. If stealing results from real need (poverty), teachers can plan with the students ways that they can borrow the items they've been stealing or earn the right to keep them. Meanwhile, the students can be praised for progress in "acting responsibly" or "respecting the property rights of others." If students have been stealing or destroying property to seek attention or express anger, teachers can help them recognize this and develop better ways to meet their needs. Here again, any positive progress the students show should be labeled and praised.

By defining problems positively, teachers give students a goal and suggestions about how to work toward it. This energizes both the teacher and the students, giving them the feeling that they are making progress. In contrast, when the problem is defined purely negatively ("You've got to stop . . ."), both teacher and student are left at an impasse. The student misbehaves and the teacher responds by criticizing and perhaps punishing. Both are left where they started, and the cycle is likely to repeat itself over and over again.

Focus on Students' School-Related Behavior.   When students show seriously disturbed behavior in school, it is usually part of a larger pattern of disturbance. Many factors contribute to the problem, including some that the teacher can do little or nothing about (parental conflict, inadequate or sadistic parent, poor living conditions). Some teachers give up hope when they hear about such things, feeling that the students will not change unless their home environments change. Other teachers become uninvited therapists, trying to change the home as well as deal with the student in the classroom. This often does more harm than good.

Students learn to play the student role by showing the behavior that teachers expect and reinforce. It is this student role that teachers should stress. Factors in the home or out-of-school environments may need to be taken into account, but they should neither be used as excuses for failing to deal with school-related misbehavior nor allowed to become focal concerns that obscure behavior change efforts.

Generally, then, teachers are advised to confine their treatment efforts to school behavior and to aspects of the home environment that are closely related to school behavior (such as asking parents to see that students get to bed early enough on nights before school or that they do their homework). Going beyond such appropriate and expected teacher concerns is risky unless the teacher has both therapeutic expertise and a good relationship with the student and the family.

Build a Close Relationship With the Student.   Student failure to respond to a reasonable and patient teacher signals that some special problem is operating. Some students are unwilling to respond because of anger or other negative emotions, while others are unable to respond because of emotions or impulses they cannot control. It is important for the teacher to build close relationships with such students as individuals, both to develop better understanding of their behavior and to earn the respect and affection that will make them want to respond.

To do this, teachers need to take time to talk with students individually, either after school or at conferences during school hours, making clear their concern about the students' welfare (not merely about their misbehavior) and willingness to help them improve. They should encourage students to talk about their problems in their own words, listening carefully and asking questions when they do not understand. The best questions are simple and open-ended. They do not put words into the students' mouths or make guesses about what is going on in their minds.

Ideally, the student will say something that suggests treatment procedures. If teacher behavior has been part of the problem (sarcasm or hostility, for example), the teacher should admit this and promise to change. If the student makes a suggestion that is reasonable, it should be accepted. For example, a seventh grader may request that he not be asked to read aloud from his seventh-grade history book, since he reads at the second-grade level. This request could be granted, provided that a plan is devised to see that the student learns to read better. If the student's suggestion cannot be accepted, the reasons should be explained. The teacher may also wish to offer suggestions. These must be presented as suggestions, however, not conclusions. Students should feel free to express their opinions about whether or not the suggestions would help. Serious, deep-rooted problems will not be solved in one day with one conference. It is sufficient as a first step if both parties communicate honestly during the conference and come away from it feeling that progress has been made. Discussions should continue until mutual understanding is reached and both parties agree to try a particular suggested solution.

With any serious problem, then, the teacher should arrange a conference and question the students to discover how they see the situation, then attempt to work out agreements about suggested solutions. Suggestions about more specific treatment of several common behavior problems are given in the following sections.

Showing Off

Some students continually seek attention by trying to impress or entertain teachers or peers. They can be enjoyable if they have the talent for the role and confine their showing off to appropriate times and places. Often, though, they are exasperating or disruptive.

The way to deal with show-offs is to give them the attention and approval they seek, but only for appropriate behavior. Ignore inappropriate behavior, or when it is too disruptive to be ignored, do not do or say anything that will call attention to it or make the student feel rejected. Thus, a comment like "We're having our lesson now" is better than "Stop acting silly." Students who seek individual attention at an awkward time should be delayed rather than refused. They should be told that the teacher will see them at a specified time, later.

When praising show-offs, praise only appropriate behaviors and specify what is being praised. This will motivate them to repeat these behaviors to gain approval. In general, show-offs need constant reassurance that they are liked and respected, and teachers should try to fill this need. However, specific praise and rewards should be reserved for appropriate behavior. Inappropriate behavior should go unrewarded and, as much as possible, unacknowledged.

Defiance

Most teachers find defiance threatening, even frightening. What is the teacher to do with students who vehemently talk back or refuse to do what they are asked to do?

To begin with, the teacher must remain calm so as not to get drawn into a power struggle. The natural tendency of most adults is to get angry and strike back with a show of force designed to show such students that "they can't get away with it." This may succeed in suppressing the immediate defiance, but it will probably be harmful in the long run, especially if it involves loss of temper by the teacher or public humiliation of the student.

Teachers who overcome the tendency to react with immediate anger will be in a good position to deal with defiance effectively. Acts of defiance make everyone in the room fearful and uneasy, including the student who rebels. The other students know that defiance may bring serious consequences, and they will be on edge, waiting to see what these will be. Teachers gain two advantages by pausing a moment before responding to defiance: (1) they gain time to control their tempers and think about what to do before acting, and (2) the mood of the defiant student is likely to change from anger and bravado to fear and contrition during this time. Therefore, it helps to ponder the situation for a few moments before responding, letting the class wait in silent anticipation.

When teachers do act, they must do so decisively, although in a calm and quiet manner. If possible, they should give a general assignment to the class and then remove the defiant student for a private conference. If this is not possible or if the defiant student refuses to leave for a conference, he or she should be told that the matter will be discussed after school. The teacher's tone and manner should communicate serious concern, but no threats or promises should be made. The defiant student and the rest of the class should know that action will be taken but should not be told exactly what it will be.

The following response would be appropriate: "John, I can see that something is very wrong here and that we'd better do something about it before it gets worse. Please step into the hall and wait for me—I'll join you in a minute." An alternative would be " . . . please sit down and think it over during the rest of the period—I'll discuss it with you after class."

Stating that the matter will be dealt with in a private conference tells the class that the teacher will handle the situation, yet does not humiliate the defiant student or incite further defiance. The teacher can even afford to let the student "get in the last word," because the matter will be taken up again later.

Defiant acts usually culminate a buildup of student anger and frustration. Difficulties at home or in relationships with peers may be part of the problem. However, the teacher is almost always part of the problem too. Students are unlikely to defy their teachers unless they resent them to some degree. Therefore, teachers must be prepared to hear defiant students out. There must be discussion, not a lecture or argument. When students claim unfair treatment, teachers must entertain the possibility that this is true. When mistakes have been made, teachers should admit them and promise to change.

It is usually best to encourage angry students to say everything they have on their minds *before* responding to the points they raise. This helps teachers to get the full picture and allows them some time to think about what they are hearing. If they try to respond to each separate point as it is raised, the discussion may turn into a series of accusations and rebuttals. Such exchanges usually leave students feeling that their specific objections have been "answered" but that they still are right in accusing the teacher of general unfairness.

With some defiant students, it may be important to review the teacher's role. Students should understand that teachers are interested primarily in teaching them, not in ordering them around or playing police officer. Regardless of the specific points raised, teachers should express concern for these students and a desire to treat them fairly. This reassurance (backed, of course, by appropriate behavior) will be more important to the students than particular responses to particular accusations.

Even serious defiance can usually be handled with one or two sessions like these, if teachers are honest in dealing with the students and if they follow up the discussion with appropriate behavior. Although unpleasant, incidents of defiance can be blessings in disguise. They bring out into the open problems that have been smoldering for a long time. Defiant acts usually have cathartic effects on students, releasing built-up tensions and leaving them more receptive to developing a constructive relationship with the teacher. Much good can come from this if the teacher takes advantage of it by remaining calm, showing concern and willingness to listen, and following up with appropriate behavior.

Aggression

Aggressive students must not be allowed to hurt classmates or damage equipment. When such harmful or destructive behavior appears, teachers should demand an end to it immediately. If the student fails to respond, the teacher should send another student for help and, if necessary and feasible, should physically restrain the student who is out of control. Most teachers rarely if ever will be required to intervene in this way, but all teachers should be prepared to do so, just in case. Such preparation should include training in techniques of restraining students and breaking up fights effectively, as well a development of clear procedures for emergency situations with the principal, other teachers, and various support staff who may be available. A good rule of thumb is that teachers' responsibilities in these situations are first to the safety of themselves and the other students, then to the assaultive student, and then to property.

While being restrained, students may respond by straining to get away, making threats, or staging temper tantrums. If so, they should be held until they regain self-control. The teacher should speak firmly but quietly, telling them to calm down and get control of themselves. The students should be reassured that the problem will be dealt with, but not until they calm down. If they insist that the teacher let go, they should be told firmly that this will happen as soon as they stop yelling and squirming. Such verbal assurance can be reinforced nonverbally by relaxing the grip as the student gradually tones down resistance.

Restraint may be required if two students are fighting and do not respond to demands that they stop. Do not try to stop a fight by getting between the participants and trying to deal with both at the same time. This will result in delay, confusion, or even the teacher getting hit. Instead, restrain one of the participants, preferably the more belligerent, or the one with whom you have less rapport, by pulling him back and away from his opponent so that he is not hit while being held (pull at the belt or waistband, leaving the arms free for self-defense). This will stop the fight, although it may be necessary to order the other participant to stay away. It is helpful if the teacher does a lot of talking at this point, calming the students down and explaining that the matter will be dealt with shortly when they comply. If the teacher does not take over here, the students are likely to exchange threats and other face-saving actions.

Humor is helpful if the teacher has the presence of mind to use it. Threats and face-saving actions are effective only when taken seriously. If teachers respond to them with smiles or little remarks to show that they are considered more funny or ridiculous than serious ("All right, let's stop blowing off steam"), they are likely to stop quickly.

Once aggressive students calm down, teachers should talk with them individually. If two students were fighting, it may be necessary to talk to both together. As usual, the teacher should begin by hearing the students out. It is important to help aggressive students see the distinction between feelings and behavior. Feelings should be accepted as legitimate or at least understandable. Students who state that they hate someone or that they are angry because of unfair treatment should be asked to state their reasons for feeling this way. The feeling itself should not be denied ("That's not nice—you must never say you hate someone.") or attacked ("What do you mean? Who do you think you are?"). If the student has been treated unfairly, the teacher should express understanding and sympathy ("I can see why you got angry.").

If angry feelings are not justified, the teacher should explain in a way that recognizes the reality of the feelings but does not legitimize them ("I know you want to be first, but the others do too. They have the same rights as you. So there's no point in getting angry because they went first. You'll have to learn to wait your turn. If you try to be first all the time, everyone will think you are selfish and won't like you as much".).

Although teachers should accept and sometimes expressly legitimize *feelings,* they should not accept *misbehavior.* They should state clearly that students will not be allowed to hit others, destroy property, or otherwise act out angry feelings in destructive ways. The students will be expected to control themselves and confine their responses to acceptable behavior.

Habitually aggressive students require resocialization to teach them new ways of dealing with their frustrations or anger. They must learn that frustration and anger do not justify aggressive behavior. They should be told to express feelings verbally rather than by acting them out and should be given specific suggestions or instructions about how to do this.

For example, students who "hit first and ask questions later" need instruction about handling frustrations and conflict. They should be urged to inhibit tendencies to strike out and taught how to resolve conflict through discussion and negotiation. They should learn to ask classmates what they are doing and why instead of assuming they are being provoked deliberately, and to express their feelings verbally when others cause them to become angry (because others may not even realize that they have made someone angry or why).

If the students are old enough to participate meaningfully, role enactments in which each takes the part of the other to reenact the situation are valuable. These should be followed with specific suggestions about how to handle situations that produce conflict. If the situations are already covered by rules, the students should be reminded of the rules. If not, rules should be suggested for the future.

Teachers should also try to help aggressive students see the consequences of their aggressive behavior, largely by appealing to the Golden Rule. Students can usually see that if they dislike others who bully, cheat, or destroy property, others will dislike and avoid them for the same reasons. It is helpful to show by examples the value of verbalizing feelings and seeking solutions to problems with the others involved instead of striking out at them. Aggressive students must learn that others will know why they are angry only if they tell them and that hitting will only make the others angry too.

If aggression results mostly from students' failure to deal with certain situations (failure to share, failure to wait one's turn, tendency to overreact to teasing or to accidental physical contact), teachers should work with them on the situational problem, stressing that part of the problem is not only the students' behavior, but also their overreactive emotions. This does not mean instructing the students to deny their feelings; anger and resentment are real. However, it does mean that they will be expected to work on controlling their feelings in frustrating situations. They must see that certain frustrations are unavoidable and that overreacting to them succeeds only in making one unhappy and unpopular.

Cases in which the student attacks others for no apparent reason are more serious. Students who do this regularly may require more professional treatment. Sometimes a child acquires a self-image as a "tough guy" and may actually want others to fear and dislike him. Even so, there are many things a teacher can do.

As with any aggressive student, the teacher should deal with aggressive acting out as it occurs and talk with the student to understand him better and to explain behavioral expectations. In addition, the teacher can cope with the problem indirectly, to help the student himself and to help the others in the class to see him in a more positive light.

First, the teacher should avoid labeling the student or reinforcing any negative label he may apply to himself. The teacher should not refer to him as a bully or announce that he is being isolated because he "can't keep his hands to himself." Such labels imply that the student is different, that there is something permanently wrong with him, or that he cannot control himself. They should be avoided in favor of statements that imply confidence that he can learn to behave acceptably.

The teacher can help the student practice a more positive role by arranging for him to play such a role toward his classmates. It might be helpful for this student to be used as a tutor to teach others useful skills that he knows (tying shoes, operating equipment, arts and crafts, music, or other talents). In reading and role-playing situations, he should be assigned parts that feature kindness, friendship, and helpfulness toward others. He would be ideal for the part of an ogre that everyone feared and disliked until they found out how good he was underneath.

Cooperative and helpful behavior can be acknowledged and praised whenever it occurs. Also, potentially serious conflicts can be nipped in the bud if teachers spot them early enough. They can turn potential fights into cooperative situations by making specific suggestions about how the students can resolve conflicts. For good measure, they can add that they are pleased to see the students cooperating. Such behaviors help change a negative self-concept and make the student see himself as someone whom others will like as a friend.

So far, we have given suggestions about what teachers *should* do with aggressive students. Before leaving this topic, it is worth discussing one frequently advocated technique that we do *not* recommend. This is the practice of providing substitute methods for expressing aggression, such as telling the student to hit a punching bag instead of another student or to act out aggression against a doll while pretending that it is the teacher. Such practices have been recommended by those psychoanalytically oriented writers who believe that angry feelings must be acted out in behavior and who see substitution as a way of doing it harmlessly. The usual rationale is that acting out angry feelings has a cathartic effect that reduces or eliminates anger. Without such a release in behavior, the anger presumably will remain and grow, eventually to be released directly.

This suggestion has a certain face validity, because most people do experience catharsis if they "get it off their chests" or "have it out." This does not mean, however, that hostile impulses *must* be acted out behaviorally. Encouraging students to act out anger against substitute objects will increase or prolong the problem, not reduce it. Instead of helping them learn to respond more maturely to frustration, this method: (1) reinforces the idea that their overreactiveness is expected, approved, and "normal"; (2) reinforces the expectation that whenever they have angry feelings they will need to act them out behaviorally; and (3) provides an inappropriate model for the rest of the class, increasing the likelihood that the problem will spread to them.

The problem is that the connection "I need to act out angry feelings—I can release them through catharsis" is merely the end point in a chain of reactions. The connections "frustration—angry feelings" and "angry feelings—act out" precede the cathartic end point. Every time the end point of the chain is reinforced, the whole chain that led up to it is reinforced. The student is reinforced not only for expressing extreme anger harmlessly but also for building up extreme anger in the first place and for believing that this emotion requires or justifies aggressive behavior.

Thus, by encouraging students to act out hostility against substitute objects, teachers merely prolong and reinforce immature emotional control. If kept up long enough, this will produce adults who are prone to temper tantrums at the slightest frustration and who spend much of their time building up and then releasing hostile feelings. This sort of person is neither very happy nor very likable and is, in a word, immature.

Teachers should not try to get students to act out all emotions. Instead, they should work on helping them to distinguish between emotions and behavior and between appropriate and inappropriate emotions. Inappropriate emotions (unjustified anger or other emotional overreactions) should be labeled as such, and the reasons why they are inappropriate should be explained. Behavior that is simply unacceptable must not be tolerated, no matter how strong the student's emotions or impulses to act out. Acceptable (and more effective) alternatives should be explained and insisted upon. All aspects of the teacher's behavior should communicate the expectation that students can and will achieve mature self-control. There should be no suggestion that they are helpless in the face of uncontrollable emotions or impulses.

Unresponsiveness

Some students lack the self-confidence to participate normally in classroom activities. They do not raise their hands to answer questions; and they copy, guess, or leave an item blank rather than ask the teacher about their seatwork. When they are called on and do not know an answer, they stare at the floor silently or perhaps mumble incoherently. Sometimes this "strategy" is successful because many teachers become uneasy and give the answer or call on someone else rather than keep such students "on the spot." Observers who see this should communicate it because teachers usually are not aware of it (Good & Brophy, 1974).

In general, fears and inhibitions about classroom participation should be treated indirectly. Attacking the problem directly by labeling it and urging the students to overcome it can backfire by making them all the more self-conscious and inhibited (much research on stuttering, for example, shows this). The teacher should stress what the students should be doing rather than what they are not doing. Questions should be asked directly and should not be prefaced with stems such as "Do you think you could . . .?" or "Do you want to . . .?" These suggest uncertainty and make it easy for the student to refuse or remain silent. Also, questions should be asked in a conversational, informal tone. If asked too formally, the question may sound like a test item and may stir up anxiety.

Questions should be accompanied by appropriate gestures and expressions to communicate that the teacher is talking to the student and expects an answer. Look at the student expectantly after asking the question. If the student answers, respond with praise or relevant feedback. If the answer is too soft, praise it but then ask the student to say it again louder, "Good! Say it louder so everyone can hear." When students appear to be about to answer, but hesitant, teachers can help by nodding their heads, forming the initial sound with their lips, or encouraging verbally, "Say it!" When students do not respond at all, teachers can give the answer and then repeat the question or ask the students to repeat the answer. If the students mumble or partially repeat, they should be asked to repeat again and then praised when they do so. All this is designed to make clear to students that they are expected to talk, to give them practice in doing so, and to reassure and reward them when they do.

Interactions with such students should be deliberately extended at times, both to give them practice at extended discussions and to combat the idea that they can keep interactions short by lying low. When such students answer initial questions correctly, teachers should sometimes ask them another question or have them elaborate on the response. When they fail the initial question, the follow-up question should be a simpler one that they can handle. In general, questions that require them to explain something in detail are the most difficult. Progressively simpler demands include questions requiring short factual answers, questions requiring students only to choose among presented alternatives, and questions that require only a yes or no response. Students who do not respond to any level of questioning can be asked to repeat things or to imitate actions. Once they begin to respond correctly, the teacher can move to more demanding levels as confidence grows (Blank, 1973).

Inhibited students need careful treatment when they do not respond. As long as they appear to be trying to answer the question, teachers should wait them out. If they begin to look anxious, as if they are worrying about being in the spotlight instead of thinking about the question, teachers should intervene by repeating the question or giving a clue. They should not call on another student or allow others to call out the answer.

Teachers should not allow students to "practice" resistance or nonresponsiveness (Blank, 1973). Anxiety or resistance should be cut off before it gets a chance to build, and the teacher should always get some kind of response. Students who do not respond to questions requiring a verbal answer can be asked to make nonverbal responses such as shaking their heads or pointing. Young children might be asked to imitate a physical action or even guided manually until they begin to do it themselves. In any case, it is important to get some form of positive response before leaving the student.

Students at all levels should be instructed to say "I don't know" rather than remain silent when they cannot respond. Many students hesitate to say "I don't know" because previous teachers implanted the idea that it is shameful, through such comments as "What do you mean you don't know?" By legitimizing "I don't know," the teacher makes it possible for students to respond verbally even when they do not know the answer.

These methods are difficult to apply in large-group situations with extremely unresponsive students who often do not say anything at all. Such students may have to be brought along slowly in individual and small-group situations first. Getting rid of strong inhibitions or fears takes time, and much progress can be undone by trying to push too far too fast. With continued progress and regular success, confidence will grow and tolerance for being "on the spot" will increase. The teacher should continue to make sure to get a response of some kind from this student every time they have an interaction and should see that the student does not become regarded as someone who does not answer and who, therefore, is no longer asked to respond.

If this type of inhibition is widespread, the teacher may be causing or contributing to it. Observers should look for signs of overvaluing correct answers and showing impatience or disgust at failure. The teacher's handling of seatwork should also be observed to see if he or she is scaring students off by criticizing instead of helping when they come with questions.

Failure to Complete Assignments

Certain students fail to complete seatwork and homework assignments. Methods for dealing with this depend on why assignments are not turned in. Some students do not turn in work because they have not been able to figure out how to do it. This is not a motivational problem; it is a teaching problem. What is needed is remedial work to help the students learn what they do not understand and move them to the point where they can do the work themselves. This may seem obvious, but students report that teachers often not only fail to provide this help to slow learners but also routinely collect seatwork assignments before they have had a chance to finish (Weinstein & Middlestadt, 1979).

Great patience and determination are needed in working with these students because they need support and encouragement just to keep trying. If the teacher criticizes them, embarrasses them before the group, or shows impatience or frustration, they will likely begin to copy from neighbors rather than continue to try to do the work themselves.

Teachers can encourage these students by pointing out the progress they are making, regardless of where they stand in relation to others in the class. Teachers will need to make time for remedial teaching with them or to plan some other remediation arrangement (see Chapter 10). In any case, slow learners need patience, more appropriate assignments, and remediation, not criticism or punishment for failing to do what they are *unable* to do.

A different type of problem is presented by students who can do the work but do not finish it or turn it in. The best way to deal with this problem is to stop it early, before it becomes entrenched. From the beginning of the year, teachers should be clear about expectations for seatwork and homework. Their purpose and importance should be explained, and the assignments should be collected, checked, and followed up with feedback and, when necessary, remedial work.

Although the teacher may wish to make open-ended assignments (such as identifying extra problems to do for extra credit or "to see if you can figure them out"), all students should have a clear-cut minimum amount of work for which they are accountable. This amount may (and often should) vary from student to student for instructional reasons, but there should be a clear understanding about what each must turn in, when it is due, and what the consequences for missing the deadline will be.

Teachers should make clear from the beginning of the year that students are expected to finish assignments before doing anything else during seatwork time. Students involved in seatwork should be monitored to see that they are working productively. The established policy must be enforced consistently so that everyone forms the habit of doing the seatwork.

Failure to turn in homework is a more difficult problem, because teachers cannot monitor and intervene if students are not working properly. They can keep track of homework being turned in, however, and can assign students who did not complete it to do so during free periods. Students who do not complete the job during free periods should be kept after school. Here again, the policy must be established from the beginning of the year that assignments are to be completed and turned in on time. If they are not, completion of the assignment will be first priority whenever the student is not involved in a lesson or other instructional activity.

Of course, this assumes that homework assignments are relevant in content and appropriate in difficulty level. If failure to turn in homework is common, the homework being assigned and the way it is monitored when it is turned in should be reviewed and adjusted.

A few students may have a problem completing homework because of pressures from job demands or a poor home situation. When this appears to be the case, the problem should be discussed at length with the student and a mutually agreeable solution should be worked out. Schools should be flexible enough to make time and space available to students who realistically cannot do homework at home. Students in such situations need help, not more trouble.

Teachers should monitor their responses to students who fail to turn in homework (especially those who say that they did the work but forgot to bring it to school), to make sure that they treat everyone fairly. It would not be appropriate, for example, to allow certain favored students to turn in the work the next day without penalty, while imposing a penalty on or refusing to accept late work from less-favored students. Teachers are often perceived to discriminate between high and low achievers in this way (Weinstein & Middlestadt, 1979).

OTHER APPROACHES TO CLASSROOM MANAGEMENT

This approach to classroom management has been eclectic, stressing principles gathered from many theories. There are a few systematic approaches that stress principles developed within one theory or point of view. Three of the most prominent are contingency contracting, cognitive behavior modification, and classroom-meeting applications of reality therapy.

Contingency Contracting

Skinner (1953) describes behavior as controlled by contingent reinforcement. Behavior that brings on or maintains reinforcement will be repeated, and behavior that is not reinforced will be extinguished. This idea is simple in theory, but it becomes complex in practice because people respond differently to the same stimuli. Some are not motivated by stimuli that most others experience as rewards, and some respond positively to stimuli that most others view as punishments. Thus, it is not possible to develop a list of rewards and another list of punishments. The same stimulus can be rewarding, punishing, or irrelevant for different people or even for the same people in different situations.

To deal with this complexity, most behavior modifiers use the Premack principle (Premack, 1965) to define reinforcers. This principle states that preferred behaviors that appear frequently under conditions of free response can be used as reinforcers to elicit and maintain behaviors that would not appear otherwise. That is, high-frequency behaviors experienced as rewarding can be used as reinforcers for less-preferred behaviors by making the opportunity to engage in the preferred behaviors contingent on performance of the less-preferred behaviors.

Applying the Premack principle, teachers can provide reinforcement when students pay attention, do their work, or keep the rules and can withhold it when they do not. This can be done unilaterally by the teacher, although students can be given a more active role through *contingency contracting*. In contingency-contracting systems, students receive reinforcement contingent on meeting work or behavioral requirements that are negotiated and then formalized into agreements between the teacher and each individual student. The form and content of contracts can vary considerably depending on the developmental levels of the students, their abilities, the kinds of reinforcers available, and many other factors. However, all contracts have stated contingencies between performance of specified behavior and delivery of specified reinforcement.

For example, teachers can determine the levels of performance (expressed as the number and types of assignments done according to specified criteria, possibly along with earning an acceptable test score) that will be required for particular grades. A specific level of performance that will require sustained effort (for a *particular* student) can be required for a grade of "A," with lesser requirements for lower grades.

Contracts for behavioral improvement can be developed using the same principles. A level of conduct that represents the most that can be expected from *this* student at *this* time can be required for the maximum reinforcement available, with less acceptable conduct levels producing less reinforcement. As students become able to control themselves more successfully, new contracts requiring better behavior can be introduced.

Contingency contracting usually works best when students are presented with a variety of attractive reinforcements. These "reinforcement menus" might include opportunities to spend time in learning centers or other enrichment activities, to go to the library or other places outside the classroom, to play games, or even just to converse with friends. Specified good behavior or acceptable completion of assignments is rewarded with so many points, and these points can be "spent" on reinforcements.

The "prices" of reinforcements may vary according to their attractiveness and the demand for them. The most attractive and popular ones are the most expensive. Occasional changes in the content of reinforcement menus or the prices for the items provide variety and help avoid satiation with the reinforcers (continued opportunities to enjoy a given reinforcer usually weaken its strength, because students come to value it less).

It is harder than it might seem to arrange contingencies so that desired behaviors are reinforced. Sometimes behavior modification attempts fail because proper contingencies are not established; at other times, the problem is in the presumed reward that is supposed to function as a reinforcer. Analyze the behavior modification attempts presented in the examples below. Are they likely to be successful? Why or why not?

1. Mrs. Bussey has set up a contingency-contracting system. Students who turn in completed and correct work assignments get tokens they can spend on reinforcers at a later time. However, the work must be complete and correct. If students come with incomplete or incorrect work, they must return to their desks and finish it correctly.
2. Mr. Cornucopia gives out goodies every Friday afternoon as a way to motivate the students to apply themselves. He sees that everyone gets something but makes sure to give the more desirable items to students who appear to have worked hard during the week. To make sure that the connection between work and reward is clear, he refers to this as "payday," and says "Good work" to each student when passing out the goodies.
3. Mrs. Calvin announces that from now on, the student who finishes the afternoon math assignment first will be allowed to dust the erasers.
4. Mr. Caries is frustrated because his students do not assume much responsibility for keeping their desks orderly. To encourage better habits, he occasionally (and unpredictably) announces that today the students who do a good job of cleaning up their desks will get candy. After allowing enough time, he goes around to check desks and gives candy to those who have neat desks.

Superficially, all four examples are similar: the teacher offers rewards to improve some performance. However, subtle differences between the examples make it likely that only Mrs. Bussey will succeed. She has arranged to have attractive reinforcers available, and students can get them only by turning in complete and correct work. Assuming that all students can do the work that is assigned to them, the contingencies are such that rewards will function as reinforcement for sustained and careful work on assignments.

Mr. Cornucopia will not succeed because there is no clear contingency between performance of the behaviors he is trying to reinforce and delivery of the reinforcements. All students get some kind of reward whether they apply themselves during the week or not, and differences in the attractiveness of rewards given to individual students depend on his unsystematic perceptions and fallible memory rather than on objective evidence of effort. Some students get richly rewarded even though they do not deserve it, and others get less than they deserve because Mr. Cornucopia does not realize how deserving they are. These students will learn that there is no clear contingency between reward and performance. After a few weeks, it is unlikely that many students will be motivated to work harder by this gimmick, even though they will enjoy the goodies.

Mrs. Calvin's scheme is almost certain to fail, for three reasons. First, she should be trying to reward effort and accomplishment, not speed. Second, the possibility for reinforcement exists for only a few students, those who can work fast enough to finish first. The others will not be affected favorably by this motivational attempt. Finally, it is unlikely that the intended reward will actually function as a reinforcer. Few students will be motivated by the opportunity to dust erasers, and even those who are will tire of this activity before too long. In other words, Mrs. Calvin is offering a weak reinforcer, susceptible to early satiation.

Mr. Caries will also fail. His reinforcements are contingent on performance of the desired behavior when they are offered, but they are offered only occasionally and he always announces this beforehand. Thus, the contingency here is not "Students who have neat desks every day will get rewarded," but "Students who clean their desks whenever Mr. Caries promises rewards will get rewarded." By always announcing the availability of rewards ahead of time, Mr. Caries eliminates their power to reinforce clean-up efforts even when they are not available.

These examples illustrate some of the problems involved in using contingency contracting in schools and especially in using it as a basic system for managing the class as a whole. The proper contingencies are hard to establish, and satiation with the available resources is a continuing problem. Although the method has been used successfully with entire classrooms (Kazdin, 1977; O'Leary & O'Leary, 1977; Robinson, Newby, & Ganzell, 1981) and even schools, most teachers will find it valuable primarily as a supplement to basic classroom management techniques, especially for students who seem to need extra incentives to keep up with their work (Macmillan & Kolvin, 1977).

Cognitive Behavior Modification

Although contingency-contracting approaches were developed by behaviorists interested in applications of the concept of reinforcement, these approaches also involved opportunities for students to participate in goal setting and self-monitoring of behavior. Experience with some of these more cognitive elements of contingency contracting led to the realization that they have important positive effects of their own, independent of the effects of reinforcement. For example, inducing students to set work output goals for themselves can lead to improved performance, especially if the goals are specific and difficult rather than vague or too easy (Rosswork, 1977). Even more powerful than inducing students to set goals is inducing them to monitor and maintain daily records of their own study behavior (Sagotsky, Patterson, & Lepper, 1978). Several studies have shown that if taught properly, students can learn to monitor their own classroom behavior more closely and control it more effectively (Glynn, Thomas, & Shee, 1973; McLaughlin, 1976; O'Leary & Dubey, 1979; Rosenbaum & Drabman, 1979).

The simplest forms of self-monitoring require students only to judge whether or not they are on task when a "beep" signal is given or a five-minute time period has elapsed on the clock. In the study by Sagotsky, Patterson, and Lepper (1978), for example, students were taught to place plus signs (on task) or minus signs (off task) in boxes on cards provided for self-recording of task engagement. Students have also been taught to record and graph the number of math problems they completed in each day's math seatwork period and to note the percentage of these problems completed correctly. With proper training, even 8-year-old students can learn to record qualitative aspects of their performance, such as the number of action words and describing words that they include in their daily compositions (Ballard & Glynn, 1975).

Typically, self-control skills are taught to students using procedures that Meichenbaum (1977) has called "cognitive behavior modification." One particularly powerful technique combines modeling with verbalized self-instructions. Rather than just tell the students what to do, the teacher demonstrates the process, not only by going through the physical motions involved but also by verbalizing the thoughts and other self-talk (self-instructions, self-monitoring, self-reinforcement) that should accompany the physical motions.

Meichenbaum and Goodman (1971) originally used the technique with cognitively impulsive students who made frequent errors on matching tasks because they responded too quickly, settling on the first response alternative that looked correct rather than taking time to examine all of the alternatives before selecting the best one. As the models "thought out loud" while demonstrating the task, they made a point of carefully observing each alternative and resisting the temptation to settle on the first one that looked correct before examining all of the rest, reminding themselves that one can be fooled by small differences in detail that are not noticed at first, and so on. Variations of this approach have been used not only to teach cognitively impulsive students to approach tasks more reflectively, but also to teach students in general to be more creative in problem solving, to help social isolates learn to initiate activities with their peers, to help aggressive students to control their anger and respond more effectively to frustration, and to help frustrated and defeated students learn to cope with failure and respond to mistakes with problem-solving efforts rather than with withdrawal or resignation.

Various approaches have in common the attempt to demystify frustrating situations for students and teach them that they can exert control over their own behavior and handle these situations effectively through rational planning and decision making.

A simple example is the "turtle" technique of Robin, Schneider, and Dolnick (1976), in which teachers teach aggressive students to assume a turtle position when upset. The students learn to place their heads on their desks, close their eyes, and clench their fists. This gives them an immediate response to use in anger-provoking situations and buys time that enables them to delay inappropriate behavior and to think about constructive solutions. Actually, the turtle position is not essential. It is a gimmick that many younger students find enjoyable, and it may also serve as a sort of crutch for students who might otherwise not be able to delay responding. In any case, the key is training students to delay impulsive responding while they gradually relax and think about constructive alternatives.

A more complex example is the program developed by Douglas, Perry, Marton, and Garson (1976) for training hyperactive students to approach seatwork tasks planfully. The modeling and verbalized self-instructions in this program were designed to enable these students to think before acting ("I must stop and think before I begin." "What plans can I try?" "How would it work if I did that?"), to monitor their performances during the task ("What shall I try next?" "Have I got it right so far?"), to check and correct mistakes ("See, I made a mistake there—I'll correct it." "Let's see, have I tried everything I can think of?"), and finally, to reinforce themselves ("I've done a pretty good job.").

A still more elaborate example is the "Think Aloud" program of Camp and Bash (1981), a structured curriculum designed to teach students to use their cognitive skills to guide their social behavior and cope with social problems. It teaches the students to pose and develop answers to four basic questions: "What is my problem?"; "How can I do it?"; "Am I using my plan?"; "How did I do?" The activities in this curriculum can be used with the class as a whole, although they were originally developed for and are probably of most value with impulsive and aggressive students taught in small groups.

Classroom Meetings

Glasser (1969) has developed an approach to classroom management that emphasizes self-control based on insight and group control based on social pressure. His ideas involve application of *reality therapy,* in which people are taught to see themselves and their actions as they really are by learning how others see them. When they find out that others react negatively to things they say and do, they usually are motivated to change. This is especially likely with students confronted with negative reactions of their classmates, because classrooms are social systems that continue throughout the school year. The desire to be accepted, combined with the knowledge that one must live with classmates for the year, constitutes a powerful motivation.

Problems are discussed during classroom meetings in which the teacher and students sit in a circle and interact as a single group. The teacher presides but functions as a group leader rather than an instructor or authority figure. Problems are presented as belonging to the class, not just to the teacher. There is continuing stress on the notion that every student has responsibilities to cooperate and help maintain a good learning environment. Students who fail to fulfill these responsibilities are warned that they will not be allowed to continue this way. On the other hand, they are led to see that they have not only the responsibility, but also the power to solve their own problems. This is the purpose of the meeting (in the case of meetings devoted to discussion of problems).

In addition to problems brought up by the teacher, the class discusses problems that students bring up in relation to themselves, other students, or the teacher. They are encouraged to speak freely. The only limitations or rules are those necessary to keep the group functioning (one person talks at a time and the others listen). The teacher may occasionally clarify or try to keep the discussion on the topic until a solution is achieved, but no one is interrupted for faultfinding, criticism, or punishment. The continuing focus is on searching for agreeable solutions, not fixing blame.

These meetings can be very effective in producing insight and changing behavior, but skill and good judgment are involved in leading them successfully. The teacher must be able to cope with unanticipated and often serious emotional reactions. Teachers who cannot shed the authority figure role or shift decision-making power from themselves to the group should not use this method. The same is true of teachers who are not prepared to deal with accusations, arguments, or emotional outbursts. Such strong emotional reactions happen regularly in such groups and provide excellent opportunities to build insight and foster psychological development, but the group leader must be able to deal with them constructively. The group meeting approach might be effective or even ideal for teachers who can tolerate and respond effectively to strong emotional expression. Even for teachers who do not want to use the technique regularly, occasional class meetings of the kind that Glasser recommends can be useful (e.g., in developing and revising classroom rules).

ANALYZING STUDENT BEHAVIOR

Many forms of problem behavior have not been discussed in this chapter: student habits that irritate or disgust the teacher, students who bait the teacher with provocative remarks, and various signs of mental or emotional disorder. These problems are hard to generalize about because they usually require specific diagnosis to determine why the students are behaving the way they are and to suggest possible treatment. Suggestions about how teachers can proceed in dealing with these problems are given below.

Finding Out What the Behavior Means

To the extent that behavior problems occur in the classroom, teachers should question the students and conduct systematic observations of them. What is the meaning of the behavior? Why does the student act this way? *Remember, surface misbehavior may be just a symptom of an underlying problem, and the symptomatic behavior may not be as important as the reasons that are producing it.*

If the behavior is just a habit, not part of a larger complex of problems, the teacher should insist that the student drop it and adopt a more appropriate behavior. This explicit improvement demand should be supported by an appropriate rationale (appeal to school rules, to social convention, or to the Golden Rule).

Where students' habits are not fundamentally immoral but merely violate the school rules, social convention, tact, good taste, or the teacher's personal preferences, this distinction should be made clear. Students should not be made to feel guilty or to believe that their habit indicates that something is seriously wrong with them. Teachers are justified in forbidding habits that are disruptive or irritating, but such habits should not be described as worse than they really are.

If the problem behavior is more serious or complex than a simple habit and the student has not given an adequate explanation for it, careful observation is needed. Observations should begin by describing the behavior more precisely. Is it a ritual or focal behavior that is repeated pretty much the same way over and over (masturbating, spitting, nose picking), or is it a more general tendency (aggression, suspiciousness, sadistic sense of humor) that is manifested in many different ways? Perhaps the description can be narrowed down. Is there a recognizable pattern? For example, do students' suspicions center around a belief that others are talking about them behind their backs, or do they think they are being picked on or cheated? If they do think others are talking about them, what do they think is being said? If students laugh inappropriately, what makes them laugh? Such information provides clues to what the behavior means.

Besides describing the behavior more specifically, observations should establish the conditions under which it occurs. Is it a chronic problem or something that started recently? Does it happen at a particular time of the day or part of the week? Does it occur when tests are given, for example, or when a student has lost a competition? Identification of such common elements in the situations in which the behavior has been observed might point to the events that trigger the reaction. In addition, sharing these observations with the students (see Rohrkemper, 1982) may produce insights that increase both the teacher's and the students' understanding of the problem behavior and also lead to useful suggestions for problem solving.

Teachers should also ask themselves what they were doing immediately before the students acted out. Perhaps they triggered the behavior by treating students unfairly or in ways that the students think are unfair. Analyses of this sort help teachers place students' behavior in context as symptoms and may help identify underlying causes. This will move teachers away from essentially negative, describe-the-problem-but-don't-do-anything-about-it approaches ("How can I get Mary to stop sulking?") and toward diagnosis and treatment ("How can I help Mary see that I am not rejecting her when I refuse her requests?").

In summary, teachers should question students and observe them systematically when they show repeated disturbing behavior. Attention should focus more on the meaning of and reasons for the behavior than on the behavior itself. Unless the behavior is an isolated, simple habit, detailed observations may be needed to discover the causes. This can be formalized in a focused case study.

Arranging a Conference

Often the simplest and best way to understand students' behavior is to talk to them about it in a conference arranged during a free period or after school. The main purpose, besides seeking information, is to show concern for the students. Teachers should note what they have observed, express concern about the students' behavior, and ask the students to explain it. The main thing is to get the students talking and then hear them out.

Students usually cannot explain fully why they act as they do, and teachers should not expect them to. If the students had such insight, they probably would not be behaving symptomatically in the first place. Instead, the hope is that clues or helpful information will emerge from the discussion. If it does produce a breakthrough, fine. If not, something is still accomplished if students come away with the knowledge that the teacher is concerned about them and wishes to help. In any case, conferences should be concluded in ways that give students a feeling of closure.

If the problem behavior has been disruptive, teachers should clarify expectations and limits, as well as reach agreements with students about any special actions to be taken. If the problem requires no special action or if it is not yet clear what action to take, teachers can conclude by telling the students that they are glad to have had a chance to discuss the problem and that they will help in any way they can if the students will let them know how.

Bringing in Parents and Other Adults

Teachers should think twice before involving parents, principals, counselors, or other adults, because this escalates the problem in the minds of all concerned and labels the student as a "problem student." The expected benefits of involving adults must be weighted against the damage that could result from such labeling.

Help may be available from a counselor, social worker, or school psychologist. By discussing the situation with such a resource person, preferably after the person has observed in the classroom several times, teachers may gain new insights or get specific suggestions. A knowledgeable principal, assistant principal, or fellow teacher might also play this role.

The resource persons' titles are less important than the quality of their observations and advice. If they are usually helpful in providing insights or suggestions about dealing with problems, teachers stand to benefit from talking with them.

Some resource people deal with students directly rather than through teachers. Again, this may or may not be helpful. There is usually little point in having students tested, for example, unless a physical problem is suspected. Knowledge of the students' scores on intelligence or personality tests usually contributes nothing to the solution of their problems. In fact, testing may lead to undesirable labeling or self-fulfilling prophecy effects.

Thus, there is little point in bringing in other adults to deal with students directly unless they can treat them effectively. Also, merely sending students to talk to counselors, vice principals, or "disciplinarians" will not do much good over the long run. If a student's behavior problem is in the classroom, it must be dealt with there.

Contacting parents about problems can also be risky. After all, to the extent that students have serious emotional or behavioral problems, their parents are probably the biggest single cause. Merely informing the parents will do no good. If teachers give parents the impression that they expect them to "do something," the parents will probably threaten or punish the student and let it go at that. Thus, teachers should not give parents this impression unless they have specific suggestions to propose.

Sometimes specific suggestions can be given, as when teachers enlist parents' help in seeing that the students get enough sleep, do their homework, or eat breakfast. When making suggestions, teachers may need to tell parents many of the things discussed in this book. The need to think of punishment as a last resort and the need for confidence and positive expectations are two particular principles that many parents violate when their children have problems.

If parents are called mostly to get information, teachers should make this clear and then state their observations and concern about the student and ask if the parents can add anything that might increase their understanding or ability to help the student. They should see how much the parents know about the problem and what their explanation for it is, if they have one. If some plan of action emerges, it should be discussed and agreed upon with the parents. The teacher and the parents should also agree on what the parents are going to tell the student about the conference.

If no particular parental action is suggested, the conference should be brought to some form of closure by the teacher ("Well, I'm glad we've had a chance to talk about George today. I think you've given me a better understanding of him. I'll keep working with him in the classroom and let you know about his progress. Meanwhile, if anything comes up that I ought to know, give me a call"). The parents should emerge from the conference knowing what to tell their child about it and what, if anything, the teacher is requesting them to do.

Bearing the Unbearable

Teachers often must cope with problems that really cannot be solved. If enough seriously disturbed students are in the room, the teacher cannot deal with all of them successfully and teach the curriculum too. When things get unbearable, something has to give; either the problem has to be whittled down or the teacher needs help from outside resources. Unfortunately, resources adequate to do the job usually are not available, and available resources usually are not successful. Parents and school disciplinarians are usually armed only with pep talks, threats, and punishment. Suspension from school merely deepens students' alienation and makes it harder for them to cope when they come back (*if* they come back). Placement in a class for the mentally retarded or emotionally disturbed, or in a reform school, although well meant and usually considered "treatment," generally is the first step toward total failure.

Genuinely therapeutic treatment is available, but unless the family is able and willing to pay high professional fees, students will likely have to go on waiting lists. If they are lucky, they may get treated a year or so later, but not immediately.

Thus, the only effective treatment that most disturbed students get must come from their classroom teachers (with the help of counselors, social workers, school psychologists, and school administrators). For students who are almost old enough to drop out of school or are in danger of being thrown out, this may be the last real chance to head off a lifelong pattern of failure and misery. It is for this reason that teachers must push themselves to their limits before giving up on any student.

SUMMARY

The key to successful classroom management lies in using the preventive techniques described in the previous chapter. Consistent use of these techniques will eliminate most problems, and the rest can be handled with techniques described in the present chapter. Many major disruptions start as minor misbehavior, so teachers should monitor the classroom continuously and know how to stop minor problems quickly and nondisruptively.

Much misbehavior can be ignored. When it is fleeting and not disruptive, there is no point in interrupting activity to call attention to it. If misbehavior is prolonged or begins to become disruptive, direct intervention is needed. When students know what they are supposed to be doing and when the nature of their misbehavior is obvious, there is no need to question them. Return them to productive activity as quickly and nondisruptively as possible, in ways that do not call attention to the misbehavior. This can be done through eye contact, touch or gesture, moving closer to the students, or calling on them.

When it is not possible to use these nondisruptive techniques, teachers should call the students' names and correct their behavior by telling them what they are supposed to be doing or reminding them of the rules. Such interventions should be brief, direct, and focused on desirable behavior. Questions, flaunting of authority, threats, and nagging should be avoided.

It is necessary to question students when misbehavior has been serious or disruptive and the teacher is unclear about the facts. Such investigations should be conducted privately, so that students will have less reason to engage in face-saving behavior. The teacher should assure all students involved that they will be heard but insist that each student speak in turn, one at a time. Questions should be confined to those seriously intended to elicit information.

Teachers should not make decisions or attempt to settle issues until they have heard everyone out. After gathering the facts, they should take action aimed at both resolving the present problem and preventing its return. This will mean clarification of expected behavior and perhaps a new rule or agreement. Ordinarily, there will be no need for punishment.

Because punishment is a stopgap control measure rather than a solution and because it involves many undesirable side effects, it should be used only as a last resort. When it is used, everyone should understand that punished students brought on the punishment through repeated misbehavior, leaving the teacher with no other choice. Appropriate forms of punishment include withdrawal or restriction of privileges, exclusion from the group, and assignments that force the students to reflect on the rules and their rationales. Punishment should be related to the offense, as brief and mild as possible, and flexible enough to allow students to redeem themselves by correcting their behavior.

A few students with long-standing and severe disturbances will require extraordinary corrective measures. Suggestions for dealing with several common types are given in this chapter. Such serious problems require careful observation and diagnosis, followed by individualized prescription and treatment. However, there are a few general principles:

1. Teachers should treat such students just as they treat other students as much as possible, so that they do not become "special cases."
2. Teachers should continually stress the positive with such students, indicating the desirable behavior they expect and communicating the expectation that the students will improve.
3. Teachers will usually have to form close individual relationships with such students, so they will like and respect them enough to want to earn respect and affection in return.
4. Teachers should concentrate on the in-school behavior of problem students, because attempts to become the students' psychotherapist or the familys' social caseworker often do more harm than good.

This chapter and the last have been eclectic, drawing ideas about classroom management from many sources. Readers wanting more information can consult sources that describe methods based on particular points of view, such as contingency contracting, cognitive behavior modification, or the reality-therapy classroom meetings approach of Glasser.

Although it is almost always useful to gather information and solicit advice, teachers should think carefully before involving anyone else in their dealings with problem students. This step may escalate the problem in the minds of everyone and lead to undesirable self-fulfilling prophecy effects. Most relevant information can be gotten by observing and questioning the students themselves, and most beneficial changes will come as a result of time spent establishing and using a good relationship. Classroom problems must be solved in the classroom, regardless of what else may exist on the outside.

SUGGESTED ACTIVITIES AND QUESTIONS

7.1. Reread the two cases presented in Chapter 1 and pinpoint the management errors that the teacher made. Then, using the contents of this chapter and your own ideas, specify how the teacher could have behaved more profitably.

7.2. Ask your instructor or in-service leader to find films or videotapes of teaching behavior and use the observation forms (Forms 7.1–7.3) that accompany this chapter to assess the teacher's managerial ability. Try to identify as many good or poor techniques as you can. When you spot ineffective techniques, suggest alternatives that the teacher could have used.

7.3. Summarize in five brief paragraphs the guidelines for dealing with the five classroom adjustment problems discussed in this chapter (showing off, defiance, aggression, unresponsiveness, and failure to complete assignments). Practice your ability to deal with these problems in role-playing situations. Specify a hypothetical problem, assign some participants to the student and teacher roles, and allow the rest to observe and provide feedback. Did the teacher deal with the problem effectively? Did he or she seem sincere? What alternatives could have been used?

7.4. Review or construct a list of student behaviors or characteristics that are most likely to embarrass you or to make you anxious. Practice how you will deal with these situations in your classroom. For example, if threats to your authority are problems for you, list student behaviors likely to touch you off and practice how you would respond. Then role-play your response with other participants. For example, how would you respond (or would you respond?) in this situation:

TEACHER: You're right, Frank, what I told you yesterday was incorrect.
HERB: (*Gleefully bellowing from the back of the room*) You're always wrong! We never know when to believe you!

7.5. Describe techniques teachers can use to eliminate minor misbehavior quickly and nondisruptively. (See also Suggested Activities and Questions, exercise 6.10.)

7.6. Why should teachers avoid threats and appeals to authority when stopping misbehavior through direct intervention?

7.7. Why do the authors not recommend the use of physical punishment?

7.8. In general, what steps can teachers follow to make exclusion from the group effective punishment (i.e., effective in reducing misbehavior)? In particular, how should teachers behave when excluding or readmitting students to group activities?

7.9. Why should teachers focus attention on students' school-related behavior rather than on their out-of-school behavior?

7.10. When is punishment necessary, and what is the best way to administer it?

7.11. A ninth-grade teacher sees Bill Thomas (without apparent provocation) grab Tim Grant's comb and throw it on the floor. Bill and Tim begin to push each other. What should the teacher do? Be specific. Write out or role-play the actual words you would use. Would you behave differently if you had not seen what preceded the pushing?

REFERENCES

Ballard, K., & Glynn, T. (1975). Behavioral self-management in story writing with elementary school children. *Journal of Applied Behavior Analysis, 8,* 387–398.

Bandura, A. (1969). *Principles of behavior modification.* New York: Holt, Rinehart and Winston.

Blank, M. (1973). *Teaching learning in the preschool: A dialogue approach.* Columbus, OH: Merrill.

Brophy, J. (1985). Teachers' expectations, motives, and goals for working with problem students. In C. Ames & R. Ames (Eds.), *Research on motivation in education. Vol. 2: The classroom milieu.* New York: Academic Press.

Brophy, J., & Evertson, C. (1978). Context variables in teaching. *Educational Psychologist, 12,* 310–316.

Brophy, J., & Rohrkemper, M. (1981). The influence of problem ownership on teachers' perceptions of and strategies for coping with problem students. *Journal of Educational Psychology, 73,* 295–311.

Camp, B., & Bash, M. (1981). *Think aloud: Increasing social and cognitive skills—a problem-solving program for children, primary level.* Champaign, IL: Research Press.

Douglas, V., Perry, P., Marton, P., & Garson, C. (1976). Assessment of a cognitive training program for hyperactive children. *Journal of Abnormal Child Psychology, 4,* 389–410.

Felmlee, D., Eder, D., & Tsui, W. (1985). Peer influence on classroom attention. *Social Psychology Quarterly, 48,* 215–226.

Glasser, W. (1969). *Schools without failure.* New York: Harper & Row.

Glasser, W. (1977). Ten steps to good discipline. *Today's Education, 66,* 61–63.

Glynn, E., Thomas, J., & Shee, S. (1973). Behavioral self-control of on-task behavior in an elementary classroom. *Journal of Applied Behavior Analysis, 6,* 105–113.

Good, T., & Brophy, J. (1974). Changing teacher and student behavior: An empirical investigation. *Journal of Educational Psychology, 66,* 390–405.

Gordon, T. (1974). *T.E.T. Teacher effectiveness training.* New York: McKay.

Hyman, I., & Wise, J. (Eds.). (1979). *Corporal punishment in American education: Readings in history, practice and alternatives.* Philadelphia: Temple University Press.

Kazdin, A. (1977). *The token economy: A review and evaluation.* New York: Plenum.

Kounin, J. (1970). *Discipline and group management in classrooms.* New York: Holt, Rinehart and Winston.

Macmillan, A., & Kolvin, I. (1977). Behaviour modification in teaching strategy: Some emergent problems and suggested solutions. *Educational Researcher, 20,* 10–21.

Meichenbaum, D. (1977). *Cognitive-behavior modification: An integrated approach.* New York: Plenum.

Meichenbaum, D., & Goodman, J. (1971). Training impulsive children to talk to themselves. *Journal of Abnormal Psychology, 77,* 115–126.

McLaughlin, T. (1976). Self-control in the classroom. *Review of Educational Research, 46,* 631–663.

O'Leary, K., & O'Leary, S. (Eds.). (1977). *Classroom management: The successful use of behavior modification* (2nd ed.). New York: Pergamon.

O'Leary, S., & Dubey, D. (1979). Applications of self-control procedures by children: A review. *Journal of Applied Behavior Analysis, 12,* 449–465.

Prawat, R., & Nickerson, J. (1985). Relationship between teacher thought and action and student affective outcomes. *Elementary School Journal, 85,* 529–540.

Premack, D. (1965). Reinforcement theory. In D. Levine (Ed.), *Nebraska symposium on motivation* (Vol. 13). Lincoln: University of Nebraska Press.

Robin, A., Schneider, M., & Dolnick, M. (1976). The turtle technique: An extended case study of self-control in the classroom. *Psychology in the Schools, 13*, 449–453.

Robinson, P., Newby, T., & Ganzell, S. (1981). A token system for a class of underachieving hyperactive children. *Journal of Applied Behavior Analysis, 14*, 307–315.

Rohrkemper, M. (1982). Teacher self-assessment. In D. Duke (Ed.), *Helping teachers manage classrooms*. Alexandria, VA: Association for Supervision and Curriculum Development.

Rosenbaum, M., & Drabman, R. (1979). Self-control training in the classroom: A review and critique. *Journal of Applied Behavior Analysis, 12*, 467–485.

Rosswork, S. (1977). Goal-setting: The effects on an academic task with varying magnitudes of incentive. *Journal of Educational Psychology, 69*, 710–715.

Sagotsky, G., Patterson, C., & Lepper, M. (1978). Training children's self-control: A field experiment in self-monitoring and goal-setting in the classroom. *Journal of Experimental Child Psychology, 25*, 242–253.

Skinner, B. (1953). *Science and human behavior*. New York: Macmillan.

Weinstein, R., & Middlestadt, S. (1979). Student perceptions of teacher interactions with male high and low achievers. *Journal of Educational Psychology, 71*, 421–431.

FORM 7.1. Teacher's Reaction to Inattention and Misbehavior

USE: When the teacher is faced with problems of inattention or misbehavior
PURPOSE: To see if teacher handles these situations appropriately
      Code the following information concerning teacher's response to mis-
behavior or to inattentiveness. Code only when teacher seems to be aware of
the problem; do not code minor problems that teacher doesn't even notice.

BEHAVIOR CATEGORIES   CODES

		A	B	C
A. TYPE OF SITUATION				
1. Total class, lesson or discussion	1.	3	3	4
2. Small group activity—problem in group	2.	3	3	4,6
3. Small group activity—problem out of group	3.	1	2	2
4. Seatwork checking or study period	4.	1	3	4
5. Other (specify)	5.	4	3	2

B. TYPE OF MISBEHAVIOR
  1. Brief, nondisruptive, should be ignored
  2. Minor, but extended or repeated. Should
     be stopped nondisruptively
  3. Disruptive, should be stopped quickly. No
     questions needed
  4. Disruptive, questions needed or advisable
  5. Other (specify)

6.	___ ___ ___
7.	___ ___ ___
8.	___ ___ ___
9.	___ ___ ___
10.	___ ___ ___
11.	___ ___ ___
12.	___ ___ ___
13.	___ ___ ___
14.	___ ___ ___
15.	___ ___ ___
16.	___ ___ ___
17.	___ ___ ___
18.	___ ___ ___
19.	___ ___ ___
20.	___ ___ ___
21.	___ ___ ___
22.	___ ___ ___
23.	___ ___ ___
24.	___ ___ ___
25.	___ ___ ___

C. TEACHER'S RESPONSE(S)
  1. Ignores (deliberately)
  2. Nonverbal; uses eye contact, gestures or
     touch, or moves near offender
  3. Praises someone else's good behavior
  4. Calls offender's name; calls for attention or
     work; gives rule reminder. No overdwelling
  5. Overdwells on misbehavior, nags
  6. Asks rhetorical or meaningless questions
  7. Asks appropriate questions—investigates publicly
  8. Investigates privately, now or later
  9. Threatens punishment if behavior is repeated
  10. Punishes (note type)
  11. Other (specify)

CHECK IF APPLICABLE
_____ 1. Teacher delays too long before acting, so problems escalate
_____ 2. Teacher identifies wrong student or fails to include all involved
_____ 3. Teacher fails to specify appropriate behavior (when this is not
             clear)
_____ 4. Teacher fails to specify rationale behind demands (when this is
             not clear)
_____ 5. Teacher attributes misbehavior to ill will, evil motives
_____ 6. Teacher describes misbehavior as a typical or unchangeable trait;
             labels student

NOTES:
      #1, 2, and 4 were all for student #12 (he seems
to be the only consistent problem as far as
management goes).

FORM 7.2. Case Study

USE: To do concentrated observations on one or a few students who are
     problems for the teacher
PURPOSE: To systematically gather information needed to understand the
     student's behavior and to make recommendations to the teacher
     Use the codes on this page to record the student's behavior and link
it to antecedent causes when possible.

A. STUDENT BEHAVIOR
   1. Pays attention or actively works at assign-
      ment
   2. Stares in space or closes eyes
   3. Fidgets, taps, amuses self
   4. Distracts others—entertains, jokes
   5. Distracts others—questions, seeks help, in-
      vestigates
   6. Distracts others—attacks or teases
   7. Leaves seat—goes to teacher
   8. Leaves seat—wanders, runs, plays
   9. Leaves seat—does approved action (what?)
   10. Leaves seat—does forbidden action (what?)
   11. Calls out answer
   12. Calls out irrelevant comment (what?)
   13. Calls out comment about teacher (what?)
   14. Calls out comment about classmate (what?)
   15. Deliberately causes disruption
   16. Destroys property (whose? what?)
   17. Leaves room without permission
   18. Other (specify)

B. APPARENT CAUSE
   What set off the behavior?
   1. No observable cause—suddenly began acting
      out
   2. Appeared stumped by work, gave up
   3. Finished work, had nothing to do
   4. Distracted by classmate (who?)
   5. Asked to respond or perform by teacher
   6. Teacher checks or asks about progress on
      assigned work
   7. Teacher calls for attention or return to work
   8. Teacher praise (for what?)
   9. Teacher criticism (for what?)
   10. Teacher praises or rewards another student
   11. Teacher criticizes or punishes another student
   12. Teacher refuses or delays permission request
   13. Other (specify)

NOTES:
     9:45 Recess.

TIME		CODES A	B
8:15	1.	1	
8:23	2.	6	1
8:24	3.	1	
8:29	4.	11	10
8:30	5.	1	
8:38	6.	6	4
8:40	7.	1	
8:47	8.	2	2
8:49	9.	1	7
8:51	10.	5	2
8:53	11.	1	6
9:00	12.	9	
9:27	13.	15	1
9:28	14.	1	9
9:34	15.	6	1
9:36	16.	1	7
9:45	17.	9	
:	18.		
:	19.		
:	20.		
:	21.		
:	22.		
:	23.		
:	24.		
:	25.		
:	26.		
:	27.		
:	28.		
:	39.		
:	30.		
:	31.		
:	32.		
:	33.		
:	34.		
:	35.		
:	36.		
:	37.		
:	38.		
:	39.		
:	40.		

Note any information relevant to the following points:

STUDENT'S EMOTIONAL RESPONSE
1. Complaints (He is disliked, picked on, left out, not getting share, unjustly blamed, ridiculed, asked to do what he can't do or he's already done):

2. Posturing Behavior (threats, obscenities, challenging or denying teacher's authority):

3. Defense Mechanisms (silence, pouting, mocking politeness or agreement, appears ashamed or angry, talks back or laughs, says "I don't care," rationalizes, blames others, tries to cajole or change subject)

    Grins while being "talked to", blames student #7 ("He hit me first").

Check if applicable:
    ✓ 1. Teacher tends to overreact to student's misbehavior
    ___ 2. Student's misbehavior usually ultimately leads to affection or reward from the teacher
    ___ 3. Student usually acts out for no apparent reason
    ✓ 4. Student usually acts out when idle or unable to do assignments
    ___ 5. Student usually acts out when distracted by another child
    ___ 6. Student usually acts out in response to the teacher's behavior.

POSITIVE BEHAVIOR
1. Note the student's changes in behavior over time. When is he most attentive? What topics or situations seem to interest him?

    Attentive throughout reading group.

2. What questions does he raise his hand to answer?

    Seeks to respond in all situations – whenever he thinks he can answer.

3. What work assignments does he diligently try to do well?

4. What activities does he select if given a choice?

Form 7.2   *(Continued)*

FORM 7.3. Teacher's Response to Problem Students

USE: When the class contains one or more students who present chronic,
*   severe problems in personal adjustment or classroom behavior*
PURPOSE: To inventory the teacher's coping strategies
*   Pick a particular problem student and check the strategies that the*
teacher uses for coping with this student.

A. GENERAL STRATEGIES

_____ 1. Control undesirable behavior through demands or threats of
              punishment
_____ 2. Offer incentives or rewards for improved behavior
_____ 3. Provide modeling, training, or other instruction designed to
              teach the student more effective ways of coping (either in
              general or in particular situations in which problem behavior is
              frequent for this student)
_____ 4. Identify and treat underlying causes believed to be
              responsible for the student's symptomatic behavior (home
              pressures, self-concept problems, etc.)
_____ 5. Provide counseling designed to increase the student's insight
              into the problem behavior and its causes or meanings
_____ 6. Attempt to change the student's troublesome attitudes or
              beliefs through logical appeal or persuasion
_____ 7. Attempt to provide encouragement, reassurance, or support
              to the student's self-concept through creating a supportive
              environment
_____ 8. Attempt to develop a close personal relationship with the
              student
_____ 9. Other (describe)

B. SPECIFIC STRATEGIES

_____ 1. Minimize conflict by intervening as seldom and as indirectly
              as possible
_____ 2. Use humor or other face-saving or tension reduction
              techniques when direct intervention is necessary

———— 3. Maintain close physical proximity or monitor the student's behavior closely

———— 4. Use time-out procedures to extinguish disruptive behavior by removing the opportunity for the student to misbehave and be reinforced for it

———— 5. Use time-out procedures to allow the student an opportunity to calm down and reflect after an outburst

———— 6. Use behavior contracts to formalize offers of reward for improved behavior

———— 7. Use modeling or role play procedures to help student learn the self talk that controls adaptive responses to frustrating or threatening situations

———— 8. Adjust work expectations or assignments if these seem inappropriate and appear to be contributing to the problem

———— 9. Adjust seat assignment, group assignment, or other social environment/peer relationship factors

———— 10. Attempt to develop peer support for the problem student

———— 11. Attempt to develop peer pressure on the problem student (to stop behaving inappropriately)

———— 12. Active listening, "I" statements, or attempts to negotiate "no-lose" solutions (Gordon's techniques)

———— 13. Attempt to get the student to recognize problem behavior, accept responsibility, and commit to a plan for improvement (Glasser's techniques)

———— 14. Contact with family members

———— 15. Involvement of mental health professionals

———— 16. Other (describe)

C. ASSESSMENT

Which of these strategies appear to be helpful, and which do not? Which might be more helpful if they were implemented more often, more systematically, or in a different way? Are there strategies that the teacher doesn't use that might be helpful?

FORM 7.3. (Continued)

CHAPTER

8 Motivation

INTRODUCTION

"You can lead a horse to water, but you can't make him drink." Teachers face the kinds of problems that are summed up in this familiar saying. Appropriate curricula and good teaching are necessary but not sufficient for insuring that students make good progress in mastering the knowledge and skills taught at school. In addition, the students must be receptive to curriculum developers' and teachers' efforts. It is the students who do the learning, and if they resist it or minimize their investment of attention and effort, not much will be accomplished. By using effective motivational strategies, however, teachers can help insure that the students will be receptive not only to academic activities but will engage in them actively and try to develop the knowledge or skills that the activities were designed to teach.

We begin our consideration of student motivation with two brief vignettes depicting tenth-grade American history teachers starting a week devoted to discussions of the Declaration of Independence and the U.S. Constitution. Read each vignette to get the gist, and then record your answers to the questions.

Classroom A

Teacher Vince Coleman begins the week with the following statement: "I hope that you read Chapter 27 carefully because it is a key chapter; in fact, questions on this chapter alone will represent about 50 percent of the next unit test. I'm going to ask a lot of questions about the facts in Chapter 27 because it covers an important part of

American history. In particular, I think that the Declaration of Independence is a key historical document that you should know 'cold.' You should also understand the Preamble to the Constitution and be able to discuss it at length. It's a well-written, important document. Let's begin by considering the important facts. First, who was the most important person involved in drafting the Declaration of Independence?"

Classroom B

Jane Strong is teaching the same material to students similar to those taught by Vince Coleman. She begins the week in the following way: "I want to discuss Chapter 27 with you, but before beginning our discussion of important ideas associated with the Declaration of Independence and its role in American history, I want to raise four questions that provide some structure for today's discussion and for the rest of this week. Write down these four questions and I'll give you some time to think about them and to talk about them in small-group discussions in just a few moments: (1) What is protest? (2) Under what circumstances is it appropriate? (3) Think about the rights and privileges that you have in this school and the constraints that also apply. If you were going to write a declaration of independence as a student in this school, what are the three or four important points that you would include in your document? (4) To what extent do you think that your view of a good school or a good government in this school is shared by other students?

"We need to consider these questions before we begin a formal discussion of the Declaration of Independence so that you can see the problems of consensus that the framers of our Constitution faced. To what extent do different individuals see government in the same way? Do they have common expectations for those services and activities that facilitate their individual needs versus those activities that inhibit the expression of their individual freedom? Tomorrow we are actually going to draft a constitution for students in this class.

"Toward the end of the week we will more formally consider the Declaration of Independence as we attempt to organize our understanding of the document in the following ways: (1) The historical background of its development; (2) the philosophical ideas that influenced its framers; (3) the individuals who drafted and signed the document and what it represented from their point of view; and (4) the continuing importance of the declaration, particularly as it affects contemporary life in American society."

Questions

Given these brief glimpses into the two classrooms, how would you answer the following questions? If you were a tenth grader, would you rather have Vince Coleman or Jane Strong as your history teacher? Why? Which teacher's students are likely to be more motivated to learn about the Declaration of Independence and the U.S. Constitution? Which teacher's students are likely to be more concerned about passing the test and getting a good grade? How might the students in Classroom A differ from the students in Classroom B in (1) describing the nature and purposes of social studies classes; (2) how they would approach the content when studying; and (3) what they would learn from the unit?

Skill in Motivating Students

Skill in motivating students to learn is obviously basic to teachers' effectiveness. Like the topic of classroom management, however, the topic of classroom motivation did not receive much systematic scholarly attention until recently, so that teachers were forced to rely on unsystematic "bag-of-tricks" approaches or on advice stemming from questionable theorizing. Much of the latter advice flowed from one of two contradictory yet frequently expressed views that are both incorrect (at least in their extreme form). The first view is that learning should be fun and that when classroom motivation problems appear it is because the teacher somehow has converted an inherently enjoyable activity into drudgery. We believe that students should find academic activities meaningful and worthwhile, but we would not expect students to typically find such activities "fun" in the same sense that recreational games and pastimes are fun. The other extreme view is that school activities are necessarily boring, unrewarding, and even aversive, so that one must rely on extrinsic rewards and punishments in order to force students to engage in these unpleasant tasks.

Recent theory and research on the topic of motivation has led to rejection of both of these extreme views in favor of a more balanced and sophisticated approach and has suggested a rich range of motivational strategies. We will summarize this theory and research here. For more information, see Ames and Ames (1984, 1985), Brophy (1983), Corno and Mandinach (1983), Corno and Rohrkemper (1985), Deci and Ryan (1985), Good and Brophy (1986), Keller (1983), Kolesnik (1978), Lepper and Greene (1978), Maehr (1984), Malone and Lepper (in press), McCombs (1984), Nicholls (1984), and Wlodkowski (1978).

BASIC MOTIVATIONAL CONCEPTS

We begin with definitions of basic motivational concepts and discussion of some key points to keep in mind when thinking about motivation in the classroom. Psychologists traditionally use motivational concepts to account for the initiation, direction, intensity, and persistence of behavior. *Motives* are hypothetical constructs explaining why people are doing what they are doing. Motives can be distinguished from related constructs such as *goals* (the immediate objectives of particular sequences of behavior) and *strategies* (the methods that the person uses to achieve the goal and thus to satisfy or at least respond to the motive). An everyday example would be a person who responds to hunger (motive) by going to a restaurant (strategy) to get food (goal). Motives, goals, and strategies are less easily distinguished in classroom learning situations that call for intentional learning of cognitive content. Here, students who adopt content mastery as their goal are likely to be operating from certain motives rather than others and are likely to use certain strategies rather than others. One can make conceptual distinctions for purposes of analysis, but in analyzing concrete examples of intentional learning in the classroom, it can be difficult to separate motives, goals, and strategies as well as to separate "motivation" from "cognition." Optimal forms of motivation to learn and cognitive strategies for accomplishing that learning tend to occur together.

Consider the vignettes presented at the beginning of this chapter. If students in the two classes responded solely to what their respective teachers chose to emphasize in introducing the material on the Declaration of Independence and the Constitution, they would develop contrasting motives, goals, and strategies. In Classroom A, Vince Coleman's students would probably be motivated primarily by a desire to do well on the unit test rather than by a desire to learn the material because of the value of doing so. Furthermore, given what Mr. Coleman said about the test, the primary goal of these students' studying would be to memorize the Declaration of Independence and the Preamble to the Constitution as well as various other facts (names, dates, etc.). Consequently, their study efforts would be likely to emphasize rote memorizing strategies (repeating the material until one can regurgitate it "by heart").

In contrast, Jane Strong's students in Classroom B are more likely to be motivated to learn about the Declaration of Independence and the Constitution because they find the information interesting and important, not just because they need it to pass a test. Furthermore, given Jane's introduction, they are likely to adopt goals and strategies that involve concentrating on the meanings and implications of the material, placing it into historical context, relating it to personal ideas and experiences, and thinking about its applications to the modern world. This is a much more broad-ranging, personalized, and meaningful way of processing and responding to the information than the rote memorizing stressed in Classroom A. It involves a broader range of goals than merely committing facts to memory and a broader range of strategies for accomplishing these goals (posing and answering questions about the material or its implications, discussing it with peers, relating the concept of student rights to the concept of citizen rights, putting oneself in the place of the framers of these documents and considering them as vehicles constructed to communicate ideas and accomplish political purposes rather than merely as text to be learned).

Students' motives, goals, and strategies developed in response to classroom activities will depend both on the nature of the activities themselves (Blumenfeld, Mergendoller, & Swarthout, in press) as well as on how the teacher presents these activities to the students. If students are motivated solely by grades or other extrinsic reward and punishment considerations, they are likely to adopt goals and associated strategies that concentrate on meeting minimum requirements that will entitle them to what they see as acceptable reward levels. They will do what they must in order to prepare for tests and then forget most of what they have learned. It is better if students find academic activities intrinsically rewarding. Even if students are intrinsically motivated, however, the academic-learning benefits that the students derive from classroom activities may be minimal if the basis for their intrinsic motivation is primarily affective or emotional (they enjoy the activity) rather than cognitive or intellectual (they find it interesting, meaningful, or worthwhile to develop the knowledge or skills that the activity is designed to teach). Consequently, it is important that teachers use strategies designed to motivate their students to learn from academic activities—to seek to gain the intended knowledge and skill benefits from these activities and to set goals and use cognitive strategies that are appropriate for doing so.

Most approaches to motivation, including the present one, fit within *expectancy* × *value theory* (Feather, 1982). This theory holds that the effort that people will be willing to expend on a task will be a product of (1) the degree to which they *expect* to be able to perform the task successfully if they apply themselves (and thus the degree to which they expect to get the rewards that successful task performance will bring), and (2) the degree to which they *value* those rewards. Effort investment is viewed as the product rather than the sum of the expectancy and value factors because it is assumed that no effort at all will be invested in a task if one factor is missing entirely, no matter how much of the other factor may be present. People do not invest their efforts on tasks that do not lead to valued outcomes even if they know that they can perform the tasks successfully; they do not invest their efforts even on highly valued tasks if they believe that they cannot succeed on these tasks no matter how hard they try. Thus, expectancy × value theories of motivation imply that teachers need both to help their students appreciate the value of school activities and make sure that the students can achieve success in these activities if they apply reasonable effort.

Until very recently, work on motivation had concentrated on expectancy issues rather than value issues (Parsons & Goff, 1980). This work has led to suggestions about how teachers can develop in their students the success expectations that are so crucial to the students' willingness to commit themselves to challenging achievement goals. Still more recently, this research has been complemented by research on task value issues (e.g., why the students should want to succeed on the tasks in the first place). Eccles and Wigfield (1985) suggest that subjective task value has three major components: (1) *attainment value* (the importance of attaining success on the task in order to affirm one's self-concept or fulfill needs for achievement, power, or prestige); (2) *intrinsic or interest value* (the enjoyment that one gets from engaging in the task); and (3) *utility value* (the role that engaging in the task may play in advancing one's career or helping one to reach other larger goals). We believe that this is a useful classification scheme, although we place more emphasis on cognitive aspects and less emphasis on affective aspects in thinking about student motivation to learn academic content. Thus, we would include the pleasure of achieving understanding or skill mastery under attainment value; we would include aesthetic appreciation of the content or skill under intrinsic or interest value; and we would include awareness of the role of learning in improving the quality of one's life or making one a better person or a better citizen under utility value.

Our treatment of motivational strategies in this chapter is organized according to these expectancy × value theory ideas. After discussing some basic assumptions and preconditions that must be in place if teachers are to be successful in motivating their students, we will discuss approaches to motivation that involve establishing and maintaining success expectations in the students. Then we will describe three sets of motivational strategies designed to enhance the subjective value that students place on school tasks: extrinsic motivational strategies, intrinsic motivational strategies, and strategies for stimulating motivation to learn.

ESSENTIAL PRECONDITIONS THAT SET THE STAGE FOR MOTIVATIONAL STRATEGIES

The following preconditions are essential to the effectiveness of all of the motivational strategies to be discussed. *No motivational strategy can succeed if these preconditions are not in effect.*

Supportive Environment

To be motivated to learn in the classroom, students need both ample opportunities to learn and steady encouragement and support of their learning efforts. Because such motivation is unlikely to develop in a chaotic classroom, it is important that the teacher use classroom organization and management skills that will successfully establish the classroom as an effective learning environment (see Chapters 6 and 7).

Furthermore, because anxious or alienated students are unlikely to develop motivation to learn academic content, it is important that this businesslike emphasis on teaching and learning the curriculum occur within a relaxed and supportive atmosphere. The teacher should be a patient, encouraging person who supports the students' learning efforts. The students should feel comfortable taking intellectual risks because they know that they will not be embarrassed or criticized if they make a mistake.

Appropriate Level of Challenge or Difficulty

Activities should be at an appropriate level of difficulty for the students. If tasks are so familiar or easy that they constitute nothing but busywork, and especially if they are so unfamiliar or difficult that the students cannot succeed on them even if they apply reasonable effort, no strategies for inducing motivation are likely to succeed. *Tasks are of appropriate difficulty level when the students are clear enough about what to do and how to do it so that they can achieve high levels of success if they apply reasonable effort.* When students encounter such tasks routinely, they will come to expect success and thus will be able to concentrate on learning the tasks without worrying about failure.

Meaningful Learning Objectives

Students will not be motivated to learn if presented with pointless or meaningless activities. Activities should be selected with worthwhile academic objectives in mind. That is, they should *teach some knowledge or skill that is worth learning,* either in its own right or as a step toward some higher objective. Activities such as the following do *not* meet this criterion: continued practice on skills that have already been mastered thoroughly; memorizing lists for no good reason; looking up and copying definitions of terms that are never used meaningfully in readings or assignments; reading material that is not presented in enough detail or integrated well enough to allow the students to develop a clear understanding of it; reading about things that are so foreign to the students' experience or described in such technical or abstract language as to make the material essentially meaningless; and working on tasks that are assigned merely to fill time rather than to fulfill worthwhile instructional objectives. Where skills must be practiced until they become smooth and automatic, such practice should occur within larger, more integrative approaches to instruction that keep the students aware of the purposes of the practice. Elementary students should get to read for information or pleasure in addition to practicing word attack skills, should get to solve problems and apply mathematics in addition to practicing number facts and computations, and should get to write prose or poetry compositions or actual correspondence with others in addition to practicing spelling and penmanship. Secondary students should learn how and why knowledge was developed in addition to acquiring the knowledge itself and should get opportunities to apply what they are learning to their own lives or to current social, political, or scientific issues.

Moderation and Variation in Strategy Use

Motivational strategies can be overused in two respects. First, the need for such strategies will vary with the situation. When content is unfamiliar and its value or meaningfulness is not obvious to the students, significant motivational effort involving several of the strategies to be described may be needed. In contrast, little or no special motivational effort may be needed when the activity involves things that students are already eager to learn. Thus, motivational efforts can be counterproductive if they are used when they are not needed, go on too long, or get carried to extremes. Second, any particular motivational strategy may lose its effectiveness if used too often or too routinely. Thus, teachers should master and use a variety of motivational strategies rather than rely on just one or two.

With these four preconditions in mind, let us consider the motivational strategies that various writers have suggested.

MOTIVATING BY MAINTAINING SUCCESS EXPECTATIONS

Much of the best-known research on motivation has focused on expectancy issues. Research on *achievement motivation* (Dweck & Elliott, 1983) has established that effort and persistence are greater in individuals who set goals of moderate difficulty (neither too hard nor too easy), seriously commit themselves to pursuing these goals rather than treat them as mere "pie-in-the-sky" hopes, and concentrate on trying to achieve success rather than on trying to avoid failure. Research on *efficacy perceptions* (Bandura, 1982; Bandura & Schunk, 1981) has shown that effort and persistence are greater in individuals who not only perceive that successful task performance will bring some reward, but also perceive that they themselves are capable of performing the task successfully and thus earning the reward (i.e., perceive that they are competent or efficacious). Research on *causal attributions* for performance suggests that effort and persistence are greater in individuals who attribute their performance to internal and controllable causes rather than to external or uncontrollable causes (Weiner, 1984).

These and related approaches suggest that teachers need to encourage their students to develop the following perceptions and attributional inferences concerning their performance at school:

> *Effort-outcome covariation.* Recognition that there is a predictable relationship between the level of effort invested in a task and the level of success or mastery that can be expected (Cooper, 1979).
>
> *Internal locus of control.* Recognition that the potential to control outcomes (the degree of success achieved) lies within themselves rather than in external factors that they cannot control (Stipek & Weisz, 1981; Thomas, 1980).

Concept of self as origin rather than pawn. Recognition that they can bring about desired outcomes through their own actions (act as origins) rather than feeling that they are pawns whose fate is determined by factors beyond their control (deCharms, 1976).

Sense of efficacy/competence. Confidence that they have the ability to succeed on a task if they choose to invest the necessary effort (Bandura, 1982; Bandura & Schunk, 1981; Schunk, 1985; Schunk & Hanson, 1985; Weisz & Cameron, 1985).

Attribution to internal, controllable causes. Tendency to attribute successes to a combination of sufficient ability and reasonable effort and to attribute failures either to insufficient effort (if this has been the case) or to confusion about what to do or reliance on inappropriate strategies for trying to do it (but not to lack of ability or to uncontrollable factors such as bad luck) (Butkowsky & Willows, 1980; Frieze, Francis, & Hanusa, 1981; Weiner, 1984; Whitley & Frieze, 1985).

Incremental concept of ability. Perception of academic ability as potential that is developed continually through learning activities rather than as a fixed level of capacity that predetermines and limits what can be accomplished (Dweck & Elliott, 1983).

Several strategies have been suggested for helping students to maintain success expectations and these associated perceptions and attributions. All of these strategies assume that the students are given tasks of appropriate difficulty and receive timely and informative feedback that is specific about the correctness of their responses and about the progress they are making toward ultimate objectives. In short, these strategies involve helping students to make and recognize genuine progress rather than misleading them or offering them only empty reassurances.

Program for Success

The simplest way to insure that students expect success is to make sure that they achieve it consistently by beginning at their level, moving in small steps, and preparing them sufficiently for each new step so that they can adjust to it without much confusion or frustration. Two points need to be made about this strategy so that it is not understood as suggesting that teachers should mostly assign unchallenging busywork.

First, we speak here of success achieved through reasonable effort that leads to gradual mastery of appropriately challenging objectives, not to quick, easy success achieved through "automatic" application of overlearned skills to overly familiar tasks. It is true that certain basic knowledge and skills will need to be practiced until mastered to a level of smooth, errorless performance, but it is also true that students should be paced through the curriculum as briskly as they can progress without undue frustration. Thus, programming for success is a means toward the end of maximizing students' achievement progress, not an end in itself.

Second, keep in mind the role of the teacher. The levels of success that students are likely to achieve on a particular task depend not only on the difficulty of the task itself, but on the degree to which the teacher prepares them for the task through advance instruction and assists their learning efforts through guidance and feedback. A task that would be too difficult for the students if they were left to their own devices might be just right when learned through active instruction by the teacher followed by supervised practice. In fact, contemporary theorists believe that instruction should focus on what is called the *zone of proximal development* (Rogoff & Wertsch, 1984; Vygotsky, 1978), which refers to the range of knowledge and skills that students are not yet ready to learn on their own but could learn with help from teachers. In summary, programming for success does not mean giving students busywork and minimizing the role of instruction. On the contrary, it means continually challenging students within their zones of proximal development yet making it possible for them to meet these challenges by providing sufficient instruction, guidance, and feedback to insure that they can attain success with reasonable effort.

This implies that teachers will typically provide extra instruction and assistance to slower student, and will monitor their progress more closely. These students will need briefer or easier assignments if they cannot succeed even with extra help and support, but even so, teachers should continue to demand that they put forth reasonable effort and progress as fast as their abilities will allow. Effective teachers do not give up on low achievers or allow them to give up on themselves.

Teach Goal Setting, Performance Appraisal, and Self-Reinforcement

Students' reactions to their own performance will depend not so much on the absolute levels of success achieved but on their perceptions of what has been achieved. Some students may not fully appreciate their own accomplishments unless helped to identify appropriate standards to use in judging their progress.

This begins with *goal setting*. Research indicates that setting goals and making a commitment to trying to reach these goals increases performance (Bandura & Schunk, 1981; Tollefson, Tracy, Johnsen, Farmer, & Buenning, 1984). Goal setting is especially effective when the goals are (1) *proximal* rather than distal (they refer to performance on a task to be attempted here and now rather than to attainment of some ultimate goal in the distant future), (2) *specific* (complete a page of math problems with no more than one error) rather than global (do a good job), and (3) *challenging* (difficult but reachable) rather than too easy or too hard.

For any particular brief assignment, meeting the instructional objective is the appropriate goal. However, for more comprehensive assignments or tests, perfect performance will not be a realistic goal for many students. These students may need help in formulating challenging but reachable goals that represent what they can expect to achieve if they consistently put forth reasonable effort. In the case of a long series of activities that ultimately leads to some distal goal, it will be important to establish specific goals for each intervening activity and make sure that students are aware of the linkages between each of these activities and achievement of the ultimate goal (Bandura & Schunk, 1981; Morgan, 1985).

Goal setting is not enough by itself; there must also be *goal commitment*. Students must take the goals seriously and commit themselves to trying to reach them. It may be necessary to negotiate goal setting with some students, or at least to provide them with guidance and stimulate them to think about their performance potential. One way to do this is to provide a list of potential goals and ask students to commit themselves to particular goals (and associated levels of effort).

Another approach is to use performance contracting, in which students formally contract for a certain level of effort or performance in exchange for specified grades or rewards (Tollefson et al., 1984). This method is time consuming and may call more attention to rewards than is desirable, but it has the advantages of insuring active teacher-student negotiation about goal setting and formalizing of student commitment to goals.

Finally, students may need help in assessing progress toward established goals by using *appropriate standards for judging levels of success*. In particular, they may need to learn to compare their work with absolute standards or with their own previous performance levels rather than with the performance levels of others. Feedback about specific responses must be accurate (errors must be labeled as such if they are to be recognized and corrected), but more general evaluative comments should provide encouragement by denoting levels of success achieved in meeting established goals or by judging accomplishments with reference to what is reasonable to expect rather than with reference to absolute perfection.

Some students will need *specific, detailed feedback* concerning both the strengths and the weaknesses of their performance (Elawar & Corno, 1985). Such students may have only a vague appreciation of when and why they have done well or poorly, so that they need not only general evaluative feedback but concepts and terms that they can use to describe their performance and evaluate it with precision. This is especially true for compositions, research projects, laboratory experiments, and other complex activities that are evaluated according to general qualitative criteria rather than by the number of answers to specific questions scored as correct or incorrect.

Students who have been working toward specific proximal goals and who have the necessary concepts and language with which to evaluate their own performance accurately will be in a position to *reinforce themselves* for the successes that they achieve. Many students will do this habitually, but others will need encouragement to check their work and take credit for their successes (that is, to attribute such successes to the fact that they had the ability and were willing to make the effort required to attain success). If necessary, teachers can focus students' attention on their progress more directly by comparing the students' current accomplishments with performance samples from earlier points in time or by having the students themselves keep scrapbooks, graphs, or other records to document their progress.

Help Students to Recognize Effort-Outcome Linkages

The following strategies are useful for developing an internal locus of control and a sense of efficacy in students and for helping them to recognize that they can achieve success if they put forth reasonable effort.

Modeling   Teachers can model beliefs about effort-outcome linkages when talking to students about their own (the teachers') learning and skill development and when demonstrating tasks by thinking out loud as they work through them. It is especially useful if, when they encounter frustration or temporary failure, teachers model confidence that they will succeed if they persist and search for a better strategy or for some error in their application of the strategies already tried (Zimmerman & Blotner, 1979).

Socialization and Feedback   Teachers can also stress effort-outcome linkages when socializing or giving feedback to students. They can explain to students that curriculum goals and instructional practices have been established with an eye toward making it possible for students to achieve success if they put forth reasonable effort. When necessary, teachers can reassure students that persistence (perhaps augmented by extra help) will eventually pay off. Some students may need strong teacher statements of confidence in their abilities or willingness by the teacher to accept slow progress so long as the students are consistently putting forth reasonable effort.

Extra socialization efforts will be needed with low achievers when grades must be assigned according to fixed common standards or comparisons with peers or norms rather than by degree of effort expended or degree of success achieved in meeting individually prescribed goals. That is, low achievers will need to be socialized to take satisfaction in receiving Bs or even Cs when such grades represent successful performance based on reasonable effort from the students involved. For some students, achieving a grade of C is an occasion for taking pride in a job well done. When this is the case, teachers should express to these students (or better yet, to the students *and* their parents) recognition of the accomplishment and appreciation of the effort it represents.

Portray Effort as Investment Rather than Risk   Students need to be made aware that learning may take time and involve confusion or mistakes, but that persistence and careful work eventually should yield knowledge or skill mastery. Furthermore, they need to realize that such mastery not only represents success on the particular task involved but provides them with knowledge or skills that will make them that much more capable of handling higher-level tasks in the future. If they should give up on a particular task because of frustration or fear of failure, they would cheat themselves out of this growth potential.

Portray Skill Development as Incremental and Domain-Specific   Students need to know that their intellectual abilities are open to improvement rather than fixed and limiting and that they possess a great many such abilities rather than just a few. This implies that difficulties in learning particular tasks usually occur not because the students lack ability or do not make an effort but because they lack experience with the particular type of task involved. With patience, persistence, and help from the teacher, the students can acquire the knowledge and skills specific to the domain that the task represents, and this domain-specific knowledge and skill development will enable them to succeed on this task and on others like it. In short, students need to realize that success depends not just on general ability but on possession and use of specific knowledge and strategies.

Focus on Mastery   In monitoring performance and giving feedback, teachers should stress the quality of students' task engagement and the degree to which they are making continuous progress toward mastery rather than comparisons with how other students are doing (McColskey & Leary, 1985). Errors should be treated as learning opportunities rather than test failures: They should lead to remedial or additional instruction followed by additional practice opportunities. Make-up exams, credit for effort, or extra-credit assignments should be used to provide struggling students with opportunities to overcome initial failures through persistent efforts.

Encouraging Effort: An Example

If students appear convinced that they cannot do the work or if they regularly try to get the teacher to do it for them, the teacher must respond in a way that stays on a fine line between two extremes. First, the teacher must repeatedly encourage the students and express the belief that they will be able to succeed with continued effort. The students' expressions of inability should not be accepted or even legitimized indirectly through such comments as "Well, at least try." The students should know that they will learn the most by doing as much as they can for as long as they can, and therefore that they should not seek help at the first sign of difficulty. On the other hand, the teacher should make it clear that he or she is available and willing to help if help is really needed.

Here is how the situation might be handled appropriately:

STUDENT: I can't do number 4.
TEACHER: What part don't you understand?
STUDENT: I just can't do it.
TEACHER: Well, I know you can do part of it because you've done the first three problems correctly. The fourth is one is similar, but just a little harder. You start out the same way, but then you have to do one extra step. Review the first three, then see if you can figure out number 4. I'll come back in a few minutes to see how you're doing.

Compare this with the following inappropriate statement.

STUDENT: I can't do number 4.
TEACHER: You can't! Why not?
STUDENT: I just can't do it.
TEACHER: Don't say you can't do it—we never say we can't do it. Did you try hard?
STUDENT: Yes, but I can't do it.
TEACHER: Well, you did the first three problems. Maybe if you worked a little longer you could do the fourth one. Why don't you do that and see what happens?

In the first example, the teacher communicated positive expectations and provided help in the form of a specific suggestion about how to proceed. Yet, the teacher did not give the answer or do the work. In the second example, the teacher communicated halfhearted and somewhat contradictory expectations and did nothing to give the student reason to believe that further effort would succeed.

For some students, even providing appropriate seatwork and giving clear instructions is not enough. They also need to be socialized to recognize and rely on their own capabilities and to respond to frustration with coping strategies rather than withdrawal or dependency.

Remedial Work With Discouraged Students

Some students will have become discouraged to the point of "failure syndrome" or "learned helplessness." Such students, who tend to give up at the first sign of difficulty or frustration, will need more intensive and individualized motivational encouragement than what will be sufficient for the class as a whole.

A few of these will be bright students who have become accustomed to consistent, easy success that they attribute to high ability (rather than to the combination of ability and effort). When such students finally encounter content that they cannot assimilate with ease, they may overreact to their difficulties and conclude that they lack ability for that particular content or task (this is especially likely to occur in elementary art or physical education classes and in secondary mathematics and science classes). Such students need to be made to see that abilities in the particular content area can be developed, that the development process will require active learning efforts rather than mere activation of already available knowledge and skills, and that the process can be expected to take some time and will involve some confusion or frustration. In this regard, it may be necessary to attack rigid or overly high standards that such students may apply to themselves, and to get them to see academic activities as opportunities to learn rather than as test situations in which they are expected to display already developed skills.

Teachers may also encounter a few "committed underachievers" who persistently set inappropriately low goals and resist "accepting responsibility for their successes" because they do not want to be expected to maintain a similarly high level of performance in the future. These students need reassurance that they can attain consistent success with reasonable effort (that is, that it will not take superhuman effort). They also may benefit from values clarification exercises and related counseling techniques designed to show them that their "helpless" behavior pattern is contrary to their own values or best interests in the long run.

Most of the students who need remedial work on their expectations, however, are low achievers of limited academic ability who have become accustomed to frustration and failure. These students are likely to benefit from the strategies used in *mastery learning* approaches: make for success likely by giving them tasks that they should be able to handle, provide them not only with the usual group instruction but also with individualized tutoring as needed, and allow them to contract for particular levels of performance and to continue to study, practice, and take tests until that level of performance is achieved (see Chapter 9 for more on mastery learning). By virtually guaranteeing success, this approach builds confidence and increases the discouraged students' willingness to take the risks involved in seriously committing themselves to challenging goals (Grabe, 1985).

Discouraged students may also benefit from "attribution-retraining" approaches (Craske, 1985; Dweck & Elliott, 1983; Fowler & Peterson, 1981; Medway & Venino, 1982) in which they are given modeling, socialization, practice, and feedback designed to teach them to (1) concentrate on the task at hand rather than worry about failure when engaged in academic activities, (2) cope by retracing their steps to find their mistake or by analyzing the problem to find another approach rather than giving up in the face of failure, and (3) attribute their failures to insufficient effort, lack of information, or reliance on ineffective strategies rather than to lack of ability. Discouraged students are especially likely to benefit from exposure to "coping models" who maintain their composure and focus on developing solutions to the problem when confronted with frustration or failure (as opposed to "success models" who sail through problems without making mistakes).

Finally, some students may need extra help because they suffer from severe *test anxiety*. Such students may learn effectively and perform well in informal, pressure-free situations but become highly anxious and perform considerably below their potential on tests or during any testlike situation in which they are aware of being monitored and evaluated. Teachers can minimize such problems by

> Avoiding time pressures unless they are truly central to the skill being taught
>
> Stressing the feedback functions rather than the evaluation or grading functions of tests in discussing tests with the students
>
> Portraying tests as opportunities to assess progress in developing knowledge and skill rather than as measures of ability
>
> Where appropriate, telling students that some problems are beyond their present achievement level so that they should not be concerned about missing them
>
> Giving pretests to accustom the students to "failure" and to provide base rates for comparison later when posttests are administered
>
> Teaching stress management skills and effective test-taking skills and attitudes

(See Hill & Wigfield, 1984; McCombs, 1984; Plass & Hill, 1986.)

Concluding Comments About Success Expectations

Teachers should bear in mind that the expectancy aspects of student motivation depend less on the degree of objective success that students achieve than on how they view their performance: what they see as possible for them to achieve with reasonable effort, whether they define this achievement as successful or not, and whether they attribute their performance to controllable factors (effort, learning effective strategies) or to uncontrollable factors (fixed general abilities, luck). Therefore, whatever their ability levels, the motivation of all students, even the most extreme cases of failure syndrome or learned helplessness, is open to reshaping through systematic socialization by teachers. Empty reassurances or a few words of encouragement will not do the job, but a combination of appropriately challenging demands with systematic socialization designed to make the students see that success can be achieved with reasonable effort should be effective.

INDUCING STUDENTS TO VALUE ACADEMIC ACTIVITIES

Within the expectancy × value approach to motivation, the value term is just as important as the expectancy term. That is, student motivation will be affected not only by expectations and attributions concerning level of performance (Can I succeed on this task? Why did I achieve the level of success that I did?) but also by attributions concerning the reasons why they are engaging in tasks in the first place and by expectations concerning goals and objectives (What am I trying to accomplish here and what benefits can I expect to obtain from my efforts?). Traditionally, teachers have been advised to supply answers to the latter questions either by offering incentives or rewards for good performance (extrinsic motivation approach) or by teaching content and designing activities that students find enjoyable (intrinsic motivation approach). We will discuss each of these familiar approaches and then turn to a third approach that we believe is deserving of more attention than it has received to date: stimulating students' motivation to learn the content and skills being taught.

EXTRINSIC MOTIVATION STRATEGIES

The extrinsic motivation strategies are in some ways the simplest, most direct, and most adaptable of the methods recommended for dealing with the value aspects of classroom motivation. Extrinsic strategies do not attempt to increase the value that students place on the task itself, but instead link task performance to delivery of consequences that the students do value. Three common forms of extrinsic motivation are rewards, emphasis on the instrumental value of tasks, and competition.

Offer Rewards as Incentives for Good Performance

Rewards are one proven way to motivate students to put forth effort, especially when the rewards are offered in advance as incentives for striving to reach specified levels of performance. Commonly used types of reward include (1) material rewards (money, prizes, trinkets, consumables), (2) activity rewards and special privileges (opportunity to play games, use special equipment, or engage in self-selected activities), (3) grades, awards, and recognition (honor rolls, hanging good papers up on the wall), (4) praise and social rewards, and (5) teacher rewards (special attention, personalized interaction, opportunities to go places or do things with the teacher).

Rewards are more effective for stimulating level of effort than quality of performance. They appear to guide behavior more effectively when there is a clear goal and a clear path to follow in striving to reach that goal than when goals are more ambiguous or when students must discover or invent strategies for responding to the task rather than merely activate familiar strategies. Thus, rewards are better used with boring or unpleasant tasks than with attractive or interesting ones, better with routine tasks than with novel ones, better with tasks intended to produce specific intentional learning than with tasks designed to encourage incidental learning or discovery, and better with tasks where speed of performance or quantity of output is of more concern than creativity, artistry, or craftsmanship. Thus, it is more appropriate to offer rewards as incentives for meeting performance standards (or performance *improvement* standards) on skills that require a great deal of drill and practice (arithmetic computation, typing, spelling) than it is for work on a major research or demonstration project.

Rewards will be effective as motivators only for those students who believe that they have a chance to get the rewards if they put forth reasonable effort. With students who lack such self-efficacy perceptions, rewards will not be effective and may even backfire by causing depression or resentment. Therefore, if rewards are to be incentives for everyone and not just the high-ability students, it will be necessary to insure that everyone has equal (or at least reasonable) access to the rewards. This may require contracting or some less formal method of individualizing criteria for successful performance.

The comments made in Chapter 6 about using rewards and praise to motivate students to conform to classroom expectations also apply to the use of these incentives to motivate students' learning efforts. In particular, it is important that incentives be offered and delivered in ways that encourage students to appreciate their developing knowledge and skills rather than just think about the reward. Teachers can do this by following the guidelines summarized in Figure 6.1.

Call Attention to the Instrumental Value of Academic Activities

Some knowledge and skills taught in school can be applied immediately in the students' lives outside of school or will be needed as "life skills" later. If students are made aware of them, these natural consequences of task mastery are likely to be more effective for motivating task engagement than the more arbitrary rewards discussed above. Thus, where possible, it is useful for teachers to note that the knowledge or skills developed by a task will be useful in enabling students to meet their own current needs, in providing them with a "ticket" to social advancement, or in preparing them for occupational success or success in life generally.

This approach is likely to be most effective if the information about the instrumental value of task mastery can be communicated to the students through concrete examples that will be both credible and memorable for them. Testimony from or anecdotes about specific individuals would be ideal, especially if these are famous people whom the students look up to, role models with whom they can easily identify (such as former students from the same school), or individuals with whom they are already familiar.

If knowledge or skills learned in school can be used in everyday life, teachers should not merely mention these uses but provide detailed modeling and examples and include questions or problems dealing with real life applications in follow-up assignments. Some students will not see the connections between school learning and applications outside of school unless they are spelled out concretely, and even students who do appreciate these connections will benefit from application exercises designed to help them learn to take advantage of them.

Structure Appropriate Competition

The opportunity to compete can add incentive and excitement to classroom activities, whether the competition is for prizes or merely for the satisfaction of winning. Competition may be either individual (students compete against everyone else) or group (students are divided into teams that compete with one another). Traditionally, competitions have been structured around test scores or other performance measures, but it also is possible to build competitive elements into ordinary instruction by including activities such as argumentative essays, debates, or simulation games that involve competition (Keller, 1983).

Several important qualifications should be kept in mind when introducing competitive elements into the classroom. First, given the risks involved in participating in classroom activities, the fact that failures occur in public, and the fact that a great deal of competition is already built into the grading system, it is questionable whether teachers should deliberately introduce additional competitive elements.

Second, competition is even more salient and distracting than rewards for most students, so it will be important to depersonalize the competition and to emphasize the content being learned rather than who won and who lost. For example, a secondary social studies teacher might divide the class into six teams and require each team to develop a campaign speech based on specified criteria. After spending one class period writing the speech as a committee, teams would spend the next period rating the campaign speeches produced by the other teams, using the specified criteria. Then, each team would be charged with the task of taking the best features from all six of the initial versions and producing an improved campaign speech that represents the class's best thinking. Such a task involves competitive elements, but it focuses most attention on the social studies content to be learned rather than on competition between individuals.

Third, the qualifications that apply to use of rewards as incentives also apply to competition. In particular, competition is more appropriate for use with routine practice tasks than with tasks calling for discovery or creativity, and it can be effective only if everyone has a good (or at least an equal) chance of winning. To insure the latter, it will be necessary to use team competition in which the teams are balanced by ability profiles or to use individual competition in which a handicapping system has been devised to equalize everyone's opportunity to win (Slavin, 1983). Handicapping systems are especially easy to develop for routine practice tasks involving skills such as spelling, basic mathematics facts, or vocabulary words. The teacher can use previous base rates as the basis for awarding points in a competition, so that any given student is competing with his or her own previous performance levels rather than directly with other students. Combined approaches that feature both a handicapping system to supply individualized criteria for scoring each student's work and an incentive system involving group rewards for winners of competitions between teams of students provide the most desirable forms of competition—they can be structured so that students cooperate in addition to competing (members of the same team help one another in preparation for the competition). These student team learning approaches are described in more detail in Chapters 9 and 10.

Finally, a root problem with competition is that it creates losers as well as winners (usually many more losers than winners, at that). Even when there is no rational reason for it, a "loser's psychology" tends to develop whenever individuals or teams lose competitions. Individuals may suffer at least temporary embarrassment or even humiliation, and those who lose consistently may suffer more permanent losses in confidence, self-concept, and enjoyment of school. Losing team members may devalue one another and scapegoat individuals that they hold responsible for the team's loss (Ames, 1984; Johnson & Johnson, 1985). Thus, teachers who are thinking about introducing competitive elements into their classrooms should be aware of the risks and take steps to minimize them by making sure that everyone has an equal chance to win, that winning is determined primarily by degree of effort (and perhaps a degree of luck) rather than by ability, that attention is focused on the task rather than on who wins and who loses, and that, in general, the emphasis is on the positive (winners are congratulated but losers are not criticized or ridiculed; the accomplishments of the class as a whole, and not just of the winners, are acknowledged).

Concluding Comments About Extrinsic Motivational Strategies

Extrinsic motivational strategies can be effective in certain circumstances, but teachers should not rely on them too heavily. If students are preoccupied with rewards or competition, they may not pay as much attention as they should to what they are supposed to be learning and may not appreciate its value. The quality of task engagement and ultimately the quality of performance or achievement are highest when students perceive themselves to be engaged in a task for their own reasons (intrinsic motivation) than when they perceive themselves to be engaged in order to please an authority figure, obtain a reward, escape punishment, or respond to some other extrinsic motivational pressure (Deci & Ryan, 1985; Lepper, 1983). More specifically, if students perceive themselves as performing a task solely to obtain a reward, they will tend to adopt a "piecework mentality" or "minimax strategy" in which they concentrate on maximizing rewards by meeting minimum standards for performance (and then moving on to something else) rather than on doing a high-quality job (Condry & Chambers, 1978; Kruglanski, 1978). As a result, they may write 300-word essays containing exactly 300 words or read only those parts of a text that they need to read in order to answer the questions on an assignment. In view of these dangers, teachers should use extrinsic approaches sparingly, keeping in mind the qualifications described above and the guidelines in Figure 6.1.

INTRINSIC MOTIVATIONAL STRATEGIES

The intrinsic motivation approach is based on the idea that teachers should select or design academic tasks that students will find inherently interesting and enjoyable, so that they will engage in these tasks willingly without need for extrinsic incentives. This is an appealing idea, although research on the characteristics of tasks that people tend to find intrinsically rewarding (Deci & Ryan, 1985; Lepper & Greene, 1978; Malone & Lepper, in press) suggests that this is difficult for teachers to accomplish in typical classroom situations.

For one thing, the simplest way to insure that people value what they are doing is to maximize their free choice and autonomy—to let them decide what to do and when and how to do it. However, schools are not recreational settings to which students come for enjoyment or entertainment. Instead, they are educational settings to which students are required to come for instruction in a prescribed curriculum. Some opportunities exist for teachers to take advantage of existing intrinsic motivation by allowing students to select activities according to their own interests, but most of the time teachers will be requiring students to engage in activities that they would not have selected on their own.

A second factor is that intrinsically rewarding activities are usually free of pressure or risk (other than risks that people assume voluntarily when they choose to engage in the activities). However, teachers' motivational attempts in the school setting are complicated by the grading system and the public nature of most teacher-student interaction. Anxiety about public embarrassment and low grades is chronic and intense enough to become a significant impediment to the learning efforts of many students (Covington & Omelich, 1985). Even where this is not a problem, students are likely to be preoccupied with maximizing their ability to predict, and if possible control, the relationship between their academic performance and their grades. This may cause them to try to avoid tasks that involve ambiguity (about what will be needed to earn high grades) or risk (due to high difficulty levels or strict grading standards) and to avoid asking questions or seeking to probe deeper into the content because they want to stick with safe, familiar routines (Doyle, 1983; Hughes, Sullivan, & Mosley, 1985). Thus, even if students find particular school activities intrinsically rewarding (or learn to do so through teacher socialization of their attitudes and beliefs), this potential for intrinsic motivation may be negated by concerns about embarrassment or failure.

Finally, teachers' efforts to motivate their students are complicated by the fact that they must act as authority figures and not just as instructors. They evaluate and grade student performance, and they propound and enforce classroom rules and expectations. In the process, they sometimes engender resentment that may interfere with their attempts to motivate and assist students' learning efforts.

Even so, teachers can take advantage of students' existing intrinsic motivation by selecting or designing classroom activities that contain elements that students are likely to find enjoyable or intrinsically rewarding. No single element will be rewarding to *all* students, but there do appear to be elements that *most* students find rewarding. Among such elements are the following.

Opportunities for Active Response

Students prefer activities that allow them to respond actively—to interact with the teacher or with one another, to manipulate materials, or in some other way to respond more actively than by listening or reading. This is one function of drill, recitation, discussion, board work, and seatwork activities. Ideally, however, students will often get active response opportunities that go beyond the simple question-answer formats seen in typical recitation and seatwork activities in order to include projects, experiments, discussions, role play, simulations, educational games, or creative applications. Language arts instruction should include dramatic readings and prose and poetry composition; mathematics instruction should include problem-solving exercises and realistic application opportunities; science instruction should include experiments and other applications or laboratory work; and social studies instruction should include debates, research projects, and simulation exercises. Such activities allow students to feel that school learning involves *doing* something, not just having something done to them.

Inclusion of Higher-Level Objectives and Divergent Questions

Even within traditional recitation and discussion formats, teachers can create more active student involvement by going beyond factual questions to stimulate their students to discuss or debate issues, to offer opinions about cause-and-effect relationships, to speculate about hypothetical situations, or to think creatively about problems. Students need to learn basic facts, concepts, and definitions, but a steady diet of activities that concentrates on these lower-level knowledge and comprehension objectives soon becomes boring. Therefore, there should be frequent activities or parts of activities devoted to higher-level objectives (application, analysis, synthesis, or evaluation of what has been learned at the knowledge and comprehension level).

Students often complain about problems in this area ("We never get to *do* anything."). So do curriculum experts ("Schools were established to promote higher level objectives—to get students to think about and use what they learn—but you wouldn't know this from visiting classrooms. Most 'discussions' are really just recitations or oral quizzes on basic facts, and seatwork usually means workbooks, dittos, or pages of computation problems."). Yet, curriculum developers usually do not provide much help to teachers in this regard, either. Curriculum packages seldom include many higher-level activities, although the teacher's manual that accompanies the program may contain suggestions for follow-up discussions or application activities. Part of the problem is that higher-level activities in the classroom are time-consuming to plan and implement, difficult to provide for within the constraints built into traditional book-and-paper curriculum materials, and difficult to evaluate by objective tests. Yet, it is important to include such activities, not only for motivational reasons but to insure that school learning is meaningfully understood and applied as intended instead of just being memorized and soon forgotten.

In addition to higher-level convergent questions designed to elicit particular correct answers, there should be divergent questions designed to elicit opinions, predictions, suggested courses of action or solutions to problems, or other divergent thinking. Such questions and related activities encourage students to respond more actively and creatively to content than do activities built around convergent questions about facts, definitions, or concepts.

The same principles apply to skills instruction. Students need to learn basic skills and often must practice these skills until they master them to the point of smooth, rapid, and "automatic" correct performance. However, at least some of this practice can be afforded by means of application opportunities. Students should not be spending most of their time practicing penmanship without getting opportunities to compose essays, for example, or other meaningful communications, and they should not continually practice mathematical computations without solving problems or applying what they are learning.

Feedback Features

Students enjoy tasks that allow them not only to respond actively but to get immediate feedback that can be used to guide subsequent responses. Such feedback features are among the reasons for the popularity of computer games and other pastimes featured in arcades (Malone & Lepper, in press). Automatic feedback features are also built into many educational toys and Montessori materials used in preschools and kindergartens, and into programmed learning materials and other "self-correcting" materials used in elementary and secondary classrooms. The same is true of computerized learning programs that allow students to respond actively and get immediate feedback.

Teachers can build feedback features into more typical classroom activities. They can provide such feedback themselves when leading the class or a small group through an activity or when circulating to supervise progress during independent seatwork times. When teachers are less available for immediate response (such as when they are teaching a small group and the rest of the students are working at their seats), they still can arrange for the students to get feedback by consulting answer keys, following instructions about how to check their work, consulting with an adult volunteer or appointed student helper, or reviewing and discussing the work in pairs or small groups.

If the feedback is positive, students will enjoy the reinforcement associated with feelings of success. If the feedback is negative, they will realize that they have not understood something and will be motivated to deal with the problem and try to improve their performance. Either way, the feedback provides an immediacy and impact to the activity. In contrast, it can be quite boring for students to work through a long seatwork assignment without getting feedback about their responses, and they may even be "practicing errors" without realizing it. Even if the work is carefully corrected and good feedback is received a day or two later, the "now" impact of immediate feedback will be lacking.

Psychologically, most students find it much more difficult and less rewarding to go back and try to relearn something that "we did already" than to respond to immediate feedback when learning something for the first time. Therefore, teachers should avoid putting students in the position of having to respond for lengthy periods of time without knowing whether or not their responses are correct. There are three basic ways to accomplish this: (1) Where possible, design or select activities that have opportunities to make responses and get immediate feedback built into them. (2) For other activities, give thorough-enough instructions and work through enough practice examples to enable the students to evaluate the correctness of their responses on their own for the most part. (3) Rather than leaving students on their own, circulate during seatwork times to supervise progress and provide immediate feedback and help to those who need it.

Incorporation of Gamelike Features into Activities

Practice and application activities for almost any kind of content can be presented as games or structured to include features typically associated with games or recreational pastimes (Keller, 1983; Malone & Lepper, in press). With a bit of imagination, ordinary seatwork assignments can be transformed into "test-yourself" challenges, puzzles, or brain teasers. Some such activities involve clear goals but require the student to solve problems, avoid traps, or overcome obstacles in order to reach the goals (such as exercises calling for students to suggest possible solutions to science or engineering problems or to find a shortcut that will substitute for a tedious mathematical procedure). Other activities challenge students to "find the problem" by identifying the goal itself in addition to developing a method for reaching the goal (many "explore and discover" activities follow this model). Some gamelike activities involve elements of suspense or hidden information that emerges as the activity is completed (puzzles that convey some message or provide the answer to some question once they are filled in). Other such activities involve a degree of randomness or some method of inducing uncertainty about what the outcome of one's performance is likely to be on any given trial (knowledge games that cover a variety of topic areas at a variety of difficulty levels that are assigned according to card draws or dice rolls—Trivial Pursuit is an example).

Note that most of these gamelike features involve presenting intellectual challenges appropriate for use with either individuals or cooperative groups. We mention this to call attention to the fact that the term *gamelike features* is intended to have a much broader meaning than the typical meaning of the term *games,* which most teachers associate specifically with team competitions (Which team will win by getting the most answers?). There is reason to believe that the gamelike features described above are likely to be both less distracting from curriculum objectives and more effective in promoting student motivation to learn than are competitive games, especially competitive games that emphasize speed in supplying memorized facts rather than integration or application of knowledge.

Opportunity for Students to Create Finished Products

Industrial psychologists have shown that workers enjoy jobs that allow them to create a product that they can point to and identify with more than jobs that do not yield such tangible evidence of the fruits of their labor. It seems likely that students will respond similarly to academic tasks. That is, they are likely to prefer tasks that have meaning or integrity in their own right over tasks that are mere subparts of some larger entity, and likely to experience a satisfying sense of completion or accomplishment when they finish such tasks. Ideally, task completion will yield a finished product that the students can use or display (a map, diagram, or other illustration; an essay or report; a scale model; a completed puzzle; or something other than just another ditto or workbook page).

Inclusion of Fantasy or Simulation Elements

If more direct applications of what is being learned are not feasible, teachers can introduce fantasy or imagination elements that will engage students' emotions or allow them to experience events vicariously. In studying poems or stories, for example, teachers can tell students about the authors' motives in writing the poems or stories or about formative experiences in the authors' lives that led to their writings. In studying scientific or mathematical principles and methods, teachers can tell students about the practical problems that needed to be solved or the personal motives of the discoverers that led to development of the knowledge or skills being taught. Or, teachers can set up role-play or simulation activities that allow students to identify with real or fictional characters or to deal with academic content in direct, personalized ways. Rather than just assign their students to read history, for example, elementary teachers can make it come alive by arranging for students to role-play Columbus and his crew debating what to do after 30 days at sea, and secondary teachers can do so by arranging for students to take the roles of the American, British, and Russian leaders meeting at Yalta.

Simulation exercises include, but are not confined to, full-scale drama, role-play, simulation games, and other "major productions." Other, more modest simulation exercises can be incorporated into everyday instruction. These include brief simulation exercises or invitations for students to bring fantasy or imagination to bear in thinking about the content they are learning. In teaching a particular mathematical procedure, for example, teachers might ask students to name problems that come up in everyday living that the mathematical procedure might be useful in solving (and then list these on the board). Secondary social studies teachers might "bring home" material on the U.S.S.R. by asking students to imagine and talk about what it would be like to seek housing in a country where the government owned all of the property or to get accurate information about world events in a country where the government controlled all of the media. Such brief fantasy or simulation exercises do not take much time or require special preparations, but they can be quite useful for stimulating students to relate to the content more personally and to take greater interest in it.

Opportunities for Students to Interact With Peers

Many students especially enjoy activities that allow them to interact with peers. Teachers can build peer-interaction opportunities into whole-class activities such as discussion, debate, role-play, or simulation. In addition, they can plan follow-up activities that allow students to work together in pairs or small groups to tutor one another, discuss issues, develop suggested solutions to problems; or work as a team preparing for a competition, participating in a simulation game, or producing some group product (a report, display, etc).

Peer-interactive activities are likely to be most effective if (1) they are sufficiently structured around curriculum objectives to make them worthwhile learning experiences and not merely occasions for socializing; and (2) conditions are arranged so that every student has a substantive role to play and must participate actively in carrying out the group's mission rather than so that one or two assertive students can dominate the interaction and do all the work while others just watch (see Chapter 10 for more information about peer-interactive activities).

Concluding Comments About Intrinsic Motivational Strategies

Schooling should be as enjoyable as it can be for both teachers and students. Therefore, whenever curriculum objectives can be met through a variety of activities, wise teachers will emphasize activities that students find rewarding and avoid the activities that they find boring or aversive. However, two important limitations on what can be accomplished through intrinsic motivational strategies should be kept in mind.

First, opportunities to use intrinsic motivational strategies in the classroom are limited. Teachers must teach the whole curriculum, not just the parts that appeal to students, and must teach factual knowledge and basic skills in addition to higher-level objectives. Opportunities to provide choice, autonomy, gamelike features, and so on are limited. Thus, even in classrooms where teachers make optimal use of these intrinsic motivational strategies, the students will still be in school rather than in a recreational setting, and all of the constraints that are built into teacher and student roles will still be in place. Learning will often be enjoyable, but it will still require concentration and effort. It will not be "fun" of the sort implied by a visit to an arcade or amusement park.

Second, although intrinsic motivational strategies should increase students' enjoyment of classroom activities, they will not in any direct way increase students' motivation to learn the content or skills being taught. Therefore, as is the case with extrinsic motivational strategies, intrinsic strategies will need to be supplemented with strategies for stimulating student motivation to learn (described in the next section). Otherwise, students may enjoy classroom activities but fail to derive the intended knowledge or skills from them.

In this connection, it is worth noting that our colloquial language for discussing intrinsic motivation is misleading. We commonly describe certain topics or tasks as "intrinsically interesting" and speak of engaging in activities "for their own sake." Taken literally, such language implies that motivation resides in activities rather than in people. In reality, people generate intrinsic motivation; it is not somehow built into topics or tasks. We study or do something not for *its* sake but for *our* sake—because it brings us pleasure, meets our needs, or in some other way provides enjoyable stimulation or satisfaction. Each of us has his or her own amount and patterning of intrinsic motivation, developed in response to our experiences and to the socialization we received from significant others in our lives. In the case of motivation to learn academic knowledge and skills, teachers are important "significant others." Therefore, rather than just confining themselves to accommodating classroom activities to students' existing motivational patterns, teachers can think in terms of shaping those motivational patterns through systematic socialization efforts designed to stimulate student motivation to learn the curriculum.

STRATEGIES FOR STIMULATING STUDENT MOTIVATION TO LEARN

By *student motivation to learn,* we mean a student tendency to find academic activities meaningful and worthwhile and to try to get the intended academic benefits from them. In contrast to intrinsic motivation, which is primarily an affective or emotional response to the activity, motivation to learn is primarily a cognitive or intellectual response involving attempts to make sense of an activity, understand information and relate it to prior knowledge, and master the skills that it promotes (Brophy, 1983; Brophy & Kher, 1986).

This definition of motivation to learn implies a distinction between learning and performance: *Learning* refers to the information processing, sense making, and comprehension or mastery advances that occur while one is acquiring knowledge or skill; *performance* refers to the demonstration of such knowledge or skill after it has been acquired. The motivational strategies to be described in this section apply not only to performance (work on tests or assignments) but also to the information-processing activities (attending to lessons, reading for understanding, comprehending instructions, putting things into one's own words) that are involved in learning content or skills in the first place. Thus, these strategies emphasize stimulating students to use thoughtful and effective information-processing and skill-building strategies when they are learning. This is quite different from merely offering them incentives for good performance later.

Student motivation to learn can be thought of both as a *general trait* and as a *situation-specific state* (Brophy, 1983; Gottfried, 1985). As a general trait, it is an enduring disposition to value learning—to approach the process of learning with effort and thought and to take pride in acquiring knowledge and skill. In specific situations, a state of motivation to learn exists when students engage purposefully in an activity and adopt the goal of trying to learn the concepts or master the skills involved. Even students who do not have much motivation to learn as a general trait may display such motivation in specific situations because they know that they need the knowledge or skills being taught or because the teacher has sparked their interest in the knowledge or made them see the importance or value of the skill.

The learning taught in schools is mostly cognitive learning—abstract concepts and verbally coded information. In order to make efficient progress in such academic learning, students need to develop and use *generative learning strategies* (Weinstein & Mayer, 1986). That is, they need to process information actively, relate it to their existing knowledge, put it into their own words, make sure that they understand it, and so on. Therefore, in the classroom context, motivating students to learn means not only stimulating them to take an interest in and see the value of what they are learning, but also providing them with guidance about how to go about learning it. It is difficult to separate strategies for motivating students to learn from strategies for effective instruction generally, although one can do so for purposes of analysis. Therefore, the following strategies are recommended for teachers who want to go beyond merely manipulating student performance through extrinsic reward and punishment, as well as go beyond trying to insure that students enjoy classroom activities, to the point of stimulating students' motivation to learn the content or skills that those activities were designed to develop.

The first three strategies are general ones that describe pervasive features of the learning environment that should be established in every classroom. These strategies are designed to develop student motivation to learn as a general personal trait. They involve socializing students to understand that the classroom is primarily a place for learning and that acquiring and applying knowledge and skills are important contributors to quality of life (not just to report card grades).

General Modeling of Motivation to Learn

Teachers should routinely model interest in learning throughout all of their interactions with their students. This modeling should encourage the students to value learning as a rewarding, self-actualizing activity that produces personal satisfaction and enriches one's life. Therefore, in addition to teaching what is in the textbooks, teachers should share their interests in current events and items of general knowledge (especially as they relate to aspects of the subject matter being taught). Teachers can call attention to current books, articles, television programs, or movies on the subject, and to examples or applications of subject matter knowledge in everyday living, in the local environment, or in current events.

By "modeling," we mean more than just calling students' attention to examples or applications of concepts taught in school. We mean that teachers should act as models by sharing their thinking about such examples or applications so that the students can see how educated people use information and concepts learned in school to understand and respond to everyday experiences in their lives and to news about current events occurring elsewhere. Without being preachy about it, teachers can relate personal experiences illustrating how language arts knowledge enables them to communicate or express themselves effectively in some important life situations, how mathematical or scientific knowledge enables them to solve every-day household-engineering or repair problems, or how social studies knowledge helps them to appreciate things they see in their travels or to understand the significance of events occurring in other parts of the world. Through teacher modeling, students should come to see how it is both stimulating and satisfying to understand (or even just to think, wonder, or make predictions about) what is happening in the world around us (see Chapter 5 for more information about modeling).

Communicating Desirable Expectations and Attributions

Besides modeling their own enthusiasm for learning, teachers should routinely communicate attitudes, beliefs, expectations, and attributions implying that the students share this enthusiasm. At minimum, this means avoiding suggestions that the students will dislike working on academic activities or will work on them only in order to get good grades or other rewards. Preferably, it means indicating to students that they are expected to be curious, to want to learn facts and understand principles clearly, to want to master skills, and to see classroom activities as meaningful, worthwhile, and applicable to their everyday lives (see Chapter 4 for more information about communicating desirable expectations).

Minimizing Performance Anxiety

Motivation to learn is likely to develop most fully in classrooms in which the students are goal oriented but relaxed enough to be able to concentrate on the task at hand without worrying about whether or not they can meet performance expectations. Teachers can accomplish this by making clear distinctions between instruction or practice activities designed to promote learning and tests designed to evaluate performance. Most classroom activities should be structured as learning experiences rather than as tests.

If instruction or practice activities include testlike events (recitation questions, practice exercises), these should be treated as opportunities for the students to work with and apply the material rather than as opportunities for the teacher to test students' mastery. If teachers expect students to engage in academic activities with motivation to learn (which implies a willingness to take intellectual risks and make mistakes), they will need to protect these students from anxiety or premature concern about performance adequacy.

Eventually, of course, teachers will have to evaluate student performance and assign grades using tests or other assessment devices. Until that point in the instructional unit, however, the emphasis should be on teaching and learning rather than on performance evaluation, and students should be encouraged to respond to questions and performance demands in terms of "Let's assess our progress and learn from our mistakes," rather than "Let's see who knows it and who doesn't." Where necessary, teachers may also want to make statements such as "We're here to learn, and you can't do that without making mistakes," or to caution students against laughing at the mistakes made by peers (see Hill & Wigfield, 1984, concerning strategies for minimizing students' test anxiety).

The three general strategies just described should be pervasive aspects of the learning environments that teachers establish in their classrooms. If used consistently, they should subtly encourage students to develop motivation to learn as a general personal trait. Furthermore, in particular learning situations, teachers can supplement these general strategies with one or more of the following specific strategies for motivating students to learn the content or skills that a particular activity teaches.

Project Intensity

Whenever they instruct, but especially when they present key explanations, teachers can use timing, nonverbal expressions and gestures, and cueing and other verbal techniques to project a level of intensity that tells students that the material is important and deserves close attention. Often, an intense presentation will begin with a direct statement of the importance of the message ("I am going to show you how to invert fractions—now pay close attention and make sure that you understand these procedures."). Then, the message itself would be presented using verbal and nonverbal public speaking techniques that convey intensity and cue attention: a slow-paced, step-by-step presentation during which key words are emphasized or underlined, unusual voice modulations or exaggerated gestures that focus attention on key terms or procedural steps, and intense scanning of the group following each step to look for signs of understanding or confusion (and to allow anyone with a question to ask it immediately). In addition to the words being spoken, everything about the teacher's tone and manner communicates to the students that what is being said is important and that they should give it full attention and be prepared to ask questions about anything that they do not understand.

Projecting intensity through slower pacing, exaggerated cueing, and related rhetorical techniques is an especially useful strategy when demonstrating procedures or problem-solving strategies (as opposed to when merely giving or reviewing information). Such demonstrations have a built in step-by-step structure that lends itself to a slow pace punctuated by exaggerated cueing, and the first- or second-person language that is used in modeling or demonstrating procedures lends itself more naturally to a high-intensity communication style than the third-person language typically used to communicate information.

Teachers will have to "pick their spots" for deliberately using an intensive communication style because they cannot be intense all the time, and even if they could, students would adjust to it so it would lose much of its effectiveness. Therefore, teachers probably should reserve their intensity for times when they want to communicate "this is important; pay especially close attention." Likely occasions for intensive communication would include: introduction of important new terms or definitions, especially those likely to be confusing to the students; demonstration of procedures and problem-solving techniques, including instructions for doing seatwork or homework assignments; instruction in concepts that the students are likely to find confusing or difficult; and instruction that requires eliminating misconceptions in addition to teaching new conceptions (and thus requires making students aware that even though they think they already understand the point at issue, in fact their "knowledge" is incorrect). Exaggerated intensity is less appropriate for more routine instructional situations, although teachers are well advised to slow the pace and be alert for signs of confusion or student desire to ask a question whenever they are covering new or complex material (Gambrell, 1983; Good & Brophy, 1986; Rowe, 1974; Swift & Gooding, 1983; Tobin & Capie, 1982).

Project Enthusiasm

Unless they are already quite familiar with the topic or assignment, students will look to their teachers for cues about how to respond to school activities. Consciously or not, teachers model attitudes and beliefs about topics and assignments, and students pick up on these cues. If teachers present the topic or assignment with enthusiasm suggesting that it is interesting, important, or worthwhile, the students are likely to adopt this same attitude (Bettencourt, Gillet, Gall, & Hull, 1983).

In suggesting that teachers project enthusiasm, we do not mean pep talks or unnecessary theatrics. Instead, we mean that teachers will identify their own reasons for being interested in the topic or for finding it meaningful or important and will project these reasons to the students when teaching about the topic. Teachers can use dramatics or forceful salesmanship if they are comfortable with these techniques, but if not, low-key but sincere statements of the value that they place on a topic or activity will be just as effective in communicating enthusiasm. Thus, a brief comment showing that the topic is food for thought or illustrating how it is interesting, unique, or different from previously studied topics may be sufficient. In short, the primary objective of projecting enthusiasm as a strategy for motivating students to learn is to induce the students to value the topic or activity, not to amuse, entertain, or excite them.

Induce Task Interest or Appreciation

Besides projecting intensity or their own personal enthusiasm, teachers can induce students' interest in or appreciation for a topic or activity by verbalizing reasons that the students should value it. If the topic or activity has connections with something that students already recognize as interesting or important, these connections should be noted. When the knowledge or skills to be taught have applications to everyday living, these applications should be mentioned, especially those that will allow students to solve problems or accomplish goals that are important to them. Teachers can also mention new or challenging aspects of activities that the students can anticipate, especially interesting or exotic aspects.

Induce Curiosity or Suspense

Teachers can stimulate curiosity or suspense by posing questions or doing "set-ups" that make students feel the need to resolve some ambiguity or obtain more information about a topic. To prepare their students to read material on the U.S.S.R., for example, teachers could ask the students if they knew that Russia is just part of the U.S.S.R., what the term "Iron Curtain" means, how many time zones there are in the U.S.S.R., or how the United States acquired Alaska. Such questions help transform "just another reading assignment" into an interesting learning experience by encouraging students to make connections between the information they will be reading and the information they already know (or think they know). Furthermore, by inducing curiosity or suspense, they make the new information food for thought rather than merely more material to be memorized. Most students will think that Russia is just another name for the U.S.S.R. and will be curious to find out about the difference once they have been alerted to the fact that a difference exists. Most students will have heard the term "Iron Curtain" but will not have thought actively about it and will become curious to read about it when stimulated to think about it in interesting ways (Is there an actual curtain? Is it made of iron? If not, why is the term used?). Similarly, it would be mind-boggling for most students to discover that the U.S.S.R. encompasses 11 time zones or that the United States purchased Alaska from Russia. These are just four basic facts found in most treatments of the history or geography of the U.S.S.R. Whether or not students will find these facts (or a great many others that could have been mentioned) interesting and will think actively about them rather than merely attempt to memorize them will depend largely on the degree to which their teachers stimulate curiosity about these facts and provide a context for thinking about their associations with existing knowledge or beliefs. This is another illustration of the point made earlier that interest does not reside in topics or activities—it resides in people.

Teachers can encourage their students to generate such interest by (1) asking them to speculate or make predictions about what they will be learning; (2) raising questions that successful completion of the activity will enable them to answer; and (3) where relevant, showing them that their existing knowledge is not complete enough to enable them to accomplish some valued objective, that their knowledge is internally inconsistent or inconsistent with the new information, or that the knowledge they presently possess in scattered form can be organized around certain general principles or powerful ideas (Malone & Lepper, in press). More generally, teachers can put their students into an active information-processing or problem-solving mode by posing interesting questions or problems that the activity will address (Keller, 1983).

Make Abstract Content More Personal, Concrete, or Familiar

Definitions, principles, and other general or abstract information may have little meaning for students unless made more concrete. One way that teachers can accomplish this is to promote personal identification with the content by relating experiences or telling anecdotes illustrating how the content applies to the lives of particular individuals (especially individuals whom the students are interested in and likely to identify with). Teachers can also make abstractions concrete by showing objects or pictures or by conducting demonstrations. They can also help students to relate new or strange content to their existing knowledge by using examples or analogies that refer to familiar concepts, objects, or events.

Sometimes the problem is not that the content would be too abstract or unfamiliar for the students to understand if it were explained sufficiently, but that the text simply does not provide enough explanation. For example, it is not enough to say that Russia exited World War I because "the revolution came and a new government was established." This brief statement does not supply enough details to enable students to understand and visualize the events surrounding the Russian Revolution. To make these events more understandable to their students, teachers would have to elaborate on the text by explaining why and (especially) how the communists and others organized political and eventually military resistance to the Czar's regime, how they killed or expelled the Czar's family and key officials, and how they established a new government. Such elaboration on the text transforms the relatively meaningless statement that "the revolution came and a new government was established" into a meaningful statement that students can explain in their own words because they can relate it to their prior knowledge and visualize the events to which it refers. Thus, they can actively process the content instead of just trying to memorize it.

As a teacher recently explained to one of the authors, a good teacher looks on a text as an outline to be elaborated, not as the entire curriculum.

Induce Dissonance or Cognitive Conflict

If the topic of a text is already familiar, students may think that they already know everything that there is to know about it and thus may read the material with little attention or thought. Teachers can counter this tendency by pointing out un-expected, incongruous, or paradoxical aspects of the content by calling attention to unusual or exotic elements, by noting exceptions to general rules or by challenging students to solve the "mystery" that underlies a paradox.

The school curriculum includes a great many "strange but true" phenomena, especially in mathematics and science. Teachers should call attention to such phenomena and get their students to begin asking themselves "How can that be?" Otherwise, students may treat new material as just more information to be absorbed without giving it much thought or even noticing the fact that it seems to contradict previously learned information.

Induce Students to Generate Their Own Motivation to Learn

Teachers can induce students to generate their own motivation to learn by asking them to think about topics or activities in relation to their own interests and preconceptions. For example, they can ask the students to identify questions about the topic that they would like to get answered, to list their particular interests in the topic, or to note things that they find to be surprising as they read. Besides generating motivation to learn in the particular situation, such exercises are useful for helping students to understand that motivation to learn must come from within themselves—that it is a property of the learner rather than the task to be learned (Ortiz, 1983).

State Learning Objectives and Provide Advance Organizers

Instructional theorists have shown that learners retain more information when their learning is goal directed and when they can structure the information to be learned around key concepts. Such theorists commonly advise teachers to introduce activi-ties by stating learning objectives and by providing advance organizers that char-acterize what will be learned in general terms that enable the learners to know what to expect and help them prepare to learn efficiently (Alexander, Frankiewicz, & Williams, 1979; Ausubel, Novak, & Hanesian, 1978; Mayer, 1979). This is good advice for motivational reasons as well. Learning objectives and advance organizers call students' attention to the nature of the task and the academic benefits that they should receive from engaging in it. This helps them to establish a learning set to use in guiding their responses to the task.

In order to be concrete and specific and to provide students with guidelines for setting goals and assessing their performance, teachers should phrase learning objectives in terms of what the students should be able to do when they complete the task successfully rather than merely describe in general terms what the task is about. Statements of learning objectives are especially important for skill development tasks, whereas advance organizers are more important for knowledge development tasks. In either case, the advance structuring prepares students for the activity by telling them what it is designed to accomplish and what prior knowledge and skills they should bring to bear in responding to it. This helps students to adopt an information-processing or problem-solving set rather than a more passive learning set when engaging in the activity.

Provide Informative Feedback

Feedback is another factor that is important from a motivational as well as a purely instructional point of view. If students are to engage themselves as active learners, they will need opportunities to assess their progress in understanding content or mastering skills—in short, opportunities to make responses and get feedback. As soon as possible after being exposed to information through reading or teacher presentation, students should be given questions or assignments that will require them to restate the information in their own words, to show that they understand the Information and can apply it successfully, or to summarize, integrate, or evaluate what they have learned. As noted previously, such response opportunities and the feedback associated with them motivate students to learn by reinforcing their sense of competence or efficacy (when learning has been successful) or by underscoring the need for further efforts (when it has not). In this regard, note the guidelines presented in Chapter 6 and earlier in the present chapter concerning when and how to provide informative feedback to students.

Model Task-Related Thinking and Problem Solving

The information-processing and problem-solving strategies needed for thinking about particular curricular content or responding to particular academic tasks will be unknown to many students unless teachers make them overt and observable by modeling them. Therefore, teachers should not confine themselves to the third-person language of expository instruction or even the second-person language of direction-giving when demonstrating skills or problem-solving strategies. In addition, teachers should model the processes involved by showing students what to do and thinking out loud as they demonstrate. Such modeling should include the thinking that goes into selecting the general approach to use, deciding on what options to take at choice points that arise during the process, checking on progress as one goes along, and making certain that one is on the right track. Such modeling should also include recovery from false starts and use of inappropriate strategies, so that students can see how one develops a successful strategy even when one was not sure about what to do at first (Diener & Dweck, 1978; Schunk & Hanson, 1985).

This kind of cognitive modeling (demonstrating by thinking out loud so that students can observe one's information-processing and problem-solving strategies) is powerful not just as an instructional device but as a way to socialize student motivation to learn. Besides enabling the teacher to model the particular strategies needed to accomplish a task, it allows the teacher to show students what it means to approach a task with motivation to learn. That is, it allows the teacher to model the general beliefs and attitudes that are associated with such motivation (patience, confidence, persistence in seeking solutions through information processing and rational decision making, benefiting from the information supplied by mistakes rather than giving up in frustration, concentrating on the task and how to respond to it rather than focusing on the self and worrying about one's limitations).

Induce Metacognitive Awareness of Learning Efforts

When motivated to learn, students do not merely let information "wash over them" and hope that some of it will stick. Instead, they process the information actively by concentrating their attention, making sure that they understand, integrating new information with existing knowledge, and encoding and storing this information in a form that will allow them to remember it and use it later. The mere intention to learn in this fashion is not sufficient to insure that such learning will occur. In addition, students must possess and use cognitive and metacognitive skills for learning and studying effectively. Therefore, when opportunities arise, teachers should train their students to be aware of their goals during task engagement, to monitor the strategies they use in pursuing these goals, to note the effects of these strategies as they are employed, and to monitor subjective responses to these unfolding events. In particular, teachers can coach their students in the following strategies for learning and studying (for more information about inducing metacognitive awareness of learning efforts, see Baker & Brown, 1984; Book, Duffy, Roehler, Meloth, & Vavrus, 1985; Good & Brophy, 1986; McCombs, 1984; Palincsar & Brown, 1984; Paris, Cross, & Lipson, 1984; Roehler & Duffy, 1984; and Weinstein & Mayer, 1985).

Actively Preparing to Learn   Teachers can train their students to prepare to learn actively by mobilizing their resources and approaching tasks in thoughtful ways: getting mentally prepared to concentrate; previewing reading or listening tasks by noting their nature and objectives; and developing plans before trying to respond to complex performance tasks. In part, this can be accomplished by planning for good introductions to tasks and good transitions between tasks. In addition, however, some students will not realize the importance of adopting an active learning set when beginning a learning task or may not know how to do so. Such students can benefit from instruction in general study skills and in particular methods of preparing for particular tasks.

Commiting Material to Memory   If material must be memorized, teachers can help their students by teaching them techniques for memorizing efficiently. Such techniques include active rehearsal; repeating, copying, or underlining key words; making notes; or using imagery or other mnemonic strategies.

Encoding or Elaborating on the Information Presented   Usually it is not appropriate (or even possible) to expect students to rely on rote memory to retain information verbatim. More typically, teachers present information to the students or assign them to read information presented in a text and then expect the students to retain the gist of the information and be able to apply it later. It helps if teachers instruct their students in methods for approaching such learning tasks using encoding or elaboration strategies that will help them to identify and retain the gist: paraphrasing and summarizing the information to put it into their own words, relating it to what they already know, and assessing their understanding by asking themselves questions about the material to see if they can answer such questions knowledgeably.

Organizing and Structuring the Content   Students also need to learn to identify or impose organizational schemes on extensive bodies of content that will allow them to structure the content by dividing it into sequences or superordinate-subordinate clusters. Teachers can train their students to note the main ideas of paragraphs, outline the material, and notice and use the structuring devices that have been built into it (lists; generalizations followed by elaborations; compare/contrast structures; historical narratives or other sequential descriptions; and presentations of rules followed by examples, questions followed by answers, or concept definitions followed by examples and nonexamples of the concept). Students who are made aware of these structural elements built into texts are more likely to be able to use them as bases for organizing and remembering what they learn (Armbruster & Anderson, 1984). Students will also benefit from instruction in effective note-taking (Carrier & Titus, 1979; Kierwa, 1985; Ladas, 1980).

Monitoring Comprehension   In giving instructions for assignments, teachers can remind their students to remain aware of the instructional objectives, the strategies that they use to pursue these objectives, the relative success of these strategies, and the remediation efforts they undertake if the strategies have not been effective. They also can teach the students (especially through modeling) strategies for coping with confusion or mistakes: backing up and rereading, looking up definitions, identifying previous places in the text where the confusing point is discussed, searching the recent progression of topics for clues to the information that has been missed or misunderstood, retracing steps to see if the strategy has been applied correctly, and generating possible alternative strategies.

Maintaining Appropriate Affect   Finally, teachers can model and instruct their students in ways of approaching academic activities with desirable affect (relaxed but alert and prepared to concentrate; ready to enjoy or at least take satisfaction in engaging in the task) and ways of avoiding undesirable affect (anger, anxiety, etc.). Such instruction should include modeling of self-reinforcement for success and of coping skills for responding to frustration or failure (reassuring self-talk, refocusing of attention on the task at hand, using the strategies listed at the end of the previous paragraph).

BUILDING MOTIVATIONAL STRATEGIES INTO INSTRUCTIONAL PLANS

Teachers who are planning courses from scratch can apply these strategies for motivating students to learn by building them directly into their curriculum and instructional plans. Teachers who are already working with given curricula and materials can use the strategies by incorporating them into their instructional plans or adjusting these plans as needed. Just as it is helpful for students to ask themselves questions about what they are learning, it is helpful for teachers to ask themselves questions about the lessons they are planning to teach or the activities they are planning to assign.

For All Activities

The following questions should be considered in planning for any academic activity. First, what are the curriculum and instructional *goals* of the activity? How do these goals translate into specific *objectives?* Why will the students be learning this information or skill? When and how might they use it after they learn it? Answers to these questions suggest information that should be conveyed to the students through the learning objectives stated when introducing the activity to them.

Before getting into the activity itself, is there a way to characterize the activity for the students using familiar, general terms that indicate its nature and provide them with organizing concepts to subsume the more specific information that will be presented? If so, such advance organizers should be communicated to the students (typically right before mentioning the learning objectives of the activity).

What are some elements of the activity that could be focused on as a means to create interest, identify application potential, or create curiosity, suspense, or dissonance? Does the activity include information that the students are likely to find interesting or build skills that they are eager to develop? Does it contain unusual or surprising information? Can the content be related to current events or events in the students' lives? Is there information that the students are likely to find surprising or difficult to believe? Are there ways to stimulate curiosity or create suspense by posing interesting questions about the content? Affirmative answers to one or more of these questions will suggest ways for teachers to capitalize on the opportunity to induce student motivation to learn by creating interest, appreciation, curiosity, suspense, or dissonance when introducing the activity.

For Listening and Reading Activities

Teachers might consider the following questions when planning activities that require students to attend to an oral presentation, watch a visual presentation, or learning by reading.

First, what aspects of the content do they (the teachers) find interesting, noteworthy, or important, and why? Answers to these questions will help teachers identify their own reasons for interest in or enthusiasm about the topic, and these reasons should be communicated to the students.

Are there personal experiences that can be related or artifacts that can be displayed in relation to the content? Are there content-related anecdotes about the experiences of others or about how the knowledge was discovered? Including such personalized aspects should spice up the presentation of the content.

Does the presentation contain sufficient variety in the cognitive levels of information communicated and the types of responses that will be demanded? Ordinarily, a presentation should not be confined to facts and terms for students to memorize, but should also include attention to skills or applications as well as to analysis, synthesis, or evaluation of the learning.

Is there provision for active response? What is the anticipated length of the presentation? If it appears that there will be too much uninterrupted lecture or reading, teachers can plan to break up the information presentation by asking questions, initiating discussion, or allowing time for students to take notes or respond to a brief assignment.

How should the students respond to the presentation or text? Should they take notes or underline key ideas? Keep particular issues or questions in mind as they listen or read? Outline the material or respond to a study guide? Note particular organizational structures to be used in learning? To the extent that teachers want students to do something more specific than just pay attention and try to get the most they can from the experience, the teachers should tell the students specifically what they want them to do, and if necessary, help by supplying questions, outlines, study guides, or information about how the material is organized.

Is there some key point that the students might easily miss if not forewarned? Are there abstractions that will not be meaningful without additional explanation or concrete examples? Are there concepts that may be troublesome because they are subtle or difficult, because they are not well explained in the text, or because they conflict with the students' prior personal experiences? If so, teachers may want to allow for extra attention to these trouble spots or to prepare students for viewing a film or reading a text by making sure that they have whatever prerequisite knowledge they will need in order to get the intended benefit from the experience.

For Activities Requiring Active Response

Teachers might consider the following questions when planning activities or assignments that require students to do something more active than just listen or read (answer questions, prepare a report, work on a project, etc.). Is the activity presented as an opportunity to apply knowledge or develop skills rather than as a test (unless it *is* a test)? When and how might the students be encouraged to ask questions or seek whatever information or help they may need?

Does the activity demand new or complex responses that should be modeled for the students? If so, what steps should be modeled at what level of detail? Are there important hypothesis-testing strategies (considering alternatives at a choice point and then selecting the correct one after reasoning or brief experimentation) or troubleshooting or repair strategies (responding to confusion or errors with diagnosis of the problem or generation of alternative strategies) that should be modeled?

When, how, and from whom will the students get feedback on their performance? What should they do if they do not understand a question or are not sure how to begin a response? What should they do when they think they are finished? How might they be encouraged to check their work or to generate and respond to questions about the work in their own words (in order to make sure that they understand the material and have gained the academic benefits that the activity was designed to produce)?

SUMMARY

The effort that students are likely to invest in an academic task will be determined by how much they value the task and the rewards associated with completing it successfully and the degree to which they expect to be able to succeed in the task and thus reap the rewards. A complete motivational program will attend to both the expectancy aspects and the value aspects of student motivation.

No motivational approach will be successful unless the following four essential preconditions are in effect: (1) the teacher organizes and manages the classroom as an efficient learning environment and creates a classroom atmosphere that is supportive of students' learning efforts; (2) students are given tasks of an appropriate difficulty level; (3) activities have been selected with worthwhile academic objectives in mind; and (4) the teacher shows moderation and variation in using motivational strategies.

Four sets of motivational strategies were reviewed in the chapter. *The first set is designed to motivate by maintaining students' success expectations and related perceptions and beliefs* (perception of covariation between effort and outcome, internal locus of control, concept of self as origin rather than pawn, sense of efficacy or competence, attribution of outcomes to internal and controllable causes, incremental concept of ability). The most basic strategy is programming for success by assigning tasks on which students can succeed if they apply reasonable effort and by instructing them thoroughly so that they know what to do and know how to do it. Other strategies include: helping students to set appropriate (proximal, specific, challenging) goals, to commit themselves to these goals, to use appropriate standards for appraising their levels of success, and to reinforce themselves for the success that they do achieve; helping students to recognize the linkages between effort and outcome through modeling, socialization, and feedback; portraying effort as an investment rather than a risk portraying skill development as incremental and domain-specific; focusing on mastery; and doing remedial work with discouraged students.

The other three sets of strategies address the *value aspects* of student motivation. The first of these three sets include *extrinsic motivation strategies,* which do not attempt to increase the value that students place on academic activities themselves but instead link task performance to delivery of consequences that the students do value. Extrinsic motivation strategies include offering rewards as incentives for good performance, calling attention to the instrumental value of academic activities (their potential for developing "life skills" or providing "tickets" to social advancement), and using individual or team competition to enhance interest in an activity. Teachers who use rewards or competition should keep in mind the undesirable side effects that these approaches can have (undermining intrinsic motivation to engage in academic activities, distracting attention from the academic goals that the activities were intended to accomplish). In this regard, the comments made about use of rewards in Chapter 6 and the guidelines summarized in Figure 6.1 should be kept in mind.

The next set of motivational strategies calls for taking advantage of students' existing *intrinsic motivation* by designing or selecting activities that contain elements that students will enjoy. These elements include: opportunities to respond more actively than by merely listening or reading; opportunities to respond to higher-level objectives and divergent questions that call for creative or challenging thought and action in relation to the content (rather than just memorizing facts or practicing basic skills); chances to perform tasks that provide immediate feedback to one's responses and thus allow opportunities to experiment and improve with practice; activities that include gamelike features such as "test-yourself" challenges, puzzles, or brain teasers; activities that allow one to create a finished product; activities that include fantasy or simulation elements; and activities that provide opportunities to interact with peers. Opportunities to use intrinsic motivational strategies are limited by the teacher's responsibility to teach the established curriculum. Furthermore, even when they can be used, intrinsic motivational strategies merely increase the likelihood that students will enjoy an activity; they do not directly stimulate the students' motivation to learn the academic content or skills that the activity was designed to develop.

To accomplish the latter goal, *strategies for stimulating student motivation to learn* are needed. Viewed either as a general personal trait or as a situation-specific state, motivation to learn is a tendency to find academic activities meaningful and worthwhile and to try to get the intended academic benefits from them. The concept emphasizes learning (acquiring information or skills in the first place) and not merely performing (activating the knowledge or skills later in an attempt to meet performance standards), and it carries cognitive implications (goal-oriented information processing, sense-making, and use of generative learning strategies) in addition to more purely motivational implications. Three general strategies describe pervasive features of the classroom learning environment that support development of student motivation to learn as a general personal trait: general modeling of the thinking and actions associated with motivation to learn, communicating expectations and attributions implying motivation to learn in the students, and creating a supportive environment for learning by minimizing the role of factors that produce performance anxiety.

Other strategies for inducing student motivation to learn are more situation-specific and would be included in the planning for particular academic activities: projecting intensity that communicates the importance of an activity; projecting enthusiasm for the topic; inducing task interest or appreciation by pointing out aspects that the students should find interesting or important; inducing curiosity or suspense by raising interesting questions that the students will get a chance to answer in the process of carrying out the activity; elaborating on vague or abstract content to make it more personal, concrete, or familiar; inducing dissonance or cognitive conflict by mentioning strange but true aspects of the content; inducing students to generate their own motivation to learn by identifying their own interests and the questions that they would like to get answers to; stating learning objectives and providing advance organizers; providing informative feedback to student responses; modeling the information-processing and problem-solving strategies that would be used when approaching the activity with motivation to learn; and inducing students' metacognitive awareness of their own learning efforts by teaching them strategies for actively preparing to learn, committing material to memory, encoding or elaborating on the information presented, organizing and structuring the content, monitoring their comprehension or mastery, and maintaining appropriate affect.

The chapter concludes with suggestions on ways that teachers can build these motivational strategies into their instructional plans by asking themselves questions about the content or skills involved in an academic activity and then using the answers to these questions as guidelines for planning motivational elements.

SUGGESTED ACTIVITIES AND QUESTIONS

8.1.   How does motivation to learn differ from intrinsic motivation to engage in classroom activities?

8.2.   To what extent do you think it necessary or advisable to use extrinsic motivation approaches (rewards, competition) in the classroom? If you intend to use extrinsic motivation approaches, what steps do you plan to take to minimize their undesirable side effects?

8.3.   As a person who chose to go into teaching, you probably were a well-adjusted student who felt comfortable in classrooms and enjoyed academic activities. Yet, you will have to cope with students who have histories of failure and find schooling to be boring or aversive. How will you cope with such students? With a friend or colleague, role-play your interaction with a student who is alienated to the point of persistent inattention to lessons and failure to complete assignments.

8.4.   Sometimes meeting the essential preconditions for developing student motivation to learn is the toughest part of motivating students, especially the preconditions calling for worthwhile learning objectives and appropriate difficulty levels. What should you do if you find that several of the activities in the workbooks that come with your adopted curriculum appear to be essentially pointless? Discuss this issue with friends or colleagues.

8.5.   What should you do if certain students in the class simply cannot handle the same material and move at the same pace as the rest of the class? What might you begin to do differently with these students and how might you explain it to them in ways that would support rather than erode their motivation to learn?

8.6.   Why do the authors make a point of distinguishing between learning and performance when talking about motivating students to *learn?*

8.7   The authors note that intrinsic motivation resides in persons rather than in topics or activities, but they talk about capitalizing on students' existing intrinsic motivation by emphasizing topics or activities that students find interesting or enjoyable. Explain this seeming contradiction.

8.8.   Similarly, the authors speak of motivation to learn as generated by learners themselves, but suggest that teachers can stimulate their students to develop such motivation to learn through general modeling and socialization and various more specific strategies. Again, explain this seeming contradiction. How can teachers stimulate the development of something that students must develop themselves?

8.9.   Explain the implications of the following statement for motivating students in the classroom: We don't do something for *its* sake, we do it for *our* sake.

8.10. How would you respond to unmotivated students who genuinely want to know why they are asked to study Shakespeare's sonnets or the history of ancient Greece?

8.11. Take any three topics in English, science, or mathematics and write a one-page introduction to each topic. In planning your introduction, consider the following questions raised in the chapter. What are some elements of the topic that could be focused on as a means to create interest, identify application potential, or create curiosity? Is there information that the students are likely to find surprising or difficult to believe? Can the content be related to current events or events in the students' lives?

8.12. Obtain students' textbooks in English, science, or mathematics and examine the exercises presented there. Given the various considerations discussed in this chapter, how satisfactory are the questions and exercises? Find three or four examples that need to be improved, and write out your strategy for improving these exercises or write different questions that have more motivational (and presumably instructional) value for the students.

REFERENCES

Alexander, L., Frankiewicz, R., & Williams, R. (1979). Facilitation of learning and retention of oral instruction using advance and post organizers. *Journal of Educational Psychology, 71,* 701–707.

Ames, C. (1984). Competitive, cooperative, and individualistic goal structures: A cognitive-motivational analysis. In R. Ames and C. Ames (Eds.), *Research on motivation in education. Vol. I: Student motivation.* New York: Academic Press.

Ames, C., & Ames, R. (Eds.). (1985). *Research on motivation in education. Vol. II: The classroom milieu.* Orlando, FL: Academic Press.

Ames, R., & Ames, C. (Eds.). (1984). *Research on motivation in education. Vol. I: Student motivation.* New York: Academic Press.

Armbruster, B., & Anderson, T. (1984). Structures of explanations in history textbooks or so what if Governor Stanford missed the spike and hit the rail? *Journal of Curriculum Studies, 16,* 181–194.

Ausubel, D., Novak, J., & Hanesian, H. (1978). *Educational psychology: A cognitive view.* New York: Holt, Rinehart and Winston.

Baker, F., & Brown, A. (1984). Metacognitive skills and reading. In P. Pearson, M. Kamil, R. Barr, & P. Mosenthal (Eds.), *Handbook of reading research.* New York: Longman.

Bandura, A. (1982). Self-efficacy mechanism in human agency. *American Psychologist, 37,* 122–147.

Bandura, A., & Schunk, D. (1981). Cultivating competence, self-efficacy, and intrinsic interest through proximal self-motivation. *Journal of Personality and Social Psychology, 41,* 586–598.

Bettencourt, E., Gillett, M., Gall, M., & Hull, R. (1983). Effects of teacher enthusiasm training on student on-task behavior and achievement. *American Educational Research Journal, 20,* 435–450.

Blumenfeld, P. C., Mergendoller, J. R., & Swarthout, D. W. (In press). Tasks as heuristics for understanding student learning and motivation. *Journal of Curriculum Studies.*

Book, C., Duffy, G., Roehler, L., Meloth, M., & Vavrus, L. (1985). A study of the relationships between teacher explanation and student metacognitive awareness during reading instruction. *Communication Education, 34,* 29–36.

Brophy, J. (1983). Conceptualizing student motivation. *Educational Psychologist, 18,* 200–215.

Brophy, J., & Kher, N. (1986). Teacher socialization as a mechanism for developing student motivation to learn. In R. Feldman (Ed.), *Social psychology applied to education.* New York: Cambridge University Press.

Butkowsky, I., & Willows, D. (1980). Cognitive-motivational characteristics of children varying in reading ability: Evidence for learned helplessness in poor readers. *Journal of Educational Psychology, 72,* 408–422.

Carrier, C., & Titus, A. (1979). The effects of notetaking: A review of studies. *Contemporary Educational Psychology, 4,* 299–314.

Condry, J., & Chambers, J. (1978). Intrinsic motivation and the process of learning. In M. Lepper and D. Greene (Eds.), *The hidden costs of reward: New perspectives on the psychology of human motivation.* Hillsdale, NJ: Erlbaum.

Cooper, H. (1979). Pygmalion grows up: A model for teacher expectation communication and performance influence. *Review of Educational Research, 49,* 389–410.

Corno, L., & Mandinach, E. (1983). The role of cognitive engagement in classroom learning and motivation. *Educational Psychologist, 18,* 88–108.

Corno, L., & Rohrkemper, M. (1985). The intrinsic motivation to learn in classrooms. In C. Ames & R. Ames (Eds.), *Research on motivation in education. Vol. II: The classroom milieu.* Orlando, FL: Academic Press.

Covington, M. V., & Omelich, C. L. (1985). Ability and effort valuation among failure-avoiding and failure-accepting students. *Journal of Educational Psychology, 77,* 446–459.

Craske, M. L. (1985). Improving persistence through observational learning and attribution retraining. *British Journal of Educational Psychology, 55,* 138–147.

deCharms, R. (1976). *Enhancing motivation: Change in the classroom.* New York: Irvington.

Deci, E., & Ryan, R. (1985). *Intrinsic motivation and self-determination in human behavior.* New York: Plenum.

Diener, D., & Dweck, C. (1978). An analysis of learned helplessness: Continuous changes in performance, strategy, and achievement cognitions following failure. *Journal of Personality and Social Psychology, 36,* 451–462.

Doyle, W. (1983). Academic work. *Review of Educational Research, 53,* 159–199.

Dweck, C., & Elliott, E. (1983). Achievement motivation. In P. Mussen (Ed.), *Handbook of Child Psychology,* 4th ed., Vol. IV: *Socialization, personality, and social development.* New York: Wiley.

Eccles, J., & Wigfield, A. (1985). Teacher expectations and student motivation. In J. B. Dusek (Ed.), *Teacher expectancies.* Hillsdale, NJ: Erlbaum.

Elawar, M. C., & Corno, L. (1985). A factorial experiment in teachers' written feedback on student homework: Changing teacher behavior a little rather than a lot. *Journal of Educational Psychology, 77,* 162–173.

Feather, N. (Ed.). (1982). *Expectations and actions.* Hillsdale, NJ: Erlbaum.

Fowler, J. W., & Peterson, P. L. (1981). Increasing reading persistence and altering attributional style of learned helpless children. *Journal of Educational Psychology, 73,* 251–260.

Frieze, I., Francis, W., & Hanusa, B. (1983). Defining success in classroom settings. In J. Levine & M. Wang (Eds.), *Teacher and student perceptions: Implications for learning.* Hillsdale, NJ: Erlbaum.

Gambrell, L. (1983). The occurrence of think-time during reading comprehension instruction. *Journal of Educational Research, 77,* 77–80.

Good, T., & Brophy, J. (1986). *Educational psychology: A realistic approach* (3rd ed.). New York: Longman.

Gottfried, A. (1985). Academic intrinsic motivation in elementary and junior high school students. *Journal of Educational Psychology, 77,* 631–645.

Grabe, M. (1985). Attributions in a mastery instructional system: Is an emphasis on effort harmful? *Contemporary Educational Psychology, 10,* 113–126.

Hill, K. T., & Wigfield, A. (1984). Test anxiety: A major educational problem and what can be done about it. *Elementary School Journal, 85,* 105–126.

Hughes, B., Sullivan, H., & Mosley, M. (1985). External evaluation, task difficulty, and continuing motivation. *Journal of Educational Research, 78,* 210–215.

Johnson, D., & Johnson, R. (1985). Motivational processes in cooperative, competitive, and individualistic learning situations. In C. Ames & R. Ames (Eds.), *Research on motivation in education. Vol. II: The classroom milieu.* Orlando, FL: Academic Press.

Keller, J. (1983). Motivational design of instruction. In C. Reigeluth (Ed.), *Instructional-design theories and models: An overview of their current status.* Hillsdale, NJ: Erlbaum.

Kierwa, K. (1985). Investigating notetaking and review: A depth of processing alternative. *Educational Psychologist, 20,* 23–32.

Kolesnik, W. (1978). *Motivation: Understanding and influencing human behavior.* Boston: Allyn and Bacon.

Kruglanski, A. (1978). Endogenous attribution and intrinsic motivation. In M. Lepper & D. Greene (Eds.), *The hidden costs of reward: New perspectives on the psychology of human motivation.* Hillsdale, NJ: Erlbaum.

Ladas, H. (1980). Summarizing research: A case study. *Review of Educational Research, 50,* 597–624.

Lepper, M. (1983). Extrinsic reward and intrinsic motivation: Implications for the classroom. In J. Levine & M. Wang (Eds.), *Teacher and student perspectives: Implications for learning.* Hillsdale, NJ: Erlbaum.

Lepper, M., & Greene, D. (Eds.). (1978). *The hidden costs of reward: New perspectives on the psychology of human motivation.* Hillsdale, NJ: Erlbaum.

Maehr, M. (1984). Meaning and motivation: Toward a theory of personal investment. In R. Ames & C. Ames (Eds.), *Research on motivation in education. Vol. I: Student motivation.* Orlando, FL: Academic Press.

Malone, T. & Lepper, M. (In press). Making learning fun: A taxonomy of intrinsic motivation for learning. In R. Snow & M. Farr (Eds.), *Aptitude, learning, and instruction: III. Conative and affective process analysis.* Hillsdale, NJ: Erlbaum.

Mayer, R. (1979). Can advance organizers influence meaningful learning? *Review of Educational Research, 49,* 371–383.

McColskey, W., & Leary, M. R. (1985). Differential effects of norm-referenced and self-referenced feedback on performance expectancies, attributions, and motivation. *Contemporary Educational Psychology, 10,* 275–284.

McCombs, B. (1984). Processes and skills underlying continuing intrinsic motivation to learn: Toward a definition of motivational skills training and interventions. *Educational Psychologist, 19,* 199–218.

Medway, F. M., & Venino, G. R. (1982). The effects of effort feedback and performance patterns on children's attribution and task persistence. *Contemporary Educational Psychology, 7,* 26–34.

Morgan, M. (1985). Self-monitoring of attained subgoals in private study. *Journal of Educational Psychology, 77,* 623–630.

Nicholls, J. (1984). Conceptions of ability and achievement motivation. In R. Ames C. Ames (Eds.), *Research on motivation in education. Vol. I: Student motivation.* Orlando, FL: Academic Press.

Ortiz, R. (1983). Generating interest in reading. *Journal of Reading, 27,* 113–119.

Palincsar, A., & Brown, A. (1984). Reciprocal teaching of comprehension-fostering and comprehension-monitoring activities. *Cognition and Instruction, 1,* 117–175.

Paris, S., Cross, D., & Lipson, M. (1984). Informed strategies for learning: A program to improve children's reading awareness and comprehension. *Journal of Educational Psychology, 76,* 1239–1252.

Parsons, J., & Goff, S. (1980). Achievement motivation and values: An alternative perspective. In L. J. Fyans (Ed.), *Achievement motivation: Recent trends in theory and research.* New York: Plenum.

Plass, J. A., & Hill, K. T. (1986). Children's achievement strategies and test performance: The role of time pressure, evaluation anxiety, and sex. *Developmental Psychology, 22,* 31–36.

Roehler, L., & Duffy, G. (1984). Direct explanation of comprehension processes. In G. Duffy, L. Roehler, &J. Mason (Eds.), *Comprehension instruction: Perspectives and suggestions.* New York: Longman.

Rogoff, B., & Wertsch, J. (Eds.). (1984). *Children's learning in the "zone" of proximal development.* San Francisco: Jossey-Bass.

Rowe, M. (1974). Pausing phenomena: Influence on quality of instruction. *Journal of Psycholinguistic Research, 3,* 203–224.

Schunk, D. H. (1985). Self-efficacy and classroom learning. *Psychology in the Schools, 22,* 208–223.

Schunk, D. H., & Hanson, A. R. (1985). Peer models: Influence on children's self-efficacy and achievement. *Journal of Educational Psychology, 77,* 313–322.

Slavin, R. (1983). *Cooperative learning.* New York: Longman.

Stipek, D., & Weiss, J. (1981). Perceived personal control and academic achievement. *Review of Educational Research, 51,* 101–137.

Swift, N., & Gooding, C. (1983). Interaction of wait-time feedback and questioning instruction on middle school science teaching. *Journal of Research in Science Teaching, 20,* 721–730.

Thomas, J. W. (1980). Agency and achievement: Self-management and self-reward. *Review of Educational Research, 30,* 213–240.

Tobin, K., & Capie, W. (1982). Relationships between classroom process variables and middle-school science achievement. *Journal of Educational Psychology, 74,* 441–454.

Tollefson, N., Tracy, D., Johnsen, E., Farmer, W., & Buenning, M. (1984). Goal setting and personal responsibility for LD adolescents. *Psychology in the Schools, 21,* 224–233.

Vygotsky, L. (1978). *Mind in society: The development of higher psychological processes.* In M. Cole, V. John-Steiner, S. Scribner, & E. Souberman, (Eds.), Cambridge, MA: Harvard University Press.

Weiner, B. (1984). Principles for a theory of student motivation and their application within an attributional framework. In R. Ames & d C. Ames (Eds.), *Research on motivation in education. Vol. I: Student motivation.* Orlando, FL: Academic Press.

Weinstein, C., & Mayer, R. (1986). The teaching of learning strategies. In M. Wittrock (Ed.), *Handbook of research on teaching* (3rd ed.). New York: Macmillan.

Weisz, J., & Cameron, A. (1985). Individual differences in the students' sense of control. In C. Ames and R. Ames (Eds.), *Research on motivation in education. Vol. II: The classroom milieu.* Orlando, FL: Academic Press.

Whitley, B. E., & Frieze, I. H. (1985). Children's causal attributions for success and failure in achievement settings: A meta-analysis. *Journal of Educational Psychology, 77,* 608–616.

Wlodkowski, R. J. (1978). *Motivation and teaching: A practical guide.* Washington, D.C.: National Education Association.

Zimmerman, B. J., & Blotner, R. (1979). Effects of model persistence and success on children's problem solving. *Journal of Educational Psychology, 71,* 508–513.

FORM 8.1. Attributing Success to Causes

USE: Whenever teacher makes a comment to explain a student's success
PURPOSE: To see whether the teacher's statements support student
confidence and motivation to learn
For each codable instance, code each causal attribution category that
applies. How does the teacher explain good performance by students?

CAUSAL ATTRIBUTION CATEGORIES   CODES
1. Effort or perseverance ("You worked hard, stuck to   1. ___   26. ___
   it")   2. ___   27. ___
2. Accurate problem representation and solution ("You   3. ___   28. ___
   developed a good plan, followed the right process")   4. ___   29. ___
3. Good progress in learning the domain ("You've really   5. ___   30. ___
   learned how to _____")
4. Native intelligence or ability ("You're smart")   6. ___   31. ___
5. Compliance ("You listened carefully, did as you were   7. ___   32. ___
   told")   8. ___   33. ___
6. Irrelevant attributes ("You're a big boy")   9. ___   34. ___
7. Cheating ("You copied." "Did someone tell you the   10 ___   35. ___
   answer?")
8. Other (specify)   11. ___   36. ___
                                                             12. ___   37. ___
NOTES: 13. ___   38. ___
                                                             14. ___   39. ___
                                                             15. ___   40. ___

                                                             16. ___   41. ___
                                                             17. ___   42. ___
                                                             18. ___   43. ___
                                                             19. ___   44. ___
                                                             20. ___   45. ___

                                                             21. ___   46. ___
                                                             22. ___   47. ___
                                                             23. ___   48. ___
                                                             24. ___   49. ___
                                                             25. ___   50. ___

FORM 8.2. Attributing Failure to Causes

USE: Whenever the teacher makes a comment to explain a student's
       failure
PURPOSE: To see whether the teacher responds to failure in ways that
        encourage the student to keep trying to master the material
        For each codable instance, code each causal attribution category that
applies. How does the teacher "explain" students' failure?

CAUSAL ATTRIBUTION CATEGORIES   CODES

1. Laziness or lack of perseverance "You didn't work at it, gave up too easily")	1. ___ 26. ___ 2. ___ 27. ___
2. Inaccurate problem representation or strategy choice ("Your efforts were misdirected because you misunderstood the task and developed a plan that doesn't address the problem at hand" or "You were on the right track and developed a good plan, but you made a mistake in carrying it out")	3. ___ 28. ___ 4. ___ 29. ___ 5. ___ 30. ___ 6. ___ 31. ___ 7. ___ 32. ___
3. Poor progress in learning the domain ("You haven't yet learned how to _____")	8. ___ 33. ___ 9. ___ 34. ___
4. Low intelligence or ability ("You can't keep up")	10. ___ 10. ___
5. Bad luck ("Looks like I picked the ones you didn't know")	11. ___ 36. ___
6. Difficult task or question ("That's a hard one, you are not ready for it yet")	12. ___ 37. ___ 13. ___ 38. ___
7. Noncompliance ("You didn't listen, didn't do as you were told")	14. ___ 39. ___ 15. ___ 40. ___
8. Irrelevant attributes	
9. Did not cheat ("See, you can't do it by yourself." "I see no one gave you the answer this time")	16. ___ 41. ___ 17. ___ 42. ___
10. Other (specify)	18. ___ 43. ___ 19. ___ 44. ___
NOTES:	20. ___ 45. ___ 21. ___ 46. ___ 22. ___ 47. ___ 23. ___ 48. ___ 24. ___ 49. ___ 25. ___ 50. ___

FORM 8.3. General Motivational Strategies

USE: *When the teacher has been observed frequently enough so that reliable information is available*

PURPOSE: *To assess the degree to which the teacher's general approach to instruction supports students' self-confidence and motivation to learn*

How regularly does the teacher follow the motivational guidelines listed below? Rate according to the following scale:

5 = *always*
4 = *most of the time*
3 = *sometimes*
2 = *occasionally*
1 = *never*

A. ESSENTIAL PRECONDITIONS

———— 1. Maintains a supportive learning environment (classroom atmosphere is businesslike but relaxed, teacher supports and encourages students' learning efforts)

———— 2. Assigns tasks at an appropriate level of difficulty (students can achieve success with reasonable effort)

———— 3. Assigns tasks with meaningful learning objectives (the tasks teach some knowledge or skill that is worth learning)

———— 4. Demonstrates moderation and variation in use of motivational strategies (does not overuse particular strategies to the point that they become counterproductive)

B. MAINTAINING STUDENTS' SUCCESS EXPECTATIONS

———— 1. Programs for success

———— 2. Helps students to develop their skills for goal setting, performance appraisal, and self-reinforcement

———— 3. Helps students to recognize effort-outcome linkages

———— 4. Portrays effort as investment rather than risk

———— 5. Portrays skill development as incremental and domain-specific (rather than as determined by fixed general abilities)

———— 6. Focuses on mastery in monitoring performance and giving feedback (stresses student's continuous progress toward mastery rather than comparisons with other students)

———— 7. If necessary, does remedial motivational work with discouraged students (to help them see that they have ability and can reach goals if they put forth reasonable effort)

C. STIMULATING STUDENTS' MOTIVATION TO LEARN

———— 1. Models own motivation to learn (portrays learning as a self-actualizing activity that produces personal satisfaction and enriches one's life)

———— 2. Communicates desirable expectations and attributions (implying that students see classroom activities as worthwhile and are eager to acquire knowledge and master skills)

———— 3 Minimizes performance anxiety (treats mistakes as understandable and expected; minimizes the threat of tests)

NOTES:

FORM 8.4. Motivational Analysis of Tasks and Activities

USE: Whenever particular classroom tasks or activities are observed
PURPOSE: To identify the motivational elements built into the task or
        activity
        Check each of the motivational elements that was included in the
observed task or activity.

A. EXTRINSIC MOTIVATION STRATEGIES

_____ 1. Offers rewards as incentives for good performance
_____ 2. Calls attention to the instrumental value of the knowledge or
             skills developed in the activity (applications to present or
             future life outside of school)
_____ 3. Structures individual or group competition for prizes or
             recognition

B. INTRINSIC MOTIVATIONAL FEATURES OF THE TASK OR ACTIVITY

_____ 1. Opportunities for active response (beyond just watching and
             listening)
_____ 2. Opportunities to answer divergent questions or work on
             higher level objectives
_____ 3. Immediate feedback to students' responses (built into the
             task itself, rather than provided by the teacher as in C.8
             below)
_____ 4. Gamelike features (the task is a game or contains gamelike
             features that make it more like a recreational activity than a
             typical academic activity)
_____ 5. Task completion involves creating a finished product for
             display or use
_____ 6. The task involves fantasy or simulation elements that engage
             students' emotions or allow them to experience events
             vicariously
_____ 7. The task provides opportunities for students to interact with
             their peers

C. TEACHER'S ATTEMPTS TO STIMULATE STUDENTS' MOTIVATION TO LEARN

——————— 1. Projects intensity (communicating that the material is important and deserves close attention)
——————— 2. Induces task interest or appreciation
——————— 3. Induces curiosity or suspense
——————— 4. Makes abstract content more personal, concrete, or familiar
——————— 5. Induces dissonance or cognitive conflict
——————— 6. Induces students to generate their own motivation to learn
——————— 7. States learning objectives or provides advance organizers
——————— 8. Provides opportunities for students to respond and get feedback (asks questions during group lessons, circulates to monitor performance during seatwork)
——————— 9. Models task-related thinking and problem solving ("thinks out loud" when working through examples)
——————— 10. Includes instruction or modeling designed to increase students' metacognitive awareness of their learning efforts in response to the task (includes information about mental preparation for learning, about the organization or structure built into the content, about how students can impose their own organizational structures on the content to help them remember it, or about how to monitor one's own comprehension and respond to confusion or mistakes)

NOTES:

FORM 8.4. (*Continued*)

9 Mastery Learning, Individualized Instruction, and Open Education

Until relatively recently in human history, only the children of the rich and powerful received formal education. This education typically took the form of private individualized tutoring. Such tutoring is the method of choice for most educational purposes, because both curriculum (what is taught) and instruction (how it is taught) can be individualized and because the teacher can provide the student with sustained personalized attention (Bloom, 1984). Unfortunately, private tutoring is too expensive for most families to afford. Consequently, as systems for mass education developed, one constant feature was an arrangement whereby each individual teacher would be responsible for working with many different students.

Colonial times featured the one-room schoolhouse, into which large numbers of students of all ages were crowded for instruction in all subjects by a single teacher who had few if any commercially prepared texts or curriculum materials to work with (Grinder & Nelsen, 1985). Except for so-called primers for reading instruction (containing the alphabet and short selections such as proverbs, catechisms, or passages from the Bible), teachers made do with slates, chalkboards, and materials (maps, books published for use by the general public) that they had purchased themselves or induced their students to bring from home. Recitations and rote memory exercises were relied on when texts or other curriculum materials were not available.

With the industrial revolution and the shift of population to the cities, schools became larger and education became more standardized and formalized. Age grouping became the basis for assigning the students to classes, curriculum guidelines and standards were established for each grade level, and teachers began working with commercial textbooks and tests. Certain common practices for organizing and managing instruction in the public schools became well established and have continued since then as the traditional model of classroom teaching: the *lock-step curriculum* with its grade-level sequencing, division of the school day into periods for teaching different subject matter, and division of instruction in each subject matter into units and lessons; group pacing, in which the whole class is moved through the same curriculum at roughly the same pace using largely the same materials and methods; and *whole-class instructional methods,* in which the teacher typically begins a lesson by reviewing prerequisite material, then introduces and develops new concepts or skills, then leads the group in a recitation or supervised practice or application activity, and then assigns seatwork or homework for students to do on their own. The teacher may occasionally teach small groups rather than the whole class (especially for beginning reading instruction) and may provide a degree of individualized instruction when "making the rounds" during individual seatwork times. However, despite these and other minor variations on the theme, the basic whole-class instruction/recitation/seatwork model has persisted as the dominant approach to public school teaching ever since it first became established, despite frequent criticism and calls for reform (Cuban, 1984; Goodlad, 1984; Grinder & Nelsen, 1985; James & Tyack, 1983).

The fact that this traditional approach persists despite its many weaknesses suggests that it has certain enduring strengths. Indeed, the approach seems to work reasonably well for students whose rates of learning and responses to commonly used instructional materials and methods are similar to those of the mythical "average student" for their grade levels. Furthermore, given that teachers must work with classes of 20 to 40 students, the traditional method, although clearly a compromise, may be the best compromise available. Other things being equal, it may enable teachers to meet more of the needs of more of their students than they could meet using any other method that is feasible given the resources and constraints that apply (the major constraints are that teachers must leave the majority of students to work without close supervision whenever they work with small groups or individuals, and that in any case, teachers cannot get around to each individual student often enough to provide effective individualized instruction).

Still, the traditional approach has important weaknesses, so that it periodically becomes the focus of criticism and calls for reform (for recent examples, see Goodlad, 1984; Sizer, 1984; and Wang & Walberg, 1985). Some critics simply do not like the traditional system and attack it as being unduly teacher dominant, rigidly structured, oriented toward passive and repetitive learning, or unimaginative and boring. Other critics acknowledge it as adequate for average students but believe that brighter students who master the curriculum more quickly should get more enrichment or accelerated pacing, that slower students should get extra instruction or more time to master the material, and that students with special instructional needs should be taught using materials or methods different from those that are suitable for the majority. Critics commonly call for more variety in educational curricula and methods and for more attempts to adapt schooling to the needs and interests of students.

In this chapter, we will discuss three reform efforts popularized in recent years that attempt to introduce fundamental changes in the traditional approach to schooling: *mastery learning, individualized instruction,* and *open education.* In the next chapter, we will discuss alternative plans for grouping students that attempt to address the weaknesses of the traditional model without introducing such fundamental changes in it as the changes associated with mastery learning, individualized instruction, and open education.

MASTERY LEARNING

Traditionally, educators discussed student individual differences in terms of IQ or general abilities or aptitudes. They simply took for granted that instruction in a given curriculum would yield a range of mastery levels, because some students would master the material quickly and easily, but others would progress only slowly and incompletely. They advised teachers to provide extra instruction and practice opportunities to slower students, but even so, the implicit expectation was that only limited progress could be expected from these students.

The notion that large differences in student ability produce large differences in curriculum mastery and nothing can be done about it began to break down in the 1960s. One reason for this was an influential article by John Carroll (1963), who argued that differences in mastery levels were produced not by inherent differences in learning potential (some students can master given material and others cannot), but by differences in the time needed to learn (some students may take longer to master the material, but they will master it if given enough time). He expressed the argument in the following equation:

$$\text{Degree of learning} = \frac{\text{time actually spent}}{\text{time needed}}$$

Carroll's model implies that all students can master the curriculum if given enough time to do so. If taken seriously, it implies that low achievement is due to the school's failure to meet students' learning needs rather than to a lack of sufficient learning abilities among low achievers. In fact, the model assumes a trade-off between learning time and individual differences in mastery (Anderson, 1985). If the schools fix learning time (allocate a fixed amount of time for teaching particular material and then move on to something else), they will maximize student individual differences in mastery levels. On the other hand, if they fix mastery levels (insure that all students are taught to a specified level of mastery), they will have to provide for individual differences in the time needed to achieve mastery. Thus, schools cannot have both fixed learning times and fixed mastery levels. The traditional model of schooling deals with this dilemma by fixing learning times and accepting individual differences in mastery levels. The mastery learning model deals with it by fixing mastery levels and accepting individual differences in learning time.

Carroll suggested that five elements determine students' rates of learning: aptitude, ability to understand instruction, task perseverance (student engaged time on the task), opportunity to learn (allocated instructional time), and quality of instruction.

Bloom (1968, 1976, 1980) elaborated on Carroll's model to develop the concept of *mastery learning*. Bloom's model includes student entry characteristics (both cognitive and affective), the learning task itself, the quality of instruction provided, and a variety of learning outcomes (level and type of achievement, rate of learning, affective outcomes). Bloom suggests that the outcome of a student's encounter with a learning task will be determined not only by the time available for learning but also by the appropriateness of the task for the learner (in terms of both its cognitive level and its affective appeal) and by the quality of the instruction provided. Learning will proceed most smoothly when students are taught effectively on tasks that they are motivated to engage in and able to master with relative ease. In suggesting guidelines for improving quality of instruction, Bloom stresses four aspects: (1) *cues* or directions about what to do, (2) active learner *participation* in the task, (3) *reinforcement* that is derived from participating in the task and experiencing success on it, and (4) *feedback/correction* from the instructor.

Bloom argues that an effective combination of good task selection, provision of sufficient time for learning, and provision of high-quality instruction should enable 80 percent of students to reach mastery levels that only the top 20 percent of students reach in traditional classrooms. This is one of the fundamental assumptions of the mastery learning approach. A second fundamental assumption is that extra time and instruction provided to slow learners when they are working on tasks that come early in a hierarchical sequence not only will allow these students to master these tasks but also will reduce the time they need to learn tasks that appear later in the sequence. For example, if students are given sufficient time and instruction to enable them to master single-digit addition, they should require less time and instruction to be able to master double-digit addition, triple-digit addition, and so on. In general, mastery of a given objective should reduce the time needed to master subsequent objectives for which the first objective is a prerequisite.

Taken together, these assumptions imply that implementing mastery learning procedures should (1) increase the percentage of students who master a given objective from about 20 percent to about 80 percent, (2) reduce the variance (individual differences) in mastery of any particular objective and of the curriculum as a whole, and (3) over time, reduce the variance in time needed to learn (because as slower students master more and more prerequisites, they will become more able to master higher level tasks in the same curriculum series with relative ease).

In moving from these general philosophical ideas toward development of particular mastery learning programs, Bloom and his colleagues borrowed ideas from the curriculum movement toward instructional objectives (Gronlund, 1985; Mager, 1962) and the instructional design movement toward task analysis, programmed instruction, and the development of individualized learning systems composed of self-contained modules (Gagné & Briggs, 1979; Reigeluth, 1983). Initial applications were at the high school and college levels where students were sophisticated and experienced at learning primarily on their own from instructional materials. Instruction from the teacher took the form of individualized tutoring. Later, however, Block and others (Block, 1974; Block & Anderson, 1975; Block & Burns, 1976) adapted the mastery learning approach for use by elementary and secondary school teachers in tandem with, rather than instead of, more traditional group-based instruction. At present, most mastery learning programs in the schools feature group-based rather than individualized instruction (Levine, 1985). Besides acceptance of basic mastery learning philosophy as described above, mastery learning programs have certain common features. Anderson (1985) suggests that the following features are essential and that all six will be found in any true mastery learning program:

1. Clearly specified learning objectives
2. Short, highly valid assessment procedures

3. Preset mastery performance standards
4. A sequence of learning units, each composed of an integral set of facts, contents, principles, and skills
5. Provision of feedback about learning progress to students
6. Provision of additional time and help to correct specified errors and misunderstandings of students who are failing to achieve the preset mastery learning standards

The heart of mastery learning is the cycle of teaching, testing, reteaching, and retesting. Students are informed of the objectives of a given unit and then receive instruction designed to enable them to master those objectives. Upon completion of instruction and related practice activities, the students receive formative evaluation tests designed to assess their mastery levels. Those who achieve preset performance standards (these usually call for passing at least 80 percent of the items on the test, although some programs require passing 90 percent or more) are certified as having mastered the unit and are not required to do further work on it. These students will then move on to the next unit, or more typically, will work on enrichment activities or activities of their own choosing until the class as a whole is ready to move on to the next unit. Meanwhile, students who did not meet mastery criteria will receive corrective instruction and additional practice opportunities and then their mastery levels will be assessed again. Theoretically, these cycles of assessment and reteaching could go on indefinitely until all students reached mastery levels, but in practice, attempts to bring students up to mastery levels usually cease after the second test administration and the class then moves on to the next unit. Thus, in practice, group-based mastery learning programs are a compromise between traditional programs that allow little if any extra time to slow learners and ideal mastery programs that would allow all learners as much time as they need. Even so, half or more of the total instructional time devoted to a unit in a typical group-based mastery program will be spent on corrective instruction with students who fail to reach mastery criteria on the formative test following initial instruction (Slavin & Karweit, 1984).

Research on Mastery Learning

The mastery learning philosophy is very appealing at first glance, but it has been attacked as being simply illogical and as impossible to implement in practice (Buss, 1976; Cox & Dunn, 1979; Greeno, 1978; Resnick, 1977). In particular, critics have suggested that individual differences in student learning ability are too stable and powerful to be compensated for by relatively minor adjustments in time allocated for teaching and learning, and that in any case, it is inappropriate to pursue the goal of reducing individual differences in student achievement levels because this can be accomplished only by holding back high achievers in addition to providing extra time and instruction to low achievers.

Research on mastery learning tends only to reinforce rather than to resolve these conflicting points of view. Comparisons of mastery learning approaches with traditional instruction typically show that achievement levels are higher in mastery classes, and that in particular, a much higher percentage of the students master content believed to be basic (Block & Burns, 1976; Guskey & Gates, 1985;

Walberg, 1984). These studies usually show affective advantages to the mastery programs as well (Guskey & Gates, 1985). Thus, in one sense, research results are highly favorable to the mastery learning approach.

However, these findings are limited or misleading in several respects. First, considerable additional learning time is required to achieve the reported gains in mastery of the material. Arrangements must be made to provide corrective instruction to students before or after school, or more typically, to provide this corrective instruction during class time and thus hold back the fast learners while the teacher works with the slow learners. Thus, critics argue that when the extra time needs are taken into account, there is little or no advantage to mastery learning at all. They claim that the extra achievement is due simply to the extra learning time provided rather than to anything else inherent in the mastery learning approach and that traditional instruction or some other approach might succeed just as well if teachers allocated the same amounts of time to teach the same units of instruction.

Another problem is that research tends not to support the key assumption that taking time to insure mastery of early objectives will reduce the time that students need to learn later objectives. Arlin (1984a) reviewed research by others on this point and concluded that it did not support the claims of mastery learning theorists, and his own studies (Arlin, 1984b; Arlin & Webster, 1983) also failed to show any decrease over time in the time needed by slow learners to master objectives (relative to the time needed by fast learners). In practice, then, it appears that mastery learning approaches do not really solve the dilemma of having to choose between fixing time allotments and accepting individual differences in mastery levels or fixing mastery levels and accepting individual differences in time to learn. Instead, they merely substitute the second choice for the first.

A third problem in interpreting research on mastery learning is that the findings are extremely variable and unfortunately, results tend to be more impressive for brief studies (lasting a week or less) involving instruction in content normally not taught at school than they are for studies of instruction in basic school subjects assessed over significant time periods (Guskey & Gates, 1985). Slavin and Karweit (1984), for example, found no advantage to mastery learning over traditional instruction in ninth-grade general mathematics classes in inner-city Philadelphia schools studied over the course of an entire semester.

Chicago's experience with mastery learning approaches illustrates the difficulties involved in implementing the mastery learning philosophy in practice. With strong support from central administration, the Chicago public schools committed themselves to a mastery learning approach to elementary reading instruction in the early 1980s (Board of Education of the City of Chicago, 1982; Jones, Friedman, Tinzmann, & Cox, 1985). The program was entitled Chicago Mastery Learning Reading (CMLR).

CMLR is a group-based mastery program developed to replace an earlier individualized continuous-progress program used in the Chicago schools. The latter program had been poorly implemented (Jones & Spady, 1985). In particular, low achievers often made little or no progress because the program called for students to progress "at their own rate," so that teachers did not feel responsible for pacing the students through the material or setting appropriate goals for them. Second, when goals were set, classroom management problems made it difficult to implement the goals. Teachers found it difficult to provide enough materials to keep all levels of students progressing and could not find the time to get around to individual students often enough to teach them effectively. The developers addressed these problems by planning CMLR as a group-based approach and training teachers in group-based mastery methods. Furthermore, they developed curriculum materials specifically designed for use with this approach, including two sets of tests to allow for both formative and summative assessment of student mastery levels. The materials and recommended instructional methods were developed with emphasis on the latest thinking in instructional design and delivery and on avoiding some of the problems that have appeared in earlier programs (lack of sufficient integration of subskills, excessive emphasis on testing and record keeping, concentration on lower-order objectives to the exclusion of higher-order objectives). In fact, the CMLR curriculum materials are now being used in many school systems.

Yet, with all of this going for it, CMLR did not succeed in Chicago. Comparisons with traditionally taught classes revealed no differences or only slight advantages to CMLR classes. Worse, initial enthusiasm about CMLR waned and was replaced with complaints about the curriculum materials and about difficulties in implementing and managing the program. In 1985, after a change in central administration, CMLR was dropped by the Chicago schools. CMLR continues to be used in over 200 school districts, however, and it could prove to be successful in at least some of them as more data become available.

Ironically, given that mastery learning approaches were developed with low achievers in mind, they appear to be especially difficult to implement in inner-city schools populated largely by low achievers. In part, this is because these schools tend to have high student-to-teacher ratios, high rates of absenteeism and transiency, high enrollments in pull-out instructional programs, fewer instructional materials, and less time for groups of teachers to coordinate planning (Jones & Spady, 1985). Also, the corrective sequence of mastery learning is designed to correct relatively minor errors or misunderstandings, whereas students in inner-city schools may have a great many serious and idiosyncratic problems needing individualized attention (Slavin & Karweit, 1984). Thus, group-paced mastery learning approaches may be both ill-suited to the needs of inner-city students and especially difficult to implement in inner-city schools.

Conclusions About Mastery Learning

Mastery approaches clearly can succeed in increasing (often dramatically) the percentage of students who reach mastery criteria on basic objectives, and they do seem to have clear benefits for low achievers. They provide extra time and instruction to enable low achievers to master more of the content than they would master otherwise, and this additional mastery is likely to bring motivational benefits as well. In particular, mastery approaches are likely to convince chronic low achievers that the old academic "game" has been replaced by a new one that gives them a chance to "win" consistently if they apply reasonable effort. Thus, at least some attempt to implement the mastery learning philosophy appears desirable.

It seems to us, however, that the emphasis should be on maximizing each student's achievement progress, even if this should mean maintaining or even increasing the range of individual differences in achievement levels. It appears that the mastery approach will not succeed in reducing the time that slow learners need to learn (relative to the time that fast learners need), so that it will be possible to reduce individual differences in achievement progress only by deliberately holding back the fast learners. This is not to say that teachers should continually push fast learners to higher curriculum levels instead of allowing them to engage in enrichment activities or other alternatives to acceleration through the curriculum. We do suggest, however, that the activities planned for fast learners should be selected for sound pedagogical reasons and not as mere time fillers designed to slow their progress through the curriculum in order to pursue the (inappropriate) goal of reducing individual differences in achievement levels. A sensible compromise to this dilemma seems to be to identify those learning objectives that seem most essential and see that all students master these objectives, while tolerating more variable performance on objectives considered less essential. Teachers can supplement the basic curriculum with enrichment opportunities, individualized learning packages, or learning centers that high achievers can use individually or in groups during times when the teachers are busy teaching low achievers.

Teachers often resist mastery learning programs because of the demands they make (Arlin, 1982). For example, Pringle (1985) notes that teachers working in district-mandated mastery programs may have to change the way that they plan and deliver courses because their lessons must reflect district requirements. The textbook, formerly the primary planning tool, becomes support material. Teachers must design their teaching to match the official objectives and assess progress toward those objectives using tests designed for the program. There may be officially sanctioned teaching techniques, elaborate recording requirements, and so on. Thus, teachers contemplating total commitment to a mastery learning approach should gather information about what is involved. A volume edited by Levine (1985) is a good place to start, along with the books and articles by Arlin, Block, and Bloom referenced in this chapter. In addition, information is available from the Clearing House on Mastery Learning that has been established at the Center for Educational Improvement at Loyola University in New Orleans.

Teachers who are not involved in district mandated mastery learning programs but wish to integrate mastery learning principles into their own individual classrooms should consider the following suggestions offered by Anderson and Block (1983):

1. *Define mastery.* Identify essential objectives, organize them sequentially, divide them into units; set mastery performance standards; and prepare formative tests designed to identify student errors and misunderstandings within units and summative tests designed to assess student learning over larger portions of the course.
2. *Plan for mastery.* Design basic materials, activities, and methods for teaching the class as a group; develop alternative materials, activities, and methods for students who still have errors or misunderstandings following the initial instruction; plan specific correction procedures in response to specific problems identified by tests; and plan enrichment activities or alternative learning opportunities for students who master the basic material quickly.
3. *Teach for mastery.* Acquaint students with the mastery approach (certification of mastery and routing into alternative activities for students whose

test scores meet criteria, reteaching and retesting for those who need it, grading according to mastery performance rather than speed); implement the instructional plan with the group as a whole; administer formative mastery tests; identify and implement alternative plans for masters and nonmasters; and insure that necessary content is covered in the time allocated.

4. *Grade for mastery.* Administer summative achievement tests and grade according to test performance without regard to how long it took for the student to reach this level.

INDIVIDUALIZED INSTRUCTION/ADAPTIVE EDUCATION

Walberg (1985) describes a range of accommodations that schools can make to students' individual differences. From this point of view, mastery learning is a relatively minor accommodation because although it allows for differences in learning time, it calls for using essentially the same methods and materials to move all students toward mastery of the same achievement goals. A more powerful form of accommodation is to retain the same achievement goals but introduce variation not only in time to learn but in the methods and materials used to accomplish this learning. The individualized instruction/adaptive education methods described in the present section take this approach, at least in theory. A still more extreme form of accommodation is to allow students to pursue different achievement goals, as well as a great deal of autonomy in deciding not only what to learn but how to learn it. The open education approach described in a later section represents this extreme level of accommodation (Walberg, 1985).

Attempts to make schooling more effective by fitting instruction to students' individual needs have traditionally been described as *individualized instruction* approaches, although the terms *adaptive instruction* or *adaptive education* have been popularized in recent years (Glaser, 1977; Wang & Walberg, 1985). All of these terms are difficult to discuss because they lack precise meaning and have been applied to programs that differ from one another in important ways (Berliner, 1985; Popkewitz, Tabachnick, & Wehlage, 1982). Some individualized instruction programs call for students to learn the same content using the same methods and materials but to progress at their own rate (such programs are similar to mastery learning programs, except that they lack the teach-test-reteach-retest cycle that typifies mastery approaches). Other individualized instruction approaches allow students to learn using different materials or methods but require them to show mastery in the same way. Still others allow demonstration of mastery in different ways (write a report, take an exam, pass an oral quiz, etc.). Thus, individualized instruction implies some degree of planned differentiation in the treatment of students in the same class, but there is a range of individualized instruction concepts and programs.

Wang and Lindvall (1984) list the following as distinguishing features of adaptive education approaches: (1) instruction based on the assessed capabilities of each student; (2) materials and procedures that permit each student to progress at a pace suited to his or her abilities and interests; (3) periodic evaluations that inform the student concerning mastery; (4) student assumption of responsibility for diagnosing present needs and abilities, planning learning activities, and evaluating mastery; (5) alternative activities and materials for aiding student acquisition of essential academic skills and content; (6) student choice in selecting educational goals, outcomes, and activities; and (7) students' assistance of one another in pursuing individual goals and cooperation in achieving group goals. Few individualized instruction or adaptive education programs have all seven of these features, but most have several of them.

Historical analyses have revealed that reformers calling for individualization or adaptation of the traditional model of schooling have been active in every educational era and that at least some of their suggestions have been adopted by about one-third of the elementary teachers but less than one-fifth of secondary teachers at any given time (Cuban, 1984). Usually these innovations call for shifting responsibility for planning and accomplishing learning from the teacher to the student and for shifting responsibility for communicating content from the teacher to instructional materials, because it is not possible for one teacher to simultaneously meet the needs of all of the students in the class (Jackson, 1985). The innovations are popularized by committed advocates (usually without data to back up the claims made), thrive briefly, and then wane. Certain elements of the innovations sometimes are retained and assimilated into traditional schooling, but the innovations are not retained as "total packages" that supplant traditional schooling. Typically, this is because the reformers give too much emphasis to social and motivational aspects and not enough to curriculum and instruction, make unwarranted assumptions about students' capabilities for independent goal setting and learning, or produce individualized curriculum materials that are focused too much on low-level isolated skills and involve too much testing or other managerial complexities (Grinder & Nelsen, 1985).

Individualization has become easier to accomplish in recent years with the development of materials and methods specifically designed to allow teachers to differentiate their instruction to different students in the class. Many of these specialized materials are augmented with audiovisual components (filmstrips, audiotaped or videotaped instruction, computer software). These materials provide instruction and practice opportunities for students who are not presently being taught or supervised directly by the teacher. Usually there is some initial assessment to determine where students should begin, and then the students work through the curriculum on their own from that point forward. In heavily individualized programs, students receive more of their content instruction from the curriculum materials than from the teacher, who acts more as a materials manager, tester, and progress monitor than as an instructor in the usual sense of the word.

Most individualized instructional materials use principles of programmed instruction, in which students are moved systematically in small steps from "entry level" of performance toward the ultimate objectives. Programs are divided into self-contained modules ready for independent use by individual students. Each module provides review of prerequisite knowledge or skills, introduction of new information and opportunities to practice by answering questions or carrying out tasks. Students are provided with immediate feedback after they make responses, and some programs have diagnostic and remediation features that allow students to skip segments that they have already mastered or to get extra instruction on material that they have not mastered by working through the regular program. Some of the best known individualized instructional approaches are described below.

Keller Plan (PSI)

Fred Keller (1968) developed a method of individualizing instruction that he called the *Personalized System of Instruction* (PSI). Others frequently refer to it as the *Keller Plan*. PSI was originally developed for use in a college psychology course and it is presently used in a variety of college courses (McKeachie & Kulik, 1975). It features self-pacing (within limits, students can go as fast or slow as they choose), mastery orientation (students move to a new unit only after mastering the previous unit to criterion), and student control of the examination schedule (students take tests when they decide that they are ready and may repeat tests as often as they need to until they reach criterion). Following initial orientation meetings, there are few if any lectures or whole-class sessions. Instead, students work individually or with one another to learn from texts or programmed materials and consult with the teacher or with assistants (called *proctors*) to get help (Keller & Sherman, 1982; Sherman, 1974).

PSI is popular with college students, or at least with those who enroll in PSI courses (Kulik, Kulik, & Carmichael, 1974; McKeachie & Kulik, 1975; Robin, 1976). These students enjoy the self-pacing, the opportunities for individualized tutoring, and the contract options that guarantee specified grades in exchange for specified levels of performance. Evaluations indicate that PSI students typically achieve as well or better than students in conventional sections of the same courses (Robin, 1976), partly because they tend to spend more time studying (Born, Davis, Whelan, & Jackson, 1972).

PSI courses work well for students who have the self-discipline and inclination to learn independently (Johnson & Ruskin, 1977). Many students dislike PSI courses and withdraw from them, however, and many others procrastinate to the point that they perform poorly or fail to earn course credit. Stiff mastery requirements may minimize the procrastination problem for some students. Robin (1976) reported that students with low grade-point averages began studying earlier and studied more often in PSI courses with 100 percent unit mastery criteria than in PSI courses using 50 percent mastery criteria. Many students were not willing to make this effort, though, and ended up withdrawing from the PSI sections. Thus, in general, PSI courses demand more self-discipline than many students are willing or able to impose.

We see additional qualifications to the applicability of PSI. For one, it is possible that the generally positive responses of most students to PSI occur in part because of its novelty. If all courses in the curriculum were organized along PSI principles, students might have difficulties finding the time or motivating themselves to put out the effort needed to earn top grades in each course.

Also, we question the feasibility of PSI for secondary and especially elementary schools. Here, most work has to be done in the classroom, where the group setting may make concentration difficult or delay or prevent contact with the teacher. Also, many students lack the learning skills (reading and following directions, checking for understanding, identifying and correcting mistakes) and independent work skills (attention span, willingness to sustain concentration on academic tasks without becoming bored or restless) that students must have if the PSI model is to work.

Thus, it appears that the PSI approach is not feasible for wholesale adoption in public school settings. However, PSI might be useful for parts of the day in certain subject matter or types of assignments, especially if teachers take time to teach their students how to operate under PSI conditions and if aides or other resource persons are available to assist with the proctoring.

Individualized Learning Systems

The 1960s and 1970s saw the development of several integrated learning systems for use in elementary and secondary schools (Talmage, 1975). One such system is *Individually Prescribed Instruction* (IPI), an omnibus learning system for elementary schools (Glaser & Rosner, 1975). In IPI classrooms, students usually learn individually using programmed packages, and the teacher's role is shifted from instructor to instructional manager. Teachers decide what programs are appropriate for their students, monitor their progress, and provide individualized help when needed. They do not need to worry about curriculum development (because materials are supplied) or selection (because this is determined by the results of diagnostic tests supplied with the program). IPI is often used in open classroom settings in elementary schools.

The *Primary Education Project* (PEP) grew out of IPI and was developed as a way to provide individualized instruction in the early elementary grades. Compared to IPI, PEP allows for more teaching of the class as a whole and includes more instruction and support designed to develop students' self-scheduling skills, independent work skills, and other skills for self-management of learning (Wang, 1981; Wang & Resnick, 1978). More recently, PEP has been supplanted by the *Adaptive Learning Environments Model* (ALEM) described below. IPI, PEP, and ALEM were all developed at the Learning Research and Development Center at the University of Pittsburgh.

The *Program for Learning in Accordance with Need* (PLAN) is another packaged program of individualized materials. It was produced by the Westinghouse Learning Corporation, the American Institutes for Research in the Behavioral Sciences, and several public school systems. Like PEP, the PLAN program not only identifies learning goals and supplies materials for students to use in working toward these goals but also provides students with opportunities to select their own goals and devise their own plans for meeting them (Flanagan et al., 1975; Quirk, 1971). In addition to the usual academic goals, the PLAN program was designed to achieve nonacademic goals such as preparing students for occupational roles and the responsibilities of citizenship, and for satisfying use of leisure time.

Individually Guided Education (IGE) is another system devised to help students learn at their own pace through activities suited to their individual needs. However, IGE is a strategy for managing instruction rather than a set of curriculum materials. Developed at the University of Wisconsin, the IGE model calls for both direct teacher instruction and student work on individualized assignments (including some individualized goal setting and self-managed learning). However, the basic learning goals are specified by local teaching staffs rather than by the program's developers, and these local teaching staffs then develop diagnostic tests to use in monitoring progress (Klausmeier, Rossmiller, & Saily, 1977; Schultz, 1974). Thus, what IGE looks like in practice and how effectively it is implemented will depend on the educational philosophies of local teaching staffs and their willingness to work together to create a coordinated program.

IGE is distinctive in that it requires major changes in school organization. A typical school will be divided into large multiage groupings of 100 to 150 students, each under the supervision of a unit leader (head teacher), other teachers, and various educational specialists. Teachers use tests, observation schedules, and work samples to assess student achievement levels, learning styles, and motivation, and then use this information to identify appropriate objectives and set up individualized instructional programs. The students are grouped according to perceived instructional needs rather than age levels and are moved into new groups or new instructional sequences depending on mastery, so there is much grouping and regrouping of students, at least in theory.

Research on Individualized Learning

Information about student achievement in individualized programs at the elementary and secondary levels is often hard to evaluate because it is usually confined to scores on criterion-referenced tests that come with the programs. Such data usually show success in meeting the objectives of the program as formulated by its developers, at least in classes where the program is considered to be well implemented. However, such data do not allow conclusions about either the absolute effectiveness or the cost effectiveness of these programs in comparison to traditional approaches (Educational Products Information Exchange, 1974).

Comparisons of individualized programs with traditional instruction typically report either no differences or very minor differences, with more variation within than between the two types of programs (Bangert, Kulik, & Kulik, 1983; Horak, 1981; Martin & Pavan, 1976). More recent evaluations of programs classified as "adaptive education" have shown more positive results favoring these programs (Wang & Lindvall, 1984; Waxman, Wang, Anderson, & Walberg, 1985), although the majority of the studies reviewed were small ones involving fewer than 150 students and the best results appear to be associated with frequent assessment, student self-management and choice, and peer cooperative arrangements rather than with reliance on individualized progress through programmed materials.

Part of the problem in evaluating individualized programs is that their implementation differs from classroom to classroom and from year to year. Even IPI, the most comprehensive and thoroughly developed model (Hambleton, 1974) has undergone continuing revision, and the other models leave a lot of room for local structuring of the program in the classroom. Thus, teachers ostensibly using the same program will act very differently from one another, and teachers in a presumably individualized program may do just as much group-based instruction and no more individualized instruction than other teachers in traditional self-contained classrooms. Many evaluation attempts did not include classroom observation data to verify whether or not the program was being implemented as the designers intended, so it is not always clear what comparisons of "individualized" and "traditional" programs mean.

There do appear to be at least some consistent differences between individualized and traditional classes. Martin and Pavan (1976) reported that more individualized and small-group work took place in schools that called themselves nongraded or individualized than in other schools. Thompson (1973) found that students in PLAN classes spent most of their time working on individual projects, whereas students in traditional classes spent most of their time in whole-class work. On the other hand, Germano and Peterson (1982) found no differences between IGE and non-IGE teachers in their use of individual student characteristics when making instructional recommendations for students, and Shimron (1976) found that slower students were off-task much more often than faster students in IPI classrooms, just as they tend to be in traditional classrooms (in theory, these time-on-task differences should disappear in truly individualized classrooms, because each student would have tasks suited to his or her individual needs and interests).

The key seems to be degree of implementation of the program developers' guidelines. Loucks (1976) found no general differences between IGE schools and other schools in second- and fourth-grade mathematics and reading achievement. However, when she classified schools according to the degree to which they were actually implementing the program as designed, she found that high-implementation schools outperformed comparison schools on three of four achievement measures. Price (1977) reported similar findings. More generally, evaluations of the IGE program (Popkewitz, Tabachnick, & Wehlage, 1982; Romberg, 1985) found that although IGE failed to bring about significant improvements in the outcomes of schooling, the problem was not so much that IGE was tried and found wanting as that IGE was never truly implemented in the majority of schools that presumably adopted the program. Most "IGE schools" never really did individualized instructional planning based on assessment data, and most did not implement multiage grouping or arrange for continuous regrouping of students in response to their current instructional needs. The IGE approach appears to work when well implemented, but good implementation requires a combination of staff competence and commitment to the IGE philosophy that appears to exist in only a minority of elementary schools.

Other individualized programs have had implementation problems similar to those experienced by IGE. It appears that these problems were due mostly to inherent difficulties in individualizing instruction in typical school settings rather than to extreme teacher resistance or similar causes. One problem was that the programs usually required extra staff and supplies that were not typically found in ordinary schools. Another was reliance on individualized materials that stressed isolated low-level skills and required students to learn on their own rather than in groups or with the teacher. As a result, oral reading was sacrificed in favor of worksheet activities concentrating on phonics subskills, creative writing was sacrificed for practice in spelling and punctuation, work with concrete manipulatives in mathematics was sacrificed for computational exercises, and science and social studies virtually disappeared (Kepler & Randall, 1977).

Slavin (1984) suggests that for any kind of instruction to be effective, four conditions must be satisfied: (1) the instruction must be high in quality, (2) the instruction must be appropriate to the students' levels, (3) the students must be motivated to work on the tasks, and (4) the students must have adequate time to learn. Slavin argues that the individualized instructional programs of the 1960s and 1970s failed to work effectively in practice because they concentrated on increasing the appropriateness of instruction but did not address the other three essential conditions. Quality of instruction was reduced because the students were not taught directly by the teacher and were instead required to learn on their own. Students were not adequately motivated because individualized instruction was often boring and seldom offered incentives for moving through the curriculum rapidly. Finally, much classroom time was spent on procedural matters (passing out materials, waiting for the teacher to check work, taking tests), to the point that time for learning was actually reduced in many cases.

Arlin (1982), Carlson (1982), Everhart (1983), and Jones et al. (1985) also provide discussion and examples of the difficulties that teachers had in implementing individualized instructional programs and the ways that what students actually experienced in the classroom fell far short of what the programs' developers had envisioned. Some of these problems are remediable: Developers can supply more and better materials to teachers, can offer a more balanced and integrative curriculum rather than overstress low level isolated skills, and can supply multimedia components that reduce the student's need to learn exclusively through reading. The basic problem, however, seems to be the student-teacher ratio. No individualized program is likely to work effectively if it depends on the teacher to simultaneously provide individualized instruction to all of the students in the class, especially if the teacher is expected to develop curriculum materials for this individualized instruction as well. So, unless they are implemented in very small classes or significant help from aides or other adult resources is available, adaptive education programs will have to rely on other strategies. Two recently developed programs that attempt to do just that are the *Adaptive Learning Environment Model* (ALEM) and *Team-Assisted Individualization* (TAI).

The Adaptive Learning Environments Model (ALEM)

ALEM is intended as a general approach to elementary-level education, and in particular, as a way to accomplish effective mainstreaming of special students into regular classrooms (Wang, 1981; Wang & Birch, 1984). It combines aspects of prescriptive instruction in basic skills with aspects of informal or open education designed to generate independent inquiry and peer cooperation (Wang, Gennari, & Waxman, 1985; Wang & Walberg, 1983). It includes five major components: (1) a basic skills curriculum consisting of highly structured and hierarchically organized learning activities along with a variety of more open-ended exploratory learning activities aimed at accommodating individual students' learning needs and interests; (2) a system for managing curricular materials and the use of teachers' and students' time; (3) a family involvement component designed to increase communication and integrate school and home learning experiences; (4) a flexible grouping and instructional team system designed to increase flexibility in use of teacher and student time, talents, and resources; and (5) a data-based staff development program that provides written plans and procedures to assist school staffs in initiating and monitoring program implementation.

ALEM is complex: It requires aides, computerized record keeping, and other specialized resources and procedures. Given these complexities and the need for frequent planning meetings and for changes in the physical space use and type of equipment included in classrooms, it might have been expected that ALEM would prove just as difficult to implement as most of its predecessors. However, data from over 100 ALEM-sponsored Project Follow-Through classrooms show convincingly that the majority of teachers implemented the ALEM program with very high fidelity to its guidelines.

There appear to be at least three reasons for this successful implementation. First, the program's developers placed great stress on implementation and developed materials and methods designed to accomplish it effectively. Second, rather than relying exclusively on materials-based individualized instruction, the program calls for introduction of new content and skills to be accomplished through whole-class or small-group instruction before students work individually. This results in a higher quality of instruction and a somewhat easier teaching adjustment than switching to a totally individualized program would. Third, ALEM contains program components designed specifically to teach students to work independently with materials and work cooperatively with peers in small groups. The students are taught how to budget their time, select goals and plan methods of attaining them, monitor their understanding as they read and make responses, check their answers for accuracy, and so on. The implementation data also indicate that ALEM classrooms reveal high rates of time on task, high rates of instructional interactions with teachers, and low rates of disruptive behavior (Wang, Gennari, & Waxman, 1985).

ALEM has shown that a complex adaptive education program can be implemented with high fidelity in a broad range of classrooms and that even primary grade students can be taught to assume a great deal of responsibility for managing their own learning. ALEM requires extra resources and extra time devoted to planning, management, and record keeping, however, so that widespread adoption in public schools seems unlikely unless further experience with the program indicates that it offers sizeable advantages over traditional instruction. Early evaluation data on ALEM are promising in that student achievement in ALEM classrooms compares favorably with national norms and with norms projected for students in the Follow-Through Program (Wang, Gennari, & Waxman, 1985), although it remains to be seen whether ALEM will produce significant advantages in student outcomes beyond those produced through traditional methods (Berliner, 1985).

Team-Assisted Individualization (TAI)

A second recently developed innovation that succeeds in avoiding many of the difficulties traditionally associated with individualized instruction programs is *Team-Assisted Individualization* (TAI), developed by Robert Slavin (1985) and his colleagues at the Johns Hopkins University, for mathematics instruction in grades 3 to 6. TAI combines direct instruction (to small, homogeneously formed groups) by the teacher, follow-up practice using programmed curriculum materials, and a student-team learning approach to seatwork management that had been developed in previous work (Slavin, 1983) on cooperative learning (to be described in Chapter 10). In an attempt to avoid the problems commonly associated with individualized programmed instruction in mathematics, TAI was developed with the following criteria in mind (Slavin, 1985): (1) the teacher would be minimally involved in routine management and checking of work; (2) the teacher would spend at least half of the period teaching students in small groups (rather than working with individuals or doing management tasks); (3) program operation would be simple enough for students in grade 3 and up to manage; (4) students would be motivated to proceed rapidly and accurately through the materials, and would not be able to do so by cheating or finding shortcuts; (5) mastery checks would be provided so that students would rarely waste time on material they had already mastered or run into serious difficulties requiring teacher help, and alternative instructional activities and parallel tests would be provided at each mastery checkpoint; (6) students would be able to check one another's work (even when the checker was not as far along in the curriculum as the student being checked); (7) the program would be simple for teachers and students to learn, inexpensive, and flexible, and it would not require aides or team teachers; and (8) by having students work in cooperative, equal-status groups, the program would establish conditions for positive attitudes toward mainstreamed academically handicapped students and among students of different racial or ethnic backgrounds.

After several cycles of development and revision, the TAI program consisted of the following components.

1. *Teams.* Students are assigned to four- or five-member teams consisting of a mix of high, average, and low achievers, boys and girls, and ethnic groups. Students receiving special education resource help for learning problems are distributed evenly among the teams. New team assignments are made every eight weeks.

2. *Placement test.* Students are pretested at the beginning of the course and placed at appropriate points in the individualized program.

3. *Curriculum materials.* During the individualized portion of the TAI process, students work with specially prepared curriculum materials that include: (*a*) an instruction sheet explaining the skill to be mastered and giving a step-by-step method for solving problems; (*b*) several skill sheets containing 20 problems each that introduce a subskill and lead the student toward final mastery of the entire skill; (*c*) formative "checkout" tests consisting of two parallel sets of 10 test items each; (*d*) a final summative test of mastery of the entire skill; and (*e*) answer sheets for the skill sheets, checkouts, and final tests.

4. *Team-study method.* Students work cooperatively in pairs or triads within their teams. Partners first exchange answer sheets and read their own instruction sheets, getting help from teammates if necessary. Then they do the first four problems on their own skill sheets and have the partner check the answers. If all four answers are correct, they go to the next skill. If any are wrong, they do the next four problems. This continues until the student gets a block of four consecutive problems correct (the student is free to ask teammates or the teacher for help if confused). When they get four in a row correct on the final skill sheet, students take Checkout A, a 10-item quiz that resembles the last skill sheet. They work on this test alone without help and then give it to a teammate for scoring. If they get eight or more items correct, the teammate signs the checkout to indicate that the student is certified to take the final test. Then the student takes the signed checkout to a student monitor from a different team to get the appropriate final test, and the monitor scores it on completion (two or three students serve as monitors each day on a rotating basis). If the student fails to get

at least eight items correct on Checkout A, the teacher is called in for diagnosis and reteaching, and the student works again on certain skill sheet items and then takes Checkout B. Remedial instruction and practice continue until the student passes a checkout test and is certified to take the final test.

5. *Team scores and team recognition.* The teacher computes team scores at the end of each week, based on the average number of units covered by each team member, with extra points for perfect or near-perfect papers. Teams that meet high performance criteria are considered Superteams, teams that meet moderate criteria are declared Greatteams, and teams that meet minimal criteria are declared Goodteams. Teams that meet Superteam or Greatteam criteria receive attractive certificates.

6. *Teaching groups.* Each day, the teacher spends half or more of the period teaching 5- to 15-minute lessons to small groups of students who are at about the same point in the curriculum. These lessons prepare students for major concepts in upcoming units and go over any points that the students are having trouble with. Teachers are instructed to emphasize concepts rather than computational procedures in their instruction, because the individualized materials are considered adequate for teaching computational procedures but not concepts.

TAI has achieved positive results in several field tests. The students have proven capable of responsibly handling the checking, self-routing, recording, and monitoring functions built into the program, and they enjoy the team reward system. Most teachers also enjoy the program and find it workable, although training procedures had to be revised to correct an early tendency for the teachers to spend too much time working with individuals and not enough with small groups. The curriculum materials also appear to be effective. Comparisons of TAI with traditional instructional methods or with other special models have yielded higher scores for the TAI groups on every comparison. The differences were significant for five of six comparisons using computation tests and for one of four comparisons using concepts and application tests. Furthermore, TAI programs showed more positive effects on social acceptance and behavior of academically handicapped mainstreamed students and improved attitudes and friendships among black and white students (Slavin, 1983).

On the whole, TAI has produced the most impressive results of all of the adaptive education programs, even though it is easier to implement than most and does not require additional instructional personnel or significant additional resources. Slavin (1985) cautions that the program is difficult to implement in inner-city classrooms containing high concentrations of students with serious reading or behavior problems where neither teachers nor students may be prepared to handle the increased responsibility and autonomy that students assume in TAI. The program is still undergoing development, however, and it is possible that procedures will be worked out for making it more manageable in classes with high concentrations of low achievers.

Computerized Instruction

Another approach to individualized instruction that appears to have the potential for avoiding the problems experienced with learning systems developed in the 1960s and 1970s is computerized instruction, especially now that microcomputers are becoming more available in classrooms. Assuming comparable instructional content, computerized instruction offers several advantages over conventional textbooks and programmed learning materials.

First, it brings novelty or at least variety to the students' school experiences, and thus is likely to be experienced as more enjoyable than conventional seatwork. Second, especially if combined with videodisc technology, it can incorporate animation, time-lapse photography, and other audiovisual techniques for communicating information and demonstrating processes in ways that are not possible through conventional print materials. Third, it can allow students to respond more actively and in more varied ways than they can respond to conventional seatwork and can provide the students with immediate feedback following their responses. Fourth, computers can be programmed to keep track of students' responses to exercises and tests, thus accumulating records for teachers to use in monitoring progress and planning remedial instruction. Fifth, it is possible to build the capacity for diagnosis and prescription into the program itself so that students are automatically routed to skip parts that they do not need and to work through remedial sequences when they have not been able to achieve mastery by working through the regular program. Sixth, programs may provide not only opportunities to practice and get feedback but also tutorial instruction and friendly encouragement similar to what the student might receive from a tutor. Finally, computerized instruction can provide opportunities for higher-level problem solving and simulation activities of the kind seldom seen in conventional seatwork or programmed individualized instruction. To the extent that these potential advantages of computerized instruction can be achieved at reasonable cost, transferring significant instructional functions from the teacher to the computer might be a feasible way of implementing individualized instruction or adaptive education principles in typical school settings (Lipson & Fisher, 1983; Taylor, 1980).

Some progress has been made already. A great variety of educational software has been developed for use with microcomputers. Early language arts instruction is being enhanced through programs such as *Write to Read* and programs designed to teach students to plan, write, and edit stories or poetry (Lawlor, 1982). Early mathematics education is being supplemented with applications of LOGO (Papert, 1980), *Turtle Geometry* (Abelson & deSessa, 1981), and other imaginative forms of computerized instruction (Davis, 1984). Social studies instruction can be enhanced with programs such as *Oregon Trail,* a simulation of a family's journey to the west in a covered wagon in 1847, or *Community Search,* a game in which student teams act as leaders of a primitive agricultural society trying to decide where and how to relocate their community to a more beneficial natural environment. Interesting tutorial programs and simulation activities have been developed for science as well (Arons, 1984). In general, there is wide interest in computerized education, new developments occur daily, and a research and development center has been established (at Harvard University) to generate and synthesize information on technological applications to education.

It remains to be seen whether computerized instruction's theoretical potential can become a practical reality. To date, reviewers interested in computer applications to ordinary classroom settings have identified several important limitations on the computer's present and potential effects (Amarel, 1983; Becker, 1982; Brophy & Hannon, 1985; Educational Products Information Exchange, 1985; Lesgold,

1983; Sloan, 1985). One major problem is availability of appropriate software. The majority of programs available even today are nothing more than electronic versions of traditional workbooks providing drill and practice on low-level skills. Once the novelty of using the computer wears off, a steady diet of these programs is likely to be just as boring as a steady diet of comparable workbook exercises and even less efficient (students with a basic grasp of the concepts and skills involved can move quickly through the workbook pages when they know how to respond and are sure that their answers are correct, but in working through a computerized version of the same exercise, they would have to take time to type in each response and then wait for confirmation before the program would allow them to go on to the next item). Also, most programs are short modules (requiring only an hour or two at most to complete) designed to provide drill and practice on just one or a small set of related skills. They are not systematically sequenced and integrated curricula designed to provide a full semester or year of instruction in a conventionally taught elementary or secondary course. Thus, teachers may have difficulty finding good software, and even when they do, they are likely to be unclear about when or how to use the program because it will not be integrated with the officially adopted curriculum objectives and materials that underlie their instruction. For this reason, most teachers tend to use computerized instruction only for enrichment with faster students or remedial drill and practice with slower students, even if they are not hampered by the problems discussed below.

Limited access to computers creates additional feasibility problems. Cost considerations (including future projections) are such that school systems are unlikely to supply typical classrooms with more than one or two microcomputers (except for classrooms equipped for instruction in computer programming). A great many more computers would be needed to implement programs that called for students to spend significant time at the computer. For example, survey data indicate that even in classrooms containing eight computers, students may spend as much as three-fourths of their time waiting for a turn at the computer (Center for Social Organization of Schools, 1984). This problem can be alleviated somewhat by having students work in small groups with a single microcomputer, although almost all of the software that is presently available was designed for use by individuals and adaptation to use by groups may sometimes be difficult.

A related problem is the trade-off between computer cost and capacity. Many of the most interesting instructional possibilities in computerized instruction require videodisc technology in addition to microcomputers, and programs that make possible the most desirable and sophisticated advances over ordinary programmed instruction (interactive simulation exercises and games; tutorial programs that provide diagnosis and corrective instruction in addition to mere drill and practice with feedback; provision for automatic record keeping and preparation of diagnostic performance summaries) require mainframe computers that are vastly more powerful and expensive than microcomputers.

Thus, at least in the near future, teachers' options for integrating computerized instruction into their classroom will be limited mostly to drill and practice programs and educational games prepared for use by individual students on microcomputers (some of which may be adaptable for use by small groups of students). Computerized instruction is not yet a solution to the practical problems involved in implementing individualized instruction in the typical classroom. On the other hand, it offers worthwhile opportunities for teachers who have access to microcomputers. An evaluation of a computerized drill and practice curriculum tested in the Los Angeles schools (Ragosta, Holland, & Jamison, 1981) found that even though the students often complained of boredom, the program had positive on mathematical computation skills. Findings were mixed for mathematical concepts and were less positive in language and reading than in mathematics.

Tucker (1983) provides useful advice on how schools can systematically prepare to make intelligent decisions about purchasing and using microcomputers. Lathrop (1982) offers guidelines (and a useful bibliography) for evaluating the quality of software. Finally, the Educational Products Information Exchange (1985) provides descriptions and critical reviews of hundreds of software products being sold for use in schools.

Conclusions About Individualized Instruction

It is difficult to generalize about programs for individualized instruction or adaptive education because of their variety and because programs as implemented in practice are often quite different from what the developers had envisioned. Programs that use poor materials, concentrating on repetitive drills on low-level isolated skills, seem clearly inadequate. So do programs that actually reduce instructional time by requiring students to spend a great deal of time handling procedural matters or simply waiting for attention from the teacher.

Programs for individualized instruction and adaptive education can also be criticized for individualizing only in terms of the time alloted for mastery rather than identifying different types of students and teaching styles (Berliner, 1985; Everhart, 1983). This criticism is valid as far as it goes: Although some of the programs reviewed here include nontraditional educational experiences (TAI's team-learning arrangements and various features of computerized instruction, for example), none of them provides guidelines for identifying different types of students, let alone supplies separate materials and guidelines for teaching these types differently.

It is not clear that this degree of individualization is actually needed, however. Research on aptitude-treatment interactions and related research seeking to establish that different types of students require different forms of instruction has not provided much support for the theorizing of individualized instruction and adaptive education advocates. Such research often indicates that slower students need more (of the same kind of) instruction than faster students do, but not that one type of student needs one kind of instruction and other types need different kinds of instruction (Cronbach & Snow, 1977). Nor does research on attempts to match instruction to students' *learning styles* support claims that such matching is necessary or will yield important advantages over traditional forms of instruction (Doyle & Rutherford, 1984). There are also some conceptual and practical problems involved in the notion of matching instruction to students' preferences. Such matching may actually reduce achievement progress even if it succeeds in improving students' attitudes toward their learning (Clark, 1982; Evertson, 1979; Peterson, 1979; Schofield, 1981).

Such complications led Good and Stipek (1983) to conclude that there is no dimension of individual differences that has unambiguous implications for instructional method. It seems most appropriate to use principles of instructional design and pedagogy to develop high-quality instructional materials and methods intended to be effective for all students rather than to set out from the beginning to develop different materials and methods for various students. Still it must be understood that some students will need more instruction or learning time than others, that students having difficulty learning may need to be retaught in a different way rather than merely to have more of the same instruction, and that teachers can include a degree of individualization within this general approach by drawing on their knowledge of their students' individual needs, interests, and learning styles.

Another criticism of individualized instruction is that although it is well suited to drill and practice in basic facts, concepts, and skills, it is not well suited to instruction in higher cognitive processes (problem solving, thinking, creativity) or to developing general dispositional states such as interests, attitudes, or values (Jackson, 1985). This criticism appears to be valid, and it is one reason why we recommend that individualized instruction requiring students to learn from curriculum materials be used in combination with, rather than instead of, whole-class or small-group instruction from the teacher.

Active instruction from the teacher has its own motivational and instructional advantages. It often saves both teachers and students a great deal of time, and teacher presentation underscores the importance of the content and provides the teacher with an opportunity to make it come alive for the students (Lipson, 1974). Also, research on factors associated with student achievement gain suggests that teachers who spend considerable time actively instructing their students get better results than teachers who rely on curriculum materials to carry the content (see Chapter 11). Active instruction from the teacher is especially important for younger students, slower students, and students who come from less-advantaged home backgrounds.

Even older, brighter students who seem to be progressing nicely through individualized learning programs can run into trouble if left on their own too long, however. Often, they do not even realize the problem. Erlwanger (1975) interviewed bright students who were consistently meeting mastery criteria on unit tests from their individualized mathematics curriculum. He found that many of them had misunderstood the material and developed mathematical concepts that were at least partly incorrect, even though they were able to get the correct answers to application exercises and test items. The students had invented their own rules of thumb, which were useful for solving particular problems but would not work (and would leave the students badly confused) later on when they encountered different applications of the concepts they were supposed to be learning.

Such findings illustrate a complaint that many teachers have voiced about individualized programs: Their students "can pass the tests but don't understand the concept." This is likely to happen if mastery criteria are set too low (70–80 percent instead of 90–100 percent) or if students continually retake the same test so that they actually memorize the answers. Even with stiffer mastery criteria and several alternate forms of each test, however, student confusion can go undetected unless teachers monitor progress closely and require students to explain concepts in their own words or show their work in detail (not just supply answers to highly structured questions).

In conclusion, we do not recommend individualized instruction if this means that students will spend most of their time working on their own trying to learn from curriculum materials. However, we do favor individualization when this means an attempt to accommodate individuals' needs within the group context and to achieve an appropriate balance of instructional activities (whole-class instruction, small-group instruction and cooperative learning activities, individual work). Even within the traditional whole-class approach, teachers can individualize to a degree by taking student interests into account in presenting content and making assignments, by asking different kinds of questions or making different kinds of assignments to different students, by allowing for student choice and autonomy when the objectives can be met in different ways, by providing enrichment activities for faster learners and extra instruction in basic skills for slower learners, and by using some of the specialized small group and individualized learning approaches discussed in the present chapter and Chapter 10.

OPEN EDUCATION

In addition to pressures for more individualization of instruction, the 1960s saw pressures to make education more student centered and to "open" it to innovations designed to meet humanistic goals (Barth, 1972; Holt, 1964; Kohl, 1969; Silberman, 1970). Critics portrayed self-contained classrooms with stationary seating as stifling and called for movement toward larger open-spaced facilities designed to be more attractive physically; to allow students more freedom of movement around the room and more variety in learning activities and settings; and to replace solid walls with movable room dividers, bookcases, area rugs, and other more flexible design elements. Prominent psychologists began to characterize students as active learners capable of creating and fulfilling their own learning needs, in contrast to earlier views stressing students' needs for external structure, supervision, and reinforcement. Glowing reports by individuals who had visited British "infant" schools (elementary schools) organized according to these principles provided further impetus for their implementation in the United States (Featherstone, 1967).

Many of these books had glaring titles (*Death at an Early Age, Crisis in the Classroom*) suggesting that American education was in crisis. This was no more true in the 1960s than in the 1980s, when reports such as *A Nation at Risk* refueled concern about public schools (ironically, criticizing many of the practices advocated by 1960s innovators and calling for a return to emphasis on basic skills).

Researchers consistently find that students *do not* describe their teachers or school experiences in negative terms (Good & Grouws, 1975; Jackson, 1968; Price, 1977). Instead, most students describe schools as "okay" places that engender satisfaction if not wild enthusiasm. This is not to argue that all schools are satisfactory, or even that being merely satisfactory is good enough. Clearly, many school situations are boring, irritating, or unlikely to develop students' interests or potential, and there are major problems with some schools (especially inner-city secondary schools).

In any case, then as now, calls for reform tended to exaggerate the sense of crisis in the schools and to advocate practices on the basis of commitment to theory rather than data from carefully conducted field tests. As a result, a great many schools incorporated principles of what became known collectively as "open education." As with individualization, it is difficult to generalize about open education because of the great range of differences among teachers who identify with this label. Consider the following examples.

Two Examples

Setting A   Jane Stoverink teams with Mary Kline, Ted Smith, and two full-time aides in teaching 102 students. The students are mostly fifth and sixth graders, although there are a few fourth graders. They come from middle-class homes and are mostly average or above in academic aptitudes. The teachers share a single large, open-space area, which is the instructional center in which most work goes on. However, groups of 25 to 30 students periodically leave the central area to go off with one teacher to a "regular" (enclosed space) room for 30- to 40- minute mathematics lessons. Students also receive regular work in reading. Each week they are assigned a vocabulary list to master and are encouraged to use the new words in a story due on Friday. They are also quizzed frequently so that the teaching staff can assess their progress in reading speed and comprehension. An hour is allocated each day for free reading. Students can select their own material for this unless they are working with a teacher on an identified deficiency. In any case, the students must complete a one-page report when they finish each book. The rest of the day they are allowed to pursue their own learning goals in the sense that they can budget time in their own way to complete self-selected (but approved) project work. They make out a tentative work plan for each week, choosing from teachers' suggestions and adding their own ideas. Within limits, they can change these schedules from day to day, although the teachers stress the importance of completing the schedules, and most students do.

Setting B   Julie Green, Maryellen Fischer, and Kay Jones also teach in an open-classroom setting. They too are responsible for about 100 mostly middle-class fifth- and sixth-grade students and are assisted by two aides. The students spend a great deal of time in teacher-structured socialization experiences. About two hours each week is spent meeting in groups of 25 to 30 (with one teacher) discussing general problems in the learning area, planning events of mutual interest, etc. Another hour each week is spent in a small-group setting (three or four students) exchanging ideas about how to deal with social problems. To develop school camaraderie and mutual trust, the students also spend an hour or so each day in familylike activities with first and second graders, in which they read to the younger students, help them with their work on projects, and generally take responsibility for them. For most of the rest of the school day, the students pursue their own learning plans. The teachers reinforce student-initiated plans and try to motivate (suggest possible ideas, etc.) the students who have no plans. They give the students general guidelines and suggested project lists, but they do not impose structure through time deadlines or require the students to structure their own work by keeping logs or work schedules. In general, students move through the curriculum haphazardly. They do tend to pick assignments suggested by the teachers, but complete them in a leisurely manner, often in cooperation with two or three friends. Those students who want to work at any particular time often have difficulty doing so because of movement of the other students around them and the high level of noise in the room.

Both of these examples involve teaching teams working with students from more than one grade level in large, well-equipped, open-space areas. Yet, they are quite different. In Setting A, the teachers value subject matter achievement and student work persistence and create an environment where these goals can be fulfilled. In Setting B, the teachers create an environment that emphasizes socialization and affective development. In yet a third "open" setting, we might have found an emphasis on stimulating students to produce creative writings and complex science projects. Clearly, to call a school or teaching unit "open" says little about the instructional activities that take place there.

Open Education: What Is It?

In response to the difficulty of defining open education, Katz (1973) has proposed several continuous dimensions to distinguish open-informal classes from traditional-formal ones. These dimensions appear in Table 9.1. As you look at the table, try to classify the two examples given above (you may want to reread them before examining Table 9.1).

The dimensions suggested by Katz are helpful in thinking about open education, but they do not lead to a single clear definition. For one thing, not all educators accept the framework proposed by Katz. Many would add or delete some of the dimensions included in Table 9.1. Furthermore, how far along the continuum must a school be, and on how many dimensions, for it to be classified as open? Which is more open, a self-contained classroom taught by an individual teacher who employs most of the principles associated with individualization and open education, or a large open-space setting in which three teachers cooperate and specialize (one handles all of the reading and language arts, another all of the mathematics, and a third all of the science and social studies) but stress large-group instruction and generally traditional methods? There are no clear answers to these questions, and in fact it is likely that settings such as both types have been classified as open in some studies but as traditional in others.

Table 9.1 COMPARISON OF OPEN AND TRADITIONAL CLASSROOMS

	Open-informal	Traditional-formal
Space	Flexible, variable	Routinized, fixed
Activities of children	Wide range	Narrow range
Origin of activity	Children's spontaneous interests	Teacher- or school-prescribed
Content or Topics	Wide range	Limited range
Use of time	Flexible, variable	Routinized, fixed
Initiation of teacher-child interaction	Child	Teacher
Teaching target	Individual child	Large or whole group
Child-child interaction	Unrestricted	Restricted

Source: Tim (Katz 1973).

Research on Open Education

Given the ambiguity about what open education means, it is not surprising that research comparing it to traditional education has produced ambiguous results. Ideally, such research should include careful observation resulting in scores classifying each classroom on the dimensions listed in Table 9.1 (and perhaps other dimensions as well). This would be followed by analysis, separately for each dimension, of the relationship between the dimension and various student outcomes. Few such studies have been done, however. Instead, most studies compared classes generally classified as open or informal with classes generally classified as traditional or formal. Classification was often based on teachers' self-reports rather than classroom observations. Even when observations were used, scores from various dimensions were typically combined rather than used to analyze each dimension separately (Marshall, 1981).

Furthermore, most studies were small (often involving only two schools or even two classes) and poorly controlled. For example, the findings of some studies seem more likely to reflect differences in teachers or students that existed prior to the experiment rather than differential effects of open versus traditional education, and the findings of many studies that seem to support open education may represent expectation and novelty effects rather than effects of the educational method itself (the effort and expense involved in switching to open education were often justified by hailing it as a revolutionary innovation and generating enthusiasm for it).

The result of all of this has been a great deal of disagreement, not only among the studies themselves but even among the reviewers of those studies. Some reviewers (Horwitz, 1979; Walberg, Schiller, & Haertel, 1979) have concluded that there are no differences between open and traditional education in effects on student achievement, but that open education improves student attitudes, self-concepts, creativity, curiosity, independence, peer cooperation, and group atmosphere. However, other reviewers have reported no trend at all (Lukasevich & Gray, 1978), minor differences favoring traditional classes on achievement measures but open classes on affective measures (Hayes & Day, 1980; Peterson, 1979), or a significant advantage to traditional classes on affective measures (Rosenshine, 1978). Our impression is that reviews merely tallied findings without considering the quality of the studies are favorable to open education, but reviews confined to the larger and better controlled studies are not. Specifically, we believe that the best evidence from overall comparisons indicates that open education is consistently inferior to traditional education in its effects on student achievement, although it may be somewhat superior to traditional education in its effects on student attitudes and other affective variables.

One study even managed to disagree with itself. Conducted in England, it involved comparing 13 third- and fourth-grade classes that had been classified as informal (open), 12 classified as mixed, and 12 classified as formal (traditional). Teachers were typed originally on the basis of their questionnaire responses, but these were later confirmed by classroom observation. Student data included achievement test scores; samples of written compositions; and measures of student motivation, anxiety, and various personality traits. The findings, reported originally in the widely publicized *Teaching Styles and Pupil Progress* (Bennett et al., 1976), were quite complex, showing different patterns on various outcome measures and for most outcomes, showing different patterns for students who differed in sex or personality type. In general, however, students in formal classrooms showed higher achievement than students in informal classrooms, whereas differences on other (nonachievement) measures were mixed in direction and minor in degree. These findings were widely publicized and caused great consternation among proponents of open education in the United States and especially in England, the home of the British Infant School philosophy. A few years later, however, criticism of the statistical methods used to cluster teachers into types led to a reanalysis of the data using new clusters (Aitkin, Bennett, & Hesketh, 1981). The new analyses yielded only mixed and minor trends, leading the authors to revoke earlier statements that the data favored formal methods and to claim that the data do not allow any general statements about formal versus informal methods.

The largest study on the topic completed to date (Hayes & Day, 1980) involved 96 third-grade classrooms in 18 public schools in North Carolina. Classes were not merely classified as open or traditional. Instead, they were scored for "degree of openness" on the basis of teacher responses to a questionnaire and observer ratings on a scale devised to measure classroom use of open-education principles. These "degree of openness" scores were then correlated with measures of student achievement, self-perceptions, and school attendance. The results were clear: None of these correlations even approached statistical significance. Degree of openness was simply unrelated to student outcome measures, either for the group of 1,648 students as a whole or for subgroups differing in sex, race, or social class.

In one of the best controlled studies on the topic, Fry and Addington (1984) compared students who had begun and continuously attended open classrooms for three years with carefully matched students who had begun and attended traditional classrooms for three years. Comparisons favored the students from the open classrooms on self-esteem and ego-strength inventories and on a self-report measure of social problem-solving skills. Unfortunately, achievement comparisons were not included in this study.

Research on Open-Space Settings

Several studies have made it clear that *open education* (referring to philosophy and teaching methods) must not be confused with *open-space* schools (referring to schools built without stationary internal walls and designed for flexible use of space). Although open education and open-space schools are often thought of as part of the same movement, there is only a small correlation between teachers' working in an open-space school and their using open-education principles (Gump, 1980). Open-space architecture is one dimension of openness that has been assessed separately from the rest. The results are mixed, although they tend toward the negative (Gump, 1980; Weinstein, 1979). Two studies that simultaneously examined both open-space versus traditional architecture and open versus traditional educational methods produced interesting and parallel sets of findings.

The first study was described in several reports by a team of investigators studying the effects of openness on 8- and 11-year-old Canadian students (Corlis & Weiss, 1973; Traub, Weiss, Fisher, & Musella, 1973; Weiss, 1973). Their sample included 30 schools, 18 serving high-socioeconomic status students and 12 serving low-socioeconomic status students. There was no effect of either architectural style or open education on achievement in high-socioeconomic status schools, but open education instructional programs were associated with *lower* achievement in the low-socioeconomic status schools. These data suggested that low-socioeconomic status students needed more structure than they received in the open-education classrooms.

Findings for creativity, curiosity, and student attitudes were mixed. The highest curiosity levels were associated with moderate degrees of openness. Students in traditionally designed schools using traditional instruction and students in open-space schools using open-education principles both had low scores on curiosity measures. Thus, the data did not support the assumption of open educators (Barth, 1982) that students are naturally highly curious and will reveal this curiosity regularly if teachers will only stay out of their way. Corlis and Weiss (1973) suggest that teachers who want to develop student curiosity will have to facilitate that development by (1) providing *fewer* materials but selecting materials carefully, and (2) providing feedback to students as they explore the new materials so that *goals* will emerge.

Lukasevich and Gray (1978) studied third graders who had been enrolled for at least two years in one of four types of schools: open facility with open instructional program, open facility with traditional instructional program, traditional facility with open instructional program, and traditional facility with traditional instructional program. In general, instructional program effects were more noticeable than architectural style effects. Achievement in reading was higher when reading was taught in a conventional style rather than an open style, regardless of classroom architectural design. In mathematics, achievement was highest for students in traditional classrooms taught in the traditional way compared to students in the other three conditions. Thus, the achievement data favored the traditional over the open approach.

Students' self-concepts concerning school subjects were higher in open-space classrooms than in self-contained classrooms, regardless of instructional style (note, however, that these higher self-concepts were not accompanied by higher achievement). Finally, self-concepts concerning convergent mental ability and social virtues were higher among students in self-contained classrooms taught in an open style and students in open-space classrooms taught in a traditional style than they were in the other two conditions.

Taken together, these studies suggest moderation rather than excess on issues of traditional versus open education. Overly regimented instruction may produce good learning gains but at some expense of student attitudes or affective development. At the other extreme, any affective gains that might result from total commitment to open education are likely to be accompanied by disappointing achievement progress.

The latter problem is especially likely when open education methods are used in open-space school settings, because students tend to spend less time on task under these conditions (Beeken & Janzen, 1978; Gump, 1980). Compared to students in traditional settings, students in open-space environments spend less time reading and writing and more time socializing with peers, traveling between locations, and handling housekeeping tasks. They have more teachers per day (because of team teaching in open-space settings) but spend less time under direct teacher supervision. These problems, in combination with the absence of data indicating important advantages for open-space settings and the fact that such settings are typically much more difficult to plan and manage than conventional classrooms, call into question the cost-effectiveness of open-space settings. Such settings can be made to work effectively, even when shared by several teachers and a great many students, but this extra teacher effort is not likely to yeild improved student outcomes. Still, certain teachers, especially those who enjoy working together as a part of a teaching team, do prefer open settings (Weinstein, 1979).

Different types of students also can be expected to react differently to open versus traditional education. Students who perceive and value a sense of internal control over the outcomes of their behavior (especially boys) are likely to prefer open classrooms, but students who prefer more control by the teacher are more satisfied in traditional classrooms (Arlin, 1975). Also, as with individualized instruction, the students most likely to thrive in open educational settings are those with both the ability and the motivation to work independently of direct teacher supervision most of the time. In contrast, open education, especially in open-space settings, presents difficulties for low achievers who need frequent teacher instruction and monitoring (Grapko, 1973), hyperactive students who have difficulty sustaining concentration (Koester & Farley, 1982), and students who lack interest or self-discipline to sustain involvement in academic activities (Solomon & Kendall, 1976).

Conclusions About Open Education

In general, we are more impressed with the potential disadvantages of open education than with its advantages. It can be made to work successfully, even in open-space settings, but only with a great deal of planning, preparation, and sophisticated group management. To the extent that desirable outcomes are achieved, they will not result from some kind of automatic student response to greater freedom or opportunity, but will be developed gradually through planning and systematic teacher behavior. This includes not only achievement but affective outcomes, as Kohler's (1973) study indicates.

Kohler compared the self-concept scores of students in open and traditional classrooms and typically found, great variation within the two groups and little difference between. To try to understand what was producing these differences, he compared what was happening in the two schools (one traditional, one open) where students reported the highest self-concepts with classroom processes in less-effective schools. The clearest difference between the effective schools and the other schools was that the effective schools had clearly defined rules concerning expected and prohibited behavior. In addition, these two schools revealed more mutual respect, acceptance of students, and demands for academic excellence. These factors are essentially the same ones that Coopersmith (1967) reported as characterizing the home environments associated with development of healthy self-concepts (structure, but with freedom to improvise within the defined limits, and with noncontingent acceptance of the child). We suspect that authenticity and respect for students are present in most school programs that call themselves open, but that academic and behavioral structure and high performance expectations are missing in many. Students need structure and limits if they are to learn to evaluate their performance objectively and to appreciate that both increased freedom and increased responsibility result from their ability to handle the self-supervision demands that accompany the autonomy granted them in open-education programs.

It seems clear that some degree of teacher structure is needed to promote both achievement gains and personal growth. The degree of structure needed will vary with the goals being pursued (subject matter achievement, for example, demands more structure than most goals) and with the ages and backgrounds of the students.

INDEPENDENT WORK AND LEARNING CENTERS

The open education movement was a classic example of the common pattern revealed in Cuban's (1984) historical analysis of trends in American education. That is, it was ushered in on a tremendous wave of enthusiasm created by committed advocates during the 1960s, was implemented (primarily at the elementary grades) in a great many schools in the late 1960s and the 1970s, lost popularity as its weaknesses became apparent, and virtually disappeared by the 1980s. However, it left legacies that have become assimilated into mainstream traditional schooling. These include more flexible furnishings and use of space in classrooms, more diversity in the kinds of activities included in curricula, more activities calling for students to work together in pairs or small groups, and establishment of learning centers where students can go to work independently or in cooperation with peers on various learning projects. We close this chapter with suggestions about how teachers can use well-chosen independent-work activities and learning-center activities to enrich instruction and adapt to individual differences.

One way for teachers to create time for working with small groups and individuals is to structure time for students to engage in interesting, creative tasks of their own choosing. Some students, especially bright high achievers, finish their work quickly. Often these students are indirectly punished (given more of the same work to do, etc.) for their rapid work. Instead, teachers should allow these students to engage in enrichment activities.

Biehler (1971) suggests a particularly good idea for older elementary students: an open-ended, personal yearbook in which the students write stories and illustrate or embellish them whenever they finish their assignments. What the students choose to put in these yearbooks is left completely up to them. Other possibilities include allowing students to read and review books on some aspect of a curriculum topic (e.g., American Indians) or to act as a resource specialist or tutor to other students. However, book reports, if overly structured, may do little to encourage reading for enjoyment and interest. Often it is useful for the teacher and the student to discuss the book, including not only the plot but also why the student liked or disliked it. Occasionally, teachers should carefully structure long periods of independent work for all students (not just those who finish quickly) and thereby create time for remediation, enrichment, and informal conversations with individuals.

The classroom can be arranged to facilitate independent study. Figure 9.1 shows how one teacher arranged her first-grade classroom. This diagram was made as the teacher instructed a reading group. Note how the room arrangement allows for both group work and independent activities. Six students are in the reading group with the teacher, and two are reading at the independent-reading table. The reading center, separated by bookcases from the rest of the room, provides a place where students can read their favorite books in comfortable privacy when they finish their work. The teacher may, at times, choose to use the reading center for independent but structured learning activity. For example, students may be asked to write reports on chosen or assigned books.

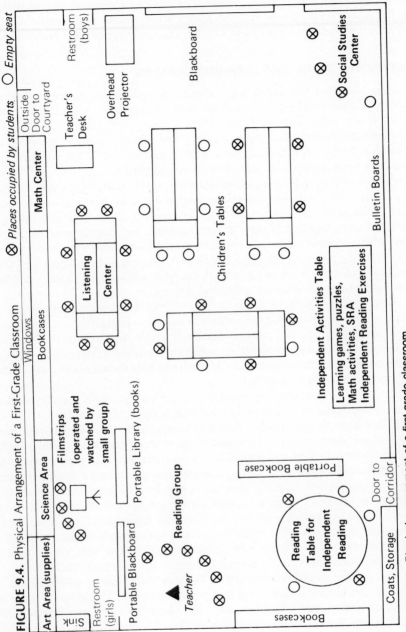

FIGURE 9.4. Physical Arrangement of a First-Grade Classroom

⊗ *Places occupied by students*   ○ *Empty seat*

Art Area (supplies) | Science Area | Windows | Bookcases | Math Center

Restroom (girls)
Sink

Portable Blackboard

Filmstrips (operated and watched by small group)

Portable Library (books)

Reading Group

Teacher

Listening Center

Children's Tables

Teacher's Desk

Overhead Projector

Blackboard

Restroom (boys)

Outside Door to Courtyard

Portable Bookcase

Reading Table for Independent Reading

Bookcases

Door to Corridor

Coats, Storage

Independent Activities Table

Learning games, puzzles, Math activities, SRA Independent Reading Exercises

Bulletin Boards

⊗ Social Studies Center

Figure 9.1 Physical arrangement of a first-grade classroom.

Eight students are working at the listening center, which is a tape recorder with eight earphones that can be wheeled from table to table. One student has passed out pencils and accompanying exercise sheets, while another is in charge of turning the tape recorder on and off. All students have been taught how to operate the recorder, and student helpers are assigned and rotated on a regular basis. Similarly, four students are viewing filmstrips without direct teacher supervision. The student in charge today runs the machine and calls on students in turn to read the story that accompanies the pictures. When the students finish watching the filmstrip and complete written exercises, they move to another activity at their seats.

When the arrangement shown in Figure 9.1 was recorded, nine students were working independently at their seats, and three were at the social studies center. Two of the latter were "buddy reading" stories about the social studies unit that had been printed by their fellow classmates while the third was painting a picture of a recent social studies field trip for the class mural. When he finished painting he crossed off his name on the social studies blackboard, and another student began painting a picture. When the teacher terminated the reading group, all students rotated to a new activity.

There are countless ways in which a classroom can be organized. Dollar (1972) suggests a room arrangement similar to the one depicted in Figure 9.2. Here, the traditional rectangular seating arrangement has been eliminated, allowing the room to be filled with several potentially exciting learning centers. A teacher who desired to do so could program most of a student's day around learning-center activities. Here is one student's schedule for an entire day. Although there would be a few other students with the same schedule, there would be many different schedules within the room. For example, another student might begin his day reading with the teacher in a reading group and end it at the listening post.

Johnny's schedule	
8:30–9:15	Math corner
9:15–9:30	Math with his group
9:30–10:00	Reading with his group
10:00–10:15	Morning recess
10:15–10:30	Social studies with entire class
10:30–11:15	Social studies in small project group
11:15–11:45	Lunch
11:45–12:15	Story center
12:15–1:00	Free selection
1:00–1:30	Math instruction with entire class
1:30–2:00	Art center
2:00–2:15	Recess
2:15–2:30	Listening post
2:30–3:00	Reading instruction—independent work at the study area

Such scheduling allows students to work at different learning centers or in different project groups; the teacher then has free time for instruction of small groups or remedial work with individuals. Although many teachers may prefer not to use centers this heavily, such centers do provide excellent independent study areas and add flexibility by increasing the variety of assignments available.

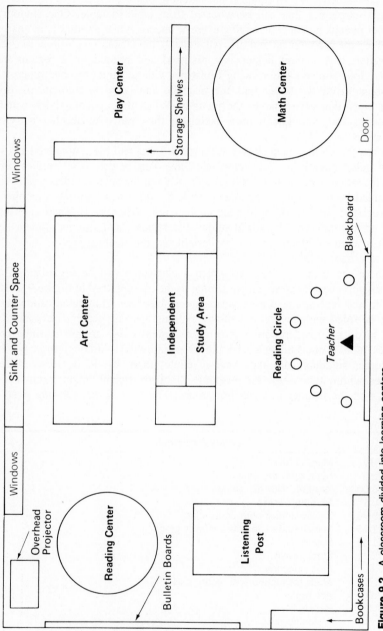

Figure 9.2 A classroom divided into learning centers.

In some classrooms, it may not be possible to set up five or six different learning centers at one time. Physical limitations (e.g., chairs bolted to the floor) may allow room for only one or two. In such cases, teachers may provide variety by setting up science and exploratory centers for a few weeks, then creative writing and mystery reading centers, and then art and historical centers. The possibilities are limited only by the teacher's imagination.

Students need to learn how to use learning centers. Like all classroom assignments, tasks at learning centers need to be clearly specified if students are expected to work on their own with minimal teacher guidance. Rules for using equipment and handing in assignments must be established. Such rules, and the activities that take place in learning centers, will vary with the ages and aptitudes of students. However, the following material from Dollar (1972) illustrates typical rules and guidelines for academic assignments.

SOCIAL STUDIES
1. Choose a card and find the book to go with it.
2. Read the book or pages listed on the card and then answer the questions on your own paper.
3. Put your papers in the yellow basket and write your name on the back of the card.
4. Answer the questions at your own desk or in the social studies corner.

READING CENTER
1. Pick a book from the shelf with a card in it.
2. Read the book.
3. Answer the questions on the card at your desk.
4. On a piece of paper put the title of the book and the number of the card. Number the questions as you answer them on your paper.
5. When you have finished, put your name on the back of the card and check your name on the chart.

PLAY CENTER
1. Only one person may hammer or saw at a time.
2. You may only use the hammer or saw between 8:00 and 8:30.
3. Leave the erector set, hammer, saw, nails, or boards in the center.
4. Clean up when you have finished.

MATH CORNER
1. There should be only three people playing math games at one time.
2. You may:
   a. play a game quietly
   b. work problems on the blackboard
   c. use the flannel board
   d. pick out what you like and return to your desk to work on it.
3. To use the math cards in the box you must:
   a. pick out any card you want
   b. work the problems on your own paper at your desk
   c. when you finish put your paper in the basket and sign the card on the back.

LISTENING POST
1. Sit down at the table—no more than seven people at a time.
2. Pick a record to listen to. Only one person should work the record player.
3. Put on the headphones.
4. Turn on the record player and listen to a story.[1]

It may be useful to have rules posted at each learning center to help the students to function quasi-independently of the teacher. Teachers can use learning centers to expose students to a variety of interesting educational tasks. Young students, for example, might be asked to do independent work by listening to a story and then responding to questions about it. The questions can be simple, "How many bears were there in the story?" or complex, "Listen to the story and then write your own ending." Teachers are free to use their own imaginations and to create material when setting up learning centers. Although companies make filmstrips, tapes, and other materials that can be used for independent work, some of the best assignments will come from spontaneous events that occur in the classroom.

For example, one day during a seventh-grade English class, the principal makes one of his frequent PA announcements. At the end of it, Joe Jordan says, loudly enough to be heard by half the class including the teacher, "Wouldn't it be great if just one day he kept his mouth shut?" After the snickering dies down, Miss Thornton's appeal to logic, "But what would happen if he made no announcements?" leads the class to conclude that nothing significant would be lost if the principal never spoke over the PA again, because teachers could make announcements. She then decides to give the following assignment for independent work. "Assume there was no television, radio, or newspaper communication for two weeks. Write a theme on one of the following topics: (1) how your life would be affected; (2) how attendance at sport events would be affected; (3) how someone wanting to buy a house would be affected; (4) how supermarkets could advertise their specials; or (5) think of your own topic and have me approve it."

Let us look at a few assignments that teachers can use in classrooms.

Some Examples

The listening post is a popular learning place in first- and second-grade classrooms. It is a table equipped with a stack of answer sheets, a can of pencils, six to eight earphones, a tape recorder, and taped stories. The stories are taken from supplementary information in the teacher's editions of textbooks, Science Research Associates' commercially produced products, or the *Weekly Reader,* or are recorded by the teacher based on special interests or incidents that have emerged in the classroom.

To avoid confusion, one student is designated as leader. After the others sit down and put on the earphones, the leader starts the tape recorder, stops it at the signal given on the tape, passes out paper and pencils for the questions, starts the tape recorder again, stops it at the end, collects the paper and pencils, rewinds the tape, and sees that the table is ready for use by the next group. To make the

---

[1]From Barry Dollar, *Humanizing classroom discipline* (New York: Harper & Row, 1972). Copyright 1972 by Barry Dollar. By permission of the publishers.

learning activity more autonomous and to provide students with quicker feedback, teachers can put the correct answers at the end of the tape. After a few drills on procedure, even first graders will be able to function independently at the listening post.

In addition to tapes and filmstrips, learning centers can be equipped with a greater variety of photocopied learning sheets. The complexity of the tasks, of course, will vary with the ages and aptitudes of the learners. For example, in the math corner on April Fool's Day, a second-grade teacher might give the students the sheet in Figure 9.3 and ask them to circle all errors that appear in the calendar (or the students could be asked to make their own calendars and see if their classmates can find the errors they included).

Many teachers have found special-feature learning centers to be useful. For example, the teacher may write an introduction to a mystery story (3 to 15 pages, the length varying with reader age and aptitude). Younger students are requested to tape record their own endings to the story, while older ones may be requested to write their own endings and compare them to those of others. At other times in the special-feature corner, the teacher may have students respond to interesting questions: "On one page respond to this question: How would you spend a million dollars? Think! Tell *why,* as well as *what* you would buy." "Relate in 200 words or less how you would feel if you (dropped, caught) the winning pass in a championship football game." "Assume that you woke up today in the year 2025. Describe what you will actually be doing in the year 2025. How old will you be then? What

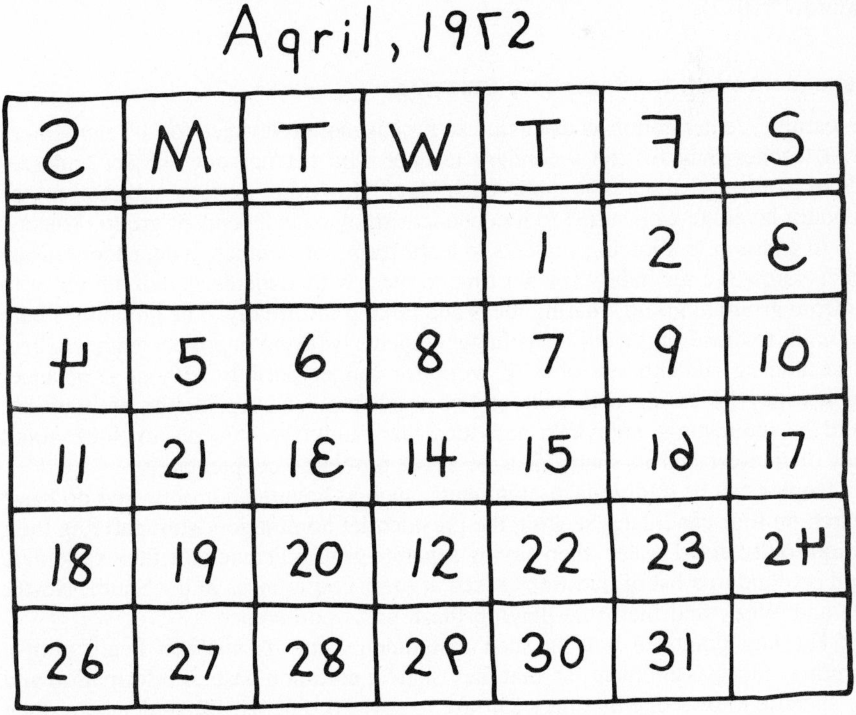

Figure 9.3 An independent work sheet.

job do you expect to hold?" The ideas presented here are only a few of the many activities that teachers can use in learning centers. The really good activities will probably be exercises you prepare especially for a class or a smaller group based on special interests you have observed.

Teachers at the same grade level can share ideas for independent learning centers. In fact, one teacher could put together several weeks of math work while another makes multiple copies of listening tapes and assignment sheets and a third works on language arts units. Such sharing enables teachers to produce high-quality units in less time, and once created, the units can be used year after year with only minor modifications (most modifications involve the addition of new units based on the spontaneous interests of students).

Similarly, a good project for preservice teachers in a college course would be to form work teams (e.g., math, social studies, reading, or science), with each group preparing from five to ten projects. In this way, students would have the chance to swap ideas and to learn how to implement the learning-center concept by actually planning sequential units and writing them into operational form. In addition, students could keep copies of all class materials and thus would be able to begin teaching with a number of ideas they could use in their own classroom learning centers.

For more suggestions about learning centers in elementary classrooms, including the design of accountability and evaluation systems and the use of individualized contracting approaches in connection with learning centers, see McCarthy (1977).

Independent Work for Secondary Students

The learning-center notion as discussed so far has more relevance for the elementary school teacher than for the secondary teacher who teaches one subject and sees students for only about one hour each day. However, certain subjects at the secondary level are well suited to independent study or independent group projects.

In addition to allowing students to learn from one another, independent group projects allow the secondary teacher time to meet with students as individuals or to pass from group to group, sharing ideas and talking informally. The guidelines here are similar to those suggested for younger students working in project teams, except that secondary students are able to work for longer periods without assistance. Students may be assigned to one- or two-week projects. Again, the assignments should be interesting, enjoyable activities that allow the students to think about topics of interest and to share ideas or solve problems cooperatively.

Topics can be traditional assignments, such as having all groups first do basic research on four candidates seeking the presidential nomination, summarizing their positions on selected issues, then having separate groups decide how their candidate would respond to a list of questions asked at press conferences in the South, North, East, and West, and then role-playing these press conferences.

The key points to note in such assignments are (1) students begin with a common reading assignment, so that they share a common base of information and have specific knowledge that they can use to solve problems, (2) students are then required to summarize their information and apply it to a particular situation (typically, they are given a choice regarding which specialty group they want to work in), and (3) they share information with other groups by presenting the views of their candidate in a general classroom discussion, where (4) they have the opportunity to receive evaluative feedback (correcting factual errors or contradictions in their position) from the teacher and fellow students.

Most students enjoy the opportunity to work independently to gather facts on a concrete problem and use the information in simulated situations. Again, organization is the key. Teachers need to structure the learning task, identify the pertinent resources, and let the students know how they will be held accountable. Of course, teachers need not structure all assignments. After students have been through the process, the teacher can solicit and use their ideas in creating new tasks. The important elements of group work are that the assignment has a clear focus (whether teacher defined or group defined), that each student is held accountable for at least part of the discussion, and that group tasks are enjoyable.

Topics need not always be traditional, content-centered assignments. Attitudes and awareness may be stimulated by combining factual knowledge with student impressions and values. For example, the above exercise involves mostly describing and reciting what political journalists have written. Other assignments might begin with content and end with expression of feelings. For example, tenth-graders in a world history class might be divided into four independent groups. Each group would be presented with summary descriptions of desirable physical and personality characteristics of women in four different countries in the 1850s. One group might then be asked to speculate about the cultural factors that led to these notions. Another might be asked to respond to such questions as: "What were the roles of women in each of these countries and to what extent were women satisfied with these roles?"

Later, group discussion could center on the frustrations that led to women's rights movements in the United States and on why some countries allowed women to assume more responsibility than others. When and under what circumstances did women become activists? How did men respond to the emerging independence of women? What is male chauvinism? Can a woman become President? What is the woman's role in contemporary American life?

Teachers who prefer not to devote much time to independent group work can still use brief assignments. Those who lecture daily or involve the entire class in daily discussion will be surprised at how effectively group assignments can enhance such a discussion. The basic procedure is as follows: (1) The previous night, the class is assigned certain pages to read. (2) At the beginning of the period, the class is broken into five small groups, each with two or three different questions to answer. (3) Each group is allowed 10 to 15 minutes to discuss their answers, look up information, and so forth. (4) The class is brought back together and the teacher calls on an individual to answer one of his or her group's questions. The teacher then encourages students from *other groups* to react to the adequacy of the answer and allows students who were in the original group to embellish the answer, defend it with logical argument, and so on.

If the teacher regularly assigns students to different groups, several good things occur. First, the students will interact regularly with many of their peers, and in discussing interesting questions about course material, will have the chance to learn from one another. Students in small groups also have more chance to talk than they do in large groups, and shy students are likely to feel more comfortable in expressing ideas in safer surroundings (when these students learn that they can express themselves and that others are interested in what they have to say, they will be more able to speak freely in front of the whole class). Students will be task oriented in these sessions when they know that any one of them may be called on to answer any one of the group's questions and that the teacher or a student in another group may ask for a clearer answer or more information. Perhaps most importantly, this procedure mobilizes students' attention, forces them to focus their thinking on relevant questions, and promotes learning. Finally, after listening and practicing their own responses, students will be interested in sharing their ideas and getting feedback from others. If the teacher models interest in the students' answers and responds to their comments constructively, the students will learn that the teacher is genuinely interested in their learning, not just quizzing them about the reading assignment.

SUMMARY

Given financial constraints that require schools to assign 20 to 40 students to each teacher, the traditional whole-class instruction/recitation/seatwork method may be the best available compromise allowing teachers to meet the most needs of the most students possible. The method is clearly a compromise with important weaknesses, however, so that each educational era spawns reformers touting innovations designed to introduce greater individualization and variety into schooling. The present chapter reviewed three such innovations popularized in the last 20 years: mastery learning, individualized instruction/adaptive education, and open education.

Mastery learning reverses the usual procedure by fixing mastery levels and allowing for individual differences in time needed to learn. Mastery procedures (especially the teach-test-reteach-retest cycle) are designed to accomplish two goals: (1) by accommodating individual differences in time needed to learn, make it possible for 80 percent of the students to attain mastery levels typically attained by only the top 20 percent of students under traditional methods; and (2) reduce individual differences in student achievement (mastery) levels by providing slower students with a solid foundation in lower-level skills that will enable them to learn higher-level skills more rapidly and thus to begin to catch up with their faster-learning peers. Research indicates that mastery programs do increase student achievement, but only by allowing extra time for a given unit of instruction. Thus, it appears inappropriate to adopt reduction in individual differences in achievement rates as an instructional goal, because this can be accomplished only by holding back higher achievers. On the other hand, mastery procedures do appear to have important instructional and motivational benefits for low achievers, and teachers may want to implement them to some degree, particularly when instructing students in content or skills considered basic to future success in school or in life generally.

Individualized instruction/adaptive education approaches are based on the philosophy that schooling should be adapted to individual differences in a variety of ways, not just in time allotted to master a fixed set of objectives. Thus, in theory at least, these approaches imply that varied objectives should be adopted for different students and that different methods and materials should be developed to make it possible to teach any particular objective in a variety of ways that accommodate different needs and interests. This sounds good in theory, but in practice, unless aides or other adults were available, it has meant heavy reliance on programmed instruction modules and related forms of continuous-progress independent seatwork. Consequently, teachers have found individualized instructional programs to be overly complex to install and manage, and the net result frequently has been reduced time on task and a lower quality of instruction than are found under typical traditional conditions.

Individually Guided Education (IGE) strategies call for a great deal of coordination and cooperation among teachers to plan a reasonable and responsive curriculum for students. When these tasks are accomplished well, the program can have positive effects. Unfortunately, these important elements of planning and coordination usually are not done sufficiently well to allow for truly effective individualized programs to be created.

More recently, adaptive education programs such as ALEM and TAI have achieved more impressive results by combining active instruction from the teacher with independent work on individualized materials and by making sure that both teachers and students were sufficiently trained to implement the program's guidelines appropriately. TAI has been especially impressive because it can be implemented after only relatively brief training and it does not require aides or team teaching. Computerized instruction may turn out to be another form of adaptive education that proves feasible under normal classroom conditions, although it is too early yet to tell. On the whole, individualized instruction/adaptive education as implemented in classrooms has fallen considerably short of the dreams of its advocates, but teachers should consider at least some adaptation of traditional instruction to accommodate individual differences, especially in allowing for drill and practice in basic knowledge and skills.

The open-education movement called for more flexibility in designing and equipping instructional settings and learning centers, more accommodation to students' interests, more opportunities for them to manage their own learning, and more choice and variety in school activities. Two separate aspects of the movement were open-space architecture and the open-education philosophy. Evaluations comparing open-space architecture with more traditional self-contained classrooms failed to support the claims of open-space architecture advocates. Comparisons of classes taught using the open-education philosophy with classes taught more traditionally have produced mixed results. In general, it appears that traditional instruction produces somewhat better *achievement* outcomes and open education produces somewhat better *affective* outcomes, but the differences within each of these two approaches tend to be much larger than average differences between them. The open-education movement has largely been supplanted by the back-to-basics movement of the 1980s, but its legacy can be seen in more flexible furnishings and use of space, the greater variety of independent activities, and the frequent presence of learning centers in today's classrooms. Learning centers and creatively designed independent work activities are ways for teachers to build more variety and enrichment into their instructional programs.

SUGGESTED ACTIVITIES AND QUESTIONS

9.1. Visit local schools or classes that purport to implement mastery learning, individualized/adaptive education, or open education. How do these settings compare with one another and with traditional classrooms in teacher roles and responsibilities, opportunities and constraints? What is expected of the students, and how do they appear to respond to these expectations? What are the trade-offs involved in these four methods? Which method (or combination of methods) do you prefer, and why?

9.2. Arrange to observe in at least one of these settings on at least five different days. Note the number and kinds of choices provided, student reaction to these choices, and the extent to which the students can handle the assignments without undue dependence on the teacher. Do the assignments seem more appropriate or interesting for some students than for others? If so, which students, and why?

9.3. Consider your own expectations as a college student. How much structure do you want, and how much freedom, in deciding what courses to take (given your goals)? Talk to others to get their views, and then design a system to manage college courses that will satisfy all students' needs. Is it possible to do so?

9.4. Often, pressure on schools to change comes from public sources (such as information that achievement scores are declining) and from parents. Seldom do changes stem from careful analyses of students' options. Should students, as consumers, be given more of a say about day-to-day school procedures and routines? Why or why not?

9.5. Think back to your high school experience. What was wrong with it? What changes should have been made? What was available and enjoyable? Would the changes that you suggest affect the aspects of schooling that you found worthwhile?

9.6. State in your own words the trade-offs involved in adopting a mastery learning approach. What is your solution to the dilemmas posed by students' individual differences in aptitudes? Can you describe and justify the trade-offs built into your solution?

9.7. Does your proposed solution involve at least some use of mastery learning procedures? If so, specify which ones and how you would implement them.

9.8. Why is it so important, whether or not you use the particular procedures associated with the mastery learning approach, to teach basic skills to the point of mastery or overlearning?

9.9. Too often the (good) idea of *individualized instruction* becomes operationalized as *independent seatwork assignments*. Is there a necessary connection here? How else might individualization be accomplished or at least approached?

9.10. Which classes (in terms of grade level and subject matter) are most amenable to individualized instruction? Why?

9.11. Both individualized and open education minimize the time that students spend getting direct instruction from the teacher and call for students to assume more responsibility for managing their own learning. Yet the authors claim that it is harder for teachers to succeed with these approaches than it is to create a successful traditional program. Why is this?

9.12. How are you likely to react to teaching in self-contained versus open-space settings? Observe and talk to teachers who work in these settings and learn about the trade-offs involved. If you were assigned to a setting that differed from the one you prefer, how could you rearrange the setting to make it more acceptable?

9.13. Describe two or three learning centers that were not already discussed in the chapter, and indicate the materials and activities that you would include in them.

9.14. With peers who share interest in teaching the same subject, prepare actual instructional material for use in learning centers.

9.15. Outline a plan (use your own ideas as well as those presented in the book) that will allow students to spend parts of each day at learning centers. Specify the room arrangement that will be required, the nature and location of learning centers, and typical schedules for groups or individual students.

REFERENCES

Abelson, H., & diSessa, A. A. (1981). *Turtle Geometry: The computer as a medium for exploring mathematics*. Cambridge, MA: MIT Press.

Aitkin, M., Bennett, S., & Hesketh, J. (1981). Teaching styles and pupil progress: A reanalysis. *British Journal of Educational Psychology, 51*, 170–186.

Amarel, M. (1983). Classrooms and computers as instructional settings. *Theory Into Practice, 22*, 260–266.

Anderson, L. W. (1985). A retrospective and prospective view of Bloom's "Learning for mastery." In M. C. Wang & H. J. Walberg (Eds.), *Adapting instruction to individual differences*. Berkeley, CA: McCutchan.

Anderson, L. W., & Block, J. (1983). The mastery learning model of teaching and learning. In T. Husen & T. Postlethwaite (Eds.), *International encyclopedia of education: Research and studies*. Oxford: Pergamon.

Arlin, M. N. (1984a). Time, equality, and mastery learning. *Review of Educational Research, 54*, 65–86.

Arlin, M. N. (1984b). Time variability in mastery learning. *American Educational Research Journal, 21*, 103–120.

Arlin, M. N. (1982). Teacher responses to student time differences in mastery learning. *American Journal of Education, 90*, 334–352.

Arlin, M. (1975). The interaction of locus of control, classroom structure, and pupil satisfaction. *Psychology in the Schools, 12*, 279–286.

Arlin, M. N., & Webster, J. (1983). Time costs of mastery learning. *Journal of Educational Psychology, 75*, 187–195.

Arons, A. (1984). Computer-based instructional dialogs in science courses. *Science, 224*, 1051–1056.

Barth, R. S. (1972). *Open education and the American school*. New York: Agathon Press.

Bangert, R. L., Kulik, J. A., & Kulik, C. C. (1983). Individualized systems of instruction in secondary schools. *Review of Educational Research, 53*, 143–158.

Becker, H. (1982). Microcomputers: Dreams and realities. *Curriculum Review, 21*, 381–385.

Beeken, D., & Janzen, H. (1978). Behavioral mapping of student activity in open-area and traditional schools. *American Educational Research Journal, 15*, 507–517.

Bennett, N., with Jordan, J., Long, G., & Wade, B. (1976). *Teaching styles and pupil progress*. Cambridge, MA: Harvard University Press.

Berliner, D. C. (1985). How is adaptive education like water in Arizona? In M. C. Wang & H. J. Walberg (Eds.), *Adapting instruction to individual differences*. Berkeley, CA: McCutchan.

Biehler, R. (1971). *Psychology applied to teaching*. Boston: Houghton-Mifflin.

Block, J. (Ed.). (1974). *Schools, society, and mastery learning*. New York: Holt, Rinehart and Winston.

Block, J., & Anderson, L. (1975). *Mastery learning in classroom instruction*. New York: Macmillan.

Block, J., & Burns, R. (1976). Mastery learning. In L. Shulman (Ed.), *Review of research in education* (Vol. 4). Itasca, IL: Peacock.

Bloom, B. (1984). The search for methods of group instruction as effective as one-to-one tutoring. *Educational Leadership, 41*(8), 4–17.

Bloom, B. (1980). *All our children learning*. Hightstown, NJ: McGraw-Hill.

Bloom, B. (1976). *Human characteristics and school learning*. New York: McGraw-Hill.

Bloom, B. (1968). Learning for mastery. (UCLA-CSEIP) *Evaluation Comment, 1* (2), 1–12.

Board of Education of the City of Chicago. (1982). *Chicago Mastery Learning Reading, Implementation Model*. Watertown, MA: Mastery Education Corporation.

Born, D., Davis, M., Whelan, D., & Jackson, D. (1972). College student study behavior in a personalized instruction course and a lecture course. Paper presented at the annual Kansas Conference on Behavior Analysis in Education, Lawrence, KS.

Brophy, J., & Hannon, P. (1985). The future of microcomputers in the classroom. *Journal of Mathematical Behavior, 4,* 47–67.

Buss, A. R. (1976). The myth of vanishing individual differences in Bloom's mastery learning. *Instructional Psychology, 3,* 4–14.

Carlson, D. (1982). "Updating" individualism and the work ethic: Corporate logic in the classroom. *Curriculum Inquiry. 12,* 125–160.

Carroll, J. (1963). A model of school learning. *Teachers College Record, 64,* 722–733.

Center for Social Organization of Schools. (1984). *School uses of microcomputers: Reports from a national survey.* (Issue No. 6, November). Baltimore: The Johns Hopkins University.

Clark, R. (1982). Antagonism between achievement and enjoyment in ATI studies. *Educational Psychologist. 17,* 92–101.

Coopersmith, S. (1967). *The antecedents of self-esteem.* San Francisco: Freeman.

Corlis, C., & Weiss, J. (1973). Curiosity and openness: Empirical testing of a basic assumption. Paper presented at the annual meeting of the American Educational Research Association, New Orleans.

Cox, W. F., & Dunn, T. G. (1979). Mastery learning: A psychological trap? *Educational Psychologist, 14,* 24–29.

Cronbach, L. J., & Snow, R. E. (1977). *Aptitudes and instructional methods.* New York: Irvington.

Cuban, L. (1984). *How teachers taught: Constancy and change in American classrooms, 1890–1980.* New York: Longman.

Davis, R. (1984). *Learning mathematics: A cognitive science approach to mathematics education.* London: Croom Helm.

Dollar, B. (1972). *Humanizing classroom discipline.* New York: Harper & Row.

Doyle, W., & Rutherford, B. (1984). Classroom research on matching learning and teaching styles. *Theory Into Practice, 23,* 20–25.

Educational Products Information Exchange (EPIE Institute). (1985). *The educational software selector (TESS).* New York: Teachers College Press.

Educational Products Information Exchange. (1974). *Evaluating instructional systems: PLAN, IGE, IPI.* (Product Report No. 58). New York: EPIE Institute.

Erlwanger, S. (1975). Case studies of children's conceptions of mathematics (Pt. I). *Journal of Children's Mathematical Behavior, 1,* 157–283.

Everhart, R. B. (1983). *Reading, writing, and resistance: Adolescence and labor in a junior high school.* Boston: Routledge and Kegan Paul.

Evertson, C. (1979). *Teacher behavior, student achievement, and student attitudes: Descriptions of selected classrooms.* Austin: Research and Development Center for Teacher Education, University of Texas.

Featherstone, J. (1967). *The primary school revolution in Great Britain.* New York: Pitman.

Flanagan, J., Shanner, W., Brudner, H., & Marker, R. (1973). An individualized instructional system: PLAN. In H. Talmage (Ed.), *Systems of individualized education.* Berkeley, CA: McCutchan.

Fry, P. S., & Addington, J. (1984). Comparison of social problem solving of children from open and traditional classrooms: A two-year longitudinal study. *Journal of Educational Psychology, 76,* 318–329.

Gagné, R., & Briggs, L. (1979). *Principles of instructional design* (2nd ed.). New York: Holt, Rinehart and Winston.

Germano, M. C., & Peterson, P. L. (1982). IGE and non-IGE teachers' use of student characteristics in making instructional decisions. *Elementary School Journal, 82,* 319–328.

Glaser, R. (1977). *Adaptive education: Individual diversity and learning*. New York: Holt, Rinehart and Winston.

Glaser, R., & Rosner, J. (1975). Adaptive environments for learning: Curriculum aspects. In H. Talmage (Ed.), *Systems of individualized education*. Berkeley, CA: McCutchan.

Good, T., & Grouws, D. (1975). *Process-product relationships in fourth-grade mathematics classrooms*. (Final Report.). Columbia: Center for the Study of Social Behavior, University of Missouri.

Good, T., & Stipek, D. (1983). Individual differences in the classroom: A psychological perspective. In G. Fenstermacher & J. Goodlad (Eds.), *Individual differences and the common curriculum. (Eighty-second yearbook of the National Society for the Study of Education, Part I.)* Chicago: University of Chicago Press.

Goodlad, J. (1984). *A place called school*. New York: McGraw-Hill.

Grapko, M. (1973). A comparison of open space concept classroom structures according to dependence/independence measures in children, teachers' awareness of children's personality variables, and children's academic progress. Paper presented at the annual meeting of the Ontario Education Research Council, Toronto.

Greeno, J. G. (1978). Review of Bloom's *Human characteristics and school learning. Journal of Educational Measurement, 15,* 67–76.

Grinder, R., & Nelsen, E. A. (1985). Individualized instruction in American pedagogy: The saga of an educational ideology and a practice in the making. In M. C. Wang & H. J. Walberg (Eds.), *Adapting instruction to individual differences*. Berkeley, CA: McCutchan.

Gronlund, N. (1985). *Stating objectives for classroom instruction* (3rd ed.). New York: Macmillan.

Gump, P. (1980). The school as a social situation. In M. Rosenzweig & L. Porter (Eds.), *Annual Review of Psychology* (Vol. 31). Palo Alto, CA: Annual Reviews Incorporated.

Guskey, T. R., & Gates, S. L. (1985). A synthesis of research on group-based mastery learning programs. Paper presented at the annual meeting of the American Educational Research Association, Chicago.

Hambleton, R. (1974). Testing and decision-making procedures for selected individualized instructional programs. *Review of Educational Research, 44,* 371–400.

Hayes, R., & Day, B. (1980). Classroom openness and the basic skills, the self-perceptions, and the school-attendance records of third-grade pupils. *Elementary School Journal, 81,* 87–96.

Holt, J. (1964). *How children fail*. New York: Pitman.

Horak, V. (1981). A meta-analysis of research findings on individualized instruction in mathematics. *Journal of Educational Research, 74,* 249–253.

Horwitz, R. (1979). Psychological effects of the "open classroom." *Review of Educational Research, 49,* 71–86.

Jackson, P. (1968). *Life in classrooms*. New York: Holt, Rinehart and Winston.

Jackson, P. W. (1985). Private lessons in public schools: Remarks on the limits of adaptive instruction. In M. C. Wang & H. J. Walberg (Eds.), *Adapting instruction to individual differences*. Berkeley, CA: McCutchan.

James, T., & Tyack, D. (1983). Learning from past efforts to reform the high school. *Phi Delta Kappan, 64,* 400–406.

Johnson, J., & Ruskin, R. (1977). *Behavioral instruction: An evaluative review*. Washington, D.C.: American Psychological Association.

Jones, B. F., Friedman, L. B., Tinzmann, M., & Cox, B. E. (1985). Guidelines for instruction-enriched mastery learning to improve comprehension. In D. Levine (Ed.), *Improving student achievement through mastery learning programs*. San Francisco: Jossey-Bass.

Jones, B. F., & Spady, W. G. (1985). Enhanced mastery learning and quality of instruction.

In D. Levine (Ed.), *Improving student achievement through mastery learning programs*. San Francisco: Jossey-Bass.

Katz, L. (1973). Research on open education: Problems and issues. In D. Hearne et al. (Eds.), *Current research and perspectives in open education*. Washington, D.C.: National Institute of Education.

Keller, F. (1968). Good-bye teacher! *Journal of Applied Behavior Analysis, 1,* 79–88.

Keller, F., & Sherman, J. (1982). *The PSI handbook: Essays on personalized instruction*. Lawrence, KS: TRI.

Kepler, K., & Randall, J. (1977). Individualization: The subversion of elementary schooling. *Elementary School Journal, 77,* 358–363.

Klausmeier, H., Rossmiller, R., & Saily, M. (Eds.). (1977). *Individually guided elementary education: Concepts and practices*. New York: Academic Press.

Koester, L., & Farley, F. (1982). Psychophysiological characteristics and school performance of children in open and traditional classrooms. *Journal of Educational Psychology, 74,* 254–263.

Kohl, H. R. (1969). *The open classroom*. New York: Random House.

Kohler, P. (1973). A comparison of open and traditional education: Conditions that promote self-concept. Paper presented at the annual meeting of the American Educational Research Association, New Orleans.

Kulik, J., Kulik, C., & Carmichael, K. (1974). The Keller Plan in science teaching. *Science, 185,* 379–384.

Lawlor, J. (Ed.) (1982). *Computers in composition instruction*. Los Angeles: Southwest Regional Laboratory for Educational Research and Development.

Lathrop, A. (1982). Courseware selection. In J. Lawlor (Ed.), *Computers in composition instruction*. Los Angeles: Southwest Regional Laboratory for Educational Research and Development.

Lesgold, A. (1983). When can computers make a difference? *Theory Into Practice, 22,* 247–252.

Levine, D. (1985). *Improving student achievement through mastery learning programs*. San Francisco: Jossey-Bass.

Lipson, J. (1974). IPI Math—an example of what's right and wrong with individualized modular programs. *Learning, March 1974,* 60–61.

Lipson, J., & Fisher, K. (1983). Technology and the classroom: Promise or threat? *Theory Into Practice, 22,* 253–259.

Loucks, S. (1976). An exploration of levels of use of an innovation and the relationship to student achievement. Paper presented at the annual meeting of the American Educational Research Association, San Francisco.

Lukasevich, A., & Gray, R. (1978). Open space, open education, and pupil performance. *Elementary School Journal, 79,* 108–114.

Mager, R. (1962). *Preparing instructional objectives*. Palo Alto, CA: Fearon.

Marshall, H. (1981). Open classrooms: Has the term outlived its usefulness? *Review of Educational Research, 51,* 181–192.

Martin, L., & Pavan, B. (1976). Current research on open space, non-grading, vertical grouping, and team teaching. *Phi Delta Kappan, 57,* 310–315.

McCarthy, M. (1977). The how and why of learning centers. *Elementary School Journal, 77,* 292–299.

McKeachie, W., & Kulik, J. (1975). Effective college training. In F. Kerlinger (Ed.), *Review of research in education*. Itasca, IL: Peacock.

Papert, S. (1980). *Mindstorms: Children, computers, and powerful ideas*. New York: Basic Books.

Peterson, P. (1979). Direct instruction reconsidered. In P. Peterson & H. Walberg (Eds.), *Research on teaching: Concepts, findings, and implications*. Berkeley, CA: McCutchan.

Popkewitz, T., Tabachnick, R., & Wehlage, G. (1982). *The myth of educational reform: A study of school responses to a program of changes*. Madison: University of Wisconsin Press.

Price, D. (1977). *The effects of Individually Guided Education (IGE) processes on achievement and attitudes of elementary school students*. Unpublished doctoral dissertation. Columbia: University of Missouri.

Pringle, P. R. (1985). Establishing a management plan for implementing mastery learning. In D. Levine (Ed.), *Improving student achievement through mastery learning programs*. San Francisco: Jossey-Bass.

Ragosta, M., Holland, P., & Jamison, D. (1981). *Computer-assisted instruction and compensatory education: The ETS/LAUSD study*. (Final Report.) Princeton, NJ: Educational Testing Service.

Quirk, T. (1971). The student in Project PLAN: A functioning program of individualized education. *Elementary School Journal, 71*, 42–54.

Reigeluth, C. M. (Ed.). (1983). *Instructional-design theories and models: An overview of their current status*. Hillsdale, NJ: Erlbaum.

Resnick, L. B. (1977). Assuming that everyone can learn anything, will some learn less? *School Review, 85*, 445–452.

Robin, A. (1976). Behavioral instruction in the college classroom. *Review of Educational Research, 46*, 313–354.

Romberg, T. (Ed.). (1985). *Toward effective schooling: The IGE experience*. Lanham, MD: University Press of America.

Rosenshine, B. (1978). Review of teaching styles and pupil progress. *American Educational Research Journal, 15*, 163–169.

Schofield, H. (1981). Teacher effects on cognitive and affective pupil outcomes in elementary school mathematics. *Journal of Educational Psychology, 73*, 462–471.

Schultz, K. (1974). *Implementation guide: I/D/E/A change program for Individually Guided Education, ages 5–12*. Dayton, OH: I/D/E/A.

Sizer, T. (1984). *Horace's compromise: The dilemma of the American high school*. Boston: Houghton-Mifflin.

Sherman, J. (Ed.). (1974). *PSI: Forty-one germinal papers*. Menlo Park, CA: W. A. Benjamin.

Shimron, J. (1976). Learning activities in individually prescribed instruction. *Instructional Science, 5*, 391–401.

Silberman, C. E. (1970). *Crisis in the classroom*. New York: Random House.

Slavin, R. E. (1985). Team-assisted individualization. In M. C. Wang & H. J. Walberg (Eds.), *Adapting instruction to individual differences*. Berkeley, CA: McCutchan.

Slavin, R. E. (1984). Component building: A strategy for research-based instructional improvement. *Elementary School Journal, 84*, 255–269.

Slavin, R. E. (1983). *Cooperative learning*. New York: Longman.

Slavin, R., & Karweit, N. (1984). Mastery learning and student teams: A factorial experiment in urban general mathematics classes. *American Educational Research Journal, 21*, 725–736.

Sloan, D. (Ed.). (1985). *The computer in education: A critical perspective*. New York: Teachers College Press.

Solomon, D., & Kendall, A. (1976). Individual characteristics and children's performance in "open" and "traditional" classroom settings. *Journal of Educational Psychology, 68*, 613–625.

Talmage, H. (Ed.). (1975). *Systems of individualized education*. Berkeley, CA: McCutchan.

Taylor, R. P. (Ed.). (1980). *The computer in the school: Tutor, tool, tutee*. New York: Teachers College Press.

Thompson, D. (1973). Evaluation of an individualized instruction program. *Elementary School Journal, 73*, 213–221.

Traub, R., Weiss, J., Fisher, C., & Musella, D. (1973). Closure on openness in education. Symposium presented at the annual meeting of the American Educational Research Association, New Orleans.

Tucker, M. (1983). Computers in schools: A plan in time saves nine. *Theory Into Practice.* 313–320.

Walberg, H. J. (1985). Instructional theories and research evidence. In M. C. Wang & H. J. Walberg (Eds.), *Adapting instruction to individual differences.* Berkeley, CA: McCutchan.

Walberg, H. J. (1984). Improving the productivity of America's schools. *Educational Leadership, 41*(8), 19–27.

Walberg, H., Schiller, D., & Haertel, G. (1979). The quiet revolution in educational research. *Phi Delta Kappan, 61,* 179–183.

Wang, M. (1981). Mainstreaming exceptional children: Some instructional design and implementation considerations. *Elementary School Journal, 18,* 195–221.

Wang, M. C., & Birch, J. W. (1984). Effective special education in regular classes. *Exceptional Children, 50,* 391–399.

Wang, M. C., Gennari, P., & Waxman, H. C. (1985). The Adaptive Learning Environments Model. In M. C. Wang & H. J. Walberg (Eds.), *Adapting instruction to individual differences.* Berkeley, CA: McCutchan.

Wang, M. C., & Lindvall, C. M. (1984). Individual differences in school learning environments: Theory, research, and design. In E. W. Gordon (Ed.), *Review of research in education* (Vol. 11). Washington, D.C.: American Educational Research Association.

Wang, M., & Resnick, L. (1978). *The Primary Education Program.* Johnstown, PA: Mafex Associates.

Wang, M. C., & Walberg, H. J. (1983). Adaptive instruction and classroom time. *American Educational Research Journal, 20,* 601–625.

Wang, M. C., & Walberg, H. J. (Eds.). (1985). *Adapting instruction to individual differences.* Berkeley: McCutchan.

Waxman, H. C., Wang, M. C., Anderson, K. A., & Walberg, H. J. (1985). *Adaptive education and student outcomes: A quantitative synthesis.* Pittsburgh: Learning and Research Development Center, University of Pittsburgh.

Weinstein, C. (1979). The physical environment of the school: A review of the research. *Review of Educational Research, 49,* 577–610.

Weiss, J. (1973). Openness and student outcomes: Some results. Paper presented at the American Educational Research Association, New Orleans.

FORM 9.1. Student Independence in Individual Work

USE: When students interact with teacher during periods of individual work assignment and/or in open settings.
PURPOSE: To see if individual students or students generally, over time, are becoming more autonomous learners.
Below is a list of student behaviors that could occur during seatwork assignments. Check each behavior as it happens.

Frequency*   Type Contact

_____   1. After beginning task, student seeks additional instructions about what to do.
_____   2. Student seeks confirmation about being on the right track ("Is this okay?").
_____   3. Student seeks substantive advice from teacher ("Is there another source that could be consulted?").
_____   4. Student seeks evaluative feedback ("What do you think about this conclusion?").
_____   5. Student tells teacher what was done and why (showing, justifying).
_____   6. Student asks teacher what to do next after completing the initial assignment (seeks direction).

*In this particular example, the scale will yield information describing the frequency of different types of contact that occur with the teacher during a given amount of time. However, codes could be entered for individual students or for types of students by assigning them a number (high achievers = 1, middle achievers = 2, and so forth).

FORM 9.2. Student Involvement in Assigned Work

USE: When some or all students are assigned individual seatwork
PURPOSE: Every two minutes, record the involvement levels of all students
*   to assess degree of student involvement in assigned work*
Number of students assigned to individual work: _____
Is teacher available to supervise assignment work? _____
Is aide(s) present to help? _____

BEHAVIOR CATEGORIES

1. Clearly involved in assigned work.

2. Can't tell—may be thinking (code this rather than 1 or 3 if there is any doubt)

3. Definitely not doing assigned or chosen work.

4. Misbehaving.

Time	*Student* *	*Number of Students in Each Involvement Category*								
2:00	____	20	1	5	2	0	3	0	4
2:02	____	18	1	5	2	2	3	0	4
2:04	____	15	1	5	2	5	3	0	4
2:06	____	15	1	4	2	5	3	1	4
____	____	____	1	____	2	____	3	____	4
____	____	____	1	____	2	____	3	____	4
____	____	____	1	____	2	____	3	____	4
____	____	____	1	____	2	____	3	____	4
____	____	____	1	____	2	____	3	____	4
____	____	____	1	____	2	____	3	____	4
____	____	____	1	____	2	____	3	____	4
____	____	____	1	____	2	____	3	____	4

*It is possible to make a rating for *all* students or for some subdivision of the class: H = high achievers; M = middle achievers; L = low achievers; G = girls; B = boys.

If several students are not involved, attempt to explain the lack of task engagement (students have finished, have given up, are waiting for the teacher, are distracted by others, no apparent reason).

FORM 9.3. Mastery Learning Checklist

USE: *In classrooms taught using mastery learning procedures*
PURPOSE: *To describe the characteristics and effects of the mastery*
learning procedures being implemented
Enter a check mark (to indicate presence) or a 0 (to indicate absence)
for each of the following components of a systematic mastery learning
approach.

COMPONENTS CHECKLIST

_____ 1. Student orientation. Do the students know what to expect from and how to operate within the mastery learning program (the teach-test-reteach-retest cycle and grading according to ultimate mastery achieved regardless of time taken to learn)?

_____ 2. Objectives. Does the unit have clear-cut mastery objectives that were used as the basis for planning the instruction and the tests?

_____ a. Were these objectives communicated clearly to the students?

_____ b. Are the objectives realistic (can most of the students reasonably be expected to reach mastery criteria within the time allotted)?

_____ 3. Initial instruction. Does the teacher provide initial instruction to the class as a whole that is sufficiently clear and complete to enable most students to move toward mastery without undue confusion or frustration?

_____ a. Does the teacher instruct the students personally (in addition to expecting them to learn on their own from reading and working on exercises)?

_____ b. Has the material been subdivided and sequenced effectively?

_____ c. Do the subunits (lessons and follow-up activities) effectively move students toward mastery of appropriately sized chunks of new material?

_____ d. Does the teacher provide sufficient instruction and modeling for assignments before releasing the students to work on the assignments independently?

_____ e. Does the teacher circulate to monitor progress on assignments and provide feedback and assistance to the students?

_____ 4. Formative evaluation. Are the students tested to assess their mastery of each significant subset of objectives?

    _____ a. Are the test items valid measures of mastery of key objectives?

    _____ b. Are all of the key objectives covered?

    _____ c. Do the items have diagnostic value (error patterns indicate the particulars of the student's confusion and his or her needs for remedial instruction)?

_____ 5. Follow up. Do nonmasters receive corrective reteaching and masters receive meaningful acceleration or enrichment opportunities?

    _____ a. Are nonmasters retaught using correction procedures designed specifically to clear up their particular confusions?

    _____ b. Does this reteaching involve methods or materials that were not used in the original instruction (so that it is not just repetition of the same instruction that the students received earlier)?

    _____ c. Are the follow-up assignments different from the assignments done originally?

    _____ d. Is retesting done with different tests rather than repetition of the same tests that the students did not pass earlier?

    _____ e. Are masters routed into worthwhile academic activities (curriculum acceleration or enrichment) rather than into busywork or nonacademic activities?

_____ 6. Summative evaluation. Are the students graded according to their mastery of the major objectives of the unit as a whole, independently of how long it took them to master these objectives?

    _____ a. Does the teacher compose and administer a summative evaluation instrument (unit test) to assess mastery of the major objectives of the unit?

    _____ b. Does the teacher grade according to scores on this test (regardless of how long it took students to be certified as masters)?

COMMENTS

Write your comments on the above issues or other relevant aspects of the teacher's implementation of mastery learning procedures. In particular: (1) Is the program succeeding in enabling at least 80 percent of the students to attain mastery levels? If not, why not? (2) Do significant numbers of students appear to be passing the formative evaluation tests even though they have not really mastered the concepts or skills being assessed? If so, what can be done about this? (3) Does the overall program provide appropriate instruction and activities for students who master objectives quickly? If not, what changes would you suggest?

Form 9.3 (Continued)

FORM 9.4. Learning Centers

USE: In classrooms containing one or more learning centers
PURPOSE: To describe the content and management of learning center
activities
Enter a check mark (to indicate presence) or a 0 (to indicate absence)
for each of the following questions.

CHECKLIST

_____ 1. Has the center been created with clear curricular objectives in mind (that is, is it designed to insure that the students learn something rather than merely to entertain them)?

_____ 2. Given the curricular goals, are the activities appropriate in difficulty level and otherwise likely to succeed in enabling the students to meet the objectives?

_____ 3. Are the activities interesting or otherwise appealing to the students?

_____ 4. Is there an appropriate amount and variety of materials and tasks (if necessary, to accommodate a range of student ability levels)?

_____ 5. Have the students been prepared (via demonstration and practice) in how to use the center?

_____ 6. Has the center been equipped with appropriate furnishings and materials?

_____ 7. Has the design and location of the center taken into account equipment storage and traffic patterns?

_____ 8. Has the teacher posted a schedule or articulated clear guidelines to enable students to know when they can or should use the center?

_____ 9. Are there clear management rules (concerning how many students may use the center at once, who should take charge of group activities, clean up and restoration of equipment, etc.)?

_____ 10. Do students know what to do when they get to the center (or can they consult clear guidelines posted at the center when they get there)?

_____ 11. Have provisions been made so that students can get feedback and check their work when they finish center activities?

_____ 12. Do the students know when and how to get help with center activities if they need it?

_____ 13. Is there a clear accountability system for center assignments (students know what they are supposed to do, know when and where to turn in completed work, and know that the work will be checked and followed up)?

_____ 14. Does the center emphasize hands-on activities that allow the students to explore or manipulate (rather than just provide more seatwork but in a different location)?

_____ 15. Have the activities been planned to allow students to work cooperatively or assist one another?

_____ 16. Does the teacher phase new activities into the center as the objectives of earlier activities are met?

COMMENTS:

CHAPTER

10 Teaching Heterogeneous Classes

We have noted that the whole-class instruction/recitation/seatwork approach that has been the dominant method used in traditional schooling is a compromise solution to the problem facing a single teacher trying to accommodate the learning needs of 20 to 40 students. We have also noted that this traditional approach functions for the most part by offering a fixed combination of instructional goals, instructional methods, and time to learn to all students, thus failing to accommodate individual differences in achievement rates and resulting in large individual differences in levels of mastery achieved. In Chapter 9, we discussed three approaches popularized in recent years as fundamental alternatives to the traditional approach: mastery learning, individualized instruction/adaptive education, and open education. In the present chapter, we will discuss several proposed solutions to the same dilemmas that are less extreme—solutions that call for adapting the traditional approach or using it in combination with other approaches rather than eliminating it entirely and replacing it with something else.

One of these proposed solutions, *between-class ability grouping,* seeks to minimize student heterogeneity by assigning students to classes on the basis of test scores so as to minimize the range of ability or achievement levels to be found in any given classroom. Other proposed solutions involve responding to whatever level of heterogeneity exists within a classroom by (1) introducing within-class ability grouping and differentiated small-group instruction; (2) differentiating, if not completely individualizing, the instruction offered and the work assigned to individual students; (3) using small-group and independent-learning activities other than traditional seatwork; and (4) sharing instructional responsibilities with the students themselves by including cooperative learning and peer-tutoring activities (that may include activities for different students).

BETWEEN-CLASS ABILITY GROUPING (TRACKING)

Between-class ability grouping involves using test scores or other information about students in order to assign them to classes that are as homogeneous as possible. Two subtypes of between-class ability grouping are common (Rosenbaum, 1980): grouping by ability or achievement levels and grouping by curriculum. *Grouping by ability or achievement levels* is more common in elementary and middle schools, where it is often called *homogeneous grouping*. To divide 69 third graders into three homogeneously grouped classes, for example, school staff would examine the most recent standardized achievement test scores available and assign the highest 23 scorers to one class, the middle 23 to a second class, and the bottom 23 to the third class. There might be some minor variations on this procedure (such as making the top class a little larger and the bottom class a little smaller, or looking for natural breaks in the distribution of achievement scores that might make for more sensible groupings than arbitrarily assigning 23 to each class), but in any case, the end result would be three classes that were each much more homogeneous in student achievement than they would have been if students had been assigned randomly or in some other fashion that yielded *heterogeneous grouping*.

Homogeneous grouping creates a top class, a bottom class, and possibly one or more others in between. Each class is taught essentially the same curriculum, but the higher-ranking classes are taught at greater depth and breadth than the low-ranking classes.

Grouping by curriculum is more frequent at the junior and especially the senior high school level. It is commonly called *tracking* in the United States and *streaming* in Great Britain. Instead of merely introducing differences in the depth and breadth of instruction in the same curriculum, tracking provides separate curricula for students in different tracks. Thus, college preparatory students take one curriculum, business/secretarial students another, vocational students another, and general education students another. Some ninth graders take algebra, some take prealgebra, some take business math, and some take general math. Assignment of students to tracks is done on the basis of test scores, grades, accumulated credits in prerequisite courses, and (usually) the wishes of the parents or the students themselves as expressed to school counselors. Like homogeneous grouping in the elementary grades, tracking in the secondary grades creates much more homogeneous classes of students than would exist if the school required all students to take the same curriculum and assigned them to classes randomly.

American educators have always been ambivalent about between-class ability grouping (Rosenbaum, 1980). It is a sensible idea in theory (reducing class heterogeneity should make it possible for teachers to meet more of their students' needs more often and thus to teach all students more effectively), but in practice, it seems less appealing. In part, this is because its effects on student achievement are weak and mixed rather than strong and positive. In addition, it appears to have undesirable affective and social effects that conflict with the nation's egalitarian traditions. Thus, although it has been and continues to be implemented widely, it tends to be accepted grudgingly as a necessity under certain circumstances rather than embraced wholeheartedly as a desirable feature of schooling. Most writers accept the need for grouping by curriculum at the senior high school level (although they often counsel keeping it to a minimum and delaying it as long as possible), but argue against grouping by ability or achievement in junior high schools and especially in middle and elementary schools.

Effects on Achievement

In theory, between-class ability grouping should improve achievement and should be equally beneficial for both low and high achievers. In fact, however, research reviews suggest only weak and mixed effects on achievement (Alexander & McDill, 1976; Barker Lunn, 1970; Esposito, 1973; Findley & Bryan, 1975; Rowan & Miracle, 1983). In a recent review of the best available evidence on between-class ability grouping in elementary schools, Slavin (1986) concludes that it has no reliable effect on student achievement at all.

The only reviewers to report a positive effect of homogeneous grouping on student achievement are Kulik and Kulik (1982), who conducted a meta-analysis of well-designed secondary-level studies and reported no effect of homogeneous grouping on low-achieving students or students representing the population as a whole, but a significant positive effect on the achievement of gifted and talented students. This conclusion at first appears to conflict with the conclusions of other reviewers, but the conflict largely disappears when several factors are taken into account. First, the Kulik and Kulik (1982) review was restricted to the secondary grades, and the studies reporting notably positive results focused on special honors courses for senior high school students. Second, although statistically significant, the effects were not large in an absolute sense. Third, within this range, effects were strongest for studies spanning 5 to 18 weeks, weaker for studies spanning 19 to 36 weeks, and nonexistent for studies spanning 37 weeks or more. This suggests a tendency for the positive effects on achievement that do occur to disappear over time. Abadzi (1985) reports the same phenomenon in an elementary-level study.

Finally, the data for the honors courses tell only part of the story. They indicate that gifted and talented students enrolled in the honors courses showed more achievement gain than similar students in heterogeneous classrooms, but they do not take into account the probability that these benefits to gifted students were balanced by detriments to the rest of the students caused by removal of significant numbers of gifted and talented academic peer leaders from their classes. Thus, even the Kulik and Kulik (1982) findings can be interpreted as consistent with the conclusion that homogeneous grouping does not improve student achievement.

Why does between-class ability grouping not produce more positive effects on student achievement? For the most part, we can only guess, because most investigators who have studied homogeneous versus heterogeneous grouping have failed to gather data on curriculum and instruction in the classrooms that might provide a basis for explaining conflicting results (Good & Marshall, 1984). One likely hypothesis, though, is that schools that adopt homogeneous grouping fail to follow through by arranging for differentiated curricula and instruction suited to the needs of each class. Johnson (1970) reported that teachers in schools that practiced homogeneous grouping were not provided with new skills or curriculum materials aimed at different levels. Also, Goldberg, Passow, and Justman (1966) found that teachers did not adjust their curricula or instruction to meet the special needs of students at different achievement levels, although some teachers of low-ability classes simply taught less content to these students and set lower achievement goals for them.

Research on the affective and social effects of homogeneous grouping suggests other reasons for its failure to fulfill its theoretical potential.

Affective and Social Effects

Critics have identified four types of negative effects that tracking is likely to have on students. First are the social labeling and teacher attitude and expectation effects reviewed in Chapter 4. Investigators have found that teachers dislike teaching low-ability classes, spend less time preparing for them, and schedule less varied, interesting, and challenging activities in them (Evertson, 1982; Finley, 1984; Keddie, 1971; Oakes, 1982). Instead of being taught via curricula or methods specifically suited to their needs, students in low-track classes frequently are not taught much at all or are merely kept quiet with busywork rather than being challenged with effective instruction.

The second problem with tracking is the undesirable peer structures that it creates in low-track classes, along with associated attitudes, work norms, and classroom atmosphere factors. In heterogeneously grouped classes, the brighter and better socially adjusted students tend to assume academic peer leadership, so that each class tends to function primarily as a learning environment and most time is spent engaged in academic activities. Under homogeneous grouping systems, however, the vast majority of these academic peer leaders are placed in upper-track classes, so that the lower-track classes become leaderless aggregations of discouraged and alienated students. Such students resent their low status and tend to respond defensively by refusing to seriously commit themselves to academic achievement goals and by deriding classmates who do (Alexander, Cook, & McDill, 1978; Metz, 1978; Persell, 1977; Rosenbaum, 1976, 1980; Schwartz, 1981).

Even if teachers assigned to low-track classes do not have undesirable attitudes and expectations, they will find it difficult to establish effective learning environments in these classes because of the defeatism, alienation, and flat-out resistance they are likely to encounter there. Similarly, those low-track students who want to learn and accomplish as much as they can will have a difficult time doing so because their classmates are likely to deride their efforts and because instructional continuity in these classes will often be disrupted. Experimental data indicate that students assigned to higher groups will achieve more than comparable students assigned to lower groups (Douglas, 1964; Tuckman & Bierman, 1971), and other studies indicate that students in classes with primarily higher-achieving classmates tend to achieve more than students in classes with primarily lower-achieving classmates (Beckerman & Good, 1981; Veldman & Sanford, 1984; see also Leiter, 1983 for mixed results).

A third factor is that assignments to homogeneous groups or tracks tend to be permanent: There is little movement from one track to another once initial assignments have been made, and the movement that does occur tends to be downward. Thus, initial placement into a low track may categorize a student permanently and close off options that would be available under other systems. Mackler (1969) conducted a longitudinal study of a Harlem school that tracked students from first grade. He found that few students assigned to the lowest first-grade class made it to the middle second-grade class, even fewer students from the middle second-grade class made it to the top third-grade class, and no student moved up to the top class after third grade. Similarly, Rosenbaum (1976) describes how tracking beginning at the junior high school level eliminates future options for students who do not get into college preparatory tracks, not only because their low-track classes are less desirable learning environments than high-track classes for the reasons described above, but also because low-track students fail to take courses that are prerequisites for other courses farther along in the system. As a result, when they begin high school these students tend to be assigned to general mathematics because they are not considered ready for algebra; their lack algebra prevents them from enrolling in other mathematics courses for which algebra is a prerequisite; and their generally weak mathematics preparation prevents them from enrolling in many science and computer courses as well. Ultimately, they graduate with a high school diploma but poor preparation for college and lack of a great many prerequisites demanded by high-quality college programs.

Thus, tracking decisions made in seventh grade or even as early as first grade may affect a student's academic progress for good or ill from that point on. This would be of less concern if students were always grouped accurately, but there is reason to believe that significant percentages of students are misclassified because of the imperfections of tests as predictors of future performance and because of the less-than-perfect reliability of such tests. This is especially likely when test data are used to group young students or students with limited facility in the language in which the test is administered.

The lack of movement from lower to higher tracks also suggests that tracking typically does not lead to adaptive instruction of low achievers. If it did, significant numbers of these students would work harder and move up to higher tracks.

In combination, these first three types of undesirable affective and social consequences of tracking have caused most educators to see tracking as undesirable and thus to call for delaying it as long as possible.

The degree to which teachers see tracking as necessary depends not only on their grade level but on their subject matter (Dar, 1985; Evans, 1985). The teachers who stress homogeneous grouping tend to teach subjects such as mathematics or foreign languages in which the content is largely abstract and arranged hierarchically. In contrast, teachers of literature, history, or other humanities and social studies subjects see the least need for homogeneous grouping, apparently because the subject matter is much less abstract and hierarchically organized. The material can be related to everyday experience and is more susceptible to commonsense explanations, so it is easier to keep a heterogeneous group of students meaningfully focused on a common topic. Teachers whose subject matter lies in between these extremes of abstraction and hierarchical organization (chemistry and biology teachers, for example) tend to place less stress on the need for homogeneous grouping than mathematics and foreign language teachers but more stress than humanities and social studies teachers.

A fourth problem with tracking made it seem especially inappropriate during the 1960s and 1970s when there was so much emphasis on achieving social equity in the schools: Tracking has the direct effect of minimizing contact during the school day between students of differing achievement levels. As a result, it also usually has the indirect effect of minimizing contact between students who differ in social class, race, or ethnicity. Consequently, national commitments to desegregation and mainstreaming (discussed below) led to a deemphasis on tracking in the 1960s and 1970s, especially prior to high school.

EDUCATIONAL EXCELLENCE AND EQUITY

School quality (*educational excellence* as it has come to be called) is a continuing concern of the general public, although the degree of attention focused on it fluctuates. By most criteria (literacy rates, percentage of the population that earn high school diplomas or college degrees, etc.), American education has been quite successful both in absolute terms and in comparison with other countries. Consequently, the general public has shown continuing commitment to the public schools and a perception that these schools are adequate, if not outstanding.

Disenchantment sets in periodically, however, either in response to the popular writings of educational critics and would-be reformers or in response to events perceived as indications of slippage in the nation's competitive position. For example, the launching into orbit of *Sputnik* by the U.S.S.R. in the 1950s, the criticism directed at mathematics and science education in the schools by leading mathematicians and scientists during the 1960s, and the economic successes achieved by the Japanese at the expense of American electronics and automobile manufacturers during the 1970s and 1980s provoked a great deal of public debate about the schools, culminating in reports such as *A Nation at Risk* and in various governmental policy decisions and program initiatives.

When fueled by concern about educational excellence, reform-oriented policies and programs tend to concentrate on cognitive rather than affective or social objectives and in particular on achievement test scores. Calls for upgrading school quality commonly include recommitment to academic objectives and standards, mandated performance objectives and associated testing programs, increases in course requirements and reductions in course options, more rigorous grading practices, more challenging curricula, and more homework. Often these changes suggested for students in general are supplemented (as they have been recently) by calls for special programs to accommodate the perceived needs of "the best and the brightest": special tracks or courses for gifted elementary students and honors courses or advanced placement for qualifying secondary students.

This "educational excellence" approach that tends to identify school quality with success in maximizing students' academic achievement levels is rejected as overly narrow by educators who wish to define school quality at least in part in terms of *educational equity:* fair and effective treatment of all students regardless of sex, race, ethnicity, socioeconomic status, or handicapping conditions. In fact, equity concerns were the primary motives underlying two of the most widespread changes introduced into the schools during the 1960s and 1970s: desegregation and mainstreaming.

Desegregation

Prior to the historic *Brown v. Board of Education* Supreme Court decision in 1954, certain states operated entirely separate school systems for black and white students, and school districts in most other states practiced de facto racial segregation by gerrymandering their school catchment zone borderlines. Following this Supreme Court decision and a great many other court rulings and related governmental directives that occurred during subsequent years, American schools gradually became less segregated. Separate schools for black students were abolished. School district lines were redrawn so as to bring together rather than separate black and white students, and if necessary (as it was in many urban school systems) to achieve racial balance, some students were bused to schools in other neighborhoods.

Assessments of the outcomes of this desegregation effort suggest mixed results. It has not necessarily produced positive attitudes or true integration of the races, but it has tended to increase social tolerance in both black and white students (Scott & McPartland, 1982). More specifically, desegregation by itself is unlikely to reduce the prejudices of either race toward the other and unlikely to increase black students' self-esteem, but it sometimes increases and rarely decreases the achievement levels of black students (Stephan, 1978).

There has been great variation in the outcomes of desegregation efforts because the success of any particular effort depends on how it is implemented. Success is more likely when school districts affirm a positive commitment to desegregation and prepare their administrators, teachers, parents, and students for smooth implementation of their policies and plans.

At this point, desegregation has largely been accomplished insofar as it can be (there are limits to what can be done, even with significant busing, in certain large cities). Consequently, attention has shifted from the legal and structural aspects of accomplishing physical desegregation to methods of addressing the equity issues it introduces: the need for multicultural awareness and fair treatment of different groups, the desire to elicit active participation of all students in classroom activities, and the attempt to get beyond mere tolerance by promoting positive, prosocial interactions among students of different racial or ethnic backgrounds.

At the school level, this requires minimizing between-class ability grouping. In most school populations, there are substantial correlations among race, socioeconomic status, and achievement level, so that between-class ability grouping in desegregated schools will have the effect of resegregating the students into largely separate classes and thus minimizing cross-racial contact. Consequently, desegregated schools are less likely to practice homogeneous grouping.

At the classroom level, the degree to which the ultimate goals of desegregation programs are likely to be accomplished will depend on the nature of the activities and organizational structures that the teacher introduces. Within-class ability grouping will tend to resegregate students, and even heavy reliance on the traditional whole-class instruction/recitation/seatwork approach or on individualized instruction approaches will minimize students' opportunities to interact with their peers. Positive attitudes and frequent cross-race interaction are more likely in classrooms in which teachers frequently use small-group projects and other peer interaction formats (Nickerson & Prawat, 1981). The cooperative learning approaches described later in this chapter have proven especially effective for improving cross-racial attitudes and behavior (Slavin, 1983).

Mainstreaming

The practice of removing students with physical, intellectual, or emotional impairments from special, segregated learning environments and returning them to regular classrooms is known as *mainstreaming*. Historically, the courts supported the view that schools could deny enrollment to students who might interfere with classroom functioning because of mental or physical handicaps, poor health, flagrant misbehavior, pregnancy, or even unconventional clothes or personal appearance (Flowers & Bolmeier, 1964). These court decisions supported the viewpoint that school is a privilege for those who fulfill specific criteria, not a right guaranteed to all.

Beginning in the 1960s, and increasingly in the 1970s, the courts began to stress public education as a universal right rather than a privilege that schools could revoke capriciously. Resistance began to develop toward the practice of placing students into special classes, even students diagnosed as having learning handicaps. Chaffin (1974) lists four reasons for this:

1. Court litigation (many parents resisted placement of their children into special classes because they viewed these classes as dumping grounds for problems rather than as improved educational settings likely to provide students with needed treatment)
2. Growing realization that labeling students as handicapped or otherwise atypical often induces undesirable expectation effects that may outweigh any advantages of special treatment
3. The equivocal findings of research on the effectiveness of special classes (such classes appear to have been successful with deaf students, but positive results are hard to find for other types of special students and especially for students with mild intellectual or emotional problems)
4. Dissatisfaction with the reliability and validity of the diagnostic procedures used to classify students as special learners (many students, especially those from minority groups, appear to have been so classified improperly)

These pressures for change culminated in Public Law 94-142, which became effective in 1977. This law directs public schools to search out and enroll all handicapped children and to educate these children in the *least-restrictive environment* in which they will be able to function and still have their special needs met. The intention is to minimize the degree to which such students will be labeled and treated as "different" and to maximize the degree to which they function as ordinary students participating in regular classes in usual ways. The following continuum of educational environments proceeds from most to least restrictive (Reynolds, 1978):

Full-time residential school
Full-time special day school
Full-time special class
Regular class plus part-time special class
Regular class plus resource room help
Regular class with assistance by itinerant specialists

Regular class with consultive assistance
Regular class only

The law calls for an individualized educational program (IEP) to be developed for each student who is recommended for special educational services. The IEP is developed by a committee that is likely to include the principal, teachers who instruct the student, a school psychologist or social worker who evaluates the student, and when feasible, a parent and the student. The IEP describes the student's present educational performance, identifies short-term learning goals and longer-term goals, and specifies a plan for achieving these goals through a combination of regular classroom teaching and specialized instruction (following the least-restrictive environment principle).

Research on regular versus special classroom placement suggests that the achievement progress of special education students will depend not so much on what kind of classroom they are assigned to as on the amount and quality of the instruction they receive there (Leinhardt & Pallay, 1982; Madden & Slavin, 1983). In general, the classroom management approaches (see Chapters 6 and 7) and instructional methods (see Chapter 11) that are effective with special education students tend to be the same ones that are effective with other students (Crawford, 1983; Larrivee, 1985), although special students may need closer supervision and more intensive instruction. Students with learning disabilities or handicaps may need individualized curricula and more one-to-one instruction from the teacher (Leinhardt & Pallay, 1982; Madden & Slavin, 1983), and students with behavior disorders may need closer supervision (Thompson, White, & Morgan, 1982). Frequently, special students will be assigned to resource rooms where they will receive instruction in basic skills from special education teachers working with only five to ten students at a time and will spend the rest of their time in the regular classroom for instruction in other academic subjects and for participation in art, music, and various expressive or recreational activities.

Most mainstreamed students will adjust well to regular classrooms if they receive acceptance and support from their teachers and peers. Teacher attitudes and expectations are critical. It is important that teachers think of mainstreamed students as "their own" and as bonafide members of the class, not as visitors on loan from the special education teachers. Conditions should be arranged to allow special students to participate as fully and equally in classroom activities as possible, and these students should be treated primarily in terms of what they can accomplish (or learn to accomplish with help) rather than with emphasis on what they cannot do because of their handicapping conditions. For more detailed suggestions about teaching handicapped students, see Gearheart and Weishahn (1984), Good and Brophy (1986), or Hewett and Watson (1979).

Conclusions About Between-Class Ability Grouping

Both desegregation and mainstreaming tend to increase the heterogeneity of school populations, and this could be taken as indicating a need for more homogeneous grouping. However, the drawbacks of between-class ability grouping appear to exceed its advantages, especially when school quality is defined in terms of equity as well as excellence. Consequently, we recommend that this form of homogeneous grouping be delayed as long as possible and be confined to grouping by curriculum rather than grouping by ability or achievement level. In other words, we see between-class ability grouping as necessary (if not ideal) when different groups of students are going to be taught different curricula, but we do not see justification for homogeneous grouping of classes by ability or achievement levels when the students are all going to be taught essentially the same curriculum, except in extreme circumstances where the range of abilities within a grade level is so large as to minimize the range of content or skills that is suitable for instruction to all of the students.

Even under conditions that compel homogeneous grouping, we recommend partial or compromise arrangements over arrangements that would segregate different groups completely. One such compromise is the so-called "Joplin Plan" and its many variations. In the original Joplin Plan, students were assigned to heterogeneous classes for most of the day but were regrouped for reading instruction across grades (the teachers all taught reading at the same time to make such regrouping possible). For example, a reading class at the fifth-grade, first-semester reading level might include high-achieving fourth graders, average-achieving fifth graders, and low-achieving sixth graders. The class would be taught as a whole class or perhaps divided into just two groups, but no more. Students would be assigned strictly according to reading achievement level (not IQ or some less-direct measure), and would be assigned to a different reading class if performance warranted it.

The Joplin Plan is complicated in one sense because it requires coordinated scheduling and cooperation among teams of teachers, but it also simplifies reading instruction by making it possible for each teacher to instruct the entire class as a group or to divide the class into only two subgroups instead of three or more. This simplifies classroom management and increases the time that students receive reading instruction directly from the teacher rather than having to work independently on seatwork assignments.

The Joplin Plan appears to have been lost in the shuffle when more extreme arrangements for nongraded classes and multiage grouping came into vogue in the 1960s and 1970s. Slavin (1986) reports that the Joplin Plan showed significant positive effects on student achievement compared to traditional homogeneous or heterogeneous class assignments within grade levels, in several studies. Slavin's review suggests that perhaps it should be brought back, at least for reading instruction in the intermediate grades.

Variations on the Joplin Plan call for regrouping of students for reading instruction within rather than across grade levels or for regrouping in subject matters other than reading. Regrouping is most likely to be beneficial for subject areas that involve hierarchically organized sequences of objectives, so that it is more likely to be used for reading and mathematics than for science or social studies.

Three first-grade teachers known to the authors devised a plan for regrouping students within grade level for both reading and mathematics instruction. Originally, students had been assigned randomly to each class. Each teacher taught and carefully observed the students in class for six weeks. Then the teachers divided the students into high, middle, and low groups for mathematics and reading instruction (the groups were not the same in each subject area). The teacher who had taken the low readers took the high mathematics students and the teacher who had taken the high readers took the low mathematics students.

Separate teacher assignments were undertaken so that students did not come to view one classroom as the dummy room and another as the brain trust room. Also, the teachers were careful to treat students as individuals even though they had been assigned together because of similar aptitudes.

The students remained with their regular teacher for all other activities (science, social studies, art, music, lunch, and recess). Consequently, these students were ability grouped for instruction in reading and mathematics, but were in mixed-ability groups for all other instruction. They worked with two or even three different teachers and yet spent most of the day with the same teacher (an arrangement that we think facilitates young students' affective growth). When a student experienced academic difficulty, all three teachers frequently had pertinent knowledge to contribute to a group planning session designed to analyze the problem and develop new strategies.

Another possibility is a plan developed in Baltimore that Findley and Bryan (1971) call *stratified heterogeneous grouping*. Under this plan, if 90 students were to be assigned to three classes, the students would be ranked according to ability or achievement test scores and then subdivided into nine groups of 10 each. Instead of assigning the top 30 students to Teacher A, the middle 30 to Teacher B, and the bottom 30 to Teacher C, the class assignment would be as follows (Group 1 contains the highest 10 ranked students, and Group 9 contains the lowest 10).

Teacher A	Teacher B	Teacher C
Group 1 (1–10)	Group 2 (11–20)	Group 3 (21–30)
Group 4 (31–40)	Group 5 (41–50)	Group 6 (51–60)
Group 7 (61–70)	Group 8 (71–80)	Group 9 (81–90)

Note the several merits of this scheme. First, there is no top or bottom section; the sections overlap, so invidious comparisons between groups are minimized. Second, each class has a narrower range than a heterogeneous class would have, so that the teachers can give special attention where it is needed without feeling unable to meet the needs of the opposite extremes. Teacher A can give special attention to the top 10 because the bottom 20 are not in the class; Teacher C can concentrate on the bottom 10, without fear of holding up the top 20. Third, each class has academic peer leaders able to stimulate one another in a fair, competitive way while giving leadership to lower groups. Note particularly that in Teacher C's class, the top group is the third ten, students who probably have been playing second fiddle to those in the top 20. Finally, no teacher has to teach a clear-cut "low group" of leaderless and alienated students.

This method is one way to achieve a mix of students at different achievement levels in each room without forcing each teacher to prepare instruction for the full range of student learning needs. We think that the plan is an interesting, workable strategy, but that two important points should be considered.

1. The groups overlap, but they are still different. Class A is still the highest group and Class C the lowest. Although Class C has many capable students, in the minds of the teachers (and the students or parents) it may become the "difficult" group to teach. Sometimes small group differences in ability become exaggerated in daily practice. When this plan is im-

plemented, it will be important to see that Class C does not become a typical "low group."

2. It is also important that teachers expect good performance from their low achievers. Although some teachers do not enjoy teaching low-ability students, these students are capable of good performance when they receive enthusiastic instruction that is appropriately matched to their aptitudes and interests. If the primary motivation for grouping is to avoid working with large numbers of low achievers, this plan probably will not work. Again, if teachers do not think that low-ability students can learn and if they are unwilling to engage in remedial activities with these students, no grouping pattern will be successful.

WITHIN-CLASS ABILITY GROUPING

Either instead of or in addition to between-class ability grouping, teachers can arrange to instruct their students in homogeneous small groups rather than rely on whole-class methods. This is done routinely for beginning reading instruction (Cazden, 1985; Hiebert, 1983) and often for elementary mathematics instruction as well (Hallinan & Sorensen, 1983).

Ability grouping within classes offers certain advantages over ability grouping between classes. First, only one teacher is involved, so that there is no need for cooperative planning and scheduling by teams of teachers. Within-class ability grouping is also more flexible in that it is easier for the teacher to vary the numbers and sizes of groups and to move students from one group to another. On the other hand, whenever the teacher is instructing a small group, provisions must be made to keep the rest of the students profitably occupied. As a result, instructional planning and classroom management are considerably more complicated than they are when the teacher uses whole-class methods. The result is that the potential advantages that within-class ability grouping offers to students (the opportunity to receive intensive small-group instruction in content and skills that are closely matched to current achievement levels) are offset by certain disadvantages (reduction in the amount of time spent being taught directly by the teacher along with a parallel increase in the amount of time spent in independent seatwork).

Most of the research on within-class grouping concerns grouping for mathematics instruction in the upper elementary grades and grouping for reading instruction in the primary grades. Research on mathematics groups in the upper elementary grades is sparse but supportive in that the few studies that do exist indicate that grouping (usually just two or three groups) is associated with higher achievement than is whole-class instruction (Slavin, 1986). Some of these studies involved special programs such as Team-Assisted Instruction (TAI), however, so it is not clear whether the achievement gains were due to the grouping arrangements or to other factors such as team competition for group rewards. Also, grouping was a novel innovation in these upper-grade mathematics classes. If such grouping should become standard practice, it might not have the same positive effects and might even raise the same concerns that have been raised about grouping for beginning reading instruction.

Remarkably, in view of the near-universal use of reading groups, there are no clear research data comparing small group versus whole class instruction in beginning reading. However, within-class ability grouping for beginning reading is often criticized on logical grounds. First, ability grouping tends to exaggerate preexisting differences in achievement rates by accelerating the progress of students in the top groups but slowing the progress of students in the bottom groups (Rowan & Miracle, 1983; Weinstein, 1976). This effect is especially pronounced when the groups are truly homogeneous and notably different from one another (Hallinan & Sorensen, 1983) and when the teacher emphasizes the distinctions between groups and treats the groups notably differently (Gamoran, 1984). Second, high groups seem to benefit not only from faster pacing but from a higher quality of instruction from the teacher (Cazden, 1985; Hiebert, 1983) and from a more desirable work orientation and higher level of attention to the lesson (Eder & Felmlee, 1984). Third, although in theory grouping should be done to meet students' individual needs and should be marked by frequent regrouping and movement of individual students between groups, in practice group membership tends to remain highly stable once groups are formed initially (Hallinan & Sorensen, 1983). Furthermore, since students spend more time with peers in their groups than they do with classmates assigned to other groups, group assignments affect peer contact and friendship patterns in addition to achievement rates, the more so as time goes on (Hallinan & Sorensen, 1985). In mixed-race classrooms where race is correlated with reading ability or achievement levels, ability grouping will result in de facto resegregation of the students, even though race as such may not be taken into account in making group assignments (Haller, 1985). Finally, ability grouping can result in the labeling effects, "low-group psychology" effects, and related undesirable expectation effects that were reviewed in Chapter 4.

Rist (1970) provides gripping examples of many of these potential problems with within-class ability grouping in a study of a class of students followed from kindergarten through the second grade. Rist noted that after just a few days in class, the kindergarten teacher began to call consistently on the same students to lead the class to the lavatory, to be in charge of the equipment, to take attendance, and so on. On the eighth day, the teacher made permanent seating arrangements.

At table 1, located closest to her own desk, she placed the children who were generally the most verbal, who approached her without apprehension, who were free of body odor, and who came from relatively higher socioeconomic backgrounds. Interviews with the teacher suggested that these groupings were based on her expectations for students' success or failure. She spontaneously verbalized low expectations for the performance of children at tables 2 and 3. Yet these children, who were shy and had trouble communicating with her, were placed farthest away from her, adding another barrier to their overcoming these problems.

Rist followed 18 of these 30 children when they were assigned to the same first-grade classroom and noted that all of those who had been placed at table 1 in kindergarten were placed at table A (the highest group) in first grade. No student who had been placed at table 2 or 3 in kindergarten was placed at table A. Those who had been at table 2 or 3 in kindergarten were placed at table B, with the exception of one placed at table C. Most of the students at table C were repeating the first grade from the previous year.

Data from the second grade revealed the same pattern. There, the teacher termed the best group the Tigers, called the middle group the Cardinals, and unbelievably, labeled the low group the Clowns. No student who had not been at table A in the first grade moved up to the Tigers. Students from tables B and C formed the Cardinals, and students repeating second grade from the previous year were the Clowns. Rist suggested that this teacher, instead of forming groups on the basis of expected performance, formed groups according to how children performed previously. He saw the slow learners as locked into a self-defeating system at this point. No matter how well a child in the low group read, he or she was now destined to remain in the low group. Other studies all suggest the same conclusion: *Rigid* ability grouping does more harm than good, especially to low-group students (Eder, 1981).

Although Rist (1970) describes an extreme case, enough problems with within-class ability grouping have been reported to cause educators to begin to question this practice and seek alternatives to it. This even includes educators concerned with beginning reading instruction, where such grouping has been standard practice. In the report *Becoming a Nation of Readers* (Anderson, Hiebert, Scott, & Wilkinson, 1985), for example, the Commission on Reading calls for reduced emphasis on oral reading in small homogeneous groups and an increased emphasis on silent reading and reading comprehension exercises. Furthermore, it suggests that teachers experiment with alternatives to homogeneous small groups as settings for accomplishing any oral reading practice that does need to be done. Some programs have accomplished this through whole-class instruction followed by silent reading and comprehension assignments during which the teacher circulates to listen to individuals read orally. Others have done so by assigning students to work in pairs, alternately taking the reader and the listener role.

It is too early to say whether such alternatives will prove more effective than teaching reading to homogeneous small groups. It is clear, however, that within-class ability grouping can have a great range of effects on students, depending on the decisions made when forming these groups in the first place and the nature of the instruction provided to the groups subsequently. We have several suggestions for teachers considering within-class ability grouping.

First, the number and composition of the groups should depend on the distributions of achievement levels and instructional needs among the students in the class. In other words, if you believe that within-class grouping is necessary to achieve homogeneity among students assigned to the same group, then make sure that such homogeneity is achieved—don't just arbitrarily divide the class into three equal-sized groups. This point may seem obvious, but Hallinan and Sorensen (1983) report that most teachers form three groups and try to keep their sizes equal, to the point that they feel it necessary to demote a student from a higher group to a lower group in order to balance out a promotion from the lower group to the higher group. Such behavior is explained in part by the availability of materials and other classroom management constraints, but many teachers probably divide the class into three equal-sized groups automatically without reflection on the purpose grouping is supposed to serve or whether it fits the needs of a particular class of students.

Second, grouping should lead to more effective meeting of instructional needs, not merely to differentiated pacing through the curriculum. Teaching will still have to be individualized within the group setting, and students who continue to have trouble will need additional instruction. This may mean simply repeating the material, but often it will mean reteaching a concept in a different way with new examples. Students who did not learn something the first time are unlikely to learn it the second time unless the teacher presents it in a new or more thorough way.

Third, group assignments should be flexible. A group should exist because it facilitates teaching and learning by placing together students with similar needs. However, a student who has mastered phonics no longer needs to be in a group that spends half of its time on phonics drills. Group assignments should be reviewed regularly with an eye toward disbanding groups that have outlived their usefulness and forming new groups to respond to current needs.

Fourth, group scheduling and instructional practices should also be flexible. When there are good instructional reasons for it, a particular group might best meet for 40 minutes on one day and 20 minutes the next day, but this will not happen if the teacher rigidly adheres to a schedule calling for each group to meet daily for 30 minutes. Also, there is no need for the teacher to continue to work with the entire group throughout the allotted time period. One way to meet individual needs within the group setting is to release students who have mastered the day's objectives and let them get started on seatwork assignments while keeping the remaining students in the group for more concentrated and individualized instruction.

Fifth, because of the potential dangers of labeling effects and because grouping affects peer contact opportunities, teachers should limit the degree to which group membership affects other aspects of students' school experiences. Members of the same reading group should not be seated together or otherwise dealt with as a group outside of the reading instruction context, and if ability grouping is used for teaching mathematics or other subjects, group assignments should be based on achievement progress in these other subjects rather than in reading.

Finally, groups should be organized and taught in ways that provide low achievers with the extra instruction that they need. For example, teachers can assign more students to high groups and fewer students to low groups, thus arranging for more intensive instruction of low achievers within the group setting (Dreeben, 1984). Or, teachers can arrange the schedule so that they spend more of their time providing direct instruction and supervision to students in the low groups (while students in the high groups spend more time working cooperatively or independently).

Planned Heterogeneous Grouping

Small groups do not have to be formed based on student ability, especially if the object of the grouping is merely to reduce the number of students to be taught together at one time and not necessarily to homogenize the group. For example, beginning reading instruction may be best conducted in small groups because it involves both slow-paced oral reading with corrections and fast-paced drills on word attack skills, two activities that are difficult to conduct with the whole class. Thus, even in classrooms composed of students of similar ability, teachers may want to conduct beginning reading instruction in the small-group setting. If so, such teachers should bear in mind that grouping can be achieved without necessarily grouping the students by ability. Often, in fact, it may make more sense to group the students randomly or on the basis of managerial considerations (e.g., separating students who tend to become disruptive when assigned to the same group).

Under some circumstances, teachers will want to make group assignments designed to achieve some kind of planned heterogeneity. For example, in activities designed to promote social awareness and acceptance, teachers might want to make sure that each group includes both sexes and whatever racial or ethnic groups are represented in the class. Such grouping is discussed in more detail in a later section of this chapter dealing with cooperative group activities. For now, we will continue with our discussion of how teachers can respond to student heterogeneity by personally providing differentiated instruction to different students. Later, the chapter will conclude with a discussion of methods that involve sharing instructional responsibilities with the students themselves through cooperative learning and student tutoring approaches.

DIFFERENTIATED INSTRUCTION

Some form of differentiated instruction to groups or individuals will be necessary when classroom composition is extremely heterogeneous. A study by Evertson, Sanford, and Emmer (1981) illustrates methods that teachers have used to cope with these difficult situations. The study focused on the ways that junior high English teachers had to adapt their instruction in heterogeneous classrooms compared to the ways that they taught more homogeneous classes. The heterogeneous classes had eight- to ten-year spreads in grade level equivalent units between the low achievers and the high achievers.

Observations revealed that all of the heterogeneous classes got off to a poor start in that the methods and materials used seemed poorly adapted to the students' interests and ability levels, and success rates in terms of completeness and correctness of assignments were poor. This pattern then continued or deteriorated further in heterogeneous classes in which the teachers lacked the managerial skills needed to respond effectively to the problem (especially the skills discussed in Chapter 6). However, after about three weeks, the more effective teachers were able to overcome these problems to some extent by using the following strategies: (1) special attention and help for lower-ability students; (2) limited use of within-class grouping and differentiated materials or assignments; (3) limited differential grading based on individualized effort and continuous progress criteria; (4) limited use of peer tutoring; and (5) frequent monitoring and provision of academic feedback to all students, coupled with mechanisms to insure student accountability for participating in lessons and completing assignments.

Due to these teachers' managerial and instructional skills, not to mention their sheer energy and determination, there was no difference in achievement gain between the heterogeneous and the homogeneous classes. Still, there were limits on what could be accomplished. The pressures of meeting the greater range of instructional needs in the heterogeneous classes left the teachers with little time for personalized interaction with the students, especially interaction concerning nonacademic topics. In the poorly managed heterogeneous classes, there were also the year-long problems of frequent student boredom or frustration due to inappropriate assignments. Probably because of these problems, ratings of student task engagement and cooperation remained lower in the heterogeneous classes throughout the year. Thus, this study illustrates that heterogeneous classes present difficulties, but that teachers can respond effectively to them by using appropriate techniques for managing the classroom and providing differentiated instruction.

The need for differentiated instruction is illustrated by Evans (1985), who presents an interesting ethnographic study of what happened when a comprehensive secondary school (grades 7–9) in England switched from the traditional streamed arrangement to mixed-ability grouping. Many of the teachers tried to persist with whole-class methods directed toward high or medium achievement levels within the class, just as they had done previously when the students had been tracked. Typically they reduced teacher-led class instruction and increased individualized work on seatwork assignments, but essentially, these teachers taught the heterogeneous groups as whole classes.

Consequently, they were forced to slow the pacing and concentrate even more than they did before on lower-level facts and skills rather than higher-level cognitive objectives, with the result that many of the brightest students were bored and many of the slowest students still had difficulty keeping up. Lacking the time to teach the latter students to the level of true mastery, the teachers would "pilot" these students through the curriculum by leading them through overly simplified paths to answers that they could give without thinking or actually learning much of anything, by frequently giving them the answers when they did not supply them, by responding to weak answers as if they indicated full understanding, and by "summarizing" answers in ways that actually elaborated on them considerably. Similarly, the teachers guided slower students through individualized seatwork assignments by simplifying directions and giving feedback in ways that converted cognitive tasks into mere procedural tasks and by often allowing students to copy answers from peers or look them up in the back of the book without truly understanding how to arrive at these answers or why they were correct. Thus, teachers who persisted with whole-class methods in highly heterogeneous classes accepted the *appearance* of progress from their slower students in the place of actual progress in mastering the curriculum. They also tended to leave high achievers underchallenged, or in the case of foreign language classes, to use the high achievers as the steering group that determined the pacing of the class as a whole through the curriculum. Here, the high achievers appeared to be the only students who enjoyed the classes or really understood the content as the year progressed.

Science teachers typically coped by emphasizing topic-centered, group-based instruction that allowed students to address common topics at a variety of levels of sophistication. All students would work on the same topic during a given unit, but the work would be divided into a number of investigatory or practical activities on which the students would work in groups (predominantly from booklets). Activities were organized to include basic work that was required and enrichment work that was optional so that the less able groups would do only the former but the more able groups could move on to the latter. Because topics were not sequenced linearly, each new topic presented new opportunities for students to learn and achieve success, yet the variety of levels of sophistication at which each topic could be addressed provided opportunities for differentiated instruction. The brighter students tended to do much more writing, for example.

The advantages of this approach were counterbalanced by management problems. The teachers found it difficult to get around often enough to supervise the progress of each group and to establish workable classroom rules and routines that would encourage students to interact about the content but at the same time discourage them from merely socializing during group-work times. Pacing tended to be determined by the high achievers within groups, so that low achievers sometimes were ignored or ended up being "piloted" by the high achievers. Sex differences in student activities also were noticeable in these science classes: The boys tended to be more assertive in planning and conducting investigations and experiments, whereas the girls were more likely to merely observe or confine their participation to recording the information. Not much truly cooperative learning occurred, at least in part because the materials and booklets were not written with that in mind and because the teachers did not train the students in cooperative learning principles.

Mathematics teachers typically shifted from whole-class to individualized instruction based on programmed learning materials and encountered the problems associated with this approach as described in the previous chapter. Most of these teachers found that they could not get around often enough to individual students (especially slow learners) to be able to teach them effectively.

Social studies teachers typically opted for a combination of whole-class instruction and individual seatwork assignments. The seatwork assignments were not individualized as in the math classes, but there usually was some differentiation of assignments according to student ability. Much of the seatwork was less effective than it could have been because of legibility problems and other deficiencies in the physical quality of the materials, and many assignments were at such low cognitive levels that they could be accomplished with little or no thinking or writing (beyond one word).

Extra materials and assignments (usually open-ended tasks) were provided for the brighter students to keep them occupied until the class as a whole was ready to move on to new content. Teachers would make rounds and deal with individuals briefly as in the individualized math classes, but there usually was less need for help in these social studies classes, so that the teachers spent less time actually talking to students once they finished whole-class instruction. Thus, both the level and the amount of instruction in social studies were reduced for most of these students compared to what occurred under the whole-class instruction approach used previously when the students were tracked.

English teachers could not be characterized in any simple way because they showed the most variability in curriculum (what they taught) and instructional method (how they taught). In general, those who emphasized basic skills (spelling, grammar, etc.) stressed low-level seatwork assignments, whereas those who emphasized higher-level language arts objectives (critical reading of prose or poetry, written compositions, etc.) relied on whole-class instruction followed by differentiated assignments.

General Principles for Differentiating Instruction

These and other experiences with teaching heterogeneous classes suggest certain general principles. First, as the range of student ability increases, the role of whole-class teaching decreases. Students in mixed-ability classes will still benefit from exchanging ideas in a large-group setting (speaking before a group, etc.). Furthermore, managerial issues, unit introductions and reviews, use of equipment, demonstration of experiments, and certain other types of information exchange will still lend themselves to whole-class presentations in mixed-ability classes. In general though, the frequency and duration of whole-class teaching will be reduced, and teachers' use of individual assignments and small-group work will increase. The following discussion focuses on ways to make individual and small-group assignments that allow students of varying ability to work on *similar projects*. Some students can read well and will do so enthusiastically; others have limited skills and interest in reading. If teachers are to allow students of mixed ability to work on similar projects, they must solve the reading problem. One strategy for doing this is to instruct students in independent reading and study skills. Another is to gather a wide assortment of materials written at varying levels of difficulty on a *few* core topics (it is unrealistic to try to acquire and store several books on every curriculum topic).

Although they read books that differ in detail or vocabulary, students can still share a common focus on historical events (the Civil War) or famous persons (Booker T. Washington, Marie Curie, Babe Ruth). Furthermore, many stories of literary significance are written with a low vocabulary demand (e.g., *Tom Sawyer*). Students reading at different grade levels could benefit from reading these books, even though the teacher may eventually ask them to respond to the books in different ways later.

Even individualized assignments that do not demand a great deal of reading must be carefully prepared with the low achiever in mind. If slow students are to comprehend written instructions and function independently, directions must be stated in very simple and explicit terms. Otherwise, teachers will spend too much time clarifying directions and responding to the managerial problems that occur when students do not know what to do. Teachers who provide directions simple enough for the least capable reader (who will use that particular activity sheet) will employ a support system that allows students to gain confidence in their independent learning skills. As this occurs, the students can be challenged with progressively more complex tasks.

Cooke (1976) suggests ways to develop individual seatwork cards for students of varying ability who are working on similar historical topics. Included in his suggestions are the following:

1. Develop a card for each topic and subtopic and require all students to complete these activities at their individual paces.
2. Develop a number of option cards that provide guidelines for more intensive subject work, special activities, etc., and allow students to choose from the option cards.
3. Do not try to develop option cards for each individual (this is unnecessary and impractical) but do produce separate option (or even core) cards for three or four ability levels.

Figures 10.1, 10.2, and 10.3 illustrate work cards prepared for three ability levels. The figures show how the same historical topic could be pursued in different ways. Figure 10.1 shows the assignment for slow 12-year-olds. Notice that it focuses on concrete details (helping the student to comprehend parts of a passage in order to find material to make comparatively simple judgments).

Figures 10.2 and 10.3 illustrate assignments for middle- and high-level students. Progressively, instructions are written in less-specific terms, students are directed to search different books, page references are omitted in favor of references to general sources or indexes, more deduction is demanded, and the use of supporting evidence for ideas is encouraged. For the most capable students, considerable initiative is required and more problem-solving questions are raised (dealing with conflicting accounts of history, etc.).

Students at all levels can benefit from problem-solving activities as well as from searching for facts and performing simple verification tasks. The work cards in Figures 10.1, 10.2, and 10.3 are presented to illustrate the relative emphasis that students of varying achievement levels need in seatwork assignments. To the extent that students who need "structure" receive and learn to handle appropriate learning assignments as depicted in Figure 10.1, they will need more assignments like those in Figures 10.2 and 10.3.

Teachers will have to decide when it is possible to keep students of mixed ability working on the same topic. Perhaps the best strategy in a subject like history is to identify core topics that all students can share and separate topics that more capable students can pursue at more complex and challenging levels. For example, all students might learn about the major battles of the Civil War, but only more capable students would be assigned to do research on the details of these battles and the leadership decisions and other factors that decided them. For more about teaching mixed-ability students in a variety of subject areas, see Evans (1985), Sands and Kerry (1982), or Wragg (1976).

Different Learning Activities for Different Students

We have emphasized the need for building different assignments around common themes to allow students of varying achievement levels to address the same content at varying levels of sophistication. More generally, we have concentrated our discussion on accommodating student differences in ability and achievement. Students also differ, however, in personal and social traits such as energy levels, assertiveness, sociability, and patience. As teachers become more proficient at matching curriculum and instruction to students' achievement levels, they may wish to introduce additional individualization by accommodating differences in students' personalities, learning styles, or preferences.

The number of student factors that could be listed for consideration by teachers is endless, so there is no point in trying to construct an exhaustive list. However, we can present guidelines for differentiated instruction of a few common student types that teachers can expect to find in most classrooms. Good and Power (1976) have identified the following five types of students:

1. *Successful students* are task oriented, academically successful, and cooperative. They typically participate actively in lessons, turn in complete and correct assignments, and create few if any discipline problems. They tend to like school and to be well liked by both teachers and peers.
2. *Social students* are more person oriented than task oriented. They have the ability to achieve but value socializing with friends more than working on assignments. They tend to have many friends and to be popular with peers, but are usually not well liked by teachers because their frequent socializing creates management problems.

HADRIAN'S WALL

This is a picture of a part of Hadrian's Wall as it is now. You can also see the ruins of the Roman fort at Housesteads.

Have a copy of *A Soldier on Hadrian's Wall* by D. Taylor on your table.

Things To Do

1. Write down these sentences and fill in the missing words. Pages 14 and 16 of *A Soldier on Hadrian's Wall* will help you.

   a. Hadrian's Wall was built from . . . . in the east to . . . . in the west. It is . . . . miles long.

   b. It was made of . . . .

   c. It measures . . . . feet high and . . . . feet thick.

   d. In front of the wall was a . . . . and behind it was a . . . .

2. Imagine that you are the Roman officer in charge of building the wall. Write a letter to a friend in Rome telling him or her what the various buildings on the wall are and what they are used for. You can find out about these buildings in your book, pp. 16–20.

3. Draw a diagram of one of the buildings in your letter. Label all the parts and sizes of it. If you prefer, make a model of it to scale.

4. Draw and color a picture showing a scene from Hadrian's Wall, perhaps an enemy attack or soldiers marching along it. From the picture on this card, imagine what it must have been like on the wall.

Figure 10.1 An example of a work card.

Work card 2

HADRIAN'S WALL

This is a picture of Hadrian's Wall today.

Read

      A Soldier on Hadrian's Wall by D. Taylor

      Roman Britain by R. Mitchell

      Roman Britain by J. Liversidge, pp. 16–33

      The Romans in Scotland by O. Thomson, Chapter 3

Things To Do

1. Answer these questions as fully as you can:

   a. Why did Hadrian build a wall across Britain?

   b. If you were an enemy of the Romans trying to break through the wall from the north, where do you think its weakest points would be? You will need to find information about the various forts and defenses along the wall.

   c. Another wall was built 20 years later by the Romans in Scotland. Which Emperor built it? Why was it built? How different was it from Hadrian's Wall?

2. Imagine that you are the Roman officer in charge of building Hadrian's Wall. Write a report to the Emperor telling him why you have decided to change the wall from turf to stone and to alter the size.

3. Draw a diagram of a cross-section of the wall, or of a fort, and label it carefully. If you prefer, make a scale model of it.

4. *Either,* as the Roman officer, write an entry for your diary describing an incident on the wall.
   Or, draw and color a picture of the incident.
   Do both of these if you wish.

Figure 10.2 An example of a work card.

HADRIAN'S WALL

Consult the books in the class history library on Roman Britain, in particular *The Roman Frontiers of Britain* by D. R. Wilson; *The Roman Imperial Army of the First and Second Centuries* by G. Webster; *The Romans in Scotland* by O. Thomson; *Handbook to the Roman Wall* by I. A. Richmond.

1. Why did Hadrian build a wall across Britain between the Solway and the Tyne? Why were no other routes suitable?

2. Find a picture of a British hill fort (e.g., Maiden Castle or Hod Hill) and compare it with Housesteads as a fortification. Illustrate your answer.

3. If you were an enemy of the Romans trying to break through the wall from the north, where do you think its weakest points would be? Why?

4. The Emperor Antoninus Pius decided to build a wall in Scotland in about A.D. 142. Imagine and write a conversation between Antoninus and his senior advisor about building the wall in Scotland in which they discuss why Hadian's Wall is no longer suitable, and in what ways the new wall should be different.

5. *Either,* make a scale model *or* draw a picture of part of Hadrian's Wall. Do both if you wish.

Figure 10.3 An example of a work card.

3. *Dependent students* frequently look to the teacher for support and encouragement and often ask for additional directions and help. Teachers generally are concerned about the academic progress of these students and do what they can to assist them. Peers may reject dependent students because they tend to be socially immature.

4. *Alienated students* are reluctant learners and potential drop-outs. Extremely alienated students reject school and everything it stands for. Some develop open hostility and create disruptions through aggression and defiance. Others withdraw, sitting in the fringes of the classroom and refusing to participate. Teachers tend to reject the ones who express alienation openly and to be indifferent toward those who express it passively.

5. *Phantom students* seem to fade into the background because they are rarely noticed or heard from. Some are shy, nervous students, while others are quiet, independent workers of average ability. They work steadily on assignments but they rarely participate actively in group activities because they do not volunteer, and are rarely involved in managerial exchanges because they do not create disruptions. Typically, neither teachers nor peers know these students very well or think about or interact with them very often. If asked to name all of their students from memory, teachers are likely to have the most difficulty remembering the names of phantom students.

After surveying the literature on these five types of students, Good and Power (1976) developed suggestions for ways that teachers might profitably introduce differentiated instruction to accommodate their different preferences and needs. Some of their suggestions are summarized in Table 10.1.

Although based partly on research, the suggestions given in Table 10.1 should be considered speculative suggestions rather than proven guidelines, for two reasons. First, accommodating students' preferences is not the same as meeting their needs. Several studies have shown that allowing students to choose their own learning methods or arranging to teach them in the ways that they prefer to be taught may produce *less* achievement gain than teaching them in some other way, even if it improves their attitudes toward the learning situation (Clark, 1982; Schofield, 1981; Solomon & Kendall, 1979). Second, accommodating students' particular personal qualities may have the effect of reinforcing these qualities, and some of them are qualities that the teacher would rather change if possible. For example, it would be easy to respond reciprocally to the behavior of phantom students and passive-withdrawn alienated students by minimizing interaction with them—never calling on them unless they raise their hand or indicate a need for help. This might even maximize the comfort of both the teacher and the students involved. However, it probably would not be in these students' best interests.

Even though such complexities must be kept in mind, the suggestions in Table 10.1 offer ideas about how teachers can introduce a degree of individualization into their instruction while basically teaching the class as a group. Some of these suggestions can be incorporated easily (such as those that involve interacting more often or more affectively with certain students), whereas others would be more difficult or time consuming to implement (such as those that call for preparing different activities or assignments for different groups of students). It may not be

Table 10.1 SUGGESTIONS FOR MEETING THE NEEDS OF FIVE DIFFERENT TYPES OF STUDENTS

	Success	Social	Dependent	Alienated	Phantom
1. Type of information needed from teacher					
a. Substantive explanation of content	Very high	Very high	High	High	High
b. Procedural directions	Low	Low	High	Moderate–high	Moderate–low
c. Socializing, emotional support, humor	Very low	Low–moderate	Moderate	Moderate (establish private rapport)	Low
2. Type of task needed					
a. Reading skills required	High	High	Low	Low	Moderate
b. Task difficulty level	Very high	High	Low–moderate	Low–moderate	Moderate
c. Abstractness level	High	Moderate	Low initially	Low initially	Moderate
d. Cognitive level	High	Moderate	Low–moderate	Low–moderate	Moderate
e. Degree of structure (specificity about what to do and how to do it)	Low	Moderate	High	High	Moderate
f. Opportunity to make active, overt responses	Not important	High	High	High	Moderate
g. Opportunity to make choices	Moderate (stress on enrichment)	Moderate (stress on choices to work with others)	Low	Moderate (stress on relevance)	Low
h. Interest value of task to student	Not important	Moderate	Low	High	Low
i. Length of task	Long	Short	Moderate	Moderate	Long

3. Type of response demanded					
a. Written	High	Low	High	Moderate	High
b. Oral	Low	High	Low	Low	Low
c. Physical	Low	Moderate	Moderate	High	Low
4. Individual vs. group settings					
a. Individual	High	Low	High	High	High
b. Group	Low	Moderate	Low	Low—moderate	Low
5. Emphasis on competition	High	Moderate	Low initially	Low	Moderate
6. Type of feedback from teacher					
a. Personal praise	Low	Low	Moderate	Moderate (private)	Low
b. Personal criticism	Low	Low	Low	Very low	Low
c. Praise of good work	Low	Moderate	Moderate	Moderate (private)	Low-moderate
d. Criticism of poor work	Moderate	Moderate	Low	Low (but communicate demand)	Low-moderate

Source: Adapted from T. Good and C. Power (1976): Designing successful classroom environments for different types of students. *Journal of Curriculum Studies, 8,* 45–60.

possible to introduce such variation into the activities and assignments planned for each particular day, but these guidelines are useful for judging the appropriateness of longer-range plans. Each week or unit should provide enough balance to deliver something for everyone rather than restrict plans to activities and assignments that are well matched to the needs of one or two subgroups but poorly matched to the needs of others.

It is never possible for a single teacher to simultaneously provide optimal curriculum and instruction to all students in the class, because different subgroups present conflicting needs and because classroom management considerations take first priority. For example, dependent students (at least until they are taught self-supervision skills and gain the confidence necessary for exercising these skills) will need close supervision and frequent teacher feedback during independent seatwork. However, wise teachers reserve the first few minutes of seatwork segments to make sure that students in general and alienated students in particular get started on their assignments. Furthermore, they learn to keep their interactions with individuals brief so that they can continue to circulate around the room and be available to students who need immediate help. All students, even the most successful, need monitoring and feedback.

Despite these complexities, teachers who have developed a workable system for instructing the whole class can then use this system as a base from which to introduce differentiated instruction for various students. In this regard, it helps if a variety of work settings or assignment formats is available and if the number of students working individually at a given time is limited so that the teacher does not have to try to provide individualized feedback to the entire class. For example, an elementary grade teacher might assign dependent, alienated, and social students to work on individualized seatwork during the early morning when these students are not involved in reading-group activities. These relatively brief times (typically two 20-minute periods) for individual work could be used profitably by these students (who may react less favorably to longer individual seatwork assignments), especially if the teacher supplies answer sheets or other self-checking devices that they can use to monitor their progress. Success students and phantom students might be engaged in brief small-group projects during these same periods. Then, after recess, the students might all be engaged in whole-class work in mathematics. In the afternoon, success students and phantom students could be assigned to spend large amounts of time in individual work while the teacher actively supervises the small-group work of other students.

However, there is only so much that can be accomplished even by experienced teachers who have developed sophisticated systems for organizing and managing instruction. Consequently, even the combination of methods we have discussed so far (ability grouping, differentiated curriculum materials and assignments, and differentiated teacher instruction) may not be enough to accommodate the diverse needs of students in heterogeneous classes. Teachers may want to take the additional step of sharing instructional responsibilities with the students themselves by using cooperative learning approaches or by arranging for students to receive tutorial assistance. At least for certain purposes and for some types of students, these may be useful alternatives or supplements to traditional methods.

COOPERATIVE LEARNING

The traditional approach calls for whole-class instruction and recitation followed by independent seatwork. Cooperative learning approaches replace independent seatwork with cooperative learning activities in which small groups (typically 4 to 6 students) work together on practice or application exercises. Thus, under cooperative learning arrangements students work with some of their peers rather than working alone on assignments, and they receive information and feedback from peers in addition to the teacher and the curriculum materials. Cooperative learning methods differ according to the task structures and incentive structures that are in effect (Slavin, 1983).

The term *task structure* refers to the nature of the task (its goal, the kinds of responses that it requires, etc.) and the specified working conditions under which the task is supposed to be accomplished. Task structures may be individual, cooperative, or competitive. *Individual task structures* require students to work on the task alone (except for help from the teacher if necessary). Traditional independent seatwork employs an individual task structure. *Cooperative task structures* require students to work cooperatively in order to meet task requirements. Assignments that call for students to assist one another in learning or to work together to produce some sort of group product involve cooperative task structures. Finally, *competitive task structures* require students to compete (either as individuals or as teams) in order to fulfill task requirements. Contests, debates, and various competitive games involve competitive task structures.

Students within groups work together under cooperative and competitive task structures that call for team competition (where members of the same team compete with other teams). Within each group, members may cooperate in working toward either group goals or individual goals. When pursuing *group goals,* the members work together to produce a single product that results from the pooled resources and shared labor of the group. For example, the group might paint a mural, assemble a collage, or prepare a skit or report to be presented to the rest of the class. When working cooperatively to reach *individual goals,* group members assist one another by discussing how to respond to questions or assignments, checking work, or providing feedback or tutorial assistance. Cooperative work toward individual goals occurs when individual students are responsible for turning in assignments but are allowed to consult with one another as they work on those assignments.

Cooperative task structures also differ according to whether or not there is task specialization. *Task specialization* is in effect when the larger task to be accomplished is divided into several subtasks and different group members work on different subtasks. When there is no task specialization, each member works on the same task. In preparing a report on a foreign country, for example, task specialization would be in effect if one group member was assigned to do the introduction, another to cover geography and climate, another to cover natural resources and the economy, and so on.

Besides differing in task structure, group activities differ in incentive structure. *Incentive structure* (also called *reward structure* or *goal structure*) refers to methods used for motivating students to perform the task. These include the nature of the incentives themselves (grades, concrete rewards, symbolic rewards) as well as the rules specifying what must be done to earn the rewards and how they will be delivered. Like task structures, incentive structures can be individual, cooperative, or competitive. Under *individual incentive structures,* any particular student's performance has no consequences for other students' chances of earning available rewards. That is, individuals are rewarded (or not) depending on whether or not they in meet prespecified performance criteria, regardless of how the rest of the class performs. Under *cooperative incentive structures,* individuals' chances of earning rewards depend not only on their own efforts but on those of other members of their group. Thus, instead of or in addition to rewarding students as individuals, the teacher rewards groups of students according to the level of performance that they have been able to achieve through their combined efforts. Finally, under *competitive incentive structures,* groups or individuals must compete for whatever rewards are available. The winners get the most desirable rewards and the losers get less desirable rewards or no rewards at all. Classes in which grades are assigned according to preset curves explicitly involve competitive incentive structures, and any classes in which grades are assigned, at least in part, on the basis of comparative performance implicitly involve competitive incentive structures.

Cooperative and competitive incentive structures can also be differentiated according to whether they involve group rewards or individual rewards. *Group rewards* are distributed equally to all members of the group. These may involve a single reward to be shared by the group (such as a prize or a treat) or may involve assigning the same reward to each group member (if the group's product receives a grade of A each group member will receive a grade of A, regardless of what that member's particular contribution to the group product might have been). *Individual rewards* are assigned differentially to individual students depending on their own personal levels of effort and performance. For example, students may be encouraged to cooperate with peers in discussing assignments and preparing for a test, but would be required to take the test individually and would be graded according to their individual performance.

Task structures and incentive structures are independent: A cooperative task structure does not necessarily imply a cooperative incentive structure, and so on. In fact, it is possible to impose any incentive structure on any task structure, although some such arrangements would be highly artificial and unusual. It is possible, for example, to require students to work on assignments alone (e.g., to use an individual task structure) but to impose a competitive reward structure by dividing students into "teams" that never work together but are rewarded partly on the basis of how well the team members do as a group on unit tests. Table 10.2 shows the combinations of task and reward structures that are typically used.

Well-Known Cooperative Learning Programs

Some of the best known and widely researched cooperative learning programs are described below. For additional information about these programs and other cooperative learning programs, see Sharan et al. (1984), Slavin (1983), or Slavin et al. (1985).

Learning Together   The Learning Together model of cooperative learning was developed by David and Roger Johnson (Johnson & Johnson, 1975; Johnson et al.,

Table 10.2 POSSIBLE COMBINATIONS OF TASK AND REWARD STRUCTURES

(all combinations are possible, but some are more typically used than others)

| | Incentive Structures | | | | |
| | I. Individual[a] | II. Cooperative[b] | | III. Competitive[c] | |
Task structures		A. Individual rewards	B. Group reward	A. Individual rewards	B. Group reward
I. *Individual.* Each student works alone.	Typical	Possible	Possible	Typical	Possible
II. *Cooperative.* Students work together or help one another.					
A. *Group goals.* Individuals cooperate to create a group product.					
1. *Undifferentiated roles.* Each student has the same task.	Possible	Possible	Typical	Possible	Typical
2. *Differentiated roles.* Different students perform different tasks.	Possible	Possible	Typical	Possible	Typical
B. *Individual goals.* Individuals help one another to fulfill their respective individual responsibilities.					
1. *Undifferentiated roles.* Each student has the same task.	Typical	Typical	Possible	Typical	Possible
2. *Differentiated roles.* Different students perform different tasks.	Typical	Typical	Possible	Typical	Possible
III. *Competitive.* The task requires students to compete.					
A. *Individual competition.*	Typical	Typical	Possible	Typical	Possible
B. *Team competition.*	Possible	Possible	Typical	Possible	Typical

[a] Reward depends strictly on one's own performance.
[b] Reward depends, at least in part, on group performance.
[c] Reward depends, at least in part, on the outcome of a competition.

1984). Early versions of this approach called for students to work together in four-or five-member heterogeneous groups on assignment sheets. The major interest was in getting students who differed in achievement level, sex, race, or ethnicity working together. The groups would hand in a single sheet and be praised as a group for working well together and for their performance on the task.

Experimentation with this approach revealed that some variations worked better than others, and eventually the Johnsons identified four basic elements that they believe should always be included in any cooperative learning activity (Johnson & Johnson, 1985b; Johnson, Johnson, Holubec, & Roy, 1984).

1. *Positive interdependence.* Students should recognize that they are interdependent with other members of their group for achieving a successful group product. Positive interdependence can be structured through mutual goals (goal interdependence); division of labor (task interdependence); dividing materials, resources, or information among group members (resource interdependence); assigning students unique roles (role interdependence); or giving group rewards (reward interdependence). By assigning separate roles or tasks or by insuring that each group member brings unique materials, resources, or information to the group task, the teacher insures that each group member will play an active role; and that it will not be possible for one or two brighter or more assertive students to dominate the interaction to the exclusion of the other students. By using mutual goals and group rewards, the teacher provides incentives for students to help other members of the group rather than just concentrate on maximizing their own performance.

2. *Face-to-face interaction among students.* Tasks that call for significant interaction among group members are preferred over tasks that can be accomplished mostly by having group members go off and work on their own.

3. *Individual accountability for mastering assigned material.* Mechanisms are needed to insure that each group member has clear objectives for which he or she will be held accountable and receives any needed assessment, feedback, or instructional assistance. It should not be possible for brighter or harder-working students to "cover" for other group members who are largely ignored or who fail to do what they are supposed to do.

4. *Instructing students in appropriate interpersonal and small-group skills.* Students cannot merely be placed together and told to cooperate. They will need instruction in effective small-group cooperation skills such as asking and answering questions, insuring that everyone participates actively and is treated with respect, and assigning tasks and organizing cooperative efforts (see Johnson & Johnson, 1982).

Group Investigation   Shlomo Sharan and his colleagues (Sharan & Sharan, 1976; Sharan et al., 1984) have developed what they call Group Investigation models in Israel that are similar to the Learning Together methods developed in the United States by the Johnsons. Group Investigation students form their own two- to six-member groups to work together using cooperative inquiry, group discussion, and cooperative planning and projects. The groups choose subtopics from a unit studied by the whole class, break these subtopics into individual tasks, and carry out the activities necessary to prepare a group report on the subtopic. Eventually, the group will make a presentation or display to communicate its findings to the class and will be evaluated based on the quality of this report.

Jigsaw   The Jigsaw approach (Aronson, Blaney, Stephan, Sikes, & Snapp, 1978) insures active individual participation and group cooperation by arranging tasks so that each group member possesses unique information and has a unique role to play. The group product cannot be completed unless each member does his or her part, just as a jigsaw puzzle cannot be completed unless each piece is included. For example, information needed to compose a biography might be broken into early life, first accomplishments, major setbacks, later life, and world events occurring during the person's lifetime. One member of each group would be given the relevant information and assigned responsibility for one of the five sections of the biography, and other group members would be assigned to other sections. Members of different groups who were working on the same section would meet together in "expert groups" to discuss their sections. Then they would return to their regular groups and take turns teaching their groupmates about their sections. Since the only way that students can learn about sections other than their own is to listen carefully to their groupmates, they are motivated to support and show interest in one another's work. The students then prepare biographies or take quizzes on the material individually.

Several cooperative learning methods have been developed by Robert Slavin and others at The Johns Hopkins University. Collectively, these methods are known as *Student Team Learning*. The four Student Team Learning methods are *TGT, STAD, Jigsaw II,* and *TAI.*

Teams-Games-Tournament (TGT)   The Teams-Games-Tournament approach (DeVries & Slavin, 1978; DeVries, Slavin, Fennessey, Edwards, & Lombardo, 1980) calls for students to work together in four- to five-member heterogeneously grouped teams to help one another master content and prepare for competitions against other teams. After the teacher presents the material to be learned, team members work together studying from worksheets. Typically they discuss the material, tutor one another, and quiz one another to assess mastery. Cooperative practice in this form continues throughout the week in preparation for tournaments held on Fridays.

For the tournaments, students are assigned to three-person tables composed of students from different teams who are similar in achievement. The three students at each table compete at academic games covering the content taught that week and practiced during team meetings. Most of these games are simply numbered questions on a ditto sheet. A student picks a number card and attempts to answer the question corresponding to that number. The student can earn points by answering questions correctly or by successfully challenging and correcting the answers of the other two students at the table. The points earned by individual students at these tournament tables are later summed to determine each team's score, and the teacher prepares a newsletter that recognizes successful teams and unusually high scores attained by individuals. The newsletter may also contain cumulative team scores if tournaments last longer than a single week. Prior to the next tournament, the teacher may reassign certain students to different tournament tables in order to keep the competition as even as possible at each table. This insures that even though the teams are heterogeneous in composition and team membership remains the same, all students begin each tournament with equal chances to earn points for their teams because they will be competing against students from other teams whose achievement is similar to theirs. This incentive structure motivates students not only to strive to master the material on their own but also to help their teammates master the material.

Student Teams—Achievement Divisions (STAD) Student Teams—Achievement Divisions (STAD) is a simplification of TGT (Slavin, 1978). It follows the same heterogeneous grouping and cooperative learning procedures as TGT but replaces the games and tournaments with a quiz. Quiz scores are translated into team competition points based on how students' individual scores compare with the scores of other students in their "achievement division" (composed of students of similar achievement), and individuals' points are combined to yield team totals. As with TGT, the achievement divisions used in STAD are adjusted periodically to keep competition even, and newsletters are published detailing team standings and publicizing noteworthy individual performances.

Both TGT and STAD combine cooperative-learning task structures with team competition and group rewards for cumulative individual performance. However, STAD depersonalizes the competitive elements. Rather than compete face-to-face against class mates at tournament tables, students in STAD classrooms try to do their best on quizzes that they take individually. They know that points will be awarded depending on how they do in comparison with peers in the same achievement division, but they do not know who these students are (teachers do not disclose achievement division membership). Over time, Slavin and his colleagues have placed more emphasis on STAD and less on TGT, both because STAD is simpler to implement and because it reduces the salience of competition.

Jigsaw II Jigsaw II is a simplification and adaptation of the original Jigsaw (Slavin, 1980b). It is simplified in that the teacher does not need to provide each student with unique materials. Instead, all students begin by reading a common narrative but then each student in the group is given a separate topic on which to become an expert. Then, as in the original Jigsaw, students who have the same topic assignments meet in expert groups to discuss them and then return to their teams to teach what they have learned to their teammates. The adaptation involves the incentive structure. The original Jigsaw called for assignment of individual grades based on quiz scores. Jigsaw II calls for the additional element of computation of team scores by summing individual scores and recognizing team accomplishments through a class newsletter.

Team-Assisted Individualization (TAI) Team-assisted individualization (TAI) was described in Chapter 9. It is an adaptation of individualized mathematics instruction that introduces cooperative learning methods and team competition with group reward, as in STAD (Slavin, 1985).

Research on Cooperative Learning Methods

There has been a great deal of research on cooperative learning methods, and several summaries are available (Johnson, Johnson, & Maruyama, 1983; Sharan, 1980; Slavin, 1980a, 1983). The results are generally quite positive, although some studies are misleading in that they begged the questions that they were supposed to be studying by using learning tasks that are necessarily done more effectively by groups than by individuals or by allowing groups to work together on tests and then assigning the group's test score to each individual (many of whom would not have scored so highly if they had been required to take the test on their own). Even with studies such as these eliminated, however, the research indicates that cooperative learning methods are feasible in many classroom situations and that they are likely to have positive effects both on achievement and on other outcome variables.

As summarized by Slavin (1983), the research results are as follows. First, the effects on achievement are quite positive. Of 41 studies conducted in regular classrooms, 26 found significantly greater learning in classes using cooperative methods and only one found significantly greater learning in a control group. Somewhat surprisingly, these achievement effects appear to be related to the use of specific group rewards based on members' individual performance rather than to the cooperative task structures used. That is, it is the group reward structures such as those used in TGT, STAD, and TAI that appear to explain positive effects on student achievement, and not the fact that students work together in groups. Consequently, the student team learning methods that include team rewards (TGT, STAD, Jigsaw II, TAI) tend to have consistently positive effects on student achievement, whereas the more purely cooperative methods (Learning Together, Group Investigation, and the original Jigsaw) are less likely to produce a significant achievement advantage over traditional techniques (Moskowitz, Malvin, Schaeffer, & Schaps, 1985; Okebukola, 1985; Slavin, 1983).

Also, methods that insure the accountability of individual group members to their groupmates produce higher achievement than methods in which it is possible for one or two students to do the work while the others take more passive roles. No study in which group members worked together to produce a single worksheet or group product has yielded positive achievement effects.

The findings on task specialization are mixed, probably because the appropriateness of task specialization varies with subject matter and the particular instructional objectives being pursued. Task specialization seems most useful in social studies and with assignments emphasizing higher-level cognitive skills (Graybeal & Stodolsky, 1985). It is difficult to use task specialization for mathematics or other linearly sequenced curricula.

There is no evidence that group competition offers advantages over other cooperative learning methods so long as arrangements are made to provide specific group rewards based on the cumulative performance of individual group members. Besides direct group competitions as in TGT and STAD, good results have been obtained by giving teams certificates for meeting preset standards independently of the performance of other teams and by using task specialization to motivate students to encourage their groupmates. Thus, although the effects of cooperative learning on achievement appear to be basically motivational, the key is not motivation to win competitions against other teams but motivation to assist one's team-mates to meet their individual goals and thus insure that the team as a whole will do well.

Achievement effects appear to be positive for all types of students, although there are some indications that black and possibly Hispanic students gain even more from cooperative learning arrangements than Anglo students do.

Effects on outcomes other than achievement are even more impressive. Cooperative learning arrangements promote friendship choices and prosocial patterns of interaction among students who differ in achievement, sex, race, or ethnicity, and they promote the acceptance of mainstreamed handicapped students by their nonhandicapped classmates. Cooperative methods also frequently have positive effects, and rarely have negative effects, on affective outcomes such as self-esteem, academic self-confidence, liking for the class, liking and feeling liked by classmates, and various measures of empathy and social cooperation.

In addition to the research summarized above comparing cooperative learning methods with traditional learning methods, there have been some studies of the effects of group composition and the nature of students' interaction during group meetings on students' achievement (Peterson, Wilkinson, Spinelli, & Swing, 1984; Swing & Peterson, 1982; Webb, 1982; Webb & Cullian, 1983). These studies typically involved groups of four students whose interactions were tape recorded for later analysis. Different studies produced somewhat different results, but three main conclusions emerge from this line of research taken as a whole.

First, whether students master the content to be learned depends not only on their entry-level achievement but on the nature of their experience in the group. Giving explanations to other group members is positively correlated with achievement, even when entry-level ability is controlled. This confirms the findings from peer-tutoring studies and other research indicating that explaining material to others is an effective learning experience for the explainer, not just the person receiving the explanation. Receiving explanations usually also correlates positively with later achievement scores, indicating that students who know what to ask about and succeed in getting their questions answered are likely to master the material. In contrast, negative correlations with achievement have been noted for asking questions without getting any response at all or receiving only a direct answer to the question without an explanation of how one arrives at the answer.

A second, related finding is that quality of interaction in small groups can be enhanced through training. Compared to those in untrained control groups, students given training in how to interact during small-group activities have been shown to spend more time on task (asking questions, giving feedback, checking answers) and to go beyond just giving answers by giving more detailed explanations designed to make sure that the listener understands the concept or process.

A third finding is that certain combinations of students seem to work better with one another than other combinations do. In mixed groups containing one high achiever, two average achievers, and one low achiever, most of the interaction involved tutoring of the low achiever by the high achiever, with the average achievers remaining relatively passive. Thus, heterogeneous small groups seemed to be relatively less effective with average achievers, at least when the students had not been trained effectively in how to interact during small-group activities.

Homogeneous groupings produced mixed results. Groups of average students worked well together, helping one another and interacting actively. However, groups in which the students either were all high achievers or all low achievers did not work well together or interact much about the academic content. Members of homogeneous high-achieving groups apparently assumed that no one would need help, and members of homogeneous low-achieving groups often became frustrated because they were unable to explain the material effectively to one another. In general, these data support the decisions of developers of cooperative learning methods to use heterogeneous groups, but they underscore the need for training the students how to act during group activities.

Controlled Conflict and Controversy in Small Groups

David and Roger Johnson and their colleagues have developed an interesting variation on small-group learning methods in which the emphasis is on a degree of controlled conflict or controversy introduced into the group rather than on group cooperation. We refer here to intellectual controversy involving conflict of opinion about academic issues, not physical aggression or other forms of personal conflict. In a general review of these issues, Johnson and Johnson (1979) found that constructively managed controversy in the classroom promotes a healthy uncertainty about the correctness of one's views, curiosity for more information, and generally better achievement. Studies conducted since then have supported this interpretation.

Smith, Johnson, and Johnson (1981) studied the learning of sixth graders about controversial issues such as whether or not strip mining should be allowed. Students were presented with material offering pro and con views on the issues and directed to study the material either individually or in small groups. Controversy groups were divided into halves representing the two sides and encouraged to debate the issues, but concurrence-seeking groups were directed to study the material together and avoid arguing. The results indicated that, compared to the other two conditions, the controversy group condition promoted not only higher achievement but a more accurate understanding of both positions on each issue, more interest in getting more information, and better attitudes toward classmates and toward the value of constructive controversy. Similarly positive results have been obtained in two subsequent studies (Johnson & Johnson, 1985a; Johnson et al., 1985). Teachers whose subjects lend themselves to controversy and debate (policy issues in social studies and science classes; interpretation issues in humanities and literature courses) should consider including controversy groups among their instructional activities.

Conclusions About Cooperative Learning Methods

Cooperative learning methods have achieved impressive results. As Slavin (1983, p. 128) puts it:

> . . . there are many important theoretical as well as practical issues yet to be resolved in research on cooperative learning. However, the research done up to the present has shown enough positive effects of cooperative learning, on a variety of outcomes, to force us to re-examine traditional instructional practices.

We can no longer ignore the potential power of the peer group, perhaps the one remaining free resource for improving schools. We can no longer see the class as 30 or more individuals whose only instructionally useful interactions are with the teacher, where peer interactions are unstructured or off-task. On the other hand, at least for achievement, we now know that simply allowing students to work together is unlikely to capture the power of the peer group to motivate students to perform; structured methods with group rewards based on group members' demonstrated learning appear to be needed. For intergroup relations, acceptance of mainstreamed students, and general interaction among students, it is not yet clear whether structured groups and group rewards are absolutely necessary, but it is clear that these outcomes can be reliably produced at the same time as achievement and other outcomes are being improved for the entire class. This is a revolutionary development for attempts to improve intergroup and cross-handicap relationships, as programs designed only to improve relationships are seen as "frills" by many school districts, and are not supported if they take time away from instruction.

We share Slavin's enthusiasm and recommend cooperative learning methods to teachers, although with certain qualifications in mind. First, it is important to view the cooperative learning approach not as a wholesale replacement of the traditional whole-class instruction/recitation/seatwork approach but instead as a variation or adaptation of this approach in which active whole-class instruction by the teacher is retained but many follow-up practice and application activities are accomplished through small-group cooperation rather than through individual seatwork. Peers are not an acceptable substitute for active instruction by the teacher as the basic method for carrying content to students. Peers can deliver effective explanations about how to respond to specific questions or assignments, but they cannot be expected to have the subject matter and pedagogical knowledge needed to provide effective advance organization and structuring of content, systematic development of key concepts, or sophisticated remedial instruction.

Second, cooperative learning approaches may be more feasible and valuable in certain classes than in others. So far, these methods have been used most frequently in (and most of the research supporting them comes from) mathematics, social studies, and language arts classes in grades 4 through 9. They may be less relevant or more difficult to implement for teachers working with primary-grade students or upper secondary-grade students, or for any teachers instructing students in writing, reading, laboratory science, or foreign languages. Also, methods that emphasize group rewards and individual accountability to other group members for one's own effort and performance (TGT, STAD, Jigsaw II, TAI) appear to be more appropriate for work in mathematics and other subjects that emphasize individual practice of specific sequenced skills. However, the other methods that emphasize group discussion and investigation, structured controversy, differentiated roles and responsibilities, or cooperative development of a group product may be more appropriate for social studies and for assignments that focus on higher-level cognitive objectives (application, problem solving, analysis, synthesis, evaluation).

Third, most of the research supporting cooperative learning methods has focused on situations where these methods were being introduced for the first time in one course or subject matter area and for a limited number of weeks.

Consequently, some of the positive results achieved must be attributed to the fact that the cooperative learning methods introduced a degree of novelty and variety into the school day. It is not yet clear what the effects would be if cooperative learning methods were institutionalized as a basic part of schooling to be found in most courses year after year. Students who are socially oriented and students who receive a lot of help from their peers would likely respond very positively to this, but other students might not. The latter include all students who enjoy working alone much of the time, as well as students who are academic leaders within teams and assume much of the responsibility for tutoring their teammates. Even students who enjoy this process in moderation might tire of it if called upon to perform it too often. Thus, there is probably some optimal level of use of cooperative-learning methods, both within any particular course and across the school day or school year as a whole.

Fourth, although it may often be important to use methods that involve group rewards and individual accountability to the group for one's effort, we advise emphasizing cooperation but deemphasizing competition in using these methods. Thus, STAD is preferable to TGT, for example. This is because, as noted in Chapters 6 and 8, competition is a form of extrinsic motivation that may distract students from basic learning goals unless handled carefully. Another problem is that competition creates losers as well as winners, and the bad feelings that result from losing competitions may undermine some of the potential contributions of small-group cooperative learning arrangements to improvements in personal and social outcomes (Ames & Felker, 1979).

Fifth, students will need to be trained to work cooperatively, especially if they are not familiar with cooperative learning approaches. Some students may not know how to act in small-group situations or may even be hostile in responding to the contributions of their peers. Consequently, teachers may need to teach their students how to share, listen, integrate the ideas of others, and handle disagreements. In the early grades, most group assignments probably should be short, highly structured, enjoyable, and unlikely to produce conflict. Students can be moved gradually into longer and more demanding tasks as their skills develop. When structured effectively, cooperative small-group activities not only produce peer support and encouragement for learning, but may result in the development of higher-quality strategies for understanding and responding to tasks than students develop when working alone (Johnson, Skon, & Johnson, 1980). In the process of discussing tasks and helping one another to learn, students discover a great deal about how to efficiently search for and identify key information, recognize what is given and what is called for in a problem, and formulate problem-solving strategies that feature systematic hypothesis testing rather than random guessing and that allow for checking of answers and identification of errors. This increases the likelihood that students will get the intended cognitive benefits, and not merely the right answers, from problem-solving exercises.

Implementation Guidelines

Johnson, Johnson, Holubec, and Roy (1984) suggest the following steps for teachers interested in implementing small-group cooperative learning methods:

Objectives
1. Specify academic and collaborative skills objectives.

Decisions
2. Decide the size of the group (typically from two to six, depending on the nature of the task, the time available, and the experience of the teacher in using small-group methods).
3. Assign students to groups (preferably by insuring heterogeneity rather than grouping by ability or allowing the students to form their own groups).
4. Arrange the room so that there is clear teacher access to each group and so that group members can meet in a circle and sit close enough to each other to be able to communicate effectively without disrupting other groups.
5. Plan instructional materials to promote interdependence (if necessary, give only one copy of the materials to each group or give each group member different materials so as to force task differentiation).
6. Assign roles to insure interdependence (assign different members complementary and interconnected roles such as summarizer-checker, researcher-runner, recorder, encourager, and observer).
7. Explain the academic task.
8. Structure positive goal interdependence and peer encouragement and support for learning (ask the group to produce a single product or use an assessment system in which individuals' rewards are based both on their own scores and on the average for the group as a whole).
9. Structure individual accountability (by using quizzes or randomly selecting group members to explain answers or present the group's conclusions).
10. Structure intergroup cooperation.
11. Explain success criteria.
12. Specify desired behaviors (define cooperative learning operationally by requesting that students take turns, use personal names, listen carefully to one another, encourage everyone to participate, etc.).

Monitoring and Intervening
13. Monitor student behavior (circulate to listen and observe groups in action; note problems in completing assignments or working cooperatively).
14. Provide task assistance.
15. Intervene to teach collaborative skills (where groups are experiencing major problems in collaborating successfully).
16. Provide closure to the lesson.

Evaluation and Processing
17. Evaluate quality and quantity of students' learning.
18. Assess how well the group functions (give feedback about how well the members worked with one another and accomplished assigned tasks and how they could improve).

ARRANGING FOR TUTORIAL ASSISTANCE TO STUDENTS

Individualized tutoring would be the optimal instructional method for achieving most academic objectives, but classroom management responsibilities severely limit teachers' opportunities to provide such tutoring. We recommend that teachers tutor their struggling students as often as they can, both by making time to get to them individually during class and by arranging to tutor them outside of class (before or after school or in between class periods) if possible. Even here, though, there are limits to what can be accomplished by even the most dedicated teachers.

Consequently, one important way for teachers to supplement the instruction that they provide is to arrange for students to be tutored by someone else. If teacher aides are available, this is one important function that they could perform. The same is true of adult volunteers in the classroom and parents or older siblings at home. To the extent that teachers structure the tutoring by providing appropriate materials and exercises and by training the tutors in how to fulfill their roles effectively, such tutoring can significantly increase the amount of instruction that slower students receive, perhaps enough to make the difference between keeping up with the class or falling hopelessly behind.

Students can also tutor one another. We have already noted that this is one benefit of student teams and other cooperative learning arrangements. Teachers can also structure such tutoring more directly by arranging for an individual tutor to work with an individual tutee. Options include *cross-age tutoring* (older students work with younger students) and *peer tutoring* (students are tutored by classmates).

Cross-Age Tutoring

Cross-age tutoring is commonly used in elementary schools, where, for example, teachers may arrange for fifth- and sixth-grade students to tutor first- and second-grade students at designated times during the week. Cross-age tutoring generally has positive effects on both the attitudes and the achievement of the students involved (Cohen, Kulik, & Kulik, 1982; Devin-Sheehan, Feldman, & Allen, 1976; Paolitto, 1976; Sharpley, Irvine, & Sharpley, 1983). Furthermore, these desirable outcomes are likely to occur not only for the tutees who receive instruction but also for the tutors who provide it. In part, this exemplifies the truism that we master material more thoroughly when we teach it to someone else than when we merely respond to it as learners.

The tutors' achievement gains may also be attributed to improved attitudes or self-concepts rather than to deeper exposure to academic content (because they are tutoring younger students on material several grade levels below their present status). Tutors often respond very positively to the responsibilities of the tutoring role. The role involves serious concern about learning academic content, and it appears to stimulate many tutors to identify more closely with the teacher and to become more concerned about their own learning. The tutoring experience may cause underachievers to take their own work more seriously, or cause antisocial students to become more appreciative of their potential for prosocial interaction with others.

Thus, tutors should not be seen merely as performing a service for the teacher. If structured properly, cross-age tutoring presents opportunities for the tutors, and not just the tutees, to derive a variety of cognitive and affective benefits. It should not be overused, however, and students (especially high achievers) should not be asked to do so much of it that they lose opportunities to do challenging or interesting work at their own level. If anything, the potential benefits of assuming the tutor role are greatest for low achievers, who rarely get the opportunity to act as the competent expert giving instruction rather than receiving it. Yet, low achievers often can play this role effectively when tutoring younger students (Bar-Eli & Raviv, 1982).

The role of tutee also presents many potential benefits. Interactions with tutors are typically friendly and experienced as enjoyable and helpful (Fogarty & Wang, 1982), and they provide a change of pace from more typical learning situations. They also provide opportunities for tutees to take a more active role in structuring their learning experiences to meet their needs by asking questions or calling for particular forms of help. This may be especially important for discouraged or alienated students accustomed to feigning competency rather than seeking help, all the more so if it generalizes to their interactions with the teacher.

Under some circumstances, students may learn more readily from student tutors than from teachers. In the case of an unresolved personality clash or communication problem between a teacher and a student, for example, the student might not only be more comfortable but also learn more during individualized instruction from an older student. Also, student tutors may use language or examples that are more easily understood than those of the teacher, or may identify learning problems more accurately because they have experienced the same problems recently.

Thomas (1970) showed the value of student tutors in his study of the relative effectiveness of fifth- and sixth-graders versus college students as tutors of second graders in reading. He found that, in general, the elementary school tutors were just as effective as the college students (seniors enrolled in a reading methods course, who had almost completed undergraduate teacher education programs).

Although they lacked both the general intellectual development and the specialized knowledge about reading instruction that the college students had, the fifth- and sixth-graders were more comfortable and spontaneous in assuming the role of tutor. Thomas stated it this way:

> In analyzing the different groups of tutors, one is struck by the differences in their approach to the tutees. The college-aged tutors seemed to be attempting to coax the tutees into liking them, into enjoying the reading materials, and into practicing the reading skills. The elementary-aged tutors, for the most part, were more direct and businesslike. They seemed to accept the fact that the tutees had problems in their school work, and seemed to feel that the tutoring sessions were for teaching those materials in front of them, not for going off in tangents and discussing matters outside the lesson.

Thomas's observations suggest that elementary-grade tutors can be as successful as adolescents or adults and that under some circumstances, they may even have certain advantages: (1) successful tutoring may demand direct instruction, and adults may tend to be too indirect; (2) the adults' vocabulary and examples may be too complex for young children to follow easily; and (3) tutors who are close in age to tutees may remember their own difficulties with materials and thus may be able to identify and respond to learning problems more effectively or maintain a patient, lesson-focused orientation longer than adults.

In general, though, adults will be more effective tutors than children, especially in supplementing nonverbal demonstrations with verbal explanations of related concepts and in helping the tutee learn the general principles that specific examples are designed to teach (Ellis & Rogoff, 1982). Thus, student tutoring is more likely to be successful when used to provide supervised practice and other follow-up to instruction originally presented by the teacher than when it is expected to stand on its own.

Peer Tutoring by Classmates

Teachers also may opt to use peer-tutoring arrangements calling for one classmate to tutor another under specified conditions. Such peer tutoring must be handled carefully, however, because it "officially" identifies the tutee as needing help on the material being tutored. Some students may resist this role because they do not believe that they need the help (Fogarty & Wang, 1982), because they are afraid of losing face before their peers, or because they believe that they know more about the material than the students who are supposed to tutor them (Rosen, Powell, Schubot, & Rollins, 1978). Problems of this sort are less likely to occur with cross-age tutoring or with tutoring that occurs within small-group cooperative learning arrangements, although they can occur even here if it is always the same students being tutored or if the teacher presents the tutoring as a remediation requirement rather than as an individualized learning opportunity.

We suggest the following guidelines for teachers considering peer tutoring.

Learning Outlook Create the mental set that *we all learn from one another*. This is more readily achieved when the teacher consistently models and points out to students how he or she learns from them. Also, the teacher can help reduce unnecessary competition by stressing that the goal is for all students to learn as much as they can and that the measure of success is how we compare to our own past performance rather than how we compare to others in the class.

Procedural Details Decisions need to be made about the following procedural matters:

1. Definite times of the day should be set aside for tutoring, so that students quickly learn that there are specific class times for helping one another (to avoid continuous disruption of the class).
2. Specific assignments need to be outlined. The teacher should mimeograph the directions each tutor is to follow each week. For example, "Johnny, this week from 8:00 to 9:00 you will work with Gay and Terry. On Monday you will use flash cards to review the 7, 8, and 9 multiplication tables. Go through each table twice with them and then get individual responses from each. The last time, write down the mistakes that each makes and return the sheet to me. On Tuesday, play audiotape Number 16

for Gay and Terry, and listen with them to the rhyming words. Then go to the word box and find the rhyming words sheet. Read the material sentence-by-sentence, and get Gay and Terry to identify the rhyming words."

3. Allow a tutor to work with one or two tutees long enough (one or two weeks) so that you can make sequential assignments and so that learning exercises are not constantly starting anew. However, switch tutoring assignments every couple of weeks to prevent "I'm your teacher" attitudes from developing.

4. Tutors should not be asked to administer real tests to tutees. One purpose of peer tutoring is to develop cooperative sharing between students. Asking tutors to quiz their tutees often defeats this purpose.

5. All students in the room should, at times, be tutors, and all should be tutees. In this way, students learn that they all can help and can benefit from one another. For example, if given the necessary answer keys, slower students can help faster ones by listening to their spelling words or administering and scoring flash card drills in math.

6. Teachers need not keep to the tutor model (one student flashes cards, the other responds) but can expand, when appropriate, to small work-team assignments (from two to eight students on a team). Shy students can be assigned to work with friendly extroverts. Students with art talents can be paired with bright but unartistic students in teams to gather facts and then represent them graphically. These combinations allow students to work together and gain interpersonal skills as well as to master the content.

7. Both learning teams and peer tutoring will take a lot of teacher time to get off to a good start, especially if students have not participated in these activities before. Take your time at first and be sure that all students understand what to do.

   The first week you ask students to tutor, model the behaviors you want. For example, pass out instructions and have all the students read them. Then tutor one or more students in accordance with the directions. Do not just describe what to do. Actually do it, modeling the appropriate behaviors.

   After this demonstration, select another two students to model the next set of directions. Then break the group into pairs and go around listening and answering questions. After a couple of practice sessions like this, most students will be able to assist others effectively, at least in repetitious drill-like activities.

   The first week you implement a peer-tutoring program you may have a loud, somewhat disorganized room as students argue over where to go or what to do. Remember that learning does not necessarily require passive, quiet students and that any teacher trying new activities will have minor adjustment problems as students learn new roles.

8. Pairing of best friends is often unwise, for several reasons: Friends tend to drift away from learning exercises; the number of classmates that a given student interacts with is reduced; and friends, in moments of anger, are more likely to become excessively critical or indulge in ridicule. Although many friends can work well together, many cannot, and the teacher should use caution in such groupings.

9. Communicate to parents that all students will both tutor and be tutored by

classmates. This is especially important in high socioeconomic status areas where some parents may become upset on learning that their child is being tutored by a neighbor's child, fearing that the neighbors will see them as inadequate parents. Needless concern can be eliminated if you communicate to parents the purpose of the tutor program in a letter or visit and point out that tutoring occurs at particular times during the day. List these times and invite the parents to visit whenever they want to do so.

SUMMARY

In this chapter, we discussed methods of adapting the traditional whole-class instruction/recitation/seatwork approach to the range of student needs likely to be found in any classroom. One popular method has been to minimize student heterogeneity by practicing *between-class ability grouping* (also known as streaming or tracking) to create homogeneously grouped classes. In theory, such grouping should enable teachers to instruct all students more effectively, but in practice, its effects are weak and mixed. Also, critics have identified four other problems with ability grouping: It can have negative social-labeling effects and teacher attitude and expectation effects on low-ability classes; it removes academic peer leaders from low-ability classes, leaving leaderless aggregations of discouraged and alienated students; assignment to tracks tends to be permanent once tracking decisions are made, so that opportunities for improvement may be eliminated for students assigned to lower tracks; and tracking counters progress toward desegregation and mainstreaming goals by minimizing contact between peers who differ in achievement levels. For these reasons, we recommend that between-class ability grouping be confined to grouping by curriculum at the high school level and that grouping by ability or achievement levels in earlier grades be avoided except in extreme circumstances. If such grouping appears to be necessary, we recommend that compromise approaches such as the Joplin Plan or the Baltimore Plan be used and that steps (such as keeping group assignments flexible) be taken to minimize the degree to which the grouping procedures lead to the undesirable outcomes described above.

A second popular strategy for coping with student heterogeneity is *within-class ability grouping,* especially for beginning reading instruction. Within-class ability grouping contains the same potential dangers as between-class ability grouping, although it can be implemented more flexibly because only one teacher is involved and it is much easier to change the number and composition of groups. We recommend that teachers minimize such within-class ability grouping (using it only when necessary to achieve homogeneity, for example, and not when the goal is merely to reduce the number of students to be taught at the same time). We also recommend that within-class ability grouping lead to differentiated instruction designed to meet particular needs rather than merely to differential pacing through the same curriculum using the same instructional methods, that group assignments be flexible and reviewed frequently, and that teachers arrange to provide low-group students with extra and more individualized instruction.

Whether or not within-class ability grouping is employed, another strategy for responding to student heterogeneity is to provide a degree of *differentiation in instruction and assignments to different students* (often with a degree of differential grading based on individualized effort and continuous progress criteria). Suggestions about how differentiated instructional materials and assignments can be used to allow various students to approach the same content from a variety of levels of sophistication were reviewed. It was noted that such differentiated instruction can be planned not only for students who vary in achievement but also for students who vary in general learning styles and preferences. Guidelines were suggested for differential instruction of success students, social students, dependent students, alienated students, and phantom students.

Besides providing differentiated instruction to groups or individual students, teachers can respond to student heterogeneity by introducing *cooperative learning methods* and by arranging for students to receive *tutorial assistance* from someone other than themselves. In addition, cooperative learning approaches and certain tutorial approaches are also desirable because they cause students to work together in prosocial interactions that foster progress toward affective outcomes in addition to achievement outcomes.

Cooperative learning approaches involve assigning students to small groups for cooperative work on group tasks (where the group members cooperate to produce a single group product) or individual tasks (where the group members help one another complete individual assignments). Successful cooperative learning programs typically feature positive interdependence of group members on one another, face-to-face interaction of group members, individual accountability for mastering assigned material, and instruction of the students in how to interact effectively during small-group activities. Incentive structures involving group rewards appear to be responsible for the achievement benefits of cooperative learning approaches (by motivating students within groups to help one another do as well as they can and thus insure that the group does as well as it can). This feature is most characteristic of the Student Team Learning approaches (TGT, STAD, Jigsaw II, TAI) that have been used mostly with practice in mathematics and other basic skills.

The affective benefits of cooperative learning approaches appear to occur either when there is an incentive structure featuring group rewards (even if students work on their own individual tasks rather than on cooperative tasks) or when the task structure is cooperative and students work together to produce a common product (often under task differentiation conditions calling for each group member to take a unique role or fulfill a unique function). Such cooperative task structures are featured in the Learning Together, Group Investigation, and original Jigsaw methods commonly used in social studies classes or in activities designed to accomplish higher-level cognitive objectives.

In contrast to most other proposed adaptations of traditional classroom teaching, cooperative learning approaches have proven to be both easy to implement and likely to yield significant advantages (both in cognitive and affective outcomes). Consequently, we recommend that most teachers make at least some use of these methods as alternatives to traditional independent seatwork to provide students with opportunities to practice and apply what they are learning.

A final method of responding to student heterogeneity is to arrange for students to receive tutorial assistance from someone other than the teacher. If the teacher has prepared appropriate instructional materials and tasks and has trained tutors effectively, tutoring by teacher aides or other adult volunteers can be an important supplement to instruction from the teacher and a valuable means of providing extra assistance to slower students. So can cross-age tutoring, in which older students tutor younger students. Research on cross-age tutoring has shown that it has benefits tutors as well as tutees. Peer-tutoring arrangements in which classmates work with one another can also be effective, but careful planning, training, and supervision are necessary to insure that the program does not prove to be more trouble than it is worth by upsetting parents or engendering resentment among students.

The wholesale alternatives to traditional instruction described in Chapter 9 (mastery learning, individualized/adaptive education, or open education) will be attractive to some teachers as responses to the dilemmas involved in teaching heterogeneous classes of students, but most teachers will prefer the less extreme adaptations of traditional instruction described in the present chapter. Any method selected for addressing these dilemmas will be a compromise involving advantages and disadvantages. However, it appears that the most generally workable arrangements rely on the traditional whole-class instruction/recitation/seatwork approach but adapt and supplement it by providing special attention and help for lower-ability students, introducing limited within-class grouping or differentiated materials or assignments, introducing limited differential grading based on individualized effort and continuous-progress criteria, making limited use of cooperative learning methods, arranging for tutorial assistance to needy students, and installing management systems (accountability mechanisms and incentive structures) to insure that all students participate in activities and complete assignments.

SUGGESTED ACTIVITIES AND QUESTIONS

10.1. If there is variation in the use of between-class ability grouping in the grade level and subject matter that you teach, arrange to observe in local schools that use heterogeneous grouping and others that use homogeneous grouping. What are the trade-offs involved, and what opportunities and constraints do they create for teachers? Which types of students (high or low achievers, phantom students versus social students) would benefit more from homogeneously grouped classes? Why?

10.2. In which setting would you prefer to teach, and why? Given that you may not have this choice, what adjustments in your preferred approach to the teacher role will you have to make if you are assigned to a school that uses the opposite grouping arrangement?

10.3. If you plan to use within-class ability grouping, state the criteria you will use to assign students to groups initially. Subsequent to these initial assignments, when and how will you schedule reassessments and arrange for regrouping?

10.4. What classes (in terms of grade level, subject matter, and student composition) are most and least appropriate for within-class ability grouping? Why?

10.5. In general, what types of students do teachers prefer to teach, and why?

10.6. Why does placing students in a higher group than their achievement suggests tend to have a positive effect on their subsequent achievement?

10.7. Why do students placed in low groups usually remain in low groups thereafter?

10.8. Do you plan to differentiate instruction or assignments that you prepare for different subgroups or individuals in your class? Why or why not?

10.9. If you do introduce differentiation, precisely what procedures will you follow and how will you explain these to the students? Given that some students will be asked to accomplish more than others, how will you handle grading?

10.10. What are the relative advantages and disadvantages of cross-age tutoring? Peer tutoring? Which types of students are most/least likely to benefit from peer tutoring (alienated, phantom, dependent)? Why?

10.11. How might you organize a cross-age student tutoring program at your school? What provisions might be made for evaluating and making adjustments in the program?

10.12. What can teachers do in advance to make peer-tutoring programs effective?

10.13. Given your preferred grade level and subject matter, are cooperative learning approaches likely to be worthwhile components of your approach to instruction? Why or why not?

10.14. Given the differences among the various cooperative learning methods described in the chapter, which would be the most appropriate for use in your preferred grade level or subject matter? Why?

10.15. If teachers group on the basis of one student characteristic (e.g., reading level), how might this affect other characteristics (dependency, sociability)? Does it make more sense to group on the basis of achievement than on the basis of personal or social traits? Why or why not?

REFERENCES

Abadzi, H. (1985). Ability grouping effects on academic achievement and self-esteem: Who performs in the long run as expected? *Journal of Educational Research, 79,* 36–40.

Alexander, K. L., Cook, M., & McDill, E. L. (1978). Curriculum tracking and educational stratification: Some further evidence. *American Sociological Review, 43,* 47–66.

Alexander, K. L., & McDill, E. L. (1976). Selection and allocation within schools: Some causes and consequences of curriculum placement. *American Sociological Review, 41,* 963–980.

Ames, C., & Felker, D. (1979). An examination of children's attributions and achievement-related evaluations in competitive, cooperative, and individualistic reward structures. *Journal of Educational Psychology, 71,* 413–420.

Anderson, R., Hiebert, E., Scott, J., & Wilkinson, I. (1985). *Becoming a nation of readers: The report of the Commission on Reading.* Washington, D.C.: National Institute of Education.

Aronson, E., Blaney, N., Stephan, C., Sikes, J., & Snapp, M. (1978). *The Jigsaw classroom.* Beverly Hills, CA: Sage.

Bar-Eli, N., & Raviv, A. (1982). Underachievers as tutors. *Journal of Educational Research, 75,* 139–143.

Barker-Lunn, J. (1970). *Streaming in the primary school.* Slough, Great Britain: National Foundation for Educational Research.

Beckerman, T., & Good, T. (1981). The classroom ratio of high- and low-aptitude students and its effect on achievement. *American Educational Research Journal, 18,* 317–327.

Cazden, C. (1985). Ability grouping and differences in reading instruction. In J. Osborn, P. Wilson, & R. Anderson (Eds.), *Reading education: Foundations for a literate America.* Lexington, MA: Lexington Books.

Chaffin, J. (1974). Will the real mainstreaming program please stand up! (or . . . Should Dunn have done it?) *Focus on Exceptional Children, 6,* 1–18.

Clark, R. (1982). Antagonism between achievement and enjoyment in ATI studies. *Educational Psychologist, 17,* 92–101.

Cohen, P., Kulik, J., & Kulik, C. (1982). Educational outcomes of tutoring: A meta-analysis of findings. *American Educational Research Journal, 19,* 237–248.

Cooke, B. (1976). Teaching history in mixed-ability groups. In E. Wragg (Ed.), *Teaching in mixed-ability groups.* London: David and Charles Ltd.

Crawford, J. (1983). A study of instructional processes in Title I classes: 1981–82. *Journal of Research and Evaluation of the Oklahoma City Public Schools, 13*(1).

Dar, Y. (1985). Teachers' attitudes toward ability grouping: Educational considerations and social organizational influences. *Interchange, 16*(2), 17–38.

Devin-Sheehan, L., Feldman, R., & Allen, V. (1976). Research on children tutoring children: A critical review. *Review of Educational Research, 46,* 355–385.

DeVries, D. L., Slavin, R. E., Edwards, K. J., & Lambardo, M. M. (1978). Teams-Games-Tournament (TGT): Review of ten classroom experiments. *Journal of Research and Development in Education, 12,* 28–38.

DeVries, D. L., Slavin, R. E., & Fennessey, G. M. (1980). *Teams-games-tournament: The team learning approach.* Englewood Cliffs, NJ: Educational Technology Publications.

Douglas, J. (1964). *The home and the school: A study of ability and attainment in the primary school.* London: McGibbon and Kee.

Dreeben, R. (1984). First-grade reading groups: Their formation and change. In P. Peterson, L. Wilkinson, & J. Hallinan (Eds.), *The social context of instruction: Group organization and group processes.* Orlando, FL: Academic Press.

Eder, D. (1981). Ability grouping as a self-fulfilling prophecy: A microanalysis of teacher-student interaction. *Sociology of Education, 54,* 151–161.

Eder, D., & Felmlee, D. (1984). Development of attention norms in ability groups. In P. Peterson, L. Wilkinson, & M. Hallinan (Eds.), *The social context of instruction: Group organization and group processes.* Orlando, FL: Academic Press.

Ellis, S., & Rogoff, B. (1982). The strategies and efficacy of child versus adult teachers. *Child Development, 53,* 730–735.

Esposito, D. (1973). Homogeneous and heterogeneous ability grouping: Principal findings and implications for evaluating and designing more effective educational environments. *Review of Educational Research, 43,* 163–179.

Evans, J. (1985). *Teaching in transition: The challenge of mixed ability grouping.* Philadelphia: Open University Press.

Evertson, C. (1982). Differences in instructional activities in higher-and lower-achieving junior high English and math classes. *Elementary School Journal, 82,* 329–350.

Evertson, C., Sanford, J., & Emmer, E. (1981). Effects of class heterogeneity in junior high school. *American Educational Research Journal, 18,* 219–232.

Findley, W. G., & Bryan, M. M. (1975). *The pros and cons of ability-grouping.* Bloomington, IN: Phi Delta Kappa.

Findley, W., & Bryan, M. (1971). *Ability grouping, 1970 status: Impact and alternatives.* Athens, GA: Center for Educational Improvement, University of Georgia.

Finley, M. (1984). Teachers and tracking in a comprehensive high school. *Sociology of Education, 57,* 233–243.

Flowers, A., & Bolmeier, E. (1964). *Law and pupil control.* Cincinnati: W. H. Anderson.

Fogarty, J., & Wang, M. (1982). An investigation of the cross-age peer tutoring process: Some implications for instructional design and motivation. *Elementary School Journal, 82,* 451–469.

Gamoran, A. (1984). Egalitarian versus elitist use of ability grouping. Paper presented at the annual meeting of the American Educational Research Association, New Orleans.

Gearheart, B., & Weishahn, M. (1984). *The exceptional student in the regular classroom* (3rd ed.). St. Louis: Mosby.

Goldberg, M., Passow, E., & Justman, J. (1966). *The effects of ability grouping.* New York: Teachers College Press.

Good, T., & Brophy, J. (1986). *Educational psychology: A realistic approach* (3rd ed.). New York: Longman.

Good, T., & Marshall, S. (1984). Do students learn more in heterogeneous or homogeneous groups? In P. Peterson, L. Wilkinson, & M. Hallinan (Eds.), *The social context of instruction: Group organization and group processes.* New York: Academic Press.

Good, T., & Power, C. (1976). Designing successful classroom environments for different types of students. *Journal of Curriculum Studies, 8,* 1–16.

Graybeal, S. S., & Stodolsky, S. S. (1985). Peer work groups in elementary schools. *American Journal of Education, 93,* 409–428.

Haller, E. J. (1985). Pupil race and elementary school ability grouping: Are teachers biased against black children? *American Educational Research Journal, 22,* 465–483.

Hallinan, M. T., & Sorensen, A. B. (1985). Ability grouping and student friendships. *American Educational Research Journal, 22,* 485–499.

Hallinan, M. T., & Sorensen, A. B. (1983). The formation and stability of instructional groups. *American Sociological Review, 48,* 838–851.

Hewett, F. M., & Watson, P. C. (1979). Classroom management and the exceptional learner. In D. L. Duke (Ed.), *Classroom management (Seventy-Eighth Yearbook of the National Society for the Study of Education, Part II.)* Chicago: University of Chicago Press.

Hiebert, E. (1983). An examination of ability grouping in reading instruction. *Reading Research Quarterly, 18,* 231–253.

Johnson, D. (1970). *The social psychology of education.* New York: Holt, Rinehart and Winston.

Johnson, D., & Johnson, R. (1985a). Classroom conflict: Controversy versus debate in learning groups. *American Educational Research Journal, 22,* 237–256.

Johnson, D., & Johnson, R. (1985b). Cooperative learning and adaptive education. In M. C. Wang & H. J. Walberg (Eds.), *Adapting instruction to individual differences.* Berkeley, CA: McCutchan.

Johnson, D., & Johnson, R. (1982). *Joining together: Group therapy and group skills.* Englewood Cliffs, NJ: Prentice-Hall.

Johnson, D., & Johnson, R. (1979). Conflict in the classroom: Controversy and learning. *Review of Educational Research, 49,* 51–70.

Johnson, D. W., & Johnson, R. T. (1975). *Learning together and alone.* Englewood Cliffs, NJ: Prentice-Hall.

Johnson, D. W., Johnson, R. T., Holubec, E. J., & Roy, P. (1984). *Circles of learning: Cooperation in the classroom.* Alexandria, VA: Association for Supervision and Curriculum Development.

Johnson, D. W., Johnson, R. T., & Maruyama, G. (1983). Interdependence and interpersonal attraction among heterogeneous and homogeneous individuals: A theoretical formulation and a meta-analysis of the research. *Review of Educational Research, 53,* 5–54.

Johnson, D., Skon, L., & Johnson, R. (1980). Effects of cooperative, competitive, and individualistic conditions on children's problem-solving performance. *American Educational Research Journal, 17,* 83–93.

Johnson, R., Brooker, C., Stutzman, J., Hultman, D., & Johnson, D. (1985). The effects of controversy, concurrence seeking, and individualistic learning on achievement and attitude change. *Journal of Research in Science Teaching, 22,* 141–152.

Keddie, N. (1971). Classroom knowledge. In F. Young (Ed.), *Knowledge and control: New directions for the sociology of education.* London: Collier-Macmillan.

Kulik, C. C., & Kulik, J. A. (1982). Effects of ability grouping on secondary school students: A meta-analysis of evaluation findings. *American Educational Research Journal, 19,* 415–428.

Larrivee, B. (1985). *Effective teaching for successful mainstreaming.* New York: Longman.

Leinhardt, G., & Pallay, A. (1982). Restrictive educational settings: Exile or haven? *Review of Educational Research, 52,* 557–578.

Leiter, J. (1983). Classroom composition and achievement gains. *Sociology of Education, 56*, 126–132.

Mackler, B. (1969). Grouping in the ghetto. *Educational and Urban Society, 2*, 80–95.

Madden, N., & Slavin, R. (1983). Mainstreaming students with mild handicaps: Academic and social outcomes. *Review of Educational Research, 53*, 519–569.

Metz, M. (1978). *Classrooms and corridors.* Berkeley, CA: University of California Press.

Moskowitz, J. M., Malvin, J. H., Schaeffer, G. A., & Schaps, E. (1985). Evaluation of Jigsaw, a cooperative learning technique. *Contemporary Educational Psychology, 10*, 104–112.

Nickerson, J. R., & Prawat, R. S. (1981). Affective interaction in racially diverse classrooms: A case study. *Elementary School Journal, 81*, 291–303.

Oakes, J. (1982). The reproduction of inequity: The content of secondary school tracking. *Urban Review, 14*, 107–120.

Okebukola, P. A. (1985). The relative effectiveness of cooperative and competitive interaction techniques in strengthening students' performance in science classes. *Science Education, 69*, 501–509.

Paolitto, D. (1976). The effect of cross-age tutoring on adolescence: An inquiry into theoretical assumptions. *Review of Educational Research, 46*, 215–238.

Persell, C. H. (1977). *Education and inequality.* New York: Free Press.

Peterson, P. L., Wilkinson, L. C., Spinelli, F. & Swing, S. R. (1984). Merging the process-product and the sociolinguistic paradigms: Research on small-group processes. In P. Peterson, L. Wilkinson, & M. Hallinan (Eds.), *Instructional groups in the classroom: Organization and processes.* New York: Academic Press.

Reynolds, M. (1978). Some final notes. In J. Grosenick & M. Reynolds (Eds.), *Teacher education: Renegotiating roles for mainstreaming.* Reston, VA: Council for Exceptional Children.

Rist, R. (1970). Student social class and teacher expectations: The self-fulfilling prophecy in ghetto education. *Harvard Educational Review, 40*, 411–451.

Rosen, S., Powell, E., Schubot, D., & Rollins, P. (1978). Competence and tutorial role as status variables affecting peer-tutoring outcomes in public school settings. *Journal of Educational Psychology, 70*, 602–612.

Rosenbaum, J. E. (1980). Social implications of educational grouping. In D. C. Berliner (Ed.), *Review of research in education* (vol. 8). Itasca, IL: Peacock.

Rosenbaum, J. E. (1976). *Making inequality.* New York: Wiley.

Rowan, S., & Miracle, A. (1983). Systems of ability grouping and the stratification of achievement in elementary schools. *Sociology of Education, 56*, 133–144.

Sands, M., & Kerry, T. (Eds.). (1982). *Mixed ability teaching.* London: Croom Helm.

Schofield, H. (1981). Teacher effects on cognitive and affective pupil outcomes in elementary school mathematics. *Journal of Educational Psychology, 73*, 462–471.

Schwartz, F. (1981). Supporting or subverting learning: Peer group patterns in four tracked schools. *Anthropology and Education Quarterly, 12*, 99–121.

Scott, R. R., & McPartland, J. M. (1982). Desegregation as national policy: Correlates of racial attitudes. *American Educational Research Journal, 19*, 397–414.

Sharan, S. (1980). Cooperative learning in small groups: Recent methods and effects on achievement, attitudes, and ethnic relations. *Review of Educational Research, 50*, 241–271.

Sharan, S., & Sharan, Y. (1976). *Small-group teaching.* Englewood Cliffs, NJ: Educational Technology Publications.

Sharan, S., et al. (1984). *Cooperative learning in the classroom: Research in desegregated schools.* Hillsdale, NJ: Erlbaum.

Sharpley, A. M., Irvine, J. W., & Sharpley, C. F. (1983). An examination of the effectiveness of a cross-age tutoring program in mathematics for elementary school children. *American Educational Research Journal, 20,* 103–111.

Slavin, R. (1986). *Ability grouping and student achievement in elementary schools: A best-evidence analysis.* Unpublished manuscript. Baltimore: Center for Effective Elementary and Middle Schools, The Johns Hopkins University.

Slavin, R. (1985). Team-Assisted Individualization: A cooperative learning solution for adaptive instruction in mathematics. In M. C. Wang & H. J. Walberg (Eds.), *Adapting instruction to individual differences.* Berkeley, CA: McCutchan.

Slavin, R. E. (1983). *Cooperative learning.* New York: Longman.

Slavin, R. E. (1980a). Cooperative learning. *Review of Educational Research, 50,* 315–342.

Slavin, R. E. (1980b). *Using student team learning* (rev. ed.). Baltimore: Center for Social Organization of Schools, The Johns Hopkins University.

Slavin, R. (1978). Student teams and achievement divisions. *Journal of Research and Development in Education, 22,* 39–49.

Slavin, R., Sharan, S., Kagan, S., Hertz-Lazarowitz, R., Webb, C., & Schmuck, R. (Eds.). (1985). *Learning to cooperate, cooperating to learn.* New York: Plenum.

Smith, K., Johnson, D., & Johnson, R. (1981). Can conflict be constructive? Controversy versus concurrence seeking in learning groups. *Journal of Educational Psychology, 73,* 651–663.

Solomon, D., & Kendall, A. (1979). *Children in classrooms: An investigation of person-environment interaction.* New York: Praeger.

Stephan, W. G. (1978). School desegregation: An evaluation of predictions made in *Brown vs. Board of Education. Psychological Bulletin, 85,* 217–238.

Swing, S. R., & Peterson, P. L. (1982). The relationship of student ability and small-group instruction to student achievement. *American Educational Research Journal, 19,* 259–274.

Thomas, J. (1970). *Tutoring strategies and effectiveness: A comparison of elementary age tutors and college tutors.* Unpublished doctoral dissertation. Austin: University of Texas.

Thompson, R. H., White, K. R., & Morgan, D. P. (1982). Teacher-student interaction patterns in classrooms with mainstreamed mildly handicapped students. *American Educational Research Journal, 19,* 220–236.

Tuckman, B., & Bierman, M. (1971). Beyond Pygmalion: Galatea in the schools. Paper presented at the annual meeting of the American Educational Research Association, New York.

Veldman, D. J., & Sanford, J. P. (1984). The influence of class ability level on student achievement and classroom behavior. *American Educational Research Journal, 21,* 629–644.

Webb, N. M. (1982). Student interaction and learning in small groups. *Review of Educational Research, 52,* 421–445.

Webb, N. M., & Cullian, L. K. (1983). Group interaction and achievement in small groups: Stability over time. *American Educational Research Journal, 20,* 411–423.

Weinstein, R. (1976). Reading group membership in first grade: Teacher behaviors and pupil experience over time. *Journal of Educational Psychology, 68,* 103–116.

Wragg, E. (Ed.). (1976). *Teaching in mixed ability groups.* London: David and Charles Limited.

FORM 10.1. Student-Managed Learning Experiences

USE: *When teacher has been observed frequently enough so that reliable information can be coded*
PURPOSE: *To see if teacher is providing opportunities for students to make choices and manage their own learning experience*
Record any information relevant to the following points:

PROVIDING CHOICES
Does the teacher include time periods or types of activities in which students can select from a variety of choices in deciding what to do or how to do it?
Only when (if) they finish seatwork. They can color or use supplementary readers.

Can you see places where provision for choice could easily be included?
Several learning centers could be created with available equipment, including some with audio-visual self-teaching equipment.

COOPERATIVE LEARNING
Does the teacher encourage students to work cooperatively in groups at times? *Top reading group (only) reads on their own at times.*

Can you see places where provision for cooperative learning could easily be included? *Other reading groups could read alone, too, or at least do flashcard drills. Teacher often has children color a picture or do some other small activity related to topics studied that day. She could plan larger, cooperative projects just as easily.*

PEER TUTORING
Does the teacher ever ask students to tutor or otherwise assist their peers?
Occasionally, if a child has been absent for a few days.

Can you see ways the teacher could arrange to do this (if he or she does not)?
Flashcard drills in both language arts and math.

FORM 10.2. Small-Group Interaction

USE: *Whenever a small group of students is working and the teacher is not a formal part of the group.*
PURPOSE: *To determine how the group spends its time*
Make a code every 15 seconds to describe what the group is doing at that moment.

Frequency   Type Contact

_____ 1. Reading (finding information etc.)
_____ 2. Manipulating equipment
_____ 3. Task discussion: general participation
_____ 4. Task discussion: one or two person dominated
_____ 5. Procedural discussion
_____ 6. Observing
_____ 7. Nontask discussion
_____ 8. Procedural dispute
_____ 9. Substantive (task relevant) dispute
_____ 10. Silence or confusion

FORM 10.3. Individual Participation in Small-Group Work

USE: *When a small group is operating and the teacher is not part of the group*
PURPOSE: *To assess the involvement and participation of individual students during small-group work*
*Observe the target student for 15 seconds and make a code. Repeat the cycle for the duration of the small-group activity.**

_____ 1. Reading (finding information)
_____ 2. Manipulating equipment (filmstrip, slide rule)
_____ 3. Participating in general discussion (telling and listening to others)
_____ 4. Listening to general discussion
_____ 5. Presents idea to group (others are listening to the target student)
_____ 6. Talking to individual (an aside: the conversation is not part of the group discussion)
_____ 7. Listening to individual (an aside: the conversation is not part of the group discussion)
_____ 8. Passive (can't tell if student is involved)
_____ 9. Misbehaving
_____ 10. Leaves group

*Note that it would be possible to use the form to code different individual students in the group (code one student for a minute, then switch to another student). Furthermore, the scale could be altered to provide information about the group. For example, the percent of the group that falls into each category could be noted.

FORM 10.4. Cooperative vs. Negative Behavior During Group Discussion

USE: Whenever small group working without the teacher
PURPOSE: To see if cooperative or negative behaviors are being practiced
*   Below is a list of student behaviors that may occur during small group work. Note each behavior as it occurs.*

Frequency   Type Contact

_____   1. Student criticizes another student (the person, not the idea).
_____   2. Student verbally states refusal to listen to another student.
_____   3. Student interrupts another student.
_____   4. Student ignores another student's request for information or clarification.
_____   5. Student defines problems as personal conflict.
_____   6. Student describes feelings.
_____   7. Student asks for feedback to his or her ideas or feelings and obtains useful feedback.
_____   8. Student asks another student to clarify and gets a clarification.
_____   9. Student defines problems as concerns to be resolved.

Describe the group behavior. Is the group on task? Operating smoothly vs. confused? Cooperative vs. conflictive? Is the discussion cumulative (students listen and build on previous statements vs. ignore previous comments)?

FORM 10.5. Teacher's Use of Ability Grouping

USE: In classrooms in which the teacher has grouped the students for small-group instruction
PURPOSE: To see if the teacher is using grouping appropriately as a means of individualizing instruction

GROUP COMPOSITION AND INSTRUCTION TIME

GROUP NAME	NUMBER OF BOYS	NUMBER OF GIRLS	START OF LESSON (TIME)	END OF LESSON (TIME)	LENGTH OF LESSON
Astronauts	3	5	8:31	9:00	29
Magicians	4	5	9:08	9:35	27
Champions	4	3	9:45	10:00	15
			:	:	

Note any information relevant to the following questions:
1. Is the class arranged so that each group is seated together as a group? *No*
2. How long have these particular groups been operating? *Since October 15*
3. Does the teacher plan to regroup? When? *Beginning of second semester*
4. Does the teacher teach the groups in the same order each day? *Yes*
5. If time for a group lesson runs short, does the teacher make it up later? *Usually not*
6. Do the groups have differential privileges regarding what they are allowed to do without special permission? *Astronauts have access to supplementary readers (considered too difficult for other two groups).*
7. If the teacher groups for more than one subject, are the groups the same or are they different? *Groups only for Reading*
8. Does the teacher show differential enthusiasm or emotion when working with the different groups? *Seemed more subdued, less involved when working with the Magicians.*

Record any descriptive or evaluative statements the teacher makes about a group.

GROUP	TEACHER'S COMMENT
Astronauts	*I'm proud of your progress — keep up the good work*
Champions	*We're almost to the end of the reader; keep up the good work and we'll finish it by Friday.*
Champions	*Let's stop reading and get ready for recess. It's time to have fun and relax.*
Astronauts	*This is the best reading group.*
Magicians	*This is the middle-achievement group in reading.*
Champions	*This is the lowest reading group.*

CHAPTER

11 Instruction

Previous chapters stressed five major aspects of teaching: expectations, modeling, management, motivation, and individualization/grouping. In this chapter, we consider a variety of topics related to instruction. Distinctions among teaching aspects are artificial, of course. Aspects of teaching that we can separate for analysis are interrelated in practice. When teachers manage classrooms, they also model prosocial behavior. Thus, we have discussed some of the material in this chapter previously. However, here we take a sharply focused look at instruction.

The material in the chapter is drawn partly from traditional theory and research on instruction and partly from recent studies of teaching. The first part of the chapter discusses information relevant to providing effective instruction in basic facts and concepts. Subsequently, we turn our attention to the issue of helping students to acquire a more active role in directing their own learning and a discussion of strategies that can help students to develop problem-solving and critical thinking skills.

There are many different approaches to instruction. Some are mutually exclusive, but most are merely different. For example, Joyce and Weil (1980) describe 23 different approaches to teaching, classified into four families or orientations (information processing, social interaction, focus on the individual person, and behavior modification). Information-processing approaches organize instruction so that material is presented in ways that learners can process and retain most easily, and there is an attempt to foster students' information-processing skills in addition to presenting information that students must process. Social interaction approaches stress the group-living aspects of schooling. Instruction is arranged so that students interact with and learn from one another as well as the teacher, and there is a concern about fostering group relations as well as instruction. Personal approaches draw on humanistic psychology to promote intellectual and emotional development (self-actualization, mental health, creativity). Finally, the behavior modification approach stresses the sequencing of activities to promote efficient learning and the shaping and control of behavior through reinforcement.

Each approach has, however, merit. It would be a mistake for a teacher to adopt any single approach exclusively. Knowledge about and consideration of the learner's frame of reference are basic to teaching, and learning by discovery appears to be a valuable way to learn. However, many things are learned much more easily when sequenced in an optimal way and taught directly by the teacher.

TEACHER BEHAVIOR AND STUDENT LEARNING

It seems intuitively obvious that for a certain learning objective with a particular group of students, some teachers will be more successful than others and some instructional methods will be more effective than others. Yet until about 1970, not much research was available on the relationships between teacher behavior and student outcomes, and the findings that were available were confusing or contradictory. For a time, in fact, it was commonly stated that learning outcomes depended almost entirely on student factors and that differences between teachers or teaching methods were trivial. The picture began to change in the late 1960s and early 1970s, due largely to increased educational research, particularly research on teacher behavior and its effects.

Researchers also introduced various methodological improvements:

1. Concentrating on in-service teachers, who had developed some consistency of method and style, rather than on preservice teachers, who were still developing their approaches to teaching
2. Using objectively measured student learning gains as the criterion of effectiveness, not subjective ratings by principals or supervisors
3. Measuring student achievement at the beginning of studies as well as the end, so that student entry level could be taken into account in evaluating the learning gains that teachers produced (previous studies often failed to control for this factor, so that the effects of differences in teacher behavior were confounded with the effects of differences in student IQ or social class)
4. Collecting data over a long enough time to allow the effects of differential teacher behavior to be evidenced in measures of student achievement (such as a term or an entire school year; previous studies were often confined to a unit or even a single lesson)
5. Collecting enough data in each classroom to develop a reliable sample of teacher behavior (10, 20, or even 40 hours of classroom observation, not just one or two brief visits)
6. Concentrating on teachers' behavior, especially behavior relating to instruction, not just on teachers' global personal characteristics
7. Measuring teacher behavior by coding specific actions as they occur and developing a detailed record of classroom events rather than relying on high-inference ratings of general traits
8. Taking into account context factors (grade level, subject matter, whole-class versus small-group versus individualized setting, student social

status, etc.) by confining studies to a single context or by separately coding and analyzing data from different contexts.

These and other improvements began to produce data indicating that some teachers and teaching methods consistently produced better results than did others. Subsequently, this work led to a series of studies, initially correlational and later experimental, that linked teacher behavior to student learning gains in basic skills (reading and mathematics). Reviewers note that this body of research supports several conclusions about basic skills instruction (Brophy & Good, 1986; Good, 1979; Medley, 1979; Rosenshine, 1983). The value of this work for policy has been examined (Shulman, 1986; Shulman & Sykes, 1983), and new questions are begining to be raised with new approaches to the study of teaching (Evertson & Green, 1986). Hence, although our knowledge of teaching continues to grow and expand, some general characteristics of teachers who offer effective basic skills instruction can be summarized.

Effective Basic Skills Instruction

Teacher Expectation/Role Definition/Sense of Efficacy   Teachers who produce greater learning gains accept the responsibility for teaching their students, believe that the students are capable of learning, and believe that they (the teachers) are capable of teaching them successfully. If students do not learn something the first time, they teach it again, and if the regular curriculum materials do not do the job, they find or make other ones. In general, these teachers display the qualities recommended in Chapter 4.

Student Opportunity to Learn   Effective teachers allocate most of their available time to instruction. Their students spend many more hours each year on academic tasks than do the students of teachers who are less concerned about promoting students' skill mastery (see Chapter 2).

Classroom Management and Organization   These teachers not only allocate most of their time to academic activities, but also organize their classrooms as effective learning environments and use group management approaches that maximize student engagement in those activities (see Chapters 6 and 7).

Curriculum Pacing   Effective teachers move through the curriculum rapidly but in small steps that minimize student frustration and allow continuous progress.

Active Teaching   These teachers actively instruct their students in large and small groups—demonstrating skills, explaining concepts, conducting participatory and practice activities, explaining assignments, and reviewing when necessary. They teach the academic content to the students rather than relying on the curriculum materials to do so. However, they do not stress just facts or skills; they also emphasize concepts and understanding.

Teaching to Mastery   Following active instruction on new content, effective teachers provide opportunities for students to practice and apply the material. They monitor each student's progress and provide feedback and remedial instruction as needed, making sure that material is mastered to the point of overlearning. This is essential in teaching basic skills, because the material is hierarchically sequenced, so success at any level usually requires not only mastery of skills taught earlier but the ability to apply them to new situations.

A Supportive Learning Environment   Despite their strong academic focus, these teachers maintain pleasant, friendly classrooms and are perceived as enthusiastic, supportive instructors.

Grade Level Differences   Successful teachers in the early grades interact frequently with individual students (although often within small-group settings) and frequently provide them with opportunities for overt practice with feedback. In the higher grades, however, students have less need for overt practice and individualized interaction with the teacher, and they are more able to learn by attending to whole-class presentations and interacting with their peers. Thus, successful teachers at these grade levels rely more on whole-class settings for introducing new material and use small groups primarily for remedial activities. They allow students to work cooperatively or independently for longer periods, although they continue to monitor progress and provide necessary assistance and feedback.

Two Examples

To illustrate this kind of instruction—and also to show how it *must be adapted* to differences in grade level, subject matter, and group setting—we have reproduced the instructions to teachers (i.e., the treatments) used in two experimental studies of teacher effectiveness. Each study involved first training teachers to use instructional principles that earlier correlational work had suggested were effective, then monitoring classrooms to assess teachers' implementation of the principles, and finally testing students to assess learning outcomes. Each study found that (1) experimental teachers implemented the recommended principles more systematically than did control teachers, who used whatever methods they had been taught previously or had developed on their own; and (2) experimental teachers produced significantly greater student learning gains than did control teachers.

Building mostly on their own earlier correlational work, Good and Grouws (1979) developed the instructional model shown in Table 11.1 for fourth-grade mathematics classes. The model is similar to traditional fourth-grade mathematics instruction in many ways, although it is more systematic. Note that it includes guidelines for time allocation to insure that mathematics is taught for about 45 minutes each day and that it calls for supplementing classroom instruction with homework assignments. Although the model calls for students to work primarily individually on seatwork and homework, it also calls for a great deal of active instruction by the teacher. New concepts are presented in detail during the development portion of the lesson, and the teacher both makes sure that the students know how to do the assignment before releasing them to work individually and reviews the assignment with them the next day. This schedule of instruction and opportunity to practice with feedback, along with frequent testing, help insure continuous progress. (For more program details, see Good, Grouws, & Ebmeier, 1983).

Anderson, Evertson, and Brophy (1979) developed a more lengthy set of guidelines for first-grade teachers to use during small-group reading instruction. Their original model contained 22 principles. Most of these were supported by their findings, although the data indicated that a few principles should be dropped and that others should be subdivided, elaborated, or otherwise revised. The revised principles (Anderson, Evertson, & Brophy, 1982) is shown in Table 11.2.

This model is similar to that of Good and Grouws in that it includes time allocation guidelines and an emphasis on active instruction by the teacher, followed by opportunities to practice and receive feedback. There are several important differences due to subject matter and grade level, however. First, first-grade reading is typically taught in small groups to facilitate provision of individualized overt practice with feedback (as noted previously, early elementary students typically need such practice, which in the case of beginning reading means taking turns reading aloud; this is much easier to accomplish in a small-group setting, even

Table 11.1 SUMMARY OF KEY INSTRUCTIONAL BEHAVIORS

Daily review (First 8 minutes except Mondays)
1. Review the concepts and skills associated with the homework
2. Collect and deal with homework assignments
3. Ask several mental computation exercises

Development (About 20 minutes)
1. Briefly focus on prerequisite skills and concepts
2. Focus on meaning and promoting student understanding by using lively explanations, demonstrations, process explanations, illustrations, and so on
3. Assess student comprehension using
   a. Process/product questions (active interaction)
   b. Controlled practice
4. Repeat and elaborate on the meaning portion as necessary

Seatwork (About 15 minutes)
1. Provide uninterrupted successful practice
2. Momentum—keep the ball rolling—get everyone involved, then sustain involvement
3. Alerting—let students know their work will be checked at the end of the period
4. Accountability—check the students' work

Homework assignment
1. Assign on a regular basis at the end of each math class except Friday's
2. Should involve about 15 minutes of work to be done at home
3. Should include one or two review problems

Special reviews
1. Weekly review/maintenance
   a. Conduct during the first 20 minutes each Monday
   b. Focus on skills and concepts covered during the previous week
2. Monthly review/maintenance
   a. Conduct every fourth Monday
   b. Focus on skills and concepts covered since last monthly review

Source: Good, T., & Grouws, D. (1979). The Missouri Mathematics Effectiveness Project: An experimental study in fourth-grade classrooms. *Journal of Educational Psychology, 75,* 821–829.

Table 11.2

General principles

1. Reading groups should be organized for efficient, sustained focus on the content.

2. All students should be not merely attentive but actively involved in the lesson.

3. Questions and tasks should be easy enough to allow the lesson to move along at a brisk pace and the students to experience consistent success.

4. Students should receive frequent opportunities to read and respond to questions and should get clear feedback about the correctness of their performance.

5. Skills should be mastered to overlearning, with new ones gradually phased in while old ones are being mastered.

6. Although instruction takes place in the group setting, monitor each individual and provide whatever instruction, feedback, or opportunities to practice that are necessary.

Specific principles

Programming for continuous progress

1. *Time*. Across the year, reading groups should average 25–30 minutes each day. The length will depend on student attention level, which varies with time of year, student ability, and the skills being taught.

2. *Academic focus*. Successful reading instruction includes not only organization and management of the reading group itself (discussed below), but also effective management of students who are working independently. Provide these students with: appropriate assignments; rules and routines to follow when they need help or information (to minimize their needs to interrupt you as you work with your reading group); and activities when they finish their work.

3. *Pace*. Both progress through the curriculum and pacing within specific activities should be brisk, producing continuous progress achieved with relative ease (small steps, high success rate).

4. *Error rate*. Expect to get correct answers to about 80 percent of your questions in reading groups. More errors can be expected when students are working on new skills (perhaps 20–30 percent). Continue with practice and review until smooth, rapid, correct performance is achieved. Review responses should be almost completely (perhaps 95 percent) correct.

Organizing the group

1. *Seating*. Arrange seating so that you can work with the reading group and monitor the rest of the class at the same time.

2. *Transitions*. Teach the students to respond immediately to a signal to move into the reading group (bringing their books or other materials) and to make quick, orderly transitions between activities.

3. *Getting started*. Start lessons quickly once the students are in the group (have your materials prepared beforehand).

Introducing lessons and activities

1. *Overviews*. Begin with an overview to provide students with a mental set and help them anticipate what they will be learning.

2. *New words*. When presenting a new word, do not merely say the word and move on. Usually, you should show the word and offer phonetic clues to help students learn to decode.

Table 11.2   (Continued)

3. *Work assignments*. Be sure that students know what to do and how to do it. Before releasing them to work on activities independently, have them demonstrate how they will accomplish these activities.

Insuring everyone's participation

1. *Ask questions*. In addition to having the students read, ask them questions about the words and materials. This helps keep students attentive during classmates' reading turns and allows you to call their attention to key concepts or meanings.

2. *Ordered turns*. Use a system, such as going in order around the group, to select students for reading or answering questions. This insures that all students participate and simplifies group management by eliminating handwaving and other attempts by students to get you to call on them.

3. *Minimize call-outs*. In general, minimize student call-outs and emphasize that students must wait their turns and respect the turns of others. Occasionally, you may want to allow call-outs, to pick up the pace or encourage interest, especially with low achievers or students who do not normally volunteer. If so, give clear instructions or devise a signal to indicate that you intend to allow call-outs at these times.

4. *Monitor individuals*. Be sure that everyone, but especially slow students, is checked, receives feedback, and achieves mastery. Ordinarily this will require questioning each student and not relying on choral responses.

Teacher questions and student answers

1. *Academic focus*. Concentrate your questions on academic content; do not ask numerous questions about personal experiences. Most questions should be about word recognition or sentence or story comprehension.

2. *Word-attack questions*. Include word-attack questions that require students to decode words or identify sounds within words.

3. *Wait for answers*. In general, wait for an answer if the student is still thinking about the question and may be able to respond. However, do not continue waiting if the student seems lost or is embarrassed or if you are losing the other students' attention.

4. *Give needed help*. If you think the student cannot respond without help but may be able to reason out the correct answer if you do help, simplify the question, rephrase the question, or give clues.

5. *Give the answer when necessary*. When the student is unable to respond, give the answer or call on someone else. In general, focus the attention of the group on the answer and not on the failure to respond.

6. *Explain the answer when necessary*. If the question requires one to develop a response by applying a chain of reasoning or step-by-step problem solving, explain the steps necessary to arrive at the answer in addition to giving the answer.

When the student responds correctly

1. *Acknowledge correctness (unless it is obvious)*. Briefly acknowledge the correctness of responses (nod positively, repeat the answer, say "right," etc.) unless it is obvious to the students that their answers are correct (such as during fast-paced drills reviewing old material).

2. *Explain the answer when necessary*. Even after correct answers, feedback that emphasizes the methods used to get answers is often appropriate. Onlookers may need this information to understand why the answer is correct.

3. *Follow-up questions*. Occasionally, you may want to address one or more follow-up questions to the same student. Such series of related questions can help the student to integrate relevant information. Or you may want to extend a line of questioning to its logical conclusion.

Table 11.2   (Continued)

Praise and criticism

1. *Praise in moderation.* Praise only occasionally (no more than perhaps 10 percent of correct responses). Frequent praise, especially if nonspecific, is probably less useful than more informative feedback.

2. *Specify what is praised.* When you do praise, specify what is being praised if this is not obvious to the student and the onlookers.

3. *Correction, not criticism.* Routinely inform students whenever they respond incorrectly, but in ways that focus on the academic content and include corrective feedback. When it is necessary to criticize (typically only about 1 percent of the time when students fail to respond correctly), be specific about what is being criticized and about desired alternative behaviors.

Source: Anderson, L., Evertson, C., & Brophy, J. (1982). Principles of small-group instruction in elementary reading. Occasional Paper No. 58. East Lansing: Institute for Research on Teaching, Michigan State University.

though it complicates classroom management). Also, many of the principles in the Anderson et al. model deal with the organization and management of the group, not just with content instruction. This is because first graders are still learning student role behaviors that fourth graders have long since mastered, so that first-grade teachers have to be more concerned about maintaining students' attention and controlling the timing and nature of their contributions to the lesson. Another difference is that the principles in Table 11.2 focus on the teacher's interaction with individual students, even though the instruction takes place in a group context. In contrast, the principles in Table 11.1 more clearly exemplify a group-based (in this case, whole-class-based) approach to instruction. Here, dealings with individuals are mostly minor variations on the main theme established by the group instruction rather than primary concerns.

These examples illustrate that even for basic skills instruction in the elementary grades, *instruction must be adapted to the subject matter, the students, and other contextual factors.* However, it is important to stress that research linking teacher behavior to student outcomes does not yield rules or simple answers to complex issues of teaching and learning (Good & Brophy, 1986; Shulman, 1986; Zumwalt, 1986). Although classroom research continues to develop support for instructional principles of varying generality, there appear to be no specific instructional behaviors that are ideal for all types of students and situations.

Different learning objectives (mastering well-defined knowledge or skills versus applying them to complex problem solving or creativity, for example) require various instructional methods, and progress toward other objectives (promoting the personal development of individuals or the social development of the class as a group) requires still other methods. Research can inform teachers about the relationships between teacher behavior and student outcomes, but teachers must decide for themselves what outcomes they wish to promote and in what order of priority.

Uses of Group-Based Instruction

The success of research linking teacher behavior to student achievement in recent years is gratifying for several reasons. First, such research reaffirms what should have been obvious all along but what some writers had tried to deny or minimize—

the fact that teachers make a difference. The research clearly shows that some teachers elicit more achievement from their students than others do, and researchers have begun to identify the classroom management and instructional behaviors associated with achievement. Also, the research helps move the field beyond testimonials and unsupported claims toward scientific statements based on credible data. Finally, the research is gratifying to most teachers because it validates, for the most part, the principles of practice that they use intuitively or developed through their own experimentation.

Compared to the feasible alternatives, teacher-led, group-based instruction appears to be an effective approach for teaching of any body of knowledge or set of skills that has been sufficiently well organized and analyzed so that it can be presented (explained, modeled) systematically and then practiced or applied during activities that call for student performance that can be evaluated and, where incorrect or imperfect, given corrective feedback.

Limits of Group-Based Instruction

This type of instruction can be used to attain most goals that teachers want to accomplish, but it also excludes many. It excludes activities with analysis, synthesis, or evaluation objectives, such as units on creative writing, projects involving conducting and reporting research, or creating a product of considerable complexity that requires diverse skills. These activities are accomplished more effectively using inquiry or guided discovery methods. Group-based instruction also excludes activities designed primarily to develop attitudes rather than knowledge or skills, like art or music appreciation units and many units in English, social studies, and physical education. Thus, teacher-led, group-based instruction may not be the primary approach used in certain courses, and even where it is the primary approach, it would ordinarily be a base to work from rather than the only method used. The teacher would shift to other methods for particular units or activities.

Because of the complexities mentioned in the previous paragraph, we prefer the term "active instruction" to the term "teacher-led, group-based instruction" and its synonyms. This is because even though we expect most lessons to be structured and led by the teacher and most instruction to be delivered to groups rather than individuals, we also expect teachers to depart from these general tendencies as instructional objectives or other circumstances dictate. Even during these departures, however, teachers should be engaged in planned, systematic activities designed to accomplish particular objectives and thus be interacting with students while monitoring and responding to their performance on assigned tasks (see Good, 1979, for more on this point). Furthermore, it is important for teachers to help students to become more active learners by helping them to acquire skills for regulating their own learning (Corno & Rohrkemper, 1985).

ADAPTING INSTRUCTION TO STUDENTS' INDIVIDUAL CHARACTERISTICS

There is no simple definition of effective teaching or good teachers. For one thing, teachers' personal attributes interact with their general competence and teaching style to determine outcomes. Teachers who are introverted and interested mostly in student achievement will be successful with achievement-oriented students but not with the less achievement-oriented. In particular, extroverted students who focus on social relationships rather than learning will find it difficult to relate to these teachers, although other teachers who are very social themselves may enjoy working with these students and manage them successfully. Other student characteristics are also important. Some teachers are quite successful with advantaged students but not with disadvantaged students, and vice versa.

Teachers may also use different approaches to accomplish the same effects. For example, there are many ways that teachers can show respect for students. One might make it a point to visit with each student each day. Another might visit students' homes or invite parents to visit the classroom. Another might take time to deal with student problems (such as a dispute over ownership of a pencil) rather than arbitrarily avoiding such problems through convenient rules (e.g., pencils with two owners are the teacher's property). Similarly, the teacher's role as a model in the classroom is important, but there are many ways to model such things as problem solving. Some teachers demonstrate for the entire class; others work with small groups; others have students model for their classmates.

Even when working from teacher-led group instruction as a base, teachers can introduce some degree of differentiation in their treatment of individual students designed to accommodate those students' personal characteristics. Some of the most important characteristics are as follows:

1. General competence and aptitude (Does the student process and comprehend information rapidly? What is the student's cognitive style?)
2. General developmental level (Is the student preoperational?)
3. Reading ability (How effectively does the student process written information?) (Often closely related to aptitude, but not always)
4. General personality adjustment (Is the student peer-oriented? Anxious? Dependent?)
5. Work mode preference and general work habits (Does the student prefer to work alone, with the whole class, or in small groups? Does he/she prefer written or verbal performances?)

Student Aptitude   Aptitude makes a difference. Brighter students can process information quickly; less capable students need more time to assimilate and integrate material. Fast students can watch a demonstration and perform; slow students need to manipulate objects themselves and need several examples. Similarly, bright students often enjoy difficult assignments; less capable students prefer easy assignments.

Student Developmental Level   The developmental stage of students has important instructional implications. Younger children's attention spans are shorter than those of older students, and they generally need relatively short lessons and frequent review. Very young children need rest periods built into the school day. Older students can benefit from longer assignments, more complex choices, and more independent work. Preoperational students need numerous concrete examples; students beyond this stage can work with abstractions and learn propositionally. Students at certain developmental stages avoid members of the opposite sex, but a few years later the opportunity to work with members of the opposite sex in small groups may be highly motivating for some learning tasks, such as those that are not very complex and do not demand total attention. Young students generally want to please adults; subsequently, peer expectations and influences rival adult influences.

Student Reading Level   Reading level may seem to be an obvious consideration, yet many teachers with students who vary considerably in reading ability try to implement individualized programs with reading assignments that are similar in difficulty. In such instances, the material will be much too demanding for some students and too easy for others. Teachers who employ many individual assignments that require students to read material, directions, and so forth on their own need to be especially alert to the need for materials that vary in reading difficulty. Teachers who use individual assignments must also consider students' general abilities and desire to work independently.

Student Personality and Work Habits   Student personality is also a major consideration in assessing whether or not a learning environment will be successful. Dependent students seek teacher structure and support; independent students want little of either. Some students want to be with peers; others are more introverted and prefer more solitude. A student's personality also influences the degree, frequency, and type of feedback that is needed or preferred.

Preferred work mode depends to some extent on student personality (dependent students prefer to be with the teacher), but some work styles are independent of personality and aptitude or cognitive style. For example, some students enjoy writing reports and stories but dislike answering questions; other students have the opposite preference. Some students prefer a variety of working assignments; other students like only one mode (whole class, individual, and so forth).

Work habits are also important considerations. Some students are careless and poorly organized. Other students are enthusiastic bookkeepers but somehow cannot put together all the associated facts and other data that they collect. If teachers want to alter such work habits, learning activities will have to be designed with this in mind. In the meantime, such activities will have to be minimized and carefully monitored.

CLASSROOM GUIDELINES

Having noted the need to adapt classroom instruction to particular learning goals and having acknowledged that a single set of rules for teaching effectively in any and all situations does not exist, it is possible to note teacher behaviors that should occur regularly in classrooms. Furthermore, it is possible to develop coding procedures that allow one to look for the presence or absence of these desirable teacher behaviors. For example, we can observe the degree to which the teacher uses modeling when it is appropriate, even though we cannot say that a particular kind of modeling is best. This applies to the variables described in this chapter as well. We can say that certain things should take place, but the frequency of their occurrence and the ways they are performed depend in part on teacher style and situational variables. These are just a few aspects of teaching that require teachers to act as *decision makers,* determining how general principles apply to their particular classrooms.

THE MATCH

A basic decision-making task is solving what Hunt (1961) has called "the problem of the match"—how to match the difficulty and interest of materials and assignments to the skills and interests of students. Typically, schooling is a compromise between prohibitively expensive individualized tutoring and the need to hold costs down. The lockstep curriculum with standardized materials at each grade level and the familiar formula of 20 to 40 students per teacher are the results. Despite their obvious weaknesses, these work reasonably well for most students but the burden of individualization is on the teacher. The variations in readiness, ability, and interests that exist in any classroom constitute problems for all teachers. The problems become more serious to the extent that students differ from the "average" students for whom the curriculum is intended. Teachers may have to supplement or even substitute for the curriculum in order to succeed (Brophy & Evertson, 1976).

Difficulty of Material

If students are to work persistently, they must be able to perform the tasks they are asked to do. Few of us work for very long if we do not enjoy success in the process. Persistence is determined largely by success experienced on similar tasks (Harter, 1978). Students' abilities to do school assignments determine the degree to which they believe they can learn independently. One important thing to look for in classrooms is the degree to which there is a match between what teachers ask students to do and what the students are capable of doing.

A major factor determining how students learn is the relationship between the demands of lessons and what students already know. The teacher's task is to provide students with progressively more difficult work, but none so difficult as to frustrate them or erode their confidence. Ideal tasks present new challenges but can be solved independently by students. In practice, this means moving along in small steps and making sure that each step is mastered. New work phases in new challenges, but these are easy for students to handle successfully. The result should be continuous work on the assignment (because students understand what they are supposed to do and can do it without becoming confused or unable to continue) and generally successful performance.

These general principles have been well known for some time, but recent research has shown that students require a *very* high success rate in order to progress efficiently. Theoretical sources disagree on this point. For example, the literature on achievement motivation suggests that a 50 percent success rate is optimal because this is the rate associated with maximal achievement motivation, at least for individuals who are oriented toward attaining success rather than avoiding failure. These data have sometimes been taken—inappropriately—to mean that classroom questions and assignments should be geared to a 50 percent success rate. Other writers have reached similar conclusions from their beliefs that higher level, or "thought," questions are more valuable than lower level, or "fact," questions or from beliefs that learning is likely to be boring or pointless if it is "too easy." On the other hand, advocates of mastery learning usually demand at least 80 percent success rates on assignments, and advocates of programmed learning expect success rates to approach 100 percent.

Classroom research supports the latter position. Recent findings indicate that teachers who program for success rates of 90 to 100 percent on assignments produce more learning than teachers who tolerate higher failure rates. This has led one group of researchers to define "academic learning time" as the time students spend engaged in academic tasks that they can complete with high rates of success (Fisher et al., 1980).

The rates to be expected for particular activities will vary with the nature of the activity and the availability of the teacher (or someone else) to monitor student progress and provide corrective feedback when necessary. For example, during group lessons in which teachers are presenting new material or attempting to challenge generally bright and successful students, the objectives may be achieved efficiently even if the students are able to answer only about 70 percent of the teacher's questions correctly. In these situations, teachers can provide corrective feedback and reexplain poorly grasped concepts as they go along, so that the students will not become overly confused or frustrated. In conducting recitations with less confident and successful students, however, the success rate probably should be 80 percent or more (Brophy & Evertson, 1976), and in review lessons covering material that has supposedly been mastered, success rates should approach 100 percent.

Very high success rates (90–100 percent) are especially important for seatwork assignments, when students are expected to work independently without frequent monitoring by or assistance from the teacher. Students given such assignments regularly will probably work on them consistently and complete them successfully. On the other hand, students consistently given assignments that are too difficult for them to handle on their own eventually will give up and become "motivation problems" (in reality, of course, the problem lies in the poor match of assignment to student achievement level and not in the students' attitudes).

To determine the match between students and tasks, you may have to observe a classroom for several visits or monitor the work of several students. However, a quick assessment can be developed by observing the variety of different books and materials being used. Even students grouped homogeneously will have different interests and academic abilities. If the entire class, or even all members of a subgroup, are treated the same, it is unlikely that the problem of match is being solved.

For example, suppose that the day's assignments for the Bluebird reading group appear on the board as follows: reading, 8:30–9:00; write the ten sentences on the board, 9:00–9:30; math work pages 61–64, 9:30–10:00. . . . In some respects, this is a good sign. The teacher is well organized and obviously has done specific planning. Also, leaving the assignment on the board is helpful for students who forget what they are supposed to do. They can consult the board without having to interrupt the teacher or their classmates. However, if all Bluebirds have the same assignment every day, there may be problems. Suppose that Robin Miller, a member of the Bluebirds, does poorly on today's math work. Tomorrow she will not be ready for pages 65–70. Instead, she needs to correct the errors in her work on pages 61–64 and, in particular, to overcome the confusion that caused those errors.

Students cannot have individualized pacing for everything, but teachers should recognize individual strengths and weaknesses and try to provide assignments accordingly. Evidence of such differentiated assignments will appear in good teachers' classrooms.

In secondary classrooms, matching task difficulty to student needs is likely to be either much easier or much harder than it is in the typical elementary classroom. It is likely to be easier in advanced courses or other situations where students are relatively homogeneous in readiness for the class, because they have self-selected themselves into the course or have been tracked through prerequisites. Here whole-class instruction without significant differentiation of assignments usually works well. In heterogeneously grouped secondary classes, however, matching instruction to students' needs can be a difficult and continuing problem. The strategies found to be effective in the study by Evertson, Sanford, and Emmer (1981) described in Chapter 10 should help (special attention and help for low achievers, some grouping or differentiation of materials and assignments, some individualization of grading criteria, peer tutoring, elaborate accountability and feedback systems). At least minimal objectives should be set for low achievers, who nevertheless may need considerable private or small-group assistance as well as urging to work to keep up through out-of-class study. The needs and abilities of high achievers can be addressed through special projects, extra-credit activities, and the like. Differentiation according to individual needs can be accomplished by exercising discretion in approving topics for and suggesting methods of accomplishing research reports and other individualized projects.

A very instructive way to determine if teachers are matching tasks to student ability is to observe slow students. In many classrooms, these students never finish their assignments, and often their failure to finish prevents them from doing other things. For example, some early elementary teachers hold show-and-tell right before lunch, and participation in show-and-tell depends on being finished with work. In fact, the work itself may be involved in the show-and-tell. If students have been working on art pictures related to a story in the reader, it may involve showing the pictures and describing them to the class. If low achievers have difficulty finishing their independent reading, many will not have pictures to share during show-and-tell. Furthermore, it is likely that these same students will be the last to finish every day, not just on one day.

More generally, it is important for students, especially slow ones, to form the habit of completing their work rather than giving up. The teacher may have to reduce the amount or difficulty of work for a while, monitor work closely and give feedback, and help slow students understand that they can finish with a positive feeling and without a sense of being overwhelmed.

Monitoring Work Involvement

After presenting appropriate materials and assignments, it is important for teachers to insure that they result in the intended learning experience. This begins with thoroughness in explaining assignments. Students should know not only what to do, but also how to do it. Unfamiliar aspects should be demonstrated, and then the students should be given opportunities to practice sample problems for themselves. It is important for teachers to monitor the students' work on sample problems and to notice and correct errors. If many students are making the same mistake, additional teaching or review is needed. This should continue until the point is cleared up (as established by student success in working additional problems, not just *apparent* understanding of the explanation).

Observers can watch teachers present assignments and can monitor the effects of presentations by observing students when they are supposed to be working. Persistent engagement in seatwork tasks (versus giving up or doing something else) is associated both with better performance on the tasks and with better general learning over the course of the school year (Fisher et al., 1980).

It may be impractical for teachers to check all students when presenting assignments, so they may have to rely on observation of a sample of students. Few teachers do this randomly. Instead, most use a *steering group:* a few students who are monitored regularly and whose understanding is used as the criterion for continuing with a presentation versus moving on to something else (Lundgren, 1972). This can be quite effective, for the same reasons that "key precincts" can be used to predict the outcomes of elections. However, the right students must be used as the steering group. In presenting assignments prior to releasing students to independent work, the steering group should be drawn mostly from the weakest students in the classroom, because making sure that *all* students understand the assignment is essential. Therefore, observers have an additional criterion to use in assessing the effectiveness of assignment presentations: Successful teachers systematically check the work of low achievers. Less successful teachers do not do this as much and may fool themselves into believing that everyone understands the assignment just because the best students do. The result is low engagement when students are released to independent work, high rates of error, and frequent failure to complete assignments.

Remedial Teaching

Remedial teaching is closely related to "the match." In both cases, teachers must recognize that problems exist and intervention is needed. If they are too concerned about moving along as quickly as possible, they may neglect, often without awareness, students who cannot keep up. Teachers often feel guilty about time spent with low achievers, because during that time they are not challenging brighter students. However, as shown in Chapters 9 and 10, there are ways to increase time spent with low achievers while at the same time helping faster students to progress through relatively autonomous, self-guided work.

There is too little remedial teaching in schools. Students who enter third grade without a good phonics background seldom learn phonics. More typically, they are given the same reading materials that other students receive, and they struggle to finish perhaps 70 pages while their classmates complete the book and move on to others. This will not do, especially with disadvantaged students. Brophy and Evertson (1976) found that a "can-do" attitude, a determination to teach, was fundamental to success with low-SES students. Teachers who achieved success with them taught a limited amount of material *thoroughly,* concentrating on teaching to overlearning rather than covering a greater amount of material only superficially. They did not hesitate to supplement or even replace curriculum materials if they proved inadequate (they often did, because most curricula are designed for middle-class children). Teachers in middle-class schools had to rely on their own resources less often, but even so, the successful ones had the same determination to attack the problem until they found a way to succeed.

Teacher commitment to the belief that every student can and will learn is basic to remedial teaching. Bereiter, Washington, Englemann, and Osborn (1969) describe what this attitude looks like in the classroom.

> The good teacher apparently intended to overteach. She hesitated to move on to another task until all the children in her group were performing adequately. The teacher who was not as good did not get as much feedback from the children. She did not seem to have the burning desire to teach every child. She let the children get by with performances that would not be acceptable to the good teacher. In one sense, the good teachers reminded one of Helen Keller's teacher as she was portrayed in *The Miracle Worker*. They felt that the children could perform and should perform if the teacher knew how to teach them. The teacher who was not so good seemed to have a mechanical view of the teaching process. It did not seem to bother her if the children did not perform well.

When looking in classrooms, note the relative concern and time devoted to remedial teaching. Is there evidence of it? Does the teacher meet with students who are experiencing difficulties?

Remedial teaching means adjusting the curriculum to the student, not vice versa. Too often the method of remedial teaching is to assign the same reading to everyone but to ask certain students only half of the questions. If the students only read at the second-grade level, they should not be expected to read a fifth- or sixth-grade text continuously and fail. As best they can, teachers should start with students where they are and advance them to more complex tasks as rapidly as possible. If teachers are not sure about deviating from the curriculum or obtaining other resources, they should consult with the principal, with reading specialists, or with remedial teachers.

Sixth graders who read at the second-grade level should get books that are written at the lower level and that cover the same topics the other students are reading about. Books about famous people and history, for example, are written with different vocabularies for various reading levels. It is valuable for the slower students if some of these alternate sources can be kept available in the classroom.

Many investigators (Fisher et al., 1980; Good & Grouws, 1977; Husen, 1967) have found that opportunity to learn is an important determinant of what is actually learned. When learning is difficult, students require not merely exposure but also opportunities to deal actively and at length with material and to practice responding to it or using it. It is this kind of active involvement that remedial teaching produces with slow learners. The result will be a reduction in exposure to content (exposure that is often too brief or shallow to be of much value for them anyway) but an increase in high-quality opportunities that result in significant learning. Remedial teaching causes slower students to deal with more content in an active way and thus to genuinely learn more.

As we saw in Chapter 9, slow learners can learn most of what faster learners achieve, but they may take as much as five times longer to do so. Usually, when instruction is paced so that individuals can master what they are ready to learn at the rates they are able to learn it, students of all ability levels learn more efficiently and general rates of achievement increase.

Remedial teaching probably brings about improvement in attitudes as well. For example, many low achievers do not attack problems in a goal-oriented, problem-solving manner. Instead, they jot down the first thing that occurs to them and hand in their papers as quickly as possible. They are afraid to look back over their work. Students who keep this up long enough eventually learn that the classroom is not a place for serious, exciting learning. Instead, it is a place where confusing things happen for mysterious reasons (Anderson, 1981).

Teachers can enhance slower students' sense of control and belief in their own ability to think by helping them see the relationships between teacher questions and specific strategies for finding answers. Many students do not see the relationships between concepts presented in textbooks (even in hierarchically sequenced subjects like mathematics), do not realize that they can eliminate their own confusion by rereading the directions or reviewing previous assignments (assuming that the text is clear and helpful), and in general do not know their own potential for figuring out how they could have found the answer. By giving them directions about the appropriate page or explaining the process involved, teachers help students learn that answering questions is a rational process involving systematic problem solving.

Students who are afraid to look back usually cope with assignments by guesswork rather than careful thinking. They do not adopt active learner roles because they do not have control over the learning situation. Remedial teaching, coupled with an appropriate match of material to student needs, is the first step in helping students become active self-evaluators.

Remedial teaching is essential if the cumulative effects of failure are to be avoided. Low achievers fall farther behind each year they remain in school. Disadvantaged students in particular require systematic remedial teaching. They often lack important skills assumed by the curriculum, and they will fall even farther behind unless these skills are developed or they are taught in ways that more realistically match their present levels. This problem arises regularly, and teachers who want to solve it will have to reteach lessons that were not learned the first time. Most of these lessons will have to be changed, not merely be retaught. Repetition alone probably will not be enough. Lessons will have to be revised by breaking them down into small steps and adding new examples and exercises.

Educators have noted that the design of instruction (sequencing of subtasks leading to the concept, principles, or other training goal) is more important in advancing learning than some of the better known psychological principles such as reinforcement (Case & Bereiter, 1984; Gagné, 1977). Revision of lessons is a vital teaching task, as is the ability to generate student enthusiasm for "something old," a review topic. If you observe a class over several days, you should see signs of review work being pursued enthusiastically by teacher and students alike. There is no reason to apologize for remedial work and every reason to engage in it.

The needs of faster students are also important. To achieve the appropriate match for all students, teachers will have to assign regularly to specialized activities for both fast and slow learners. Perhaps 20 to 50 percent of the day should be spent in recycling work with low achievers and enrichment work with high achievers. These figures will increase as the ages of the students and their capacities for independent work increase (assuming that the students are in mixed-ability, self-contained classrooms).

GROUP INSTRUCTION

Presentation of information to the class assembled as a group is an important part of teaching. Several aspects of this task have shown consistent relationships with student learning. These include clarity and enthusiasm in teacher presentations, the use of a variety of teaching methods, and the maintenance of student attention.

Clarity

Clarity in the teacher's presentations is essential if students are to understand concepts and work assignments. Does the teacher communicate the objectives of the lesson clearly? Do lectures begin without introductions or end without summaries, lack organization to provide structure and highlight main points, or otherwise lack sufficient clarity to enable students to follow them without confusion?

McCaleb and White (1980) have identified five aspects of clarity that observers can attend to in the classroom:

1. *Understanding*. This is a prerequisite to clarity and involves matching the information to be learned to the learner's present knowledge. Does the teacher:
   a. Determine students' existing familiarity with the information presented?
   b. Use terms that are unambiguous and within the students' experience?
   c. Clarify and explain terms that are potentially confusing?
2. *Structuring*. This involves organizing the material to promote a clear presentation: stating the purpose, reviewing main ideas, and providing transitions between sections. Does the teacher:
   a. Establish the purpose of the lesson?
   b. Preview the organization of the lesson?
   c. Include internal summaries and a final review?
3. *Sequencing*. This involves arranging the information in an order conducive to learning, typically by gradually increasing the difficulty or complexity of the material. Does the teacher order the lesson in a logical way, appropriate to the content and the learners?
4. *Explaining*. This refers to explaining principles and relating them to facts through examples, illustrations, or analogies. Does the teacher:
   a. Define major concepts?
   b. Give examples to illustrate these concepts?
   c. Use examples that are accurate and concrete as well as abstract?
5. *Presenting*. This refers to volume, pacing, articulation, and other speech mechanics. Does the teacher:
   a. Articulate words clearly and project speech loudly enough?
   b. Pace the various sections of the presentation at rates conducive to understanding?
   c. Support the verbal content with appropriate nonverbal communication and visual aids?

Others have written more extensively about some of the aspects of clarity identified by McCaleb and White. For example, Ausubel's (1963) concept of advance organizers is useful in thinking about how to structure presentations. Advance organizers tell students what they will be learning before the instruction begins. For example, before describing 20 penalties that can occur during hockey games, a physical education instructor could provide a way to organize the information: "Today we are going to discuss penalties that might be called during hockey games. We will discuss the differences between minor and major penalties and describe 15 minor penalties and 5 major penalties. At the end of the period, I will show you 20 slides and ask you to name the penalty illustrated and state whether it is major or minor."

Advance organizers give students a structure to which they can relate the specifics presented in the teaching of reading. They can expand this structure as they identify relevant concepts and information. Without such a structure, the material may seem fragmented, much like listening to a random list of unrelated sentences. A clear explanation of the nature of the assignment helps students to focus on the main ideas and order their thoughts effectively. This is because we are more likely to find what we need if we know what we are looking for. Therefore, before lecturing, teachers should tell students what they will be expected to learn from the lecture and why it is important for them to know this information. After lectures, they should summarize the main points in a few simple sentences. Providing a clear introduction and a strong summary takes little planning and presentation time, but it can make a big difference in the degree to which students remember essential facts and concepts (Luiten, Ames, & Ackerson, 1970; Schuck, 1981).

For extended presentations, periodic internal summaries of subparts may be needed in addition to a major summary at the end. Rosenshine (1968) discusses in general the value of these kinds of internal summaries and in particular the "rule-example-rule" approach, in which a summary statement is given both before and after a series of examples. He also stresses the importance of "explaining links"— prepositions or conjunctions that indicate when the teacher is giving the cause, means, or purpose of an event or idea. Words and phrases such as "because," "in order to," If . . . then," "therefore," and "consequently" make explicit the causal linkages between phrases or sentences in ways that might not be clear without such language. For example, consider the following sentences:

1. Chicago became the major city in the Midwest and the hub of the nation's railroad transportation system.
2. Because of its central location, Chicago became the hub of the nation's railroad transportation system.

The first example presents the relevant facts but does not make explicit the linkage between them, as the second example does. If asked, "Why did Chicago become the hub of the transportation system?" most students taught with the second example would respond, "Because of its central location," but many students taught with the first example would respond, "Because it is a big city," or in some other way that would indicate failure to appreciate the linkage between a city's geographical location and the role it plays in a nation's transportation system.

In addition to these organization factors, presentations or questions can lack clarity because of vague or confusing language. Smith and Land (1981) review several studies indicating that the effectiveness of presentations is reduced by the presence of *vagueness terms* and *mazes*. They have identified nine categories of vagueness terms:

1. Ambiguous designation (somehow, somewhere, conditions, other)
2. Negated intensifiers (not many, not very)
3. Approximation (about, almost, kind of, pretty much, sort of)
4. "Bluffing" and recovery (actually, and so forth, anyway, as you know, basically, in other words, to make a long story short, you know)
5. Error admission (excuse me, I'm sorry, I guess, I'm not sure)
6. Indeterminate quantification (a bunch, a couple, a few, a lot, a little, some, several)
7. Multiplicity (aspects, kinds of, sort of, type of)
8. Possibility (chances are, could be, maybe, perhaps)
9. Probability (frequently, generally, often, probably, sometimes, usually)

They give the following as a brief example indicating how vagueness terms can distract from the intended content of a message. The vagueness terms are italicized.

> This mathematics lesson *might* enable you to understand *a little more* about *some things we usually* call number patterns. *Maybe* before we get to *probably* the main idea of the lesson, you should review *a few* prerequisite concepts. *Actually*, the first concept you need to review is positive integers. *As you know*, a positive integer is any whole number greater than zero.

Mazes refer to false starts or halts during speech, redundantly spoken words, or tangles of words. The mazes are italicized in the following example.

> This mathematics lesson will *enab* . . . will get you to understand *number, uh,* number patterns. Before we get to the *main idea of the,* main idea of the lesson, you need to review *four conc* . . . four prerequisite concepts. A positive *number* . . . integer is any whole *integer, uh,* number greater than zero.

In addition to looking for such problems in teachers' presentations to students, observers can study the effects of the presentation on the students themselves. The students' facial expressions, and especially their questions or responses to the teacher's questions, should indicate that they have received the message that the teacher intended to communicate. Frequent evidence of student frustration, confusion, or misunderstanding suggests problems in teacher clarity (see Cruickshank, 1985, for related information about students' perceptions of teacher clarity).

Enthusiasm

When teachers are enthusiastic about their subject matter, students are likely to pay attention and develop enthusiasm of their own. Ultimately, they also are more likely to achieve at higher levels (Rosenshine, 1970; Rosenshine & Furst, 1973). There is a bit of Tom Sawyer in all of us. In particular, young people develop interests through modeling others, including teachers. If teachers appear to enjoy knowledge in general and specific subject matter in particular, students are likely to develop similar interests. If the teacher shows no enthusiasm, students probably will not either (if the teacher does not like to paint fences, why should the students?). Teacher enthusiasm is important even to college students, who frequently stress it in explaining why they like certain instructors and do not like others (Costin, Greenough, & Menges, 1971). In fact, students and observers are prone to over-value enthusiasm and to rate enthusiastic instructors highly even when their presentations lack substance or clarity (McCaleb & White, 1980).

Like clarity, enthusiasm is a general teacher characteristic that is difficult to describe in specific terms. However, qualities such as alertness, vigor, interest, movement, and voice inflection are important. Enthusiastic teachers are alive in the room; they show surprise, suspense, joy, and other feelings in their voices; and they make material interesting to students by relating it to their experiences and showing that they themselves are interested in it.

Because of television, today's teachers must have the dramatic qualities of actors. Presentations to today's students often are met with a chorus of "We've done that before" or "We've seen that before." Studies of children watching *Sesame Street* have revealed that they do not attend to "talking heads" for long. However, they do pay attention to an adult voice when it is accompanied by an animated figure, such as a bouncing chart or some puppets. Apparently, some children learn to tune out adults who stand relatively motionless while giving information, even before they enter school (Lesser, 1974).

Tom Sawyer-like characteristics have always been important for teaching, and if TV and kindergarten experiences have reduced students' interest in school, these factors are more important now than ever. In particular, teachers should be enthusiastic when reviewing or having students try to improve on things done in the past. Many teachers do this regularly and well. Bereiter et al. (1969) provide this account:

> When a good teacher pointed to a picture and said, "What's this?" she expected all children to respond. If they didn't respond, she would perhaps smile and say, "I didn't hear you. What's this?" By now all of the children were responding. She would smile, cock her head and say, "I didn't hear you." Now the children would let out a veritable roar. The teacher would acknowledge, "Now I hear you," and proceed with the next task, with virtually 100% of them responding. Basically her approach was to stop and introduce some kind of gimmick if the children— all of them—were not responding or paying attention. She did not bludgeon the children, she "conned" them. It seemed obvious that they understood her rules; she would not go on until they performed. It seemed that they liked performing because when they performed well she acted pleased.

Apparently, there are at least two major aspects of enthusiasm. The first is conveying sincere interest in the subject. This involves modeling, and even shy teachers should be able to demonstrate it. The other aspect is vigor and dynamics. Teachers who lack a dynamic voice and manner can compensate with other techniques. For example, three days in advance, the teacher can announce that, "On Thursday we will role-play the Scopes trial." This can be followed with information that builds interest and suspense. During the intervening days, this will help provide motivation for activities planned as preparation for the "big event." The teacher could ask students to imagine themselves in the places of historical persons: "Put yourself in the place of William Jennings Bryan and analyze the feelings, values, and attitudes of people in that small Tennessee town. What arguments would you advance? What types of witnesses (pastors, medical experts, whomever) would you want to use?" Seatwork and homework assignments could also be related to the project: "Tomorrow we will select jurors for the trial. Before doing this, we need to find out the basis on which the prosecutor and defense attorney can reject witnesses. . . ."

Of course, teachers must be enthusiastic about everyday topics and lessons as well, not just those related to special events. This is done by continually modeling enthusiasm in the very process of teaching, in the way that material is presented: calling attention to new information or skills, presenting tasks as positive challenges rather than unwelcome chores, challenging students to test themselves when they try to solve problems or apply new skills, and personalizing information by showing how it relates to students' everyday lives and interests.

Using Lecture and Recitation Teaching Methods Effectively

Research on teaching reveals that a degree of variety (along with clarity and enthusiasm) is important for maintaining student interest and attention and ultimately for producing higher achievement (Rosenshine & Furst, 1973). Systematic use of a variety of techniques produces better results than heavy reliance on any one technique, even a good one. Appropriate variety makes it easier for students to sustain attention over long periods of time. Lectures mixed with small-group work, panel discussions, debates, and other devices add spice to classroom life. For years, writers have debated the relative merits of lecturing versus discovery approaches that minimize teacher structuring and rely on independent learning by students. Despite much evidence, neither approach is established clearly as better than the other, and neither is likely to be.

The lecture approach has been criticized as follows:

1. Lectures deny students the opportunity to practice social skills.
2. Lectures make the implicit assumption that all learners need the same information, and this usually is incorrect.
3. Lectures often exceed students' attention spans, so that they begin to "tune out."
4. Lectures only convey information; they do not affect attitudes or promote skill development.
5. Students can read facts on their own—why waste time with lectures?

Most of us have known teachers whose lectures were ineffective because they were dull, vague, or simply too frequent and too long. However, the lecture method has much to recommend it, assuming that lectures are well organized, up to date, and presented appropriately (Gage & Berliner, 1979; McLeish, 1976). Ausubel (1963), among others, has pointed out that effective lectures provide students with information that it would take hours for them to collect. He and others would ask, "Why force students to search for information for hours when a lecture will allow them to get it quickly and then move on to application or problem solving?" Obviously this point has merit. The important question is not "Should we lecture?" but "When should we lecture?"

Various authors (Davis & Alexander, 1977; Gage & Berliner, 1984; Henson, 1980; Hoover, 1968; McMann, 1979) suggest that the lecture method is appropriate in the following situations:

1. When the objective is to present information.
2. When the information is not available in a textbook or some other readily accessible source.
3. When the material must be organized and presented in a particular way for the students.
4. When it is necessary to arouse interest in the subject.
5. When it is necessary to provide an introduction to a topic that the students will then read about on their own or to provide instructions about learning a task.
6. When the information is original or must be integrated from a number of different sources.
7. When material needs to be summarized or synthesized (following a discussion or inquiry process).
8. When the text or curriculum materials need updating or other elaboration.
9. When the teacher wants to present alternate points of view or interpretations or to clarify issues in preparation for discussion or debate.
10. When the teacher wants to provide supplementary explanations of material that students are likely to have difficulty learning on their own.

These points are well taken. Good lectures and presentations at these times do seem preferable to available alternatives. Furthermore, some of the criticisms of lecture methods can be met without abandoning the methods themselves. For example, consider the criticisms that lecture methods do not allow students to learn actively or assist the students to develop social skills. Teachers could adjust to this while retaining the advantages of lectures by giving short lectures (perhaps 15 minutes) to structure problems and provide students with necessary information, and then breaking the class into small problem-solving groups. Teachers who can lecture in an interesting, enthusiastic way that clarifies issues and helps students to raise questions that they can then try to answer themselves are providing valuable learning experiences. Lectures should be viewed not merely as convenient devices for presenting information but also as ways to stimulate interest and raise questions that students will want to address later in groups or independent activities.

The lecture method can be an appropriate teaching strategy if used for an appropriate purpose. Just how effective it will be will depend on the care and skill with which the lecture is prepared. We believe that effective "information" lectures (1) start with advance organizers or previews that include general principles, outlines, or questions that establish a learning set; (2) briefly describe the objectives and alert the students to new or key concepts; (3) present new material in small steps organized logically and sequenced in ways that are easy to follow; (4) elicit student response regularly in order to stimulate active learning and insure that each step is mastered before moving to the next; (5) finish with a review of the main points, stressing general integrative concepts; and (6) follow up the presentation with questions or assignments that require students to encode the material in their own words and apply or extend it to new contexts.

Other Presentation Modes

Classroom discussions and small-group activities not only provide variety but also help students develop skills in expressing themselves orally and in working with other students on joint projects. Students assigned to work in small groups (5 to 15 students) can practice communication skills and solve problems. Small groups allow students to participate in problem-centered discussion, and many students are more comfortable expressing themselves in small groups than in whole-class activities. Also, many more students are able to practice communication skills than would be possible in a single large group.

Motivation and interest often are affected positively when teachers involve students in small-group activities, provide them with interesting projects, and supply them with clear procedural guidelines for accomplishing goals. Small-group work, *if well planned,* complements whole-class lecture/recitation activities nicely by allowing students to learn in more social and active ways (see also the material in Chapter 10 on student teams and other recently developed small-group methods).

Inquiry Approach

Just as teachers can vary the mode of classroom learning (whole class, small group, individualized), teachers can also vary in whether they present key concepts to students or allow the students to discover them on their own. To be successful, inquiry or discovery learning approaches have to fulfill all the criteria we discussed earlier in this chapter (i.e., the "match" has to be considered) and the experiment or activity students are to solve or to engage in needs to be carefully planned.

Collins and Stevens (1983) present an approach to instructional design that focuses on the use of questioning and inquiry teaching strategies to bring about higher-level cognitive objectives and discovery learning. They describe ten instructional strategies: (1) selecting positive and negative examples, (2) varying case studies systematically, (3) selecting counterexamples, (4) generating hypothetical cases, (5) forming hypotheses, (6) testing hypotheses, (7) considering alternative predictions, (8) entrapping students, (9) tracing consequences to a contradiction, and (10) questioning authority.

Collins and Stevens focus on selecting and sequencing examples so as to create dissonance or curiosity in students and thus set the stage for inquiry-oriented discussion rather than emphasize using examples to teach concepts through efficient didactic instruction. The strategy of generating hypothetical cases is used to challenge students' reasoning or force them to take into account factors that they are presently ignoring.

In this inquiry approach, students are challenged to form and evaluate hypotheses rather than given rules or principles and are prodded to consider alternative predictions whenever they jump to conclusions without adequately considering alternatives. The strategy of entrapping students is used to reveal the inadequacies of erroneous preconceptions. Entrapment involves using the students' own thinking to show how it leads to incorrect predictions or conclusions. Tracing consequences to a contradiction is a similar strategy. Finally, the strategy of questioning authority involves training students to think for themselves rather than rely on the teacher or the book for correct answers.

In addition to discussing these instructional strategies, Collins and Stevens (1983) present rules for structuring and sequencing dialogues with students designed to achieve particular objectives. We mention their work briefly here to underscore the point that thoughtful planning is just as important for discovery and inquiry approaches to instruction as it is for other methods of teaching. Hence, classroom observers and/or teachers need to be attentive to the degree that students understand their role and the procedures and criteria students are to use as they try to discover key principles.

Conducting Discussions

Although drill and recitation occur frequently in classrooms, true group discussion is rare (Dillon, 1984). Even activities that teachers call "discussion" tend to be recitations in which teachers ask questions and students respond by reciting what they already know or are presently learning. Relatively few such activities are actual discussions in which the teacher and students, working as a group, share opinions in order to clarify issues, relate new knowledge to their prior knowledge or experience, or attempt to answer a question or solve a problem.

In order to structure and conduct such discussions, teachers must adopt a different role from the one they play in drill and recitation activities. Instead of acting as the primary source of information and the authority figure who determines whether answers are correct or incorrect, the teacher is a discussion leader who structures the discussion by establishing a focus, setting boundaries, and facilitating interaction. In other respects, the teacher assumes a less dominant and less judgmental role. The discussion may begin in a question-and-answer format, but it should gradually evolve into an exchange of views in which students respond to one another as well as to the teacher and respond to statements as well as to questions.

If ideas are being collected, the teacher should record them (by listing them on the board or on an overhead projector, for example) but should not evaluate them. Once the discussion is established, the teacher may wish to participate in it periodically in order to point out connections between ideas, identify similarities or contrasts, request clarification or elaboration, invite students to respond to one another, summarize progress achieved so far, or suggest and test for possible consensus as it develops. However, the teacher does not attempt to push the group toward some previously determined set of conclusions (if the teacher were to do this, the activity would be a guided discovery lesson rather than a discussion).

The pace of discussions is notably slower than that of recitations, with longer periods of silence between speech. These periods provide participants with opportunities to consider what has been said and to formulate responses to it.

Dillon (1981) illustrates that teachers' statements can be just as effective as questions for producing lengthy and insightful student responses during discussions. Dillon (1978) also notes that questions may impede discussions at times, especially closed-ended questions that call for brief responses or questions that are perceived as attempts to test students rather than to solicit their ideas. To avoid this problem,

Dillon (1979) lists six *alternatives to questioning* that teachers can use to sustain discussions:

1. *Declarative statements.* In discussing the effects of war on the domestic economy, the teacher might respond to a student's statement by thinking "When the war broke out, unemployment dropped." The teacher could introduce this idea into the discussion by stating it directly rather than putting it into the form of a question such as "What happens to the unemployment rate in war time?" or "What causes a drop in unemployment?" The statement provides information that the students will have to accommodate and respond to; compared to a question, however, it invites longer and more varied responses.

2. *Declarative restatements.* Teachers can show students that they have attended to and understood what the students have said by occasionally summarizing. Such summarizing may be useful to the class as a whole, and in addition, psychotherapists using nondirective counseling techniques have found that reflecting people's statements to them tends to stimulate additional and deeper responding.

3. *Indirect questions.* When a direct question might sound challenging or rejecting, the teacher can make a statement such as "I wonder what makes you think that" or "I was just thinking about whether or not that would make any difference." Such indirect questions might stimulate further thinking without generating anxiety.

4. *Imperatives.* Similarly, statements such as "Tell us more about that" or "Perhaps you could give some examples" are less threatening than direct requests for the same information.

5. *Student questions.* Rather than asking all of the questions themselves, teachers can encourage students to ask questions in response to statements made by their classmates.

6. *Deliberate silence.* Sometimes the best response to a statement is to remain silent for several seconds in order to allow students to absorb the content and formulate follow-up questions or comments.

In general, if teachers expect an activity to involve genuine discussion and not merely recitation, they will have to make this fact clear to students and alter their own behavior accordingly.

Maintaining Student Attention

Clarity, enthusiasm, and variety in instructional techniques promote achievement primarily by helping teachers elicit and maintain students' attention. Students must attend to and think about learning tasks if they are to master them. A useful focal point for examining classrooms is to assess students' attention to learning tasks. Considering what we know about attention span, it is not reasonable to expect students to be attentive at all times. Pencils have to be sharpened, resource books have to be returned, and many other factors reduce student attentiveness (hunger, need to go to the bathroom, distractions from outside the room). The question we try to answer about student attention is the following: What percentage of the students are actively paying attention or involved in their work? Teachers should be able to create learning environments in which 80 to 90 percent of the students are attending at any given time.

Students need not be sitting quietly at their desks. They can be reading books on the floor, drawing at an easel in an art corner, or talking with other students about a group project. The only important consideration is whether or not they are involved in productive work.

Older students might be listening attentively or thinking about a problem even though they appear to be gazing out the window or staring blankly at the floor. Younger ones are likely to be doing what they appear to be doing. A useful means of studying classrooms, then, especially in the early grades, is to determine the percentage of students who appear to be involved in learning tasks, using indices such as the following:

1. When the teacher gives directions, how many students watch?
2. When the teacher finishes, how many students begin work?
3. When students are supposed to be working at their desks, how many are writing or reading?
4. When the teacher works with a reading group or subgroup, what percentage of the rest of the class remains working?

Interpretations of data on students' classroom attention have to be made with care. First graders can be paying attention even though they may be squirming. Reflective students may spend time organizing their work and thinking about it before they begin to write. However, if large numbers of students do not begin work promptly, something is wrong (unclear directions, lack of interest, etc.).

The authors have observed classrooms in which 70 to 80 percent of the students were sitting quietly but doing nothing productive. Situations like this occur most often when teachers who are strict disciplinarians conduct small-group lessons. If seatwork assignments are inadequate because faster students have nothing to do after they finish working and/or slower students give up, many students will be off-task. If the teacher has used strict disciplinary tactics to teach them not to make noise or get out of their seats, they have nothing to do but sit there. Teachers who control less rigidly but also fail to plan appropriate seatwork assignments typically have 20 to 30 percent of the class misbehaving (talking to other students who are trying to work, walking around the room aimlessly, pinching neighbors) and a high percentage of the rest merely sitting.

In general, good teachers have a high percentage of their students working on learning tasks most of the time. Teachers who do not should examine their behavior and seek ways to improve. Perhaps they are accepting inattention: They may describe and label it but do nothing to change it. For example, when explaining an assignment, a teacher may say, "I notice that several of you are not paying attention; when we start our seatwork, you will be at my desk, asking for directions." The teacher may then continue to explain the seatwork. After the explanation, it is likely that several students will in fact come up to the desk to ask questions.

Teachers must intervene when students are inattentive. A good way to examine how teachers demand attention is to observe what happens when students continually call out answers without really listening to the questions, perhaps even before the teacher finishes asking them. It is also instructive to see how often students answer a different question from the one asked by the teacher or have their hands up before the teacher asks a question. In these situations, do teachers recognize and deal with the problem or are they oblivious to it? Do they remind the class to listen to the question? If not, what do they do, and what are the effects?

It is also useful to observe how much time students spend doing nothing. Teachers are often unaware of the extent of this problem and need to be alerted to it if they are to reduce it. Students should not be sitting in their seats, bored, with nothing to do. The appearance of attention does not guarantee that students are engaged in purposeful activity, but it suggests that at least minimal conditions for learning are met and that it is possible for learning to take place. Attention is measurable and is associated with achievement.

Ideally, of course, assessment of students' responses to activities should go beyond mere attention to consider whether or not the students are obtaining the intended meaning from listening to the teacher or reading materials. Research by Anderson (1981), Peterson and Swing (1982), and Winne and Marx (1982) shows that even attentive and well-motivated students can be badly confused about material they are supposed to be learning. To uncover such confusion, it usually is necessary not only to monitor students for apparent attention but also to question them about their understanding and to monitor their written work.

QUESTIONING

Teacher questioning is a popular area of classroom research, partly because it is among the easiest of teacher behaviors to observe and code reliably. There are many classification schemes that categorize questions (and usually order them into some kind of hierarchy) and many studies that involve relating types of teacher questions to students' achievement. Despite this, and despite well-publicized and accepted claims that divergent questions are better than convergent questions, that high-level or complex questions are better than low-level or simple questions, and that thought questions are better than fact questions, *actual findings* are mixed, and most reviewers conclude that measures of type or level of question do not correlate consistently with learning gains (Brophy & Good, 1986; Dunkin & Biddle, 1974; Rosenshine & Furst, 1973; Winne, 1979).

Some studies even have found that rates of low-level, factual questions correlate positively with achievement gain but that rates of more complex or abstract questions do not (Dillon, 1981; Soar, 1973; Stallings, 1975). Most such findings come from studies of instruction of disadvantaged students in early elementary grades, where schooling concentrates on mastery of basic skills. Under these circumstances, complex or abstract questions are seldom helpful.

In contrast to the confusing and unpromising data concerning types or levels of questions, several studies show that the frequency of academic questions is related to learning (Brophy & Evertson, 1976; Soar, 1973; Stallings, 1975). There are probably at least two reasons for this. First, teachers who have high rates of academic questions usually have well-organized and well-managed classes and spend most of their time actively teaching their students during academic activities. Other teachers are either poorly organized or choose to spend time pursuing nonacademic goals. Thus, high frequencies of questions mean, among other things, that a class spends most of its time in learning-related activities. A second reason is that teachers who question frequently tend to supplement lectures, demonstrations, reading, and seatwork activities with recitations, discussions, and other opportunities for students to express themselves orally. This not only adds variety but also appears to be valuable in its own right.

Much advice about questioning techniques is available. Most of it is based not on research but on logical analyses of the strengths and weaknesses of different types of questions with reference to instructional goals. Such analysis is useful because the appropriateness of questions depends on the purpose of the exercise and the characteristics of the students. For example, a teacher may ask questions to see if students are ready for an impending discussion, to determine if they have achieved learning objectives, to arouse their interest, or to stimulate critical thinking. A good question for arousing interest may not be a good question for assessing learning.

Questions to Avoid

Groisser (1964) also discusses certain questioning habits that often lead to unproductive student responses. He describes four types of questions that are particularly misused: (1) yes-no questions, (2) tugging questions, (3) guessing questions, and (4) leading questions.

Yes-No   Groisser advises against excessive use of yes-no questions because they typically are asked only as warm-ups for other questions. For example, the teacher asks, "Was Hannibal a clever soldier?" After a student answers, the teacher says, "Why?" or "Explain your reason." Groisser believes that these initial yes-no questions confuse the lesson focus and waste time, so that it is better to ask the real question in the first place.

We see two additional dangers in yes-no questions or other questions that involve a *simple choice between alternatives* ("Was it Hamilton or Jackson?"). First, such questions encourage guessing, because students will be right 50 percent of the time even when they have no idea of the correct answer. Holt (1964) describes vividly how students read teachers like traffic lights in such situations and how students quickly change their answers at the slightest teacher frown. When a teacher asks too many of these questions, students are apt to develop devious strategies to get the teacher to cue the answer instead of concentrating on the question itself.

The other disadvantage of yes-no and simple choice questions is that they have *low diagnostic power*. One valuable aspect of student responses, whether correct or incorrect, is that they cue teachers about the most appropriate way to proceed. Unfortunately, because of the guesswork factor, responses to simple choice questions do not provide much of a basis for deciding whether or not students know the material. Choice questions sometimes are useful for low-achieving or shy students who have a difficult time responding. They are relatively simple to answer, and this type of warm-up often helps these students respond better to more substantive questions that follow. For most instructional purposes, however, these questions should be avoided.

Tugging   Tugging questions or statements often follow a halting or incomplete student response ("Well, come on." "Yes . . . ?"). Tugging questions essentially say "Tell me more." These questions provide no help to students who are unable to respond and may be perceived as nagging or bullying. Brophy and Evertson (1976) found that it was best for teachers to give students the answer when they were unable to respond and unwise to try to elicit it by pumping them, because students would give the answer if they knew it. When teachers do stay with a student, it is better to provide some kind of help rather than to continue to demand the answer. This study was conducted in second and third grades, where most questions are factual ones that students either can or cannot answer. At higher grade levels, where questions become more complex and varying degrees of completeness and specificity in answers are possible, rephrasing and giving clues are more likely to result in improved student response.

When students have responded correctly but incompletely, teachers are more likely to get additional information if they ask new, more specific questions than if they continue to ask: "What else?" "What's another reason?" and so forth. For example, a teacher might ask, "Why did the Pilgrims live in a fort?" A student might respond, "They built a fort to protect themselves from the Indians and from animals." If the teacher wants the student to focus on the advantages of community living, the next question should cue the student to this aspect of Pilgrim life: "What advantages did the Pilgrims gain from living in a group?"

Guessing   Guessing questions require students to guess or reason about a question, either because they do not have the facts ("How far do you think it is from New York to Denver?" "How many business firms have offices on Wall Street?") or because the question has no correct answer ("In the song *Houston,* why do you think Dean Martin wanted to go there?" "How many games does a National Football League team have to win in order to make the playoffs?"). Guessing questions can be useful in capturing students' imagination and involving them in discussions. However, if such questions are overused or used inappropriately, they encourage students to guess and respond thoughtlessly rather than to think.

The value of guessing questions depends on how they are used. If the teacher just wants a guess, the question is probably pointless. However, if the teacher wants students to formulate hypotheses and make realistic estimates based on limited information, such questions can be valuable. The game *Twenty Questions* is an excellent case in point, especially for younger elementary students. If the teacher allows aimless guessing, the game will have little value. However, if the teacher models the game, demonstrating problem-solving strategies, it can be a valuable learning experience.

Similarly, secondary mathematics students may learn to enjoy working with abstract formulas when the formulas are introduced with questions like, "How many games will the Cardinals have to win if they are to win the pennant? Let's see, in the past 10 years the range has been . . ." or "How could we figure the formula? They have a six-game lead with 22 games remaining."

Guessing questions are useful if they are related to teaching strategies that help students think rationally and systematically and if they are designed ultimately to elicit a thoughtful response. Guessing questions that to encourage impulsive or irrational thought are self-defeating. The momentary enthusiasm such questions may generate is not worth the risk of teaching students inappropriate attitudes or habits.

Leading Leading questions (such as, "Don't you agree?") and other rhetorical questions ("Johnny, you want to read about the Pilgrims, don't you?") should be avoided. They reinforce student dependence on the teacher. *Questions should be asked only if the teacher really wants a response.* Avoidance of such rhetorical and meaningless questions helps students develop the expectation that when the teacher asks a question, something important and interesting is about to happen.

Characteristics of Good Questions

Although the complete definition of a good question depends on context, certain guidelines can be applied to most questions. Groisser (1964) indicates that good questions are (1) clear, (2) purposeful, (3) brief, (4) natural and adapted to the level of the class, and (5) thought provoking. Elaboration of these descriptions follows:

Clear Questions should precisely describe the specific points to which students are to respond. Vague questions can be responded to in many ways (too many), and their ambiguous nature confuses students. For example, Groisser writes:

> If a teacher of Spanish wished to call attention to the tense of a verb in a sentence on the board and asked, "What do you see here?" the student would not know exactly what was being called for. Better to ask, "What tense is used in this clause?"

Vague questions often result in wasted time as students ask the teacher to clarify or rephrase. They fail to identify the specific attack point ("What's wrong with football?" versus "Why do so many college players never receive a degree?" or "What about beer?" versus "Should 16-year-olds be allowed to drink beer?").

Questions can also be unclear if they are asked as part of an uninterrupted series. Groisser writes of a teacher who,

> . . . in discussing the War of 1812 asks, in one continuous statement, "Why did we go to war? As a merchant, how would you feel? How was our trade hurt by the Napoleonic War?" The teacher is trying to clarify his first question and to focus thinking upon an economic cause of the war. In his attempt, he actually confuses.

This teacher would have been more effective asking a clear, straightforward question to begin with ("What was the cause of the War of 1812?"), waiting for the students to respond, and then probing for economic causes if students failed to mention them. Teachers often ask two or three questions in one or rephrase their original question a number of times. When faced with such a series of questions, students do not know what the teacher is asking. Even if the questions are answered as the teacher hoped, many students will not profit from hearing the answers because they are confused or distracted by the questions.

The usefulness of clear and specific (highly focused) questions has been shown in some experimental situations (Rosenshine, 1968; Wright & Nuthall, 1970). *Questions should clearly cue students to respond along specific lines.* This does not mean that the teacher cues the answer; it means that the teacher communicates the specific question to which the student is asked to respond.

Brief   Questions should be brief. Long questions are often unclear. The longer the question, the more difficult it is to understand.

Natural   Questions should be phrased in natural, simple language (as opposed to pedantic, textbook language) and should be adapted to the level of the class. If students do not understand the question, they cannot do what the teacher wants.

This does not mean that teachers should avoid unfamiliar words. Students benefit from learning new words that teachers introduce clearly. Clear teacher modeling of sophisticated verbal communication helps students to develop this ability. However, teachers must consider students' vocabularies. When teachers introduce new words, they should immediately clarify them and teach students to use the words.

Purposeful   Purposeful questions help achieve the lesson's intent. Question series that are not planned in advance are seldom purposeful (this is why it is useful to write out questions that will be asked later during class discussion). Teachers who improvise most of their questions will ask many irrelevant and confusing questions that work against achievement of their own goals.

Sequenced   If questions are intended as teaching devices and not merely as oral test items, they should be asked in carefully planned *sequences* with teachers obtaining answers to each question and integrating each answer with previously discussed material before moving to the next question. Initial questions should lead students to identify or review essential facts. These questions can be followed with ones that ask students to refine understanding of the information and apply the knowledge to real or hypothetical problems ("Now that we have identified the properties of these six types of wood, which would you use to build a canoe? A huge sailboat?"). Planning will help insure an orderly progression through the sequences of objectives. Of course, it is not necessary that teachers adhere rigidly to a prepared sequence of questions. Other worthwhile topics may be opened up by pupil questions, and these should be pursued.

Logical thinking about sequences of questions indicates that researchers' emphasis on the cognitive level of questions is misplaced. At a certain point in a class discussion, factual questions are important. At other times, questions of value and priority are essential and factual questions are inappropriate. Although there are few empirical data on this point, researchers who wish to understand and to improve instruction should attempt to study the interconnectedness of questions.

We emphasize that the sequence and the meaningfulness of information exchange are of critical importance and not the cognitive level of the question per se. For example, in Table 11.3 it is clear that a sequence of questions, even relatively "low-level" factual questions, can lead to a meaningful exchange of information and to insight. In this sequence, the teacher is helping students to understand the historical events that preceded the Boston Tea Party and is trying to illustrate that different events can be seen in different ways depending on one's perspective. Here, key information is being tied to the concept of monopoly and representative taxation, and the questions of fact that are being raised are helping students to *understand* the historical significance of activities. For example, the question, what was the tea worth?—a simple fact question—should help students to realize that in colonial times tea was extraordinarily valuable. The fact that they were willing to dump the tea into the harbor rather than taking the tea home indicated how outraged the citizens were. Similarly, the question, who participated in the Boston Tea Party? is trying to get at the fact that a wide range of citizens participated in the demonstration.

In the unreasonable sequence, the fact questions asked are often trivial and are not really used to logically examination of what the Boston Tea Party represented. For example, questions about the number of ships that were in the harbor and colonial dress during the tea party seem to represent teachers' interest in whether or not the students had read the book quite carefully. Although such questions may be of value occasionally, overemphasizing trivial detail is counterproductive in most circumstances. Although questions evaluating students' knowledge of Townshend Duties and Coercive Acts might be important if they were being used to teach students the antecedent and subsequent effects of the Boston Tea Party, in the sequence in which they appear in Table 11.4 these questions seem to be designed to determine whether or not the students had read the material rather than playing an instrumental role in an important sequence of questions. Hence, we believe that too much emphasis is placed on the apparent cognitive level of questions asked rather than the role that a particular question plays in stimulating discussion and debate. Although distinctions in the cognitive levels of questions can be useful by providing a basis for teachers to think about the cognitive demands that they place on students, we think that to little attention has been given to the *sequence* of questions and that in the long run an analysis of one's sequence of questions is more important than information about the cognitive level of questions.

Thought Provoking   Good questions are thought provoking. Especially in discussions, questions should arouse strong, thoughtful responses from students, such as "I never thought of that before," or "I want to find the answer to that question." Discussion questions should force students to think about facts and to integrate and

Table 11.3   A REASONABLE QUESTIONING SEQUENCE

1. What was the Boston Tea Party?
2. What events preceded the Boston Tea Party?
3. What is a monopoly?
4. Under what conditions might a monopoly be justified?
5. Do we provide favorable circumstances for certain industries in this country that make it difficult for foreign countries to compete?
6. What did the Boston Tea Party mean to British citizens? To American citizens?
7. Who participated in the Boston Tea Party?
8. How much was the tea worth?

Table 11.4   AN UNREASONABLE SEQUENCE

1. What was the Boston Tea Party?
2. How many ships containing tea were in the harbor?
3. How did the colonials dress when they entered the ships to destroy the tea?
4. Define Townshend Duties.
5. Define Coercive Acts.
6. Who was Thomas Hutchenson?
7. On what date did the Boston Tea Party occur?

apply them. Discussions should help students to clarify their ideas and to analyze or synthesize facts in addition to listing them.

Fact questions often are needed to see if students possess information basic to the discussion or to bring out relevant facts before posing more abstract questions. Other questions should require students to use the information rather than just recite it and should motivate them to want to respond. This is especially true as students move into the upper elementary and secondary grades.

Groisser suggests that questions should be planned, logical, and sequential; addressed to the class; followed by pauses that allow students time to think; balanced between fact and thought questions; distributed widely; be asked conversationally; not repeated; and sometimes asked in such a way that directs students to respond to classmates' answers.

The first two points have already been discussed. Both are logical and appeal to common sense. The third point suggests addressing most questions to the entire class before calling on a student to respond: ask the question, allow students time to think, and then call on someone. This way, everyone in the class is responsible for the answer. If teachers name a student to respond before asking a question or call on a student as soon as they finish asking the question, only the student who is named is responsible for answering. Other students are less likely to try to answer it.

Groisser notes at least three situations in which it is practical to call on a student before asking a question: (1) the teacher wants to draw an inattentive student back into the lesson, (2) the teacher wants to ask a follow-up question of a student who has just responded, or (3) the teacher is calling on a shy student who may be "shocked" if called on without warning.

Groisser's point that students need time to think seems self-evident but actually raises several complicated issues. First, the optimal wait-time seems likely to vary with the question and the situation. A question calling for students to solve a complex problem or give an opinion about a complex issue requires a much longer wait-time than a question asking for a specific fact that a student either does or does not know. Similarly, a question asked in the process of introducing new material to students would ordinarily require a longer wait-time than a question asked as part of a fast-paced review or drill.

Wait-Time

Good questioning behavior requires allowing students sufficient time to think about and to respond to questions. Rowe (1974a, 1974b) reported data that at the time seemed remarkable: After asking questions, the teachers she observed waited less than one second before calling on someone to respond. Furthermore, even after calling on a student, they waited only about a second for the student to give the answer before supplying it themselves, calling on someone else, or rephrasing the question or giving clues. Such findings do not seem to make sense because they suggest that the teachers minimized the value of their questions by failing to give students time to think so that their questions could have the desired effect on student thinking.

Rowe followed up these observations by training teachers, to see what would happen if they extended their wait-times from less than one second to three to five seconds. Surprisingly, most of the teachers found this difficult to do, and some never did succeed. However, in the classrooms of teachers who extended their wait-times to three to five seconds, the following desirable changes occurred:

1. Increase in the average length of student responses.
2. Increase in unsolicited but appropriate student responses.
3. Decrease in failures to respond.
4. Increase in speculative responses.
5. Increase in student-to-student comparisons of data.
6. Increase in statements that involved drawing inferences from evidence.
7. Increase in student-initiated questions.
8. A greater variety of verbal contributions to lessons by students.

In short, Rowe found that longer wait-times led to more active participation in lessons by a larger percentage of the students, coupled with an increase in the quality of this participation. Subsequent research (reviewed in Tobin, 1983*a*, 1983*b*) replicates and extends these findings. In particular, this research verifies that increasing wait-time leads to longer and higher-quality student responses to teacher questions and participation by a greater number of students (Rowe, 1986; Swift & Gooding, 1983; Tobin & Capie, 1982). These effects are most notable on the less able students in the class.

Subsequent research has verified Rowe's finding that many teachers experience difficulty in extending their wait-times. For example, DeTure (1979) found that even after training, no teacher attained an average wait-time longer than 1.8 seconds. Why should this be? The matter has not been researched, but it seems likely that the answer lies in the pressures on teachers to maintain lesson pacing and student attention. Some teachers may be reluctant to extend their wait-times because they fear, with justification in some cases, that they may lose student attention or even lose control of the class if they do. This is one of many illustrations of how good classroom management and good instruction are mutually dependent and supportive of each other, and it also illustrates one of the continuing dilemmas that require teacher decision making and adjustment to the immediate situation. Wait-times of three to five seconds are generally preferable to shorter wait-times because they allow more thinking by more students, but the teacher may have to use shorter wait-times when the class is restive or when time is running out and it is necessary to finish the lesson quickly.

Even without training, most teachers adjust wait-times at least to some degree according to the type of question asked. They are likely to wait longer, for example, following higher-level questions (especially analysis and synthesis questions) than following lower-level questions (Arnold, Atwood, & Rogers, 1974). Furthermore, the causal linkages between question level and wait-time seem to work in both directions. In addition to noting effects on students, some of the investigators who trained teachers to increase wait-times noted that this change also led to interaction patterns in which the teachers asked fewer questions per time-unit than before, but more questions at higher cognitive levels (Fagan, Hassler, & Szabo, 1981; Rice, 1977).

Thus, in general, we should expect interactions featuring mostly lower-level questions to move at a quicker pace with shorter wait-times compared to inter-actions featuring higher-level questions. *The appropriateness of these pacing and wait-time factors depends on the objectives of the activity.* Thus, although most studies in which teachers were trained to slow the pace and extend wait-time have produced positive outcomes, these studies have focused on intermediate and upper grade levels and on instruction in abstract or difficult material. Anshutz (1975) reported no science achievement differences between short and long wait-times for students in grades 3 and 4, and Riley (1980) reported interaction effects on science achievement in grades 1 through 5. A decrease in achievement occurred when wait-time was extended from medium to long for low-level questions, whereas an increase in achievement was noted when wait-time was extended for high and mixed cognitive level questions.

These studies show that pacing and wait-time should be suited to the questions being asked and ultimately to the objectives these questions are designed to ac-complish. A fast pace and short wait-times are appropriate for drill or review activities covering specific facts. However, if questions are intended to stimulate students to think about material and formulate original responses rather than merely to retrieve information from memory, it is important to allow time for these effects to occur. This is especially true for complex or involved questions. Students may need several seconds merely to process such questions before they can even begin to formulate responses to them. When a slow pace and thoughtful responding are desired, teachers should not only adjust their wait-times but make their objectives clear to the students. Unless cued, some students may not realize that they are supposed to formulate an original response rather than search their memories for something taught to them explicitly, and some may think that the teacher is looking for speed rather than quality of response.

Distribute Questions to a Range of Students

Groisser and Loughlin both suggest that teachers should distribute questions widely rather than allow a few students to answer most of them. The idea is that students will learn more if they are actively involved in discussions than if they sit passively day after day without participating. We all know reticent students who rarely par-ticipate in discussions but still get excellent grades, but most students benefit from opportunities to practice oral communication skills, and distributing response opportunities helps keep students attentive and accountable. Also, teachers who restrict their questions primarily to a small group of active (and usually high-achieving) students are likely to communicate undesirable expectations (Good & Brophy, 1974) and generally to be less aware and less effective.

Repeating Questions and Answers

Another point Groisser and Loughlin note is that questions normally should not be repeated (assuming that they are audible and clearly expressed). Teachers who continually repeat and rephrase questions teach students that they need not pay attention because teachers will always repeat the question if they should call on another student. This also is a sign of poor preparation and disorganized thinking.

Similarly, many teachers have an annoying habit of regularly repeating students' responses: "John has told us that there were three fundamental reasons for the Civil War. First he suggested . . ." This wastes time, lessens the perceived value of students' responses, and fails to hold students accountable for attending to what their classmates say.

Again, there are exceptions. Occasionally it is advisable to repeat answers when working with young students in drill recitations. Statements such as "Yes, two plus two equal four" or "The tallest block is the red one" acknowledge that the student is correct and model speaking in complete sentences. The latter feature is also a useful way to restate important points that some students might have forgotten (if there was a long delay between the question and the answer, for example). In general, repetition of answers is appropriate when teachers are working with young children, when the questions deal with rote memory of factual material, or when the answers are short.

Another occasion when it is appropriate to repeat an answer is when the teacher rephrases the answer somewhat in order to summarize important material. This should not be done too frequently, though, to avoid indirectly teaching students that "The teacher always says it better than we can." Also, although teacher summaries are important, teachers should also encourage students to summarize discussions and to describe how classmates' comments are related.

Feedback About Responses

Students should receive information about the correctness or incorrectness of their responses. This is especially important for low achievers. In general, feedback is important both to motivate students and to produce learning. Feedback lets students know how they are doing or how much progress has been made. This probably seems obvious, but teachers sometimes fail to give feedback, especially to low achievers (Brophy & Good, 1974).

Unless it is understood that no response indicates correctness, teachers should give some sort of response every time students answer questions. Feedback need not be long or elaborate, although sometimes it will have to be. Often a head nod or a short comment like "Right" is all that is needed to tell students that they are on the right track. Also, teachers do not always have to provide feedback personally. They can give students answer sheets so that they can assess their own work or can allow students to provide feedback to one another.

Reasons for Questioning

Some types of questions suggest to students that the teacher is more interested in quizzing them than in sharing or discussing information (see Dillon, 1978). Does the teacher present questions as challenges or as threats? Teachers who question students in harsh terms are likely to threaten them and make it difficult for them to share their thinking. Usually, questions should stress the exchange of information: The teacher is trying to assess knowledge, and the student's answer, whether correct or not, conveys information. It allows the teacher to make decisions: Do the students understand? Can they go on to the next exercise? Do they need review? Questions that present interesting challenges and stimulate friendly exchanges of information are likely to maximize motivation and yield productive answers. They should be honest questions asked because the teacher wants to see if the student understands the material, not aggressive questions asked in the spirit of "Say something and then I will tell you why you are wrong."

That is what Groisser means when he suggests that questions should be asked conversationally. He also suggests that allowing students to respond to one another is helpful for demonstrating teacher interest in obtaining student discussion. Groisser writes:

> Many teachers seize upon the first answer given and react to it at once with a comment or with another question . . . It is more desirable, where possible, to ask a question, accept two or three answers, and then proceed. This pattern tends to produce sustaining responses, variety, and enrichment. It encourages volunteering, contributes to group cooperation, and approaches a more realistic social situation.

Such techniques model teacher interest in the exchange of information about a topic (as opposed to pushing for the right answer) and indicate that there is not always a single correct answer. Students are likely to listen more carefully to one another if they are called on to respond to one another's answers occasionally. Wright and Nuthall (1970) found that teachers who redirected questions to other students during science lessons got better achievement than those who did not. Having pupils react to one another's responses apparently is valuable in some situations, especially in the higher elementary grades. With young students (preschool to second grade), this technique may be too tedious and time consuming to be worth the trouble.

TEACHING FOR CONCEPTUAL CHANGE

Not surprisingly, students often have misconceptions about various scientific and mathematical concepts prior to instruction in those same concepts (Helm & Novak, 1983). One purpose of instruction is to alter such misconceptions and to help students understand scientific phenomena. However, there is evidence that students' misconceptions often persist despite instruction.

Some writers contend that misconceptions persist because they make sense to students as they experience the world. Smith and Lott (1983) noted in one empirical study that students' misconceptions continued to exist after instruction partly because teachers did not adequately identify students' basic misunderstandings prior to instruction.

Posner, Strike, Hewson, and Gertzog (1982) argue that four conditions must be satisfied if students are to change in their understanding of central concepts: (1)

dissatisfaction with existing conceptions must be induced, (2) the new conception must be intelligible, (3) the new conception must be initially plausible, and (4) the new conception must appear fruitful.

Although the need for conceptual change teaching is relevant to a variety of subjects, our discussion focuses on science—an area where there has been some interesting empirical work. As a case in point, Smith and Anderson (1984) describe a study and present an interpretive discussion of students' misconceptions. They note that recent developments in cognitive psychology, linguistics, and artificial intelligence have lead to new insights in the field of cognitive science. Findings from recent studies in cognition help to organize these insights. First, recent research suggests that although humans are infinitely flexible in the way in which they can use information (much more inventive and creative than any computer), the working memory of the human mind is quite limited in comparison to even an inexpensive computer. Considering that humans have a relatively limited short-term memory (we can only think about a few things at the same time), we are quite susceptible to information overload. Second, preexisting cognitive structure plays an important role in perception and comprehension. What is noticed and how it is interpreted are partly determined by cognitive structures that exist prior to an experience. New experiences are filtered through preexisting cognitive structures.

According to Smith and Anderson, an important result of recent research is the discovery of how often these cognitive structures are inadequate or incorrect. For example, it is clear that students in high school chemistry courses can often balance chemical equations but have little or no understanding of what the symbols represent. Similarly, mathematics students can often solve problems successfully although they cannot conceptualize and interpret the meanings of their computations. Thus, it is easy for teachers to assume that students have understood an experiment or a general concept because they can complete tasks that are associated with such understanding; however, more detailed questioning of the students often reveals that the instruction did not alter their preexisting, inadequate conceptions.

For example, Smith and Anderson pretested students' scientific conceptions about light and plants as producers of their own food and found that students had important misconceptions about both areas. Furthermore, posttesting revealed that *less than a quarter* of the students had dropped these misconceptions and acquired the correct scientific conceptions following units of instruction on these topics. Analyses of classroom instruction documented ways in which students' misconceptions contributed to these results by affecting both students' interpretation of instruction and their behavior.

One of the crucial experiments in the plant unit involved growing plants in the light and in the dark. Students' observations that the plants in the dark began to grow and then wilted were designed to set the stage for an explanation of photosynthesis. The scientific conception is that the plants in the dark died because they could not engage in photosynthesis without light, and photosynthesis was their only source of food after the food stored in the seeds was used up. However, the students' misconceptions caused them to interpret the experiment differently. Because they assumed that food for plants is water and the other materials taken in from the environment, most students saw no connection between the experiment and the issue of where plants get their food. Instead, students interpreted the pale appearance of the plants in the dark as support for their misconceptions—namely, plants need light in order to stay green and healthy (the investigators also note that certain practical aspects of the project may pose additional difficulties of interpretation for students, because in the hands of fifth graders, plants in the dark sometimes live longer than plants in the light!).

Through classroom observations, observations of teacher planning, and interviews with teachers, Smith and Anderson found that teachers also had misconceptions. In contrast to students, whose misconceptions concerned the *science content,* teachers' misconceptions were essentially *instructional* and *pedagogical.* The teachers observed were characterized as exhibiting one of three approaches to the teaching of science: activity-driven teaching, didactic teaching, and discovery teaching. Although there were major differences in these approaches, none of the 14 teachers was particularly successful in getting students to abandon their misconceptions in favor of more appropriate scientific theories. Activity-driven teachers focused primarily on activities to be carried out in the classroom (textbook assignments, demonstrations, experiments, etc.). These teachers seemed to think that the activities would teach the content. They assumed that by following the recommendations in the teacher's guide, students would learn automatically. Unfortunately, because of a lack of careful attention to the important elements of instruction, activity-driven teachers often unknowingly modified or deleted crucial parts of the program, making it difficult if not impossible for students to discover the intended concepts.

Teachers who used a didactic style presented information directly to students and regarded the text as a repository of knowledge to be taught. These teachers did not suspect that students had misconceptions or see a need to be certain that students had interpreted the information as intended. They remained unaware of students' misconceptions throughout the unit and taught in a way that did not allow students to express their own thinking. As a result these teachers denied themselves the opportunity to become aware of students' misconceptions.

Discovery-oriented teachers also had difficulty correcting students' misconceptions. These teachers tried to avoid telling answers to their students and instead encouraged the students to develop their own ideas about the results of the plant-growing experiment. However, ambiguities in the teacher's guide about how to conduct this experiment and the teachers' perception that SCIS was strictly a discovery program prevented these teachers from understanding the nature of "invention" as intended by the SCIS developers. The SCIS teachers' guide calls for *direct presentation* of the concept of photosynthesis during the "invention" portion of the SCIS learning cycle.

Since discovery teachers were also unaware of the importance of students' misconceptions, they did not understand the need to challenge and direct students' attention to key concepts. These teachers frequently asked students to interpret their own observations in open-ended ways when the teacher's guide suggested questions that would lead students to consider specific theoretical issues. In the absence of direct information and feedback from their teachers, most students *used their misconceptions* as the basis for interpreting the plant-growing experiments.

The investigators thus concluded that all three teaching styles were inadequate for producing conceptual change. However, they also concluded that simply providing teachers with information about their students' misconceptions or the inappro-priate teaching techniques they used would not be sufficient to change teaching. For example, the SCIS teachers had difficulties because they failed to make use of information that was already in the teacher's guide. Thus, teachers' beliefs about discovery learning and their own cognitive structures affected how they interpreted assignments and suggestions in the teacher's guide. *Teachers must attend to how students perceive and structure concepts if they are to help students achieve adequate conceptual understanding.*

ACTIVE STUDENT LEARNING

We have argued that successful teachers are very active in the classroom, providing appropriate motivation, instruction, and resources to students. However, we also believe that *students need to be active learners,* learning not only how to respond successfully to the challenges and questions teachers and textbooks raise but also to raise their own questions and to use teachers and other resources as they pursue self-defined goals. Thus, teachers need to help students acquire skills for indepen-dent learning and practice those skills in problem-solving and critical-thinking exercises.

Types of Learning Strategies

There are certain relatively generic skills which, if mastered thoroughly and used consistently and appropriately, can facilitate learning in a broad range of situations. Reading with speed, accuracy, and comprehension is one such generic skill. Others include logical reasoning, critical thinking, problem solving, "learning to learn" skills, and study skills. Ideas about conceptualizing and teaching such skills have been around for a long time. Recently, however, with the emphasis on cognition and human information processing, a great deal of research has been done on the development and functioning of effective learning strategies and on how these strategies may be taught to individuals who do not use them spontaneously.

In a review of this work, Weinstein and Mayer (1986) identify the following five general types of learning strategies:

1. *Rehearsal strategies* involve repeating material by either saying or writing it or by focusing attention on key parts of it. For brief rote-learning tasks, rehearsal may involve nothing more than repeating the material aloud as an aid to memorizing it. For more complex tasks such as learning from lectures, rehearsal might involve repeating key terms aloud, copying the material, or underlining important parts.
2. *Elaboration strategies* include making connections between the new mate-rial and more familiar material. For rote-learning tasks, elaboration strat-egies would include forming mental images to associate with the material and generating sentences that relate the terms to be learned to one another or to more familiar terms. For more complex meaningful learning tasks, elaboration strategies would include paraphrasing, summarizing, creating analogies, taking notes that go beyond verbatim repetition to extend or comment on the material, answering questions, and describing how the new information relates to existing knowledge.

3. *Organizational strategies* require students to impose structure on the material by subdividing it into parts and identifying superordinate-subordinate relationships. For simple rote learning tasks, organizational strategies involve breaking lists into subgroups. Organizational strategies for complex meaningful learning tasks would include outlining the text or creating diagrams showing relationships among the concepts. Teachers can help students to organize material by providing them with skeleton outlines around which they can systematically integrate information. For example, a teacher discussing careers in science in a seventh-grade life science class might distribute the outline presented in Table 11.5 as a way of helping students to take notes effectively.

4. *Comprehension-monitoring strategies* include remaining aware of what one is trying to accomplish during a learning task, keeping track of the strategies one uses and the degree of success achieved with them, and adjusting behavior accordingly. Comprehension-monitoring strategies include noting and taking action when one does not understand something, self-questioning to check understanding, and modifying strategies if necessary.

5. *Affective strategies* involve eliminating undesirable affect and getting ready to learn. They include establishing and maintaining motivation, focusing attention, maintaining concentration, managing performance anxiety, and managing time effectively.

Table 11.5   OUTLINE FOR STUDENT NOTE-TAKING ON THE TOPIC OF CAREERS IN THE BIOLOGICAL SCIENCES

I. Major career fields in the biological sciences
   A. Botanists
   B. Zoologists
   C. Entomologists
   D. Microbiologists
   E. Anatomists
   F. Physiologists
   G. Geneticists
   H. Emerging areas of "synthesis"
II. Employment opportunities
   A. Universities and colleges
   B. Federal government
   C. Private industry
      1. Hospitals
      2. Clinics
      3. Laboratories
      4. Research foundations
III. Working conditions
   A. Qualifications—necessary training
   B. Prospects for employment
   C. Income/fringe benefits
   D. Degree of mobility
IV. References for additional information
   A. History of field
   B. Training programs
   C. Career opportunities

In this section we cannot review all of these learning strategies; detailed information is available elsewhere (Good & Brophy, 1986; Weinstein & Mayer, 1986). Here we want to discuss one learning strategy—reading with comprehension—in some detail because we believe that helping students to read critically and with understanding is the first step in helping them to solve problems and to think critically.

Strategy Training

In many strategy-training experiments, younger or poorer readers are trained to use the strategies that more skilled readers employ, usually with at least some success and sometimes with quite remarkable results. Students trained to use such strategies usually do not function as effectively as students who develop the strategies spontaneously, but they do learn to read with better comprehension than before. Often the training needs to be quite detailed; simply giving students a little general information is not enough. Some of the promising research in this area is described next.

Elementary School   Paris, Cross, and Lipson (1984) developed a training program entitled Informed Strategies for Learning (ISL) that is designed to increase third- and fifth-graders' awareness and use of effective reading strategies. The program contains 14 weekly modules that illustrate the strategies concretely and show students the effort required, when to use a strategy, and the benefits to be expected from strategy use. Students first observe models using the strategies and then practice the strategies themselves along with guidance and feedback from the teacher. Strategies are explained and illustrated using metaphors familiar to the students. For example, the lesson on evaluating tasks to discover clues to the topic, length, and difficulty of a passage uses the metaphor "Be a reading detective." Comprehension-monitoring strategies are made comprehensible by analogies to traffic signs like the following: "Stop—say the meaning in your own words." "Dead end—go back and reread the parts you don't understand."

Intermediate Grades   Hansen and Pearson (1983) improved fourth-graders' reading comprehension using a program that featured strategy training and practice in answering questions. The strategy training involved story introductions in which students were asked to relate what they knew from prior knowledge to situations like those that the upcoming story characters would experience, predict what the protagonist would do when confronted with these critical situations in the story, write down their prior knowledge answers on one sheet of paper and their predictions on another, and then combine the two to demonstrate that reading involves combining what one knows with what is in a text. Following these preparations, students read the story and compared their predictions with what actually occurred.

The other part of the treatment involved changing the nature of the questions asked of the students following story reading. Typically, students are asked about 80 percent factual questions and only 20 percent inferential questions. In this study, the literal questions were removed and the students were asked only inferential questions. Evaluation data showed that this combination of strategy training with practice in responding to inferential questions improved the reading comprehension of the experimental students over that of control students taught in traditional ways. The treatment was especially effective with poor readers.

Roehler and Duffy (1984) and Book, Duffy, Roehler, Meloth, and Vavrus (1985) trained intermediate-grade teachers to provide explicit, detailed instruction in comprehension strategies to their low-reading-group students. The strategies are the ones typically taught in these grades, such as identifying the main idea or using a dictionary, but they are taught much more explicitly and thoroughly than usual. Teachers are trained to explain the nature of each skill, tell when and why it is used, model by verbalizing the mental processes that occur when using it, point out sequential aspects and salient features of the processes involved, and then provide students with opportunities to use the skill and see its effectiveness for themselves. Following instruction, students are interviewed to determine whether or not they can state in their own words what they learned, how one uses a strategy, and why it is important to know how to use it. Evaluation data reveal modest improvements in student awareness of how the reading process works and how to use the strategies taught.

Secondary School Andre and Anderson (1978–1979) studied three groups of high school students—a group trained to generate questions about the main points of the text, a group directed to ask such main idea questions but not trained in strategies for doing so, and a group that simply read and reread the material. The data revealed that the trained group outperformed the other groups and that the self-questioning treatment was especially effective with students having low and medium verbal ability.

Palincsar and Brown (1984) taught four comprehension-fostering and comprehension-monitoring strategies to seventh-grade poor comprehenders. These strategies included summarizing (self-review), questioning, clarifying, and predicting. They used a reciprocal teaching method, in which the teacher initially did most of the modeling and explaining but then gradually turned the instructional responsibilities over to the students themselves. Students eventually took turns acting as the teacher and leading small-group discussions of the texts being read.

When beginning a passage, the teacher would note the title and ask for predictions about the content of the passage. Then the group would read the first segment silently and the "student teacher" would ask a question about it, summarize it, and then offer a prediction or ask for clarification if appropriate. If necessary, the adult teacher provided guidance to the student teacher by prompting, "What questions do you think a teacher might ask here?," instructing, "Remember, a summary is a shortened version; it doesn't include detail," or modifying the activity, "If you are having a hard time thinking of a question, why don't you summarize first?" The adult teacher also provided feedback concerning the quality and specificity of questions, the logic involved in making predictions, and so on.

This treatment produced sizable gains on criterion tests of comprehension, reliable maintenance of these gains over time, and improvement that generalized to other comprehension tests and transferred to novel tasks. A follow-up study in which ordinary classroom teachers rather than the experimenters functioned as instructors produced similarly impressive results.

We believe that efforts to help students read critically and organize information in ways that enable them to understand (or identify what they do not understand) are critical aspects of teaching. Students also need to solve problems and think critically if they are to be active learners.

PROVIDING STUDENTS WITH OPPORTUNITIES FOR SELF-EVALUATION

In addition to teaching students various strategies that they can use to make their own learning more active and more focused, teachers can also use a process in the classroom that encourages and values student self-evaluation.

Providing for Self-Evaluation

Students should be taught to evaluate their own work. This skill will be needed if they are to become independent, autonomous learners. We live in the midst of an information explosion and in an age when computers help us solve problems, but people still must identify the problems and evaluate the information they gather. If anything, the need to evaluate one's work, assess one's inadequacies, and determine what is needed to correct the situation (i.e., to define problems) is greater than ever. Yet schools still emphasize presenting information (Covington & Beery, 1976), and students need the chance to learn and practice self-evaluation skills (Corno & Rohrkemper, 1985).

Classrooms tend to be places for action, not reflection, unless teachers involve students in reflection and decision making. A few ways that this might be done are:

Students Explain Their Thinking   Even when their answers are correct, students are occasionally asked to explain how they arrived at an answer. Asking students to explain themselves only when they have responded incorrectly implies that the teacher is interested only in the answer, not the thinking process behind it or other things related to it.

Students Evaluate Their Own or Others' Work   This can be done in a variety of ways. When a student answers a question, the teacher can ask other students to react instead of reacting immediately. The teacher can have students critique their own papers, asking them to pick out the strongest parts and explain why they are particularly good or to explain why the weakest parts are weak and how they can be improved. Students can exchange papers and try to improve them by adding ideas or arguments not considered by the authors.

Of course, allowing students to react to the papers of classmates must be handled carefully. Students should not critique one another until they have had practice in critiquing themselves. Even here, it is advisable to restrict the scope of evaluation to something simple, such as "List two ideas that might make the paper better." This will eliminate the problems that occur when students are overwhelmed by too many "helpful" comments, reduce pressures on those who have difficulty thinking up improvements, and require those who can think of many improvements to concentrate on quality rather than quantity.

Such assignments are useful in teaching students the value of sharing information and in demonstrating that there is no one right way to prepare a paper. They also help students learn to think about their work rather than turn in assignment after assignment without reflection. Repeated over time, this also helps students to see their progress. For example, an effective technique for early elementary students is to let them compare handwriting exercises done early in the year with others done later.

Students Make Decisions   These can be relatively simple decisions about assignments or larger decisions involving planning. In any case, there should be genuine opportunities for decision making by students.

For those who have not been trained in self-evaluation, teachers may have to ask simple questions, accept students the way they are, and help them develop skills as rapidly as possible. The ability to criticize oneself openly and without defensiveness is learned. Teachers can help foster it by creating opportunities for students to make decisions and by helping them to evaluate decisions that are proposed or tried out.

Teachers Respond to Students' Questions About Academic Content   Such questions signal student desire to learn about the topic. Teachers can influence learning significantly by taking time to deal with such questions in depth by giving the desired information or by providing students with resources and ways to pursue the question on their own.

Students Question the Teacher's Opinions and the Content of the Curriculum   Students should not learn the curriculum blindly without questioning any interpretations made in the book or by the teacher. They should learn that statements are not necessarily true just because they appear in books and should learn to separate facts from interpretations or hypotheses. They should also be encouraged to make interpretations on their own.

Teachers should model this attitude, along with the notion that students can "play with" the curriculum by considering it from different points of view. They should occasionally ask students to question certain points and should express their own disagreements with the text when they have them. Also, teachers should take care to separate their own opinions and interpretations from established fact, thus encouraging students to take issue with them as well. Finally, when students do give their opinions, teachers can help them evaluate their thinking by asking them to explain their reasons and perhaps by questioning or debating them. All of these things help develop recognition that complex issues may not have any single interpretation and that the validity of interpretations depends on the logic and evidence that can be brought to bear in their support, not on the authority or aggressiveness of the people who support them. Along these lines, it is sometimes useful to review "mistakes" that key figures in history have made, particularly the mistakes made by persons who are usually regarded in favorable terms. This helps students to see that even individuals who are usually good thinkers and decision makers make mistakes in some areas.

PROBLEM-SOLVING STRATEGIES AND THINKING SKILLS

Besides being able to read with comprehension and study efficiently, students need to learn to solve problems effectively. We refer here not only to problems in mathematics but to problems in any subject area, and more generally, to any situation in which a person perceives a discrepancy between his or her present state and a desired goal state and desires to take action to eliminate that discrepancy.

Educators have long been interested in studying problem solving and identifying ways to teach people to solve problems effectively. Pessimists, impressed by limitations on transfer effects and the expert problem solver's need for broad experience and considerable domain-specific knowledge, believe that problem solving cannot be taught directly, although students will benefit from frequent opportunities to develop their problem-solving skills through practice. Optimists, on the other hand, believe that problem-solving skills can be developed more directly by identifying effective problem-solving heuristics and teaching them to students.

Some Examples of Recommended Strategies

Polya (1957) offered the following guidelines for problem solving in a famous book entitled *How to Solve It:*

1. *Understand the problem.* Identify what information is given or known, and what is required.
2. *Devise a plan.* Look for connections between the given information and the unknown that might help solve the problem. Does the information seem to fit a general principle or a familiar algorithm? Is the problem analogous to a simple or more familiar problem that might provide guidelines for solving it?
3. *Carry out the plan.* Once a clear plan has been formulated, carry it out step by step, checking to make sure that each step has been included and done correctly.
4. *Look back.* Check the accuracy or usefulness of the obtained result by making sure that it does in fact solve the problem and that it fits with all of the other information given. If the result checks out, review the result itself and the method of obtaining it for information that may be useful in solving other problems in the future.

Bransford and Stein (1985) describe the IDEAL method of problem solving:

1. *I*dentify the problem.
2. *D*efine it.
3. *E*xplore possible strategies for solving it.
4. *A*ct on these strategies.
5. *L*ook at the effects of your efforts.

Contemporary Cognitive Views of Problem Solving

Contemporary views of problem solving have been influenced heavily by the human information-processing approach to learning and cognition and especially by research that compares novice to expert problem solvers (Mayer, 1983; Tuma & Reif, 1980). This work shows that expert problem solvers do not generate a large number of hypotheses and then test each one systematically. Instead, they conceptualize a problem by identifying key features and relating them to background knowledge or schemas and then identify a single hypothesis or a small number of promising hypotheses for further testing. Physicians diagnosing medical problems, for example, do not begin by attempting to list every conceivable source of a patient's symptoms. Instead, they ask questions designed to narrow the search quickly to one or a small number of probable diagnoses and then pursue these hypotheses (Elstein, Shulman, & Sprafka, 1978). At least when utilized by experts with sufficient experience and knowledge to know what they are doing, this approach is much quicker and easier than the classical approach because it minimizes the time spent, and usually wasted, in checking out incorrect hypotheses.

Accurate representation of the problem in the first place is the key to the success of the method used by experts. If key features of the problem are recognized accurately and related to appropriate background knowledge or problem-solving schemas, the result is likely to be a quick and successful solution. However, if a problem is represented inappropriately, the problem-solving efforts based on this representation will fail and the person essentially will have to begin all over again.

Cyert (1980) suggests the following heuristics (drawn from the work of Rubenstein, 1975): (1) Keep the big picture in mind without getting lost in details; (2) avoid committing yourself too early to a particular hypothesis when it is just one of several promising hypotheses worth considering; (3) create models to simplify the problem by using words, images, symbols, or equations; (4) try to change the representation of the problem if the present one does not seem to be working; (5) use the information to generate questions that you can ask yourself and attempt to answer; (6) be flexible and willing to question the credibility of your premises; (7) try working backwards from possible solutions; (8) keep track of various partial solutions that you may eventually be able to combine; (9) use analogies and metaphors; and (10) talk about the problem.

To the extent that you expect your students to be able to apply what they learn rather than merely to remember it, you will need to provide them with frequent application exercises and opportunities to solve problems. Furthermore, most students will require instruction in the problem-solving process. The specifics of this instruction will vary with grade level and subject matter, but it should include such heuristics as reading a problem carefully and paraphrasing it into one's own words; identifying the information given and the information desired as well as the possible linkages between these problem elements; separating relevant from irrelevant information, representing the problem clearly and sketching the general plan of attack before applying formulas or performing calculations; and developing a workable problem space by dividing the problem into a series of subproblems, reasoning by analogy from more familiar problems, working backwards from possible solutions, or substituting specific examples for abstract symbols. Such instruction should include first-person modeling with thinking aloud in addition to typical lecturing, and should proceed to coaching, guided practice, students' reflection on and assessment of their strategies, and other activities designed to increase students' metacognitive awareness of the processes involved in solving problems successfully.

Teaching Thinking Skills

In a sense, the entire educational enterprise is an attempt to teach students how to think by first presenting them with important knowledge and skills and then giving them opportunities to apply, analyze, synthesize, or evaluate this information. The developments discussed above (work on reading comprehension and problem solving) can be seen as even more directly designed to stimulate thinking, or at least to stimulate a more thoughtful approach to learning. The most direct approach, however, has been to identify key elements of the thinking process itself and teach these directly to students.

The classical approach to training sdtudents to think involved curricular emphasis on subjects such as Latin, philosophy, mathematics, and science. Although Thorndike (1924) showed long ago that this approach does not yield generalized improvements in mental functioning, it continues to be emphasized even today.

A more focused variation of this same general approach is to emphasize instruction in thinking skills and means of developing knowledge. One approach to the teaching of thinking skills is coursework in logic—the use of formal rules of inference to develop conclusions from established premises. Courses in logic teach students to deduce implications from premises and evaluate whether or not conclusions follow from the premises given. For example, given the premises that all humans require food and that movie stars are human, it would be logical to deduce that movie stars require food but not to deduce that all humans are movie stars.

A related form of instruction is training in critical thinking skills for evaluating the credibility of information. Critical thinking skills include assessing the validity of authors' premises and the soundness of their logic in developing conclusions from those premises, identifying authors' purposes in writing the material (distinguishing attempts to be complete and objective from attempts to sway the reader toward particular conclusions), distinguishing relevant from irrelevant information, recognizing and counteracting the effects of rhetorical devices that appeal to emotion rather than evidence (glittering generalities, name calling, testimonials, or "just plain folks" appeals, and stacking the cards by presenting only favorable facts and suppressing unfavorable facts), and distinguishing fact from opinion (Devine, 1981).

Programs for Teaching Thinking Skills

Not content with attempts to build more emphasis on thinking into instruction in traditional subject matter areas, some authors have developed programs designed specifically to develop students' thinking skills.

The CoRT Program   DeBono (1983, 1985) developed the CoRT program. CoRT is an acronym that stands for Cognitive Research Trust, an organization located in Cambridge, England. This program consists of 60 lessons on thinking intended for 9- to 11-year olds, although it has been used with both younger and older students as well. The program focuses on thinking skills that will help students to function better in their lives outside school. Consequently, the lessons concentrate on life events such as deciding on a career or how to spend one's vacation, moving to a new house, or changing to a new job. Instruction focuses on thinking and decision making.

The first lesson in CoRT teaches a scanning skill known as PMI. To introduce PMI, the teacher invites the students to consider the merits of some idea (e.g., that students should be paid five dollars a week for coming to school or that basic foods should be supplied free to everyone) by thinking about the implications of the idea and categorizing them into three sets labeled: *P*lus (good points or desirable implications); *M*inus (bad points or undesirable implications); and *I*nteresting (implications that are neither good nor bad but are nevertheless interesting and worth noting). This method helps students to clarify their thinking about an issue and to state the reasons underlying the decisions they make.

As the program progresses, additional tools for thinking and decision making are added. Students are encouraged to consider multiple aspects of issues before settling on solutions and to get information from others through brainstorming and related mechanisms.

The Instrumental Enrichment Program Feuerstein and his colleagues (Feuerstein, Rand, Hoffman, & Miller, 1980; Feuerstein et al., 1985) have developed the Instrumental Enrichment Program for students nine or older. The program was originally intended as a special education tool for use with disadvantaged students or students suffering from cognitive deficiencies or learning disabilities. Its goal was to change the cognitive structures of these students and transform them into autonomous, independent thinkers capable of initiating and elaborating ideas. As the program became further elaborated and better known, it was used with average students as well.

The program encourages cognitive activities such as perceptual organization of information, problem representation, planning, goal analysis, and restructuring of problems when existing plans are not working. It uses a series of progressively more demanding paper-and-pencil exercises that encourage learners to discover relationships, rules, principles, operations, and strategies. The tasks were designed on the basis of analyses of the processes involved in mental activities, and many of them resemble the tasks used in psychometric tests and laboratory learning experiments. There are some puzzles and brainteasers as well, but in general the program is a bridge between approaches based on thinking concerning curriculum content and approaches that try to develop thinking through content-free exercises.

Conclusions: Teaching Thinking Skills

These programs for teaching thinking skills are two possible means of responding to the criticism that schooling concentrates too much on knowledge and comprehension of specific information and not enough on higher-level cognitive objectives. If their goals and procedures appeal to you, you may wish to investigate them and incorporate them into your teaching. We believe that these goals are critically important; however, there is little research that indicates how to achieve them in classrooms. Thus, despite the enthusiasm with which these programs have been received by some educators, their efficacy remains to be demonstrated. The data that do exist suggest positive but limited effects. Also, bear in mind that even when programs are successful in developing certain general thinking or problem-solving skills, possession of such skills will not eliminate the need for broad experience and domain-specific knowledge necessary to be an expert in any particular area of application.

SUGGESTED ACTIVITIES AND QUESTIONS

11.1. Several aspects of teaching were discussed in this chapter; however, no summary synthesizing this information was provided. Show your mastery of the important aspects of the chapter by writing your own summary in a couple of typewritten pages. Compare your summary with the summaries made by classmates or fellow teachers.

11.2. What are some of the advantages and disadvantages involved when students are asked to summarize material on their own?

11.3. Plan a brief (15-minute) discussion. Write out the sequence of questions you will use to advance the discussion fruitfully, applying the criteria suggested in this chapter for asking effective oral questions. Role-play your discussion if you have the opportunity to do so.

11.4. The criteria for questions presented in this chapter were designed to aid teachers in asking *oral* questions effectively. In general, these criteria apply to written questions as well, but there are some exceptions. Try to identify other guidelines or criteria that are applicable only to written questions. In what important ways do written and oral questions differ?

11.5. Review and revise (as necessary) the statements you made after reading Chapter 1, when you attempted to identify teaching behaviors and characteristics that are signs of effective teaching. How much has your view of effective teaching changed?

11.6. You have now completed reading the substantive chapters of this book that describe effective teaching. What important aspects of teacher and student behavior have been neglected in this book? Why do you believe these behaviors are important? What information do you need as a teacher that the book has not addressed? Compare your list with lists made by others.

11.7. Role-play the process of introducing and ending lessons *enthusiastically* and with *clarity*. Describe the classroom situation (age of students, etc.) so that others may provide you with appropriate feedback.

11.8. Why should students be allowed to talk freely about opinions that differ from those of the teacher's or the book?

11.9. Select some of the forms at the end of the chapter and use them in observing real or simulated teaching.

11.10. Discuss (with classmates or fellow teachers) specific ways in which you as a teacher can increase opportunities for students to engage in self-evaluation.

11.11. Why is it important that students assume responsibility for evaluating their own learning?

11.12. What does the term *match* refer to?

11.13. Give concrete examples of instances when lecturing might be desirable.

11.14. Why is it impossible to give a precise definition of an *effective teacher?*

11.15. Why does active teaching, in which the teacher presents the content to the students and structures their subsequent practice and application exercises, generally produce more learning than approaches in which students are encouraged to learn on their own or from one another?

11.16. How should teachers' questioning and feedback strategies in recitations differ from those in discussions?

11.17. Define *conceptual change teaching* in your own words. Why is more time for instruction not always effective?

11.18. How important is it to teach thinking skills to students? In an instructional week, how much time should be given to helping students learn how to learn versus learning content?

REFERENCES

Anderson, L. (1981). Short-term student responses to classroom instruction. *Elementary School Journal, 82,* 97–108.

Anderson, L., Evertson, C., & Brophy, J. (1982). *Principles of small-group instruction in elementary reading.* Occasional Paper No. 58. East Lansing: Institute for Research on Teaching, Michigan State University.

Anderson, L., Evertson, C., & Brophy, J. (1979). An experimental study of effective teaching in first-grade reading groups. *Elementary School Journal, 79,* 193–223.

Andre, M., & Anderson, T. (1978–1979). The development and evaluation of a self-questioning study technique. *Reading Research Quarterly, 14,* 605–623.

Anshutz, R. (1975). An investigation of wait-time and questioning techniques as an instructional variable for science methods students microteaching elementary school children. (Doctoral dissertation, University of Kansas, 1973). *Dissertation Abstracts International, 35,* 5978A.

Arnold, D., Atwood, R., & Rogers, V. (1974). Question and response levels and lapse time intervals. *Journal of Experimental Education, 43,* 11–15.

Ausubel, D. (1963). *The psychology of meaningful verbal learning: An introduction to school learning.* New York: Grune & Stratton.

Bereiter, C., Washington, E., Engelmann, S., & Osborn, J. (1969). *Research and development programs on preschool disadvantaged children.* Final report, OE Contract 6-10-235, Project No. 5-1181. Washington, DC: U.S. Department of Health, Education, and Welfare, Office of Education, Bureau of Research.

Book, C., Duffy, G., Roehler, L., Meloth, M., & Vavrus, L. (1985). A study of the relationships between teacher explanation and student metacognitive awareness during reading instruction. *Communication Education, 34,* 29–36.

Bransford, J., & Stein, B. (1985). *The IDEAL problem solver.* San Francisco: Freeman.

Brophy, J., & Evertson, C. (1976). *Learning from teaching: A developmental perspective.* Boston: Allyn & Bacon.

Brophy, J., & Good, T. (1986). Teacher behavior and student achievement. In M. Wittrock (Ed.), *Handbook of research on teaching* (3rd ed.). New York: Macmillan.

Brophy, J., & Good, T. (1974). *Teacher-student relationships: Causes and consequences.* New York: Holt, Rinehart and Winston.

Case, R., & Bereiter, C. (1984). From behaviourism to cognitive behaviourism to cognitive development: Steps in the evolution of instructional design. *Instructional Science, 13,* 141–158.

Collins, A., & Stevens, A. (1983). A cognitive theory of inquiry teaching. In C. Reigeluth (Ed.), *Instructional-design theories and models: An overview of their current status.* Hillsdale, NJ: Erlbaum.

Corno, L., & Rohrkemper, M. (1985). Self-regulated learning. In R. Ames & C. Ames (Eds.), *Research in motivation in education* (Vol. 2). Orlando, FL: Academic Press.

Costin, F., Greenough, W., & Menges, R. (1971). Student ratings of college teaching: Reliability, validity, and usefulness. *Review of Educational Research, 41,* 511–535.

Covington, M., & Beery, R. (1976). *Self-worth and school learning.* New York: Holt, Rinehart and Winston.

Cruickshank, D. (1985). Applying research on teacher clarity. *Journal of Teacher Education, 36,* 44–48.

Cyert, R. (1980). Problem solving and educational policy. In D. Tuma & F. Reif (Eds.), *Problem solving and education: Issues in teaching and research.* Hillsdale, NJ: Erlbaum.

Davis, R., & Alexander, L. (1977). *The lecture method.* East Lansing: Instructional Media Center, Michigan State University.

deBono, E. (1985). The CoRT thinking program. In J. Segal, S. Chipman, & R. Glaser (Eds.), *Thinking and learning skills. Vol. 1: Relating instruction to research.* Hillsdale, NJ: Erlbaum.

deBono, E. (1983). The direct teaching of thinking as a skill. *Phi Delta Kappan, 64,* 703–708.

DeTure, L. (1979). Relative effects of modeling on the acquisition of wait-time by preservice elementary teachers and concommitant changes in dialogue patterns. *Journal of Research in Science Teaching, 16,* 553–562.

Devine, T. (1981). *Teaching study skills: A guide for teachers.* Boston: Allyn and Bacon.

Dillon, J. (1984). Research on questioning and discussion. *Educational Leadership, 42*(3), 50–56.

Dillon, J. (1981). Duration of response to teacher questions and statements. *Contemporary Educational Psychology, 6,* 1–11.

Dillon, J. (1979). Alternatives to questioning. *High School Journal, 62,* 217–222.

Dillon, J. (1978). Using questions to depress student thought. *School Review, 87,* 50–63.

Dunkin, M., & Biddle, B. (1974). *The study of teaching.* New York: Holt, Rinehart and Winston.

Elstein, A., Shulman, L., & Sprafka, S. (1978). *Medical problem solving: An analysis of clinical reasoning.* Cambridge, MA: Harvard University Press.

Evertson, C., & Green, J. (1986). Observation as inquiry and method. In M. Wittrock (Ed.), *Handbook of research on teaching* (3rd ed.). New York: Macmillan.

Evertson, C., Sanford, J., & Emmer, E. (1981). Effects of class heterogeneity in junior high school. *American Educational Research Journal, 18,* 219–232.

Fagan, E., Hassler, D., & Szabo, M. (1981). Evaluation of questioning strategies in language arts instruction. *Research in the Teaching of English, 15,* 267–273.

Feuerstein, R., Rand, Y., Hoffman, M., & Miller, R. (1980). *Instrumental enrichment: An intervention program for cognitive modifiability.* Baltimore: University Park Press.

Feuerstein, R., et al. (1985). Instrumental enrichment, an intervention program for structural cognitive modifiability: Theory and practice. In J. Segal, S. Chipman, & R. Glaser (Eds.), *Thinking and learning skills. Vol. 1: Relating instruction to research.* Hillsdale, NJ: Erlbaum.

Fisher, C., Berliner, D., Filby, N., Marliave, R., Cahen, L., & Dishaw, M. (1980). Teaching behaviors, academic learning time, and student achievement: An overview. In C. Denham & A. Lieberman (Eds.), *Time to learn.* Washington, DC: National Institute of Education.

Gage, N., & Berliner, D. (1984). *Educational psychology* (3rd ed.). Boston: Houghton Mifflin.

Gage, N., & Berliner, D. (1979). *Educational psychology* (2nd ed.). Chicago: Rand McNally.

Gagné, R. (1977). *The conditions of learning* (3rd ed.). New York: Holt, Rinehart and Winston.

Good, T. (1979). Teacher effectiveness in the elementary school: What we know about it now. *Journal of Teacher Education, 30,* 52–64.

Good, T., & Brophy, J. (1986). School effects. In M. Wittrock (Ed.), *Handbook of research on teaching* (3rd ed.). New York: Macmillan.

Good, T., & Brophy, J. (1974). Changing teacher and student behavior: An empirical investigation. *Journal of Educational Psychology, 66,* 390–405.

Good, T., & Grouws, D. (1979). The Missouri Mathematics Effectiveness Project: An experimental study in fourth-grade classrooms. *Journal of Educational Psychology, 71,* 355–362.

Good, T., & Grouws, D. (1977). Teaching effects: A process-product study in fourth-grade mathematics classrooms. *Journal of Teacher Education, 28,* 49–54.

Good, T., Grouws, D., & Ebmeier, H. (1983). *Active mathematics teaching*. New York: Longman.

Groisser, P. (1964). *How to use the fine art of questioning*. New York: Teachers' Practical Press.

Hansen, J., & Pearson, P. (1983). An instructional study: Improving the inferential comprehension of fourth-grade good and poor readers. *Journal of Educational Psychology, 75*, 821–829.

Harter, S. (1978). Effectance motivation reconsidered: Toward a developmental model. *Human Development, 21*, 34–64.

Helm, H., & Novak, J. (Eds.). (1983). *Proceedings of the international seminar on misconceptions in science and mathematics*. Ithaca, NY: Cornell University.

Henson, K. (1980). What's the use of lecturing? *High School Journal, 64*, 115–119.

Holt, J. (1964). *How children fail*. New York: Pitman.

Hoover, K. (1968). *Learning and teaching in the secondary school: Improved instructional practice*. Boston: Allyn & Bacon.

Hunt, J. (1961). *Intelligence and experience*. New York: Ronald Press.

Husen, T. (Ed.). (1967). *International study of achievement in mathematics: A comparison of twelve countries* (Vol. 2). New York: Wiley.

Joyce, B., & Weil, M. (1980). *Models of teaching* (2nd ed.). Englewood Cliffs, NJ: Prentice-Hall.

Lesser, G. (1974). *Children and television: Lessons from "Sesame Street."* New York: Random House.

Luiten, J., Ames, W., & Ackerson, G. (1970). A meta-analysis of the effects of advance organizers on learning and retention. *American Educational Research Journal, 17*, 211–218.

Lundgren, U. (1972). *Frame factors and the teaching process*. Stockholm: Almqvist and Wiksell.

Mayer, R. (1983). *Thinking, problem solving, and cognition*. San Francisco: Freeman.

McCaleb, J., & White, J. (1980). Critical dimensions in evaluating teacher clarity. *Journal of Classroom Interaction, 15*, 27–30.

McLeish, J. (1976). The lecture method. In N. Gage (Ed.), *The psychology of teaching methods (Part I). (Seventy-fifth Yearbook of the National Society for the Study of Education.)* Chicago: University of Chicago Press.

McMann, F. (1979). In defense of lecture. *Social Studies, 70*, 270–274.

Medley, D. (1979). The effectiveness of teachers. In P. Peterson & H. Walberg (Eds.), *Research on teaching: Concepts, findings, and implications*. Berkeley, CA: McCutchan.

Palincsar, A., & Brown, A. (1984). Reciprocal teaching of comprehension-fostering and comprehension-monitoring activities. *Cognition and Instruction, 1*, 117–175.

Paris, S., Cross, D., & Lipson, M. (1984). Informed strategies for learning: A program to improve children's reading awareness and comprehension. *Journal of Educational Psychology, 76*, 1239–1252.

Peterson, P., & Swing, S. (1982). Beyond time on task: Students' reports of their thought processes during classroom instruction. *Elementary School Journal, 82*, 481–491.

Polya, G. (1957). *How to solve it* (2nd ed.). Princeton: Princeton University Press.

Posner, G., Strike, K., Hewson, K., & Gertzog, W. (1982). Accommodation of a scientific conception: Toward a theory of conceptual change. *Science Education, 66*, 211–228.

Rice, D. (1977). The effect of question-asking instruction on preservice elementary science teachers. *Journal of Research in Science Teaching, 14*, 353–359.

Riley, J. (1980). The effects of teachers' wait-time and cognitive questioning level on pupil science achievement. Paper presented at the annual meeting of the National Association for Research in Science Teaching, Boston.

Roehler, L., & Duffy, G. (1984). Direct explanation of comprehension processes. In G. Duffy, L. Roehler, & J. Mason (Eds.), *Comprehension instruction: Perspectives and suggestions*. New York: Longman.

Rosenshine, B. (1983). Teaching functions in instructional programs. *Elementary School Journal, 83*, 335–351.

Rosenshine, B. (1970). Enthusiastic teaching: A research review. *School Review, 78*, 499–514.

Rosenshine, B. (1968). To explain: A review of research. *Educational Leadership, 26*, 275–280.

Rosenshine, B., & Furst, N. (1973). The use of direct observation to study teaching. In R. Travers (Ed.), *Second handbook of research on teaching*. Chicago: Rand McNally.

Rowe, M. (1986). Wait time: Slowing down may be a way of speeding up! *Journal of Teacher Education, 37*, 43–50.

Rowe, M. (1974a). Science, silence, and sanctions. *Science and Children, 6*, 11–13.

Rowe, M. (1974b). Wait-time and rewards as instructional variables, their influence on language, logic, and fate control: Part I—Wait time. *Journal of Research in Science Teaching, 11*, 81–94.

Rubenstein, N. (1975). *Patterns of problem solving*. Englewood Cliffs, NJ: Prentice-Hall.

Schuck, R. (1981). The impact of set induction on student achievement and retention. *Journal of Educational Research, 74*, 227–232.

Shulman, L. (1986). Paradigms and research programs in the study of teaching: A contemporary perspective. In M. Wittrock (Ed.), *Handbook of research on teaching* (3rd ed.). New York: Macmillan.

Shulman, L., & Sykes, G. (Eds.). (1983). *Handbook of research on teaching and policy*. New York: Longman.

Smith, E., & Anderson, C. (1984). *The planning and teaching intermediate science study: Final report*. East Lansing: Institute for Research on Teaching, Michigan State University.

Smith, L., & Lott, G. (1983). *Ways of going wrong in teaching for conceptual change*. Research Series No. 139. East Lansing: Institute for Research on Teaching, Michigan State University.

Smith, E., & Land, M. (1981). Low-inference verbal behaviors related to teacher clarity. *Journal of Classroom Interaction, 17*, 37–42.

Soar, R. (1973). *Follow through classroom process measurement and pupil growth: Final Report*. Gainesville: College of Education, University of Florida.

Stallings, J. (1975). Implementation and child effects of teaching practices in Follow-Through classrooms. *Monographs of the Society for Research in Child Development, 40*, Nos. 7–8, Serial No. 163.

Swift, J., & Gooding, C. (1983). Interaction of wait-time feedback and questioning instruction on middle school science teaching. *Journal of Research in Science Teaching, 20*, 721–730.

Thorndike, E. (1924). Mental discipline in high school studies. *Journal of Educational Psychology, 15*, 1–22, 83–98.

Tobin, K. (1983a). The influence of wait-time on classroom learning. *European Journal of Science Education, 5*(1), 35–48.

Tobin, K. (1983b). Management of time in classrooms. In B. Fraser (Ed.), *Classroom management*. Bentley, Australia: Western Australian Institute of Technology.

Tobin, K., & Capie, W. (1982). Relationships between classroom process variables and middle-school science achievement. *Journal of Educational Psychology, 74*, 441–454.

Tuma, D., & Reif, F. (Eds.). (1980). *Problem solving and education: Issues in teaching and research*. Hillsdale, NJ: Erlbaum.

Weinstein, C., & Mayer, R. (1986). The teaching of learning strategies. In M. Wittrock (Ed.), *Handbook of research on teaching* (3rd ed.). New York: Macmillan.

Winne, P. (1979). Experiments relating teachers' use of higher cognitive questions to student achievement. *Review of Educational Research, 49,* 13–49.

Winne, P., & Marx, R. (1982). Students' and teachers' views of thinking processes for classroom learning. *Elementary School Journal, 82,* 493–518.

Wright, C., & Nuthall, G. (1970). The relationships between teacher behaviors and pupil achievement in three experimental elementary science lessons. *American Educational Research Journal, 7,* 477–492.

Zumwalt, K. (Ed.). (1986). *Improving teaching.* (The 1986 ASCD Yearbook). Alexandria, VA: Association for Supervision and Curriculum Development.

FORM 11.1. Variety of Teaching Methods

USE: *Whenever the class is involved in curriculum-related activities*
PURPOSE: *To see if teacher uses a variety of methods in teaching the cur-*
riculum
Each time the teacher changes activities, code the time and the type of
activity.

	CODES			
BEHAVIOR CATEGORIES	START			ELAPSED
A. OBJECTIVES	TIME	A	B	TIME

A. OBJECTIVES

What is teacher doing?
1. Introduce new material
2. Review old material
3. Give or review test
4. Preview or directions for next assignment
5. Checking seatwork in progress
6. Other (specify)

B. METHODS

What methods are used to accomplish objectives?
1. Demonstration or diagram at blackboard
2. Lecture
3. Prepared handouts (diagrams or teaching aids)
4. Media (filmstrip, slides, tape, record, etc.)
5. Questioning students to check understanding
6. Inviting and responding to student questions
7. Focused discussion (prepared, sequenced questions)
8. Unfocused discussion (rambling, no specific objective)
9. Students take turns reading or reciting
10. Drill (flashcards, math tables, chorus questions)
11. Practical exercise or experiment
12. Seatwork or homework assignment
13. Field trip, visit
14. Game, contest
15. Other (specify)

#	START TIME	A	B	ELAPSED TIME
1.	8 :30	2	5	10
2.	8 :40	1	1	10
3.	8 :50	4	1,3	5
4.	8 :55	transition		5
5.	9 :00	2	5	8
6.	9 :08	1	1	11
7.	9 :19	4	1,3	5
8.	9 :24	transition		6
9.	9 :30	2	5	10
10.	9 :50	1	1	12
11.	10 :02	4	1,3	8
12.	10 :10	transition		5
13.	10 :15	Recess		15
14.	10 :30	transition		3
15.	10 :33	1	7	27
16.	11 :00	2	10,14	25
17.	11 :25	transition		5
18.	11 :30	Lunch		
19.	:			
20.	:			
21.	:			
22.	:			
23.	:			
24.	:			
25.	:			
26.	:			
27.	:			
28.	:			
29.	:			
30.	:			
31.	:			
32.	:			
33.	:			
34.	:			
35.	:			
36.	:			
37.	:			
38.	:			
39.	:			
40.	:			

NOTES:

1—11: Reading groups
15: Social studies
16: Spelling (Went around room twice, then had spelling bee)

FORM 10.2. Seatwork

USE: Whenever part or all of the class is doing assigned seatwork
PURPOSE: To see if seatwork appears appropriate to students' needs and interests

WORK INVOLVEMENT
At fixed intervals (every 3 minutes, for example), scan the group and note the number of students working productively, in neutral, or misbehaving.

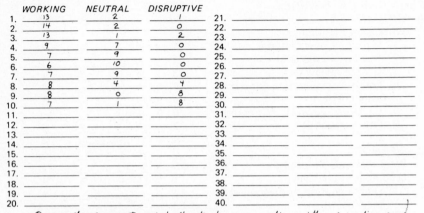

	WORKING	NEUTRAL	DISRUPTIVE				
1.	13	2	1	21.			
2.	14	2	0	22.			
3.	13	1	2	23.			
4.	9	7	0	24.			
5.	7	9	0	25.			
6.	6	10	0	26.			
7.	7	9	0	27.			
8.	8	4	4	28.			
9.	8	0	8	29.			
10.	7	1	8	30.			
11.				31.			
12.				32.			
13.				33.			
14.				34.			
15.				35.			
16.				36.			
17.				37.			
18.				38.			
19.				39.			
20.				40.			

During this 30-minute period the teacher was working with one reading group.
The work-involvement coding refers to the other 16 students who were working
independently.

APPROPRIATENESS OF ASSIGNMENTS
What seems to be the problem with students who are not productively involved? (Check statements that apply.)
_____ 1. Assignment is too short or too easy—students finish quickly and do not have other work to do.
_____ 2. Assignment is boring, repetitive, monotonous.
__✓__ 3. Assignment is too hard—students can't get started or continually need help.
_____ 4. All of the above—assignments are not differentiated to match student needs.
The Stars seemed too confused to get started.

DISTRACTIONS
What distracts students from seatwork? What do they attend to or do when not working?
Disruptions, especially by #12

STUDENT ATTITUDES
What clues to student attitudes are observable during seatwork periods? When students can't get an answer do they concentrate or seek help, or do they merely copy from a neighbor? How do they act when the teacher's back is turned? Do they notice? Do they make noises and gestures? Do they seem to be amused by the teacher? Fear him? Respect him?

#12 "passes licks" when he thinks he can get away with it. Problems
occur when others strike back and disruption spreads.
  Other kids mostly concentrate on work.

FORM 11.3. Feedback to Correct Answers

USE: In discussion and recitation situations when students are answering questions
PURPOSE: To see if teacher is giving appropriate feedback to students about the adequacy of their responses
When a student answers correctly, code as many categories as apply to the teacher's feedback response.

BEHAVIOR CATEGORIES
1. Praises
2. Nods, repeats answer, says "Yes," "That's right," "Okay," etc.
3. No feedback—goes on to something else
4. Ambiguous—doesn't indicate whether or not answer is acceptable
5. Asks a student or the class whether answer is correct
6. Asks someone else to answer the same question
7. New question—asks same student another question
8. Other (specify)

NOTES:

Both praised answers were called out by # 19, a high-achieving student.

CODES

1.	2	26.	__
2.	2	27.	__
3.	2	28.	__
4.	2	29.	__
5.	3	30.	__
6.	2	31.	__
7.	7	32.	__
8.	2	33.	__
9.	2	34.	__
10.	3	35.	__
11.	2	36.	__
12.	2	37.	__
13.	1	38.	__
14.	2	39.	__
15.	2	40.	__
16.	1	41.	__
17.	2	42.	__
18.	2	43.	__
19.	2	44.	__
20.	__	45.	__
21.	__	46.	__
22.	__	47.	__
23.	__	48.	__
24.	__	49.	__
25.	__	50.	__

FORM 11.4. Feedback When Student Fails to Answer Correctly

USE: *In discussion and recitation situations when students are answering
        questions*
PURPOSE: *To see if teacher is giving appropriate feedback to students about
        the adequacy of their responses*
        When a student is unable to answer a question, or answers it incorrectly,
code *as many categories as apply to the teacher's feedback response.*

BEHAVIOR CATEGORIES
1. Criticizes
2. Says "No," "That's not right," etc.
3. No feedback—goes on to something else
4. Ambiguous—doesn't indicate whether or not answer is acceptable
5. Asks a student or the class whether answer is correct
6. Asks someone else to answer the question
7. Repeats question to same student, prompts (Well?" "Do you know?" etc.)
8. Gives a clue or rephrases question to make it easier
9. Asks same student an entirely new question
10. Answers question for the student
11. Answers question and also gives explanation or rationale for answer
12. Gives explanation or rationale for why student's answer was not correct
13. Praises student for good attempt or guess
14. Other (specify)

CODES

1.	_2_	26.	___
2.	_2,6_	27.	___
3.	_2,8_	28.	___
4.	_2,10_	29.	___
5.	_2,10_	30.	___
6.	_2,12_	31.	___
7.	___	32.	___
8.	___	33.	___
9.	___	34.	___
10.	___	35.	___
11.	___	36.	___
12.	___	37.	___
13.	___	38.	___
14.	___	39.	___
15.	___	40.	___
16.	___	41.	___
17.	___	42.	___
18.	___	43.	___
19.	___	44.	___
20.	___	45.	___
21.	___	46.	___
22.	___	47.	___
23.	___	48.	___
24.	___	49.	___
25.	___	50.	___

FORM 11.5. Assigning Seatwork and Homework

USE: *When teacher presents a seatwork or homework assignment*
PURPOSE: *To see if teacher's instructions are clear and complete*
Each time teacher presents seatwork or homework, code as many behavior categories as apply.

BEHAVIOR CATEGORIES

CODES

A. *DEMONSTRATIONS AND EXAMPLE PROBLEMS*
   1. No demonstration was needed or given
   2. No demonstration was given, although one was needed
   3. Teacher demonstrated or called on students to do so. Activity was demonstrated in proper sequence, with no steps left out
   4. Demonstration was poorly sequenced, or steps were left out
   5. Each step was verbally described while being demonstrated
   6. More verbal description should have accompanied the demonstration
   7. Demonstration too long or complex; should have been broken into parts

B. *CHECKING FOR UNDERSTANDING*
   1. The teacher never asked whether directions were understood
   2. The teacher asked if the students understood, and no one said he or she didn't
   3. The teacher called on one or more volunteers to demonstrate understanding
   4. The teacher called on one or more non-volunteers to demonstrate understanding
   5. The teacher failed to call on any low achievers (bottom 1/3 of group) to see if they understood

C. *DEALING WITH CONFUSION*
   How did the teacher respond if one or more students was confused?
   1. No one was confused
   2. The teacher repeated directions and demonstrations, made sure everyone understood
   3. The teacher repeated directions and demonstrations, but didn't make sure everyone understood
   4. The teacher promised individual help to those who needed it before starting work
   5. The teacher delayed giving help ("Try to do it yourself first")
   6. The teacher told students to get help from other students
   7. The teacher failed to deal with the problem directly, student remained confused, teacher never specifically told him what to do about it

D. *CLARITY ABOUT SPECIFICS OF ASSIGNMENT*
   1. Students were not clear about which problem or pages were assigned
   2. Students were not clear about what was required or optional
   3. Students were not clear about what to do if they needed help
   4. Students were not clear about what was allowed if they finished

	A	B	C	D
1.	3,5	2	1	___
2.	3,5	2	1	___
3.	3,5	2	1	___
4.	___	___	___	___
5.	___	___	___	___
6.	___	___	___	___
7.	___	___	___	___
8.	___	___	___	___
9.	___	___	___	___
10.	___	___	___	___
11.	___	___	___	___
12.	___	___	___	___
13.	___	___	___	___
14.	___	___	___	___
15.	___	___	___	___
16.	___	___	___	___
17.	___	___	___	___
18.	___	___	___	___
19.	___	___	___	___
20.	___	___	___	___
21.	___	___	___	___
22.	___	___	___	___
23.	___	___	___	___
24.	___	___	___	___
25.	___	___	___	___
26.	___	___	___	___
27.	___	___	___	___
28.	___	___	___	___
29.	___	___	___	___
30.	___	___	___	___
31.	___	___	___	___
32.	___	___	___	___
33.	___	___	___	___
34.	___	___	___	___
35.	___	___	___	___
36.	___	___	___	___
37.	___	___	___	___
38.	___	___	___	___
39.	___	___	___	___
40.	___	___	___	___

FORM 11.6. Questioning Techniques

USE: *When teacher is asking class or group questions*
PURPOSE: *To see if teacher is following principles for good questioning practices*
For each question, code the following categories:

BEHAVIOR CATEGORIES

CODES

A. *TYPE OF QUESTION ASKED*
 1. Academic: Factual. Seeks specific correct response
 2. Academic: Opinion. Seeks opinion on a complex issue where there is no clear-cut response
 3. Nonacademic: Question deals with personal, procedural, or disciplinary matters rather than curriculum

B. *TYPE OF RESPONSE REQUIRED*
 1. Thought question. Student must reason through to a conclusion or explain something at length
 2. Fact question. Student must provide fact(s) from memory
 3. Choice question. Requires only a yes-no or either-or response

C. *SELECTION OF RESPONDENT*
 1. Names child before asking question
 2. Calls on volunteer (after asking question)
 3. Calls on nonvolunteer (after asking question)

D. *PAUSE (AFTER ASKING QUESTION)*
 1. Paused a few seconds before calling on student
 2. Failed to pause before calling on student
 3. Not applicable; teacher named student before asking question

E. *TONE AND MANNER IN PRESENTING QUESTION*
 1. Question presented as challenge or stimulation
 2. Question presented matter-of-factly
 3. Question presented as threat or test

	A	B	C	D	E
1.	1	2	2	1	2
2.	1	2	2	1	2
3.	1	3	2	1	2
4.	1	2	2	1	2
5.	1	2	2	1	2
6.	1	3	2	1	2
7.	1	2	2	1	2
8.	2	1	2	1	1
9.	1	2	2	1	2
10.	1	2	2	1	2
11.	1	2	2	1	2
12.	1	2	2	1	2
13.	—	—	—	—	—
14.	—	—	—	—	—
15.	—	—	—	—	—
16.	—	—	—	—	—
17.	—	—	—	—	—
18.	—	—	—	—	—
19.	—	—	—	—	—
20.	—	—	—	—	—
21.	—	—	—	—	—
22.	—	—	—	—	—
23.	—	—	—	—	—
24.	—	—	—	—	—
25.	—	—	—	—	—
26.	—	—	—	—	—
27.	—	—	—	—	—
28.	—	—	—	—	—
29.	—	—	—	—	—
30.	—	—	—	—	—
31.	—	—	—	—	—
32.	—	—	—	—	—
33.	—	—	—	—	—
34.	—	—	—	—	—
35.	—	—	—	—	—
36.	—	—	—	—	—
37.	—	—	—	—	—
38.	—	—	—	—	—
39.	—	—	—	—	—
40.	—	—	—	—	—

Record any information relevant to the following:
Multiple Questions. Tally the number of times the teacher:
1. Repeats or rephrases question before calling on anyone *II*

2. Asks two or more questions at the same time *0*

Sequence. Were questions integrated into an orderly sequence, or did they seem to be random or unrelated?
Teacher seemed to be following sequence given in manual (led up to next history unit).
Did students themselves pose questions? *No*

Was there student-student interaction? How much? *None*

When appropriate, did the teacher redirect questions to several students, or ask students to evaluate their own or others' responses? *No*

FORM 11.7. Ending Lessons and Activities

USE: Whenever the teacher brings a lesson or activity to an end
PURPOSE: To describe the strategies used to end the lessons or activities
    Each time that the teacher ends a lesson or activity, describe the
lesson or activity and code each of the behavior categories that applies.

BEHAVIOR CATEGORIES
LESSON OR ACTIVITY
CODES

1. Summarizes the main points
2. Questions the students on the main points
3. Allows the students to ask questions
4. Praises students for their performance
5. Criticizes students for their performance
6. Motivates students for follow-up assignment
7. Describes connections between current activity and past or future activities
8. Warns or reminds students of forthcoming test
9. Tells students what they are expected to remember or how they are expected to use what has been taught during this activity
10. Makes transition into new or follow-up activity without bringing clear-cut closure to the first activity
11. Runs short of time: Activity is ended by bell
12. Completes planned activity early; fills in with games, busywork assignments, or student free time
13. Other (describe below)

1. _____ 1. __
2. _____ 2. __
3. _____ 3. __
4. _____ 4. __
5. _____ 5. __
6. _____ 6. __
7. _____ 7. __
8. _____ 8. __
9. _____ 9. __
10. _____ 10. __
11. _____ 11. __
12. _____ 12. __
13. _____ 13. __
14. _____ 14. __
15. _____ 15. __
16. _____ 16. __
17. _____ 17. __
18. _____ 18. __
19. _____ 19. __
20. _____ 20. __
21. _____ 21. __
22. _____ 22. __
23. _____ 23. __
24. _____ 24. __
25. _____ 25. __

COMMENTS:

FORM 11.8. Teacher Lectures, Presentations, and Demonstrations

USE: When the teacher lectures, presents information, or demonstrates
skills to the class
PURPOSE: To assess the effectiveness of the presentation
Enter a checkmark for each of the following features that was
included effectively in the presentation, and a 0 for each feature that was
omitted or handled ineffectively. Add your comments below, emphasizing
constructive suggestions for improvement.

CHECKLIST

INTRODUCTION

_____ 1. States purpose or objectives
_____ 2. Gives overview or advance organizer
_____ 3. Distributes a study guide or instructs the students concerning
how they are expected to respond (what notes to take, etc.)

BODY OF PRESENTATION

_____ 4. Is well prepared; speaks fluently without hesitation or
confusion
_____ 5. Projects enthusiasm for the material
_____ 6. Maintains eye contact with the students
_____ 7. Speaks at an appropriate pace (neither too fast nor too slow)
_____ 8. Speaks with appropriate voice modulation (rather than a
monotone)
_____ 9. Uses appropriate expressions, movements, and gestures
(rather than speaking woodenly)
_____ 10. Content is well structured and sequenced
_____ 11. New terms are clearly defined
_____ 12. Key concepts or terms are emphasized (preferably not only
verbally but by holding up or pointing to examples, writing or
underlining on the board or overhead projector, etc.)
_____ 13. Includes appropriate analogies or examples that are effective
in enabling students to relate the new to the familiar and the
abstract to the concrete
_____ 14. Where appropriate, facts are distinguished from opinions
_____ 15. Where appropriate, lengthy presentations are divided into
recognizable segments, with clear transitions between
segments and minisummaries concluding each segment
_____ 16. Where necessary, questions the students following each
major segment of a lengthy presentation (rather than waiting
until the end)
_____ 17. Monitors student response; is encouraging and responsive
regarding student questions and comments on the material

CONCLUSION

_____ 18. Concludes with summary or integration of the presentation
_____ 19. Invites student questions or comments
_____ 20. Follows up on the presentation by making a transition into a
recitation activity, a follow-up assignment, or some other
activity that will allow the students an opportunity to practice
or apply the material

COMMENTS:

CHAPTER

12 Improving Classroom Teaching

We have described a variety of behaviors that should appear in the classroom and provided ways of measuring their presence or absence. We hope that teachers have been stimulated to look at their behavior and make plans for improving. In this chapter, we will present some guidelines for in-service training and self-improvement.

In this book we have provided practical interpretations of important research, theory, concepts, and findings that have value for classroom teachers. This information needs to be integrated with your personality and teaching style and applied in a specific teaching context. The ideas, although practical and useful, are not presented as a method of teaching. Our view of these ideas is similar to that of Biddle and Anderson (1986, p. 246) when they describe the role of theories in research on teaching:

> They provide a synthesis and explanation for findings to date, they suggest predictions that we might make for teaching contexts we have not yet examined, they make explicit the assumptions with which we think about events, and they provide tools we can use to think about and comprehend the confusing phenomena of teaching.

In this book, we also describe ways of looking at teaching and suggested alternative hypotheses about how to structure classrooms in ways that facilitate student achievement and affective growth.

In this chapter, we stress "going beyond extant information" by learning about teaching through personal reflection on experience, as well as using others' ideasto gain insight into one's teaching. However, others' informed opinions and feedback must be used in combination with other information about classroom behavior—not as a "pat" answer. There are some exciting developments occurring in teaching

523

today—a growing willingness of citizens to accept the importance and complexity of teaching and a willingness of some administrators to share with teachers responsibility for evaluation and staff development programs. In this chapter we discuss ways to make these programs work effectively and to foster teachers' professional growth.

The chapter begins with a discussion of personal, individual programs of self-growth and of informal study groups of volunteer teachers and then discusses self-improvement programs in the context of staff development that occurs as part of a school system's official in-service program.

Remember, the perfect teacher does not exist. All of us can refine skills, discard ineffective tactics, and develop new ones. Some teachers are excellent lecturers and classroom managers but are only average in stimulating independent student work and leading class discussion. None of us will ever be a perfect teacher, few will even be excellent in all aspects of teaching, but all of us can become better teachers than we presently are. This, the continual process of improving our teaching skills, is the essence of professional teaching.

Teachers, like everyone else, are sometimes unwilling to engage in self-evaluation. Is this because they are not committed to their profession or are unwilling to do the extra work necessary to improve their skills? Is it because they feel that they already function at optimal effectiveness? We doubt it. We think teachers will seek opportunities to evaluate and improve their teaching if acceptable and useful methods for doing so are available. The fact that we have written this book attests to our belief in teachers' willingness to participate in self-evaluation and benefit from it. However, certain obstacles minimize self-improvement in some teachers. These must be removed if continual improvement is to take place.

THE SOCIALIZATION PROCESS

Teachers are hindered in their efforts to improve their teaching skills for several basic reasons. Perhaps the most fundamental problem is the socialization process they have gone through. Most of us have seldom engaged in self-criticism or self-evaluation designed not only to uncover weaknesses but also to eliminate such weaknesses. Most of us have occasionally engaged in destructive self-criticism; however, we seldom link criticism with constructive plans designed to improve our skills.

In part, we act this way because our past socialization (especially our experience in schools) has not helped us to develop the needed skills. For example, has a teacher ever returned an "A" paper to you with these instructions: "Basically, your paper is very sound; however, I have identified a few flaws and I am sure you will find additional ways to improve the paper when you reread it. Eliminate the weaknesses that I have indicated and improve the paper in new ways that you discover by *thinking* about it again." Certainly, most of us have had to rewrite papers, but seldom A papers, and seldom have we been asked to rethink a paper and incorporate new ideas of our own into it.

Typically, we redo assignments because they are "inferior" and we repeat them only to incorporate someone else's criticism. Indeed, school seldom allowed most of us time to *think* about what we were doing. We were too busy finishing assignments to think about them. Remember the feeling of relief when major tasks or final exams were completed? No matter how well or poorly we think we have performed, we feel relieved when we hand in the paper because we are finished. We no longer have control over the paper, and we do not have to think about it any more.

Socialization in schools tends to emphasize *do not look back, keep moving forward*. Although the advice to move forward is sound, only by examining our past and present performances can we monitor progress and determine if we are moving forward or merely traveling in circles. Relatively little of this reflection is done in most schools.

A second difficulty is that school experience has often emphasized analytical thinking, not synthesis. The following behavior in a tenth-grade social studies classroom represents analytical thinking:

> TEACHER: John, what's wrong with electing members of Congress every two years?
>
> JOHN: (*Hesitatingly and in a soft tone*) Well, ah, I think that they spend too much time trying to be reelected. (*John notices the teacher beaming and nodding, so he begins to speak more confidently and loudly.*) Since they face reelection every two years, they have to always seek money for reelection. Since they build their campaign chest primarily with funds from the people who financed their original candidacy, they owe these people a double debt. It is hard for them to be their own person.
>
> TEACHER: Good answer, John. Carol, what did John imply when he said, "be their own person?"
>
> CAROL: Well, that the candidates' debts to the people who have given money and their continual dependency upon them, ah, since they have to be elected every two years, put them in such a position that they may cater to these people's needs. But even if members of Congress are strong, the two-year election procedure is bad because they continue to run, make speeches, raise money, and have little time to do their real job.

Although such discussions are important, they seldom go beyond criticizing or defining the problem. For example, the teacher might continue this discussion by pointing out the desirability of controlling campaign spending and making the sources of contributions public knowledge and then challenging students to go beyond common solutions that *others* have suggested. Seldom do classes develop their own unique solutions to problems. Yet this is the meaning of synthesis: taking the facts and readdressing the problem in a different fashion.

For example, the teacher might "playfully" suggest that senators, even though they are elected for six-year terms, spend much time running for reelection and that most of their decisions are made on the basis of "How does it affect my chances for reelection?" The teacher could suggest that politicians might still spend more time running for office than running the office even if their terms were for ten years. The teacher could also call for students to suggest ways in which elected federal representatives could be held accountable to their local and national constituencies: "Should daily logs of their activities be kept? What are the pros and cons? Should they hold regular office hours for the public? Should they spend a designated number of days in the district or state they represent? How can a broader set of candidates [nonlawyers] be encouraged?"

Demands are seldom made on students for original, practical suggestions. Some teachers who stimulate this type of thinking from their students, but most teaching emphasizes analysis per se. Fortunately, in recent years there has been increased emphasis on process approaches and problem-solving activity. Still, most teachers were socialized in schools that demanded and rewarded analytical thinking. This heavy emphasis on criticism gave most of us plenty of practice in pinpointing weaknesses but comparatively little practice in developing constructive alternatives.

Evaluation that we experienced in schools was external and nonconstructive. The way it was handled told us "where we stood," not "how we could improve." Thus, we tended to avoid evaluation. (For example, in Spanish class, if we had time to thoroughly translate the first two pages, we waved our hands vigorously to volunteer at the beginning of a lesson. However, we slumped in our chairs and hid behind our neighbor's head late in the period unless we knew the material thoroughly.) Since evaluation was so strongly associated with negative consequences, it often evoked the attitude of "I'm going to be exposed," not "I'm going to receive new information." Evaluation made us anxious. Our past socialization provided little training or inclination for self-evaluation.

Yet another factor that has limited teachers' ability to improve is the fact that teacher education programs have not assisted students to develop collegiality skills. Hence, in addition to the fact that teachers have not had training in self-evaluation, it appears that too few teacher education programs provide explicit training in collegial relationships and the opportunity to learn through feedback from others. As Copeland and Jamgochian (1985) note, for preservice and in-service teachers need more opportunities to see models of interactive colleague relationships and to practice giving and receiving feedback.

EXPERIMENTING AND GROWING

Teachers are unique individuals with different strengths and weaknesses. You have to develop a style that allows you to express yourself and motivate students in your own way.

To achieve your own style, you may have to search and experiment with different teaching methods before you develop a style that is comfortable and right for you. We have stressed the desirability of using a variety of teaching methods because students have different learning needs and are often stimulated by different teaching techniques. However, teaching techniques are justified if, and only if, they work in the classroom. They work when you feel comfortable using them and when students learn and respond positively to classroom assignments. If you systematically try an approach for a reasonable amount of time and it does not work for you in your classroom, *then discard the approach and develop other techniques*. There is no need to teach the way your cooperating teacher did (he or she may have been a poor model) or the way you think you "should" teach, without regard to your own feelings or to the responses of your students. However, as we note in Chapter 5, the pressure to model the cooperating teacher's behavior can be considerable and data suggest that some teachers are unduly affected by their supervisors.

If you are to improve your teaching, you must be willing to critically examine your classroom behavior and that of your students and to try new ways of teaching when the present ones are not working. After identifying a basically satisfying style, successful teachers continue to experiment with new behaviors. Good teachers continually try to find new ways to instruct to students.

TEACHING IS DIFFICULT

Few teachers will be excellent in all aspects of teaching. Too often, teachers enter the classroom with unrealistically high expectations ("I will capture the interest of every student at every moment, and every lesson I teach will be completely successful"), so that when outcomes do not match expectations, they become depressed and disappointed. When this occurs, there is a tendency to blame students for one's own inability to spark a response. If the difficulty continues, teachers may withdraw and begin to justify and rationalize their behavior rather than to search for new styles of teaching. This occurs in part because teachers do not realize that other teachers also have difficulties. All teachers occasionally teach lessons that fail, say the wrong thing to students, and so forth. Teaching is difficult! Teachers must not become complacent about mistakes, but must identify them and try to eliminate them.

Like everyone else, teachers tend to talk about successes, not failures. Thus, some teachers, especially new ones, may become anxious and discouraged when they have trouble because they hear nothing but the good or interesting things that other teachers are doing. Some beginners fully expect to be accomplished teachers by October of their first year! These teachers experience feelings of disappointment and ineptness when they do not achieve easy success. They are reluctant to ask veteran teachers for help because they feel it would be an admission of failure and a disgrace.

If you have thoughts like these, dismiss them, because they are nonsense. Teaching is difficult, challenging, and exciting work, but it takes time to develop and refine teaching skills. Most experienced teachers are sympathetic to the problems of beginning teachers and are glad to help. However, few of us like to be approached by someone who says, "Tell me what to do." It is much better to approach other teachers by telling them that you have a teaching problem and would like to exchange ideas with them and benefit from their experience. Remember that all teachers, even veteran teachers, have classroom problems from time to time and that the appropriate strategy is not to hide mistakes (as we learn to do as students) but to seek help and to solve the problems.

In Table 12.1, Posner summarizes some of the questions that you might want to ask your cooperating teacher. He suggests that you select a time when the cooperating teacher is alone in the classroom and when outside distractions are minimal. He also suggests that some of the questions might be best left until a future meeting when you have established a better working relationship with the cooperating teacher.

How to Identify Good Teaching

Teachers must decide what is "good" practice by observing the effects of their behavior on students. (Do tests reveal appropriate learning? Do lectures lead students to raise their own questions? Do students appear to enjoy activities? Do

Table 12.1   CONFERENCE QUESTIONS WITH THE COOPERATING TEACHER

1. I've noticed some special areas in your room. (*Specify one of them.*) What do you and the students do in this area? Who gets to use it? How are they selected? (*Repeat for each area.*)

2. Did you arrange the room this way? (*If no*) Who did? (*If yes*) What were you trying to do with this arrangement? How long has it been this way?

3. Did you put up the posters, pictures, exhibits, etc., on the walls and bulletin boards? (*If no*) Who did? (*If yes*) What was the purpose? When did you put them up? ((*May be different for each poster.*)

4. I've been looking through the textbook. How was it selected and by whom? How do you like it? What are its strengths? Weaknesses? Is it successful with some kids but not with others? (*Repeat this set of questions for each text.*)

5. I also looked over the worksheets and quizzes you've been using. Did you write them? (*If no*) Where did you get them? (*If yes*) When did you make them up? Did you base them on anything in particular? Are you happy with them?

6. I enjoyed the lesson(s) that I observed. When I compared your lesson plan with the actual lesson, I noticed that you did not follow your plan precisely. (*This question is used only if you noticed some discrepancies.*) What caused you to modify your plan?

7. What rules do you expect students in your class to follow? (*Probe: rules for waiting their turn to speak and to receive help, rules for moving around the classroom, leaving the classroom, being on time, what to do when finished working , working together, resolving conflicts among students, homework, forms to follow, procedures for work, language, noises, who may speak, etc.*) Does the school have rules or regulations with which you disagree? (*If yes*) Why do you disagree? Do you follow them anyway? Which rules are the most important to you? How do you handle infractions? Do some students break rules more than others? Tell me about those kids.

8. Do parents ever visit the classroom? (*If no*) Would you like them to? (*If yes*) Are you pleased that they do? How can parents be of most help to you as a teacher? How can they hinder you? Should parents be involved in selection of school books? What about in hiring teachers?

9. Does the school or the district have a curriculum? Are you expected to follow it? Do you? Did you have any say in it? Do you ever depart from it?

10. Do your students' (*or "children's," for primary grades*) interests affect your teaching methods? (*If yes*) In what ways? What about the content, do their interests affect it? Do they have any say in what they study? (*If yes*) In what ways?

11. What sorts of students do you teach? Are there different groups? Could you describe the groups? Do you devote more time to certain students? Do you expect all of them to assume the same degree of responsibility for their learning? Do you use different criteria to evaluate different students? Do you find the diversity among them to be a major problem?

12. How friendly are you with the children? Do you tell them much about yourself? What do you think is the proper role for a teacher?

13. Do you try to develop a sense of competition in your class? How important is cooperation among students ? What do you use to motivate the kids? (*Probe: grades, interest and curiosity, comparison of one child's work with another's, fear*)

14. Do you ever let the kids know your political views? Do you think that the schools are doing a pretty good job or do they need to change drastically? Are you trying to help kids fit into the society as it is, or would you like to equip them to reform society?

Table 12.1   (Continued)

15. How important are the *3 Rs* to you? What about the children's emotional needs, are they important? What about things like problem-solving skills and creativity—are they important? What is the relative importance of these various goals?

16. Do you ever try to relate one subject matter (e.g., science) with another that you or another teacher teaches? Or do you think that different subject matters should be treated separately?

17. Most people have days in their work when they go home feeling especially good because the day and its activities were particularly rewarding. What makes a good day in teaching for you?

18. How do you tell how well you are doing as a teacher? That is, what things provide you with evidence that you're doing a good job?

19. Suppose you accidently happened to overhear a group of your former students discussing you as a teacher. What kinds of things would you like to hear them saying?

20. Why did you ask to have a student teacher (*or aide, depending upon your role*)?

21. What do you expect from me?

Source: Posner, G. (1985). *Field experience: A guide to reflective teaching.* New York: Longman.

anonymously administered questionnaires show student satisfaction?) There is no single formula specifying good teaching because research has not yielded definite teaching behaviors that are always clearly related to student achievement (Brophy & Good, 1986; Dunkin & Biddle, 1974; Shulman, 1986) and because achievement is only one of many student outcomes that must be considered. The advice given in this book is based on available research, but we often go beyond these data in order to make suggestions. These statements are not intended to tell you how to teach but rather to provide you with a way of looking a classroom life.

There are many materials that teachers can use effectively in in-service programs that attempt to improve instruction. It is impossible to list all books that discuss the concerns of teachers, but we can mention a few central references.

Reviews of research on teaching are extremely valuable because they critically examine what is known about teaching and call for more research on explicit questions. These reviews show that very few teaching behaviors are invariably related to student achievement. However, research evidence collected in the past decade has provided practical findings and concepts that are of immense value in planning instructional programs. This knowledge is summarized in references such as the *Handbook of Research on Teaching* (3rd edition, Wittrock, 1986), the *Handbook of Reading Research* (Pearson, Barr, Kamil, & Rosenthal, 1984), and *Becoming a Nation of Readers* (Anderson, Hiebert, Scott, & Wilkinson, 1985). Research findings can be to analyze practice (e.g., Stallings, 1986) and are especially useful to teachers who want to engage in self-study programs when they realize that although empirical data provide direction, they have to assume the responsibility for evaluating the effectiveness of their own classroom behavior (Good & Weinstein, 1986; Shulman & Sykes, 1983; Zumwalt, 1986).

An excellent source for a teacher who wants to learn about findings from research on teaching. is the *Handbook of Research on Teaching* (3rd edition, Wittrock, 1986). The volume covers a wide range of topics that are discussed comprehensively and critically. Among many valuable topics discussed are The Cultures of Teaching (Feiman-Nemser & Floden); Teaching Functions (Rosenshine & Stevens); Paradigms and Research Programs in the Study of Teaching: A Contemporary Perspective (Shulman). Also in the *Handbook of Research on Teaching* are several chapters on adapting teaching to differences among learners (e.g., Teaching Creative and Gifted Learners: Torrance) as well as research and discussion on various subject-matter topics (e.g., Research on Teaching Social Studies: Armento).

We think that beginning teachers will find especially useful the section of the *Handbook* on Research on Teaching and Teachers. Here, detailed ideas about how teachers teach are presented as well as information about how teachers think about teaching (e.g., Teachers' Thought Processes: Clark & Peterson). Invaluable advice is presented throughout the *Handbook*. For example, most beginning teachers would find discussions of the beginning teacher's adjustment to teaching to be both fascinating and useful (see, for example, The Cultures of Teaching: Feiman-Nemser & Floden).

Lanier (1986) provides a careful history of teacher education and the role of the teacher in society. Such background reading is critical for a teacher who wants to understand the political, professional, and economic conditions that have prevented teaching from becoming a profession. As we move into an era that emphasizes the need to recognize the importance of teachers and the need for more professional opportunities (i.e., career ladders, master teachers), it is important to understand decisions and forces that have prevented the professionalization of teaching in the past. Knowledge of history may prevent the profession—and committed teachers who remain in teaching—from repeating past mistakes. Shulman and Sykes (1983) have edited a volume that discusses the value of recent research for improving schools and classrooms but also points out the problems that occur when simple policy directives are issued to teachers and school administrators on the basis of that research. An understanding of these policy issues helps to provide teachers with a rich background that can inform the decisions that they make in the classroom.

Teachers can use these sources to stimulate thinking about classroom behavior and to develop plans for experimenting. However, we are perhaps putting the cart before the horse. Before changing, the teacher needs to assess present behavior.

How to Start Self-Evaluation

The starting point is to evaluate your present teaching and to make definite plans (changing certain behaviors, trying new instructional styles) for the future. Go back through this book and list, on three separate sheets of paper: (1) behaviors that you think you perform capably, (2) those that you need to work on or that you have not tried, and (3) those that you are not sure how capably you perform. Take the first list and store it in your desk so that you can examine it from time to time and can add to the list as you make progress. This list represents progress that you have made as a teacher.

For example, you may note on this list that you already ask a variety of factual and higher-order questions and that you ask questions before calling on students. On your list for "needs work," you may note a tendency not to follow through on warnings and inconsistency as a classroom manager. After a few hours of thinking about strengths and weaknesses, you will have a general outline of your ability as a teacher. Now you are ready to begin work on the list of needed improvements and to plan remediation so that you can move one or more items from the "needs work" list to the "okay" list in the near future.

You may not know how well you perform in some of the areas mentioned in this book. Perhaps you are not sure if you emphasize the intrinsic interest that lessons hold for students rather than threaten "Pay attention or you'll fail the exam." Monitor your behavior as best you can and begin to assign these areas to the "okay" or "needs work" sheets as soon as you can.

Take time to assess yourself carefully, then, and make a list of your strengths and weaknesses. Naturally, your list will differ somewhat from the one that your students would make of you or that an observer would make after spending two weeks in your class. Which one of these descriptions is the most objective is a question that has no simple answer. In some situations, the students' list might be a truer   picture. However, even your own list can be a useful guide in making decisions if you can view yourself openly.

If you have trouble making decisions about where to start, you might want to arrange to have a teacher or supervisor whom you respect visit your class and make suggestions. Alternatively, you could listen to a tape-recorded session of your class. As we have argued in this book, it is sometimes difficult to identify problems in classrooms because so much happens so quickly. Hence, it may take some time before you can identify a place where you want to start.

Make Explicit Plans

Teachers who attempt to improve their teaching must be able to decide what they want to do and how to determine if their plans are working. Too often, our halfhearted New Year's resolutions are never acted upon because they are vague. Resolutions such as "I want to be a better driver," "I want to help the community more," or "I want to be a more enthusiastic teacher" are seldom accomplished simply because they are not concrete suggestions that guide behavior.

The following resolutions are much more likely to result in behavioral change because they specify the desired change: "On long trips, I plan to stop and relax for ten minutes every two hours," "I plan to devote ten hours a week from September through November to working on the community chest drive," "I want to tell students why a lesson is important before it begins and model my sincere interest in the content."

These statements indicate how the individual is to behave in order to reach a goal. If the person stops for ten minutes after driving for two hours, the goal has been met; thus, self-evaluation is easy. Self-evaluation is relatively simple in many teaching situations. However, certain aspects of teacher behavior are more difficult to evaluate. For instance, teachers frequently set goals for students as well as for themselves. The teacher may say, "I want to tell students why a lesson is important before it begins and to model my sincere interest in the content so that more students will pay attention and not engage in long private conversations with their neighbors." In this case, teachers need to evaluate both their own behavior and the behavior of their students.

In judging the behavior of students, teachers can see if students appear to pay attention and if they refrain from extended private conversations during the lesson. However, if teachers' goals become more complex and the evaluation more demanding, they will need to watch videotapes or seek the assistance of observers (see, for example, Stallings, 1986) to help them assess their progress. These topics will be discussed later in the chapter.

The message here is simple. If you do not know specific behaviors that you want to change, you are unlikely to improve. Teachers need to state goals in explicit language. Careful statement of a goal accomplishes two objectives: (1) the teacher knows exactly what behavior he or she is trying to effect and (2) the teacher can easily assess progress by examining actual behavior in comparison with the goal. The key is to state goals in terms of explicit, observable behaviors.

Action

After taking a look at yourself and stating explicit behavioral goals, the next step is to choose two or three behaviors that you want to change or new ones you want to try. Be careful in your zeal not to attempt to change too many things at once. Changing behavior, even our own, takes careful work, and it is easy to become overwhelmed and discouraged when we attempt to change too much too rapidly. Therefore, take a few things at a time and carefully monitor your progress.

For example, if you attempt to call on students randomly, you may have to write out the names of students in advance on flash cards so you can shuffle through the stack. Always calling on students who have their hands up is a difficult habit to break. Again, most people make more progress in the long run by changing only one or a few behaviors at a time, moving to new ones only when the newly acquired behaviors become firmly established habits.

After you decide upon concrete goals and implement the change for a couple of days, start to monitor the class for feedback about effectiveness of the change. For example, after you introduce lessons in ways that make it clear to students why the lesson is important to them, try to assess whether more students follow the directions or seem interested. Similarly, if you start to call on students to react to fellow students' responses, note if students seem to pay greater attention to the discussion topic.

Remember, the strategies listed in this book are not always appropriate; their effectiveness depends upon stimulating desirable student responses. Strategies that you invent yourself should be evaluated in the same way: what effect do they have on student behavior and attitudes?

SELF-STUDY

Teachers who want to examine their classroom behavior independently might consider the following questions, which include *some* of the important points teachers should consider (the questions and the case study that follows are adapted from Good, Biddle, & Brophy, 1975).

Do my low- and high-achievement students indicate that I have equal interest in them?

When I ask questions, what percentage of the time do students respond with the correct answer?

How long do I wait for students to respond if they do not respond immediately? Is this figure different for high- and low-achieving students?

What percentage of my day is actually spent in instructional activities as opposed to procedural activities, bookkeeping, and so on?

Are there some students who need help but rarely seek me out to discuss academic material? Which students initiate contact with me and which ones do not? Why?

How much time do I spend with individual students in a given day?

How much time do I spend in math, social studies, language arts? Do student achievement gains reflect time spent?

Are undesirable sex roles communicated in the classroom?

How does the achievement of my students at the end of the year compare with the achievement of similar students of other teachers or teams of teachers?

How often do I get requests from students to tailor an assignment to their interests?

How much time do students in my class spend on their homework? More or less than I expected?

How do students study for exams? In groups, individually, in pairs? Does it seem to make any difference?

How interesting do students rate various lessons or unit assignments? Does this interest fluctuate as a function of gender or achievement level? Does this interest relate to homework or unit test performance?

Answers to such questions would provide teachers with information about aspects of their classrooms that they might want to change. That is, the results would lead to selected treatments and follow-up evaluations. Teachers might next ask questions such as:

1. Can I raise the average amount of time I spend with individual low achievers during mathematics from two minutes to five minutes a day? What effect, if any, would this have on their attitudes, achievement, and attention spans (when they work independently)?
2. When I allow students to choose one of two homework assignments, do their study habits, performance levels, and/or attitudes change?
3. When I implement learning centers and peer-tutoring activities, do I have more time to work with individual students? How do measures of work involvement (attention spans) collected on students in tutoring pairs and learning centers compare with measures collected on students working independently in previous years?

Classroom Example: Increasing Effectiveness

Let us consider an example to see how a teacher could use information to increase instructional effectiveness. Assume that sixth-grade teacher Joe Bean's students do well in all subjects but math. Their performance in math is not terrible, but it is noticeably lower than their achievement in other subjects. Joe is puzzled by this. He enjoys teaching math and feels well qualified to do so. His concern about mathematics instruction is compounded by the fact that student attitudes measured earlier in the year were generally positive toward him and the instructional program. However, math drew the most criticism when students commented on specific subject areas.

Concerned about his students' low achievement and relatively negative attitudes toward math, Joe decides to obtain anonymous information from students about the specific problems they encounter in math and about ways in which the program might be improved. He is discouraged to find that much of the information he has collected is contradictory (what some students prefer is disliked by others) or does not lead to suggestions for action (students do not believe that the math period is too long). However, one theme is evident in the comments of several students: "I often don't know what I'm supposed to do for my assignments in class"; "When we start a new unit in class I'm always lost"; "I don't understand my work until you explain it the next day."

Subsequently, Joe notices that students engage in more neutral or aimless activity when working on math assignments than at any other time during the day. Joe decides that he does not spend enough time explaining material and assignments (modeling how to do problems, explaining how the work relates to preceding work) before he has students begin work on assignments.

If students had expressed generally low interest, Joe might have considered peer tutoring or devising a mathematics learning center to add novelty and provide more time for him to work with individuals. However, students' self-reports ("Often I'm confused, but after a period of time I catch on") match his own observations that the problem is not motivational (boredom), but a lack of direction. Joe's plan is to increase his ratio of explanation and modeling to practice work, especially at the beginning of a unit, and to see if this will improve students' attitudes and achievement.

Remember that Joe's plan is only a hypothesis, a hunch about how to proceed. The only criterion by which to judge his plan is its effect on student performance. Too often plans become "answers" without consideration of their effects on students. We stress that collecting information will suggest ways in which instruction might be improved, but information does not guarantee solutions. Joe might find that some other factor (assignments too long, feedback inadequate) is related more directly to student achievement. By evaluating his attempts to alter classroom processes through the examination of students' products (achievements and attitudes, eventually he will find procedures that work in this class.

You Are Not Alone

Teachers may wish to begin their evaluation and, for a while, to work independently. However, all teachers will benefit from talking with others and sharing ideas about classroom teaching and should begin to do this when they are ready to receive feedback.

Many school districts now have videotape equipment. If you are fortunate enough to have access to such equipment, arrange to have one or two of your typical lessons videotaped. Do not attempt to construct special units or to review old material. Teach your regularly scheduled lessons in your normal fashion. Then, when you start your assessment program, you do not have to depend on memory but can view yourself on tape and assess your weak and strong points. After a couple of weeks, make arrangements to retape your behavior in similar lessons so you can watch for signs of progress in your behavior and in the responses of students.

If your school does not have video equipment, check with your principal to see if the central office has the equipment. In many school districts, equipment is available for loan but often goes unused. Central school officials are usually delighted to loan video equipment. (If a school makes repeated requests, it is sometimes possible for equipment to be assigned to it permanently.) If it is impossible to secure video equipment, cassette audio recorders are readily available and can be used to collect useful information about the verbalizations of teachers and students.

Teachers can use other sources to get relevant feedback. For example, many elementary school teachers work in team-teaching or nongraded situations where it is easy to arrange for another teacher to watch them for a half hour or so. Similarly, teachers can use student teachers, student observers, and parents, on occasion. Secondary teachers can make arrangements to trade weekly visits with other teachers during free periods.

In arrangements that are not a part of a regular in-service training program, it is usually best to tell the observer exactly what to look for. Prepare an observation form (or use some of those included in this book). There is so much to see in the classroom that observers may not notice the things that the teacher would like to receive feedback about. Teachers are *decision makers* and, in planning improvement, should decide which weaknesses to work on first. Observers, of course, can always volunteer additional information.

Curriculum supervisors can also provide teachers with relevant feedback. Most supervisors are delighted when teachers request observations. Often, supervisory visits are as frustrating for supervisors as for teachers (see, for example, McDaniel, 1981). Since supervisors may not know the goals of a particular lesson or how it fits into a unit, it is difficult for them to provide helpful feedback. However, armed with a specific request, supervisors can provide information about areas of interest to the teacher.

Students are another source of information. Informal conversations and anonymously administered questionnaires will provide teachers with useful feedback (see, for example, Rohrkemper, 1981; Weinstein, 1983; Wittrock, 1986). Teachers who have never solicited student comment may be dismayed at first when they see the variety of comments. Students have unique perspectives, and different students may label the same behavior as a weakness or a strength. However, if you look over their responses carefully, you can usually identify some items that most students label as good or bad. Then you can take action on these points of agreement.

We have found that student feedback is most useful if it is given anonymously. Also, rather than ask for global comments or ratings, it is usually better to ask for specific reactions. One method is to request a list of three or more strengths and three or more weaknesses from each student. This forces students to be specific and to provide a more balanced critique than do global, free-response methods.

It is beyond the scope of this book to discuss strategies for obtaining student feedback; detailed information is available elsewhere and there are various standardized instruments for obtaining student feedback. Anderson (1983) provides extensive coverage of affective assessment in school settings, including definitions of key affective dimensions, observational and self-report measures that can be used to gather affective data, procedures for developing new affective measures, and strategies for interpreting affective data.

Still, there are several ways in which teachers can gain useful information from students in relatively easy ways. For example, teachers could ask students questions such as the following:

I. A.   If there were three things I could change about individual study units, I would change
      1.
      2.
      3.

  B.   The two assignments I have most (least) enjoyed this year are
      1.
      2.

  C.   The part of the school I most like (dislike) is
      1.

  D.   If I could change any two things about chemistry, they would be
      1.
      2.

II. A.   Compared to other art projects I have done this year, I like landscape design better 1
      __ 2 __ 3 __ 4 __ 5 __ 6 __ less.

  B.   Compared to individual work, I like group work (on science or other particular areas)
      better 1 __ 2 __ 3 __ 4 __ 5 __ 6 __ less.

III. A.   On the next science unit,
      1. I want to work alone.
      2. I want to work with the teacher.
      3. I want to work with one or two friends.
      4. I want to work with a group.

  B.   40 minutes in math class each day is
      1. Too much.
      2. About right.
      3. Not enough

		Always	Some- times	Never
IV.	Does time go quickly in school?	—	—	—
	Do most of your classmates like you?	—	—	—
	Do you feel free to say what you feel in class?	—	—	—
	Do you like to talk in class discussions?	—	—	—
	Do you have enough time to finish schoolwork?	—	—	—
	Does the teacher listen when you have a problem?	—	—	—
	Does the teacher give clear directions?	—	—	—
	Does the teacher give help when you need it?	—	—	—
	Does the teacher embarrass you when you give a wrong answer?	—	—	—

Each of the four formats illustrated above has advantages and disadvantages. Type IV questions can be completed by very young students and yield a good survey of student attitudes. Type I questions are more likely to yield decision-making information, and they may be used as a natural follow-up to "problems" identified by type IV questions. Type II and type III formats can be used for both diagnosis and surveying. The best format depends on program goals and the ages of the students. Question content is determined by what the classroom teacher believes to be important goals.

Information from students gives teachers at least a glimpse of how the students see the classroom world. To obtain accurate and useful information, ask the students to respond anonymously. Teachers who collect information frequently should demonstrate to students the usefulness of this information; that is, they should call the students' attention to program changes made in response to student feedback. Under most circumstances, sampling elementary children's attitudes more than once a month is unnecessary.

Self-Study Groups as a Base for In-Service Education

Teachers can often use regularly scheduled in-service time for work in self-improvement groups. This procedure is especially useful when in-service meeting time is devoted to small-group work with teachers who share common problems. In elementary schools, for instance, teachers at each grade level can meet together. In secondary schools, teachers can be subdivided into small groups according to the subject taught (social studies, mathematics, English, etc.) so that they may discuss common problems. Small groups provide an excellent place for teachers to receive feedback and suggestions from peers.

Different goals call for different groupings. For example, if one is trying to achieve more curriculum continuity so that students' time is not wasted in overly redundant assignments, then it makes sense for teachers in contiguous grades to work together. However, if the goal is to allow teachers in elementary and secondary settings to realize that some of their simple assumptions about what occurs at other levels do not apply, then it will be important to exchange across different grade levels. If content is emphasized, then teachers of the same subject matter taught should confer. To promote the exchange of information about teaching style or climate, teachers at various grade levels and in different subject areas are needed. Similarly, there are circumstances when beginning teachers should meet together (where they will feel free to express problems) and there are times when experienced teachers should meet with beginning teachers (i.e., to offer the benefit of experience in responding to problems).

Self-improvement teams may wish regularly to view and provide feedback about one another's tapes of classroom teaching. In particular, a teacher can get peers to provide information about those aspects of teaching behavior of special interest to the teacher. This procedure is in marked contrast to the typical in-service program or consultation that provides teachers with training, information, or evaluative feedback on issues that the consultant wishes to talk about. Teachers are not always interested in these topics. Many staff development programs are designed by persons outside schools to "fix" teachers' deficiencies as these persons perceive them.

Teachers meeting in small study groups can structure in-service programs that are meaningful to them. Research by Spencer (1984) suggests that too often teachers view in-service activities as unrelated to their teaching needs. Teachers need to assume initiative and to assist in planning and evaluating in-service activities. Although some principals may resist teachers' assistance in planning in-service work, most principals will be delighted to respond to teachers' initiatives.

In general, participation in self-study groups should be voluntary. The desirability of a voluntary program is probably self-evident. Nothing hurts a program that involves the sharing of information more than persons who participate solely because they have to do so. Consideration should be given, however, to those teachers who want to join a study group at some point but who are not ready to do so at the beginning of the year. It is perfectly reasonable for teachers to want to assess their own behavior and develop their own goals before joining a self-improvement group. Teachers should have a chance to join self-study groups when they are ready to do so.

Three rules should be kept in mind when in-service groups begin to function. The first one we have mentioned previously—*group structure and feedback exist to provide teachers with information that augments their personal self-development.* The group provides a unique viewpoint and resources to give teachers information regarding behaviors about which they want to receive feedback. Thus, *teachers function as decision makers, planning their own developmental goals.* The group functions as a barometer, telling teachers how they look to them and suggesting alternative ways to reach the goals that teachers have set. Teachers in the group will, of course, have their own viewpoints and each will react in terms of his or her own strengths, weaknesses, and preferences.

The teacher tells the group what his or her current goals are and outlines what behaviors and techniques the other teachers should examine when they view the teacher's videotape or come into the classroom to observe. Also, as previously mentioned, when a teacher or a group of teachers begins to engage in self-improvement activities, there is a tendency to do too much at once. Initially, the individual teacher should limit improvement areas to a few, so that full attention can be directed toward work on these new skills. Correspondingly, the group should help the teacher by restricting their comments to these designated behaviors. After the group has functioned for a few weeks, then the "video teacher of the week" may begin to ask the group to focus on all dimensions of teaching that were exhibited in the film. When the teacher is ready for such feedback, the group can help the teacher to learn more about how others react to his or her teaching.

The second rule to follow, then, especially in the group's formative weeks, is not to overwhelm the teacher with information. Restricting discussion to a few areas will help, and it may be useful to limit the number of comments that each group member makes. We can profit from only so much information at a given time, particularly negative feedback. No matter how competent and resilient a teacher may be, receiving notice of 50 mistakes will tend to make the teacher give up (at least psychologically). Negative comments do not tell the individual how to improve and tend to immobilize behavior.

In-service groups may benefit from such an artificial rule as: each participant writes out a reaction to the two or three major strengths and the two or three major weaknesses of the presentation. This guideline limits the information that a teacher receives initially, but it does focus the teacher's attention on a small, manageable list of "points to consider." The guideline also allows the teacher to have in writing (for future review) the basic reactions of each participant to the lesson.

Useful feedback should not only provide teachers with a rough assessment of their strengths and weaknesses but should also focus on specific ways to improve teaching. Ensuing discussions should emphasize alternative procedures that teachers might use to produce more desirable student responses. Effective in-service sessions allow teachers to receive both realistic reactions (positive and negative) to their performance on the behaviors in question and direct assistance in the form of information about alternative behaviors to use in the future. In-service self-study groups should not only evaluate present teaching but should also provide direction for subsequent teaching.

A third rule to bear in mind is to be honest. Self-study groups lose their effectiveness when individuals engage in either of two participatory styles: Pollyanna and Get-the-Guest. Too many teachers are unwilling to criticize another teacher's behavior, perhaps because they are afraid that openness and frankness will lead other teachers to respond in kind when they are being evaluated, or because they believe that the teacher will be hurt by an honest reaction. Such masking of reactions is self-defeating. Teachers can improve only if they get honest, objective comments about their behavior. Criticism followed by new ideas or approaches that may improve present practice is the best way the group can assist a teacher in self-development. To be sure, the group should reinforce the good things that a teacher does. We all like to know when we have done well, and it is especially important that we receive praise and encouragement when we improve. If a teacher has been working on a technique for a few weeks and shows improvement, let the teacher know about the improvement as well as ways to continue it. But it is still important to note major weaknesses. If there is no critical comment, there is no impetus or direction for change.

The other undesirable participant role is that of the carping critic who criticizes excessively and thoughtlessly. Perhaps such behavior is motivated by the need for self-protection ("If everybody looks bad, I'll be okay"). Perhaps such teachers are just insensitive to the needs of others. At any rate, their behavior rarely does any good, and participants who cannot deliver criticism tactfully and who cannot link criticism with positive suggestions should be encouraged and helped by other group members to develop these skills. When participants are not willing to temper excessive criticism, they should not continue in the group, for their presence generally generates a great deal of hostility and prevents the development of an atmosphere that is marked by the sharing of information and by positive planning to improve classroom instruction.

There is growing interest in making teaching assessment and feedback (whether for development or evaluation) more sensitive to individual teachers' needs and interests. Indeed, this emphasis is necessary if staff development programs are to help teachers improve their performance. In their book, *Marching to Different Drummers,* Guild and Garger (1985) raise issues associated with various teaching styles and discuss the value of such information for teacher supervision and staff development. For example, drawing upon the work of Witkin, Moore, Goodenough, and Cox (1977), Guild and Garger illustrate how administrators' knowledge and understanding of teachers' field dependence–field independence is valuable in designing supervisory conferences with individual teachers (see Tables 12.2

through 12.5). They argue that teachers and administrators who respect each others' styles can be more helpful to one another. We believe that these principles apply to communication among teachers as well. For example, research on individual differences strongly suggests that various teachers want different types of information from other teachers about their classroom performance. In any staff development program, teachers must be able to obtain the information that they want from other teachers.

OPPORTUNITIES TO OBSERVE AND GET FEEDBACK CAN IMPROVE INSTRUCTION

Eash and Rasher (1977) report that a school district's in-service program to help teachers individualize instruction was aided by classroom observation. Such training was useful in helping teachers cope with greater diversity in students brought about by a desegregation program and in improving student achievement in the district. Supervisory personnel needed additional training for their new roles because observation does not automatically improve instruction. It is useful only when conducted by competent persons who have a systematic way of looking at classroom behavior.

Feedback from students also can be useful in changing teacher behavior, but again, good results are not automatic. Several studies show that teachers do not change their behavior simply because they receive information. They need information about teaching behavior or goals that are important to them if the information is to be useful in changing their behavior. Too often, evaluation forms completed by high school and college students do not reflect teachers' goals. Or they

Table 12.2   HOW STUDENTS LEARN

Field dependence	Field independence
Perceive globally	Perceive analytically
Experience in a global fashion, adhere to structures as given	Experience in an articulated fashion, impose structure or restrictions
Make broad general distinctions among concepts, see relationships	Make specific concept distinctions, see little overlap
Have a social orientation to the world	Have an impersonal orientation to the world
Learn material with social content best	Learn social material only as an intentional task
Attend best to material relevant to own experience	Interested in new concepts for their own sake
Seek externally defined goals and reinforcements	Have self-defined goals and reinforcements
Want organization to be provided	Can self-structure situations
More affected by criticism	Less affected by criticism
Use spectator approach to concept attainment	Use hypothesis testing approach to attain concepts

Source: Guild, P., & Garger, S. (1985). *Marching to different drummers.* Alexandria, VA: Association for Supervision and Curriculum Development.

Table 12.3 HOW TEACHERS TEACH

Field dependence	Field independence
Strong in establishing a warm and personal learning environment, emphasize personal aspects of instruction	Strong in organizing and guiding student learning, emphasize cognitive aspects of instruction
Prefer teaching situations that allow interaction and discussion with students	Prefer impersonal teaching methods such as lecture and problem solving
Use questions to check on student learning following instruction	Use questions to introduce topics and following student answers
More student-centered	More teacher-centered
Provide less feedback, avoid negative evaluation	Give specific corrective feedback, use negative evaluation

Source: Guild, P., & Garger, S. (1985). *Marching to different drummers.* Alexandria, VA: Association for Supervision and Curriculum Development.

Table 12.4 WHAT TEACHERS EXPECT FROM AN ADMINISTRATOR

Field dependence	Field independence
To give warmth, personal interest, support	To focus on tasks
To provide guidance, to model	To allow independence and flexibility
To seek their opinions in making decisions	To make decisions based on analysis of the problem
To like them	To be knowledgeable about curriculum and instruction
To have an open door	To maintain professional distance
To "practice what they preach"	To be professionally experienced in appropriate content areas
To use tones and body language to support words	To give messages directly and articulately

Source: Guild, P., & Garger, S. (1985). *Marching to different drummers.* Alexandria, VA: Association for Supervision and Curriculum Development.

Table 12.5 HOW TEACHERS WANT TO BE EVALUATED

Field dependence	Field independence
With an emphasis on class "climate," interpersonal relationships, and quality of student-teacher interaction	With an emphasis on accuracy of content, adherence to learning objectives and assessment of learning
With a narrative report and personal discussion	With a specific list of criteria
With consideration of student and parent comments	With consideration of academic achievement and test scores
With credit for "effort" and for trying	With evidence and facts to support comments

Source: Guild, P., & Garger, S. (1985). *Marching to different drummers.* Alexandria, VA: Association for Supervision and Curriculum Development.

ask questions that are so global or inadequate (e.g., the student does not have the information necessary for responding) that teachers reject the feedback as meaningless.

When teachers are given specific and accurate information from students, especially when teacher participation is voluntary, they can use it to improve instruction. For example, Pambookian (1976) reports that a discrepancy between teachers' perceptions of teaching and feedback from students can motivate teachers to alter instructional behavior. He argues that if the discrepancy is large, there will be motivation for the teacher to change behavior. (We also suspect that the discrepancy should involve a goal that is important to the teacher.)

Pambookian found that when a group of college teachers was informed about such discrepancies, they changed their teaching behavior. Instructors with student ratings lower than their own ratings improved their teaching the most. If student feedback is to have optimal value, teachers must be involved in the construction of the evaluative instruments to see that questions of personal importance are included, and instruments need to be *changed* occasionally to present teachers with information about different aspects of their behavior. Teachers also can use feedback from classroom observation to modify their behavior. Much inappropriate teaching occurs because teachers are unaware of their behavior.

In interviews with teachers, Good and Brophy (1974) found that many aspects of differential teacher behavior toward high and low achievers were unknown to teachers. This was especially the case with qualitative variables (e.g., What percentage of the time did teachers "stay with" or "give up" on students generally? On high- and low-achievement students?).

When teachers were presented with specific information about their behavior that both intrigued and bothered them, they wanted to change their behavior. Subsequent observation illustrated that teachers did change their behavior, and there were signs that students were beginning to alter their behavior as a result of changed teacher behavior.

An especially good illustration of the use of observation to improve teaching comes from a program directed by Martin and Kerman (see Martin, 1973). The project, *Equal Opportunity in the Classroom,* attempted to help teachers become aware of self-defeating treatment of low-achieving students and learn new ways to interact with these students. First, teachers were presented with detailed information about teacher expectation research. Then they discussed how subtle, unproductive differences in behavior toward high and low achievers that might be taking place in their own classrooms. They were then trained in skills that were easy to use and observe.

Many of these skills were based on the Brophy-Good Dyadic Observation System (Brophy & Good, 1970), but several others were added by the project team. The key was that teachers were trained not only to treat low-achieving students in specific ways, but also to observe and code these behaviors. In addition to the training, teachers had the opportunity to observe and be observed by fellow teachers.

Teacher reports about the project were enthusiastic. In particular, they found it stimulating to be observed by other teachers (and get feedback from them) and to have a chance to observe other teachers themselves. Watching other teachers is a valuable way to *see* new techniques.

Observational data illustrated that teachers in the project treated low achievers much differently than did control teachers (i.e., teachers who did not participate in the project). The attitudes of low-achieving students in the classrooms of trained teachers were better than those of low-achieving students in control classrooms. Furthermore, the *reading achievement* of both high- and low-achieving students was better in the project classrooms.

Experimental evidence that teachers' learning can be assisted by the involvement of other teachers comes from research conducted by Ascione and Borg (1980). In this effort to train teachers in programs designed to improve students' self-concepts and their involvement in assigned classroom tasks, the researchers had pairs of teachers listen to tapes of one another's teaching and provide feedback. Teachers studied skills presented in a training module, then completed written exercises involving simulated teaching situations, and then practiced the skills in their own classrooms. Teachers made audiotapes of their classrooms and allowed other teachers to critique them. Although the specific effects of teacher-teacher feedback are not clear (i.e., the teachers received training in addition to feedback from other teachers), this research does suggest that teachers can provide realistic and helpful feedback to other teachers (Ascione & Borg, 1980; Borg & Ascione, 1982).

Stallings (1986) also argues that peers' observation and analysis of teachers' behavior can lead to greater understanding of the classroom and to hypotheses about ways that teachers might improve. She notes that detailed observational information can make teachers more aware of their own behavior and prepare them to work with other teachers in small groups to solve selective classroom problems identified by the observations. Thus, teachers can be researchers in their own classrooms and can use other teachers to help them solve to their own problems. Readers who are interested in detailed information about such a program can find it elsewhere (Stallings, 1986); however, the material presented in Figure 12.1 suggests the type of information that teachers need about their classrooms. This figure shows an observational profile of a teacher's classroom and specifies how time is spent in various activities. The specific interaction patterns that the teacher uses are shown in Figure 12.2, which profiles teacher-student interaction.

Stallings notes that her program shows teachers how to analyze student behavior and their own teaching methods. Also, she attempts to develop a peer climate in which teachers feel safe enough to try something new, risk failure, and try again. In this sense, her program recognizes that change is difficult to introduce into complex classroom settings and that sometimes teachers' initial attempts will lead to failure, but that teachers can learn from failure, plan again, and attempt new strategies. Thus, program the helps teachers feel competent and professional.

Additional support for our contention that teachers will change if their attention is called to the need for change is provided by Moore and Schaut (1975). One of their experiments involved observing teacher and student behaviors on the variables of interest before and after treatment. Thirty-six teachers were divided into experimental and control groups. During the study, teachers were given information about their behavior with ten randomly selected students. The observers focused on students' lack of attention and teachers' responses to it. Experimental teachers gave more attention to inattentive students than did control teachers. After the experiment, the student inattention rate was only 5 percent for the experimental group but 23 percent for the control group. Furthermore, the experimental teachers interacted

Observation variables	Criterion	% of Time spent — Criterion	% of Time spent — Betty's class	Goal
Teacher involved in				
Monitoring silent reading	X	15.00	.00	Monitoring: 35% or less
Monitoring written work	X	20.00	36.00	
Reading aloud	X	6.00	.00	Interactive instruction: 50% or more
Instruction/explanation	X	25.00	10.00	
Discussion/review assignments	X	10.00	13.00	
Practice drill	X	4.00	.00	
Taking test/quiz	X	5.00	.00	
Classroom management with students	X	2.50	.00	Organizing: 15% or less
Making assignments	X	10.00	20.00	
Organizing—teacher alone	X	2.50	18.00	
Social interaction with students	X	.00	.00	
Student uninvolved	X	.00	.00	
Providing discipline	X	.00	3.00	
Students involved in				
Reading silently	X	15.00	2.00	Seatwork: 35% or less
Written assignments	X	20.00	55.00	
Reading aloud	X	6.00	.00	Interactive instruction: 50% or more
Receiving instructions/explanations	X	25.00	26.00	
Discussion/review	X	10.00	12.00	
Practice drill	X	4.00	7.00	
Taking test/quiz	X	5.00	6.00	
Social interaction	X	.00	14.00	Off-task: 6% or less
Student uninvolved	X	.00	12.00	
Being disciplined	X	.00	3.00	
Classroom management	X	5.00	.00	Organizing: 15% or less
Receiving assignments	X	10.00	10.00	

Figure 12.1 Observation profile of Betty Brown's classroom. [*Source*: Stallings, J. (1986). Using time effectively: A self-analytic approach. In K. Zumwalt (Ed.), *Improving teaching*. 1986 ASCD Yearbook. Alexandria, VA.]

Variables	Criterion, percent	Betty's class, percent	Recommended
001 All academic statements	80.00	65.28	Increase
002 All organizing or managing statements	15.00	30.76	Decrease
003 All behavior statements	3.00	3.83	OK
004 All social statements	2.00	.00	OK
005 Total for discrete variables	100.00	100.00	
006 Teacher instructs/explains	12.00	15.45	OK
007 Teacher asks direct questions or commands	10.00	4.00	Increase
008 Teacher asks clarifying questions	3.00	.13	Increase
009 Teacher asks open-ended questions	3.00	.79	Increase
010 Student asks academic questions	2.00	1.32	OK
011 Teacher calls upon new students (academic)	6.00	5.02	OK
012 Students respond academically	15.00	5.00	Increase
013 Student shout-outs/initiates remarks	.00	7.39	Decrease
014 Student doesn't know answer	1.00	.13	OK
015 Student refuses to answer	.00	.00	OK
016 All praise	8.00	2.00	Increase
017 Teacher praises or supports academic responses	6.00	2.00	Increase
018 Teacher praises behavior	2.00	.00	Increase
019 Teacher corrects academic responses	6.00	4.35	Increase
020 Teacher corrects with guidance	4.00	.00	Increase
021 Teacher corrects behavior	2.00	3.03	Decrease
022 Teacher monitoring academic work	6.00	10.96	Decrease
023 All written work	10.00	.00	OK
024 Students read aloud	1.00	4.62	OK
025 Teacher reads aloud	1.00	2.24	OK
026 Teacher working alone	3.00	6.00	Decrease
027 Intrusions	.00	3.14	Decrease
028 Teacher involved with visitor	.00	2.20	Decrease
029 Positive interactions	4.00	.52	Increase
030 Negative interactions	.00	1.50	Decrease
031 Teacher touching	5.00	.00	Increase
032 Teacher movement	3.00	1.12	Increase
033 All activity-related comments or actions	16.00	9.77	OK
034 Student organizing comments	1.00	.13	OK
035 Student academic comments	3.00	.13	OK
036 Teacher organizing comments	5.00	1.98	OK
037 Students academic discussion	7.00	7.66	Increase
038 Students cooperative group academic discussion	5.00	.00	Increase
Total Number of Interactions for Teacher 905			

Figure 12.2 Interaction profile of Betty Brown. [*Source:* Stallings, J. (1986). Using time effectively: A self-analytic approach. In K. Zumwalt (Ed.), *Improving teaching.* 1986 ASCD Yearbook. Alexandria, VA.

with inattentive students one-and-a-half times more than the control teachers did. Such data strongly suggest that feedback to teachers can change their behavior and that of their students. However, again we want to emphasize that feedback does not change teacher behavior automatically.

Kepler (1977) also stresses that teacher awareness of classroom behavior does not necessarily lead to more appropriate behavior on the part of the teacher. Although it is clear that descriptive feedback to teachers is an important first step in understanding classroom behavior, it is not an answer per se. Much more information is needed about the ways in which feedback can be presented to teachers to optimize its value. Furthermore, more information is needed about those personal characteristics of teachers that make them more or less likely to benefit from feedback.

Lanier (1986) reviews research that indicates that collaboration among teachers is often undermined by the actual conditions of work. She notes that sometimes teachers are taught various collaborative strategies in in-service programs but in practice do not have the opportunity to use what they have been taught. For example, teachers are taught how to do cooperative planning but are not given time during the school day to plan cooperatively. She notes that if in-service is to be effective, certain important (and expensive but necessary) changes would have to occur in work conditions. For example, induction programs for new teachers would require administrators and veteran teachers to give more attention to the potential and competence of beginning teachers. She further argues, "More extensive and coherent staff development programs would require giving up the notion that experience by itself is an adequate teacher of teachers. Finally, the lack of progression in the teaching career would have to be confronted and challenged, as indeed it is being challenged in many states today" (p. 563). We agree and in the selections that follow, we will discuss the importance of having teachers play a more central role in regulating their professional development.

PROFESSIONAL COLLABORATION

Following the important work of Martin (1973), there is increasing recognition of the need to involve teachers as colleagues in a variety of educational programs. Recent literature indicates that teachers are collaborating more often with professors in conducting classroom research (for example, Lieberman, 1986), and there is greater recognition of the need for teacher education programs to encourage teachers to seek opportunities and develop skills for professional exchanges with colleagues (e.g., De Bevoise, 1986; Zumwalt, 1985). Evidence shows that teachers find such professional opportunities stimulating and rewarding (e.g., Bradford, 1986; Marwood, McMullen, & Murry, 1986; Nelson, 1986; Schmuck, 1986). However, structure and follow-up appear to be important parts of successful staff development efforts. Joyce (1981) systematically studied career and staff development and argues that all of the following elements should be included in good staff development programs.

1. Presentation of theory or description of teaching skills or strategies
2. Modeling or demonstration of teaching skills or strategies
3. Practice in simulated and real classroom settings

4. Structured and open-ended feedback about performance
5. Coaching for application—in-classroom, hands-on assistance with the problems of transferring new knowledge and skills to the classroom

Based on studies of teaching as well as review of the literature, Joyce (1981) estimates that fewer than 20 percent of the trainees master the skills of a training program if they do not receive feedback about their performance and if they are not directly coached in how to apply new skills. Thus, it is important that teachers learn to apply new skills in their particular classroom or school setting. This condition is often missing in staff development programs. Although he emphasizes feedback and coaching, Joyce (1981) believes that all five steps presented above should be present in an effective staff development program.

TEACHING MATERIALS: ANOTHER BASE FOR PROFESSIONAL EXCHANGE

We have emphasized teacher-student interactions in this chapter not only because they are important, but because they are often of special interest to many beginning teachers who have pressing questions about their relationships with students (Will I be liked? Can I control students?). Also, we have focused on teachers' classroom behavior because it is often difficult for teachers to be aware of their behavior because they interact with so many students under hurried and varied conditions. However, there are many other aspects of classrooms that teachers could profitably increase their knowledge about. These include curriculum materials and assignments.

Teachers might profitably exchange ideas about textbooks, seatwork assignments, learning stations, learning kits, computer labs, problem sets, quizzes, tests, homework assignments, unit reports, etc. Teachers who examine the questions and student exercises prepared by commercial publishers may discover that the curriculum task imposed by these materials is merely to memorize what is read—because in many cases a high percentage of the questions are factual.

After examining seventh-grade science teaching and the science curriculum, Mitman, Mergendoller, Packer, and Marchman (1984) conclude that too little attention is given to the process of science (actually conducting experiments, making and testing inferences) and too much time is spent on low-level memorization. Their work suggests that it is valuable to study the curriculum materials that students use in the classroom. For example, Table 12.6 illustrates one strategy for analyzing review questions that appear in students' texts.

In addition to analyzing materials, teachers can also be of considerable value to one another by developing and sharing materials. For example, teachers might design clever ways to begin selected science units with experiments or assignments that are of practical value to students. Developing such units takes time and if teachers shared responsibilities they could have more time to develop a few themes in greater depth. In most schools, teachers working in isolation are so busy getting ready for the next day or unit that they do not have sufficient time for curriculum development. Similarly, considering the vast amount of time that students spend in seatwork and the generally low quality of tasks that students work on, this seems an especially advantageous way for teachers to collaborate (e.g., write better questions

Table 12.6   ANALYZING END-OF-CHAPTER QUESTIONS

Textbook chapters typically end with review or summary questions/exercises. The purpose of this analysis is to judge the demands of these questions/exercises. Two aspects of the questions/exercises will be considered. First, the analysis examines the mode of response required. Here, the continuum ranges from items for which the student simply marks "t" for true and "f" for false to questions that ask the student to write a coherent well-structured expository essay. Second, the analysis examines the connection between the questions/exercises and the preceding text prose. There is a range for this aspect also, with questions that ask for answers that can be obtained directly from the text at one end and questions requiring original analysis at the other end.

Directions: For this analysis, you are to focus on all the chapters that contain the portions of the text associated with each of the two topics (i.e., the chapters containing the parts you've examined for the previous three analyses). In some instances there may be more than one chapter involved for each topic. Read each chapter even if this entails reading parts that are not directly on the topic. *It is important to read thoroughly because part of the analysis entails assessing the link between the questions and the text.* Next, turn to the review questions/exercises at the end of each chapter. (Do *not* include suggested investigative activities). Read each question and categorize it according to the mode of response required. Then examine the same question in terms of its relationship to the text, going back to the text to see what relevant information is provided. The categories under *mode of response* and *relationship to text* are as follows.

Mode of Response: There are four main categories for this dimension: (1) Verbal Restricted, (2) Verbal Extended, (3) Numerical Calculations, and (4) Figural. Category 1, verbal restricted, is further subdivided into five subcategories: (i) Matching, (ii) True/False, (iii) Fill-in/Label,

The mode of response categorization may raise the issue of what the unit of the question/exercise is. Take the following example:

6. How does the nervous system in man function in
    a. recognition of the environment?
    b. interpretation of the environment?
    c. response to the environment?

The text treats this as one item but there are three questions given, each requiring a separate, if related, answer. Thus, you would code this as three separate questions. Another example to consider is one problem where the student is asked to match 10 scientific terms with their definitions. Here, you would treat this as 10 separate questions.

Relationship to Text: For this dimension, you are asked to decide which of the following three categories best characterizes each question or exercise: (1) Textually Explicit, (2) Textually Implicit, or (3) Scripturally Implicit. (This taxonomy was developed by Pearson & Johnson, 1978.) Textually explicit questions have answers that are right there on a page of text. Other reading educators might refer to such questions as "literal comprehension" questions. Textually implicit questions have answers that are derived from the text but in an indirect sense. There is some degree of inference necessary for the reader to generate the answers. The point to stress is that the relationship between the question and the answer is to some degree an implicit one. Finally, "scripturally" implicit questions ask the reader to use his or her own script (prior knowledge and general reasoning) to come up with an answer. These are called, in terms of other reading frameworks, critical/evaluative items. Again, it is important to emphasize that it is necessary to study the text in order to make these categorizations.

(iv) Multiple-Choice, and (v) Short Answer. These are all self-explanatory, save the last, which is defined to mean questions that can be answered well by writing one simple sentence. Category 2, verbal extended, is broken into two subcategories: (i) paragraph and (ii) essay/report. Paragraph is defined to mean a question where a good answer would require a set of at least two sentences, all addressing a common idea. Essay/report refers to a question where a good answer would entail two or more paragraphs, each addressing a slightly different idea. Here, it is likely that the question will specify that an essay or report is necessary. The third main category is Numerical Calculations. This refers to questions where the main task is to perform a mathematical operation, even if the answer is expressed verbally. The fourth main category is Figural. This includes all problems where the main task is to make a drawing or graph data. In deciding what a "good" answer to any question consists of, you will have to use your own judgment. If a teacher's edition is available to you, it may be very helpful to see what model answers it gives.

Source: Mitman, A., Mergendoller, J., Packer, M., & Marchman, V. (1984). *Scientific literacy in seventh-grade life science: A study of perceptions and learning outcomes.* Final Report. San Francisco: Far West Laboratory for Educational Research and Development..

for students to respond to individually, design activities that allow students to compare and contrast their work).

TEACHER CENTERS

Teacher centers became popular in the 1970s and provided means of enriching the training of pre- and in-service teachers. However, teacher centers are difficult to define because of the many ways in which they operate. Centers have been created for a variety of reasons (legislative mandate, voluntary program in a school district, formal working agreements between universities and school districts, etc.).

Teacher centers could be used to provide the type of peer feedback–based in-service training that we described above. The teacher center movement has provided both human and material resources that can be used to improve teaching. Still, teachers will have to be sure that programs fulfill their individual needs and respond to their questions rather than subtly pressure them to conform to a "popular style."

Feiman (1977) presents an interesting account of the historical forces that led to the development of teacher centers and some of the major differences among these centers today. Teachers interested in the formation of a teacher center would benefit from reflecting on the distinctions that Feiman makes, because such distinctions may help teachers to focus on what they hope to achieve. The three major types of teacher centers identified by Feiman are behavioral centers, humanistic centers, and developmental centers.

In brief, *behavioral centers* focus on specific teaching behaviors and basically are concerned with helping teachers to improve classroom performance. Teachers are provided with a chance to view training films and the like in order to develop technical skills. In the *humanistic centers,* it is assumed that teacher development will occur naturally as long as teachers get the feedback they want in a supportive environment. *Developmental centers* share many concerns with the humanistic centers (e.g., teachers must learn at their own pace, teachers must begin at their own starting point). However, in the developmental centers, less time is spent trading practical advice and more time is used to encourage initiative (i.e., fewer short-term spontaneous encounters and less emphasis on responding to immediate needs and more on creating awareness of fundamental needs and problems).

The notion of a teacher center is an important concept—a place where teachers can receive and give help. Unfortunately, the cutback in federal funds has led to the elimination of teacher centers in some locations; in others, local funds have enabled the programs to continue. Even so, the philosophy of teacher center movements has been captured in some staff development programs (see, for example, Caldwell, 1985) and may influence the directions followed in new staff development programs.

The report *What works: Research About Teaching and Learning* (1986) notes that although high student achievement occurs more often in schools that possess high faculty morale and a shared sense of responsibility, in too many schools, most teachers are alone in their efforts to improve instruction. In some studies, as many as 45 percent of the teachers report *no* contact with other teachers during a school day and another 32 percent report having only infrequent contact with colleagues. The lack of opportunity to share experiences, to get new ideas, or to obtain supportmay increase teacher alienation and isolation and undermine efforts to obtain appropriate information in schools. Hence, there seems to be a growing realization that school districts' in-service programs need to offer teachers increased opportunity to interact with peers.

THE GROWING IMPORTANCE OF STAFF DEVELOPMENT

The ideas presented earlier in this chapter are organized and written as informal suggestions that a group of teachers at a school might implement. However, self-improvement programs can be an important part of an official district inservice program. Fenstermacher and Berliner (1985) note that staff development today is not the same as the in-service education of earlier decades, when teachers were thought to have primary responsibility for their professional development and self-renewal. As Fenstermacher and Berliner point out, today's teachers function in a complex environment of policy, law, regulation, special programs, and various professional associations. Modern staff development usually involves groups of teachers working together with specialists, supervisors, administrators, parents, and university personnel. In some school districts, a large percentage of the school budget is spent on staff development.

Despite its perceived importance, planning for staff development in some school districts is not as systematic as it should be, and too often it is a one-time undertaking (a speaker is brought in but relatively little follow-up occurs after the speaker leaves). Although there is growing interest in broadening the concept of staff development and including teachers more in the decision-making process, Fenstermacher and Berliner argue that there is still too little attention to the effects of in-service training. Accordingly, they provide an extensive plan for evaluating staff development (Fenstermacher & Berliner, 1985).

Improving the Entire School

As we argued earlier, a staff development program should first help teachers to satisfy their *individual needs and concerns*. Once these needs have been responded to satisfactorily by inservice programs, teachers can address broader school programs through cooperative inservice programs. Ultimately, staff development should lead to the improvement of the entire teaching staff at a school. Working collectively to improve is a potent determinant of the value of a staff development program. As a case in point, after studying staff development programs, Little (1981) writes, "First, the school as a work place proves extraordinarily powerful. Without denying differences in individuals' skills, interests, commitment, curiosity, or persistence, the prevailing patterns of interactions and interpretations in each building demonstrably create certain possibilities and set certain limits" (p. 9). "We are led from a focus on professional improvement as an individual enterprise to improvement as particularly an organizational phenomenon. Some schools sustained shared expectations (norms) both for extensive collegial work and for analysis and evaluation of and experimentation with their practices; continuous improvement is a shared undertaking at schools, and these schools are the most adaptable and successful of the schools we have studied" (p. 10).

There is evidence that collegial goal setting, problem solving, and performance feedback can improve teachers' skills as well as their willingness to experiment (Darling-Hammond & Wise, 1985; Little, 1982). As Darling-Hammond and Wise (1985) note, in an approach that depends on providing incentives for professionalizing teaching, evaluation must rely on people and judgments rather than on standardized tests of achievement. Such an approach assumes that teachers will become more capable by engaging in the joint construction of goals, definition of standards of good practice, mutual criticism, and commitment to self-improvement and inquiry.

Along these same lines, McDonnell (1985) argues that staff development programs must help teachers and principals to participate in experiences that provide them with more than just expertise and information. Although acknowledging that the effective schools and effective teaching literature provides considerable guidance for teachers and that this important information ought to be part of any in-service activity, McDonnell feels that school improvement projects should also have a strong affective component. That is, such programs need to boost morale, raise expectations, and maintain higher expectations. She notes that high morale and positive expectations are critical to creating an effective school; therefore, staff development programs need to help principals and teachers to develop more technical skills but also to feel good about using those competencies in a school setting.

STAFF DEVELOPMENT IN EFFECTIVE SCHOOLS

That the way that resources in schools are utilized and the ways in which teachers are encouraged to interact with one another help to predict the overall effectiveness of a school (Good & Brophy, 1986; Little, 1981, 1982; Purkey & Smith, 1983, 1985). Hence, it is important to consider how best to develop the collective talent of teachers as well as the talents of individual teachers. As has been argued elsewhere (Good & Weinstein, 1986), it is important to think about school and classroom processes at the same time, trying to identify processes and interrelationships that facilitate or hinder goals at each level. What are the ways in which schools can focus on high-quality instruction at the same time that individual classrooms are helping students to develop their talents as effectively as possible? Although much is known about effective classroom teaching, we need to know much more about how we can utilize the entire school as a learning environment—how can we improve the opportunities for practice, display, and reward of learning accomplishments and how best can opportunities such as school newspapers and journals, as well as processes such as school-wide assemblies and recognition, be used to supplement the efforts of teachers in individual classrooms (Good & Weinstein, 1986)? Although much research remains to be conducted in this area, already some practical, innovative ideas for improving schools have started to emerge (Deal, 1985).

However, the focus in this textbook is on individual teachers and teachers' ability to communicate with other teachers in the building. We think that one of the things that teachers will have to be able to do if they are going to be effective in the classroom is to help others collectively build a favorable school environment. Still, the first and most basic contribution that individual teachers can make is to develop an effective environment in their own classrooms, to help other teachers understand what they are doing, and work to understand what, in turn, other teachers are doing in their classrooms. We strongly feel that there is no need for teachers in the same building or the same school system to utilize highly similar styles and practices. That is, although there are some general principles of instruction that should be applied in every classroom, there are clearly many different ways to instruct effectively. Through working with peers it is possible to exchange ideas and to improve instruction; the goal is not to match or to model someone else's behavior. If schools are to significantly affect student outcomes, however, teachers must be cognizant of how other teachers in the same school teach (Good & Brophy, 1986; Good & Weinstein, 1986).

It is not uncommon, for example, to visit schools in which seatwork assignments and general class assignments for fifth-grade students are less demanding than work that third-grade students receive. Furthermore, students in lower grades often have more choices in books that they read, more freedom to work with other students, and more opportunities to plan work assignments than do students in higher grades. Similarly, in some secondary programs, students in the seventh grade write original essays; whereas, ninth graders only answer questions about various works of history and English. We feel that such discrepancies not only fail to challenge students to become progressively more independent and self-reliant, but may lower older students' motivation for and interest in schoolwork. Unfortunately, many teachers fail to provide enjoyable and appropriately challenging classroom assignments because they are unaware of what practices other teachers in the same school use.

What we are discussing here is broader than teachers simply sharing information, although the exchange of information is vital. We are also referring to a sense of community among teachers who are attempting to develop appropriate, positive expectations for all students and to challenge and stimulate students by use of information obtained in carefully planned and coordinated discussions with other teachers, in-service training, etc.

However, increased time for interaction does not necessarily lead to more insight and improved teaching. We believe that teachers should have regular time built into their schedules to confer with other teachers and to exchange strategies for enhancing student learning and motivation. For example, Table 12.7 summarizes some of the topics that teachers might discuss. More focused discussion of students, materials, and learning should result from more time for teacher interaction.

The Principal as Facilitator

The school principal and auxiliary school personnel (e.g., the school psychologist, supervisors, etc.) can also share ideas with teachers. One clear mandate from effective schools literature is that principals need to be active leaders and to support the instructional improvement efforts of teachers. However, it is important to have realistic expectations for principals' job functions, because it is clear that principals are busy simply running their schools and that a typical day is filled with many conflicts and interruptions. If teachers are interested in additional assistance and if administrators are able and willing to play a facilitative rather than merely an evaluative role, then it is possible for principals and teachers to work together to improve instruction. Principals are valuable instructional leaders when they create opportunities for teachers to improve their skills by observing teachers and providing systematic feedback.

Table 12.7 STAGES OF INTERACTION CONTEXT

1. Nonteaching duties
   a. Clerical routines (attendance, forms)
   b. Simple management routines (lineup, etc.)
   c. Playground supervision
   d. Lunchroom supervision
2. Materials
   a. Seatwork assignments
   b. Homework assignments
   c. Laboratory assignments
   d. Daily quizzes
   e. Unit tests
3. School-level meetings
   a. Committee meetings
   b. Before- and after-school duties
   c. Extracurricular activities
   d. Ceremonies, special events
4. Preactive teaching
   a. Lesson plans
   b. Evaluation plans
5. Adult relationships
   a. Principals
   b. Other teachers
   c. Parents
   d. Secretaries
   e. Other building staff members
   f. Outside administrators
   g. Board members
   h. Representatives of teacher organizations
6. Classroom management
   a. Getting/maintaining attention
   b. Responding to student misbehavior
   c. Task management—time allocation during seatwork
   d. Interruptions
   e. Student record keeping
7. Teacher behavior
   a. Lesson introduction
   b. Quality of teacher explanations
   c. Quality of questions asked
   d. Pace of lesson
   e. Appropriateness of assigned task
8. Student learning
   a. Student-initiated questions
   b. Student explanations
   c. Student responses
   d. Student understanding
   e. Student interest
9. Explanatory mechanisms
   a. Motivation theory
   b. Development theory
   c. Learning theory
   d. Instructional theory
   e. Classroom management/organization theory
   f. Research on teaching

Perhaps most important, the principal can play a valuable role in the in-service development of teachers by soliciting funds to buy appropriate video equipment and by scheduling videotaping so that optimum use can be made of it. For example, it may be necessary for first- and second-grade teachers to have different in-service training days than other teachers so that all groups will have video equipment available to replay their tapes or the tapes of other teachers. Thus, the principal can create the conditions that self-improvement groups need to function well.

Films or videotapes of teaching behavior that lend themselves to critical analysis are available. Principals may obtain these, show them to small groups of teachers, and allow teachers to code behavior and suggest alternative teaching methods. Although this procedure will help teachers to develop skill in objectively examining behavior, the principal should not force teachers to stay at this level very long. It is important to arrange for pairs of teachers to visit each other for at least a half-hour each week. The sooner teachers receive feedback, the sooner they can begin to plan improvement strategies.

Teacher Involvement

When teachers find in-service training programs boring and a waste of time, it is usually because the programs are unrelated to their needs. Much time and effort are currently being spent to develop curricula that are inherently more interesting to students and allow students to pursue topics independently. Perhaps corresponding emphasis should be placed on identifying ways for teachers to become more active in the development of in-service training programs that meet their needs and interests rather than subjecting them to a passive role. We believe that allowing teachers to use in-service time to engage in independent self-improvement activities, either as individuals or in groups, would be valuable.

After teachers begin to work on self-improvement, they are in a position to advise the principal as to the type of university consultant who would facilitate their program. Teachers given the freedom and responsibility for planning their own in-service training typically take the task quite seriously and work earnestly to develop useful programs. As a resource specialist and general facilitator, the principal can aid immeasurably by supplying teachers with copies of recent books and journals that focus on classroom practice (e.g., *Educational Leadership, Elementary School Journal, Phi Delta Kappan, Theory Into Practice, Today's Education, Instructor,* etc.) and can provide access to journals that present new models and empirical studies of classrooms (e.g., *American Educational Research Journal, Journal of Educational Psychology, Sociology of Education*). The best way principals can influence and encourage the development of teachers is to have a genuine interest in their self-development and to search for and experiment with ways of becoming better principals.

Many principals have been trained primarily as managers rather than as instructional leaders; hence, some of them do not have the skills necessary to observe teachers and to provide them with information about their classroom behavior. As is made clear in the report, *What Works: Research About Teaching and Learning* (1986), teachers welcome suggestions about how to improve their work but they rarely receive them—the average teacher is visited by a supervisor only once a year and then receives only very general and vague feedback about teaching performance. In contrast, principals who are good supervisors frequently visit classrooms and help teachers to improve by giving relevant feedback that is of interest and value to teachers. Such principals make themselves available to teachers and allow teachers to come to them without being branded as "weak" because they seek help. Principals need to develop skills for this role by reading recent books on teaching, curriculum, and supervision. Still, even principals who are adequate observers will often find that they can gain by allowing teachers to assume more responsibility for self-evaluation and for taking further steps to improve their own teaching.

Principals' Feedback to Individual Teachers

An interesting research area of the future will involve determining how principals influence the instructional behavior of teachers in their schools. How do they communicate expectations and establish instructional priorities? If principals encourage teachers to determine their own instructional goals, how do principals become aware of each teacher's goals and how do they monitor and provide feedback about progress? Dwyer, Lee, Rowan, and Bossert (1982) provide a helpful profile that characterizes effective principals as *active*. Considering that effective principals are more visible to teachers and students in their schools, it is important to know whether or not their decisions and actions are related to student progress. For example, when and how often do principals visit particular classrooms? Do successful principals spend more time with teachers they believe to be average, or do they observe less capable teachers more closely? How specific is the feedback they provide to teachers? On what topics do conferences focus? Do effective principals discuss curriculum and instruction or do they talk only about general issues of classroom management, resources, and human relations?

Just as some teachers expect too little from certain pupils, some principals likely expect too little from certain teachers. It would be valuable to study how principals communicate expectations to teachers (e.g., the classes or students assigned to a teacher, the committees or duties assigned, the way requests for supplies are handled, the frequency and degree of formality of observational visits, etc.) and to determine how principals vary in their ability to communicate in positive and helpful ways with teachers.

Though there is no research on this issue, we suspect that more effective principals visit teachers and are willing to discuss with teachers issues of content, student learning, and specific instructional problems. What is critical is not the frequency of teacher-principal interaction but the nature of the interaction and whether or not it leads to more thoughtful instruction. Table 12.8 illustrates that principals can communicate their expectations to teachers in various ways.

Principals as Evaluators

Principals in many school districts have to evaluate teachers as well as provide supervision and in-service education programs. It is beyond the purpose of this book to discuss the principal's role as evaluator. However, we do want to make a few brief comments about evaluation problems. Part of the difficulty in evaluating teachers is that we have too little information about teacher behaviors that consistently relate to desired student outcomes in predictable ways. In some areas (e.g., student achievement in basic subjects), extensive empirical findings can be used to study teacher effectiveness systematically. Such information could, if properly and judiciously used, help to identify teachers who need assistance. For certain student affective outcomes, we have much useful information (see Slavin, 1983, for a comprehensive discussion of the effects of cooperative team learning on interpersonal perceptions), and in other areas, formative work is under way (see Anderson & Prawat, 1983, for a discussion of issues associated with students learning self-responsibility). However, there is a paucity of information about how classroom processes relate to most affective goals and many important cognitive goals (e.g., problem solving). In this book, we have reviewed research fingings (time, expectations, management, motivation, instruction) that should be of considerable value to principals who must evaluate teachers. However, this information should be discussed so that teachers and principals reach broad agreement on how such findings can be applied appropriately in the classroom.

As we have pointed out repeatedly, there are many types of effectiveness, and process indicators can sometimes be very misleading. Students who appear to be on task may not really be thinking about assigned work. Some teachers may take more time than others to introduce a concept or to establish classroom rules and hence

Table 12.8 PRINCIPALS' COMMUNICATION OF COMPETENCY EXPECTATIONS TO INDIVIDUAL TEACHERS

1. Classroom visitation
   a. Frequency of classroom visitation
   b. Frequency of feedback conferences
   c. Types of exchanges—social vs. instructional
   d. Content focus (to the extent that interactions focus on instruction, what is the focus of interactions?)
2. Opportunity to have contact with other teachers
   a. Be visited by other teachers
   b. Visit other teachers
   c. Visit teachers in other schools
   d. Planning time with other teachers
3. Resource allocation
   a. Equipment budget
   b. Materials budget
   c. Free time/extra assignments
   d. Availability of substitutes so teachers can participate in in service workshops
   e. Active voice in how in service funds will be used
4. Leadership roles
   a. Principal selects teacher to represent school at district or state meeting
   b. Teacher serves as chair of committee (e.g., textbook selection)
   c. Principal solicits teachers' opinions privately and publicly
5. Curriculum teaching assignment
   a. Principal assigns teachers advanced section
   b. Principal assigns honor students to these teachers
   c. Teacher has free period at advantageous time

may appear to be ineffective. However, these teachers may be able to cover subsequent content more quickly and with fewer interruptions because they have given students a thorough preparation. A particularly strong caveat comes from Doyle (1983), who reports that teachers who are poor managers (using the criteria of recent classroom management research) nevertheless obtain high student achievement. Although it is unlikely that many such teachers exist, it is noteworthy that some teachers can compensate for poor management skills so that they still have positive effects on student achievement.

Virtually all the concepts generated by classroom research have to be interpreted and applied to particular classrooms. Teachers can wait too long for students to respond as well as not long enough, and there can be too much alerting and accountability as well as too little. Again, we argue that concepts (e.g., wait-time, action zone, controlled practice) enable teachers, supervisors, and principals to examine more aspects of teaching and to assess more extensively why a particular classroom is or is not effective. Nevertheless, to be used well, concepts must be related to instructional goals and learners' needs (Zumwalt, 1986).

Principals' Central Role: Stimulate Professional Growth

Clearly, improvement efforts can be initiated by the school district or principals, and teachers can be observed in terms of their progress toward these goals as well as toward their own goals. Indeed, there is some evidence that teacher alignment (agreement on school goals and practices) can have a positive influence on student achievement (see, for example, Rutter, Maughan, Mortimore, Ouston, & Smith, 1979). The information presented in this book is organized at the teacher or classroom level rather than at the school level, and we believe that any analysis of school effectiveness should begin with a careful examination of classroom behavior. Other recent reviewers of the school effectiveness literature also emphasize observing and understanding classroom behavior (see, for example, Rowan, Bossert, & Dwyer, 1983). Still, we think it is important that teachers and principals have some knowledge of the effective schools literature (see Purkey & Smith, 1983), and this information needs to be coordinated with classroom improvement strategies.

After a thorough analysis of recent teaching and school research and its policy implications, Shulman (1983) concludes that the classroom teacher is the key to school effectiveness. Hence, although principals must think of building a school climate and a school program, they cannot lose sight of the need for teachers to have flexibility and to function as decision makers. Shulman stresses that the literature on effective schools is meaningless if teachers are not afforded some autonomy in making decisions about how to teach. We agree with him that principals can help classrooms function more smoothly by making teaching more satisfying and stimulating—a profession rather than an occupation that requires only a few classroom skills change.

Furthermore, we believe that it is important that principals effectively involve teachers in discussing and planning school change as well as change in individual classrooms. Schlechty and Vance (1983) argue that virtually all of the research on effective schools indicates that schools in which teachers engage in considerable job-related discussion and have the opportunity to share in decisions about instructional programs and staff development are more effective than schools in which decisions are made by rule-bound bureaucratic procedures. However, these authors point out that these same studies of effective schooling indicate that relatively few schools allow teachers to participate in decision making. They argue that the way schools are typically managed and organized means that teaching does not attract the most talented people available, nor do schools obtain optimal performance from those who are currently teaching.

EMERGING ROLES AND ISSUES

In order to prepare for and/or to be effective educators, we feel that teachers of today and tomorrow will have to deal with three important issues. These issues concern the attempt to find differentiated career roles for teachers (master teacher program), the increased involvement of teachers in evaluation, and the growing use of beginning teacher evaluation programs.

The Master Teacher

There is currently a great deal of interest in differentiating the work of teaching and in designating some teachers as master teachers. In part, this effort is intended to attract and retain good teachers and to reward teachers for effectiveness. As Zumwalt (1985) notes, however, the concept of master teacher means different things to different people, and the concept is implemented in various schools in diverse ways. Table 12.9 shows that master teacher programs can serve various purposes and that teachers can also be designated as master teachers and rewarded in diverse ways.

Griffin (1985) notes that current national concern for the quality of teaching is accompanied by the recognition that teachers are not compensated sufficiently for the important and complex work that they do. He argues that the interest in finding ways to increase teacher compensation recognizes that improving schooling is largely dependent on the knowledge and skill of individual teachers and that to insure high levels of knowledge and skill, it will be necessary to increase compensation.

Master teacher programs have a long history. They have been tried in a variety of settings and have worked in some places but have failed miserably in others. Success depends partly on the criteria that are used to evaluate teachers.

According to Griffin (1985), there are two dominant ways to describe and identify a master teacher. The first conception is based on a "better than" assumption. In this conception, one teacher engages in essentially the same activities as another but is judged to be better at accomplishing those activities than the other. This approach, as Griffin notes, raises questions and dilemmas associated with specification of criteria to determine who can perform a particular task better than someone else. It brings into question issues of measurement including objectivity, validity, and reliability of human judgments in a complex social situation.

Doyle (1985) notes that this definition tends to create a narrow set of criteria for differentiating effective teachers. That is, under pressure to identify teachers

Table 12.9 MASTER TEACHER: SOME SAMPLE VARIATIONS

Category	Criteria

Purpose	Recognizing teachers:
	  To attract teachers to district/state/profession
	  To increase teacher effectiveness
	  To prevent burnout
	  To retain good teachers
	Providing career advancement opportunities (for same reasons as in recognition)
	Meeting specific educational needs (e.g., curriculum development, evaluation, staff development)
	Being responsive to external and/or internal demands

Selection criteria	Seniority/years of teaching
	Test scores (professional knowledge, subject-matter knowledge)
	Educational requirements
	Attendance record
	Evaluation as effective teacher:
	  Student test scores
	  Observation (general or specific criteria, such as "time on task")
	  Nominations (self, peers, students, parents, administrators)
	Specialized skills/knowledge (e.g., curriculum development, supervision, evaluation)
	Professional portfolio
	Interview
	Proposal for project, research, etc.
	Desire to take on additional responsibilities/time commitment

Selection decision	Objective criteria, ratings Committee of one or more of following: peers, administrators, students, parents, outside consultants
N	Set *N* or % at any given time Maximum *N* or % at any given time *N* to vary depending on demographics/finances/teachers who meet criteria

Reward	Title
	Money:
	  Merit award (lump sum or accumulative)
	  Tied to additional responsibilities
	Hierarchical (career ladder) or nonhierarchical
	Additional responsibilities
	Materials, supplies, teacher aides
	Opportunity to work 11–12 month contract
	Sabbaticals
	Staff development opportunities

Responsibilities	None (recognition only) Added responsibilities (e.g., curriculum developer, staff developer, diagnostician, program evaluator, researcher) Released from full-time teaching or "add-on" (after hours, vacations, summer months)

Source: Zumwalt, K. (1985). The master teacher concept: Implications for teacher education. *Elementary School Journal, 86,* 45–54.

who are better than other teachers, there is a tendency to reify and to over-apply classroom research. Although noting the value of research and its usefulness, especially in the context of the teaching that has actually been studied, Doyle notes that a narrow definition will create more problems than it solves. Specifically, he argues that an approach that attempts to find the "better than" teachers using research will miss some excellent teachers if criteria for judging teachers are based only on current knowledge about effective teaching. He notes that it is also possible to have false positives, that is, teachers who fit the profile of an effective teacher but who are not really effective.

According to Doyle (1984, p. 31), "This problem is especially serious when management indicators are the primary basis for judging teaching ability. It is quite possible for a teacher to achieve high work involvement and student productivity by simplifying task demands to the point that students learn very little. This possibility does not nullify the importance of management in teaching, but it underscores the need to include information about instructional practices and curriculum content in assessing effectiveness."

Griffin notes that a second conception of the master teacher is based on a "more than" perspective. In this view, the master teacher is one who may or may not engage in traditional teaching but who also performs specialized functions in schools and classrooms (National Education Association, 1983). For example, the master teacher may plan curriculum for a group of other teachers, monitor student progress, formulate and administer evaluation schemes, or serve as a mentor by helping beginning teachers with special instructional or curricular issues.

Griffin contends that master teacher plans may increase the professional status of teachers. However, he believes that this can happen only if these plans move away from narrow definitions of teaching and associated tasks and provide greater freedom for teachers to make curriculum decisions. Specifically, he argues that proposals that differentiate among teachers on the basis of varied role expectations have more promise than ones based on the assumption that a few teachers can perform a limited number teaching tasks better than others.

Doyle (1985) defines master teachers as those who consistently design tasks that convey the curriculum to students in appropriate ways and orchestrate these tasks successfully in a complex classroom environment. Effective teaching, from Doyle's point of view, is more than modeling a master teacher. It consists of the constructive adaptation of instruction to specific contexts. This conception of effectiveness holds that mastery includes a knowledge and skill base that is accessible to all practitioners rather than residing in the magic qualities of a few extraordinary teachers. Furthermore, Doyle suggests that identifying mastery is a task involving a full complement of professional knowledge and judgment, not a simple application of a few discrete indicators that might be used in a checklist.

Caldwell (1985) describes one school district's attempt at a professional development/master teacher program in which master teachers serve as staff development leaders. This program has three goals: (1) to provide knowledge of and experience with research-based, effective teaching practices; (2) to build commitment to and support for teachers' professional growth; and (3) to reward, recognize, and reinforce excellent teachers and to afford these teachers the opportunity for continued professional growth.

Workshop activities (led by master teachers) are organized in five major areas: content analysis, diagnosis, prescription, instruction, and evaluation. More specifically, activities include making content decisions, designing instruction, helping students to develop self-direction, and using learning, motivational, and reinforcement principles effectively in the classroom.

Caldwell notes that master teachers differ from regular teachers in two ways. First, master teachers have performed effectively in their own classrooms. Second, they receive specialized training and support in order to assist them in thinking through the issues associated with helping other teachers. She notes that as the program continues, its goals will broaden and that this initial effort will serve as a model as other teachers are identified and have the chance to use their competencies more fully. As the district's needs and goals change, its staff development program will change also; however, the program will continue to be based on the need to provide respect, recognition, and reinforcement for excellence in teaching.

BEGINNING TEACHERS

As Veenman (1984) notes, the transition from preservice to in-service teaching can be a traumatic experience as teachers move from the ideal world of the college classroom to the reality of everyday teaching. For a variety of reasons, teachers may experience role adjustment problems. They may be poorly trained in teacher preparation programs and develop unrealistic expectations, so that they do not perceive that teaching is a demanding and difficult but doable and rewarding job. We have emphasized (beginning in Chapter 1) that classrooms are complex settings that demand decision making and the application of general principles to particular classroom situations.

New teachers may experience some problems because they have had only general training and are thus not ready for a specific job in a specific school. For example, as a student teacher one may be in an inner-city first-grade classroom but then be assigned to teach full-time in a sixth-grade class in a suburban school district. For this reason, we recommend that teachers in training spend time in various types of schools. After learning about their first assignments, new teachers should talk with other teachers who teach at the same grade level.

There are other reasons why teachers may have difficulties when they start to teach, and there are some "problems" that teachers cannot prepare for in advance. First-year teachers are not only becoming teachers and learning to deal with students, parents, and other adults, they are also assuming new responsibilities (making new friends, paying off loans, etc.). Thus, anxiety and role conflict are expected when one becomes a full-time teacher.

Becoming a teacher affects individuals in different ways, but it is clear that some teachers alter their behavior after their initial teaching experiences. For example, Bergmann et al. (1976) found that 57 percent of beginning teachers reported that they changed their initial student-focused teaching to a more traditional instructional model. A more student-centered style is not necessarily wrong, but most new teachers do not have the necessary management skills to maintain a student-centered instructional approach. Moskowitz and Hayman (1974) report that many beginning teachers ignore too much misbehavior (almost in the hope that, if not acknowledged, it will disappear). Similarly, Fogarty, Wang, and Creek (1982) found beginning teachers less able to respond to the immediate, spontaneous reactions of students. In a growing number of states, beginning teachers have to participate in state-mandated beginning teacher programs and the evaluation criteria used in these programs may not match those in university training programs. (For a discussion of state-mandated beginning teacher programs, see Hoffman, Edward, O'Neal, Barnes, & Paulissen, 1986.)

Reported Problems

Veenman (1984) reviews the problems of beginning teachers that are reported in 83 studies. From each study the 15 most serious problems reported were selected, and then a comparison was made across all studies. The most serious problem reported by new classroom teachers was *discipline*. The next most salient problem was *motivating* students. Other frequently reported problems were dealing with individual differences among students, assessing students, and communicating with parents.

Despite the fact that many teachers report problems, it should be clear that most teachers enter teaching successfully. Several studies (Broeders, 1980; deVoss & Dibella, 1981; Edmonds & Bessai, 1979; Tisher, Fyfield, & Taylor 1979) report that over 80 percent of beginning teachers are satisfied with their schools.

Different Needs

Beginning teachers with different skills and various needs will react to teaching in different ways. For example, Glassberg (1980) found that more mature beginning teachers emphasized the need to understand individual students and to be flexible, whereas less mature beginning teachers held a more restricted view of teaching.

There are several models for analyzing the developmental level of teachers (e.g., Hunt & Joyce, 1981; Sprinthall & Thies-Sprinthall, 1983). The first explicit theory describing teacher development was proposed by Fuller (1969) and further elaborated by Fuller and Bown (1975). The first stage of teaching is concern with *survival*. Will I be liked? Can I control students? Will others think I am a good teacher? The second stage is concern with the *teaching situation* (methods, materials, etc.) and the third stage reflects concern with *students* (their learning and needs). In theory the early self-centered concerns are seen as less mature than later, more student-centered concerns. It seems reasonable to assert that until teachers deal with early concerns (Will I survive? Can I refine my teaching skills?), they will have less time to respond to individual students' needs.

We believe that realistic materials (such as this textbook), relevant experience, content knowledge, and good supervision (i.e., during student teaching) can help many students to at least be past the survival stage when they enter the classroom as regular teachers. Teachers will need to work through a variety of personal (Will anybody listen to me?) and teaching concerns (how to use the computer, how to structure small-group instruction) before they will be able to devote most of their attention to the effects of teaching (i.e., student learning).

We believe that the advice and strategies for self-growth provided in this chapter are useful for all teachers, even those who have taught successfully for several years. However, the recommendations are especially important for beginning teachers. Unfortunately, too many teachers who experience difficulty deny their problems (at least to others) and fail to avail themselves of the experience of certain other teachers and supervisors. New teachers need to use some discretion in deciding which teachers to approach for information; some teachers are better sources of information and are more empathic than others, and as we suggested earlier in the chapter, student teachers and beginning teachers need to exercise tact when they ask for suggestions and information. However, a broader, more pervasive problem is failing to obtain help.

Teachers—experienced as well as inexperienced—benefit from the exchange of information about teaching. Through exchanging information teachers can develop a sense of purpose and support from other teachers as well as gain specific information about improving instruction (Little, 1981). New teachers especially could benefit greatly by visiting with experienced, successful teachers who teach at the same grade level in order to gain invaluable advice about strategies for beginning and ending lessons, content assignments that enhance thinking skills, and assignments for presenting content that students find both meaningful and enjoyable.

INDUCTION PROGRAMS FOR BEGINNING TEACHERS

Presently there is a great deal of interest in programs that provide special assistance to or assessment of teachers, especially first-year teachers. Proponents of these programs believe that new teachers will improve their teaching because of the support and assistance they receive and that eventually education will be improved in enduring, important ways.

In some states, legislators have mandated programs for beginning teachers in order to eliminate incompetent teachers before they receive tenure. However, reports indicate that very few incompetent teachers are actually being "weeded out" (Huling-Austin, 1985). Other beginning teacher programs were created to help teachers become more professional and adjust successfully to the complex demands of teaching. In some states and districts, programs serve both of these functions at the same time.

In the long run, we believe that successful induction programs can help teachers to remain in teaching and adapt to its demands. The retention of promising beginning teachers is extremely important because when these teachers leave the profession, a large investment of time and resources is lost. There are not enough qualified teachers to staff public schools adequately. Indeed, the National Center for Education Statistics estimates that the demand for new teachers between 1986 and 1990 should reach about 197,000 teachers per year, which is more than the number of college students planning to enter teacher education programs. As Huling-Austin (1985) notes, this situation is likely to last through the year 2000 and may worsen due to high retirement rates, increased curriculum requirements in public schools, shifting demographics, expanded career options for educated women, mandated reductions in class size, and increasingly rigorous teacher credentialing standards.

Huling-Austin (1986) notes that induction programs can help in five general areas: (1) improve the teaching performance of beginning teachers (assuming that teachers are provided with ongoing support and assistance), (2) increase the retention rate of promising beginning teachers during the induction year, (3) help to screen out the least promising teachers (if the programs provide means of doing so), (4) promote the personal and professional well-being of teachers by fostering each teacher's professional self-esteem, and (5) satisfy mandated requirements related to induction and certification. She notes, however, that it is *unreasonable* to expect induction programs to (1) overcome major problems in the school context such as when teachers are misplaced (teaching in an area that they have not been trained for) or when teachers face overcrowded classrooms or have too many preparations to make; (2) develop into successful teachers those who enter the classroom without the necessary background, ability and personal characteristics that are required to be competent professionals; (3) substantially improve the long-range retention of teachers in the field, if additional changes are not made in the broader educational system as well (improved status in the eyes of society, better salaries and working conditions). Thus, it is reasonable to assume that under certain circumstances induction programs will assist beginning teachers as they adjust to the professional demands of teaching and as they grow in their commitments to teaching as well as in their ability to communicate effectively with students. However, these programs are not magic. Independent of broader social understanding and support, they can only accomplish so much. Thus, what counts is the quality of induction programs, not just the presence of a program in the school district.

Principals' Roles in Induction Programs

Huling-Austin and Emmer (1985) outline useful ways in which principals can help first-year teachers to adjust to teaching and subsequently to remain in teaching:

1. Principals should provide first-year teachers with as much preparation time as possible. Although all principals recognize the benefits of hiring teachers as soon as possible, it is important that new teachers be furnished with their course schedules and have copies of the textbooks that they are going to use and any other information useful in planning for the school year.
2. Principals need to be realistic about assignment of courses and extra-curricular duties to new teachers. Senior teachers often want to teach the most desirable courses (algebra rather than general math) and as a result, beginning teachers are often left with the most difficult assignments and the least interesting courses. It is important to allow beginning teachers some choices in what they teach so that they might maintain their interest in teaching and find teaching more satisfying.
3. Each beginning teacher should be assigned an appropriate support teacher. More important, teachers who are assigned as mentors must be willing to take on the responsibility of helping a beginning teacher. The mentor teacher should teach the same subject or grade level as the first-year teacher. In addition, mentor teachers should be trained for this role.
4. Before the school year begins, the principal should introduce first-year

teachers to other teachers in the school. At the secondary level, a new teacher should also meet the department chairperson. Special luncheons or seminars are two means of encouraging communication among teachers.

5. Principals should conduct a first-year teacher orientation at their schools. Although most schools have orientation sessions, principals rarely have special orientations for first-year teachers. Such sessions allow the principal to provide new teachers with detailed information about administrative procedures that other teachers are already familiar with. Huling-Austin and Emmer recommend that principals have a series of meetings with first-year teachers, beginning one morning a week for the first six weeks of school, to discuss counseling, testing, contact with parents, and general instructional issues.

6. They also recommend that principals be highly visible during the first few days of classes and accessible to new teachers. Although principals are extremely busy at the beginning of the school year, it is important for them to make time to discuss issues of concern to beginning teachers.

Mentor Teachers' Role in Induction Programs

In many districts experienced and successful teachers are appointed to help beginning teachers adjust to their role in the school. Mentor teachers need to realize that beginning teachers' needs may be different from their own (for more information about mentor/beginning teacher relationships, see Galvez-Hjornevik, 1986; Huffman & Leak, 1986). This is true not only in terms of focus (beginning teachers have more concerns about self and classroom management, whereas, more mature teachers have more concerns about student learning) but also in process (beginning teachers may need to think about teaching somewhat differently until they develop a better understanding of content and procedures). The following discussion should illustrate the value of planning for classroom teaching and highlight potential differences between beginning and more experienced teachers. We use the example of planning, but many other aspects of classroom life also show differences between beginning and more experienced teachers.

Planning Models

Considering that teachers develop and use different types of plans, what models describe how teachers do, in fact, plan? For many years, those writing on the topic of planning cited Ralph Tyler's (1950) work as a good example of appropriate planning for classroom instruction. Tyler's linear model consists of four steps: (1) specify objectives, (2) select learning activities, (3) organize learning activities, and (4) specify evaluation procedures. For many years this model was accepted at face value, and it was not until the 1970s that researchers started to examine directly the planning process that teachers used and to compare what teachers actually did with what was prescribed.

In one of the first studies of teacher planning, Taylor (1970) examined how teachers planned syllabi for courses in British secondary schools. Using group discussions with teachers and a questionnaire as well as an actual examination of the course syllabi, Taylor concluded that the most common theme in teachers' course planning was the centrality of the pupil. Teachers' thinking about planning was organized around pupil needs, abilities, and interests. Following the pupil as a central point in the planning process were subject matter, general goals, and teaching methods. In planning, teachers appeared to place little importance on evaluation and the relationship between their own courses and the curriculum as a whole. Given such findings, Taylor concluded that when planning curriculum, teachers should start with the content to be taught and accompanying important issues (e.g., time, resources, etc.). Furthermore, teachers should consider pupils' interests and attitudes, aims and purposes of the course, learning situations to be created, the philosophy of the course, the criteria for judging the course, the degree of pupil interest fostered by the course, and finally, evaluation of the course.

Later, Yinger (1977) developed a theoretical model of the process of teacher planning. He views teacher planning as beginning with a discovery cycle in which the teacher's goals, as well as knowledge and experience, produce an initial "problem conception" worthy of continual refinement. The second stage in Yinger's model is problem formulation and solution. Yinger argues that the procedure for carrying out such a process is the design cycle, and that problem solving as a design process involves progressive elaboration of plans over time. Elaboration, investigation, and adaptation are the phases through which teachers formulate their plans. The third stage of his planning model involves implementation, evaluation, and eventual routinization of the plan. According to Yinger, evaluation and routinization contribute to a teacher's knowledge and experience, which in turn can play a major role in the teacher's future planning.

As Clark and Peterson (1986) note, a significant aspect of Yinger's conceptualization is that it is a cyclical (dynamic) rather than a linear model. The cycle Yinger proposes is similar to the processes that are believed to go on in the work of architects, physicians, artists, and other professionals. His position symbolizes that schooling is not a series of unrelated planning-teaching episodes, but that each planning stage can be influenced by prior planning and teaching experiences and that each teaching event can influence future planning. Mentor teachers can help beginning teachers by sharing with them examples of how they have had to change units to meet the needs of different classes and by stressing that planning is never final, but rather is a dynamic on-going process.

Borko and Niles (in press) discuss the implications of classroom research for teachers-in-training (e.g., preservice teachers). They argue that preservice teachers can learn from research that planning typically focuses on subject matter and the selection of corresponding activities, and that teachers pay relatively little attention to objectives or evaluation. However, they note that if teachers are to use this information appropriately, they must understand *why* experienced teachers plan this way and why their plans include certain elements and exclude others. According to Borko and Niles, experienced teachers do not specify objectives because they are implied in the materials and in curriculum guides. However, preservice teachers have not had as many opportunities as experienced teachers to work with these objectives and most likely will need to focus more on them. Similarly, in noting the lack of research that evaluates experienced teachers' planning, preservice teachers should realize that it is natural for experienced teachers to use more indirect means to determine which students have reached objectives for a particular lesson. Experienced teachers have a broader range of experience and a variety of procedures for receiving and interpreting information from students (e.g., the way they ask questions, examination of seatwork, etc.). Borko and Niles conclude that Tyler's model, which includes objectives and evaluation, may have more relevance for preservice teachers than for experienced teachers. Hence, it may be important for less experienced teachers to begin with a formal model for planning and later to adapt that model to their own classes. Mentor teachers need to expect and to accept the fact that beginning teachers may use different models.

Too Much Planning?

The concept of excessive planning is an important one for *preservice* teachers. Experienced teachers told Borko and Niles that student teachers should learn to *plan thoroughly*. By emphasizing thorough planning, experienced teachers mean developing more than enough activities for a given time period; they do not imply the specification of a detailed, *rigid* script (I will ask this question and, if given this student answer, will follow it with this question, etc.). In fact, experienced teachers discouraged their proteges from using detailed scripts. Recent planning research supports this advice. That is, appropriate thorough planning (even over-planning to a certain extent) may be of value, but not when it entails the rigid construction of detailed scripts that can hinder the spontaneity and fluency of lessons. Plans are valuable to the extent that they provide organization and direction for the teacher and students in the class; however, they can cause teachers to react rigidly to students and may impede creative responding and learning in the classroom. Simply put, plans need to be thorough but not rigid.

Practical Ideas About Planning

As we have seen, teachers need to plan proactively if they are to be successful in the classroom. There are many different strategies that teachers can use to plan, but we believe that it is best to start with a few simple, straightforward ideas about what you want to accomplish and then later develop more elaborate plans about what you will do at different stages in the lesson. Table 12.10, shows a preliminary planning sheet (Posner, 1985) that provides a framework for organizing the initial questions that you might want to ask as you begin to plan for a particular unit. Subsequently, a more detailed plan (see Table 12.11) could be developed that answers more questions and tries to integrate the learning unit more fully. The initial plan helps you to understand your unit goals. When you examine this plan, you undoubtedly will discover some issues that merit more attention. Ultimately, then, you need to develop a plan that will allow you to respond to these issues. Clearly, any plan must be adapted to a particular situation on a given day, but a plan should provide one with confidence and a good base for teaching a unit. As we have stressed before, mentor teachers can be of considerable benefit to beginning teachers by sharing their planning outlines and discussing how they prepare for teaching.

It is beyond the scope of this book to discuss mentor-beginning teacher relationships in detail (for extended discussions, see Galvez-Hjornevik, 1986). We feel that the idea of providing a mentor who assists is a good one, especially if the mentor is sensitive to the advice presented earlier in this chapter: That is, good mentors allow beginning teachers to structure their own self-improvement plans and help by providing appropriate feedback; mentors are obstacles when they insist (explicitly or implicitly) that beginning teachers teach the way they do or when they fail to realize that beginning teachers legitimately have different concerns than more experienced teachers do.

Zeichner and Tabachnick (1985) note that there are some advantages to the loose supervision of first-year teachers. For example, some of the first-year teachers that they observed were able to maintain their own style—their own perspective despite a differing school philosophy (Tabachnick & Zeichner, 1984). Hence, mentors, supervisors, and principals should offer teachers assistance, but beginning teachers (and student teachers, for that matter) should allowed an independent role in adapting content and designing classroom environments.

Table 12.10 PRELIMINARY PLANNING SHEET

Planning element	Planning question	Preliminary answers (plans)
I. Direction		
1. Activity	What activity do you plan to initiate or lead?	
2. Objectives	What are the students supposed to learn from the activity?	
3. Entry characteristics	What prior skills and understandings do you expect the learners to bring to the lesson?	
II. Specifics (use separate sheet for specifics as necessary)		
4. Content	What specific content will you cover?	
5. Procedures	What specifically will you and the learners do during the activity?	
6. Results	What results do you expect?	
III. Provisions		
7. Resources	What facilities and materials will you and the learners need in order to carry out the activity?	
8. Feedback	How will you and the learners be provided with feedback regarding their progress?	
9. Time	How long will the activity take?	
10. Follow-up	What activities will you assign as a means of extending or reinforcing the lesson?	

Source: Posner, G. (1985). *Field experience: A guide to reflective teaching.* New York: Longman.

**Table 12.11 REFINING PRELIMINARY PLANS: RESOLUTION OF PLANNING
DILEMMAS**

Planning element	Dilemmas	Your resolutions for this lesson
1. Activity	What teacher role does the activity require (e.g., source of information, facilitator, adversary)? One activity for whole class or different activities for different groups? Does the activity entail intrinsic or extrinsic motivation? Does the activity entail passive or active learning? Does the activity entail cooperative, competitive, or individualistic learning?	
2. Objectives	Are there different objectives for different learners or groups of learners? Do the objectives describe observable behaviors or internal processes and states? Is there some mastery level included and how was it determined?	
3. Entry characteristics	Will the learners' prior knowledge and understandings determine groupings? Will differences in learners' backgrounds be ignored, remediated, or compensated? Do you describe the differences in terms of prerequisite skills or prior beliefs and understandings?	
4. Content	For what type of learner is the content directed with regard to level of abstraction, prerequisites, interest, etc.? Does your content outline imply rote or meaningful learning?	
5. Procedures	How will you guide the activity? Through written or spoken instructions? Through imitation? How much help will learners need and how will you distribute access to help? Who determines the procedures? The book? The learners? You? To what extent will you provide for individualization of instruction? And what do you mean by this phrase? Do your procedures focus on observable behaviors or internal operations?	
6. Results	How open ended? How important are correct answers? Are there criteria for acceptable products? What other parameters?	

Table 12.11 *(Continued)*

	What receives more attention: the form or the substance of product/result?
	If form is important, do you emphasize neatness, format, packaging, or what?
	Is the result a product of individual, group, or teacher work?
	Is the result reported by individuals or groups?
	Do learners have to show work in progress, i.e., how they got the results or just final product/answer?
7. Resources	Who chooses materials and how are they chosen? Are there enough materials and facilities for everyone? If not, who and what determines access to them?
	Are materials available for learners at different levels?
	Are the materials primarily manipulative or literary?
8. Feedback	Who provides feedback to learners? The teacher? The answer book? Peers? The situation itself or each learner himself or herself?
	What decisions hinge on feedback to learners? Grades? Revision of products?
	Does feedback to learners serve as reinforcement of self-correction?
	How will you get feedback on your teaching? From test results, products of work, participation in class, nonverbal cues, or what?
9. Time	Who determines pacing? Predetermined by teacher or teacher's guide? By teacher based on a steering group of learners? By learners?
	Will all learners have the same amount of time, or will pace vary?
10. Follow-up	Will follow-up activity be done in class or as homework?
	Will follow-up activity be required or just suggested?
	Will follow-up be literary or manipulative?
	Will it be the same for all learners?
	Will it have right answers or be open-minded?
	How will learners get feedback on it?
	Is its purpose to reinforce or extend the lesson?
	Will all learners have equal access to whatever resources are required for doing the follow-up?

Source: Posner, G. (1985). *Field experience: A guide to reflective teaching.* New York: Longman.

TEACHER EVALUATION

As Wise, Darling-Hammond, McLaughlin, and Bernstein (1985) note, a well-designed teacher evaluation procedure provides an important communication link between the school system and teachers. It achieves this by specifying the conditions of teachers' work and by helping the school system to structure, manage, and reward the work of its teachers.

Clearly, much of the initiative for examining the issues of merit and extra compensation for teachers can be attributed to the National Commission on Excellence in Education's report, *A Nation at Risk: The Imperative for Educational Reform* (1983). For example, this report states that "persons preparing to teach should be required to meet high educational standards, to demonstrate an aptitude for teaching, and to demonstrate competence in an academic discipline. . . . salaries for the teaching profession should be increased and should be professionally competitive, market-sensitive, and performance-based. Salary, promotion, tenure, and retention decisions should be tied to an effective evaluation system that includes peer review so that superior teachers can be rewarded, average ones encouraged, and poor ones either improved or terminated" (p. 30). We will question some of these assumptions later in the chapter.

Wise et al. (1985) studied teacher evaluation practices with an interest in analyzing how teacher evaluation can be used to improve personnel decisions and staff development. Their study began with a review of the literature and a preliminary survey of 32 school districts in order to find districts with highly developed evaluation practices. They discovered that relatively few districts had highly developed teacher evaluation systems and that even fewer used results of evaluation to make personnel decisions or to plan staff development. Most school systems must therefore develop teacher evaluation systems before they can begin to think about innovative personnel practices.

After the initial screening process, Wise et al. selected for intensive analysis four districts that had diverse but effective teacher evaluation systems: Salt Lake City, Utah; Lake Washington, Washington; Greenwich, Connecticut; and Toledo, Ohio. Wise et al. found that despite differences between the evaluation systems, there were four important common features across the four districts: (1) top-level leadership and institutional resources were applied to the evaluation process, (2) evaluators charged with the task of implementing the evaluation system had the necessary expertise to perform their task, (3) administrator-teacher collaboration enabled a common understanding of evaluation goals and processes, and (4) the evaluation process was compatible with the district's overall goals and organizational context. Wise et al. argue that systematic attention to these four factors— organizational commitment, evaluator competence, collaboration, and purposeful compatibility—is essential if evaluation is to be a meaningful process rather than a meaningless ritual. They further note that although these factors are straightforward and self-evident requisites for effective evaluation, they are not easily accomplished and are often overlooked in the pressure that local administrators feel to develop the "perfect" criteria for teacher evaluation. The authors also point out that districts must tailor evaluation systems to their unique circumstances. Still, their general conclusions and recommendations provide a useful means of considering the problems of evaluation.

First, Wise et al. (1985) conclude that *to succeed, a teacher evaluation system must suit the educational goals, management style, conception of teaching, and community values of a school district.* This statement suggests that a school district that values uniformity of instruction and emphasizes standardized testing as the most appropriate way to measure goal attainment should not adopt a teacher evaluation system that allows multiple definitions of teaching success. A district that values multiple outcomes of teaching and learning should not use standardized test scores as the only or even the primary criterion for evaluating teachers. Although these conclusions almost seem self-evident, it is not uncommon to find school districts in which the measure of evaluation differs notably from the official philosophy of the school district.

Second, *administrator and teacher-leader commitment to evaluation is necessary.* Wise et al. stress that successful teacher evaluation systems require that top school administrators and the leaders of the teachers' organizations be committed to evaluation and that the school district allocate resources for evaluation. Too many educators believe that good teacher evaluation requires no more than the "right" checklist. After considering various forms and choosing one, they then discuss relatively minor details and attempt to implement the system. In contrast, Wise et al. found that the *form* and *procedures* of the relatively few successful teacher evaluation systems vary little from those of the less successful systems. What does distinguish successful systems are the seriousness of purpose and the intensity of implementation. Because evaluation is both a difficult and an uncomfortable activity, explicit procedures are required to insure that it receives high priority. Without such district and teacher support, evaluators tend to put evaluation aside for more immediate and perhaps less important activities.

Third, Wise et al. (1985) concluded that *a school district must decide the main purpose of its teacher evaluation system and then match the process to the purpose.* Teacher evaluation can serve many purposes, and a school district may be tempted to try to serve too many goals with one group of evaluators who use a single instrument. For example, the goal of evaluation might be to eliminate incompetent teachers or it might be to reward teachers who are especially innovative in the classroom. It is unlikely that these two goals—and the many other potential goals—could be satisfied with a single instrument. A single teacher evaluation process can serve only one goal well.

Fourth, *to sustain resource commitments and political support, teacher evaluation must be seen as useful, which in turn depends on the efficient use of resources to achieve reliability, validity, and cost-effectiveness.* If an evaluation system is to produce meaningful data, resources must be used to carefully train and select those who implement the system process. Perhaps there are better ways for the district to spend these funds. The cost of evaluation can be determined several ways. For example, the effects of teacher evaluation may be assessed in terms of the cost of terminating an ineffective teacher or the percentage of teachers dismissed because of poor teaching. However, Wise et al. also contend that some of the most important effects may be indirect: Does the community believe that the school district is doing something about incompetent teachers? Does the district have a means of communicating performance expectations to teachers? Are good teachers recognized and encouraged? In the long run, these issues may be more important than the most immediate results of an evaluation system. In our opinion, one of the most important results of an evaluation system concerns whether or not teachers become more aware of resources, including peers, that they can use to analyze and design instruction. That is, does the system enable teachers to obtain information about ways in which they can improve their teaching, and do they find teaching more satisfying and rewarding as a result of the system?

Finally, Wise et al. (1985) conclude that *teacher involvement and responsibility improve the quality of teacher evaluation.* The case studies of Wise et al. provide strong support for the argument that peer review and peer assistance greatly strengthen school districts' capacity to supervise teachers. Teachers who serve in differentiated staff roles give their peers the kind of leadership and assistance that can promote the development of high professional standards and the dissemination of information about various curriculum and instructional issues. They noted that in the four successful school districts, expert teachers provided curricular advice and classroom assistance, and that teachers in general played a more professional role than in districts that controled teachers through bureaucratic channels.

In concluding their case study, Wise et al. argue that the use of expert teachers is the only practical way to give specialized and useful help to teachers who need it. They feel that expert teachers should be selected on the basis of their competence as teachers and their ability as well as their interest in providing supervision and assistance to other teachers. They argue strongly that school districts should involve teachers' organizations in the design, review, and maintenance of teacher evaluation in order to enhance the fairness and effectiveness of the process. However, they note that peer review shifts the teacher's and administration's role from an adversarial to a participatory one. This shift increases not only teachers' rights but also their responsibilities. It mandates that administrators share power but also gives administrators more freedom and authority to implement decisions once they are jointly made.

Wise et al. (1985) contend that quality control through the enforcement of a professional standard of practice differs from quality control that is obtained through prescribed curricula and standardized testing. Both approaches contain risks. Namely, a standardized definition of good teaching and explicit recommendations for how teachers ought to teach make teaching less attractive, which in turn lowers the quality of the teaching force. This, in turn, causes school districts to become even more prescriptive in their attempts to monitor teachers' behavior. On the other hand, the professional approach depends on teachers' judgments and places more importance on the development of teacher-responsive practices than on the definition of standardized practice. In time, such a system eliminates teachers who are unable or unwilling to develop competence instead of controlling their damage by specific standards through practice.

In arguing for the professional approach, Wise et al. summarize their case: "It assumes that others will become more capable by engaging in the joint construction of goals, definition of standards of good practice, mutual criticism, and commitment to ongoing inquiry. It supposes that investing in staff development, career incentives, and evaluation (i.e., in teachers themselves) will improve the quality of teaching. . . . we recommend, therefore, that: the school district should hold teachers accountable to standards of practice that compel them to make appropriate instructional decisions on behalf of their students" (p. 119).

In Tables 12.12 and 12.13 and Figs. 12.3 and 12.4, the reader can find the evaluation devices that were used in the four successful school districts that Wise et al. studied. Recall, however, that the evaluation forms successful school districts used did not differ notably from forms used by less successful school districts. Rather, the intensity and integrity of the process were important.

We agree with Dillon-Peterson (1986), who argues that administrators need to trust teachers to know what is good for them and to allow teachers to have more opportunity for planning and evaluating in-service programs. Similarly, we suspect that teachers can assume more responsibility for self-growth and for self-evaluation when given appropriate training, support, and time. Although administrators have considerable responsibility for teacher evaluation, we believe that effective administrators will involve teachers in this process and will use their professional knowledge to good advantage.

DO LOOK BACK

The intent of this chapter is to encourage teachers to look at their classroom behavior and to plan ways to make instruction more meaningful and exciting. Stress

Table 12.12   SALT LAKE TEACHERS ASSOCIATION TEACHER EVAULATION CRITERIA

1. Determines standards of expected student performance
   a. Preassessment (diagnosis)
   b. Competencies expected at a given level
   c. Determine individual needs
   d. Expected goals for student achievement
   e. Evaluation of goals
2. Provides learning environment
   a. Availability of resources personnel
   b. Availability of variety of resource materials
   c. Physical organization and learning process
   d. Positive attitude toward students
   e. All students can learn
   f. Teacher shows enthusiasm and commitment for the subject taught
   g. Student behavior demonstrates acceptance of learning experience
3. Demonstrates appropriate student control
   a. Evidence that student knows what to do
   b. Evidence that student is working at task
   c. Evidence of positive responses from students because of adults' demonstration of fairness, acceptance, respect, flexibility, etc.
   d. Appropriate control in crisis
   e. Anticipate and avoid crisis
4. Demonstrates appropriate strategies for teaching
   a. Demonstrates techniques that are appropriate to different levels of learning
   b. Adjusts techniques to different learning styles
   c. Uses variety of techniques to teach specific skill or concept
   d. Gives directions that are clear, concise, and appropriate to the student learning level
   e. Establishes two-way communication with students and utilizes feedback to determine teaching strategies
   f. Demonstrates a purpose has been determined for the instruction

Source: Wise et al. (1985). Teacher evaluation: A study of effective practices. *Elementary School Journal, 86,* 61–119.

Table 12.13 GREENWICH GUIDELINES FOR PROFESSIONAL PERFORMANCE

I. Professional competence
  A. Classroom instruction
    1. Shows good extent and quality of basic preparation
    2. Exhibits knowledge that is current
    3. Shows evidence of planning and good organization
    4. Recognizes differences in capacities and interests of students
    5. Uses instructional techniques that are current, resourceful, and challenging
    6. Enriches the daily program through a variety of interests
    7. Conducts class with poise and self-assurance
    8. Makes a sound evaluation of each student, using reliable tools of measurement
    9. Conducts activities consistent with and supportive of the school system's philosophy
  B. Human relationships
    1. Shows understanding, interest, and concern for students' emotional, social, and physical characteristics
    2. Develops in students a respect for learning
    3. Develops in students a consideration of the rights, feelings, and ideas of others
    4. Achieves pupil control through wise and careful guidance
    5. Works cooperatively with other staff members
    6. Recognizes and respects individual differences among staff members
    7. Communicates with parents
    8. Interprets educational programs, procedures, and plans to the public

    9. Shows an awareness of community activities
    10. Respects the confidential nature of professional information
    11. Recognizes the effect of personal appearance on the learning environment
    12. Functions in a controlled and effective manner under pressure
II. Professional attitudes
  A. Growth
    1. Avails self of opportunities to improve professionally
    2. Keeps abreast of the professional literature and current methodology
    3. Seeks assistance when needed
    4. Accepts and uses constructive suggestions
    5. Shares techniques and pertinent materials with other teachers
    6. Recognizes strengths and limitations
  B. Responsibilities
    1. Accepts responsibilities
    2. Knows and uses channels of authority
    3. Meets obligations (promptly and thoroughly)
    4. Speaks and writes clearly and accurately
    5. Maintains, within reasonable limits, physical and mental health needed to meet professional responsibilities
    6. Has mature understanding of own and others' problems
    7. Seeks to understand different sides of a question
    8. Seeks facts before reaching conclusions
    9. Conducts self in an ethical manner

Source: Wise et al. (1985). Teacher evaluation: A study of effective practices. *Elementary School Journal, 86,* 61–119.

has been placed on the fact that objective, improvement-oriented self-evaluation is difficult for many of us to engage in because we have not been trained to do it. Any significant new experience is always a challenge, and self-evaluation is no exception. Your first efforts to examine your own behavior openly will be difficult and perhaps frustrating. However, such analysis, if it is attempted one step at a time and linked to strategies for improving behavior, will lead to self-growth and the satisfaction that accompanies becoming more effective.

This book was written to encourage you to examine your behavior and to assume responsibility for your development. Observation forms and materials are included in the book to help you assess your behavior and plan new instructional strategies, but ultimately you and only you can evaluate the effects of your teaching. Do not avoid your responsibility by uncritically accepting someone else's advice or teaching philosophy.

Remember, a teaching strategy is good when two basic conditions are satisfied: (1) students learn the material they are supposed to master and (2) find the learning process so interesting and enjoyable that they initiate efforts on their own and can progressively assume more responsibility for planning and evaluating their work.

It is up to you to identify teaching behaviors that meet these criteria and to combine them into a teaching style with which you feel so comfortable that you look forward to class and to teaching. You are the teacher, and *you* must assume responsibility for establishing a learning atmosphere that is stimulating and exciting for yourself as well as for your students. If you do not enjoy class, your students will not either!

SUMMARY

In this chapter, we have urged readers to assess their strengths and weaknesses as teachers by collecting objective information on their classroom behavior and its effects on students. A good way to begin is to consider the concepts and guidelines presented throughout this book, listing those that you use effectively, those that need work or are untried, and those about which you ned more information. The latter
can be reduced by arranging to obtain feedback. Teachers can collect feedback about some behaviors by keeping records, consulting their students, or arranging to be audiotaped or videotaped. For many behaviors, however, it will be necessary to arrange to be observed by someone (typically, a principal, supervisor, or fellow teacher) who agrees to visit the classroom and conduct focused observation designed to obtain objective information about the behaviors of interest to the teacher.

Observational feedback is also important in providing teachers with information about the effects of behaviors they are trying for the first time and about their improvement in areas that need work. Suggestions are offered for enlisting the help of teacher centers and principals in self-improvement efforts and, in particular, for working with teachers in cooperative self-help groups. The group approach is likely to be especially valuable if each teacher sets individual priorities and goals, focuses on a few behaviors at a time, and receives balanced and honest feedback. Self-help programs following these guidelines have been popular with teachers and effective

Preobservation Conference Date _____

Teacher Objective				

Observation Date _____	Satisfactory	Needs Improvement	Unsatisfactory	COMMENTS
Criterion 1. Instructional Skill	----	----	----	
1.1 Plans instruction				
1.1.1 Identifies the learning needs				
1.1.2 Teaches the curriculum				
1.1.3 Develops plans				
1.2 Implements the planned objectives/experiences				
1.2.1 Gives clear instruction				
1.2.2 Assist student to develop work habits and study skills				
1.2.3 Gives assistance	----	----	----	
Criterion 2. Classroom Management	----	----	----	
2.1 Develop classroom procedures				
2.2 Organizes the physical setting				
2.3 Prepares materials				
2.4 Exercises care for physical safety and mental health of students	----	----	----	
2.5 Maintains records appropriate to level/subject				
2.6 Maintains records as required by law, District and building				
2.7 Organizes individual small group, or large group learning experiences	----	----	----	

Figure 12.3 Lake Washington School District No. 414 evaluation of certified teachers: evaluative criteria checklist. [*Source*: Wise et al. (1985). Teacher evaluation: A study of effective practices. *Elementary School Journal, 86*, 61–119.]

Criterion 3. The Handling of Student Discipline and Attendant Problems	----	----	----	
3.2 Follows disciplinary procedures				
3.2 Encourages self-discipline				
3.3 Recognizes conditions, develops and implements strategies				
3.4 Makes known to student clear parameters for pupil conduct				
3.5 Deals consistently and fairly with student(s)				
3.6 Enlists assistance	----	----	----	
Criterion 4. Interest in Teaching Pupils	----	----	----	
4.1 Develops rapport with students				
4.2 Recognizes the unique characteristics of each student				
4.3 Guides learning	----	----	----	
Criterion 5. Effort Toward Improvement When Needed	----	----	----	
5.1 Continually assesses self				
5.2 Acknowledges recommendations	----	----	----	
Criterion 6. Knowledge of Subject Matter	----	----	----	
6.1 Keeps abreast of new developments and ideas				
6.2 Relates subject matter to general body of knowledge	----	----	----	
Criterion 7. Professional Preparation and Scholarship	----	----	----	
7.1 Possesses and maintains academic background				

Signature of Evaluator	Date	Signature of Person Being Evaluated	Date

(Both signatures are required. Signing of this instrument acknowledges participation in, but not necessarily concurrence with, evaluation conference.)

Provide a copy of this report to the employee.

Figure 12.3 *(Continued)*

TEACHER SUMMARY EVALUATION REPORT

Name _____ School _____ Date _____

Grade or
Subject _____

Period of
Sept-Dec ☐

Period of
Jan-March ☐

Amount of time spent in observation _____

Check on March and Dec Report	Check on March Report Only	Contract Status
☐ Outstanding	☐ Recommended for second one-year contract	☐ First-year contract
	☐ Recommended for initial four-year contract	☐ Second-year contract
☐ Satisfactory	☐ Recommended for third one-year contract	☐ Four year-contract
☐ Unsatisfactory	☐ Not recommended for reappointment	☐ One year-contract
		☐ Continuing contract

	Out-standing	Satis-factory	Unsatis-factory
I. TEACHING PROCEDURES			
A. Skill in planning			
B. Assessment and evaluation skills			
C. Resourceful use of instructional material			
D. Skill in using motivating techniques			
E. Skill in questioning techniques			
F. Skill in making assignments			
G. Ability to recognize and provide for individual differences			
H. Skill in developing good work-study habits			
I. Voice quality			
II. CLASSROOM MANAGEMENT			
A. Effective classroom facilitation and control			
B. Effective interaction with pupils			
C. Efficient classroom routine			
III. KNOWLEDGE OF SUBJECT			
IV. PERSONAL CHARACTERISTICS AND PROFESSIONAL RESPONSIBILITY			
A. Shows a genuine interest in teaching			
B. Appropriate interaction with pupils			
C. Is reasonable, fair and impartial in dealing with students			
D. Personal appearance			
E. Skill in adapting to change			
F. Adheres to accepted policies and procedures of the Toledo Public Schools			
G. Accepts responsibility both inside and outside the classroom			
H. Has a cooperative approach toward parents and school personnel			
I. Is punctual			

Evaluator's Signature   Teacher's Signature   Principal's Signature

Evaluator's Position

Date of Conference _____

(See opposite side of page for directions)

Figure 12.4 Toledo evaluation forms: (*a*) teacher summary evaluation report; (*b*) four-year cointract evaluation report. [*Source:* Wise et al. (1985). Teacher evaluation: A study of effective practices. *Elementary School Journal, 86,* 61–119.]

```
┌─────────────────────────────────────────────────────────────────┐
│                                                                   │
│              FOUR-YEAR CONTRACT EVALUATION FORM                   │
│                                                                   │
│  All teachers serving in their fourth year of a four-year limited │
│  contract will be evaluated. A copy of the completed evaluation   │
│  form must be on file in the Office of Personnel, room 102 on or  │
│  before March 15, 1983. The following teacher is employed under a │
│  limited contract which expires June, 1983                        │
│                                                                   │
│  Name _____   School _____    │
│  Grade/Subject _____    Date _____    │
│                                                                   │
│    I. TEACHING TECHNIQUES          High              Low          │
│       Includes planning and        ┌─┬─┬─┬─┬─┬─┬─┐                 │
│       organizing; skill in         └─┴─┴─┴─┴─┴─┴─┘                 │
│       presenting subject; ability                                 │
│       to motivate; recognition of                                 │
│       individual differences; and                                 │
│       ability to develop good work                                │
│       habits and attitudes, etc.                                  │
│                                                                   │
│   II. CLASSROOM CONTROL            High              Low          │
│       Includes rapport with pupils; ┌─┬─┬─┬─┬─┬─┬─┐                │
│       respect for rules; atmosphere └─┴─┴─┴─┴─┴─┴─┘               │
│       for learning; and efficient                                 │
│       routines, etc.                                              │
│                                                                   │
│  III. KNOWLEDGE OF SUBJECT         High              Low          │
│                                    ┌─┬─┬─┬─┬─┬─┬─┐                 │
│                                    └─┴─┴─┴─┴─┴─┴─┘                 │
│                                                                   │
│   IV. PERSONAL CHARACTERISTICS     High              Low          │
│       Includes responsibility,     ┌─┬─┬─┬─┬─┬─┬─┐                 │
│       dependability, interest,     └─┴─┴─┴─┴─┴─┴─┘                 │
│       enthusiasm, effective speech,                               │
│       personal appearance, health                                 │
│       and emotional stability.                                    │
│                                                                   │
│       (If necessary, use reverse side for additional comments.)   │
│  ─────────────────────────────────────────────────────────────── │
│  RECOMMENDED FOR A FOUR          YES _____  NO _____          │
│  YEAR CONTRACT                                                    │
│                                                                   │
│  _____    _____     │
│       Teacher's signature             Principal's signature       │
│                                                                   │
│  Copy to: Executive Director                                      │
│           School Office                                           │
│           Teacher                                                 │
│           Office of Personnel                                     │
│                                                                   │
│  48                                                               │
│  intrv. 2/81                                                      │
└─────────────────────────────────────────────────────────────────┘
```

Figure 12.4 *(Continued)*

in helping them to increase their awareness of and control over their classroom behavior. We have also argued that it is appropriate that at least a part of a school district's in-service program be organized around the needs of individual teachers and designed to promote professional satisfaction and growth.

Finally, we have discussed three current trends that affect teachers: master teacher programs, beginning teacher induction programs, and increased involvement of teachers in evaluating other teachers.

SUGGESTED ACTIVITIES AND QUESTIONS

12.1. Make a list of all books and ideas that you want to explore in the near future. Please do not limit your selection to materials listed in this text. Rank the three things you most want to learn. This will serve as your in-service map. Compare your notes with other teachers' and if you have similar interests, share material and collectively urge the principal to design in-service programs that will satisfy these needs.

12.2. Make a list of your teaching strengths and weaknesses. Make specific plans to improve your two weakest areas.

12.3. Read the cases in the Appendix and see if you can pinpoint the teaching strengths and weaknesses that appear there. Compare your ratings with those made by others.

12.4. What are the possible advantages and disadvantages of using parents or retired but capable adults as observers to supply teachers with information about their behavior?

12.5. Why is it difficult for most of us to engage in self-evaluation?

12.6. Why do teachers benefit more from critical but specific prescriptive feedback than they do from vague positive feedback?

12.7. How can the school principal facilitate the development of effective in-service programs?

12.8. How can teachers initiate self-improvement programs?

12.9. Should young teachers seek advice from veteran teachers? If so, under what circumstances and in what manner?

12.10. As a teacher, how can you help your students to develop skills and attitudes for examining their own work nondefensively?

12.11. What are some of the dangers involved in having teachers evaluate other teachers? What are the advantages of peer evaluation?

12.12. What are your views about master teachers? What criteria are most important for teachers to satisfy if they are to become master teachers? What percentage of teachers should be able to become master teachers—only a few or most? Why do you feel this way?

12.13. Reread the narrative that appears at the end of Chapter 1. If this teacher were a member of your self-study team, what advice would you offer? Be specific.

12.14. What is the role of research in defining effective teaching? Can teachers be effective in one school district and not in another? How likely is it that teachers might vary in effectiveness because districts use different evaluative criteria?

12.15. We have stressed the need for you to seek evaluative comments and to analyze your behavior if you are to grow and to improve. In that spirit, we seek your evaluative comments about this book. We would like to know how useful it is from your perspective and about any deficiencies it may have that can be remedied in future editions. We encourage you to write us (Tom Good, College of Education, University of Missouri-Columbia; Jere Brophy, College of Education, Michigan State University-East Lansing) with your comments and suggestions (What was your general reaction to the book? Is it relevant to teachers and future teachers? What topics are omitted that you feel should be in future editions? What advice or suggestions did you disagree with, and why? Did we communicate negative expectations or provide contradictory advice, and if so, where and how? Were there sections of the book that you found to be especially helpful, and why?). We will be delighted to receive your suggestions and criticisms, and your comments will be given serious consideration when a new edition of this book is written.

REFERENCES

Anderson, C. (1983). The causal structure of situations: The generation of plausible causal attributions as a function of the type of event situation. *Journal of Experimental Social Psychology, 19,* 185–203.

Anderson, L., & Prawat, L. (1983). Responsibility in the classroom: A synthesis of research on teaching self-control. *Educational Leadership, 12,* 343–356.

Anderson, R., Hiebert, E., Scott, J., & Wilkinson, I. (1985). *Becoming a nation of readers: The report of the Commission on Reading.* Washington, DC: National Institute of Education.

Ascione, F., & Borg, W. (1980). Effects of a training program on teacher behavior and handicapped children's self-concepts. *Journal of Psychology, 104,* 53–65.

Bergmann, C., Bernath, L., Hohmann, I., Krieger, R., Mendel, G., & Theobald, G. (1976). *Schwierigkeiten fuer junger Lehrer in der Berufspraxis.* Giessen: Zentrum fuer Lehrerausbildung der Justus Liegig-Universitaet.

Biddle, B., & Anderson, D. (1986). Theory, methods, knowledge, and research on teaching. In M. Wittrock (Ed.), *Handbook of research on teaching* (3rd ed.). New York: Macmillan.

Borg, W., & Ascione, F. (1982). Classroom management in elementary mainstreaming classrooms. *Journal of Educational Psychology, 74,* 85–95.

Borko, H., & Niles, J. (In press). Descriptions of teacher planning: Ideas for teachers and researchers. In V. Koehler (Ed.), *Educators' handbook: A research perspective.* New York: Longman.

Bradford, D. (1986). The metropolitan teaching effectiveness cadre. *Educational Leadership, 43,* 53–55.

Broeders, A. (1980). *Beginnende leerkrachten: Werksituatie en arbeidssatisfactie.* Doctoraalscriptie. Instituut voor Onderwijskunde, K. U. Nijmegen.

Brophy, J., & Good, T. (1986). Teacher behavior and student achievement. In M. Wittrock (Ed.), *Handbook of research on teaching* (3rd ed.). New York: Macmillan.

Brophy, J., & Good, T. (1970). The Brophy-Good dyadic interaction system. In A. Simon & E. Boyer (Eds.), *Mirrors for behavior: An anthology of observation instruments continued.* 1970 Supplement (Vols. A and B). Philadelphia: Research for Better Schools, Inc.

Caldwell, S. (1985). The master teacher as staff developer. *Elementary School Journal, 86,* 55–60.

Clark, C., & Peterson, P. (1986). Teachers' thought processes. In M. Wittrock (Ed.), *Handbook of research on teaching* (3rd ed.). New York: Macmillan.

Copeland, W., & Jamgoschian, R. (1985). Colleague training and peer review. *Journal of Teacher Education, 36,* 18–21.

Darling-Hammond, L., & Wise, A. (1985). Beyond standardization: State standards and school improvement. *Elementary School Journal, 85,* 315–336.

De Bevoise, W. (1986). Collaboration: Some principles of Bridgework. *Educational Leadership, 43,* 9–12.

deVoss, G., & Dibella, R. (1981). *Follow-up of 1979–80 graduates at the Ohio State University's College of Education Teacher Certification Program*. Columbus: Ohio State University, College of Education.

Deal, T. (1985). The symbolism of effective schools. *Elementary School Journal, 85*, 601–620.

Dillon-Peterson, B. (1986). Trusting teachers to know what is good for them. In K. Zumwalt (Ed.), *Improving teaching*. Alexandria, VA: ASCD Yearbook.

Doyle, W. (1985). Effective teaching and the concept of master teacher. *Elementary School Journal, 86*, 27–34.

Doyle, W. (1984). How is order achieved in classrooms: An interim report. *Journal of Curriculum Studies, 16*, 259–277.

Doyle, W. (1983). How order is achieved in classrooms. Paper presented at the annual meeting of the American Educational Research Association, Montreal, Canada.

Dunkin, M., & Biddle, B. (1974). *The study of teaching*. New York: Holt, Rinehart and Winston.

Dwyer, D., Lee, G., Rowan, B., & Bossert, S. (1982). *The principal's role in instructional management: Five participant observation studies of principals in action*. San Francisco: Far West Laboratory.

Eash, M., & Rasher, S. (1977). Mandated desegregation and improved achievement: Longitudinal study. *Phi Delta Kappan, 58*, 394–397.

Edmonds, E., & Bessai, F. (1979). *First class: A survey of Canadian teachers in their first year of service*. Charlottetown: University of Prince Edward Island.

Feiman, S. (1977). Evaluating teacher centers. *School Review, 85*, 395–411.

Fenstermacher, G., & Berliner, D. (1985). Determining the value of staff development. *Elementary School Journal, 85*, 281–314.

Fogarty, J., Wang, M., & Creek, R. (1982). A descriptive study of experienced and novice teachers' interactive instructional decision process. Paper presented at the annual meeting of the American Educational Research Association, New York.

Fuller, F. (1969). Concerns of teachers: A developmental conceptualization. *American Educational Research Journal, 6*, 207–226.

Fuller, F., & Bown, O. (1975). Becoming a teacher. In K. Ryan (Ed.), *Teacher education. (Seventy-fourth Yearbook of the National Society for the Study of Education)*. Chicago: University of Chicago Press.

Galvez-Hjornevik, C. (1986). Mentoring among teachers: A review of the literature. *Journal of Teacher Education, 37*, 6–11.

Glassberg, S. (1980). A view of the beginning teacher from a developmental perspective. Paper presented at the annual meeting of the American Educational Research Association, Boston.

Good, T., Biddle, B., & Brophy, J. (1975). *Teachers make a difference*. New York: Holt, Rinehart and Winston.

Good, T., & Brophy, J. (1986). School effects. In M. Wittrock (Ed.), *Handbook of research on teaching* (3rd ed.). New York: Macmillan.

Good, T., & Brophy, J. (1974). Changing teacher and student behavior: An empirical investigation. *Journal of Educational Psychology, 66*, 390–405.

Good, T., & Weinstein, R. (1986). Teacher expectations: A framework for exploring classrooms. In K. Zumwalt (Ed.), *Improving teaching*. 1986 ASCD Yearbook. Alexandria, VA: Association for Supervision and curriculum development..

Griffin, G. (1985). The school as a workplace and the master teacher concept. *Elementary School Journal, 86*, 1–16.

Guild, P., & Garger, S. (1985). *Marching to different drummers*. Alexandria, VA: Association for Supervision and Curriculum Development.

Hoffman, J., Edward, S., O'Neal, F., Barnes, S., & Paulissen, M. (1986). A study of state-mandated beginning teacher programs. *Journal of Teacher Education, 37,* 16–21.

Huffman, G., & Leak, F. (1986). Beginning teachers' perceptions of mentors. *Journal of Teacher Education, 37,* 22–25.

Huling-Austin, L. (1986). What can and cannot reasonably be expected from teacher induction programs. *Journal of Teacher Education, 37,* 2–5.

Huling-Austin, L. (1985). *The low budget/almost no budget approach to interactive research and development: An implementation game plan.* Austin, TX: Research and Development Center for Teacher Education.

Huling-Austin, L., & Emmer, E. (1985). *First days of school: A good beginning.* Report No. 7206. Austin: University of Texas, Research and Development Center for Teacher Education.

Hunt, D., & Joyce, B. (1981). Teacher trainee personality and initial teaching style. In B. Joyce, C. Brown, & L. Peck (Eds.), *Flexibility in teaching.* New York: Longman.

Joyce, B. (1981). A memorandum for the future. In B. Dillon-Peterson (Ed.), *Staff development/organization development.* Alexandria, VA: Association for Supervision and Curriculum Development.

Kepler, K. (1977). Descriptive feedback: Increasing teacher awareness, adopting research techniques. Paper presented at the annual meeting of the American Educational Research Association, New York.

Lanier, J. (1986). Research on teacher education (with J. Little). In M. Wittrock (Ed.), *Handbook of research on teaching* (3rd ed.). New York: Macmillan.

Lieberman, A. (1986). Collaborative research: Working with, not working on . . . *Educational Leadership, 43,* 28–33.

Little, J. (1982). Norms of collegiality and experimentation: Workplace conditions of school success. *American Educational Research Journal, 19,* 325–340.

Little, J. (1981). School success and staff development in urban desegregated schools: A summary of recently completed research. Paper presented at the annual meeting of the American Educational Research Association, Los Angeles.

Martin, M. (1973). *Equal opportunity in the classroom.* ESEA, Title III: Session A Report. Los Angeles: County Superintendent of Schools, Division of Compensatory and Intergroup Programs.

Marwood, L., McMullen, F., & Murray, D. (1986). Learnball league: Teacher-to-teacher staff development. *Educational Leadership, 43,* 56–59.

McDaniel, T. (1981). The supervisors' lot: Dilemmas by the dozen. *Educational Leadership, 38,* 518–520.

McDonnell, L. (1985). Implementing low-cost school improvement strategies. *Elementary School Journal, 85,* 423–438.

Mitman, A., Mergendoller, J., Packer, M., & Marchman, V. (1984). *Scientific literacy in seventh-grade life science: A study of perceptions and learning outcomes. Final Report.* San Francisco: Far West Laboratory for Education Research and Development..

Moore, J., & Schaut, J. (1975). An evaluation of the effects of conceptually appropriate feedback on teacher and student behavior. Paper presented at the Association for Teacher Education Conference, New Orleans.

Moskowitz, G., & Hayman, J. (1974). Interaction patterns of first-year, typical, and "best" teachers in inner-city schools. *Journal of Educational Research, 67,* 224–230.

National Commission on Excellence in Education. (1983). *A Nation at Risk: The imperative for educational reform.* Washington, DC: National Institute of Education.

National Education Association. (June 1983). Statement by the National Education Association on excellence in education. Paper presented to the House Budget Committee Task Force on Education and Employment, Washington, DC.

Nelson, B. (1986). Collaboration for colleagueship: A program in support of teachers. *Educational Leadership, 43,* 50–52.

Pambookian, H. (1976). Discrepancy between instructor and student evaluation of instruction: Effect on instruction. *Instructional Science, 5,* 63–75.

Pearson, D., Barr, R., Kamil, M., & Mosenthal, P. (Eds.) (1984). *Handbook of reading research.* New York: Longman.

Posner, G. (1985). *Field experience: A guide to reflective teaching.* New York: Longman.

Purkey, S., & Smith, M. (1985). School reform: The district policy implications of the effective schools literature. *Elementary School Journal, 85,* 353–390.

Purkey, S., & Smith, M. (1983). Effective schools: A review. *Elementary School Journal, 83,* 427–452.

Rodriguez, S., & Johnstone, K. (1986). Staff development through a collegial support group model. In K. Zumwalt (Ed.), *Improving teaching.* 1986 ASCD Yearbook. Alexandria, VA.

Rohrkemper, M. (1981). *Classroom perspective study: An investigation of differential perceptions of classroom events.* Unpublished doctoral dissertation. East Lansing: Michigan State University.

Rowan, B., Bossert, S., & Dwyer, D. (1983). Research on effective schools: A cautionary note. *Educational Researcher, 12,* 24–31.

Rutter, M., Maughan, B., Mortimore, P., Ouston, J., & Smith, A. (1979). *Fifteen thousand hours: Secondary schools and their effects on children.* Cambridge, MA: Harvard University Press.

Schlechty, P., & Vance, B. (1983). Recruitment, selection, and retention: The shape of the teaching force. *Elementary School Journal, 83,* 469–487.

Schmuck, P. (1986). Networking: A new word, a different game. *Educational Leadership, 43,* 60–61.

Shulman, L. (1986). Paradigms and research programs in the study of teaching: A contemporary perspective. In M. Wittrock (Ed.). *Handbook of research on teaching* (3rd ed.). New York: Macmillan.

Shulman, L. (1983). Autonomy and obligation: The remote control of teaching. In L. Shulman & G. Sykes (Eds.), *Handbook of teaching and policy.* New York: Longman.

Shulman, L, & Sykes, G. (Eds.), (1983). *Handbook of teaching and policy.* New York: Longman.

Slavin, R. (1983). *Cooperative learning.* New York: Longman.

Spencer, D. (1984). The home and school lives of women teachers: Implications for staff development. *Elementary School Journal, 84,* 299–314.

Sprinthall, N., & Thies-Sprinthall, L. (1983). The teacher as an adult learner: A cognitive-developmental view. In G. A. Griffin (Ed.), *Staff development. (Eighty-second Yearbook of the National Society for the Study of Education.)* Chicago: University of Chicago Press.

Stallings, J. (1986). Using time effectively: A self-analytic approach. In K. Zumwalt (Ed.), *Improving teaching.* 1986 ASCD Yearbook. Alexandria, VA.

Tabachnick, R., & Zeichner, K. (1984). The impact of the student teaching experience on the development of teacher perspectives. *Journal of Teacher Education, 35,* 28–36.

Taylor, C. (1970). The expectations of Pygmalion's creators. *Educational Leadership, 28,* 161–164.

Tisher, R., Fyfield, J., & Taylor, S. (1979). *Beginning to teach: The induction of beginning teachers in Australia* (Vols. 1 and 2). Canberra: Australian Government Publishing Service.

Tyler, R. (1950). *Basic principles of curriculum and instruction.* Chicago: University of Chicago Press.

Veenman, S. (1984). Perceived problems of beginning teachers. *Review of Educational Research, 54*(2), 143–178.

Weinstein, R. (1983). Student perceptions of schooling. *Elementary School Journal, 83,* 287–312.

What works: Research about teaching and learning. (1986). Washington, DC: U.S. Department of Education, Office of Educational Research and Improvement.

Wise, A., Darling-Hammond, L., McLaughlin, M., & Bernstein, H. (1985). Teacher evaluation: A study of effective practices. *Elementary School Journal, 86,* 61–119.

Witkin, H., Moore, C., Goodenough, D., & Cox, P. (1977). Field-dependent and field-independent cognitive styles and their educational implications. *Review of Educational Research, 47,* 1–64.

Wittrock, M. (1986). Students' thought processes. In M. Wittrock (Ed.), *Handbook or research on teaching* (3rd ed.). New York: Macmillan.

Yinger, R. (1977). A study of teacher planning: Description and theory development using ethnographies and information processing methods. Unpublished dissertation. East Lansing: Michigan State University.

Zeichner, K., & Tabachnick, R. (1985). The development of teacher perspectives: Social strategies and institutional control in the socialization of beginning teachers. *Journal of Education for Teachers, 7,* 1–25.

Zumwalt, K. (Ed.). (1986). *Improving teaching.* Alexandria, VA: ASCD Yearbook, 1986.

Zumwalt, K. (1985). The master teacher concept: Implications for teacher education. *Elementary School Journal, 86,* 45–54.

Practice
Examples

This Appendix includes six brief examples of classroom life in elementary school and junior and senior high schools.[1] These fictional case studies will give you an opportunity to apply the material you have mastered in this book. Try to identify the teaching strengths and weaknesses that appear in the episodes that follow and to suggest alternative ways in which the teacher could have behaved to improve the class discussion. Then compare your insights with those of your classmates.

EXAMPLE 1

Charles Kerr had done his student teaching at the high school level; in college he majored in social studies and physical education. He accepted a position as a seventh-grade teacher (and coach of the seventh-grade basketball and football teams) temporarily while waiting for an opening on the coaching staff in the high schools. He teaches in a predominantly middle-class school and he has good social rapport with his students.

> TEACHER: Class, today we are going to talk about the upcoming presidential election. The actual election is not for a whole year, but some individuals, senators mainly, have already announced themselves as candidates. Tom, tell me why people like the senators from Maine and Ohio have said they are going to run for President this soon.
>
> TOM: Because they don't want the President to stay in office any more.
>
> TEACHER: A lot of people don't want that, but they aren't running; there's a good reason you haven't thought of yet; try again.
>
> TOM: I don't know; I don't care much about the election.

[1] We acknowledge the capable assistance of Kathy Paredes in preparing the first draft version of some of the examples.

EXAMPLE 1   **589**

TEACHER: Well, you should care; it won't be too long before you can vote and you need to be aware. Susanne, what reason can you come up with?

SUSANNE: Maybe people don't know them very well.

TEACHER: That's right. They need the advance publicity. Brian, what kind of elections are held in each state before the general election?

BRIAN: Preliminary?

TEACHER: The word's primary—but that was close enough. Craig, who can run in the primary?

CRAIG: Republicans and Democrats.

TEACHER: And that's it? Suppose I wanted to run and I'm neither one of those mentioned, then what?

BRIAN: You couldn't do it.

TEACHER: (*Impatiently*) Jane, stop shuffling your feet that way—do you think I could run for President if I wanted?

JANE: I suppose so.

TEACHER: You don't sound very definite in your opinion; be decisive and tell me yes or no.

JANE: Yes!

TEACHER: All right—don't be wishy-washy in your opinions. Now, Tony, who would you like to see run for President?

TONY: The mayor of New York.

TEACHER: How about you, Janette?

JANETTE: The honorable senator from Texas.

TEACHER: Why?

JANETTE: Because he's attractive and colorful.

TEACHER: (*Sarcastically*) Girls don't think logically sometimes. Bobby, could you give me a more intelligent reason than Janette?

BOBBY: Because he has had lots of experience.

TEACHER: In my opinion, I don't think that counts for much, but at least you are thinking along the right lines. Danny, what will be a major issue in this campaign?

DANNY: Crime.

TEACHER: (*With a loud, urgent voice*) Crime is always an issue; there's something else you should concern yourself about as an issue; I'll give you another chance.

BARBARA: (*Calling out*) Won't the economy be an issue?

TEACHER: I'll ask the questions, Barbara, and you think of some good answers! Danny, have you thought of it yet?

DANNY: Probably the economy and foreign policy.

TEACHER: Certainly. Rob, since you have been doing so much commenting to everyone around you back there, tell me, should we fight other people's wars? What should our foreign policy be with respect to small wars?

ROB: If they need the help and can't defend themselves.

TEACHER: Does that really sound sensible to you? Do you want to go to some distant part of the world and get killed?

ROB: No, but I don't think we should let other powers move in and take what they want either.

TEACHER: Of course not, but I don't think we should get involved in foreign affairs to the point of war and you shouldn't listen to anybody who tells you we should. Back to the issues: We decided the war should be over and that we should get out no matter what the cost; there are a few more issues you might hear a lot about. Yes, Margaret?

MARGARET: Don't you think the war is just about over now and will be by the election?

TEACHER: No, I don't; if I did think so, I wouldn't have brought it up here; pay attention! We only have eight minutes more before the bell rings and then you can do what you want to do. Pay attention to the discussion and quit moving around. Now let's get back to my question. Tim?

TIM: There aren't enough jobs for everyone.

TEACHER: No, there aren't. I wanted to teach high school, but there are already too many of those teachers; so don't decide to be a high school teacher because there may not be a job for you.

CONNIE: You mean I shouldn't become a teacher?

TEACHER: I would consider something else where there might be more job openings. What I would like you to do is find some resource material that will tell you more about the elections and what we can expect in the way of candidates and issues. John, when we go to the library where might you look to find this information?

JOHN: Magazines.

TEACHER: Yes, which ones?

JOHN: *Time, Newsweek.*

TEACHER: Good, where else, Leslie?

LESLIE: Newspapers.

TEACHER: Which ones?

LESLIE: Local newspapers.

TEACHER: You had better go farther than that. Why should you look at more than one newspaper, Mike?

MIKE: Our paper might not have anything in it about elections.

TEACHER: No. The reason is that different papers have various views of the candidates. I want you to have two different viewpoints in your papers. Now, I want you to write a good paper on what we have discussed today, using reliable resources. If you have forgotten the style you are to use, get out the instruction sheet I gave you a few weeks ago and follow it point by point. Tomorrow you are going to defend your positions to the class. The class will attempt to refute your arguments. So write them carefully or else your poor logic will embarrass you.

EXAMPLE 2

Linda Law is teaching for a second year at Thornton Junior High School. The students at Thornton come from upper middle-class homes and Linda teaches social studies to the brightest group of ninth-grade students. Today she is deviating from her normal lesson plans in order to discuss the Tasaday tribe that resides in the Philippine Rain Forest.

TEACHER: Class, yesterday I told you that we would postpone our scheduled small-group work so that we could discuss the Tasadays. Two or three days ago Charles mentioned the Tasadays as an example of persons who were isolated from society. Most of you had never heard of the Tasadays but were anxious to have more information, so yesterday I gave you a basic fact sheet and a few review questions to think about. I'm interested in discussing this material with you and discussing questions that you want to raise. It's amazing! Just think, a Stone Age tribe in today's world. What an exciting opportunity to learn about the way people used to live! Joan, I want you to start the discussion by sharing with the class what you thought was the most intriguing fact uncovered.

EXAMPLE 2   **591**

JOAN: (*In a shy, shaky voice*) Oh, that they had never fought with other tribes or among themselves. Here we are, modern people, and we fight continuously and often for silly reasons.

SID: (*Breaking in*) Yeah, I agree with Joannie; that is remarkable. You know, we have talked about human's aggressive nature, and this finding suggests that perhaps it isn't so.

SALLY: (*Calling out*) You know, Sid, that's an interesting point!

TEACHER: Why is that an interesting point, Sally?

SALLY: (*Looks at the floor and remains silent*)

TEACHER: Why do you think these people don't fight, Sally?

SALLY: (*Remains silent*)

TEACHER: Sally, do they have any reason to fight?

SALLY: No, I guess not. All their needs . . . you know, food and clothing, can be found in the forest and they can make their own tools.

TEACHER: Yes, Sally, I think those are good reasons. Class, does anyone else want to add anything on this particular point? (*She calls on Ron, who has his hand up.*)

RON: You know what I think it is that makes the difference, well, my dad says it is money. He says that if these Tasadays find out about money, there will be greed, corruption, and war, all in short order.

TEACHER: Ron, can you explain in more detail why money would lead to deterioration in life there?

RON: (*With enthusiasm*) Well, because now there's no direct competition. It's people against nature and what one person does is no loss to another.

TONY: (*Calling out*) Not if food or something is in short supply!

TEACHER: Tony, that's a good point, but please wait until Ron finishes his remarks. Go ahead, Ron.

RON: Well, money might lead to specialization and some people would build huts and others would hunt and exchange their wares for money, and eventually they would want more money to buy more things and competition would lead to aggressive behavior.

TEACHER: Thank you, Ron, that's an interesting answer. Now, Tony, do you want to add anything else?

TONY: No, nothing except that Ron's making a lot of generalizations that aren't supported. You know, the Tasadays might have specialized labor forces. Now there's nothing in the article I read about this.

TEACHER: That's good thinking, Tony. Class, how could we find out if the Tasadays have a specialized labor force?

MARY: (*Called on by the teacher*) Well, we could write a letter to Dr. Fox, the chief anthropologist at the National Museum, and ask him.

TEACHER: Excellent, Mary. Would you write a letter tonight and tomorrow read it to the class and then we'll send it.

MARY: Okay. (*The teacher notices Bill and Sandra whispering in a back corner of the room and as she asks the next question, she walks halfway down the aisle. They stop talking.*)

TEACHER: What dangers do the Tasadays face now that they have been discovered?

TOM: (*Calling out*) I think the biggest problem they face will be the threat of loggers, who are clearing the forest, and the less primitive tribes, who have been driven farther into the forest by the loggers.

TEACHER: Why is this a problem, Tom?

TOM: Well, they might destroy the tribe. You know, these less primitive tribes might attack or enslave the Tasadays.

TEACHER: Okay, Tom. Let's see if there are other opinions. Sam, what do you think about Tom's answer?

SAM: Well, I do think that those other natives and the loggers are threats, but personally I feel that the Tasadays' real danger is sickness. Remember how, I think it was on Easter Island, natives were wiped out by diseases that they had no immunity to. I think they might be wiped out in an epidemic.

TEACHER: What kind of an epidemic, Sam?

SAM: Well, it could be anything, TB, you know, anything.

TEACHER: Class, what do you think? If an epidemic occurred, what disease would most likely be involved?

CLASS: (*No response*)

TEACHER: Okay, class, let's write this question down in our notebooks and find an answer tomorrow. I'm stumped, too, so I'll look for the answer tonight as part of my homework. I'm going to allow ten minutes more for this discussion, and then we'll have to stop for lunch. I wish we had more time to discuss this topic; perhaps we can spend more time tomorrow. In the last ten minutes, I'd like to discuss your questions. What are they? Call them out and I'll write them on the board.

ARLENE: I was surprised that the oldest of these people were in their middle forties and the average height was only five feet. It looks like living an active outdoor life, they would be healthy and big. What's wrong with their diet?

MARY JANE: I'm interested in a lot of their superstitious behavior. For example, why do they feel that to have white teeth is to be like an animal?

EXAMPLE 3

Mrs. Jackson taught school for two years, in 1970–1971, then retired to rear a family. Now that her children are older, she has decided to return to the classroom and has received a teaching position in a large city school. Her third-grade class is composed of equal numbers of black, Oriental, Mexican-American, and Anglo children whose parents work but are still very involved in the school's activities. Previously, Mrs. Jackson had taught in an upper-middle-class school, and although she had adapted her lesson plans to the changes in curriculum, she had not expected to have to change her approach to teaching since children, their behavior, and their needs remain pretty much the same over the years. Today, she is reviewing multiplication tables with the class, working with everyone the first 20 minutes, and then dividing the children into four groups to complete their assigned independent work. The teacher sits with one group and helps them with their lesson.

TEACHER: Today, children, let's review our 8 and 9 times tables; whichever group can give me all the answers perfectly will be able to use the math games during independent work instead of having to do the exercises in the book. John, what is 8×9?

JOHN: 72.

TEACHER: Tim, 8×0?

TIM: 8.

TEACHER: Wrong, tell me what 8×1 is?

TIM: 8.

TEACHER: Yes, now you should know what 8×0 is.

TIM: (*No response*)

EXAMPLE 3   **593**

TEACHER: Tim lost the contest for group 3.

JAN: (*Calls out*) Why didn't you ask me, I know the answer!

TEACHER: I'm glad that you do, so you can teach Tim and your group will win next time. I'm going to ask Terri what 8 × 2 is.

TERRI: 16.

TEACHER: Mark, what is 8 × 4?

MARK: 32.

TEACHER: Lynn, 8 × 6?

LYNN: 48.

TEACHER: Judy, 8 × 10?

JUDY: 56. No. Wait a minute. (*Teacher pauses and gives her time to come up with another answer.*) It's 80, isn't it?

TEACHER: Yes, it is. Jeff, give me the correct answer to this one, and your group will have a perfect score; what is 8 × 11?

JEFF: (*Thinks a minute and Carrie, from another group, calls out.*)

CARRIE: 88!

TEACHER: Carrie, it was not your turn and now I'm not going to give your group a chance to win. I'm sure Jeff knew the answer and so his group has done the best so far. Now, Linda, let's see how well your group will do; what is 9 × 3?

LINDA: 28. No! 27.

TEACHER: Are you sure?

LINDA: I think so.

TEACHER: You must be positive; either it is 27 or it isn't. Class?

CLASS: Yes!

TEACHER: All right, Chuck, you don't seem to be listening so I will ask you the next one. What is 9 × 6?

CHUCK: (*Counting on his fingers silently*)

TEACHER: We haven't got time to wait for you to get the answer that way and that's not the way I taught you to do multiplication. Let's see if your friend Bobby can do better.

BOBBY: (*Looks at Marilyn without giving any response.*)

TEACHER: Marilyn is not going to give you the answer; this was something you were supposed to learn for homework last night. Did you do it?

BOBBY: Yes.

TEACHER: Well, since you did the work, you should be able to answer my question. Again, what is 9 × 6?

BOBBY: I can't remember.

TEACHER: Marilyn, do you know?

MARILYN: 56?

TEACHER: (*Exasperated*) For as many times as we have done these tables, I don't know why you can't learn them. I think this group will have to go back and do some work in the second-grade math book until they are ready to learn what everybody else is doing. (*Class laughs.*) Now, let's look at our chart here and everyone together will recite the tables twice. (*Class reads down the chart.*)

TEACHER: I have written the pages and directions for each group on the board. Terri, your group may get the games out because you know your tables. Matthew, read me what your group is to do.

MATTHEW: "Find the products (*Matt falters on word, teacher gives it to him*) and factors" (*Doesn't know word*).

TEACHER: How can you expect to do the work if you can't read the directions? I guess

I had better read it. Now does everyone understand? (*No comment from group*) All right, go to work, and I don't want any interruptions while I'm working with Tim's group. Chuck, you get out the second-grade books and start on the pages that I have written up here. I'm sure you understand what all of you have to do.

TEACHER: Will the monitors pass out paper? John, if you don't think you can do the job without chatting with your friends, you had better give the papers to someone else. Elaine and Mike, I like the way you are sitting—ready to go to work! Let's see how quietly we can all do our work today. (*With group 3*)

TEACHER: Carrie, you're a good thinker, do this problem on the board for me. (*Carrie does it correctly.*)

TEACHER: That's good. Darryl, you try this one—(2 × 3) × 6. (*Darryl works it out.*)

TEACHER: I'll finish it for you and then tell me what I did to get the answer. [*Writes (2 × 6) × 3.*]

DARRYL: You just changed the parentheses.

TEACHER: Will I get the same answer? (*Chorus: "Yes!"*) Paula, you make up a problem of your own and Ted will figure it out. (*She does.*)

TED: What is 7 × 4?

TEACHER: Ted, we just went all through this; now do the best you can. (*Ted does and gets the wrong answer.*)

TEACHER: I guess Paula will have to do it herself. Tonight I'm going to give you extra homework so that you will know this type of problem perfectly.

EXAMPLE 4

Matt Davidson teaches American literature at a predominantly middle-class high school. The seniors in his class at Windsor Hills have been doing some concentrated study of Mark Twain's writings. They are of above-average intelligence and have previously read two other novels by Twain.

TEACHER: Class, I know I didn't give you as much time to read *The Adventures of Huckleberry Finn* as we might ordinarily take; however, since you are familiar with Twain's style, his settings, and characters, I knew you would be able to grasp the content and motives in the story without much trouble. *Huckleberry Finn* is considered to be a classic today, a real artistic work of fiction. Stylistically, why is this book considered to be a masterpiece, John?

JOHN: He used a setting in Missouri and adapted the narrative to the dialects common to that place and time.

TEACHER: Good. Was there one dialect only?

JOHN: No, I think maybe there were two.

TEACHER: Actually, there were several—Huck and Tom's, Jim's, Aunt Sally's, and others. Dialect was a necessary ingredient in the fiction of the time. What sets the mood, what gives the structure to the story?

TERRI: (*Calling out*) The time.

TEACHER: Could be, to a small extent, but not what I had in mind, Terri. Where is the setting?

TERRI: St. Petersburg, Missouri. (*Teacher notices Matt drawing on a piece of paper and looks at him as Terri responds. When Matt looks up, the teacher catches his eye and Matt puts away his paper.*)

TEACHER: All right. Could Twain have taken Huck to Phoenix, Arizona, and related the story exactly the same? How about that, Tim?

EXAMPLE 4   **595**

TIM: I guess not; there's no Mississippi River in Phoenix.

TEACHER: Exactly. Develop that thought further, Tim—keep in mind the author himself.

TIM: Twain grew up in Hannibal and he probably saw much of what he wrote about.

TEACHER: You're right there. Did you want to add something, Melissa?

MELISSA: The story is probably semiautobiographical, then, with a few names and places changed.

TEACHER: Yes, I think so too.

MARK: (*Calling out*) There probably weren't any slaves in Phoenix, either, so Jim might have not been in the story.

LARRY: (*Calling out*) There might have been.

TEACHER: I think Mark is pretty close to the truth in what he said, Larry, but that's something for you to look into. So locale is important. Now, what is the book about—is it just about a boy going down the river, Lynne?

LYNNE: It's an adventure story.

TEACHER: Could you lend a little more depth of thought to your answer? Is it just a comedy?

LYNNE: A thoughtful one.

ED: (*Calling out*) It has a more serious element—satire.

TEACHER: I don't think we've discussed satire and I'm glad you brought it up. What is your definition of satire?

ED: Well, for instance, Aunt Sally and Aunt Polly always pretended to be so virtuous and Christianlike, but they were willing to sell Jim back into slavery. Huck wanted to get away from all the hypocrisy and fraud.

TEACHER: Very good! But Huck had a hard time coping with this. What one particular quality or emotion did Huck have, as opposed to say, Tom, Linda?

LINDA: (*Reading her book*) He was smarter?

TEACHER: That's not so much a quality—this is something he feels.

DUANE: (*Calling out*) Sad, about the way people treat each other.

TEACHER: That's more what I was looking for, Linda. He was sensitive. Whom was he most sensitive about, Carol?

CAROL: Tom, I guess.

TEACHER: Oh, no. He accepted Tom for what he was—a foolish little kid. The story revolves around Huck and one other person. Who, Bobby?

BOBBY: It was Jim. Huck knew slavery was wrong and was disturbed by it. Mr. Davidson, was slavery over yet?

TEACHER: No, this takes place in 1850, and slaves were not emancipated until the end of the Civil War in 1865. Your answer is correct. The way Tom treated Jim always hurt his feelings; that hurt Huck, too. Chris, did Jim reciprocate this treatment toward the boys by being cruel in some manner?

CHRIS: I think he did.

TEACHER: Give me an instance.

CHRIS: (*No response*)

TEACHER: Can you remember anything Jim did on the raft?

CHRIS: (*No response*)

TEACHER: Did you read the book?

CHRIS: No.

TEACHER: I think it's important you read it and I'm sure you will find it very captivating. Susann, who is the most admirable character?

SUSANN: Jim, because he was always loyal and dedicated to Huck no matter what.

GERRY: (*Calling out*) No, I think it was Huck because he was always wrestling with his conscience and knew things were wrong.

TEACHER: Both answers are correct and show good reasoning. There is never one necessarily right answer when discussing literature—it's a matter of your interpretation as you read it and see it. Who are the villains? Kevin?

KEVIN: The most obvious are the Duke and the Dauphin.

TEACHER: Why, Leslie?

LESLIE: (*Rustling through the pages*)

TEACHER: You don't need to look it up; just give me your impression of their characters.

LESLIE: They pretended to be royalty and Shakespearean actors, but they really lied and cheated people out of their money.

TEACHER: Right. Huck's father was something of a villain, and the Grangerfords and Shepherdsons were certainly not the most upstanding citizens. Turn to page 254 and read this short passage with me. I think this pretty well summarizes Huck's feelings: "But I reckon I got to light out for the territory ahead of the rest, because Aunt Sally she's going to adopt me and civilize me, and I can't stand it. I been there before."

TEACHER: A very important concept is contained here. Who can discover what it is? Yes, Marilyn?

MARILYN: He doesn't want to have any part of fancy clothing, going to school or church, or eating off a plate.

TEACHER: Yes, he wants his freedom. Let's do a little deeper analysis of Huck's character. I'm going to put some questions on the board and you tell me as best you can what Huck really thought about the Grangerfords, about slavery, about the Duke and Dauphin, and so forth. How did he confront and deal with these people?

EXAMPLE 5

Joan Maxwell has been teaching the first grade for seven years in a small rural community school. Her students are children of primarily farm and ranch workers of lower-middle-class background. Joan and her husband both received their degrees from a large university and now operate a lucrative business in the area. Joan is introducing a science lesson today; it's late fall and the children have been asked to bring in some leaves to show changes in leaf colors from season to season. The class has previously discussed seasonal changes and what weather patterns occur during these times.

TEACHER: Boys and girls, let's first review what we talked about last week when we were writing our stories about different seasons.

SHARI: (*Calling out*) Do we have to do this? Why can't we do something fun instead of doing something we don't like?

TEACHER: We can't always do things we enjoy. Carol, do you remember how many seasons we have in a year?

CAROL: Three.

TEACHER: No, we wrote more stories than just three-think for a minute.

CAROL: Four.

TEACHER: All right, now can you name them for me?

CAROL: Fall, winter, summer . . .

TEACHER: Didn't you write four stories?

CAROL: I don't remember.

TEACHER: (*Forcefully, and with some irritation*) You may have to go back and write them again. Who knows the fourth season? Can somebody in my special Cardinal group respond? John, you answer.

EXAMPLE 5   **597**

JOHN: Fall, winter, spring, and summer.

TEACHER: Good thinking! It helps us to remember seasons sometimes if we think about important holidays that come during them. Tim, in what season does Christmas come?

TIM: (*No response*)

TEACHER: You weren't listening. I want you to put those leaves in your desk and not touch them again till it's time. Cory, when does Christmas come?

CORY: In the winter.

TEACHER: How do you know it's winter, Mark?

MARK: Because of the snow and ice and rain . . .

TEACHER: Does it snow here?

MARK: No.

TEACHER: How do you know it's winter, then?

MARK: (*No response*)

MARY: (*Calling out*) It snows at Christmas where I used to live.

TEACHER: Mary, if you have something to say, will you please raise your hand? (*She does.*) Now what did you say?

MARY: Where I used to live it did snow, but not anymore.

TEACHER: Right! In some places it does snow and not others. Clarence, why wouldn't it snow here?

CLARENCE: Because it's too warm?

TEACHER: It's not warm here! I told you this before a couple of times. (*Turns to Tim*) I asked you once before to put those away and you can't seem to keep your hands on the desk, so I'm going to take them away from you and when we do our project you will have to sit and watch! Don't anyone else do what Tim did. Now, let's talk more about the fall season and get some good ideas for our story. What is another word for the fall season? Lynne?

LYNNE: Halloween.

TEACHER: I didn't ask you to give me a holiday, a word.

LYNNE: I can't think of it.

TEACHER: I'm going to write it on the board and see if Bobby can pronounce it for me.

BOBBY: (*No response*)

TEACHER: This is a big word, Bobby. I'll help you.

JUDY: (*Calling out*) Autumn!

TEACHER: (*Turns to Judy*) Is your name Bobby?

JUDY: No.

TEACHER: Then don't take other children's turns. Now, Bobby, say the word. (*He does.*) I think this is a good word to write in your dictionaries. Get them out and let's do it now.

JANE: I don't have a pencil.

TEACHER: That is something you are supposed to take care of yourself. Borrow one or stay in at recess and write it then. Let's look at these pictures of leaves as they look in the fall and spring. Mary Kay, can you tell me one thing that is different about these two pictures?

MARY KAY: The leaves are different colors.

TEACHER: Good. Tell me some of the colors.

MARY KAY: In spring, they are bright green.

TEACHER: Right. Joe, how about the other ones?

JOE: They are brown and orange and purple.

TEACHER: I don't see any purple—you've got your colors mixed up. Tony?

TONY: It's more red.

TEACHER: Yes. Steve, we are finished writing in our dictionaries; put it away. You can finish at recess with Jane. Some people in our class are very slow writers. Take out your leaves now. Mark, how does that leaf feel in your hand?

MARK: It feels dry and rough like old bread. (*Class laughs.*)

TEACHER: Don't be silly! How did it get so dry? Marilyn?

MARILYN: It fell off the tree.

TEACHER: Yes, a leaf needs the tree to stay alive. Is that right, Dave?

DAVE: You could put it in water and it would stay alive.

TEACHER: Not for long. Martha, what else can you tell me about these leaves?

MARTHA: I don't have one.

TEACHER: I don't know what to do about children who can't remember their homework assignments. You will never be good students if you don't think about these things. Mike, what do you see in the leaves?

MIKE: Lines running through.

TEACHER: We call those lines *veins*. Are all leaves the same shape?

MIKE: No, my leaf came from a sycamore tree and it has soft corners, not sharp ones.

TEACHER: That's good. I think you will be able to write an interesting story. Two holidays come during the fall; who can name one? Terri?

TERRI: Halloween.

TEACHER: That's one; Jeff, do you know another?

JEFF: (*No response*)

TEACHER: It comes in November and we have a school holiday.

JEFF: Easter?

TEACHER: No, that is in the spring; we have turkey for dinner this day.

CHORUS: Thanksgiving.

TEACHER: Now, do you remember, Jeff? I would like you to write about Thanksgiving in your story; then you won't forget again. Now we are ready to put on the board the vocabulary words that we will use for our story and pictures. (*Teacher notices Shari, Jim, and Rick exchanging their books but she ignores their misbehavior.*)

TEACHER: Ed, you come up here and Sally come up here and help me print our vocabulary words on the board. Ed, you print these four words (*Hands him a list*) and Sally, you print these four (*Hands her a second list*).

TEACHER: What are you kids doing in that corner? Shari, Rick, Jim, Terri, Kim stop fighting over those books. (*All the children in the class turn to look at them.*)

RICK: Mrs. Maxwell, it's all Kim's fault.

KIM: It is not. I wasn't doing anything. Shari, Rick, and Jim have been fooling around but I've been trying to listen.

TEACHER: Quiet down, all of you. You all stay in for recess and we'll discuss it then.

KIM: Not me!

TEACHER: Yes, all of you.

KIM: (*Mutters to her friend.*) It's not fair.

TEACHER: Kim, what did you say?

KIM: Nothing.

TEACHER: That's more like it.

TEACHER: Okay, Ed, put your words up.

ED: I've lost the list. . . . (*Class roars with laughter.*)

EXAMPLE 6   **599**

EXAMPLE 6

Judy Burden is in her sixth year of teaching at Owensboro High School. She teaches in a high school that serves the entire community of 30,000. Although the high school has a full range of students, one of her courses, Advanced Consumer Education, is a special course for honors students.

Read the dialogue that follows and try to identify aspects of the discussion that the teacher may not have been aware of. What strengths and weaknesses do you see in the teaching?

MRS. BURDEN: As you know after writing papers on inflation, maintaining purchasing power is a key concept of any investment program. Last week we discussed insurance and savings programs—the "safety valves" of our programs. This week we want to discuss two potential investment sources that offer greater growth potential and greater risk. These two, as you know, are stocks and real estate. During the next two periods we will discuss stocks, and then we will spend two days on real estate. On Friday you will begin drawing up your individual investment portfolios. Eventually, you will each "invest" $10,000 in stocks. I hope that during the college years you can keep track of your "paper" investments and periodically buy and sell. I hope the exercise will be useful not only in teaching you the language and mechanics of investing but also in helping you to develop a personal investment philosophy and an awareness of the risks that investing involves. Let's review some of the basic concepts in your reading material before we start using them. Ted, define the price-earning ratio concept.

TED: That's easy. It's essentially the amount investors are willing to pay for earnings. If stock X is paying a higher dividend than stock Y and both are the same price, the price-to-earnings ratio for stock Y would be higher. People buying stock Y would believe its future payoff would be better than that of stock X.

MRS. BURDEN: Ralph, what does Ted mean when he says future payoff?

RALPH: Stocks have two forms of payoff: dividend interest and capital gains. He's talking about capital gains.

MRS. BURDEN: Rick, define capital gains.

RICK: I'm not sure of a precise definition. It's basically the rate of return on your investment.

MRS. BURDEN: (*With some irritation*) You should read the material more closely, Rick.

FRANK: (*Interrupting*) I know, Mrs. Burden.

MRS. BURDEN: Okay, Frank, tell us.

FRANK: It's the percentage of the principal amount employed to obtain a profit. If, for example, I buy stock in Headache Cure, Inc., at $100 per share and sell it for $150, my capital gain would be 50 percent.

MRS. BURDEN: That's okay as far as you go, Frank, but that might be misleading. For example, if you held the stock for 2 months and sold it for $150 it would be fantastic, but if you held the stock for 18 years and sold it for $150 it would be considerably less attractive. Ted, how could you take this into account?

TED: (*Looks at the floor and shrugs his shoulders.*)

MRS. BURDEN: Alice, can you help Ted out?

ALICE: I'm not sure how to do it. But I can see why it would be important to do so.

MRS. BURDEN: Can anyone tell me how to do this? (*Scans the room for 15 seconds and continues.*) Well, the trick is that you must figure the *annual* rate of yield, not just the yield. Reread this in your test, and tomorrow be sure that you can calculate an annual rate of yield on an investment. Okay, let's go on. Rick, what problems does one have in determining the value of a common stock?

RICK: Lots! There simply isn't any way to build a solid base for valuation. Let's go back to the capital gain question. I've put my thoughts in order now. There's an old saying on Wall Street that a stock is worth ten times current earnings. And based on all stocks, this figure proves to be an acceptable figure for the market as a whole. But it is grossly inadequate for individual stocks.

MRS. BURDEN: You're right, Rick, you can't use rule-of-thumb for valuing an individual stock. The fact that stocks are basically worth ten times their earning power isn't useful for picking stocks. Sometimes stocks are worth twenty or thirty times their present earning power. But what can you do to estimate the value of a stock? Ralph, what are some ways that occur to you?

RALPH: Well, one way is to compare the price-earnings ratios for stocks of other companies in the same industry.

MRS. BURDEN: Okay, that's one way. Ted, how about another way?

TED: Stable earnings are worth more than unstable earnings.

MRS. BURDEN: Right, Ted! Frank, what does Ted mean by stable earnings?

FRANK: (*Looks at the floor.*)

MRS. BURDEN: Better read the book tonight, Frank. Also, tonight I want everyone to read the paper and find the ten highest priced stocks. Now let's continue. Mary, how do you figure a reasonable rate of return for an investment? . . .

Name Index

Abadzi, H., 406
Abelson, H., 370
Ackerson, G., 477
Adams, G., 129
Adams, R., 29, 30, 49
Addington, J., 378
Ahlbrand, W., 29
Airasian, P., 127
Aitkin, M., 378
Alexander, K., 406, 407
Alexander, L., 334
Alhajri, A., 30, 49
Alleman-Brooks, J., 31
Allen, V., 443
Allington, R., 128, 140
Amarel, M., 370
Amato, J., 128
Ames, C., 237, 307, 321, 441
Ames, R., 237, 307
Ames, W., 477
Anderson, A., 237
Anderson, C., 222, 497, 536
Anderson, D., 523
Anderson, H., 226
Anderson, K., 364
Anderson, L., 2, 31, 177, 220, 222, 239, 244, 246,
    354, 355, 359, 463, 466, 475, 481, 486, 556
Anderson, R., 247, 417, 529
Anderson, T., 118, 131, 337, 502
Anderson-Levitt, K., 27, 62
Andre, M., 502
Anshutz, R., 494
Anttonen, R., 119, 127
Archer, P., 127
Arlin, M., 357, 359, 366, 380
Armbruster, B., 337
Arnold, D., 494
Arons, A., 370
Aronson, E., 435
Ascione, F., 223, 226, 542
Ashton, P., 141
Atwood, R., 494
Ausubel, D., 334, 477, 480

Babad, E., 129, 138
Baker, F., 336
Ballard, K., 290
Bandura, A., 174, 176, 218, 269, 311, 312, 313
Bangert, R., 364

Bar-Eli, N., 444
Barger, S., 127
Barker-Lunn, J., 406
Barnes, S., 562
Baron, R., 127, 128, 129
Barr, R., 529
Barth, R., 374, 379
Bash, M., 291
Baum, M., 239
Becker, H., 43, 45, 370
Beckerman, T., 407
Beeken, D., 379
Beery, R., 503
Beez, W., 118, 129
Bellack, A., 239
Benevento, A., 143
Bennett, N., 377, 378
Bereiter, C., 474, 475, 479
Bergmann, C., 561
Berliner, D., 34, 35, 360, 367, 372, 480, 481, 550
Bernstein, H., 571
Bessai, F., 562
Bettencourt, E., 332
Biddle, B., 29, 30, 49, 238, 486, 523, 529, 532
Biehler, R., 381
Bierman, M., 407
Birch, J., 366
Blakey, M., 128, 129
Blanck, P., 129
Blaney, N., 435
Blank, M., 284
Block, J., 355, 356, 359
Bloom, B., 352, 354, 355, 359
Blotner, R., 314
Blumenfeld, P., 34, 92, 134, 239, 308
Bognar, C., 127
Bolen, D., 143
Boles, K., 27, 47
Bolmeier, E., 411
Bond, R., 143
Book, C., 336, 502
Borg, W., 28, 29, 223, 226, 542
Borko, H., 127, 142, 566, 567
Born, D., 362
Bossert, J., 33, 136
Bossert, S., 555, 557
Bowers, K., 129
Bown, O., 562
Bozsik, B., 128, 140

Bradford, D., 546
Bransford, J., 505
Brattesani, K., 131, 135, 137
Braun, C., 118, 127
Brewer, H., 226
Brickman, P., 143
Briggs, L., 355
Brody, N., 129
Broeders, A., 562
Brookover, W., 142, 143, 239
Brophy, J., 14, 27, 28, 29, 30, 31, 32, 33, 34, 37,
    38, 43, 75, 84, 97, 118, 121, 124, 126, 127,
    128, 129, 130, 131, 136, 137, 138, 140, 141,
    143, 144, 147, 189, 193, 195, 197, 219, 222,
    226, 234, 238, 239, 241, 244, 268, 273, 276,
    284, 307, 328, 332, 336, 412, 461, 463, 466,
    470, 471, 473, 486, 488, 494, 495, 501, 529,
    532, 541, 542, 551, 552
Brown, A., 336, 502
Brubaker, N., 31
Bryan, J., 174
Bryan, M., 406, 414
Buchmann, M., 36
Buenning, M., 313
Burkhart, R., 47
Burnham, J., 118
Burns, R., 355, 356
Burstein, L., 69
Buss, A., 356
Butcher, R., 127
Butkowsky, I., 312
Button, C., 129

Cahen, L., 129
Caldwell, J., 35, 127
Caldwell, S., 550, 560, 561
Cameron, A., 312
Camp, B., 291
Capie, W., 332, 493
Carew, J., 31, 195
Carlson, D., 366
Carmichael, K., 362
Carrier, C., 337
Carroll, John, 354
Carter, K., 41, 42
Case, R., 475
Cazden, C., 415, 416
Chaffin, J., 411
Chaikin, A., 129
Chambers, J., 237, 322
Channon, G., 27
Chase, C., 62
Claiborn, W., 118
Clark, C., 10, 566
Clark, R., 372, 427
Clements, B., 222, 223, 224, 230
Coates, T., 59
Cohen, A., 129
Cohen, P., 443
Collins, A., 482, 483
Condry, J., 237, 322
Conn, L., 131
Cook, M., 407
Cooke, B., 422
Cooper, H., 32, 33, 56, 116, 117, 118, 119, 127,
    128, 129, 131, 133, 136, 138, 142, 311
Coopersmith, S., 380

Copeland, W., 526
Corlis, C., 378, 379
Cornbleth, C., 129
Corno, L., 231, 307, 314, 467, 503
Costin, F., 479
Covington, M., 323, 503
Cox, P., 539
Cox, W., 356, 357
Crano, W., 135
Craske, M., 317
Crawford, J., 239, 412
Creek, R., 562
Cronbach, L., 372
Cross, D., 336, 501
Cruickshank, D., 478
Cuban, L., 29, 353, 361, 381
Cullian, L., 438
Cyert, R., 506

Dar, Y., 408
Darley, J., 131
Darling-Hammond, L., 551, 571
Darracott, C., 129
Davidson, W., 239
Davis, M., 362
Davis, O., 128, 129
Davis, R., 370, 481
Day, B., 377, 378
Deal, T., 551
deBono, E., 507
De Bevoise, W., 546
deCharms, R., 312
Deci, E., 237, 307, 322
Dembo, M., 41
Derlega, V., 129
DeSessa, A., 370
DeTure, L., 493
Devin-Sheehan, L., 443
Devine, T., 507
DeVoss, G., 562
DeVries, D., 435
Dibella, R., 562
Diener, D., 336
Dillon, J., 483, 484, 486, 495
Dillon-Peterson, B., 574
Dinkmeyer, D., 201
Dollar, B., 383, 385, 386
Dolnick, M., 290
Dornbusch, S., 47, 128, 239
Douglas, J., 407
Douglas, V., 290
Doyle, W., 1, 2, 18, 41, 42, 106, 119, 134, 177,
    216, 217, 219, 250, 323, 372, 557, 560
Drabman, R., 289
Dreeben, R., 418
Duffy, G., 31, 148, 336, 502
Dunkin, M., 238, 486, 529
Dunn, T., 356
Durkin, D., 29
Dusek, J., 118, 127
Dweck, C., 134, 138, 239, 311, 312, 317, 336
Dwyer, D., 555, 557

Eash, M., 539
Ebmeier, H., 29, 34, 179, 463
Eccles, J., 34, 126, 134, 138, 309
Eden, D., 236

Eder, D., 140, 261, 416, 417
Edmonds, E., 562
Edmonds, R., 143
Edward, S., 562
Edwards, K., 435
Egan, O., 127
Ehman, L., 56
Elawar, M., 314
Elliott, E., 134, 138, 311, 312, 317
Ellis, S., 445
Elstein, A., 506
Emmer, E., 2, 18, 28, 29, 69, 89, 106, 177, 220,
    222, 223, 224, 226, 229, 230, 231, 419, 472,
    564, 565
Emmons, B., 143
Engel, M., 33, 46
Engelmann, S., 474
Enna, B., 239
Epstein, J., 43, 45
Erickson, F., 60, 98
Erlwanger, S., 373
Espinosa, R., 128
Esposito, D., 406
Evans, J., 408, 420, 423
Everhart, R., 366, 372
Evertson, C., 2, 18, 29, 60, 61, 69, 70, 92, 110,
    111, 138, 141, 142, 148, 177, 220, 222, 223,
    224, 225, 226, 230, 234, 239, 244, 273, 372,
    407, 419, 461, 463, 466, 470, 471, 472, 473,
    486, 488

Fagan, E., 494
Fanelli, G., 183
Farley, F., 380
Farley, J., 143
Farmer, W., 313
Fazio, R., 131
Feather, N., 308
Featherstone, J., 374
Feiman, S., 549
Feldman, R., 443
Felker, D., 441
Felmlee, D., 261, 416
Fennema, E., 33
Fennessey, G., 435
Fenstermacher, G., 550
Fernandez, C., 128
Feuerstein, R., 508
Findley, M., 32
Findley, W., 406, 414
Finley, M., 142, 407
Finn, J., 129
Firestone, G., 129
Fisher, C., 35, 233, 234, 378, 471, 473, 474
Fisher, K., 370
Flanagan, J., 363
Flavell, J., 179
Fleming, E., 119, 127
Florio, S., 39, 98, 99
Flowers, A., 411
Fogarty, J., 444, 445, 562
Fowler, J., 317
Francis, W., 312
Frankiewicz, R., 334
Freedman, S., 27, 47
Freeman, D., 37
Friedman, L., 357

Frieze, I., 312
Fry, P., 378
Fuller, F., 49, 562
Furst, N., 478, 480, 486
Fyfield, J., 562

Gage, N., 480, 481
Gagné, R., 355, 475
Gall, M., 332
Galvez-Hjornevik, C., 565, 567
Gambrell, L., 233, 332
Gamoran, A., 416
Gantt, W., 233
Ganzell, S., 289
Garger, S., 539, 540
Garson, C., 290
Gates, S., 356, 357
Gearhart, B., 412
Gennari, P., 366, 367
Germano, M., 365
Gertzog, W., 496
Gillett, M., 332
Given, B., 129
Glaser, R., 360, 363
Glassberg, S., 562
Glasser, W., 266, 267, 268, 291, 292, 296
Glynn, E., 289
Glynn, T., 290
Goetz, J., 96, 98
Goff, S., 309
Goldberg, M., 406
Goldenberg, C., 124, 125
Good, T., 14, 28, 29, 32, 33, 35, 43, 56, 57, 75, 84,
    97, 116, 117, 118, 121, 126, 127, 128, 129,
    130, 131, 134, 136, 137, 140, 142, 143, 179,
    195, 219, 244, 247, 284, 307, 332, 336, 372,
    374, 406, 407, 412, 423, 427, 429, 461, 462,
    463, 466, 467, 474, 486, 494, 495, 501, 529,
    532, 541, 542, 551, 552
Goodenough, D., 534
Gooding, C., 332, 493
Goodlad, J., 353
Goodman, J., 290
Gordon, T., 266, 268
Gottfried, A., 328
Grabe, M., 317
Graeber, A., 35
Graham, S., 128, 129, 134
Grant, L., 33, 34
Grapko, M., 380
Gray, R., 377, 379
Graybeal, S., 437
Green, J., 60, 61, 69, 70, 92, 110, 111, 461
Greenberg, H., 62
Greene, D., 237, 307, 322
Greeno, J., 356
Greenough, W., 479
Greenwood, G., 57
Griffin, G., 47, 48, 56, 558, 560
Grinder, R., 352, 353, 361
Groisser, P., 487, 489, 492
Gronlund, N., 355
Grouws, D., 29, 179, 244, 374, 462, 463,
    474
Grusec, J., 143
Guild, P., 539, 540
Gump, P., 378, 379

Gump, T., 74, 106
Guskey, T., 356, 357

Haertel, G., 377
Haller, E., 416
Hallinan, M., 415, 416, 417
Hambleton, R., 364
Hancock, G., 119
Handley, J., 33, 34
Hanesian, H., 334
Hannon, P., 371
Hansen, J., 501
Hanson, A., 312, 336
Hanusa, B., 312
Harter, S., 470
Haskett, M., 140
Haskins, R., 140
Hassler, D., 494
Hauserman, N., 143
Hayes, R., 377, 378
Hayman, J., 562
Heapy, N., 129
Heathers, G., 142
Helm, H., 496
Henry, J., 195
Henson, K., 481
Hesketh, J., 378
Hess, R., 179, 189
Hewett, F., 412
Hewson, K., 496
Hiebert, E., 140, 415, 416, 417, 529
Hill, K., 318, 330
Hill, P., 37, 39
Hinkel, G., 35
Hoffman, J., 562
Hoffman, M., 189, 508
Hoge, R., 127
Holland, P., 372
Holt, J., 374, 487
Holubec, E., 433, 441
Hoover, K., 481
Horak, V., 364
Horn, T., 136
Horwitz, R., 377
Hudgins, B., 29
Huffman, G., 565
Hughes, B., 323
Huitt, W., 35
Huling-Austin, L., 563, 564, 565
Hull, R., 332
Humphreys, L., 135
Hunt, D., 562
Hunt, J., 470
Husen, T., 474
Hutslar, S., 129
Hyde, J., 32
Hyman, R., 239, 269

Inbar, J., 129, 138
Irvine, J., 443
Izu, T., 127

Jacklin, L., 32
Jackson, P., 26, 27, 31, 47, 217, 361, 362, 373, 374
Jacobson, L., 117, 118
James, T., 353
Jamgoschian, R., 526

Jamison, D., 372
Janzen, H., 379
Jeter, J., 128, 129
Johnsen, E., 313
Johnson, D., 202, 321, 406, 432, 433, 437, 439, 441
Johnson, J., 362
Johnson, R., 321, 432, 433, 437, 439, 441
Johnson, S., 129
Jones, B., 357, 358, 366
Jones, R., 120
Jones, V., 129
Jorgenson, G., 37, 233
Joseph, G., 127
Joyce, B., 459, 546, 562
Justman, J., 406

Kamil, M., 529
Karper, W., 129
Karweit, N., 356, 357, 358
Katz, L., 376
Kazdin, A., 289
Keddie, N., 142, 407
Keller, A., 28
Keller, F., 362
Keller, J., 307, 320, 325, 333
Kendall, A., 380, 427
Kepler, K., 365, 545
Kerman, S., 143
Kerry, T., 423
Kester, S., 129
Kher, N., 30, 328
Kierwa, K., 337
Kifer, E., 119
Kimbrough, J., 37, 39
Klausmeier, H., 364
Kleinfeld, J., 59, 128, 239
Kliebard, H., 239
Koester, L., 380
Kohl, H., 374
Kohlberg, L., 189
Kohler, P., 380
Kolesnik, W., 307
Kolvin, I., 289
Kounin, J., 218, 219, 220, 233, 240, 243, 260, 272
Kraut, R., 143
Kruglanski, A., 237, 322
Kuczynski, L., 143
Kulik, C., 362, 364, 406, 443
Kulik, J., 362, 364, 406, 443

Ladas, H., 337
Lahaderne, J., 31
Lampert, M., 17
Land, M., 477
Langer, E., 143
Lanier, J., 530, 545
Larrivee, B., 412
Lathrop, A., 372
Lawlor, J., 370
Leacock, E., 34, 142
Leak, F., 565
Leary, M., 325
LeCompte, M., 96, 98
Lee, G., 555
Leinhardt, G., 3, 33, 46, 412
Leiter, J., 407

Lepper, M., 143, 237, 289, 290, 307, 322, 324, 325, 333
Lesgold, A., 371
Lesser, G., 479
Letchworth, J., 129
Levine, D., 129, 355, 359
Leyser, Y., 200, 201
Lickona, T., 189
Lieberman, A., 545
Lightfoot, S., 31, 195
Lindvall, C., 360, 364
Linn, R., 69
Lipson, J., 370, 373
Lipson, M., 336, 501
Little, J., 550, 551, 563
Lombardo, M., 435
Lott, G., 496
Loucks, S., 365
Loughlin, R., 494, 495
Luginbuhl, J., 129
Luiten, J., 477
Lukasevich, A., 377, 379
Lundgren, U., 473

Maccoby, E., 32, 189
Mackler, B., 407
Macmillan, A., 289
Madaus, G., 127
Madden, M., 412
Maehr, M., 129, 307
Mager, R., 355
Malone, T., 307, 322, 324, 325, 333
Malvin, J., 437
Mandinach, E., 307
Manning, B., 49
Marchman, V., 546, 548
Marrett, C., 31
Marshall, H., 14, 110, 111, 112, 118, 131, 135, 137, 140, 377
Marshall, S., 406
Martin, J., 189, 223
Martin, L., 364, 365
Martin, M., 541, 545
Martinek, T., 129
Marton, P., 290
Maruyama, G., 437
Marwood, L., 546
Marx, R., 486
Mason, E., 128
Maughan, B., 557
Mayer, R., 329, 334, 336, 499, 501, 505
McCaleb, J., 476, 477, 479
McCarthy, M., 388
McColskey, W., 315
McCombs, B., 307, 318, 336
McDaniel, T., 535
McDill, E., 406, 407
McDonnel, L., 551
McGraw, M., 138
McIntyre, L., 148
McKeachie, W., 362
McLaughlin, M., 571
McLaughlin, T., 289
McLeish, J., 480
McMann, F., 481
McMullen, F., 546
McNeil, J., 46

McPartland, J., 410
Medinnus, G., 129
Medley, D., 47, 461
Medway, F., 127, 317
Meece, J., 239
Mehan, H., 239
Meichenbaum, D., 129, 290
Mellon, P., 135
Meloth, M., 336, 502
Mendoza, S., 129
Menges, R., 479
Mergendoller, J., 308, 546, 548
Merton, R., 116
Metz, M., 148, 407
Meyer, W., 128, 239
Middlestadt, S., 43, 285, 286
Miller, R., 143, 508
Millet, G., 69, 92
Miracle, A., 406, 416
Mitman, A., 127, 546, 548
Monk, M., 127, 137
Montessori, M., 237
Moore, C., 539
Moore, J., 545
Moore, L., 143
Moore, O., 237
Morgan, D., 412
Morgan, M., 313
Morris, L., 34
Morse, L., 33
Mortimore, P., 557
Mosher, R., 189
Moskowitz, G., 437, 562
Mosley, M., 323
Motta, R., 33
Murry, D., 546
Musella, D., 378

Nash, R., 216
Nash, S., 56
Natriello, G., 47, 128, 239
Nelsen, E., 351, 352, 353
Nelson, B., 546
Nelson, S., 239
Newby, T., 289
Nicholls, J., 307
Nickerson, J., 276, 410
Niles, J., 566, 567
Novak, J., 334, 496
Nuthall, G., 490, 496

Oakes, J., 407
Okebukola, P., 437
O'Leary, K., 218, 289
O'Leary, S., 218, 289
Oliver, W., 46
Omelich, C., 323
O'Neal, F., 562
Ortiz, R., 334
Osborn, J., 247, 248, 474
Ouston, J., 557

Packer, M., 546, 548
Page, S., 129
Palardy, J., 119
Palincsar, A., 336, 502
Pambookian, H., 46, 541

Paolitto, B., 443
Papert, S., 370
Paredes, K., 587
Paris, S., 336, 501
Parsons, J., 309
Passow, E., 406
Patterson, C., 289, 290
Paulissen, M., 562
Pavan, B., 364, 365
Pearson, D., 529
Pedulla, J., 127
Perrott, E., 180
Perry, D., 189
Perry, L., 189
Perry, P., 290
Persell, C., 127, 128, 131, 407
Peterson, P., 10, 33, 35, 42, 67, 127, 317, 365, 372, 377, 438, 486, 501, 566
Pflaum, S., 140
Piaget, J., 191, 237
Pintrich, P., 239
Plass, J., 318
Polya, G., 505
Popkewitz, T., 360, 365
Posner, G., 56, 496, 527, 529, 567, 568, 570
Powell, E., 445
Power, C., 423, 427, 429
Prawat, R., 276, 410, 556
Premack, D., 287
Price, D., 365, 374
Pringle, P., 359
Proctor, C., 143
Purkey, S., 551, 557
Putnam, J., 226

Quirk, T., 363

Ragosta, M., 372
Ramey, C., 140
Rand, Y., 508
Randall, J., 365
Rasher, S., 539
Raudenbush, S., 127, 135
Raviv, A., 444
Reif, F., 505
Reigeluth, C., 355
Rejeski, W., 129
Resnick, L., 356, 363
Rest, J., 189
Reynolds, M., 411
Rice, D., 494
Riggs, J., 144
Riley, J., 494
Rist, R., 129, 416, 417
Roark, A., 201
Robin, A., 290, 362
Robinson, P., 289
Roehler, L., 336, 502
Rogers, V., 494
Rogoff, B., 313, 445
Rohrkemper, M., 43, 65, 193, 231, 268, 293, 307, 467, 503, 535
Rolison, M., 127
Rollins, P., 445
Romberg, T., 365
Rosen, S., 445
Rosenbaum, J., 142, 405, 407, 408

Rosenbaum, M., 289
Rosenholtz, S., 47, 136
Rosenshine, B., 238, 327, 461, 477, 478, 480, 486, 490
Rosenthal, R., 117, 118, 128, 129, 135, 138
Rosner, J., 363
Ross, R., 129
Rossmiller, R., 364
Rosswork, S., 289
Rotter, J., 183
Rowan, B., 406, 555, 557
Rowan, S., 406, 416
Rowe, M., 46, 49, 117, 128, 129, 332, 492, 493
Roy, P., 433, 441
Rubovits, P., 129
Rushton, J., 143
Ruskin, R., 362
Rutherford, B., 372
Rutter, M., 143, 557
Ryan, R., 237, 307, 322

Sagotsky, G., 289, 290
Saily, M., 364
Sands, M., 423
Sanford, J., 222, 223, 224, 230, 407, 419, 472
Schachter, S., 177
Schaeffer, G., 437
Schaps, E., 437
Schaut, J., 545
Schiller, D., 377
Schlechty, P., 558
Schmidt, W., 36
Schmuck, P., 546
Schneider, M., 290
Schofield, H., 372, 427
Schrank, W., 118
Schubot, D., 445
Schuck, R., 477
Schultz, K., 364
Schunk, D., 311, 312, 313, 336
Schwartz, F., 407
Scott, J., 417, 529
Scott, R., 410
Seaver, W., 128
Sedlak, M., 142
Seewald, A., 33, 46
Shaftel, F., 201
Shaftel, G., 201
Sharan, S., 432, 433, 437
Sharan, Y., 433
Sharpley, A., 443
Shavelson, R., 69, 127, 142
Shee, S., 289
Sherman, J., 362
Shimron, J., 365
Short, G., 127
Shulman, 461, 466, 506, 529, 530, 557
Sieber, R., 2
Siegel, B., 57
Siess, T., 129
Sigler, E., 129
Sikes, J., 128, 129, 435
Silberman, C., 374
Simmons, B., 33
Simpson, C., 136
Simutis, Z., 143
Sizer, T., 353
Skinner, B., 287

Skon, L., 441
Slavin, R., 321, 356, 358, 365, 367, 369, 406, 410,
    412, 413, 415, 431, 432, 435, 436, 437, 439,
    440, 556
Sloan, D., 371
Smith, A., 557
Smith, D., 3
Smith, E., 477, 497
Smith, F., 129, 239
Smith, K., 439
Smith, L., 496
Smith, M., 135, 136, 551, 557
Smylie, M., 47
Snapp, M., 435
Snow, R., 118, 372
Snyder, M., 129, 138
Soar, R., 486
Solomon, D., 380, 427
Sorensen, A., 415, 416, 417
Spady, W., 357, 358
Spector, P., 129
Spencer, D., 27, 62, 537
Spencer-Hall, D., 40, 62, 67
Spinelli, F., 438
Spradley, J., 65, 98
Sprafka, S., 506
Sprinthall, N., 562
Stallings, J., 35, 36, 486, 529, 532, 542
Stanford, G., 200, 201
Stein, B., 505
Stephan, W., 410
Stern, P., 142
Stevens, A., 482, 483
Stipek, D., 311, 372
Stodolsky, S., 437
Strike, K., 496
Stubbs, J., 135
Stuck, M., 37
Sullivan, H., 200, 323
Swann, W., 129, 138
Swarthout, D., 308
Swift, J., 493
Swift, N., 332
Swing, S., 35, 42, 67, 438, 486
Sykes, G., 461, 529, 530
Szabo, M., 494

Tabachnick, R., 360, 365, 568
Talmage, H., 363
Taylor, C., 118, 128, 137, 565, 566
Taylor, R., 370
Taylor, S., 562
Thies-Sprinthall, L., 562
Thomas, J., 136, 289, 311, 444
Thompson, D., 365
Thompson, R., 412
Thoresen, C., 59
Thorndike, E., 507
Tinzmann, M., 357
Tisher, R., 562
Titus, A., 337
Tobin, K., 332, 493
Tollefson, N., 313, 314
Tom, D., 119, 127, 138
Toner, I., 143
Tracy, D., 313
Traub, R., 378
Tsui, W., 261

Tucker, M., 372
Tuckman, B., 46, 407
Tuma, D., 505
Tyack, D., 353
Tyler, R., 565

Unruh, R., 129

Vance, B., 558
Vane, J., 33
Vavrus, L., 336, 502
Veenman, S., 561, 562
Veldman, D., 407
Venino, G., 317
Vygotsky, L., 313

Walbek, N., 174
Walberg, H., 353, 357, 360, 364, 366, 377
Walden, T., 140
Wang, M., 353, 360, 363, 364, 366, 367, 444, 455,
    562
Washington, E., 474
Watson, P., 412
Waxman, H., 364, 366, 367
Webb, N., 69, 438
Webster, J., 357
Wehlage, G., 360, 365
Weil, M., 459
Weiner, B., 311, 312
Weinstein, C., 329, 336, 378, 380, 499, 501
Weinstein, R., 14, 43, 56, 65, 110, 111, 112, 118,
    128, 130, 131, 135, 136, 137, 139, 142, 239,
    285, 286, 416, 529, 535, 551, 552
Weishahn, M., 412
Weiss, J., 378, 379
Weisz, J., 311, 312
Wertsch, J., 313
Wessels, K., 239
West, C., 118, 131
Whelan, D., 362
White, J., 476, 477, 479
White, K., 412
Whitley, B., 312
Wigfield, A., 126, 134, 138, 309, 318, 330
Wilkinson, I., 417, 529
Wilkinson, L., 31, 34, 438
Williams, R., 334
Willis, B., 129, 189
Willows, D., 312
Wilson, B., 136
Wilson, R., 233
Winne, P., 29, 486
Wise, A., 551, 571, 572, 573, 574, 575
Wise, J., 269
Witkin, H., 539
Wittrock, M., 61, 529, 535
Wlodkowski, R., 307
Wolfson, B., 56
Worsham, M., 222, 230
Wright, C., 490, 496
Wyne, M., 37

Yinger, R., 566

Zeichner, K., 568
Zimmerman, B., 314
Ziomek, R., 34
Zuckerman, M., 131
Zumwalt, K., 56, 466, 529, 546, 557, 558, 559

Subject Index

Ability grouping, 404–410, 412–419, 447
Academic learning time, 35–36
Achievement motivation, 311
Action system knowledge, 3
Action zone, classroom, 30, 49
Active student learning, 499–503
Adaptive education, 360, 390, 404
Adaptive instruction, 360
Adaptive Learning Environments Model (ALEM), 363, 366–367, 391
Administrators, school, 294–295, 535, 540, 552, 555–558, 564–565
Affective learning strategies, 500
Aggression among students, 280–283
ALEM (Adaptive Learning Environments Model), 363, 366–367, 391
Answers, student, 262, 323, 339–340. *See also* Questions
Assignments. *See* Homework; Seatwork
Attainment value, 309
Attention, student
  coding, 89–90
  dealing with minor inattention, 260–262
  maintaining, 221, 240, 242–245, 484–486
Attribution theory models, 134–135

Back-to-basics movement, 391
Behavioral centers, 549
Behavioral contacts, 87–88
Behavior modification, 287, 289–291, 296, 459–460
Between-class ability grouping, 404–410, 412–415, 447
Bias, 59–63, 71–72
Brophy-Good Dyadic Interaction System, 75, 84–88, 97, 542

Chicago Mastery Learning Reading (CMLR), 357–358
Children. *See* Students
Classroom Dimensions Observation System, 110–115
Classrooms
  boring, 142–143
  complexity of, 1–2, 26–54
  describing and interpreting, 1–2, 16–17, 26–27, 55–115. *See also* Observation
  examples of, 587–599
  instruction in. *See* Instruction; Teaching, improving
  life of, 1–25, 195–196, 587–599
  management of. *See* Management, classroom
  meetings in, 287, 291–292, 296

Classrooms *(cont'd)*
  misbehavior in. *See* Misbehavior
  motivation in. *See* Motivation
  seeing in. *See* Observation
  students in. *See* Students
  teachers in. *See* Teachers
  teaching in. *See* Instruction; Teaching, improving
  time, use in, 18–22, 34–36
Coding, 75–84, 106–110. *See also* Observation systems
Cognitive behavior modification, 287, 289–291, 296
Competition, structuring, 320–322
Comprehension-monitoring learning strategies, 500
Computerized instruction, 369–372
Conceptual change, teaching for, 496–499
Conferences, 293–295
Conflict resolution, 266–268. *See also* Management, classroom
Context effects, 135–139
Contingency contracting, 287–289, 296
Cooperative learning
  conclusions about, 439–441
  controlled conflict and controversy, 439
  general description, 431–432, 448
  Group Investigation models, 435, 437, 443, 448
  implementation guidelines, 441–442
  Jigsaw approaches, 435–437, 440, 448
  Learning Together model, 432–433, 437, 448
  research on, 437–439
  Student Teams—Achievement divisions (STAD), 435–437, 440–441, 448
  Team Assisted Individualization (TAI), 366–369, 391, 415, 435–437, 440, 448
  Teams-Games-Tournament (TGT) approach, 435–437, 440–441, 448
  See also Group-based instruction
CoRT (Cognitive Research Trust) program, 507–508
Counselors, 294–295
Credibility, teacher, 9, 190–191
Cross-age tutoring, 443–445, 449
Cueing and reinforcing appropriate behavior, 234–240, 287, 314
Curiosity, modeling, 187–188, 332

Demonstrations, effective, 178–181
Desegregation, 409–410, 412, 447
Developmental centers, 549
Differentiated instruction, 419–430, 447
Disciplinary contacts, 87–88
Discipline. *See* Management, classroom

Educational equity, 409–415
Educational ethnography, 39–40, 96–106
Educational excellence, 409
Efficacy perceptions, 311
Effort-outcome linkages, 311–316
Elaboration learning strategies, 499
Emmer Observation System, 88–92, 97
Emotional control, modeling, 198–200
Enthusiasm, teacher, 478–480
Ethnographic studies, 39–40, 96–106
Examples of classroom life, 587–499
Exclusion from group, as punishment, 271–272, 296
Expectancy × value theory, 308–309
Expectations, teacher
  communication of, 128–134
  effects of, 135–147, 461
  examples of, 14–16, 122–126
  formation of, 116–128
  gender, student, 15, 32–34
  measuring of, 161–172
  negative, avoiding, 144–152
  as self-fulfilling prophecies, 116–126
  student perceptions of, 130–131
Extrinsic motivation strategies, 319–322, 340
Eye contact, 201–202

Feedback
  observer-to-teacher, 46–50, 534–535, 539–545, 555–556. *See also* Observation
  student-to-teacher, 48, 535–536
  teacher-to-student, 8, 314–315, 324–325, 335, 495. *See also* Motivation
Fighting among students, 280–283. *See also* Misbehavior

Gender and achievement patterns, 15, 32–34
Generative learning strategies, 329
Gesture and touch, 262
Glasser's Ten Steps to Good Discipline, 266–268
Goals, 307–308, 313
Gordon's Teacher Effectiveness Training, 266–268
Group-based instruction
  attention, maintaining, 484–486
  clarity, 476–478
  cooperative learning. *See* Cooperative learning
  discussions, 483–484
  enthusiasm, 478–480
  heterogeneous classes. *See* Heterogeneous classes
  inquiry approach, 482–483
  lecture and recitation methods, 480–482
  limits of, 467
  research on, 466–467
Grouping, 404–419, 447. *See also* Heterogeneous classes
Group Investigation models, 433, 435, 437, 448
Groups
  climate of, 195–196, 274
  exclusion from, 271–272, 296
  formation of, 404–419, 447. *See also* Heterogeneous classes
  instruction of. *See* Cooperative learning; Group-based instruction
  teacher expectation effects on, 139–141. *See also* Expectations, teacher

Handicapped children, 411–412

Heterogeneous classes
  between-class ability grouping (tracking), 404–410, 412–415
  educational excellence and equity, 409–415
  instruction of, 419–430, 447. *See also* Cooperative learning; Group-based instruction
  tutoring, 443–447
  within-class ability grouping, 415–419, 447
Heterogeneous grouping, 405–406, 408, 414, 418
Homework
  extra, as punishment, 270
  failure to complete, 285–286
  meaningful, 249–251, 463
Homogeneous grouping, 405–408, 412–415, 447
Humanistic centers, 549
Hyperactive students, 290–291, 380

IGE (Individually Guided Education), 363–365, 391
Imitation, 175–176. *See also* Modeling
Inattention, minor, dealing with, 260–262. *See also* Attention, student
Independent activities, student, 231–234, 249–250
Independent work and learning centers, 381
  examples of, 386–388
  for secondary students, 388–390
Individualized instruction, 352–354, 360–374, 390–391, 404
  Adaptive Learning Environments Model (ALEM), 366–367
  computerized instruction, 369–372
  conclusions about, 372–374
  individualized learning systems, 363–366
  Keller Plan (PSI), 362–363
  Team-Assisted Individualization (TAI), 366–369, 391, 415, 435–437, 440, 448
Indivdually Guided Education (IGE), 363–365, 391
Individually Prescribed Instruction (IPI), 363–365
Information-processing approaches to teaching, 459
In-service training, 43, 46, 50, 536–539, 549–550. *See also* Staff development
Instruction, 10–14
  active student learning, encouraging, 499–503
  adapting to students' characteristics, 467–469
  classroom guidelines, 469–470
  for conceptual change, 496–499
  demonstrations, effective, 178–181
  differentiated, 419–430, 447
  group. *See* Cooperative learning; Group-based instruction
  of heterogeneous classes. *See* Heterogeneous classes
  improving. *See* Teaching, improving
  individualized. *See* Individualized instruction
  the "match," 470–476
  of problem-solving and thinking skills, 504–509
  questioning. *See* Questions
  student self-evaluation, 503–504
  teacher behavior and student learning, 460–467. *See also* Expectations, teacher
Instrumental Enrichment Program, 508
Internal locus of control, 311, 314
Intrinsic or interest value, 309
Intrinsic motivational strategies, 322–328, 341
Investigations, conducting, 265–266
IPI (Individually Prescribed Instruction), 363–365

Jigsaw approaches, 435–437, 440, 448
Joplin Plan, 413, 447

Keller Plan (PSI), 362–363

Learning
 centers, 391
 cooperative. *See* Cooperative learning
 definition of, 328
 objectives, 310–311, 334–335
 motivation for. *See* Motivation
 strategies, 499–503
Learning Together model, 432–433, 437, 448
Listening, active, 266
Listening habits, modeling, 198
Lock-step curriculum, 353, 470
Logical thinking, modeling, 181–185, 335–336
Low achievers, 31–32, 55, 246–247, 295, 358, 380,
  406–407, 495

Mainstreaming, 409, 411–412, 447
Management, classroom, 9–10, 286–292, 461
 attention, getting and holding. *See* Attention,
  student
 conflict resolution, 266–268
 coping with problems, 260–304
 cues and reinforcement, 234–240, 287, 314, 319,
  321
 by developmental level, 273–275
 essential teacher attitudes, 226–228
 general principles, 228–234
 investigations, conducting, 265–266
 misbehavior, disruptive or prolonged, dealing with,
  263–268, 274, 276–286
 misbehavior, minor, dealing with, 231–232,
  260–262, 266–268
 as motivation and problem prevention, 218–226,
  310
 punishment. *See* Punishment
 rules, establishing, 222, 228–231, 263
 seatwork. *See* Seatwork
 socialization of students, 275–276
 student behavior, analyzing, 292–295
Master teachers, 558–561
Mastery learning, 315–317, 352–360, 390, 404,
  461–462, 471
 conclusions about, 358–360
 research on, 356–358
Microcomputers, 370
Misbehavior
 inappropriate intervention, 264–265
 investigating, 265–266
 major problems, 263–268, 274, 276–286
 minor problems, 231–232, 260–262, 266–268
 punishment. *See* Punishment
Modeling, 173–215, 314, 329–330
 awareness of, 174–178
 beliefs about subject matter, 185–187, 330
 curiosity, 187–188, 332
 emotional control, 198–200
 listening and communication habits, 198
 logical thinking, 181–185, 335–336, 504–508
 respect for others, 193–195
 role-playing techniques, 200–204, 326–327
 socialization through, 143–144, 189–204, 275–276,
  315
 teaching through, 178–188, 479
Modeling effects, 176–177
Momentum, 220

Motivation, 8, 30, 218–226, 305–351
 basic concepts of, 307–309
 extrinsic strategies, 319–322, 340
 instructional plans, incorporating motivational
  strategies in, 338–340
 intrinsic strategies, 322–328, 341
 to learn, 328–338, 341
 preconditions for, 309–311
 strategies of, 311–340
 by success expectations, 311–318, 340
Motives, 307–308

Objectives, learning, 310–311, 334–335
Observation, 55–115, 539–545
 benefits of, 1, 2, 55–56
 bias, 59–63, 71, 72
 case study techniques, 60–68
 coding, 75–84, 106–110. *See also* Observation
  systems
 feedback. *See* Feedback
 frequency data, 83, 95
 interpreting, 59–60, 81, 83
 planning for, 68–72
 problems with, 56–57
 reliability of, 60–63, 69–70, 77
 by students, 535–536
 of students, 293
 systems for. *See* Observation systems
 of teachers, 46–48, 50, 59
Observation systems
 Blumenfeld and Miller method, 92–96
 Brophy-Good Dyadic Interaction System, 75, 84–88,
  97, 542
 Classroom Dimensions Observation System,
  110–115
 coding academic activities and tasks, 106–110
 Emmer Observation System, 88–92, 97
 ethnography, 39–40, 96–106
 qualitative approaches, 96–98
 teacher attitudes and expectations, 161–172
Open education, 352–354, 374–381, 391, 404
 conclusions about, 380–381
 defining, 376
 examples of, 375–376
 research on, 377–380
Open-space schools, 378–380, 391
Organizational learning strategies, 500
Overlapping, 219
Overreactive teachers, 137–138

Parents, communication with, 43–45, 294–295
Peer tutoring, 443, 445–447
PEP (Primary Education Project), 363
Performance, 328
Performance anxiety, 330–331
Personal approaches to teaching, 459–460
Personalized System of Instruction (PSI), 362–363
Physical punishment, 269–270
PLAN (Program for Learning in Accordance with
  Need), 363
Practice examples, 587–599
Praise, 197, 238–240
Preservice training, 43, 46, 50, 549, 561–570
Primary Education Project (PEP), 363
Principals, 294–295, 535, 540, 552, 555–558,
  564–565
Proactive teachers, 137
Probing techniques, 12–13

Problem behavior. *See* Misbehavior
Problem prevention and solving. *See* Management, classroom
Problem-solving behavior, modeling, 181–185, 335–336, 504–508
Procedural contacts, 87–88
Professional collaboration, 545–549
Program for Learning in Accordance with Need (PLAN), 363
Programmed instruction, 361
PSI (Personalized System of Instruction), 362–363
Psychologists, school, 294–295
Pull-out instruction, 37–40
Punishment
  effective, 270–272
  exclusion from the group, 271–272, 296
  extra work, 270, 296
  inappropriate, 269–270
  physical, 269–270
  verbal attacks, 269
  when to punish, 268–269, 272–273, 296
  withdrawal of privileges, 271, 296

Qualitative data-collection approaches, 96–98
Questions, 11–13, 29–30, 486–496
  alternatives to, 484
  avoiding certain types of, 487
  factual, 11–13, 29–30, 486
  feedback on responses, 495. *See also* Feedback
  good, characteristics of, 486–487, 489–492
  guessing, 487–489
  higher-level, 30, 323–324, 486
  indirect, 484
  leading, 487, 489
  reasons for, 495–496
  repeating, 495
  rhetorical, 10, 265–266
  student, 14, 484, 504
  thought, 30
  tugging, 487–488
  wait time, 55, 492–494
  yes-no, 487

Race, 34, 274
Reactive teachers, 137
Reality therapy, 287, 291, 296
Reform efforts. *See* Individualized instruction; Mastery learning; Open education
Rehearsal learning strategies, 499
Reinforcing appropriate behavior, 234–240, 287, 314, 319, 321
Remedial work, 317–318, 473–476
Respect for others, modeling, 193–195
Responses, student, 262, 323, 339–340. *See also* Questions
Rewards. *See* Reinforcing appropriate behavior
Risk, 42
Role-play (simulation activities), 200–204, 326–327
Rules, establishing, 222, 228–231, 263

Seating patterns, 30, 261
Seatwork, 30–31, 245–251, 290–291, 353, 370, 463
  extra, as punishment, 270
  failure to complete, 285–286
  inappropriate, 149
  meaningful, 233–234, 249–251
Self-fulfilling prophecies. *See* Expectations, teacher
Setting effects, 135–139

Showing off, 278
Signal continuity, 220
Simulation activities (role play), 200–204, 326–327
Small groups. *See* Groups
Social interaction approaches to teaching, 459
Socialization, 143–144, 189–204, 275–276, 315
Social workers, 294–295
Software, educational, 370
Special education students, 411–412
STAD (Student Teams—Achievement Divisions), 435–437, 440–441, 448
Staff development, 550–558. *See also* In-service training
Stratified heterogeneous grouping, 414
Streaming, 405, 447
Student engaged time, 35
Students
  accountability of, 243–245
  active learning, 499–503
  behavior, analyzing, 292–295
  defiance of teachers, 278–280
  effects on teachers, 40–43
  fighting among, 280–283
  gender, 15, 32–34
  heterogeneous. *See* Heterogeneous classes
  low achievers, 31–32, 55, 246–247, 295, 358, 380, 406–407, 495
  management of. *See* Management, classroom
  misbehavior of. *See* Misbehavior
  motivation of. *See* Motivation
  out-of-school environments, 277
  perceptions of differential teacher treatment, 130–131. *See also* Expectations, teacher
  personal and social development, 143–144, 189–204
  questions of, 14, 484, 504. *See also* Questions
  responses of, 262, 323, 339–340. *See also* Expectations, teacher
  self-evaluation, 503–504, 530–539
  teaching of. *See* Instruction; Teaching, improving
  unresponsiveness of, 283–285
Student teachers, 47–48
Student Team Learning, 435, 448
Student Teams—Achievement Divisions (STAD), 435–437, 440–441, 448
Success expectations, motivation by maintaining, 311–318, 340
Supervisors, 294–295, 535, 540, 552, 555–558, 564–565
Sustaining expectation effects, 117. *See also* Expectations, teacher

TAI (Team-Assisted Individualization), 366–369, 391, 415, 435–437, 440, 448
Teacher centers, 549–550
Teacher Effectiveness Training (Gordon), 226–228
Teachers, 1–4
  attitudes of, 147–152
  awareness (unawareness) of classroom behavior, 26–54
  beginning, 561–570
  credibility of, 9, 190–191
  effectiveness of, 1, 26, 221–222, 460–466. *See also* Management, classroom
  enthusiasm of, 478–480
  evaluation of, 571–576. *See also* Observation
  expectations of. *See* Expectations, teacher

Teachers *(cont'd)*
    experimenting and growing, 526–532. *See also*
        Teaching, improving
    feedback about classroom behavior, 46–50. *See also*
        Observation
    instruction methods. *See* Instruction; Teaching,
        improving
    management of classrooms. *See* Management,
        classroom
    modeling, use of. *See* Modeling
    motivating students. *See* Motivation
    observation of, 46–48, 50, 59. *See also* Observation
    personal characteristics, effects of, 136–139,
        219–220
    self-evaluation, 530–539
    socialization of, 524–526
    student, 47–48
    students, showing interest in, 196–198. *See also*
        Students
Teaching. *See* Instruction; Teaching, improving
Teaching, improving, 523–586
    beginning teachers, 561–570
    emerging roles and issues, 558–561
    evaluation of teachers, 571–576
    experimenting and growing, 526–532
    materials, sharing, 546–549
    observation, usefulness of, 534–536, 539–545
    professional collaboration, 545–549
    self-evaluation, 530–539
    socialization process, problems caused by, 524–
        526
    staff development programs, 550–558
    teaching centers, 549–550
    See also Instruction
Team-Assisted Individualization (TAI), 366–369, 391,
    415, 435–437, 440, 448

Teams-Games-Tournament (TGT) approach, 435–437,
    440–441, 448
Ten Steps to Good Discipline (Glasser), 266–268
TGT (Teams-Games-Tournament) approach, 435–437,
    440–441, 448
Thinking skills, 181–185, 335–336, 504–508
Time use in classrooms, 18–22, 34–36
Touch and gesture, 262
Tracking, 405, 407–408, 447
Traditional approach to education, 351–353, 376–378,
    404, 449
Training, teacher, 43, 46, 50, 222, 549, 561–570. *See
    also* Teaching, improving
Truancy, 274
"Turtle" technique, 290
Tutorial assistance
    cross-age tutoring, 443–445, 449
    peer tutoring by classmates, 443, 445–447

Utility value, 309

Vandalism, 274
Verbal punishment, 269
Videodisc technology, 370

Wait time, 55, 492–494
Whole-class instructional methods, 353, 404, 447
Withdrawal, student, 274
Withdrawal of privileges, as punishment, 271,
    296
Within-class ability grouping, 415–419, 447
"With-it-ness," 219, 260
Work-related contacts, 87–88

Zone of proximal development, 313

70 032